The Local Network Handbook

Edited by George R. Davis
Editor-in-chief,
Data Communications Magazine

McGraw Hill Publications Company
1221 Avenue of the Americas
New York, New York 10020

The Local Network Handbook

Edited by George R. Davis
Editor-in-chief,
Data Communications Magazine

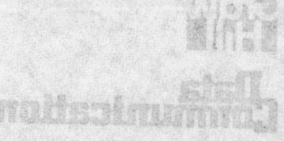

Data
Communications

McGraw-Hill Publications Company
1221 Avenue of the Americas
New York, New York 10020

Data Communications BOOK SERIES

- *Basics of Data Communications.* Edited by Harry R. Karp. 1976, 303 pp., softcover.
- *Data Communications Procurement Manual.* By Gilbert Held. 1979, 150 pp., clothbound.
- *Practical Applications of Data Communications.* Edited by Harry R. Karp. 1980, 424 pp., softcover.
- *Fiber Optics and Lightwave Communications Vocabulary.* Edited by Dennis Bodson. 1981, 149 pp., softcover.
- *McGraw Hill's Compilation of Data Communications Standards (Edition II).* Edited by Harold C. Folts. 1982, 1923 pp., clothbound.
- *Teletext and Videotex in the United States: Market Potential, Technology, and Public Policy Issues.* By J. Tydeman, H. Lipinski, R. Alder, M. Nyhan, L. Zwimpfer. 1982, 312 pp., clothbound.

Cover design by Cathy Canzani, Designworks

Copyright © 1982, by McGraw-Hill, Inc. All rights reserved. Printed in the United States of America. Except as permitted under the United States Copyright Act of 1976, no part of this publication may be reproduced or distributed in any form or by any means, or stored in a data base or retrieval system, without the prior written permission of the publisher.

Second printing: April 1983

Third printing: January 1984

Library of Congress Cataloging in Publication Data
Main entry under title:

The Local network handbook.

Includes index.
1. Computer networks. I. Davis, George R.

TK5105.5.L6 1982	001.64'404	82-10068
TK5105.5.16 1982	001.64'404	82-10068

ISBN 0-07-606831-5

Table of Contents

iv Introduction

1 SECTION I TECHNOLOGY

2 Concepts, strategies for local data network architectures *R. H. Sherman, M. G. Gable,* and *G. McClure*

11 Local Networking: The missing link emerges *Ken Hardwick* and *William Federbusch*

20 Local networks consensus: High speed *Peter Hsi* and *Tsvi Lissack*

31 A user speaks out: Broadband or baseband for local nets? *Thomas E. Krutsch*

39 13 Often-asked questions about broadband *Edward Cooper*

43 How fiber optics reduces a private net's growing pains *Richard C. McCaskill*

48 Making a case for token passing in local networks *C. C. Kenneth Miller* and *D. M. Thompson*

54 Overcoming local and long-haul incompatibility *R. H. Sherman, M. G. Gable,* and *A. Chung*

61 SECTION II SOFTWARE

62 Dynamic reconfiguration by a local network's operating system *Robert Coyne*

71 Unix: An operating system that means business *Wendy Rauch-Hindin*

78 A programming language for networks *Paul A. D. de Maine*

85 SECTION III EQUIPMENT

86 Minicomputers' network roles *Edwin E. Mier*

101 Finesse versus force in bolstering micros' capabilities *John Wharton* and *Lionel Smith*

110 Microtalk's maxi applications could benefit companies *Frank J. Derfler*

113 The new network roles of the statistical mux *Joseph Visvader*

121 The new breed—switching muxes *Thomas H. Scholl*

126 A buyers guide to today's versatile statistical multiplexers *James H. Scharen-Guivel* and *A. A. Carlson*

144 How to keep terminal users honest *Alan Berman*

149 SECTION IV IMPLEMENTATION

150 Implementing Ethernet from soup to nuts *Jeffrey Mason* and *Gregory Shaw*

157 The first all-in-one local network *Didier S. Castueil, Domenic L. Giovachino,* and *Dennis L. Lengyel*

165 LSI devices control loop-mode SDLC data links *John Beaston*

173 SECTION V APPLICATIONS

174 Data Communications in the office *Edwin E. Mier* and *J. Peter Schmader*

189 Which technology will rule the automated office? *Wendy Rauch-Hindin*

202 Universities are setting trends in data communications nets *Wendy Rauch-Hindin*

213 Bank finds proven methods lead to successful network *Frederick S. Haines*

221 SECTION VI SELECTION

222 The many faces of local networking *Kenneth J. Thurber* and *Harvey A. Freeman*

230 Build a local network on proven software *Dale Way*

234 Inside Wang's local net architecture *Mark Stahlman*

240 Ring nets: Passing the token in local networking circles *Richard E. Sterry*

244 The microcomputer connection to local networks *Joe Malone*

248 A low-speed local net for under $100 per station *Robert Bosen*

251 Net/One's answer to packet and circuit switching *John M. Davidson*

255 Index

256 Original Publication Dates

Introduction

You will find two kinds of articles in this book. First are those that describe local network techniques, technologies, applications, and choices. The others, articles not directly related to local networking when they were first published, are included because the equipment or software they describe has found wide use in installed local networks. Such is the case, for instance, with the articles concerning multiplexers. Although multiplexers were originally designed to promote efficiency in long-haul data communications networks, they are being used increasingly in local network installations. Since minicomputers and microcomputers are serving as local network nodes, articles describing their latest capabilities are included as well. Several articles, particularly those concerning applications, go beyond local network technology. These are here since the modern communications specialist can not put all his eggs in one basket. The article, "Which technology will rule the automated office," for example, compares local networking solutions with several other approaches.

The book has been divided into six sections. Section I details local network technology with a number of articles examining the overall concept of local networking and others zeroing in on specific approaches. Section II deals with software. Here you will find articles describing the software techniques that are being employed on today's local networks. If anything is holding local networking back from its predicted explosion it is a lack of higher-level applications and data transport software. As you will see in Section II, up to now most local network software has been "borrowed" from long-haul network technology. In fact, the article "Dynamic reconfiguration by a local network operating system" describes one of the few examples of software actually designed for local environments. Section III deals with equipment. Here the reader will find articles describing the latest in minicomputers, microcomputers, and multiplexers, along with an interesting piece concerning terminal security. These article represent a good cross-section of actual equipment being used on local networks. Implementation of local networks is the subject of Section IV. These articles discuss actual implementation efforts that will make the reader aware of the scope and expected results of such undertakings. Applications and application possibilities are found in Section V. Here an attempt was made to select articles that deal with real world problems and solutions. Section VI, is called "Selection" because it presents the reader with a broadview of different available local network products. It starts by detailing the different choices, and continues with an examination of the most popular ones on the market today.

It is necessary to clear up two misconceptions about local networks. Misconception number one is that a PBX is a local network. PBXs and CBXs are often touted as alternatives—in some cases as viable ones—to local networks, but their centrally controlled architecture and dedicated-line concept makes them unsuitable for resource sharing. It is resource sharing above all else that makes local networks cost and operationally effective.

What is a local network? Since there are several answers to that, it is necessary to define a set of ingredients that is generally held to make up a local network. The first ingredient is a common medium, usually shared by all user stations. Next is wide bandwith, which translates to high-speed interactions. A local network must have rapid multi-addressing or broadcasting capability, and it must have distributed control for flexibility. It must be able to offer distributed processing, host-to-host and host-to-peripheral transparent communications. It is also necessary that a local network be capable of providing remote job entry and at least file transfer (if not full distributed database capability), database management, and access to long haul networks. Its range varies. It is not the area that defines a local network, but its high speed connection capabilities. If properly amplified, a local network has no range limitation. However, its common medium usually limits it to within a building or within an area in and around several buildings located near each other.

The second misconception is that local networking is inexpensive. You will read examples in this book that describe low-cost local networking, but those offerings are limited in scope. Full-fledged local networking, capable of performing the tasks detailed above, vary in price. Per-station connection costs (a station ranges from a microcomputer operating as an intelligent terminal to a minicomputer with peripherals like printers and hard-disk memory) start at about $1,000. Remember that the $1,000 average minimum is the cost of the network connection only; the equipment attached to the network is not included. Much has been written about the $100-per-station hook-up cost predicted for local networks. However, until the large-scale integrated circuit manufacturers bring their latest generation into production the cost will remain in the $1,000 range. Keep in mind, too, that even when the new local networking chips are ready, there will still be software costs. No one is predicting a rapid decline in that area. It is likely then, that local-network connection costs will not decline in one fell swoop, but rather if they decline at all it will be a gradual process.

IV

Section 1

Local Network
Technology
Technology
Technology
Technology
Technology
Technology
Technology
Technology
Technology
Technology
Technology
Technology
Technology

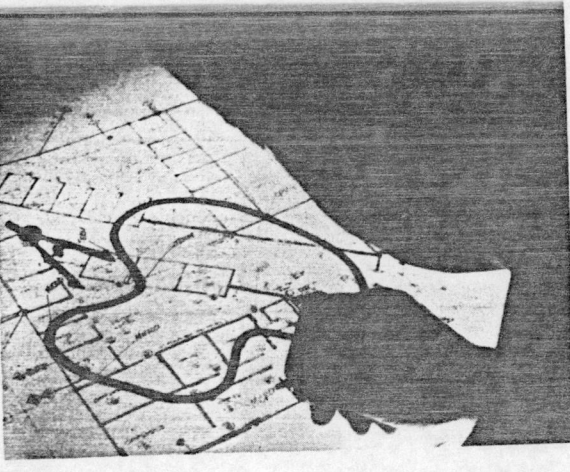

Small is different

Concepts, strategies for local data network architectures

R.H. Sherman, M.G. Gable, and G. McClure, Ford Motor Co.
Research Laboratory, Dearborn, Mich.

For a data communications network covering a limited area, what's needed is a new architecture embracing contention, propagation delay, functionality

The number of microcomputers and minicomputers employed in process control applications has vastly increased over the past few years. Recently, a few organizations have expanded these applications toward fully distributed networks employing high-speed channels, with all users located in the same building complex.

Since the control for these networks is local, no central computer can bottleneck the data communications. Thus, higher data rates than those associated with larger networks are possible, since information is processed only by the communicating computers.

Local data network architectures—the backbones of these systems—are designed to implement functional control of several different process control environments. One local network architecture (LNA), used in Ford Motor Co.'s Research Laboratory in Dearborn, Mich., is typical of this new breed of architecture.

The requirements for an LNA-based process control network are more comprehensive than the requirements for conventional networks because of the wide use of heterogenous computers in Ford's manufacturing environment. Besides handling a wide mix of computers, the network is fully decentralized, with no single node more important than any other. Also, the net-

work's file system is decentralized and can contain automatic recovery features. A common protocol exists among all processors, which range from mainframes to microcomputers.

Historically, process control networks have been organized into star, multidrop, or ring configurations.

In a star configuration, one computer forms the center, acting as the network control (master), with separate lines to all other computers (slaves). These networks can be hierarchical, since a slave computer to one star can be a master computer for a different star.

One computer also forms the center of the network control in a multidrop scheme. In this configuration, a line is "dropped" to the other computers from a trunk. Communications are handled by polling (sequencing from one computer to another). Communication between computers is possible only by sending messages through the polling computer.

With a ring configuration, each computer is linked to two other computers in a loop arrangement. Messages from one computer to another are passed along by intermediate computers, which retransmit the messages. Usually, in a ring, a network master exists to delete messages that have not been acknowledged as received. Several difficulties arise when these configu-

1 Packet collisions

Wait. The retransmission delay (RD) in CSMA is the sum of packet n's collision time (y), packet n's normalized length (1), and the medium's delay/packet time ratio (a).

When both collision and carrier are sensed (CSMA/CD), the RD is simply equal to the average arrival time of the first data packet which collides with packet zero.

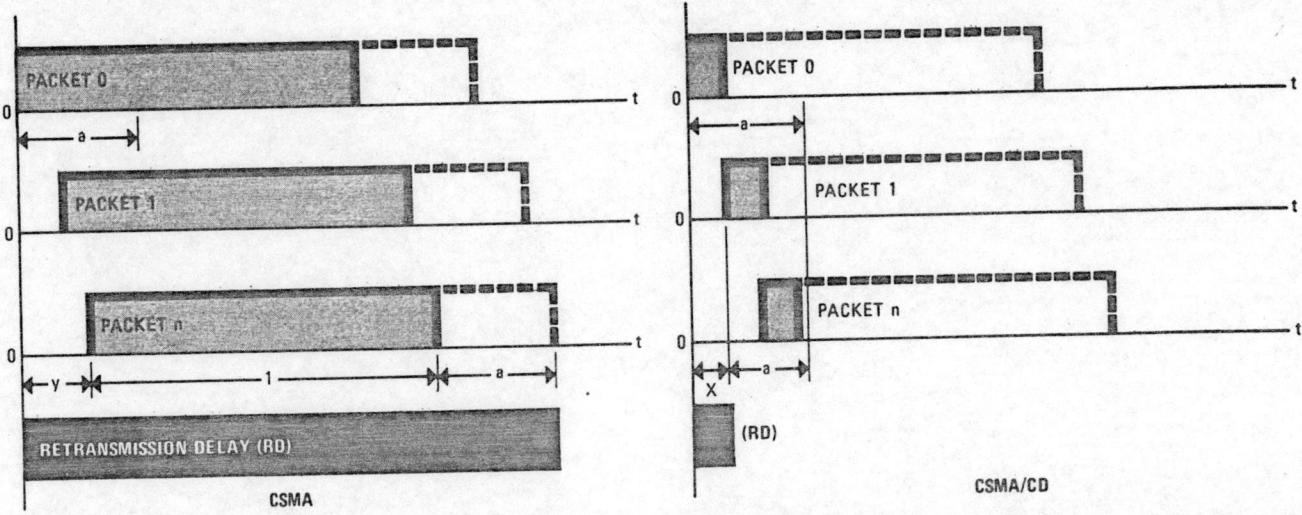

rations are considered for a manufacturing control system like the one used by Ford. None of these networks adapt well to full or partial communications failures. In the star, when a master fails, slave computers go off-line. To avoid the effect of a master failure, redundancy is required at all levels in the star's hierarchical control system. In the multidrop arrangement, if a polling computer fails, no other computers can communicate. In the ring network configuration, any computer failure inhibits communications.

Local data networks are better suited to a manufacturing control environment because they decentralize control communications with contention techniques. All computers share one medium, such as coaxial cable or a radio frequency, and the contention for the medium is locally handled by each computer.

One such network, the Aloha (Ref. 1) system, uses a broadcast channel with transmissions occurring at random. A refinement of the Aloha scheme, called Slotted Aloha (Ref. 2), provides a time slot for transmission which is shared by several computers. Transmission can only be initiated at the beginning of each time slot.

Network Systems Corp. (Ref. 3) uses a carrier-sense-multiple-access (CSMA) technique for contention. Retransmissions in CSMA are based on individually assigned time delays. To detect simultaneous transmissions, a message checksum is used. The average packet delay is decreased by increasing the transmission rate.

Yet another contention method is found in Ethernet (Ref. 4), used by Xerox. Ethernet handles contention by a carrier-sense-multiple-access scheme with collision detection CSMA/CD. Transmission in Ethernet is permitted only when an idle line (no carrier) is sensed. However, two or more computers may sense the idle

line simultaneously, due to the propagation delay of the line. In this case, a message collision may result. If a collision is detected, the transmitters stop transmitting and wait a random amount of time, weighted by the network traffic, before retransmitting.

Contention comparisons

The choice of a contention scheme involves an analytical analysis, using models and simulation results which are available for several access methods. To begin the analysis, assume a Poisson traffic model in which the user can detect both carrier and collision. The channel can employ a nonpersistent protocol, which schedules packets in the following way. If the channel is idle, the packet is transmitted; if the channel is busy, the packet is rescheduled for transmission at some later time according to a delay distribution function which satisfies the Poisson traffic model.

In contrast to the nonpersistent user, a 1-persistent approach (Ref. 5) can be used. With this method, the packet is transmitted with probability-one (no delay before attempting retransmission) when an idle channel is sensed. The left side of Figure 1 depicts packets colliding in a CSMA scheme; while the right side shows packets truncated by the action of the collision-detection logic. The throughput equation denoted by S for a nonpersistent CSMA without collision detection is:

$$S = \frac{Ge^{-aG}}{G(1+2a-ae^{-aG})+2e^{-aG}-e^{-2aG}} \quad (1)$$

where G is the arrival rate of new and rescheduled packets per normalized packet time, and a is the ratio of propagation delay to packet time. The duration for a successful packet transmission is $1+a$, and the average duration of idle is $1/G$. The minimum packet re-

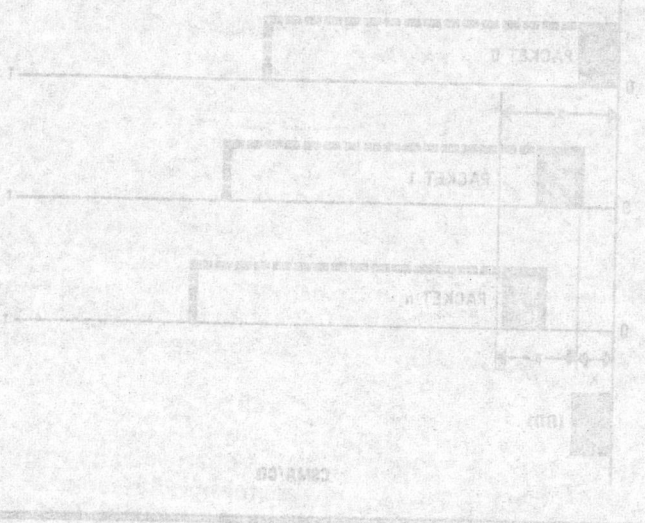

transmission delay (RD) is illustrated by the solid color bar in Figure 1.

In the case where the user can sense both collision and carrier, the minimum retransmission delay is equal to X, the average time for arrival of the first packet that collides with packet 0, as illustrated in the right portion of Figure 1. The channel will be clear after all truncated packets have traveled for the total propagation delay time. To derive the distribution function consider:

X = arrival time of the colliding packet

P(X > x) = P (no arrival during time x, and at least one arrival during a − x)

$$P(X>x) = e^{-Gx}(1 - e^{-G(a-x)})$$

$$P(X>x) = e^{-Gx} - e^{-aG}$$

Then:

$$P(X \le x) = 1 - P(X>x) = 1 - e^{-Gx} + e^{-aG}$$

Hence, the density function is:

$$\frac{d\ f(x)}{dx} = Ge^{-Gx} \qquad (2)$$

The average of X is therefore:

$$\overline{X} = \frac{1}{G} - \frac{e^{-aG}}{G} - ae^{-aG} \qquad (3)$$

The average duration of an unsuccessful packet is $\overline{X} + a$, and that for a transmission of a packet without conflict is $1 + a$. Therefore, the throughput equation for the nonpersistent CSMA with collision detection (CSMA/CD) protocol is:

$$S = \frac{Ge^{-aG}}{(1+a)(Ge^{-aG}) + (1+aG)(1 - e^{-aG})^2 + 1} \qquad (4)$$

In Figure 2 for a equal to 0.01, a plot of S versus G for various random access modes shows the relative performance of each. For large G, note that CSMA/CD is superior to other modes of operation. A channel capacity of approximately 0.952 can be obtained with CSMA/CD compared to only 0.815 for a nonpersistent CSMA approach.

Further, it is possible to trade off packet size, transmission rate, and propagation delay to obtain an acceptable level of performance. An analysis of throughput relative to the ratio a reveals that, as a becomes large, the throughput of the channel is reduced (Fig.

2 Comparing access methods

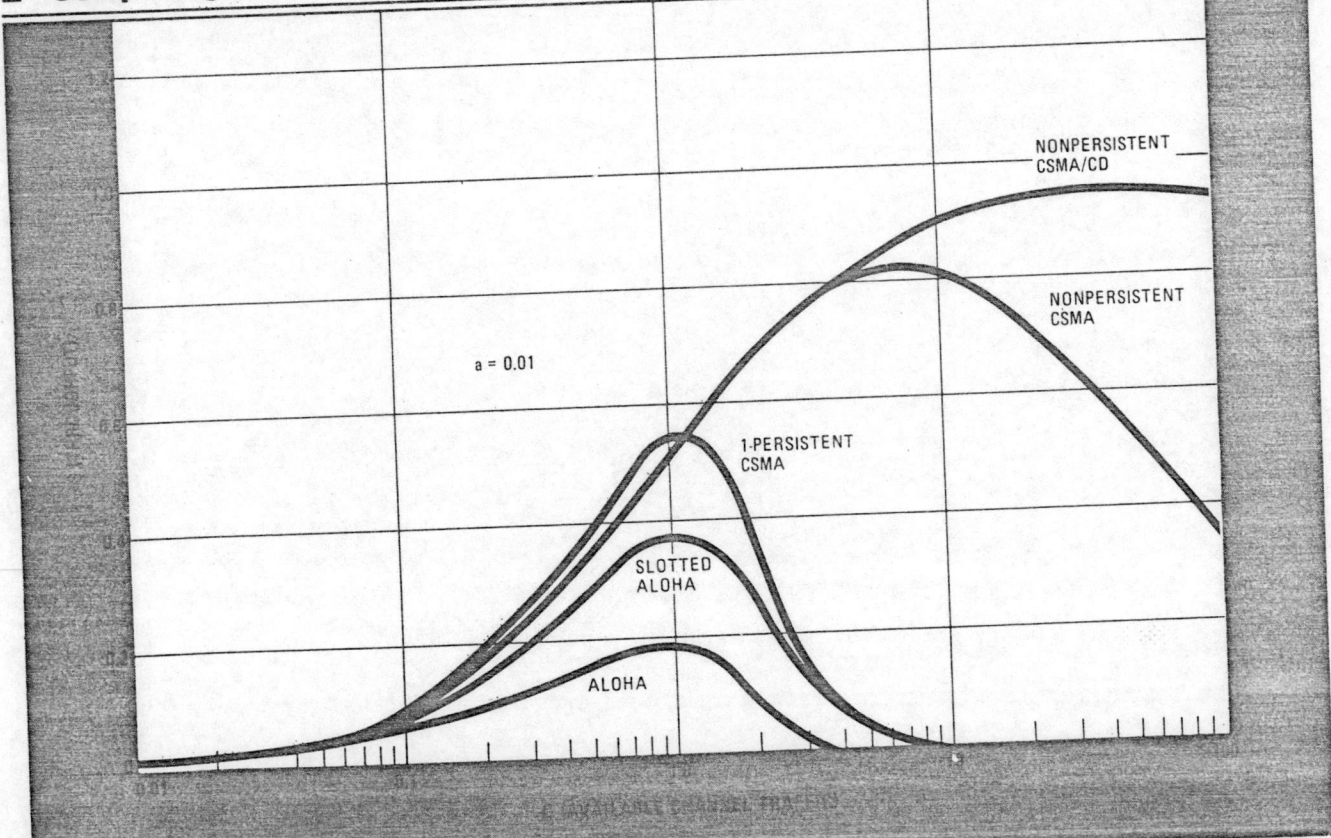

Fixed a. For a given propagation/packet-length ratio, CSMA/CD with a nonpersistent protocol yields the maximum throughput. As with most contention schemes, the throughput goes to zero when the system loading becomes too large, but note the slow rate of CSMA/CD's decline to zero. Parameters in this graph are normalized.

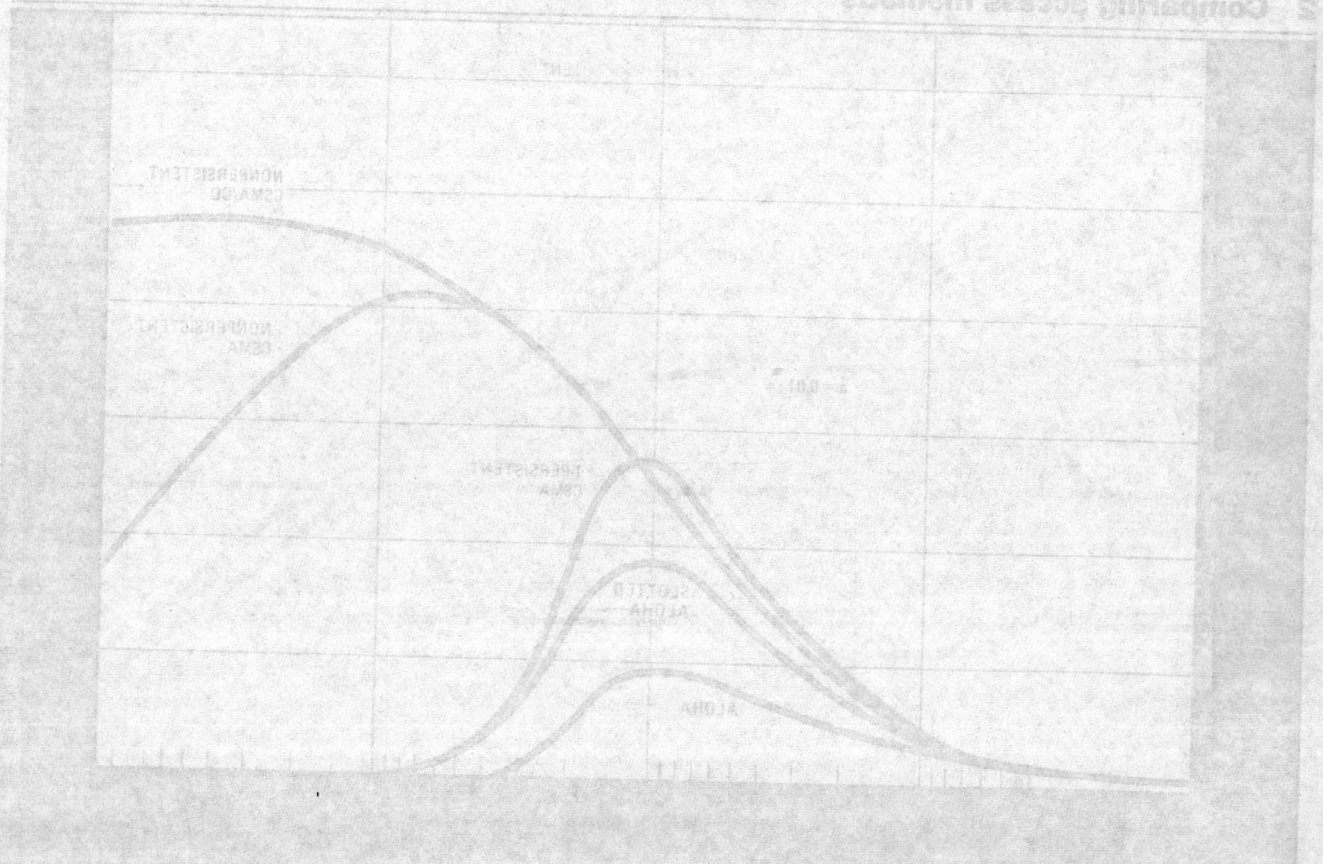

3). Hence, to effectively employ a carrier-sense-multiple-access scheme, it is necessary to maintain an a of about 0.01. Ford's LNA network uses a transmission rate of 1 Mbit/s with a maximum packet of 1K bits.

Collision detection is not performed directly on the encoded or modulated signal. If a design employs the amplitude or phase relationship of the transmitted signal for detection collision, it will probably be very sensitive to noise. In LNA, a band-spreading modulation technique is employed, which encoded the data using a ternary (base three) code of length six. The decoder classifies all 729 possible combinations of the code.

The correlation properties of this code permit collision detection to be performed by the *exclusive-OR* function of the data transmitted and decoded by the receiver. The encoded signal also incorporates timing information which makes it possible to extract the data rate from the waveform to avoid problems with conventional clock synchronization techniques.

Coaxial cable medium

LNA uses the Ethernet CSMA/CD contention approach for a process control application, but with a slight modification. Communications connections in LNA are made between processes, instead of between hosts and terminals. Ford's communications channel— a branching bidirectional-passive tapped coaxial cable, shared in a multi-access scheme—is operated in a packet-switched mode. The number of users, limited by signal attenuation, and the number of port addresses is always less than 256. The transceiver amplification stages permit 25 dB (decibels) signal attenuation. This permits combinations of passive branching and non-directional taps. The propagation delay between any source-to-destination pair is a relatively small fraction of the overall network propagation delay.

The Ford net is designed for use in product testing, machine monitoring, power tool monitoring, product functional control, maintenance dispatching and energy management. With LNA, several of these applications can coexist on the network within one plant.

LNA is realized by using a communications interface between the user and coaxial cable. The choice of coaxial cable over more exotic media, such as fiber optic cable, is made for several reasons. Coaxial cable has a proven reliability, and while fiber optic cable users boast of excellent performance, in the manufacturing industry these applications are still limited. More importantly, coax is still less expensive than fiber optic cable, especially in large volume. The block diagram,

3 Changing propagation delay

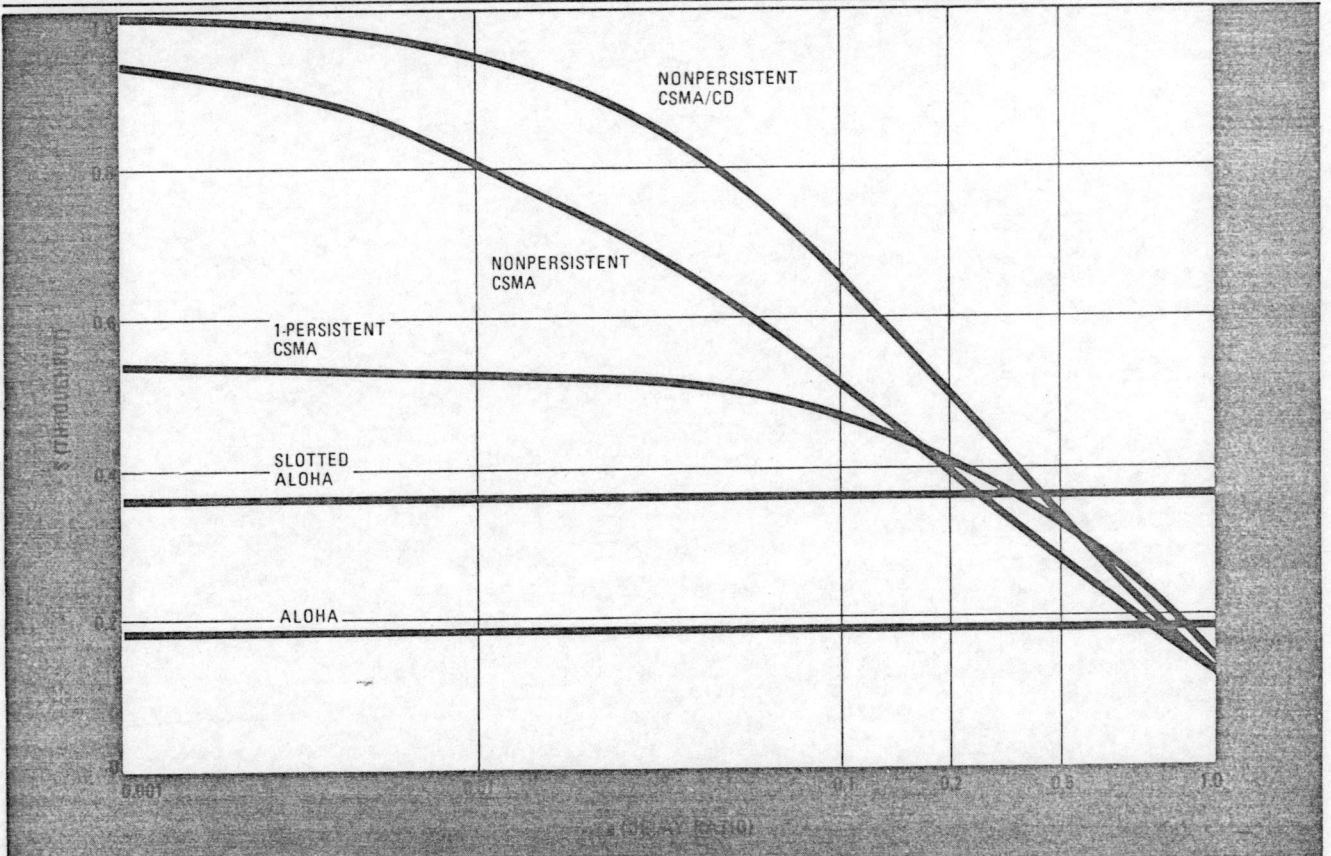

Varying a. As a increases, network throughput falls, for any of the CSMA arrangements. For effective CSMA or CSMA/CD operation, a should be equal to, or less than 0.01. Keep in mind that a change in the ratio a can come about because of a change in the transmission medium's delay or a change in the time duration of the packet.

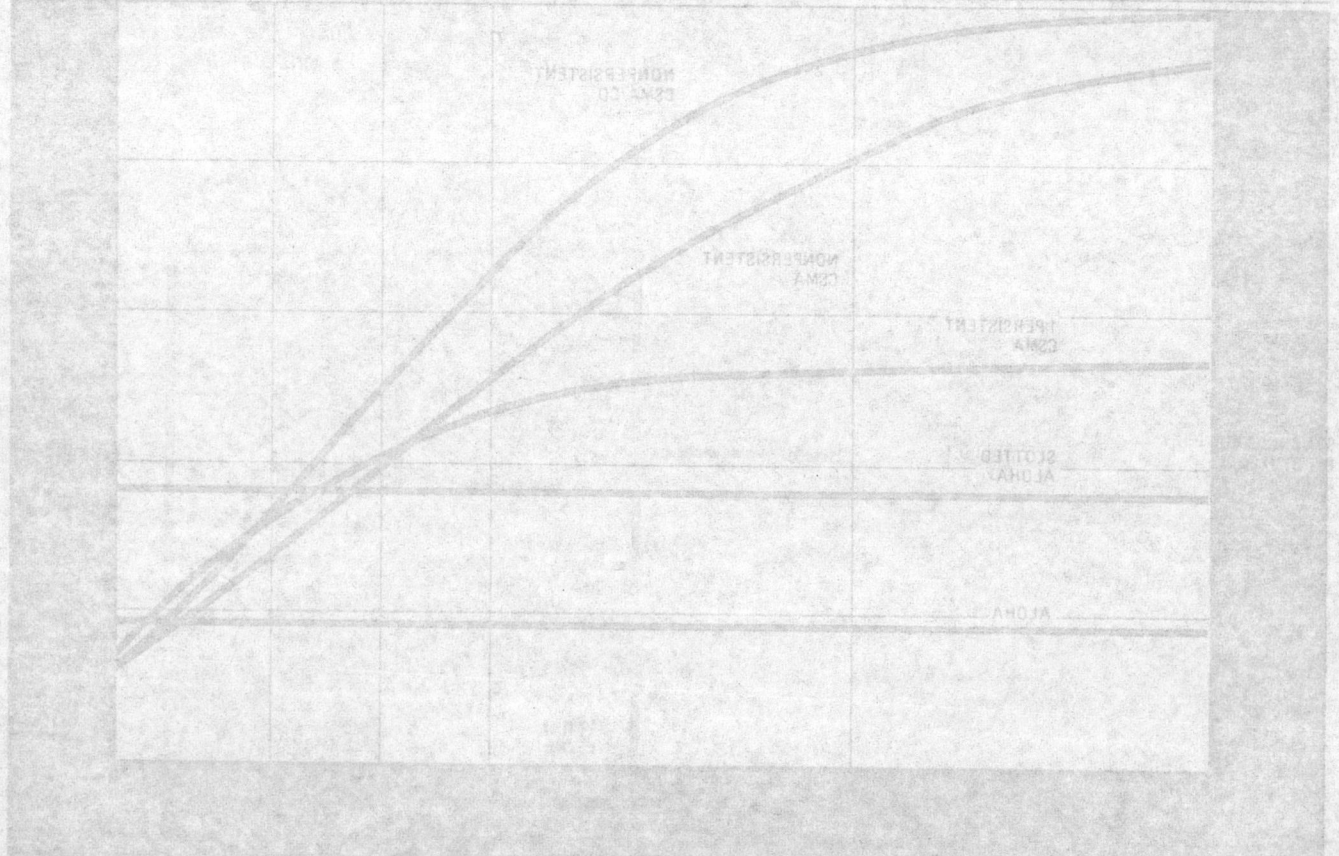

Figure 4, illustrates the communications interface and its functions. The user accesses the interface through either a RS-232-C port or an eight-bit parallel port. The transceiver performs all the contention logic. The adapter contains a communications microcomputer which controls the logical message flows. The network includes a PDP-10 (DEC) computer, a microcomputer-controlled engine dynamometer test stand, a data-acquisition microcomputer on a machine tool, and a monitor computer.

Six-level structure

LNA provides: a scheme for resource allocations, a process naming function, and a means to initiate connections. Network addresses and resources are maintained by the user. When a process needs a resource, it can easily find it. Also, a new process can name itself in the network. For automatic handling of resource allocations, generic names must exist. These generic names for processes in the network are translated to network addresses by a LOG process. The LOG is a dynamic bookkeeping procedure which achieves resource management through a CATALOG—a file which contains both the generic name and the network addresses of processes and resources. Associated with

these names are resource costs, access privileges, and present attachments. For network reliability the LOG process and the CATALOG can be partially or completely replicated.

A CATALOG-update algorithm deletes network addresses when connections cannot be established. After recovering from a network fault, the LOG restores a state of agreement between replicated CATALOGs.

The architecture's organizational levels, shown in Figure 5, range from a user-level to a physical link level. In Ford's LNA-network the entire architecture is implemented, although the two highest levels—user and system processes—are still in the experimental stage.

The basic entity in the LNA-based network is a process. Processes communicate with other processes, and with machines, operators, and test stands in the manufacturing system. Process levels exist for both user and system jobs. System-level processes include mechanisms for task scheduling, communications, input/output device interfacing, and procedures to manage system resources such as files. User processes communicate with system processes to create an environment for operation of conventional applications.

File or message transfers between a set of processes are the responsibility of the communicating layers;

4 Interface block diagram

Logic. The logic for the carrier-sense-multiple-access with collision detection is implemented in the Ford network at the transceiver, which receives its input from a synchro-nous-communications port which is connected to the coaxial-cable network medium. The error checking is carried out at the LNA architecture's link-protocol level.

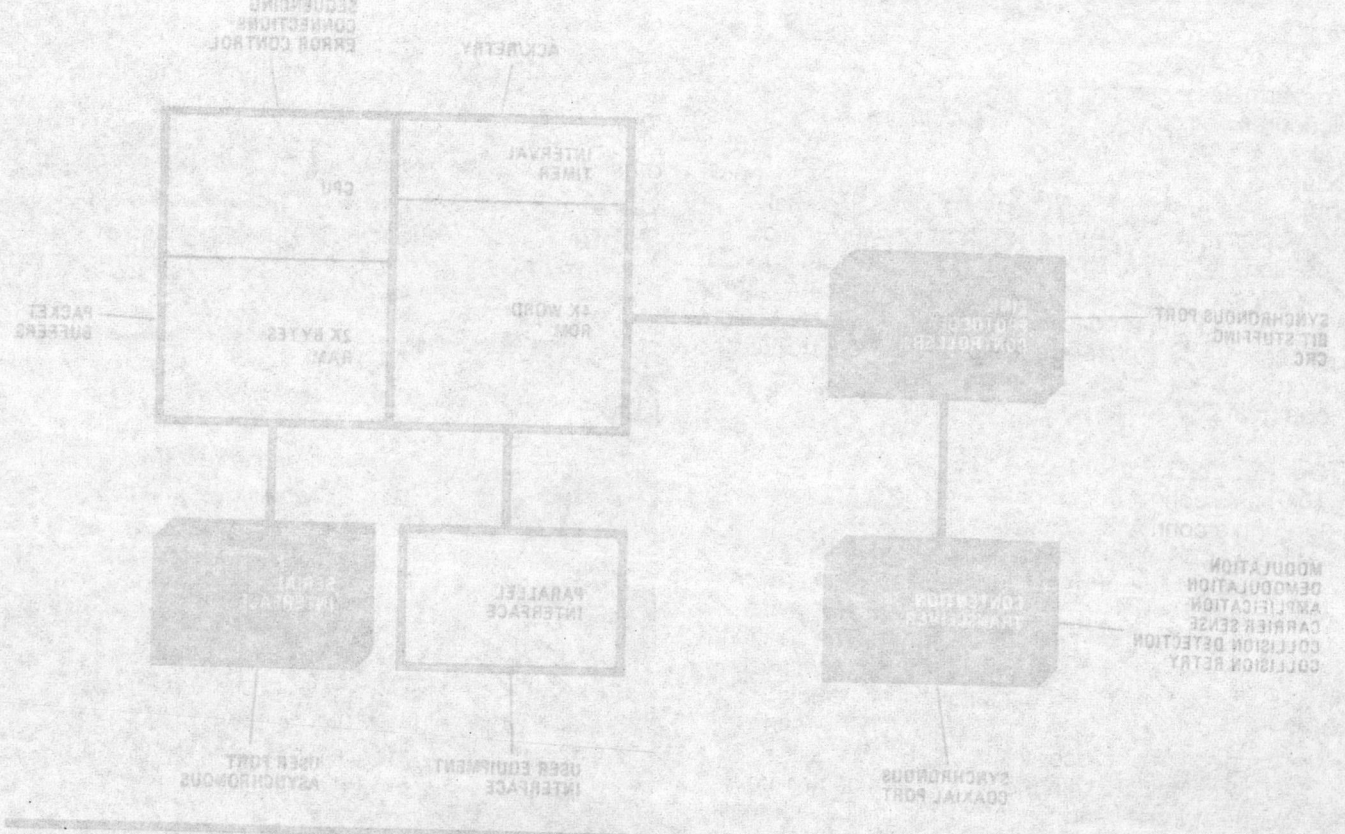

5 Functional layering

Organization. *Six levels are defined in LNA, each with a unique role. The contention-control level, for instance, is responsible for the network's port-to-port message traffic.*

LNA FUNCTIONAL LEVELS

APPLICATION PROGRAMS
- USER PROCESS (USER FUNCTIONS)
- SYSTEM PROCESS (SYSTEM FUNCTIONS)
  - FILE CONTROL
  - DEVICE SERVICES
- LOGICAL LINK PROTOCOL

COM PROCESS
- DATA PROCESS
- ROUTING PATH
- CONTROL
  - CONNECTION CONTROL
  - PACKET PROTOCOL
  - PHYSICAL LINK PROTOCOL

nevertheless, certain standard process-exchange procedures and formats are included in the network. These allow the user process to retrieve, store, and append data files, as well as to run certain utility software packages. The procedures also permit the user to make the necessary process-to-process connections and disconnections in a logical manner.

One example of a system process used to allocate and de-allocate processes and files is the LOG. The LOG process also controls access to the network addresses by users, thus controlling network security. The LOG command language is shown in Table 1.

Connection control

The basic connection of processes is established through a connection control function called COM. COM defines a port which is a unique network address and controls port-to-port message transfers. Associated with each port is at least one unique job. Ports are dynamically allocated and de-allocated. The COM function performs message-to-packet parsing, packet sequencing, buffering, and selection, positive acknowledgment, cyclic redundancy checking (CRC), and initial connection of processes.

To communicate with the connection control COM, a unique string is used to identify the logical link messages. The commands, which start with $COM ($ de-

notes a control character), are followed by a parameter list. These parameters are used to specify the initial connections, find the error conditions, test the operations, and impart special personality characteristics. The personality for buffer transmission is described by three statements which characterize how messages should be fragmented. These commands define the maximum packet length (LENG), maximum time before sending data (TIME), and a packet delimiter (DLMT).

Logging in

A user enters the network by logging in with his source network name (LOGI). Connections are established by assigning the destination network name (ASGN). The source and destination names are network addresses consisting of three bytes: the port identification (ID), the segment number (used to identify a specific local network when two or more local networks are connected through a gateway), and the user identification. For destinations on other segments, an entire route may be entered. The route is called the pathname and consists of gateway port identifiers, followed by the final destination name.

Three characters are reserved for network addresses:

* = the port name of the LOG process
? = don't care name of a port, process, or segment.
! = unassigned name of a port, process, or segment.

These characters are used to match the destination name of a packet with the name of a user. Either the unique name or a don't-care name must exist for the packet to be accepted. The assigned name is used in establishing a packet's destination. The assigned name can be changed by incoming packets to permit remote control of connections.

This logical-link protocol allows the user to define the data flow, routing, and path control to the COM process. The packet carries data from one port to another. Its length is variable from zero to 128 characters;

Table 1 The LOG process language

COMMAND	TASK
QU MARY LOCATION	FIND THE NETWORK ADDRESS OF THE GENERIC NAME PROCESS, IF IT EXISTS
QU MARY ENTER	ENTER INTO THE CATALOG THE GENERIC NAME PROCESS WITH ITS NETWORK ADDRESS
QU MARY EXIT	REMOVE FROM THE CATALOG THE NETWORK ADDRESS OF THE GENERIC NAME
QU MARY ATT FRED	ATTACH THE NAMED PROCESS TO THE REQUESTING GENERIC PROCESS
QU MARY DET FRED	DETACH THE GENERIC NAME PROCESS FROM THE REQUESTING PROCESS
QU MARY COST	PROVIDE THE NETWORK RESOURCE COST OF THE GENERIC NAME PROCESS

6 Laboratory automation

Distributed. *One application of Ford's LNA-based network is engine dynamometer testing. A microprocessor on the stand collects engine performance data and communicates the information to the network's datalogger and file computer. If the file computer fails, the datalogger will continue to acquire and store data on the test.*

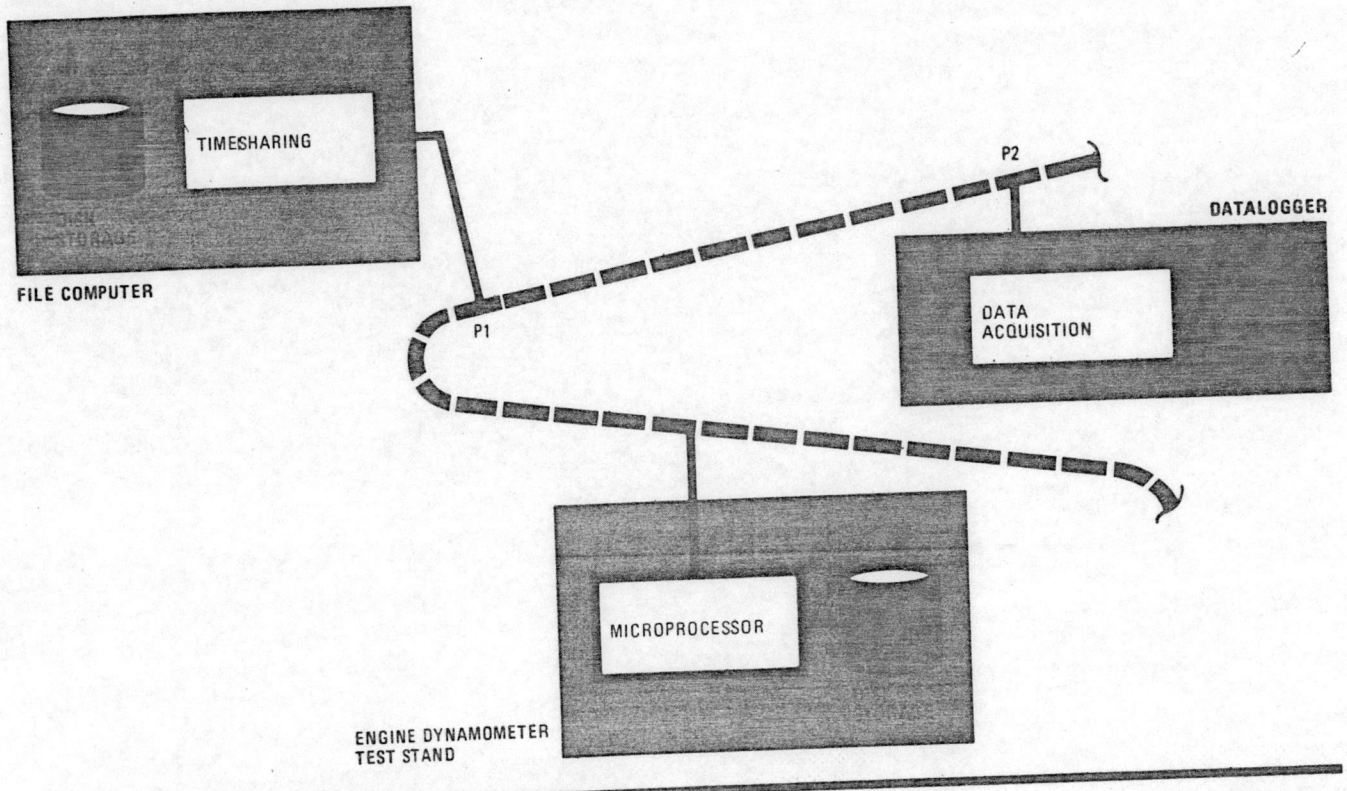

the packet format contains a link-protocol flag, a packet header, a data body, a CRC link-protocol check field, and a flag. The packet header is composed of the destination address, source address, and control field. The destination and source address fields are free-formatted, allowing gateway port names to be appended and deleted from the pathname.

Identification plan

The port name identifies individual adapters. The segment name is used for packet routing between local networks as it is in the link protocol. The user name identifies a specific process within a multiprocessing resource.

The physical link carries both the data and link control characters and must distinguish between them. Polynomial error encoding and decoding, synchronization, and information encoding for data transparency are all handled by the physical link protocol. These functions are performed by employing the CRC/CCITT error polynomial, the SDLC (IBM's synchronous data link control) flag for synchronization and bit-stuffing for data transparency.

Consider as an example LNA, the network shown in Figure 6. The engine dynamometer test stand uses a microcomputer to interact with an operator, to acquire data and to store data into a file. When a file-system

fault occurs, the datalogger can continue as usual without altering its acquisition procedures. The backup computer can store the data into its file and restore the primary file when the fault is cleared. A normal connection is made as shown in Table 2.

The datalogger enters the network with the network address, $p2S1U1$, where $p2$ is the eight-bit port name, $U1$ is the eight-bit user process name, and $S1$ is segment 1, (local network 1). The datalogger assigns the destination address for the data as $p1S1U1$. The file computer enters with its network address, $p1S1?$.

When data is sent, the packet is received by the file computer since $U1$ matches the don't care field, $?$, which is then converted to the $U1$ field. The COM sends an acknowledgment, using only port names since the segment is known. On completion of the data transfer a # is sent as an acknowledgment to the datalogger. The file computer unassigns itself by entering $p1S1?$ which allows other users to access the file system.

Automatic fault detection

An example of the logical link messages used in automatic fault detection and recovery is given in Table 3. The datalogger operates as in the earlier case; however, assume a communications fault is sensed by the backup computer. The backup computer immediately

renames itself and takes on the role of the original file computer. End-to-end acknowledgements protect against lost packets during logical switching.

As an example of using the LOG process, consider the datalogger which doesn't know its network address, as shown in Table 4. The datalogger asks the LOG process for a network address by using its generic name Mary.

Mary's name is found to be p1S1U2 and the information returned to the datalogger. Next the location of John is requested and the reply received. An assignment to John's network address is made. This example shows the capabilities of acquiring network addresses from the LOG process.

Wide area LNA

When LNA networks are connected through gateways a wide area LNA results. The LNA's protocol is designed to accommodate interconnection of local networks. The gateway corresponds to two segments connected by a link such as a leased line. This approach can be particularly attractive when the link is a satellite which forms the backbone of the wide area LNA.

The major distinction between local networks, wide area local networks and global networks is the level or routing complexity. In local networks there is no routing, since all users have access to the packet destination name. In wide area local networks, simple routing is done by gateways. In a global network, front-end processors contain routing tables, protocol translation, and program buffer allocation and communicate with neighboring front-end processors for routing table updates.

Gateway functions between local networks include path building, address filtering, and fault control. Path building is the modification of the packet header during transmission of packets across a gateway. The gateway name in the destination field is deleted and the

Table 2   Normal process connection

DATALOGGER	COM PROCESSES	FILE SYSTEM
LOGI=p2S1U1		LOGI=p1S1?
ASGN=p1S1U1		
	p1S1U1;p2s1U1;0W;DATA →	
	← – p2;p1;0A;	
DATA	p1S1U1;p2S1U1;1W;DATA –→	DATA
	← – p2;p1;1A;	
	•	
SENT	•	RECEIVED
	•	
RECEIVED	← – p1S1U1;p2S1U1;0W;#	# SENT
	p1;p2;0A; – →	
		LOGI=p1S1?

Table 3   Fault recovery

DATALOGGER	FILE SYSTEM	BACKUP
LOGI=p2S1U1	LOGI=p1S1U1	
ASGN=p1S1U1		
DATA	DATA	
SENT →	RECEIVED	
	"CRASH"	
	– – →	"CRASH SENSED"
		LOGI=p1S1?
		DATA
DATA		RECEIVED
SENT	– – →	
	"BACK ON-LINE"	
	LOGI=!S1!	
	ASGN=p1S1!	LOGI=p1S1?
	FILE SYSTEM UP – – →	DATA
		RECEIVED
		← – – BACKUP OFF-LINE
		LOGI=!S1!
	LOGI=p1S1?	
DATA	DATA	
SENT →	RECEIVED	

gateway name on the opposite segment is appended to the beginning of the source field. The gateway name is simply the port address, since this name is unique on each segment.

Address filtering is the process of recognizing a message that is to be transmitted across a gateway. This can be done for two types of packets.

The first has a pathname which is the complete route of the packet containing all gateway port addresses. The second type has only the three destination names: port, segment, and user process name. Notice that gateways have no knowledge of the network topology.

Fault control is provided both by error detection through time-outs on positive acknowledgments, and by error correction through gateway broadcasts for alternate routes. Unlike global networks, alternate routes are found by exploiting the broadcast nature of the contention medium, not by using routing tables.

Gateway routing

To illustrate the gateway strategy, consider a message sent from process U1 to process U2 in Figure 7. The destination name is a pathname which is received by the gateway, G1, as:

p2p1S2U2;p1S1U1;0W;data

which is acknowledged by the gateway as:

p1;p2;0A;

The gateway performs path building by removing

Table 4 The LOG process

DATALOGGER	COM PROCESSES	LOG PROCESS
LOG!=!S1U2		LOG!="S1!
ASGN="S1!		
OU MARY ATT →	*S1!;!S1U2;0W;data	
	← ─ !;*;0A;	
		LOG!="S1U1
		ASGN=!S1U2
	← ─ ─ p1S1U2;*!U1;1W;data	MARY LOCATION p1S1U2
	*;p1;1A; ─ ─ →	
LOG!=p1S1U2		
OU JOHN		
LOCATION ─ ─ →	*S1U1;p1S1U2;2W;data	
	← ─ ─ p1;*;2A;	
	← ─ ─ p1S1U2;*!U1;3W;data	JOHN LOCATION p2S1U1
	*;p1;3A; ─ ─ →	
ASGN=p2S1U1		

G1's name (p2 on segment S2) from the destination and appending the return pathname, p3, onto the source name field. Thus:

p1S2U2;p3p1S1U1;0W;data

This packet is acknowledged by the com of user U2 as:

p3;p1;0A;

If the same transaction between U1 and U2 occurs without U1's knowing the pathname, then the message destination need only contain the network address. U1 sends the following message as seen by the gateway:

p1S2U2;p1S1U1;0W;data

which is acknowledged as:

p1;p2;0A

and retransmitted by the gateway, since S2 does not match the present segment, as:

p1S2U2;p3p1S1U1;0W; data

The message is received by U2 and acknowledged as:

p3;p1;0A

Now U2 has the entire route to U1 which is used to send from U1 to U2:

p3p1S1U1;p1S2U2;0W;data

Upon receiving the message at U1 the entire pathname is acquired:

p1S1U1;p2p1S2U2;0W;data

The address filtering, illustrated above, takes advantage of the medium when multiple gateways are on the same segment. Redundant paths from one user to another allow multiple packets to be received with a decision strategy to select the route.

One decision strategy is to select the route of the first packet received. Additional copies of the same packet are rejected, since the sequence number is the same. All packets with sequence numbers less than or equal to the current number are acknowledged. When a gateway does not receive an acknowledgment from another gateway along a route, the gateway can remove the pathname up to the final destination, and use the address filtering technique described above. A level count can be used to control the depth of search in the network. File control protects against lost packets. ∎

References

1. N. Abramson, *The Aloha System- Another Alternative for Computer Communications*, R75-170, IEE Computer Society, Long Beach, Calif., 1975.
2. L. G. Roberts, *Extensions of Packet Communication Technology to a Hand-Held Personal Terminal*, AFIPS Conf. Proceedings, 1972 Spring Joint Computer Conference 40, 295-298.
3. Network Systems Corp., *Systems Description: Series A Network Adapters*, Pub. No. A01-000-00, Brooklyn Center, Minn., 1976.
4. R.M. Metcalfe and D.R. Boggs, *Ethernet: Distributed Packet Switching for Local Computer Networks*, Comm. of the ACM, July 1976, Vol. 19, No. 7, pp. 395-404.
5. L. Kleinrock, *Queuing Systems, Vol II: Computer Applications*, John Wiley and Sons, 1976.

7 Gateway

Interconnect. Gateways allow two or more local networks to communicate. Here, Fred uses the gateway to establish a datapath for a message transaction with Mary.

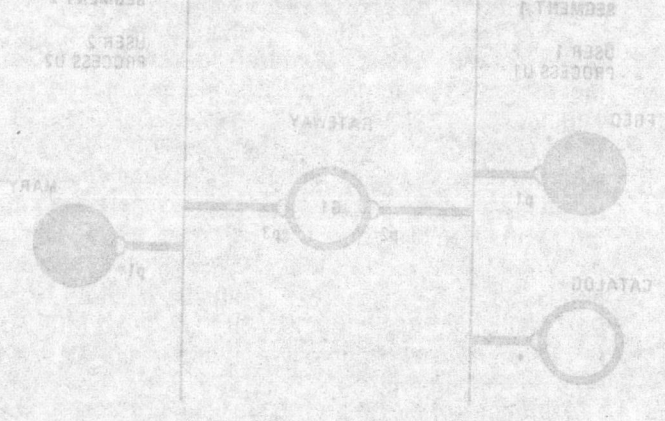

Local networking: The missing link emerges

Ken Hardwick and William Federbusch,
Network Systems Corporation, Minneapolis, Minn.

Within a decade, the local network has evolved from a simple channel coupler between two processors into a multinodal, high-speed bus that requires no centralized control.

Few areas in the data communications world have seen as much recent technological innovation and new commercial offerings. Local network development has primarily responded to users' demands for greater transmission speed and capacity. Although common carrier communications is adequate for most remote-job-entry (RJE) terminals, interactive terminals, and clustered terminal controllers, independently programmable computers need to exchange data at channel, not common carrier, speeds.

Local networks are also meeting users' requirements for enhanced responsiveness. In the process-control environment, for example, a manufacturing operation could fail if exceptional conditions are not relayed to another minicomputer within milliseconds. In addition, since the costs of individual computer systems have plunged dramatically in recent years, users have begun to add computers at central sites to provide redundancy and extra processing power.

More and more users are implementing minis as the feasibility of a dedicated computer is realized. Yet, although the cost of these computers is decreasing, the price of high-performance peripherals such as impact printers and high-capacity disk drives remains relatively high. Also, as the cost and complexity of maintaining databases continues to grow, the need for high-speed local network links to allow these many small, fast computers to access and share the valuable peripheral resources becomes obvious.

In an elementary form, local networks have been around for some time. Since the early 1960s, computer manufacturers have provided "channel couplers" between large-scale processors, "channel interfaces" between mainframes and minicomputers, and "parallel interfaces" between minicomputers (Fig. 1). Examples of these are the IBM Channel-to-Channel Adapter that couples the input/output channels of two IBM central processing units (CPUs), Digital Equipment Corporation's (DEC) DX-11 interface that allows a PDP-11 to appear to be a peripheral on an IBM selector or byte multiplexer channel, and the DEC DA-11B interface that allows two PDP-11s to exchange blocks of data at channel speeds of roughly 1.5 Mbit/s.

These types of connections offer two main advantages. The processor's data transfer rate is about as fast as can be expected, and the incremental cost of adding the "network" is small relative to the cost of the processors themselves. There are, however, several inherent disadvantages. First, the distance covered by these local links is small—generally no more than 200 feet, and often less than 100 feet. Also, such a link is designed to have only a certain type of processor at each end. As most manufacturers are reluctant to support digital interfaces that attach to a competitor's processor, there is generally a limited inventory of available channel interfaces.

Another problem is that these links are essentially half-duplex—only one end of the link can be in control

1. Local communications. *In its simplest and oldest form, local networking consisted of a single point-to-point channel connection between two colocated processors*

[CPU] —DATA CHANNEL— [CHANNEL COUPLER] —DATA CHANNEL— [CPU]

at any instant. The parallel digital medium precludes both ends from transmitting at the same time, and, therefore, software must be designed to arbitrate which processor controls the link. Also, this kind of link is only point-to-point. If another processor is added to this configuration, a separate channel interface must be attached to every processor that the new computer will access. To have all computers "talk" to one another requires an unfeasible number of channel interfaces.

Although the point-to-point local connection is simple compared to the complex networks now available, it helps illustrate some fundamental differences between high-speed local networking and remote communications networking. One of the most common applications of IBM's Channel-to-Channel (CTC) Adapter is its use with the JES3 job-entry subsystem (Fig. 2).

This type of small local network is unworkable without a link with the speed of the CTC adapter. A remote communications link between the CPUs could typically not handle a large CPU's batched job traffic.

A noteworthy factor is that this local network calls for the specialization of the network processors. One CPU, the global processor, is responsible for all the mechanics of batch processing. Another CPU, the local processor, actually executes the batched jobs that are passed to it by the global CPU. The effect is that the facility's total power is greater than if the two processors were running independently. Each processor can use the resources (RJE terminals, databases) attached to the other computer, which is a real benefit of local networking: it provides a facility of many computers that effectively behave like a single computer "system" to the end user.

Because of the point-to-point properties of these interprocessor links, the "star" network topology has become the most prevalent. In a star network, all nodes attach to a central machine (Fig. 3.). Data received by the central computer is either processed internally or forwarded to another node for processing. One primary advantage of such a network is that it can be easily mixed with remote communications links. Since most remote lines funnel into a central CPU, data can be easily forwarded to a node that resides at the end of a common carrier line. Where distance permits, a sufficiently active network node may have its remote communications link replaced with a channel interface and a high-speed line driver that can cover limited distances at rates of 50 kbit/s, 230 kbit/s, and in some cases up to 1 Mbit/s.

The star network, though, has many significant problems. For example, all compatibility headaches are placed into the central computer. Sophisticated software that can receive and send data on a variety of communications and channel interfaces must be written for the central computer. And the addition of a new type of interface frequently requires software changes that affect the network's stability. Also, the process of relaying data messages at channel speeds can significantly affect performance of the central computer.

The major problem, however, is that the entire network stops whenever the central computer goes down. In other communications networks, machine failure can frequently be circumvented if the front-end processors can switch communications to another computer, or if users can switch communications lines to a different front-end processor. For star configurations, however, this switching becomes progressively difficult because more and more local attachments are typically made to the central computer. A final problem is that the expandability of this network is restricted—most central processors accommodate only a limited number of channel interfaces.

Users can make the star network sufficiently reliable by having the central computer simply relay data between computers, or by making this central node a simple, preprogrammed device that performs only specific functions of communications, routing, and so on.

One typical example is the "shared-disk" configuration, a method of sharing access to a set of disk drives between two or more computers (Fig. 4). Note that a disk shared between computers provides many attributes of a local network in that:
- Data moves to and from the central node at data channel speeds.
- Data placed in the central node (the disk) can be retrieved by any other node.
- Attached computers can be effectively located up to several hundred feet apart.

---

2. Specialized processing. *Local communications permits the specialization of processors. This IBM configuration includes back-end and front-end processing.*

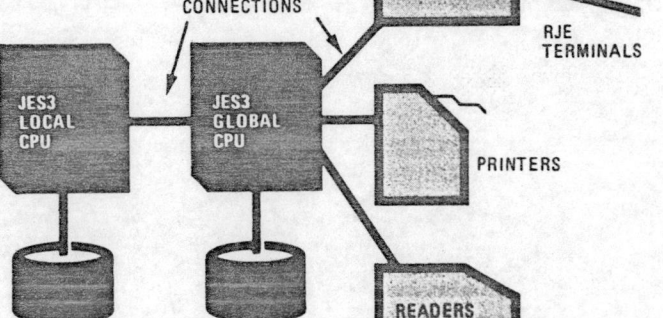

Many current large-scale processors, such as the Honeywell Level 66 and Univac 1100 series, are designed to incorporate the star topology local network. Both manufacturers wanted to provide a computer system to which users could add large-scale instruction processors and I/O processors at will to configure a system with the desired power (Fig. 5). All instruction and I/O processors in the Honeywell configuration attach to an eight-port system control unit (SCU) that controls access to the memory and to the other processors. The SCU also permits each processor to signal (via interrupts) any other processor at microsecond speeds that it should examine the common memory. Preset parameters in memory determine the desired action to be performed and designate, for example, which batched jobs are dispatchable at that instant.

Separate entities

A significant step in the development of local networking was the network's becoming a facility separate from the discrete computers attached to it, rather than just a series of links connecting individual computers. The initial design objectives (which remain critical even today) were threefold.

1. The local network connections should allow data to move directly from one node to another without intervention by intermediate host processors. This essentially establishes local network communications on a peer-to-peer basis, where no single CPU is responsible for all communications.

2. Data enters the network in a standard format. This means that adding a new type of processor to the local network requires a hardware and software interface between the new host and the local network. With this interface, the new processor should be able to communicate with any network node.

3. Since both efficient throughput and high responsiveness are goals of the local network, it must be able to allocate data-transmission capacity on a demand—

rather than on a partitioned—basis. Traffic between any two nodes on a local network tends to be "bursty," in the same sense that data traffic volume between a CPU and a disk drive varies greatly over a period of time. At the same time, the network must ensure that a single node with high traffic requirements does not lock out other network nodes.

Enter the ring

Incorporating these separate design objectives gave birth to the "ring networks." Probably the most publicized was built at the University of Cambridge in England, beginning in 1974. The ring itself (Fig. 6) consisted of a set of "repeaters" connected in a loop by a pair of twisted-pair wires. The loop continuously circulated a pair of "packets" at a raw bit rate of 10 Mbits/s. Each packet contained 2 bytes of information plus routing and control information, which was constantly examined by each repeater.

If a node on the ring wanted to transmit, it waited until it detected a passing packet that was empty. It then forwarded the packet while inserting its own routing information and data. The packet then made a complete circuit on the ring and returned to the originator, where it would have been marked as copied, or rejected, by the receiving node. The original sender then marked the packet as empty and forwarded it on the ring so that another node could use it.

The repeaters were not powered by the processor nodes but by d.c. voltage injected at several points onto the network. This minimized the possibility of a repeater failure. A station unit informed the repeater when data was to be sent and received, and provided the data, in parallel digital form, to the "access box," which interfaced to the host computer.

The ring architecture realizes most goals of the local network. Data can proceed more or less directly to the intended destination at about 3 or 4 Mbits/s, which is adequate for most applications. Users found that they

---

3. Star topology. Until recently, point-to-point channel connections, radiating in a star from a central CPU, were the only local network configurations. Besides locally attached processors, typically from the same computer vendor, a front-end communications processor was required for any extensive remote communications.

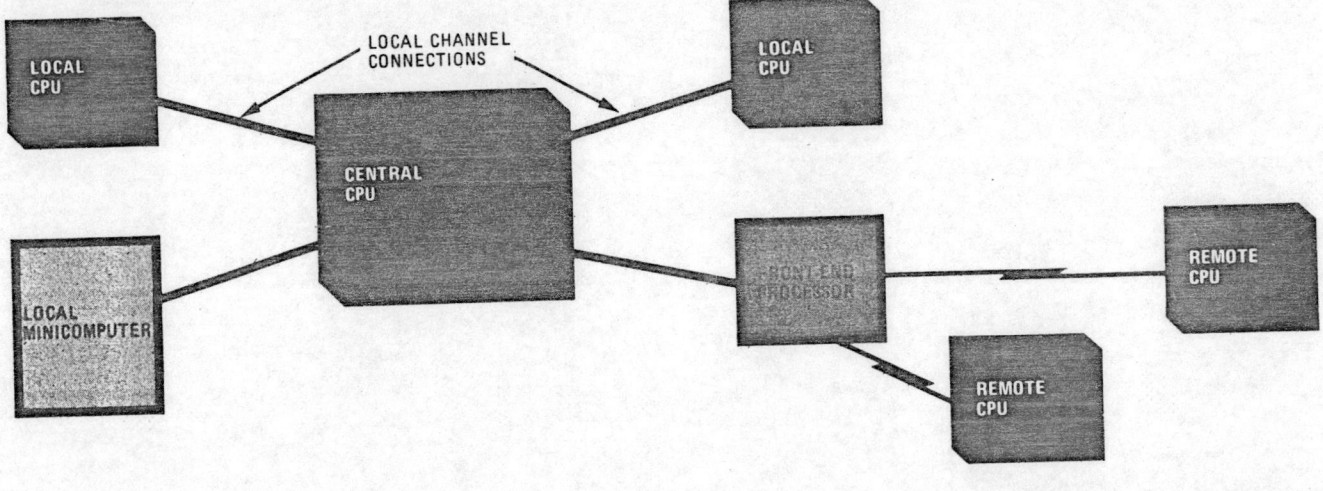

13

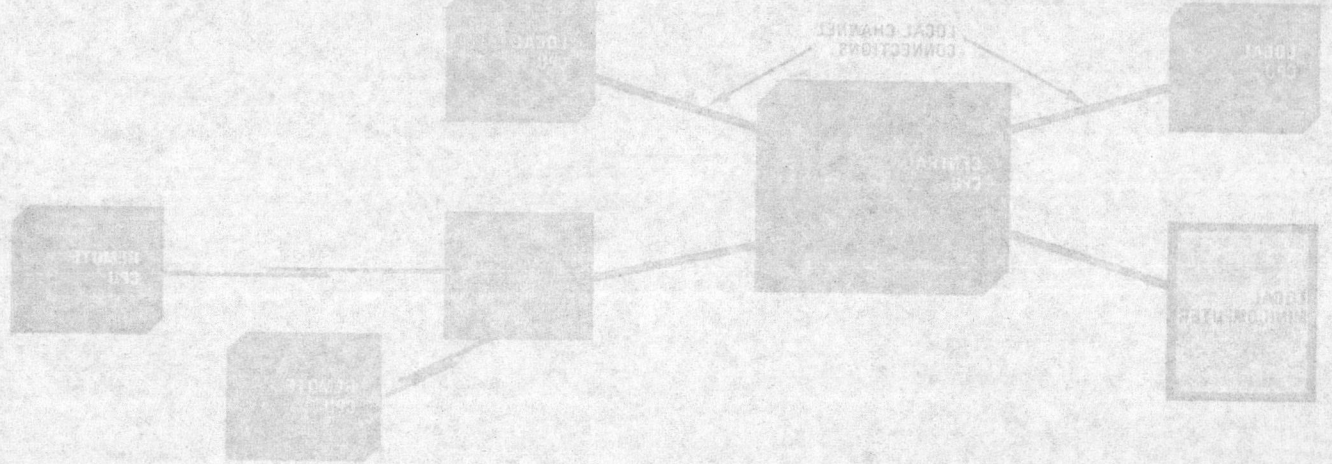

4. Shared disk. Besides specialization, local communications facilitates resource sharing, wherein several CPUs, performing similar tasks, share common peripherals.

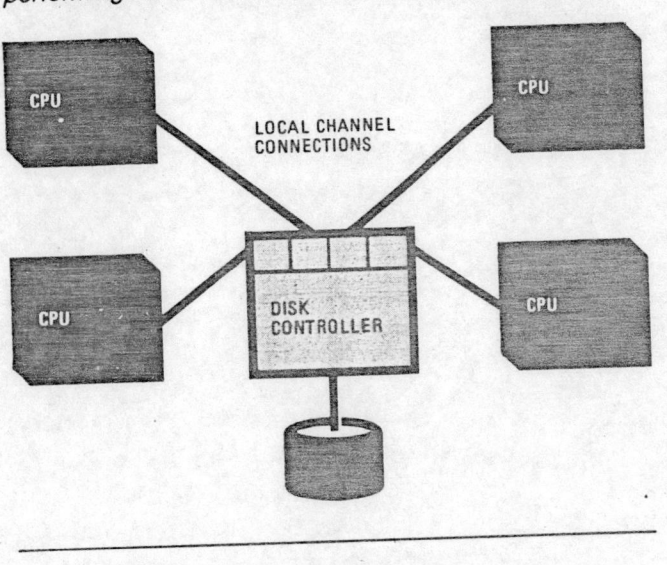

or circumvent their failures. Various refinements have since been added to the Cambridge ring to detect the point of failure. Other network designs have attempted to centralize the ring so that all repairs can be performed from a single location.

The bus connection

A different type of local network is achieving commercial acceptance today. Network nodes, connected by a linear "bus," can broadcast data directly to the destination. All other nodes simply ignore the broadcast data and await their turns to broadcast. A principal advantage of the bus architecture is that all nodes on the bus are "passive"; that is, if one node fails, it will simply fail to send or receive its signals—all other activity remains uninterrupted.

Local bus networks can be divided into two classes: "digital" (or parallel) and "serial." The digital bus (Fig. 7) is an evolutionary extension of the modularity found in modern computer design. Each computer on a digital bus network has an interface that drives an external data bus. The computer node can request the use of the bus and place a word of data on it, along with its destination address. Interfaces generally allow each attached computer to send or receive a block of data to or from any other computer on the bus.

Two commercially available digital buses are Tandem Computers' Dynabus, a high-speed link between separate Tandem computers in the same physical cabinet, and Digital Equipment Corporation's PDP-11 local network offering, PCL-11, which can interconnect up to 32 PDP-11 computers.

The Dynabus, for example, allows one computer to check its work in progress and send current status

achieved higher network performance by improving the communications link between the repeaters—typically by replacing the twisted pairs with coaxial cable. Depending on the adaptability of the access box, adding a new processor to the network interrupts network service only briefly.

The major disadvantage of the ring network is that a failure of any single repeater or communications link will cause the entire network to fail. Furthermore, these repeaters and links are often geographically distributed, so it is not always possible to immediately repair

5. Superstar. This configuration, representative of the Honeywell Level 66 multiprocessor system, exploits the local star network. Instead of a central CPU, a System Control Unit (SCU) handles local "routing" between CPUs and I/O controllers. Such a local network facilitates redundancy should any single CPU or I/O controller fail.

Information to another computer at 100 Mbit/s. Up to four Tandem computers can be attached in this way.

With the PCL-11, a master unit dynamically allocates transmission time so that several computers' transmissions can be time-division multiplexed simultaneously. If the master node fails, another "dormant" master, in a different computer, automatically assumes control.

Microprocessor and integrated circuit manufacturers are realizing that sophisticated control systems can be similarly structured. Each microprocessor is a module that performs a specialized part of the overall control application. Newer microprocessor architectures essentially establish "local buses" that control the memory and peripherals of a single microprocessor and a "global bus" that allows these separate microprocessors to share global memory, send status information directly to one another, and add new microprocessors as needed for expansion.

All-digital bus networks essentially allow independently operating computer systems to share resources efficiently. They make it easy for users to expand the system to the maximum allowable number of nodes on the bus and are also very responsive—processors can exchange crucial data in microseconds. However, they have two significant disadvantages. First, digital buses limit the network link to the maximum distance that these digital signals can travel, generally no more than 100 feet. Second, although they are relatively easy to implement when all nodes on the network are the same type, if the kinds of processors vary widely, interfacing is more difficult.

The network story serializes

Although the digital (or parallel) bus architecture has many attractive aspects, its extremely limited distance makes it generally unsuitable for a local network that is intended to connect most existing, in-place computers. The most successful technique to date for extending the bus distance is to use a single strand of coaxial cable instead of a set of digital signal lines (or "ribbon" cable). When the network is idle, no signal is present on the coaxial cable, and when a node on the local network chooses to transmit, it transmits a stream of data in bit-serial mode (Fig. 8). The data is broadcast throughout the length of the cable. The destination adapter analyzes the data, recognizes its address, and forwards it to the attached host. All other nodes on the serial bus ignore the data. Like those on the digital bus, all nodes are passive—they need not be operational for the network to function.

Coaxial cable as the transmission medium allows much higher bit transmission rates than do twisted pairs or other transmission lines. Data can travel at speeds of 50 Mbit/s for a distance of 1 mile over some networks. Since it takes a relatively long time for a signal to propagate down the cable, it is generally best to send a rather large data block, or packet, between two nodes on the serial bus before control is relinquished to another set of nodes.

A significant problem, however, is determining which node is entitled, at any given time, to broadcast on the serial bus. Most current serial bus systems resolve con-

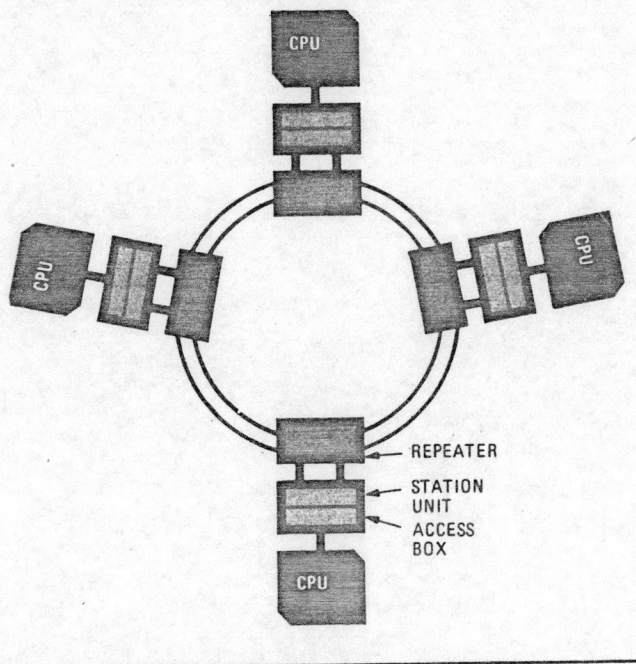

6. The Cambridge "Ring." The ring—a passive topology requiring no central control unit —has evolved from this model, developed in Cambridge, England.

tention through a technique called CSMA (Carrier Sense Multiple Access). If the bus is idle, any node can transmit as soon as it is ready. If a node becomes ready to transmit when another node is active, it detects the signal passing on the coaxial cable (carrier sense) and refrains from transmitting until the current transmission is complete.

An occasional "collision" between transmitting nodes is inevitable. This occurs when two nodes begin transmission at essentially the same time, and each is initially blind to the other's signals. Various serial-bus implementations use different means of detecting a collision and determining the order of retransmission. Most call for a predefined or random timeout before retransmission is again attempted.

Xerox entry

Only recently have commercial local networking products become available for general public use. One such offering from Xerox, Ethernet, facilitates communications between local office-types of processors.

Ethernet was developed for internal use at the Xerox Palo Alto Research Laboratories in 1976 to link a set of single-user minicomputers that were scattered throughout the research center. Ethernet provided a means for these minis (and their associated researchers) to exchange programs, data, and access specialized peripherals rapidly and dynamically.

The Ethernet serial-bus local network consists of a single coaxial cable that is multidropped at each of up to 32 processors. Each processor has a network interface module that buffers and formats messages, and can broadcast data on the cable in bursts at megabit-per-second rates. The data is in fixed-length pack-

The network story continues

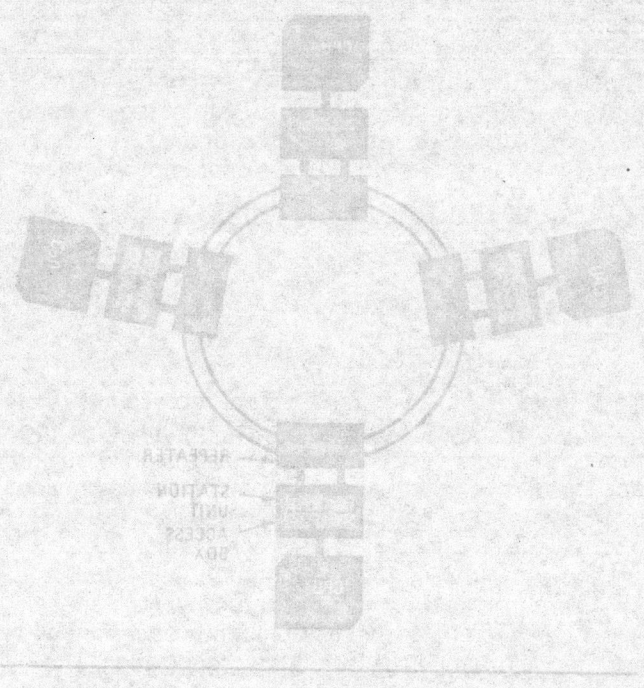

7. Parallel bus. *Several vendors today support local communications between like processors over a digital, or parallel, bus. It is severely limited in distance.*

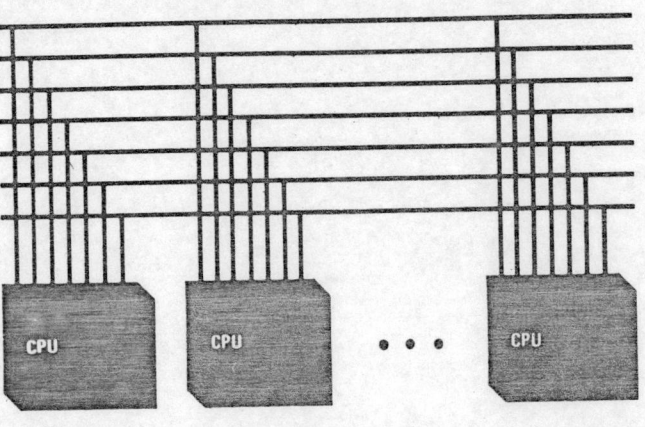

ets that contain address information in the header. The packet size is currently about 256 bytes.

Ethernet handles contention through the use of a "listen-while-talk" feature. Whenever a node is broadcasting, it also monitors the signal for interference from another node. If two nodes pick the same time to transmit, then both will detect the other's interference and cease transmission. Each node delays for a random time interval and retransmits if the other node's transmission is not detected first.

Ethernet is commercially available as part of the Xerox 860 word processing system. When a network of Xerox 860s is connected with Ethernet, any word processor can be accessed by any word processing terminal in the same area. Xerox is presently developing Ethernet interfaces to other computers and recently announced joint development plans with Intel Corporation and DEC.

Networking different hosts
User demand for a local network that interconnects processors from several vendors has increased significantly in recent years. One of the few commercial offerings that supports this is Hyperchannel, developed by Network Systems Corporation in 1976. Like Ethernet, it is a serial-bus architecture, but with different design goals. It was designed to handle the data-movement needs of large-scale mainframes and large minicomputers and to support communications at high computer-data-channel rates.

The Hyperchannel bus is a single strand of coaxial cable, up to a mile long, that can be multidropped at up to 64 different locations. Each computer site has a "network adapter" that interfaces the cable and functions as a high-speed controller on the computer's data channel. An adapter can broadcast on the cable in "frames" that vary in size from 12 to about 4.1K bytes.

The Hyperchannel contention scheme allows a large number of contending adapters (and computers) to automatically rank their transmission sequence in about the time needed to propagate a signal down the cable. If two nodes broadcast at the same time, a collision occurs, but both continue transmitting the entire contents of their frames (which requires only milliseconds, even for a 4-kbyte frame). However, each destination network adapter must return a "response frame" the instant it successfully receives a frame. Therefore, the collision results in an erroneous frame that the destination node ignores. Both of the contending transmitters detect the absence of the response frame in the time needed for the signal to propagate from one end of the coaxial cable to the other, and that adapter predetermined to have the highest priority transmits again. The other adapter may resume transmission after the transmit and response frames have been successfully sent.

Advantages and applications
Both Hyperchannel and Ethernet are representative of passive, serial local networks—a communications tool that users are discovering offers many advantages and applications. The high-speed communications provides users with new networking approaches, such as specializing the functions of various computers.

Say an organization has four computers, not all of which are from the same manufacturer. One of these has a database that must be constantly accessed and updated by many branches of the organization. The classic configuration would require that all batched jobs affecting or using the database be run on the database machine. Furthermore, all on-line inquiry and updating of the database would run on a teleprocessing module installed on the database machine. This one machine would soon become enormous just to handle all computing functions (communications, queuing, and so on) not directly related to accessing the database.

An alternative would be to have copies of the database in several different machines. This would present severe database-management problems because the capability for correctly updating all copies of the database is not yet commercially available.

Local networking could solve this problem by placing in another machine a module dedicated to receiving requests for database service over the local network. This software would handle the data requests, access the database machine more efficiently, and return the results over the local network. Applications such as on-line inquiry could access the database through the local network in the same time they could access the database resident in the on-line computer. Batch programs can perform massive database updates over the local network because network transmission is frequently as fast as local peripherals. Not only can the database machine be much smaller because of its reduced computing requirements, but database management is still centralized in a single computer.

Another example of computer specialization is the on-line machine designed to service all on-line activity destined for the database machine. This machine, because of its dedicated function, can efficiently handle a large number of remote terminals. In addition, since the local network can, in some cases, handle the me-

16

chanics of moving data between different computer types, the user can employ different manufacturers' machines for these various functions.

Masstor Systems Corporation in Sunnyvale, Calif., has commercially implemented this concept of "back-end" file processing. It markets an IBM-compatible mainframe with specialized file- and database-management software that runs under the IBM MVS (Multiple Virtual Storage) operating system. The Masstor processor uses a serial local network to connect processors at a user's site. Masstor software permits IBM and Univac users to access this global database and file system while retaining many of the standard programming languages and utilities (support programs, such as diagnostics) in the user's existing CPUs.

Other organizations are also using computers as sophisticated front-end processors to other machines. For example, Boeing Computer Services, a large commercial service bureau, provides an enhanced Control Data Corporation (CDC) Cyber processing facility to its users through a local network. A pair of IBM 3031 computers run the JES3 RJE system, which administers a network of 200 to 300 RJE terminals and performs all input and output operations. The 3031s are attached to a complex of six CDC Cyber 175s. When a Cyber computer is available, the 3031 sends it a queued CDC job, which is then run to completion. The resultant output is sent back to the 3031, where it is queued for printing and punching on the appropriate RJE terminal.

The division of functions is very clean—all network administration can be handled by the IBM computer. The CDC systems do not get involved in remote I/O and spooling. CDC programming efforts can be concentrated on the performance and function relating to execution of batched jobs. If a new batch processing computer (such as the Cray-1 planned for delivery this summer) arrives, it can take advantage of the RJE network as soon as the batch processing software in the new computer is ready. As enhancements to JES3 such as SNA protocols and NJE (network job entry) become available, they will be automatically extended to the CDC computer users.

The local network permits a type of distributed computing different from the industry standard. Rather than channeling menial computing chores away from a central processing unit (CPU), it turns a set of basically autonomous CPUs into "modules" in an integrated "system," which reverses the administrative complexity of distributed systems. Since applications and data can be centrally managed, the user has greater control over the organization's computing facilities.

Developing media
Local networking applications will continue to proliferate, as will the technology employed for local transmission. To date, the primary transmission medium for local networks has been either twisted-pair cable or simple (baseband) coxial cable. However, two new media have recently attracted attention in the high-speed communications field: fiber-optic and CATV (cable television), or broadband, cable.

Lightwave technology will mushroom throughout the 1980s because of these major attractions:
■ Its potential bandwidth is virtually unlimited. Current fiber-optic transceivers can work in the 100-Mbit/s range, and their performance is expected to improve considerably in the next 10 years.
■ Fiber-optic cable is virtually invulnerable to outside interference or "tapping" by unauthorized listeners (at the present time).
■ Fiber-optic cable is much lighter and more compact than coaxial cable of the same bandwidth and, although about equal in price right now, promises to be much cheaper as mass production increases.

Fiber optics will probably become the best medium for point-to-point applications within the next few years. Current manufacturing can produce a 5-mile fiber-optic link that can transfer data at 44.7 Mbit/s. These characteristics will make fiber optics an attractive alternative for high-speed communications for distances between 100 feet and about 10 miles. This range may even be extended as repeating equipment is further developed.

Still problems
However, one problem with fiber optics in a multinode local network is that the fiber-optic link is essentially a point-to-point medium. And as long as fiber optics is restricted to a single source and destination, then either the ring or the star local networking topologies must be used. And as we have seen, both are vulnerable to a single failure.

Researchers in lightwave transmission are working on two ways to enhance the versatility of this medium. The first involves a device called a "star coupler" that allows an incoming signal to be evenly split among a set of outgoing lines. The data flow through the network still basically follows a star pattern, but at least the central point—the site most vulnerable to failure—would be a reliably passive component.

The second, and more promising, line of research involves a "splitter" that allows a node attached to the splitter to divert a fraction of the optical signal for analysis. Currently, no such device has been reliably fabricated, but it is only a matter of time before it can be produced in quantity.

Serial-bus network developers generally agree that the migration from coaxial to new fiber-optic cable will be simple. There are, of course, no changes required to any nodal software because the transmission medium is transparent to the attached processors. Digital-to-fiber-optic interfaces are already generally available, and new products such as fiber-optic multiplexers are emerging regularly.

Broadband, the other developing medium, is attractive because users can multiplex digital, voice, and video signals on a single communications carrier. On a broadband cable used for computer communications, a frequency range of about 150 MHz, (or 150 Mbit/s, if all traffic is data) can be allocated.

Broadband networks are potentially a fine solution to users who need to carry a mixture of low- and medium-speed links (100 kbit/s or less) between their com-

8. Serial transmission. *Coaxial cable carrying digital information is the method used in serial-bus networks, such as Xerox's Ethernet and NSC's Hyperchannel.*

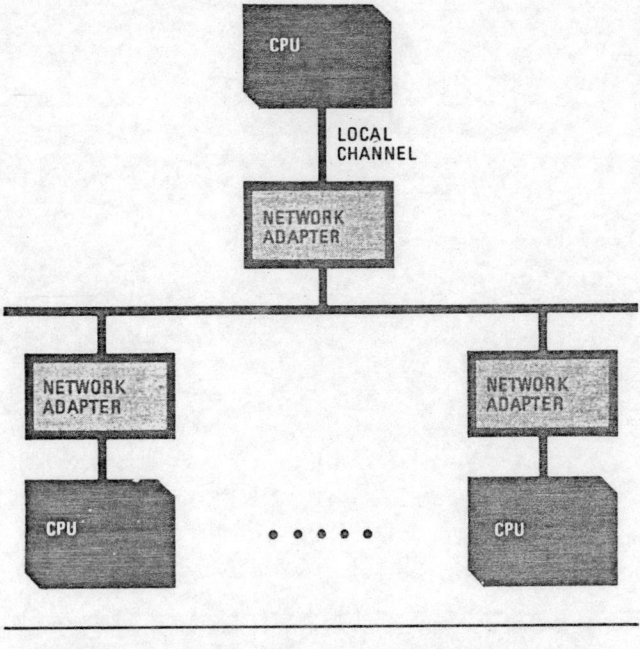

puters and terminals. However, since each communications channel on a broadband network is more or less fixed, the broadband network can accommodate only very few point-to-point links that run at data-channel speeds of, say, 10 Mbit/s or more.

Since there is presently no facility to change broadband network frequencies on demand, these high-speed communications links cannot be shared. Future broadband enhancements will probably add the capability to permit any node on the cable to easily alter its sending/receiving frequency, thereby permitting several users to share fixed-frequency channels.

Broadband cable, like fiber-optic cable, is merely an alternative medium to baseband, or serial, coaxial cable and requires no significant change to the operation or software load of the network nodes. However, broadband employs CATV, not digital, technology, and this means that any interface to the broadband cable requires an RF (radio frequency) modem to perform the digital-to-RF conversion. While these modems vary significantly in price, depending on efficiency, the sheer number required in a local network with many nodes might prohibit the implementation of this medium for some time to come. It might to argued, however, that the RF transmission used for broadband could be the most viable technology for future-office-type networks—where not only digital data but analog voice and video will need to be carried as well.

Regional and global nodes
The next logical step in the functional evolution of local networks is extending their range to include regional and global nodes. Today, there is a trend toward distributing the processing function geographically. And this pertains not only to applications and batch pro-

cessing but also to database management. Since the interdependency of regional databases is becoming more important, high-speed communications service is vital. "Integrated" database-management systems are increasing in sophistication, and, in the not-too-distant future, fully distributed database packages, employing high-speed local and remote communications links, will be commercially available.

To effectively implement high-speed data transmission, there must be an efficient local distribution mechanism that can be extended over high-speed remote links. Traditionally, distribution mechanisms such as front-end processors immediately cause an I/O bottleneck. All data received from remote locations must pass through a front-end processor, then be either stored or processed by one CPU, or distributed via short-haul modems, channel-to-channel links, or an off-line medium (such as tape) for further processing.

The bus architecture scheme lends itself well to this local distribution requirement. Since all major computing entities (such as CPUs and peripheral controllers) can be directly connected to the bus, data entered on the local network is instantly available to the destination node for processing, without switching or storing.

Several extension options that permit high-speed communications service are becoming a reality. The regional alternatives (services addressed to a geographical radius of approximately 30 miles between nodes) that are generally available today are:
■ Common carrier services, which are generally available in the 50-kbit/s range and require implementation of a front-end processor or multiplexer. Depending on the application, they can use switched or dedicated facilities. However, no common carrier service can presently distribute data locally at high speeds within a bus architecture scheme (Fig. 9). These facilities are essentially point-to-point connections between regional nodes, and data distribution within the node is the user's responsibility, typically relegated to a single front end or CPU.
■ Broadband facilities that, in conjunction with an appropriate RF modem, can be extended to interface with high-speed T-1 carrier facilities, or microwave service (see "Broadband technology magnifies local networking capability", DATA COMMUNICATIONS, February 1980, p. 61). Again, these require appropriate broadband modems and front-end processors to access the local computing processors.
■ Baseband coaxial facilities, which provide a high-speed local-distribution mechanism. In local networks such as Hyperchannel, link adapters can provide direct digital connection to either T-1 (1.5-Mbit/s) or T-3 (44.7-Mbit/s) microwave service. The remote link adapter is similar to a local adapter in that it appears to the network as just another node and is transparent to the application. The advantage of this is that the direct digital connect facility between all computing entities interfaces to the local network at each regional site (Fig. 10).

As these high-speed communication facilities proliferate (digital microwave radio units are now available from companies such as Collins Radio and Farinon

18

9. Intersite communications. *Situations requiring inter-processor communications between geographically dispersed sites, each with several processors, are prevalent* *today. An efficient local networking scheme is required to handle interprocessor communications in the same site and to interface to remote carriers and remote sites.*

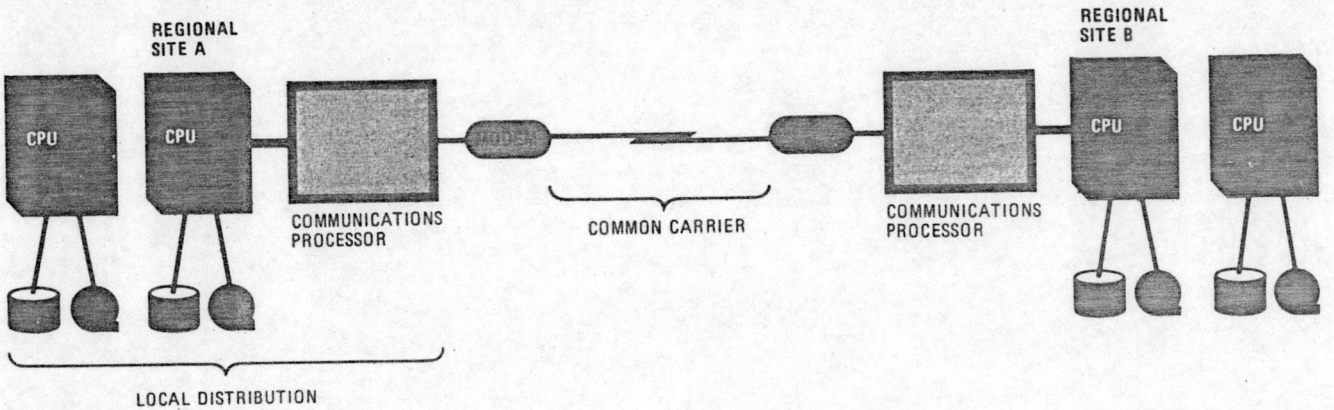

Electric and are being developed by Bell Northern Research), and as function, space, and security problems become more acute, the trend toward "regionalizing" computing centers will no doubt accelerate rapidly.

Global nodes
Not only are users establishing regional nodes, but for the same reasons, many are requiring connection to remote, or global, nodes. Recent attention has focused on a variety of existing or projected communications services, such as SBS, XTEN, AT&T's ACS, GTE Telenet, and Tymnet. Each offers (or proposes to offer) integrated "data, voice, and image" communications. From a broad perspective, the technology exists today to transmit vast amounts of data at very high speeds,

but questions remain as to how to interface to and utilize these services efficiently and economically. Again, we see the applicability of the bus architecture scheme. Since the direction of future communications services is toward employing digital transmission technology, the digital, serial-bus local network seems an ideal method of distributing data to regional nodes.

The success of communications service vendors (whether they be the common carrier, computer manufacturers, or independents) in developing facilities for network integration will be one key to survival in this rapidly growing and already complex field. Local networking is only a part, it is true, but a part that has only recently come of age in tying together remote teleprocessing networks with multiprocessor sites. ▪

10. Universal interconnection. *In the near future, local networking will support resource sharing and high-speed communications between regional CPU clusters. Such* *networks will offer redundancy or specialization, as the user requires. Network adapters not shown in the diagram will provide for common communications protocols.*

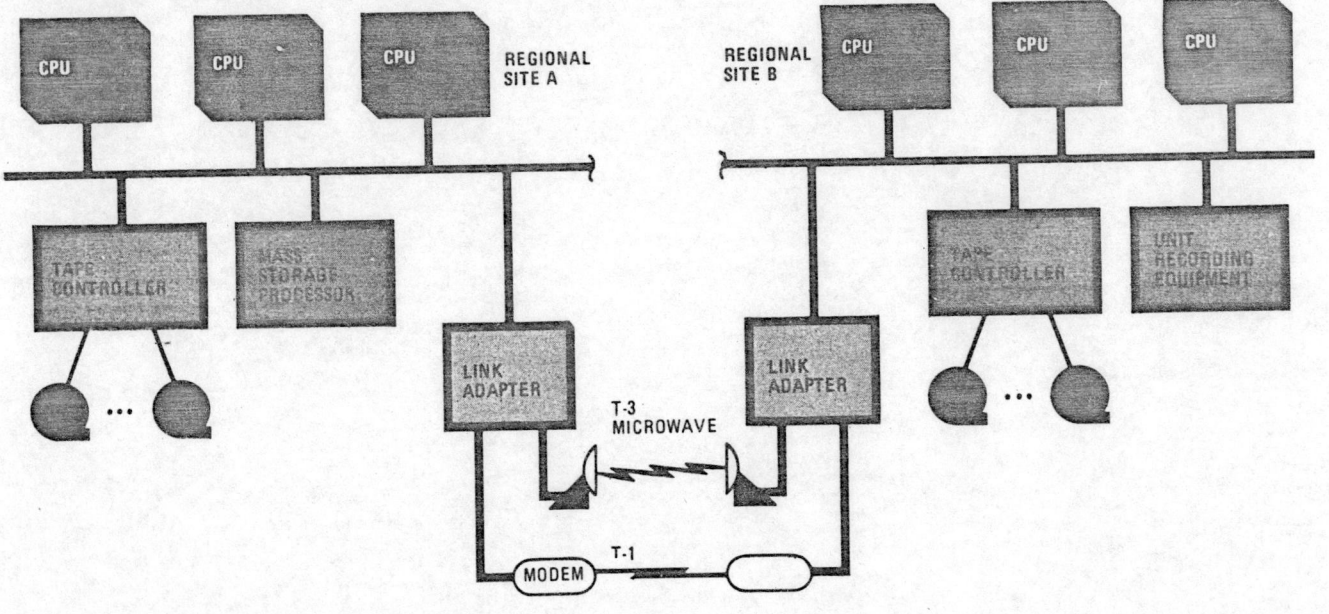

19

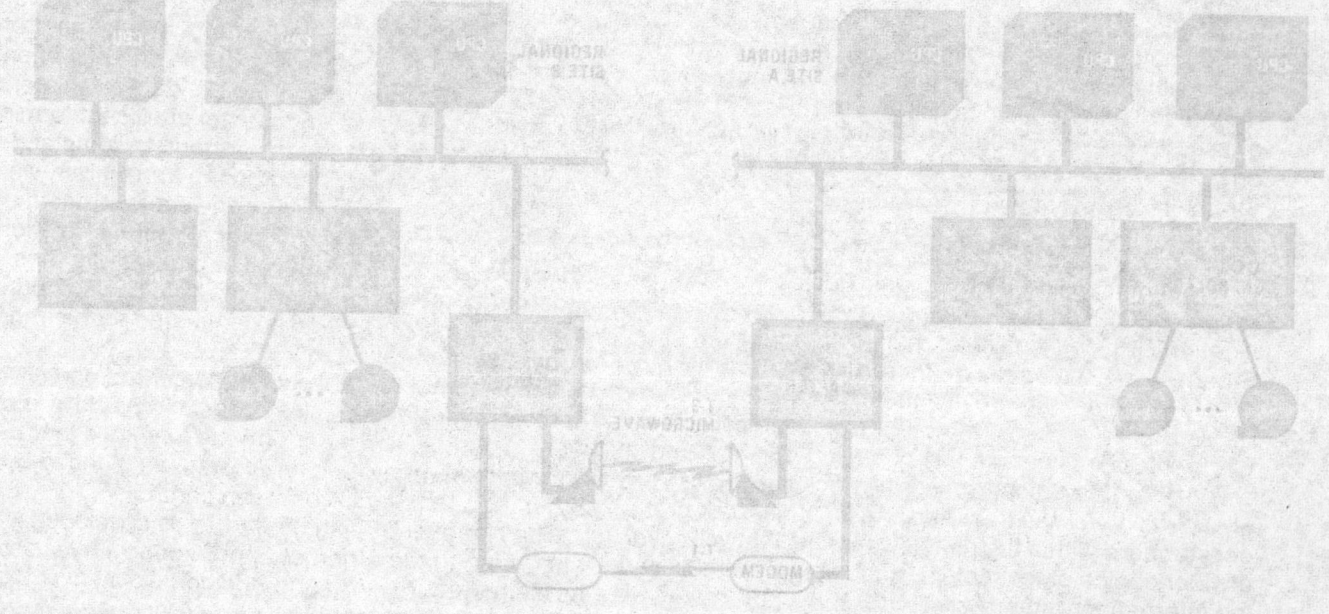

Peter Hsi and Tsvi Lissack, Network Analysis Corporation, Great Neck, N.Y.

Local networks' consensus: High speed

A look at five local networks and two proposed standards reveals vital differences—especially in access protocols and link control.

The coaxial-cable-based, bus-oriented architecture has emerged as one of the most promising candidates for general-purpose local networks. Since the early pioneering efforts of the experimental Ethernet at Xerox Corporation, many coaxial-cable-based local networks have either come under development or been proposed. Yet, although these local networks are similar to the original Ethernet in their basic design, they vary in their actual hardware and software implementations because of the different user devices and applications they support.

There are many unsettled issues surrounding modern local networks: Should the link-level protocol be responsible for reliable communications? How can the addressing capability be extended up to gateways or remote bus interface units (BIUs) and down to ports or user devices connected to a BIU? Should we adopt an enhanced version of an existing standard link protocol (such as ADCCP or HDLC) for local bus networks? None of the current proprietary network protocols is able to answer all these issues satisfactorily.

A recent move by Xerox, Digital Equipment Corporation (DEC), and Intel to jointly develop protocol specifications for local networks, based on Xerox's Ethernet, may well set a de facto standard for the industry in the near future. On the other hand, the standards bodies, such as the Institute of Electrical and Electronics Engineers (IEEE) or the International Federation of Information Processing Societies (IFIPS), are also pushing for the adoption of a local-network protocol standard within the next few months that will cover a wider choice of technologies and comply with existing international standards.

Will there ever be a consensus?

Through a comparison of five major local networks—Xerox's Ethernet, NBSnet at the National Bureau of Standards, Fordnet at Ford Aerospace and Communications Corporation, Hyperbus at Network Systems Corporation, and Mitrenet at Mitre Corporation—and the two proposed standards, the authors point out the pros and cons of each configuration. Such an examination is necessary to provoke dialog among network vendors and standards bodies with regard to internetwork and protocol compatibility problems and to provide a base for the eventual adoption of a common local-network protocol standard.

Ethernet was initially developed at the Xerox Corporation Palo Alto Research Center (PARC). The prototype network is coaxial-cable-based and bus-oriented, provides bandwidth for a 3-Mbit/s data rate, interconnects up to 255 minicomputers or intelligent terminals, and spans a linear distance of about 1 kilometer. Figure 1A shows its overall structure. The transceiver, which drives and receives signals on the cable, detects signal collisions, and maintains electrical-ground isolation, is attached to the colocated cable by pressure taps. The Ethernet controller resides in the host minicomputer or intelligent terminal and is connected to the transceiver by a twisted-pair cable.

The Ethernet controller is implemented partially in hardware, partially in microcode, and partially in software. Together, they perform the functions that transfer packets—the basic unit of data exchanged by two Ethernet controllers—between controllers.

The National Bureau of Standards developed NBSnet according to the Ethernet approach, to serve users on its Gaithersburg, Md., and Boulder, Colo., campuses. NBSnet emphasizes serial, asynchronous service at

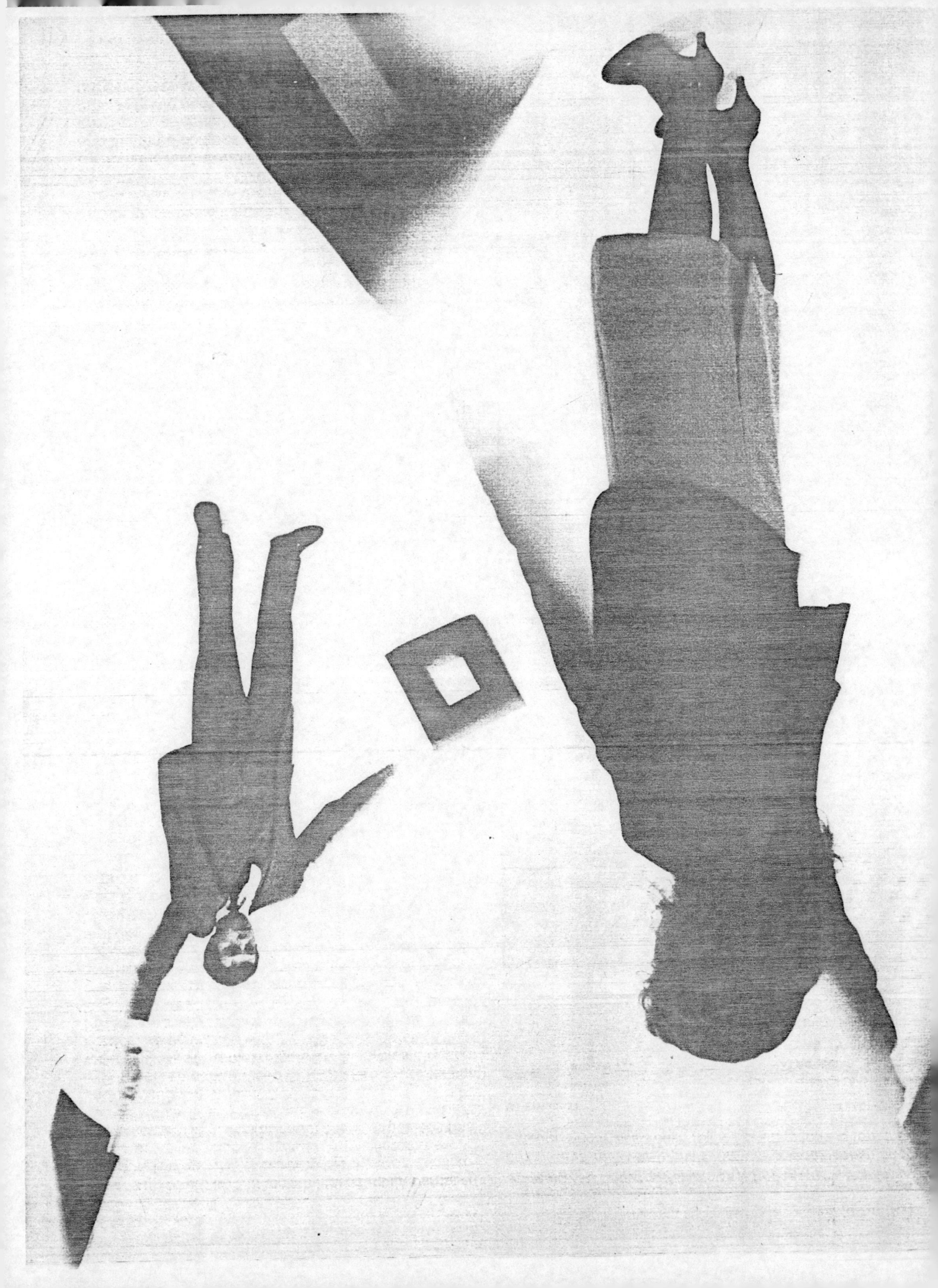

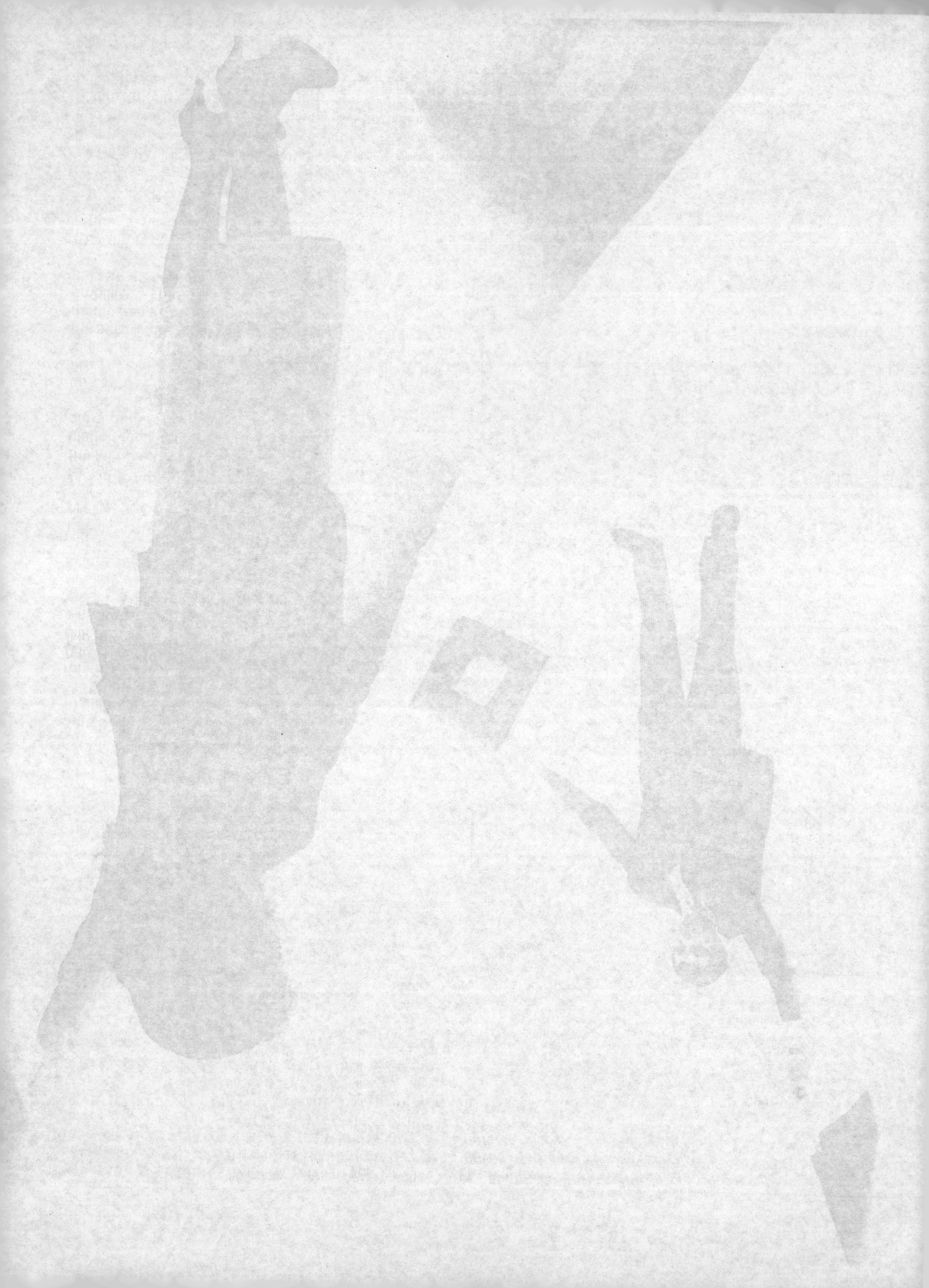

speeds up to 9.6 kbit/s to terminal users and small computers (Fig. 1B). Its building blocks are the microprocessor-based nodes, called terminal interface equipments (TIEs), that connect the user devices to a coaxial cable. The NBSnet cable operates at 1 Mbit/s and can support at least 2,000 user nodes.

Fordnet is a cable-based 0.8-Mbit/s broadcast network similar to Ethernet. Figure 1C illustrates a typical Fordnet configuration with two host computers (DEC PDP-11s here) interconnected by a coaxial cable and local network adapters (LNAs). Each LNA is composed of a Z80 microprocessor and a coaxial-cable transceiver. The LNA is attached to the host's I/O channel (DEC's Unibus) and appears to be an ordinary peripheral device. The Fordnet design philosophy is to use LNAs as network front ends to offload protocol software from the host computer and to permit interconnection of devices from different vendors.

Interfacing the bus

Network Systems Corporation is currently developing Hyperbus, a cable-based commercial local network designed to interconnect different manufacturers' terminals or computers through devices known as bus interface units. The BIUs contain microprocessors and data buffers. Various BIU models implement interfaces to different families of devices.

The bus operates at 1 Mbit/s and accommodates multidrops over distances of several thousand feet (Fig. 1D). The bus-allocation method is significantly different from other access-control schemes: More elaborate priority access provides preferential treatment for different types of messages or BIUs. Preproduction deliveries of Hyperbus are expected to begin in late 1980.

The Mitre Corporation has also implemented a cable-based local network using an Ethernet-like contention discipline. This method, used by NBSnet and Fordnet, employs microprocessor-based nodes as the interface for subscriber devices. But unlike NBSnet or Fordnet, the Mitre network uses an RF (radio-frequency) modulation technique rather than baseband signaling to carry data on the cable.

The Mitre network requires two parallel channels, one outbound and one inbound, as shown in Figure 1E. The bus interface unit contains modems and digital logic that support the network protocol and interface the subscriber's devices. Standard CATV components—such as cables, four-way taps, splitters, and amplifiers—handle signal distribution. Mitrenet operates at 1.2 Mbit/s.

Bus characteristics

Although all five local networks are based on coaxial cables, their actual hardware implementations vary. The table summarizes the major bus characteristics of each network and those of the standards proposed by both the IEEE Local Network Standards Committee and the three-company accord formed by DEC, Intel, and Xerox, referred to as DIX. Since the terminology differs among networks and standards, all interface units between cable and user devices are called bus

1. Network architectures. (A) Ethernet's transceiver drives and receives signals on its coaxial cable and detects signal collisions. (B) NBSnet is based on the

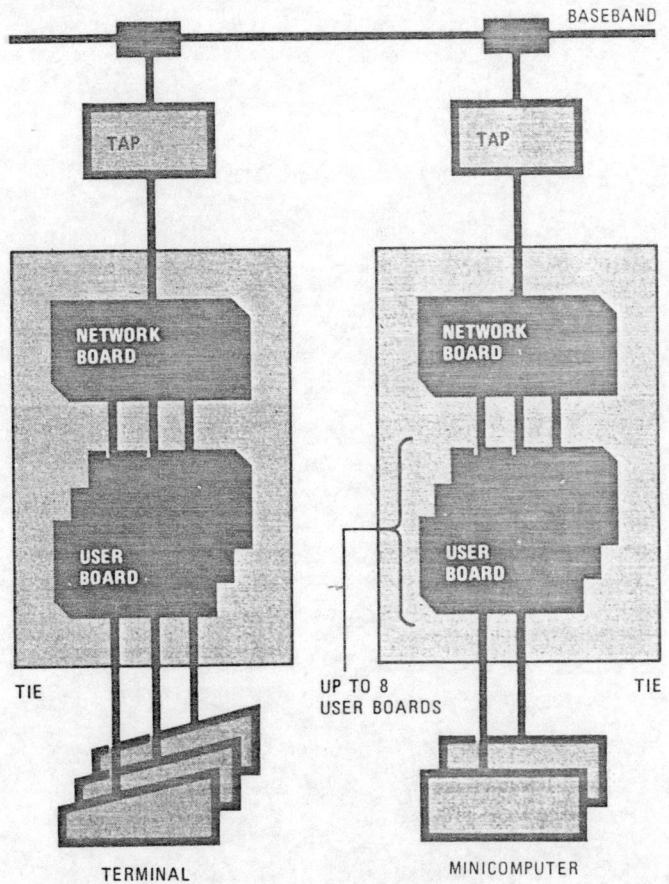

Ethernet approach. (C) Fordnet is a broadcast network. (D) Hyperbus is designed to interconnect devices from different vendors. (E) Mitrenet uses RF modulation.

(C) FORDNET

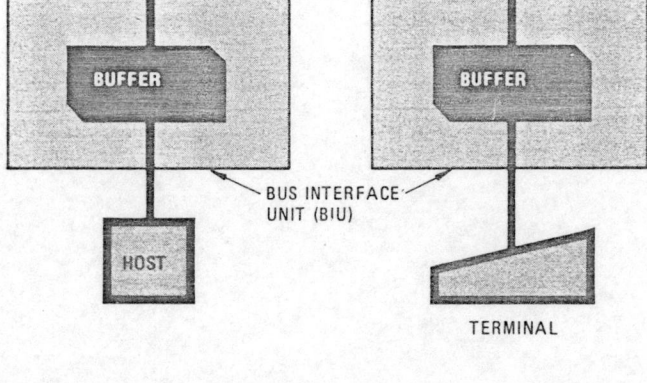

(D) HYPERBUS

(E) MITRENET

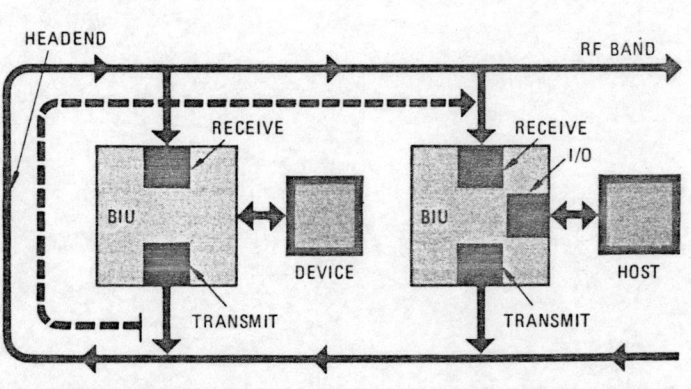

interface units for consistency in this article.

Two types of cable arrangements are used: single or dual cable. Mitrenet employs a dual-cable structure, as shown in Figure 1E. One cable is used to transmit data, the other to receive. Both are connected at one end and passively terminated at the other. No repeater or other head-end equipment is used.

The other networks employ a single-cable architecture, passively terminated at both ends. There are no significant differences between the choices of these two approaches, except that the dual-cable architecture offers double the bandwidth and can take advantage of the well-developed unidirectional CATV components for signal distribution. This is an important consideration for users who require RF broadband transmission. Since the major cost in cable transmission is conduit installation, the second cable is a minor expense compared with the capability and growth potential it provides.

In some of the local networks (see table), data is transmitted at baseband (not modulated on a carrier frequency). Data on the cable is phase-encoded (Manchester code), whereby each bit cell is divided into two complementary halves (Fig. 2). There is always a transition in the middle of the bit cell: A positive-going transition corresponds to a binary 1, and a negative-going transition to a 0. This kind of coding enables self-clocking; that is, the received data generates the receiver clock. It also eliminates d.c. components in the signal.

Mitrenet has CATV-RF transmission, which modulates data by a carrier frequency between 5 and 300 MHz before transmission onto the cable. The advantages of RF transmission are that it minimizes the phase and amplitude distortion present in baseband transmission and avoids most low-frequency noise. Because of its broad bandwidth, data-transfer rates on RF cable are limited by the digital logic in the network interface unit rather than by the transmission method itself. Although the RF cable's bandwidth facilitates future growth, the RF components are about three times as expensive as baseband's. Therefore, for applications with data rates up to 3 Mbit/s and cable lengths less than 1 kilometer, baseband design seems appropriate. For applications that require high bandwidth or simultaneous use of the cable for purposes other than data exchange—such as voice and video—the RF broadband approach is clearly a better choice.

Access protocols

Except for Hyperbus, all the networks and the proposed standards have similar methods for each BIU to access the cable on a contention basis. Known as carrier-sense multiple access/collision detection (CSMA/CD), this scheme involves three operations: carrier sense, collision detection, and backoff.

During carrier sense (also known as "listen before talk") operation, each BIU monitors the channel prior to transmission. If it senses the presence of carrier frequency on the bus, the BIU is refrained from transmitting until the channel is free again. The second operation is collision-detection, also known as "listen while talk." Each transmitting station monitors the channel

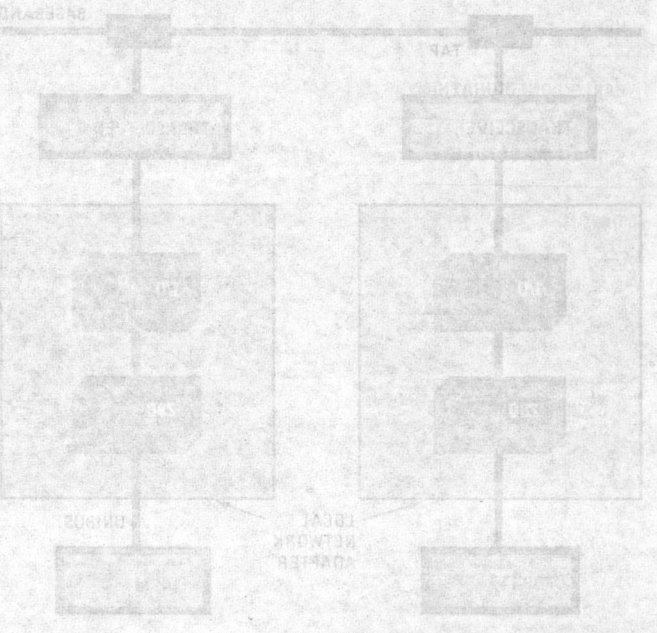

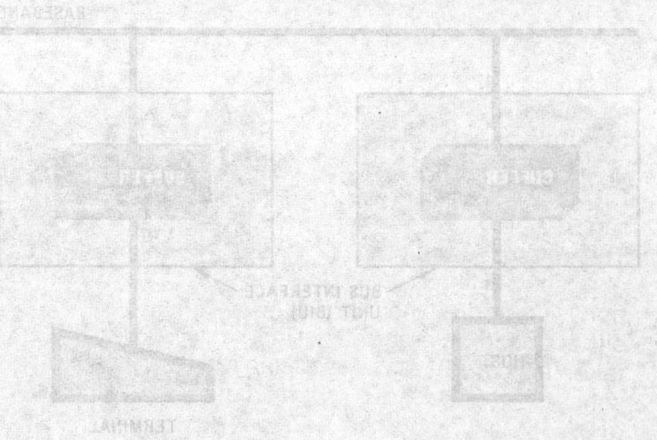

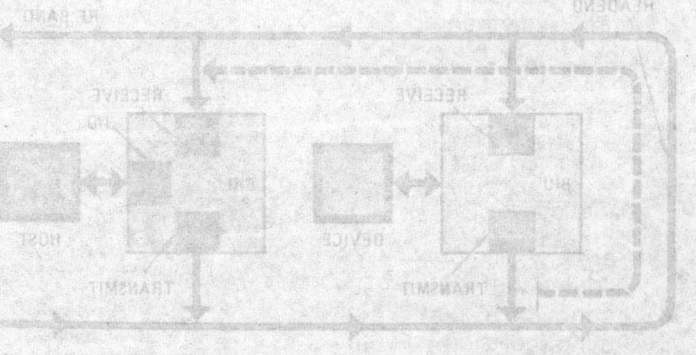

Bus characteristics

	ETHERNET	NBSNET	FORDNET	HYPERBUS	MITRENET
VENDOR/DEVELOPER	XEROX	NBS	FORD	NSC	MITRE
CABLE CONFIGURATION	SINGLE	SINGLE	SINGLE	SINGLE	DUAL
SIGNAL STRUCTURE	BASEBAND	BASEBAND	BASEBAND	BASEBAND	RF BROADBAND
DATA ENCODING	MANCHESTER	MANCHESTER	B.S.B. PCM	MANCHESTER	MODULATED SIGNAL
DATA RATE (MBIT/S)	3.0	1.0	0.8	1.0	1.2
CABLE LENGTH	1 KILOMETER	1.5 KILOMETERS	3 KILOMETERS	1 KILOMETER	N/A
NUMBER OF DROPS PER CABLE	255	2,000	255	256	N/A
ACCESS PROTOCOL	CSMA/CD	CSMA/CD	CSMA/CD	MODIFIED CSMA	CSMA/CD
BACKOFF ALGORITHM	BINARY— EXPONENTIAL	RANDOM TABLE	DETERMINISTIC ALGORITHM	PRIORITY	UNIFORM RANDOM DELAY
FORCED COLLISION	YES	YES	NO	NO	NO
PRIORITY ACCESS	NO	NO	YES	YES	NO

N/A = INFORMATION NOT AVAILABLE   B.S.B. PCM = BAND-SPREAD-BINARY PULSE-CODE MODULATION

while it is transmitting and aborts the transmission immediately if it detects destructive interference because of data collision.

The final operation is backoff. When a transmitting BIU detects a data collision, it waits or backs off for a random period of time before retransmitting the frame. The collision can be resolved if each colliding BIU chooses a different backoff period. Typically, the duration is computed independently by the colliding BIUs, either based on a predetermined backoff algorithm or taken from a table. The resulting CSMA/CD access scheme yields very high channel utilization—in excess of 90 percent of channel capacity—during light traffic with low access delay. The probability of deference (busy bus) or collision is typically less than 1 percent.

There are variations in the actual implementation of the access method among the five networks. In Mitrenet, since the transmission is accomplished at RF, the presence of the carrier on the bus is detected by an analog circuit. The other networks use Manchester encoding, so "carrier" is detected by the presence of signal transitions on the cable.

All local networks except Hyperbus have implemented a collision-detection process, which compares the received signal with the transmitted signal. If there are any discrepancies between those signals, it is assumed that there was a collision or some other error condition. Ethernet and NBSnet also transmit a jamming (collision-forcing) signal onto the bus of about one round-trip-delay time when collision is detected.

This alerts the participants involved in the collision and forces them to retransmit. In Hyperbus, the collision (or other discrepancy) is detected through lack of acknowledgment from the receiver.

An important distinction among these access protocols is the backoff algorithm. Ethernet's binary exponential backoff algorithm causes the average retransmission interval to increase automatically every time a collision takes place. For example, when a collision occurs, a retransmission timer is set to a random value chosen uniformly between 0 and $(2^n - 1)\Delta$, where n is the number of retries and Δ is some unit of time. Typically, Δ is chosen to be the round-trip propagation delay on the cable.

In NBSnet, the backoff values are chosen from a look-up table (based on a deterministic algorithm), allowing a few short-interval retries followed by longer waits. In Fordnet, a deterministic algorithm is used to compute the waiting period determined by the propagation delay between two interfering transceivers and the difference in time between their initial transmissions. In Mitrenet, the backoff values are chosen from a pseudorandom interval whose mean is approximately 400 microseconds.

The selection of any one particular backoff algorithm is often a trade-off between the performance and the complexity of implementation. However, a backoff algorithm that can be readily implemented in hardware will reduce processing requirements.

There are drawbacks in the CSMA/CD protocols

DIX	IEEE
DEC, INTEL, XEROX	IEEE
SINGLE	SINGLE
BASEBAND	BASEBAND/ RF BROADBAND
MANCHESTER	NOT YET DECIDED
10	1–20
500 METERS	500 METERS (MINIMUM)
100	150 PER KILOMETER (NOMINAL)
CSMA/CD	CSMA/CD
BINARY—EXPONENTIAL	N/A
YES	YES
NO	LIKELY

implemented in the four local networks. In Ethernet, NBSnet, and Mitrenet, no priority mechanism is built into the access protocol. Therefore, frames with different urgencies receive the same treatment when accessing the bus. It is more efficient to provide bus access by priority so that the timeliness of data is reflected at the low-level access mechanism.

Another drawback is that carrier sense causes a BIU to defer its transmission until the cable is freed. Since BIUs do not transmit at random times after deferring, the probability of collision immediately after a frame transmission is much higher, because two or more BIUs may have deferred during the busy period. This is especially true under heavy traffic. The waiting BIUs will initiate transmission, collide, and then retransmit at random intervals resulting in extra delays. Such a situation can be alleviated by implementing an additional back-off algorithm whenever the cable is sensed to be busy. This approach is also known as p-persistent or nonpersistent CSMA. Not one of the four networks has implemented this feature.

Hyperbus's access protocol differs from the others. It employs two modes of operation: free-flow and priority. During the free-flow mode, the BIU is free to transmit when the channel is idle and detects collisions by the absence of an acknowledgment.

Once any BIU has transmitted, the network enters the priority mode. Here, the cable is reserved for a time period after each transmission to allow acknowledgment. If there is a collision in the free-flow mode, the

acknowledgment will not be present, and all BIUs then enter the priority mode to resolve the contention.

There are three priority classes: alert, normal, and background. Each BIU at every priority level is assigned a unit-time transmission slot, which is equal to the signal propagation delay on the cable times the distance between the BIU and the next BIU. After a complete scan of all the time slots in the three priority levels, if no transmission occurs, the network returns to the free-flow mode. Once a BIU has transmitted in a time slot of any priority level, the network reenters the acknowledgment phase of the priority mode.

This complex scheme provides access to the cable by priority and allows marginal improvement of channel use during heavy traffic. However, increased channel utilization is usually of secondary importance in local networks, where capacity is rather inexpensive and the BIU is kept as simple as possible.

Link-control protocols
Each of the five local networks has developed its own low-level protocol for exchanging data between bus interface units through the cable. These low-level protocol functions are simpler versions of the standard data-link-control procedures, such as SDLC or HDLC. However, since cable is basically a broadcasting medium, these standard protocols must be enhanced to take advantage of the one-to-many or many-to-many environments. For example, a broadcast address, which is recognized by all BIUs on the cable, would be a desirable feature in the link protocol.

On the other hand, the unique characteristics of cable transmission, such as high data rate and low propagation delay, allow simplification of protocol design. In some cases, the complex buffer-management, flow-control, and network-congestion-control mechanisms, which are necessary in a long-haul network, could be replaced by simpler schemes, because the interactions between the sender and receiver are almost instantaneous.

Figure 3 compares the formats of the basic data units handled by each link protocol. In Fordnet, Hyperbus, Mitrenet, and the IEEE standard, the basic data unit is called a frame, a term used by most standard protocols, such as HDLC and X.25, to indicate a link-controlled data block. In Ethernet, NBSnet, and the DIX standard, this data unit is called a packet, which usually means the data units routed between nodes in a packet-switching network. In this article, the basic data unit is called a frame.

Each network has a different framing mechanism to indicate the beginning and end of a frame (Fig. 3). Ethernet uses a single bit for recovering the clock at the beginning of each frame. The end of a frame is detected by the absence of transitions in the bit cell in both Ethernet and NBSnet. Such a framing mechanism would not seem very reliable, depending as it does on one bit's transition—which could be caused by noise. Besides, it is specific to the Manchester code and may not work with other types of coding schemes, such as NRZI (non-return-to-zero-inverted) coding.

In Fordnet and Hyperbus, traditional HDLC flags

2. Bit encoding. *Most of the local networks use Manchester (phase) encoding for which each bit period is divided into two complementary halves. A positive-going transition in the middle of the bit period corresponds to a binary 1; a negative-going transition, to a 0. This coding allows self-clocking and eliminates d.c. components.*

delimit a frame. The data bits enclosed by the leading and trailing flags are also subject to the bit-stuffing process (to distinguish a flag from data) to provide data transparency. This framing mechanism has an integrity problem, because a single bit error may cause an entire frame to be delimited incorrectly. However, such problems can be alleviated by using double flags in the beginning and end of every frame, as implemented in Hyperbus's frames.

Mitrenet uses a byte count in the frame header to determine the length of a frame. The advantage of doing so is that a bit reversal in the middle of the frame will not delimit the frame. However, errors in the byte count field can cause incorrect frame delimiting. Also, this frame structure is incompatible with most bit-oriented protocols.

The framing and synchronization in the DEC-Intel-Xerox standard is done through a long preamble (64 bits) at the beginning of a frame. The end of a frame is delimited through detection of the loss of carrier within 1 bit-time after the last data transition. Again, this framing mechanism works only when a self-clocking coding is used. The DIX standard also specifies a minimum frame spacing of 9.6 microseconds, to provide time for the receiver to reset.

The proposed IEEE standard moves the framing and synchronization issue away from the link-control protocol. Instead, a separate physical protocol sublayer handles all media access and interface protocols between link and medium, including framing and synchronization. This approach allows the link protocol to be defined transparent to a specific network topology, transmission medium, data rate, or access method. The framing and synchronization can therefore be done with a specific scheme that is optimized to a given transmission medium, such as baseband cable, CATV cable, or fiber-optic cable.

Addressing

Four networks employ two address fields: TO ADDRESS and FROM ADDRESS. Fordnet uses three address fields: two TO ADDRESS and one FROM ADDRESS. Ethernet and Fordnet use an 8-bit address field, which limits the number of direct network addresses on one cable to 256, while the others use 16 bits, which accommodate up to 65,536 addresses. Clearly, a large address space

allows more flexible addressing schemes or direct addressing to the physical ports or attached devices.

The five networks provide at least two addressing modes: point-to-point and broadcast. Typically, the broadcast address is all binary 1s in the TO ADDRESS field and is received by all bus interface units. Some networks such as Hyperbus dedicate the first 8 bits to the bus interface unit's address and the second 8 bits for internal port address or device address. Ethernet and Hyberbus have implemented the group addressing capability (simultaneous transmission to a selected group of bus interface units), which is desirable for local-network-related applications such as electronic mail and teleconferencing.

Enhanced addressing

Both the DIX and the IEEE standards adopt the two-address-field format. However, the address-field size is significantly larger than that of the existing network implementations. Such a large field permits great flexibility in addressing.

The DIX standard has a fixed 48-bit address field that provides 2^{47} physical addresses, one broadcast address, and $2^{47} - 1$ group addresses—close to 300 trillion addresses. It is therefore possible both to assign each device its own unique address, called a Universal Product Code (UPC), instead of BIU addressing or tap (or equivalent) addressing, and to more easily change the network configuration.

The proposed IEEE standard allows three different address-field sizes (two, four, or six 8-bit bytes) through the use of the address-extension bit. The address-extension bit is the most significant bit of each 16-bit field, and it indicates whether the address field should be extended into the next 2 bytes. The standard provides 2^{45} physical addresses, one broadcast address, and $2^{45} - 1$ group addresses. In a 6-byte address format, the address space between 2^{30} and 2^{45} is allocated for UPC address administration.

The functional capabilities of the proposed IEEE standard exceed those of the DEC-Intel-Xerox standard. The IEEE standard offers more flexible provisions for network implementation. The DIX standard can be regarded as a subset of the IEEE standard (except for the address-extension bit).

Basically, there are two approaches to error control

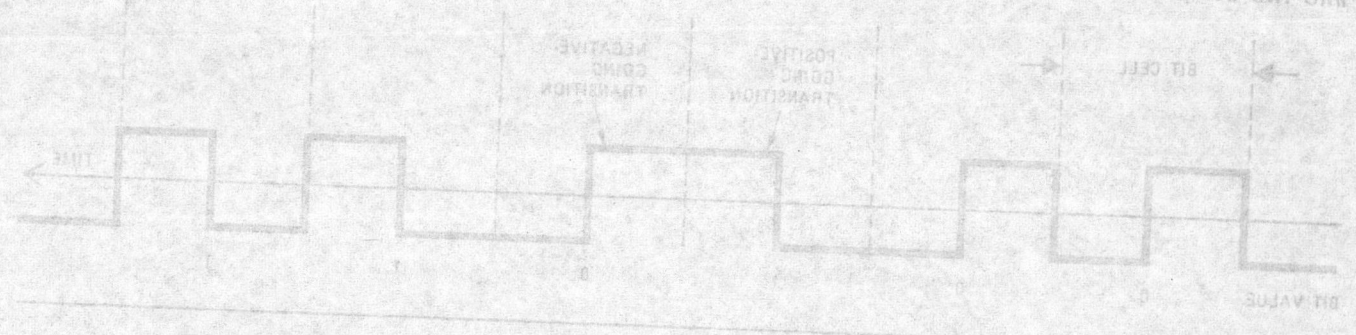

3. Fielding the format. How the local networks' link protocols handle the format of a basic data unit is illustrated here. Each employs a different framing mechanism to indicate the beginning and end of every frame. The proposed IEEE standard moves the framing and synchronization issue away from the link-control protocol.

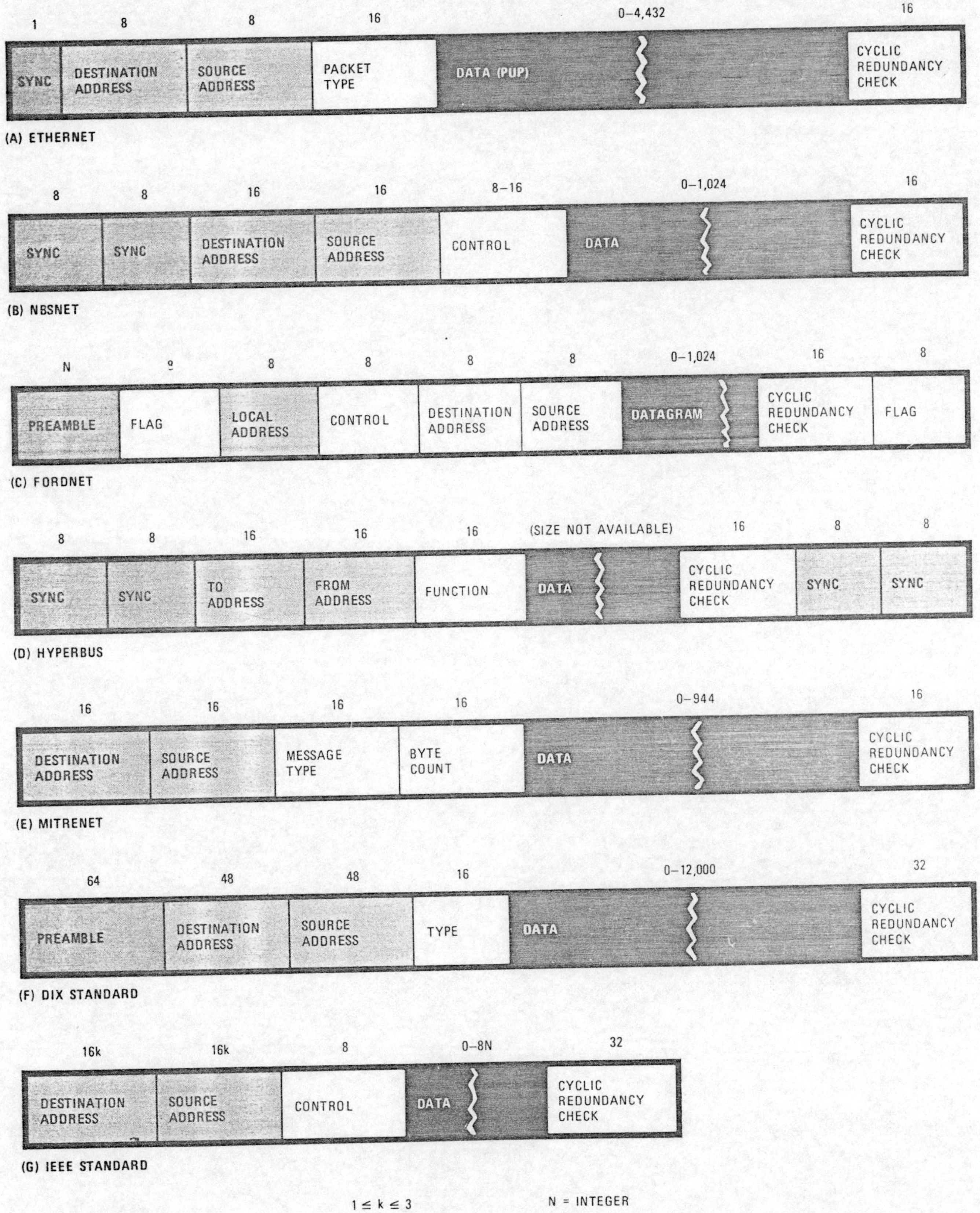

1	8	8	16	0–4,432	16
SYNC	DESTINATION ADDRESS	SOURCE ADDRESS	PACKET TYPE	DATA (PUP)	CYCLIC REDUNDANCY CHECK

(A) ETHERNET

8	8	16	16	8–16	0–1,024	16
SYNC	SYNC	DESTINATION ADDRESS	SOURCE ADDRESS	CONTROL	DATA	CYCLIC REDUNDANCY CHECK

(B) NBSNET

N	8	8	8	8	8	0–1,024	16	8
PREAMBLE	FLAG	LOCAL ADDRESS	CONTROL	DESTINATION ADDRESS	SOURCE ADDRESS	DATAGRAM	CYCLIC REDUNDANCY CHECK	FLAG

(C) FORDNET

8	8	16	16	16	(SIZE NOT AVAILABLE)	16	8	8
SYNC	SYNC	TO ADDRESS	FROM ADDRESS	FUNCTION	DATA	CYCLIC REDUNDANCY CHECK	SYNC	SYNC

(D) HYPERBUS

16	16	16	16	0–944	16
DESTINATION ADDRESS	SOURCE ADDRESS	MESSAGE TYPE	BYTE COUNT	DATA	CYCLIC REDUNDANCY CHECK

(E) MITRENET

64	48	48	16	0–12,000	32
PREAMBLE	DESTINATION ADDRESS	SOURCE ADDRESS	TYPE	DATA	CYCLIC REDUNDANCY CHECK

(F) DIX STANDARD

16k	16k	8	0–8N	32
DESTINATION ADDRESS	SOURCE ADDRESS	CONTROL	DATA	CYCLIC REDUNDANCY CHECK

(G) IEEE STANDARD

$1 \leq k \leq 3$ N = INTEGER

at the link level. In Ethernet, the link protocol does not assume responsibility for reliable data transport. Each data frame is protected from transmission errors by a 16-bit cyclic redundancy checking (CRC) error-detecting code, although no acknowledgment is sent at link level for each frame correctly received. An erroneous frame is simply discarded. A higher-level protocol (datagram) handles acknowledgment and retransmission, only if required by high-level applications.

The other networks have implemented stop-and-wait error-control procedures, which require that each frame be acknowledged before the next frame is transmitted. Each network frame is protected by a 16-bit CRC error-detecting code. Every network has tailored its version of stop-and-wait error control to its specific applications. For example, in NBSnet, the retransmission timeout interval is taken from tables. This allows several short-interval retries followed by longer waits. It also allows fewer retries during the initial connection stage than in normal data transmission.

Generally speaking, the Ethernet approach, which moves the responsibility for reliable communications to higher-level protocols, has significantly simplified the link-protocol design, because the bulk of a traditional link control involves such functions as acknowledgment, retransmission, and timeout. It also allows tailoring reliability to applications and placing error recovery where it will do the most good.

However, this approach is successful only if the transmission medium provides a reasonably low bit error rate. Otherwise, the excessive overhead of acknowledgment and retransmission at the network-level protocol will severely degrade the overall network performance. Therefore, this approach may not work if twisted wires, instead of coaxial cable, are the basic transmission medium. Besides, since this scheme deviates significantly from most standard link-control procedures, compatibility problems can occur when the local networks are connected to other types of communications networks.

On the other hand, the stop-and-wait error-control mechanisms of the other four networks were developed in an ad hoc manner. None of them are compatible with most standard link-control procedures or allow flexible handling of data traffic with different error-control requirements. For example, the stop-and-wait protocol may not be suitable for certain traffic types, such as digitized voice or video signals, because of their required timeliness; it is better to receive a frame with a few transmission errors than to wait for the retransmission of an entire frame.

An ideal link-error-control mechanism for a local network should be able to handle both error-controlled and non-error-controlled traffic. It should also conform as much as possible to the accepted link-control-procedure standards for ready interface to existing communications networks.

The proposed IEEE standard has adopted this approach in handling error control and defines two types of link operations. In type 1 operation, the frames are not acknowledged, nor is there any flow control or error recovery at link level. In type 2, the frame transfer is

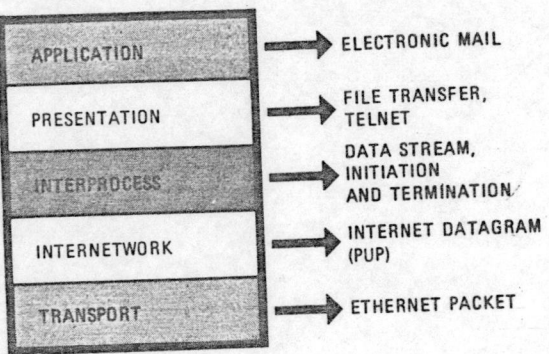

(A) ETHERNET PROTOCOL HIERARCHY

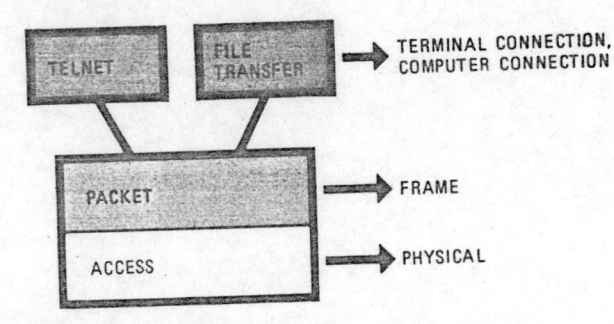

(B) NBSNET PROTOCOL HIERARCHY

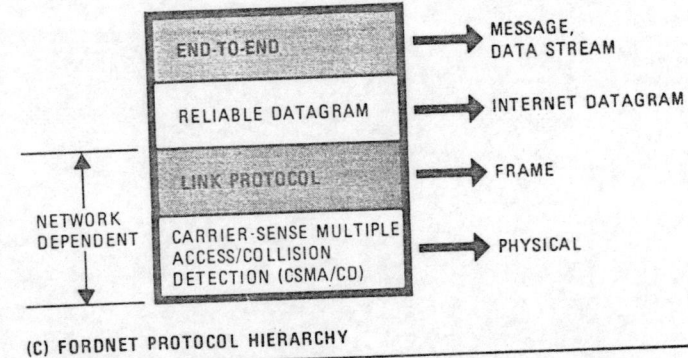

(C) FORDNET PROTOCOL HIERARCHY

handled by a point-to-point, balanced link-control procedure. This procedure provides acknowledgment, sequencing, error recovery, and flow control, similar to the asynchronous balanced-mode operation of the HDLC protocol.

Note that both the DIX and IEEE standards use a 32-bit CRC, instead of 16 bits. This provides better error-detection capability.

Controlling the flow

Because of the high data rate of the cable and the incompatible input/output rates of the user devices, local networks need a mechanism to prevent buffer overflow. In general, most networks have implemented three stages of flow-control procedures: The data flow between sending or receiving devices and the bus interface units is decoupled from the internal data flow between two bus interface units.

Double data buffers—one for cable interface and one for user-device interface—are required as bus

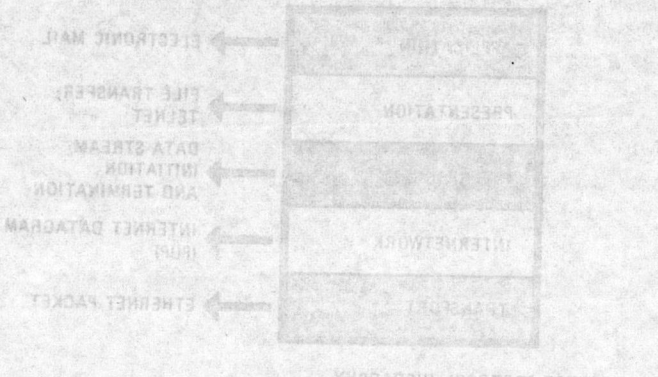

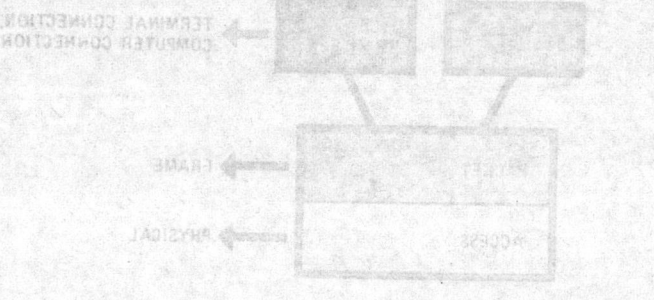

4. Protocol hierarchies. Ethernet and Fordnet have implemented a reliable-datagram protocol. NBSnet has two high-level protocols: Telnet and file transfer. The datagram is a common denominator of several network-level protocols. The BIU encapsulates and decapsulates the datagram, allowing its fragmentation and reassembly. The RF-modulated Mitrenet has implemented a variety of end-to-end and high-level protocols that are built on the flexible transport and access protocols. Are the DIX and IEEE protocols the standards of the future?

CONFERENCE

NAME SERVICE   BROADCAST   FILE ACCESS   VIRTUAL CIRCUIT

TRANSMISSION-CONTROL PROTOCOL   DATAGRAM   CONNECTION   DATA STREAM

FLEXIBLE TRANSPORT

LOW-LEVEL ACCESS

(D) MITRENET PROTOCOL HIERARCHY

interface units. This arrangement allows independent flow-control mechanisms for the two BIU functions. For example, the data flow between user equipment and the bus interface unit can be controlled through out-of-band RS-232-C signals.

For flow control, NBSnet includes a buffer-status bit in the frame header. When the receiving buffer is full, a status bit is set in the ACK frame and the sender suspends transmission until the bit is reset.

Fordnet implements a special global flow-control scheme, analogous to a traffic-light operation, to avoid congestion. Each bus interface unit maintains a flow-control table that records the buffer loads of every other bus interface unit on the cable. The tables are constantly updated by ACK, NACK, or ANNOUNCE (update) frames, which are broadcast to all bus interface units. When the total buffer load is less than 75 percent, it is a "green light" (all datagrams can enter the network). When the total load is between 75 and 85 percent, it is a "yellow light" (encourage expeditious processing).

When the total load exceeds 85 percent, it is a "red light" (only an emergency datagram is allowed to enter the network in this case).

In Mitrenet, the buffer status is combined with the ACK frame. If the receiver sends ACK, the buffer is available; if it withholds ACK, the buffer is full. However, such a scheme may result in excessive retransmission of data frames. In Ethernet, the flow control is handled through a high-level (datagram) protocol.

The local networks' flow-control mechanisms (except Fordnet's) provide adequate control on a per-link basis (where a link is represented by a source-destination BIU pair). Although the trade-off in a specific implementation is between performance and implementation complexity, because of the multipoint network environment, it is now possible for a single BIU to receive data from several BIUs (over several distinct links) in rapid succession.

The control mechanism on a per-link basis may not provide sufficient control of the incoming data flow,

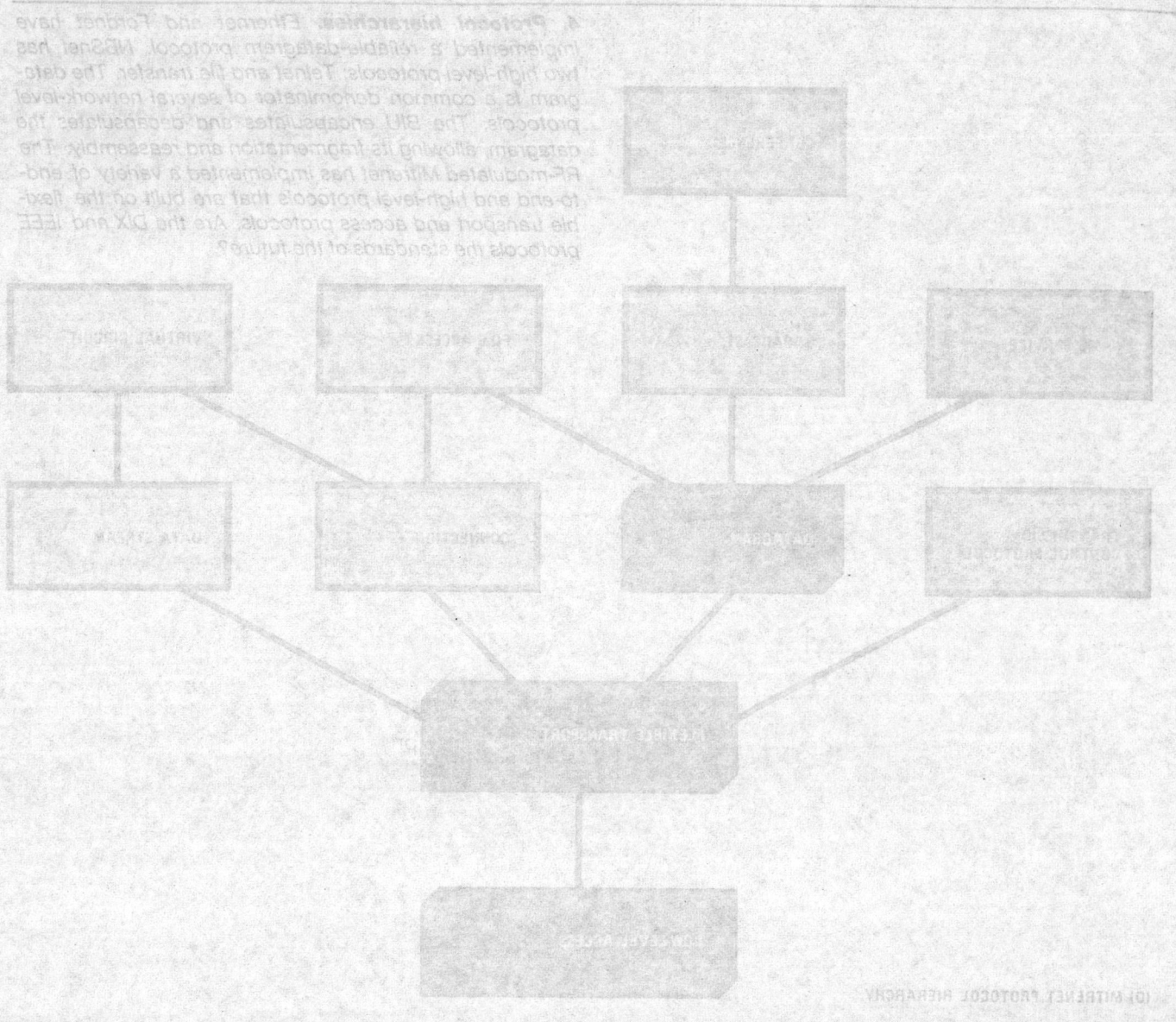

because the resources at a BIU (such as its buffer) can be shared by all links. Ideally, a global flow control—similar to the Fordnet implementation—would be built into the link protocol on top of the per-link flow control. Such a proposal is now under consideration by the IEEE standards committee.

High-level protocols

Among the five local networks, Ethernet and Fordnet have implemented a reliable datagram protocol (having additional mechanisms to assure delivery) on top of the link-level protocol for internetwork transport. The Ethernet internetwork datagram is known as PARC Universal Packet (PUP), a standard data packet common to all Ethernets. Each PUP is independently addressed and protected by its own software CRC error-detecting code. Acknowledgments and retransmissions are done at the datagram level to guarantee the transport function. Therefore, a PUP can be routed from the source through several interconnected Ethernets to the destination.

In each network, a PUP is encapsulated by the link-level packet, permitting it to be carried transparently. All other high-level communications protocols, such as connections and streams transactions (sequence of file records), are based on PUP and are strictly a matter of agreement among the communicating applications. In the prototype Ethernet, various high-level protocols have been implemented on top of the PUP protocol—such as the electronic mail application—as shown in the protocol hierarchy of Figure 4A.

NBSnet has implemented two high-level protocols: Telnet (for terminal handling) and file transfer (Fig 4B). Figure 4C shows the Fordnet high-level protocol hierarchy. The datagram is a common denominator of several network-level protocols.

The bus interface unit performs address translation from another network's host address to a local-network address. It encapsulates and decapsulates the datagram, allowing its fragmentation and reassembly. The reliable datagram guarantees no errors or duplication at the receiving bus interface unit.

Mitrenet has implemented a variety of end-to-end and high-level protocols that are built on the flexible transport protocol and the access protocol (Fig. 4D). The details of the high-level protocols for Hyperbus are not available.

To take full advantage of the cable-bus communications network, more standard high-level protocols—including network transport, end-to-end, session, and presentation level (Fig. 4A)—must be developed. Since these high-level protocols generally are not affected by the peculiarity of the transmission medium, there is no reason why standard high-level protocols in many long-haul packet-switching networks cannot be implemented in local networks. This would not only reduce protocol development efforts but also allow for ready interface between long-haul and local networks.

Because of signal attenuation and propagation delay, most local network cable lengths are restricted to a few kilometers. To cover a wider area would require more than one network cable. Each cable forms a sub-network and is interconnected with other subnetworks through various "bridges" or gateways. Ethernet has proposed at least three types of bridges for interconnecting cable subnetworks:

1. Frame repeater. This simple unbuffered repeater reproduces the frame from one cable to another, extends the signal coverage, and enriches the network topology with little or no extra delay.

2. Frame filter. This is a buffered frame repeater. A simple address filter allows frames to be passed from one cable to another only if the destination BIU is on the cable past the bridge. This reduces the number of BIUs contending on each cable while still allowing full access to all the BIUs within the same address space. Each frame filter accesses the bus according to the same CSMA/CD discipline as other buffer interface units. Therefore, additional delay may be introduced when crossing the bridge.

3. Media translator. This frame-level protocol translator allows each subnetwork to have independent address space and link protocol. The internet-work datagram is decapsulated and encapsulated at the translator before being forwarded to another cable. Such a translator usually has to buffer the entire frame.

The Ethernet gateway, or bridge, provides an interface between local networks and other types of communications networks, such as a long-haul, packet-switching network. Since the protocol structure may be completely different in the other network, it is necessary to provide transport as well as high-level protocol translation at the gateway.

Detailed information about gateway connections for the other four networks is not available. The functional roles of a gateway, in terms of the responsibility for end-to-end accountability, routing, and flow control, remain to be clearly specified. More work in this area needs to be done to facilitate ready interconnection of local and long-haul communications networks—a vital extension of the technology. ∎

References

1. John F. Shoch, *An Annotated Bibliography on Local Computer Networks*, 2d. ed., Xerox Corporation, Palo Alto Research Center, Calif., February 1980.
2. Robert M. Metcalfe and David R. Boggs, "Ethernet: Distributed Packet Switching for Local Computer Networks," *Communications of the Association for Computing Machinery*, New York, N.Y., July 1976.
3. Robert J. Carpenter and Joseph Sonol Jr., "Serving Users with a Local Area Network," Proceedings of the Local Area Communications Network Symposium, Boston, May 1979.
4. Kenneth J. Biba and Jeffrey W. Yeh, "Fordnet: A Front-End Approach to Local Computer Networks," Proceedings of the Local Area Communications Network Symposium, Boston, May 1979.
5. G. S. Christensen, "Design Objectives, Hyperbus General Facilities," Technical Report, Network Systems Corporation, Brooklyn Center, Minn., June 1979.
6. G. T. Hopkins, "A Bus Communication System," Mitre Technical Report, MTR-3515, The Mitre Corporation, Bedford, Mass., November 1977.

A user speaks out: Broadband or baseband for local nets?

Thomas E. Krutsch, Security Pacific National Bank, Glendale, Calif.

Which coaxial-cable approach is most convenient and reliable? The author examines the strengths and weaknesses of the two technologies.

Networking trends foretell that the coaxial-cable bus topology will be the widespread choice for general-purpose local information networks. And although many users agree that coaxial cable is the best medium, it remains to be seen whether baseband or broadband emerges as the predominant technology.

The bus design has several advantages over a centralized configuration of conventional communications networks. A new or relocated device may be connected to any conveniently located network-access point without necessitating physical changes to the network. Also, portions of the bus may be extended with relative ease to serve devices not originally included in the network; expanding centralized setups requires multiple cable runs back to the switching equipment. A bus-based design makes it possible for numerous relatively "bursty" devices to share, as needed, a common, high-capacity transmission link economically. In addition, it enables the distribution of the necessary intelligence for control of the network among many intelligent bus-interface units. This can decrease or eliminate the number of network components, possibly increasing the fault tolerance of the total network.

A local network contains several characteristic elements, not the least of which is the transmission medium. The transmission medium must be rugged, able to endure a lifetime of manhandling by construction and maintenance personnel and by users who pull it through conduits and step on it—all this, while remaining highly reliable. The medium must be immune to noise and maintain low data loss, enabling it to be used

for reasonable distances at adequate data rates, with a minimum number of amplifiers and repeaters. According to many users, coaxial cable best satisfies these needs (see "Which transmission medium?").

Since numerous devices can share a common cable bus, it is necessary to multiplex the data passing over it. One technique used is time-division multiplexing (TDM). The form of TDM generally used in baseband local networks allows multiple access, with the bandwidth of the transmission medium being shared as needed. Examples of networks using TDM modulation are Net/One, (Ungermann-Bass), Ethernet (Xerox Corporation), and Hyperbus and Hyperchannel (Network Systems Corporation).

Frequency-division multiplexing (FDM) is used in broadband local networks and is much like the multiplexing technique used for years in conventional analog microwave networks and in CATV. An FDM local network can be almost identical to a CATV distribution scheme (see "Local networks' consensus: High speed," DATA COMMUNICATIONS, December 1980, p. 56).

One advantage of a broadband network is that, unlike TDM-based networks, it can carry analog as well as digital information. For example, numerous channels of full-bandwidth video (used in teleconferencing and building-security applications) could be distributed, along with data. Another advantage is its ability to accommodate multiple, special-purpose applications on a noninterfering basis, even to the extent of containing subnetworks operating on TDM principles.

A disadvantage is the need for radio-frequency (RF)

Which transmission medium?

Twisted pair. Twisted pair has the advantage of relative low cost but has several serious disadvantages. Single twisted pair lacks the physical ruggedness required by a local network. It tends to both emit and pick up electrical noise and possesses relatively unpredictable impedance characteristics under conditions of practical use, resulting in relatively low data rates.

Optical fiber. Near the opposite end of the bandwidth spectrum lies optical fiber. The fiber itself offers digital bandwidths up to many hundreds of megabits per second. Practical lightwave transmitter/receivers already yield 100-Mbit/s performance in point-to-point applications, and higher speeds are expected in the future. A major difficulty in using optical fiber to form a practical bus configuration is that a great number of bus taps and couplers are necessary. Unfortunately, the science of fiber optics and the communications marketplace have not yet come together to make available couplers and taps with adequate low loss, high reliability, and low cost.

Coaxial cable. Coaxial cable has been in use for many years, in numerous applications which impose requirements similar to local networks'. Its advantage is that many types of coaxial cable, connectors, splitters, and taps are available, and installation and maintenance personnel are familiar with its use. Coaxial cable is the medium generally used in modern local networks.

---

modems, which are often more expensive than the relatively simple transceivers used in baseband schemes. Moreover, since these modems often have components that do not readily lend themselves to LSI (large-scale integration) or VSLI (very-large-scale integration), their cost may remain high relative to that of their baseband counterparts. Another disadvantage is that the propagation delay through a broadband network is likely to be much greater than that in a baseband network.

Subnetworks on a cable

FDM/TDM networks are a subdivision of the FDM classification and use a combination of the two techniques. Into this category fall LocalNet (Network Resources Corporation), Cablenet (Amdax Corporation), and Mitrenet (Mitre Corporation). Although designed basically like a broadband (FDM) network, FDM/TDM networks contain, in effect, one or more subnetworks, each of which operates internally according to TDM principles.

The communicating devices belonging to each subnetwork are equipped with bus-interface units much like those used with baseband (TDM) networks, except that they incorporate RF modems whose outputs are compatible with the frequency plan of the broadband network. These bus-interface units buffer data from their respective devices just as in a pure TDM network and enact access protocols similarly.

An important difference is that in a TDM network, the interface units occupy the entire cable bandwidth during transmission. In an FDM/TDM network, they occupy only that portion of the bandwidth allotted to them by the network designer, leaving the remainder for other uses. Just as in a TDM network, the interface units may be used to communicate between otherwise incompatible devices. In such a network, the cable bandwidth might be divided into a number of different user groups, with several independent subnetworks provided for the various groups. These could coexist in real time with numerous virtual point-to-point and multipoint circuits, depending on network requirements. Since such a network is basically an FDM design, numerous bands could be reserved for video or additional analog services.

In a typical baseband network, there is essentially a single communications channel, which all using devices can access. Network control is generally distributed among the many interface units that share the network. Consequently, it is the network-access protocol that stands between efficient network operation and chaos.

One access scheme, token passing, ensures relatively tight control over the network. It achieves "fairness"; that is, there is little possibility that any one device or interface unit will hog more than its share of bus capacity. It also eliminates the inefficiency caused by collisions between contending bus-interface units. A priority-access arrangement can be used, with designated interface units being sent the token more often than others.

But there are also disadvantages to token passing. Bandwidth is not entirely available on demand, and there is overhead associated with passing the token. Therefore, if the control token is passed to each interface unit in turn, including those that have nothing to send, then those that do have traffic to send will have somewhat less network capacity at their disposal. Token passing also requires error recovery mechanisms that enable the network to recognize and recover from the effects of garbled or lost tokens and from the failure of an interface unit to forward the token.

Most baseband local networks, including Net/One, Ethernet, Hyperbus, and Hyperchannel, use contention-type control. The bandwidth of the bus is available on demand, so that contention is well suited to environments in which each device using the network possesses bursty (low-duty-cycle) traffic characteristics.

A basic contention-based access protocol is carrier-sense multiple access with collision detection (CSMA/CD). Under this protocol, the interface unit through which each communicating device is connected to the network first "listens" to the bus (senses carrier) to see if it is free before transmitting its own accumulated frame. A contention-based access protocol for control of either a baseband or a broadband network involves trade-offs between speed, frame size, maximum allowable round-trip propagation delay throughout the network, and efficiency.

A priority-access scheme can refine contention: Each interface unit is pre-assigned a fixed value that must effectively be added to the random-retry interval

that it computes on detecting a collision. The interface unit with the lowest pre-assigned fixed value will have the shortest retry interval, giving it the highest priority in beginning the retransmission of its packet. To maintain efficiency during peak traffic periods, the interface units can adjust the length of their retry intervals upward as the frequency of collisions increases. This operation is known as back-off.

Independent paths
Unlike baseband networks, broadband networks may possess a physical focal point (the head-end facility) at which amplification and frequency translation take place. However, this does not necessarily mean that control of the network is centralized.

With broadband networks, a great many simultaneous, independent communications paths are possible in real time, and it is not necessary to depend on an access protocol to mediate between numerous interface units vying for time on the bus. An FDM network, like conventional communications media, simply supplies a transparent communications medium. Any conventional circuit configuration (that is, point-to-point or multipoint) may be implemented using broadband cable by substituting RF modems for the conventional modems or line drivers. Then control may be imposed through conventional communications link protocols [such as binary synchronous communications (BSC) and synchronous data link control (SDLC)] enacted by the communicating devices themselves.

A network-control technique unique to broadband networks uses frequency separation between channels. However, rather than using a static, semipermanent frequency assignment, the channels are allocated dynamically, through the use of frequency-agile RF modems. Such a network may use a contention channel for requests for channel allocation and demand-allocated dedicated channels for the actual traffic.

Figure 1 compares typical baseband and broadband networks configured to supply communications services under the same physical circumstances. In the baseband network shown in Figure 1A, each cable segment follows the bus layout, with the main cable itself connected to each transceiver serving a network-access point. Active repeaters are required to regenerate the signal when the desired cable length is greater than the maximum allowed (typically 500 to 1,200 meters) or when the maximum number of transceivers per cable segment (typically from 100 to 250) would otherwise be exceeded.

Repeaters can lend flexibility to baseband-network design. Although passive bus splitters cannot be used in baseband networks, active repeaters can connect several cable segments to form a tree or star configuration. However, only a small number of repeaters may be allowed between any two communicating stations. Regardless of the physical layout eventually reached with baseband and broadband, the logical design is still considered to be that of a bus.

Since there are propagation time limits beyond which the access protocol loses efficiency, the number of cable segments that can be connected by simple re-

peaters is restricted. To extend the network beyond these limits, the network must be divided in two, with the portions separated by a buffered repeater, or filter repeater. Unlike the simple repeater, it ignores (filters) all frames that do not bear the address of a device on the other portion of the network. When a frame bearing an appropriate address is detected, it is momentarily stored while the buffered repeater acquires control of the adjacent portion of the network for which the frame is intended. It is then sent, just as if the buffered repeater were a bus-interface unit originating a frame. (While buffered repeaters are supported as a concept by most local-network vendors, there are no known buffered repeaters available for purchase at this time.)

Besides enlarging the allowable physical extent of a baseband network, buffered repeaters can be useful in alleviating network congestion when much of the traffic is between stations on the same subnetwork. A buffered repeater could place this subnetwork into semi-isolation, freeing the remainder of the network from the higher-density traffic.

The broadband layout in Figure 1B shows the same topology as the baseband layout (Fig. 1A). One obvious difference is the broadband's retransmission facility. In single-cable broadband local networks, the retransmission facility receives information from communicating devices on the low-frequency end of the spectrum and retransmits it to all devices on the spectrum's high end. A second difference is that there are no repeaters used on the cable; CATV amplifiers can be employed if necessary (see "Broadband technology magnifies local network capability," DATA COMMUNICATIONS, February 1980, p. 61).

Guidelines for bus selection
In choosing the type of coaxial cable suitable for a network, the user must evaluate design trade-offs, including size, ruggedness, electrical loss, ease of handling, and cost. In commercial CATV distribution systems, which cover long distances, requirements generally dictate that different types of cable be used for various parts of the "tree" layout. The trunk would be composed of cable with very good electrical characteristics, including very low loss, to minimize the number of amplifiers required. Such cable is generally from 0.7 to 1 inch in diameter, with a shield of solid aluminum. More loss can be tolerated in the cables extending from the trunk, known as feeder cables, so that less-expensive cable with a smaller diameter and a braided-foil shield might be used. Still more loss is acceptable in the drop cables extending to each network-access point. In broadband communications networks with shorter distances, three types of cable may not be necessary.

It is easier to start up a small-scale network using baseband than using broadband. The minimum baseband configuration is no more than two baseband transceivers, two bus interface units (which might already exist within certain office equipment), and a length of terminated coaxial cable.

A broadband network, on the other hand, typically requires a greater initial commitment, particularly if it

1. Brief comparison. *Baseband cable leaves and enters area A at the same point and doubles back on itself. One branch heads to area B, and the other to area D. A* *repeater is used in area C to avoid the doubling back. The broadband areas show drop cables extending from the main cable to users. An amplifier boosts signal levels.*

(A) BASEBAND

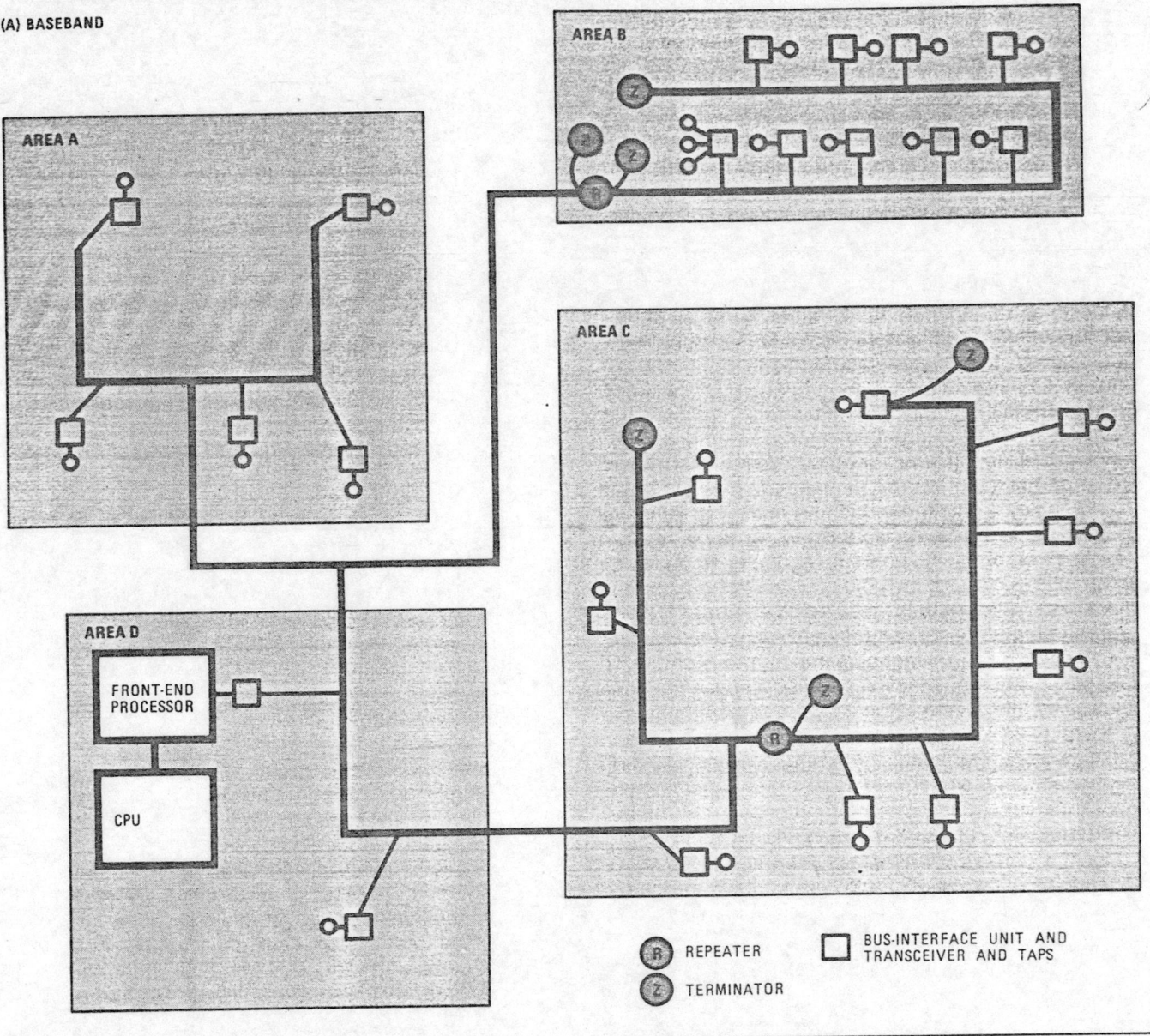

will handle analog video and if it is to offer maximum future adaptability. The network should be designed by competent personnel, with attention paid to RF power levels at various points and the likely location and ultimate number of access points. The location of the retransmission facility (if used) must be planned, and its equipment purchased and installed. Once in place, the network must be aligned, with frequency and amplitude equalized and standing wave ratios taken, among other things.

Baseband capacity and performance
Baseband/TDM and broadband/FDM have different strengths and limitations in their capacity and performance. General-purpose baseband networks accept

data at rates ranging from approximately 4 to 10 Mbit/s. The effective network throughput must always be less, for several reasons.

One reason is the way user devices share the bus. Under the CSMA/CD access protocol, frame collisions will inevitably occur, requiring back-off and retransmission. The collision rate—and its consequences—depend on several factors, including the degree of network loading, the frame length, the time required for a frame to be propagated throughout the network, and the possible existence of a priority-access scheme. Studies of one local network using CSMA/CD indicate that when the total traffic load that devices are trying to send rises above 100 percent of the bus transfer rate, actual bus use remains above 95 percent.

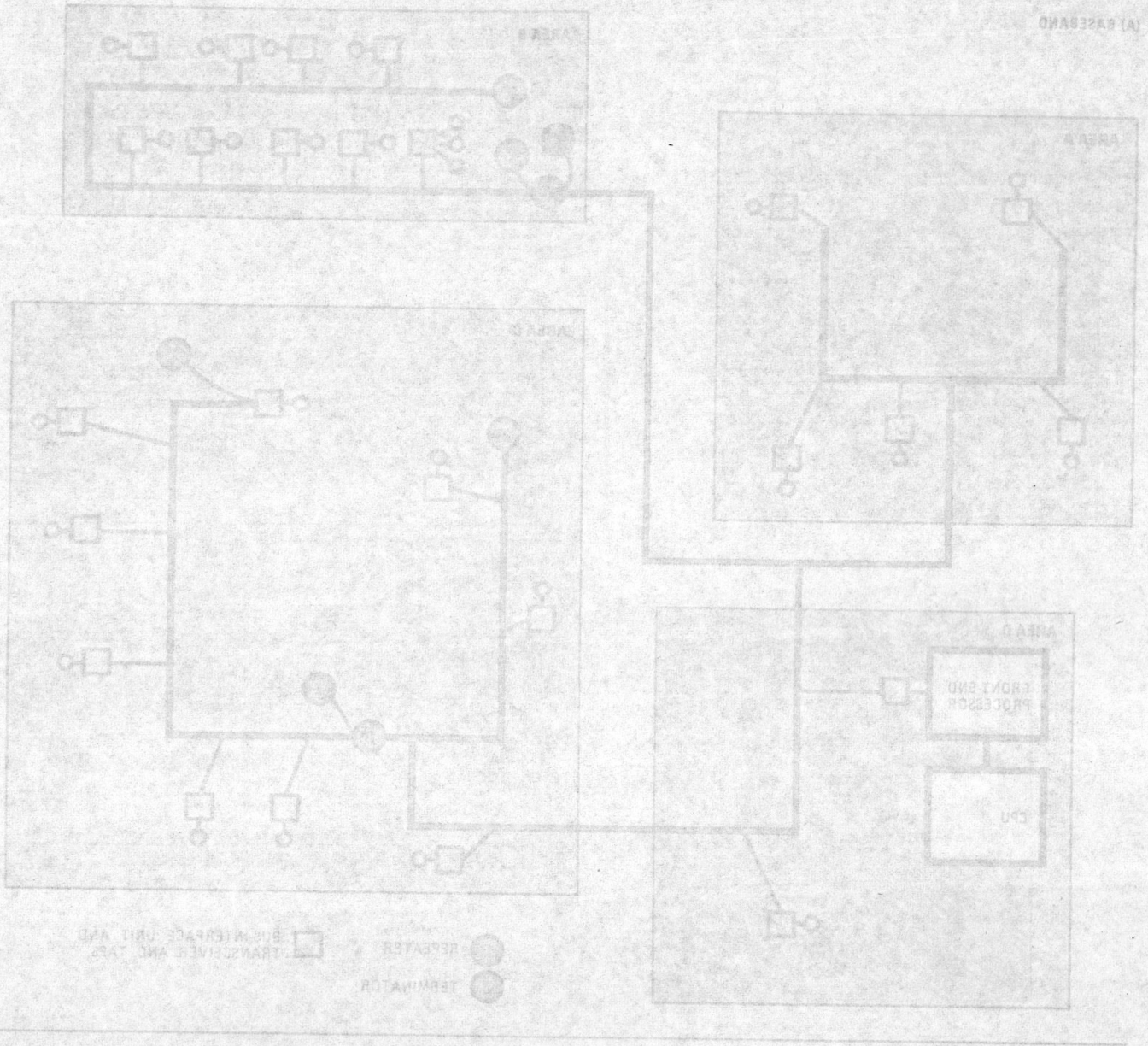

(B) BROADBAND

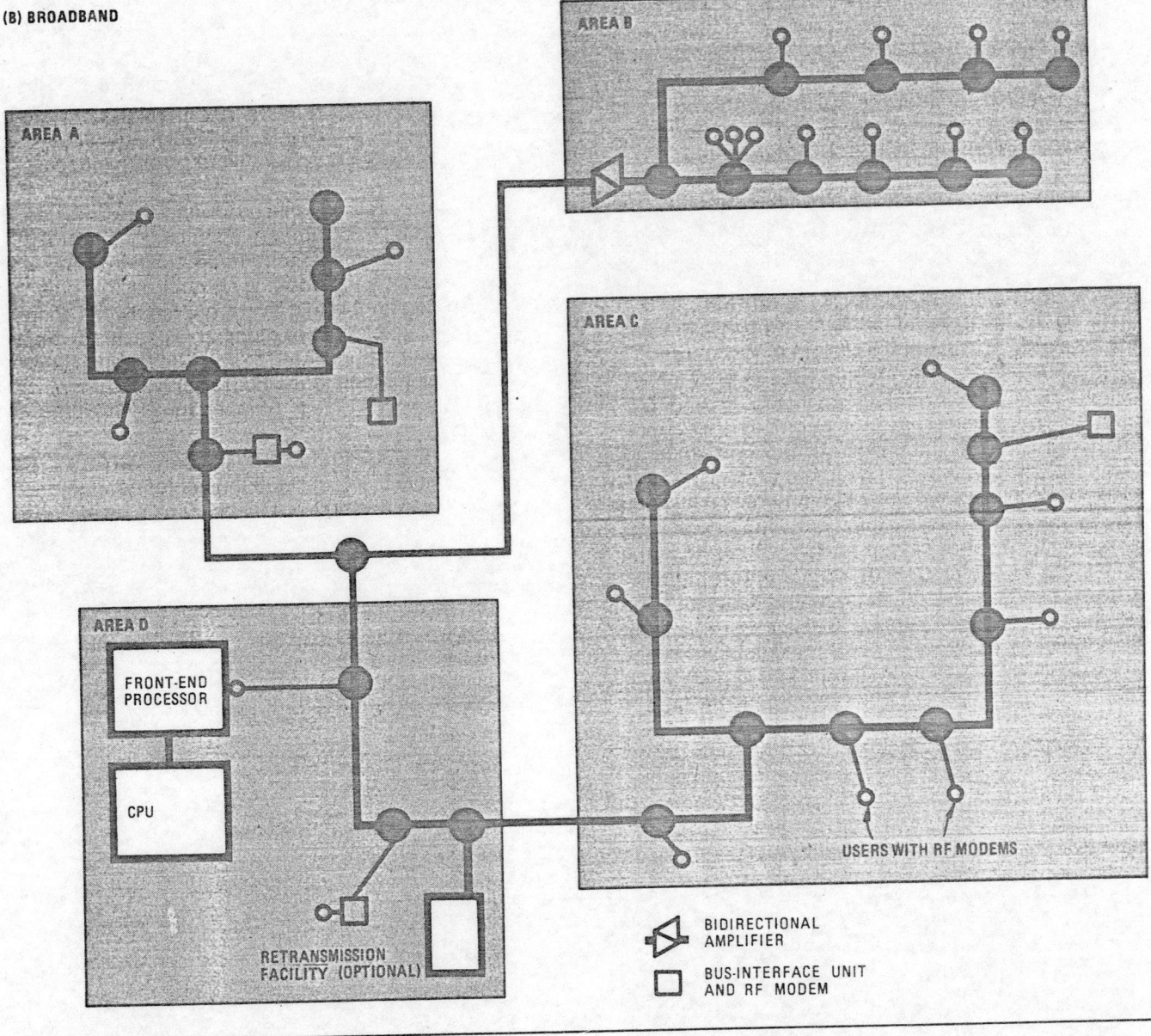

AREA B

AREA A

AREA C

AREA D

FRONT-END
PROCESSOR

CPU

RETRANSMISSION
FACILITY (OPTIONAL)

USERS WITH RF MODEMS

BIDIRECTIONAL
AMPLIFIER

BUS-INTERFACE UNIT
AND RF MODEM

All the bits counted toward bus use do not represent user data, however. A more serious factor lowering effective network throughput is overhead from various sources. On one local network, which did not require an acknowledgment for each frame successfully received, approximately 21 percent of all bits transiting the bus during actual use represented overhead traceable to the network and internetwork environment itself. (This figure is influenced by a great many variables and should be taken only as a very rough indicator of the network's expected performance.)

Effective bus throughput is only one aspect of baseband network capacity. Another, and one that more directly concerns each network user, is the maximum data rate that the network can accept from and deliver to an individual device. The interface unit often imposes limitations that may be more severe than expected from looking at network specifications.

Still another performance issue is delay. The length of this period depends on a number of factors. When a contention access protocol is used, this delay may vary with network conditions and may also be imposed "unfairly"; that is, last-in/first-out contention may occur during high-traffic periods. When a token-passing access protocol is used, the delay tends to be more constant and predictable.

A local network's capacity and performance can be greatly influenced by the characteristics of the traffic applied to it. For instance, the efficiency of a network using contention can be greatly reduced if it is used to

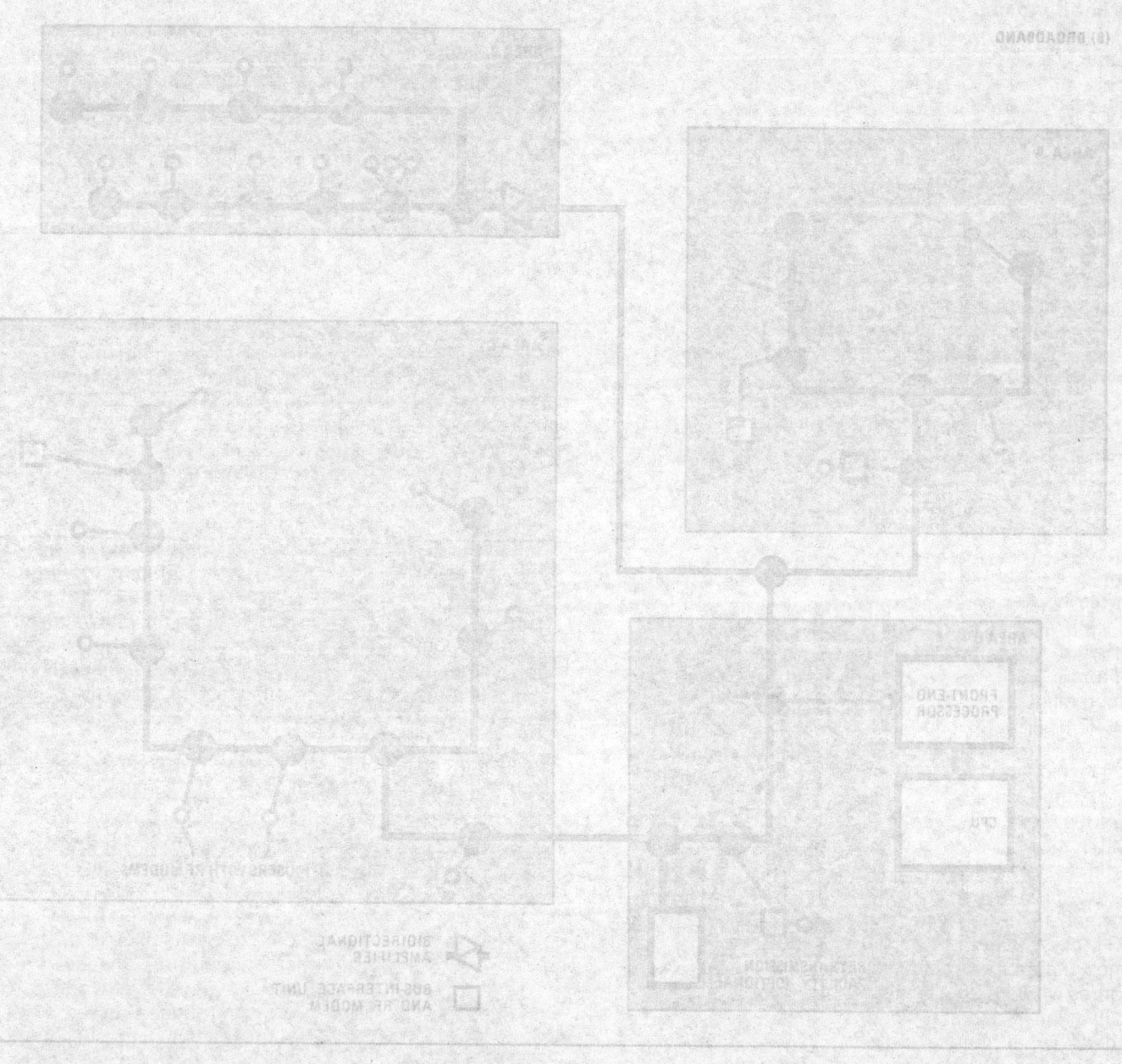

serve devices generating short frames at a high duty cycle, in contrast to "bursty," low-duty-cycle traffic.

Broadband capacity

The first step in evaluating the capacity of a broadband network is to consider its total bandwidth: the complete range of frequencies usable for information transmission. The greater the bandwidth of the network or of one channel, the greater the potential information-carrying capacity. Typical single-cable broadband networks have bandwidths of approximately 250 MHz.

The second step is evaluating the modems' use of the bandwidth. RF modems accept the data from the communicating device and convert it into RF signals, whose frequencies lie within a pre-assigned portion of the bus's total bandwidth. The range of the frequencies used by the modem constitute its bandwidth. As a general rule, the higher a modem's transmission speed, the larger the amount of bandwidth it will occupy.

RF modems presently provide speeds from a few bits per second to several megabits per second. (A few bits per second is unusual, but there are RF modems in building-monitoring setups that operate at 1 bit every several seconds.) The amount of bandwidth required by each modem depends not only on its speed but on its bandwidth efficiency. For instance, two modems from different manufacturers, each capable of a data rate of 1.5 Mbit/s, may occupy bandwidths from 1.5 Mhz to 6 MHz. Of course, the more efficient the modem, the greater its cost—in this case, by a factor of about 3. RF modems of lower maximum speeds tend to be relatively less bandwidth-efficient. For instance, modems capable of 19.2 kbit/s may require bandwidths in the neighborhood of 100 kHz.

The ultimate digital capacity of a broadband network, then, depends on the available network bandwidth and the efficiency of the modems. For example, with multiple 1.5-Mbit/s modems, a single-cable broadband network of 250-MHz bandwidth would have a maximum digital capacity approaching 250 Mbit/s, if the relatively efficient modems were used, or about 63 Mbit/s, with the inefficient (but less-expensive) ones. If a double-cable design were used, the above figures would be more than doubled.

Evaluating capacity becomes more complicated when a broadband network serves video and facsimile applications, as well as digital data. Full-bandwidth video is the service most demanding of bandwidth, with each video channel occupying 6 Mhz. For two-way video as used in teleconferencing, 12 MHz is required.

Vulnerability to failure

Every communications network has areas of vulnerability to accidental or deliberately caused failure. Most conventional networks, for instance, have multiple parallel communications links converging on a central point at which switching equipment is located. This type of network is relatively immune to serious consequences resulting from the failure of a single link, since such a failure would tend to impact only a single user of a single service. On the other hand, such a conventional network is vulnerable to problems affecting the centralized switching equipment, particularly since such equipment is complex enough to be difficult to troubleshoot, and its expense generally prevents it from being provided in fully redundant form.

The vulnerabilities of a bus-based network are reversed. There is no centralized switching equipment serving the entire network. In the case of broadband networks, the relativley low expense of the head-end equipment permits redundancy, and its simplicity promotes high reliability and rapid fault isolation. Instead, a bus-based network is vulnerable to problems affecting the bus.

The cable generally used in baseband networks has 50-ohm impedance, comprises a combination braided-foil shield, and is in the neighborhood of 0.4 inch in diameter. Since the tree topology is not possible on a single cable segment within a baseband network, there are no couplers, splitters, or drop cables. Instead, the main cable itself is connected to each baseband transceiver. The connection to the bus is generally made with a pressure-type of tap. To make the connection, the bus cable is pierced and "cored" with a special tool, and the tap is clamped onto the cable while a sharp point makes contact with the center conductor.

The baseband transceiver must generally be attached directly to the tap to minimize the length of the "stub." There are several advantages to these arrangements. The cable is fairly flexible and easily handled (although the minimum bend radius can be a problem), making for convenient installation. A tap may be installed at nearly any point along the cable (subject to spacing limitations), lending adaptability, since the location of possible future taps along the cable need not be anticipated.

However, if a vital main cable is stepped on, pinched, twisted, and kinked, its electrical characteristics may be altered at the damaged point, causing an impedance mismatch. When a frame, beginning to be propagated along the cable, encounters an impedance mismatch, several abnormalities occur. A portion of its transmission power (how much depends on the degree of mismatch) is reflected from the mismatch, back toward the bus-interface unit that transmitted the frame. The nonreflected portion of the signal continues past the damaged point with reduced power. If of sufficient magnitude, these reflections can result in each bus-interface unit detecting an apparent collision (with itself) each time it attempts to transmit.

The impedance mismatch resulting from the disconnection of a section of cable or loss of a segment termination has a similar effect. Since this problem disrupts all communication on that portion of the network not isolated by a buffered repeater, it appears that there is no rapid and effective way of isolating the problem, short of time-domain reflectometry, possibly after turning off each affected interface unit to prevent interference from the attempted frame transmission. Using a time-domain reflectometer, a technician sends an electrical pulse along the cable. The pulse detects any fault it encounters. A portion of the pulse is reflected back to the reflectometer, hence its name. The amount of time from the pulse emission to its arrival

2. Redundancy. *A bus-interface unit (BIU) or communicating device is connected to only one cable at a time. If one cable fails, its output is switched to the second cable.*

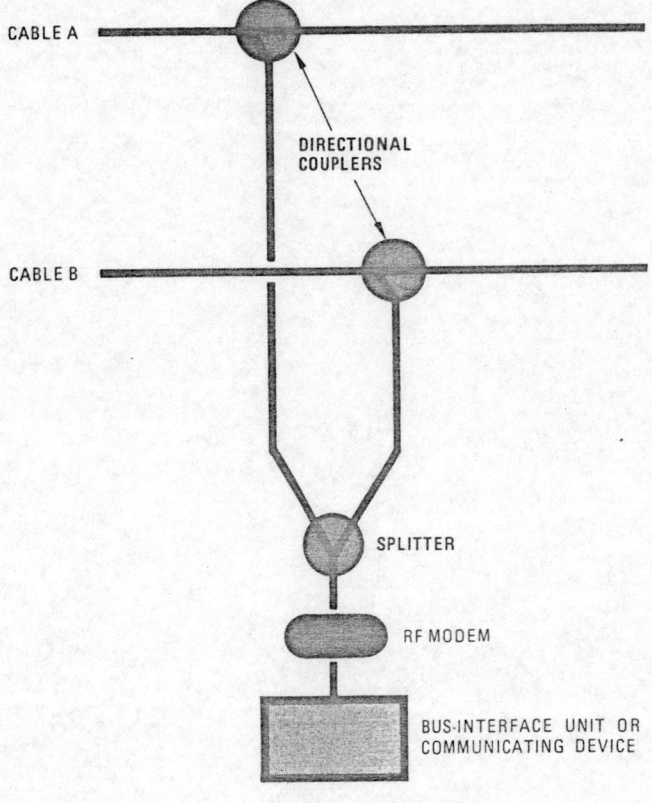

CABLE A

DIRECTIONAL COUPLERS

CABLE B

SPLITTER

RF MODEM

BUS-INTERFACE UNIT OR COMMUNICATING DEVICE

---

back at the reflectometer is measured to gauge the distance to the fault, whereon the technician can plan remedial action. In actual practice, sections of cable will probably have to be systematically disconnected and terminated, until the interface units on remaining cable sections cease detecting constant spurious collisions and begin to function normally. The precise location of the damaged point along the affected section would then have to be determined, and the damage repaired, or the entire cable section replaced.

A large baseband network, consisting of multiple subnetworks connected by buffered repeaters, would not be totally disabled by such a failure, since the problem would not extend beyond the buffered repeaters into adjoining subnetworks. Portions of the network on either side of the affected subnetwork would be totally isolated, however. The susceptibility of baseband networks to problems of this kind in actual large-scale use remains to be seen.

Broadband cable has 75-ohm impedance. The trunk cable may be semi-rigid with a shield of solid aluminum and may range in diameter from approximately 0.4 inch to 1.1 inches. It is less apt to be damaged than the baseband bus cable because of its ruggedness and its distance from the connections to each network-access point. In other words, less trunk cable is used, and it can be better protected.

In a mid-split broadband network equipped with bus-

interface units employing a CSMA/CD access protocol, the modem of each interface unit uses one frequency in transmitting and "listens" for a different frequency in receiving. This means that in case of an impedance mismatch, the reflection of a transmitted signal back to its source would not be "heard" by the modem and would not be interpreted as a collision by the interface unit. To affect the network, a cable would have to be damaged badly enough to reduce the signal level passing through the damaged point so that other modems could not satisfactorily receive it after it had been frequency-shifted and retransmitted. If this occurred, only that portion of the network on the "downstream" (from the retransmission facility) side of the damaged point would be adversely affected. The rest of the network would continue to operate.

Ways around problems

With both baseband and broadband networks, there are procedures to reduce cable damage and similar failures and to minimize their consequences. One is simply to place the cable in conduit when it passes through areas particularly vulnerable to damage. Another is to plan for "inevitable" failures by building in serviceability during network design. This includes devising means to rapidly detect and bypass a damaged section of cable or other fault.

In baseband networks, a physical layout that segments the cable permits rapid fault isolation. Multiple cable segments radiating from a single point allow users to systematically disconnect cable segments so as to identify the segment with the failure. Once the affected segment has been bypassed, the remainder of the network can resume normal operation while the fault on the disconnected segment is pinpointed. Each cable segment should be broken into sections, by placing the appropriate connectors at intervals on the cable, to facilitate this process.

Also, users might limit the number of transceivers placed on each segment to some figure below the allowed maximum to minimize the impact of disconnecting a segment and to ease the task of locating the source of the failure. In this case, the decrease in reliability due to the use of greater numbers of repeaters would have to be weighed against the expected bene-

---

3. Amplified reliability. *Duplicate broadband amplifiers are used for continuous operation. If one amplifier fails, however, the collective output level will drop.*

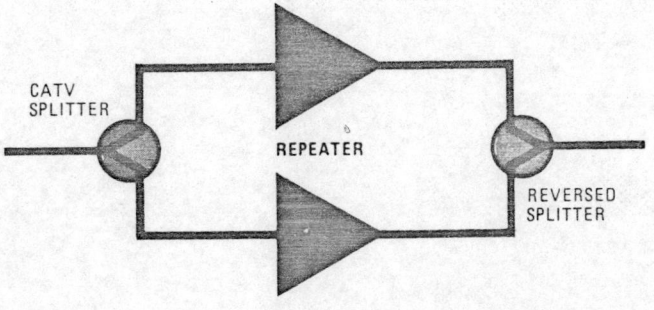

CATV SPLITTER

REPEATER

REVERSED SPLITTER

37

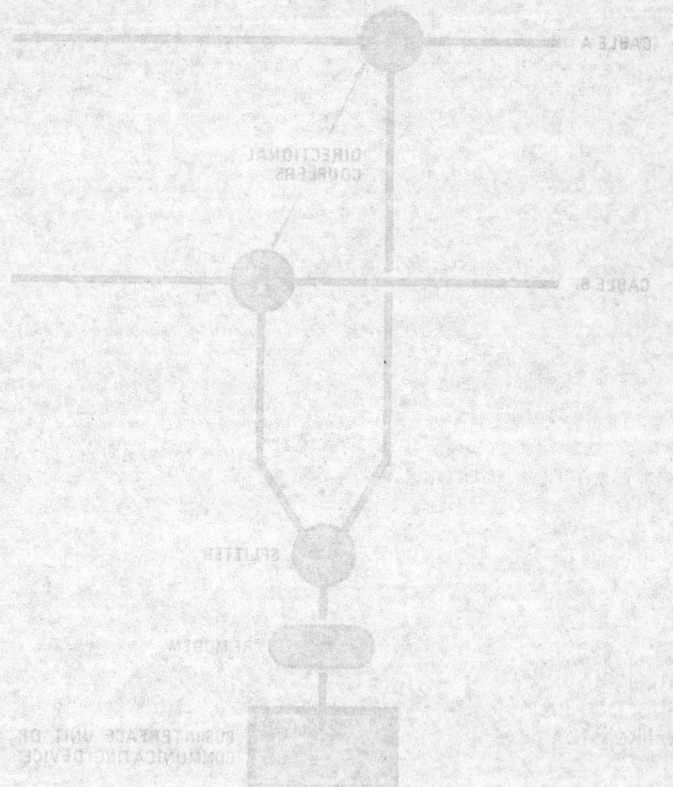

fits resulting from a reduction of the MTTR (mean time to repair). Also, the use of time-domain reflectometry (TDR) would indicate to maintenance personnel both the magnitude of any cable discontinuity and its distance along the cable from the test equipment. If TDR were used, accurate cable routing and transceiver-placement records would have to be maintained to relate the output of the test equipment to the physical location of the fault.

The best insurance against serious consequences resulting from damage to the bus might be a redundant cable. This redundancy can be provided in several ways, one of which is illustrated in Figure 2.

Unfortunately, in the baseband realm, only one network (Hyperchannel) currently provides the capability of a backup cable, and the location of the transceivers can cause problems. They are often deliberately placed in somewhat inaccessible locations (such as above a false ceiling) to discourage accidental or deliberate tampering or damage. This means that manually making the change from one bus to the other might be difficult unless redundant transceivers were also provided, with one permanently attached to each bus. Users would then manually change their bus-interface units from one transceiver to the other in the event of a failure. If redundant cables are used, it is wise to consider the principle of diverse routing, which provides enough physical separation of cables so that an accident or other occurrence causing damage to one would not be likely to affect the other.

Network control

The equipment common to both baseband networks and broadband networks includes active devices such as amplifiers, power supplies, modulators, and repeaters—the failure of which would affect all or large portions of the network. In a broadband network, the common equipment is generally located at the cable head-end, at the retransmission facility. This location also serves as a convenient central point for network technical control. Standard CATV components are generally used, taking advantage of the maturity of the technology and reliability of the equipment. Statistics gathered by one CATV operator indicated a mean time between failures for amplifiers of over 48,000 hours and for power supplies of over 100,000 hours, although typical figures are somewhat lower.

In spite of this reliability, it is wise to provide a full complement of backup equipment, along with adequate patching facilities, test equipment, and training. During network design, when possible, an attempt should be made to place all active equipment within the head-end and technical-control facility, to facilitate fault isolation. However, if the number of network-access points or the distances involved are great enough, it may be necessary to locate amplifiers remote from the head-end facility.

Such amplifiers can be powered from the cable itself, by power supplies located at the retransmission facility, so that it is not necessary to obtain power externally in areas where commercial power backup may not be readily available. If such an amplifier fails, only the portion of the network "downstream" from the cable head-end would likely be affected, with the remainder of the network operating normally. Depending on the reliability requirements of the network, parallel redundant amplifiers could be used, as illustrated in Figure 3.

Other problems

Dedicated equipment is that which is devoted to the use of relatively few communicating devices, and whose failure would generally not seriously disrupt large portions of the network. The bus-interface unit used in both baseband pure TDM and FDM/TDM networks typically supplies bus access to form one to four communicating devices. Although reliability figures on interface units are not readily available, the fact that they use the same technology as typical microcomputers, and are of approximately the same complexity, may be a rough indicator as to their reliability. The baseband transceiver is a piece of dedicated equipment unique to baseband networks. Again, reliability figures are not readily available, but their simplicity is a point in their favor in this regard.

Since in baseband networks each interface unit or transceiver occupies the entire bus bandwidth when transmitting, and since baseband transceivers are generally connected directly to the bus without isolation, baseband networks are potentially vulnerable to two types of dedicated equipment failure which could occasionally impact the entire network: streaming and impedance changes.

A streaming-terminal condition occurs when a terminal on a multidrop line does not wait to be polled, insteand transmitting in a continuous stream. When this occurs, data from all other terminals on the line becomes unintelligible and useless. On a baseband network, a streaming bus-interface unit that ignored the normal access protocol would disable the network, but transceivers are equipped to prevent this.

Of course, the bus-interface units used in an FDM/TDM network could fail in a similar way. Even though the consequences would not be as serious, since only the bandwidth accessible to the RF modem is affected, an independent fail-safe timing circuit is desirable.

The second potentially serious problem concerns the baseband transceiver, which normally presents a high impedance to the bus. Since it is generally connected directly to the bus cable, any individual transceiver failure (such as a shorted transistor or faulty drive circuitry) that resulted in anything other than the normal high impedance could cause reflections that would disable the entire network, just as in the case of a damaged bus cable. Here also, locating a faulty transceiver could be difficult.

RF modems, because of features such as loopback switches, can assist in problem diagnosis. They are connected to the bus through CATV taps. Since each RF modem has access to only a specific frequency band, a modem failure which resulted in, say, constant carrier being transmitted (rather than controlled carrier) would affect only a particular frequency band, rather than the entire network. ∎

Edward Cooper, Sytek Inc., Sunnyvale, Calif.

13 often-asked questions about broadband

How much basic information do you know about the technology used in many of today's local networks? One broadband provider answers many common user questions.

Once only the technological property of the cable television (CATV) industry, broadband has in recent years become increasingly attractive to data communications users for local networking applications. [See related story, p. 127 and DATA COMMUNICATIONS, February 1980, p. 61.] But because CATV and data communications are relatively new partners, many users are still somewhat confused by the radio-frequency (RF)-based technology that offers multichannel, megabit-range communications. In the following article, some of the often-asked questions about broadband are answered. Scattered throughout the article are a number of common design symbols used in sketching broadband networks.

Perhaps before going any further, one basic question should be addressed: Where did the word broadband originate? Although its precise origin is somewhat fuzzy, the word was first used by the cable television industry during the 1950s to distinguish radio-frequency distribution's capabilities from those of such narrowband media as twisted pair, and even from baseband, another common local network medium.

1 Does the FCC have to approve a broadband local network?

A broadband local network falls under the heading of a master antenna television (MATV) distribution system, which does not require FCC approval. So the FCC regulations for the CATV community do not apply to the broadband local network user.

2 How difficult are broadband networks to design?

Broadband networking, and its RF technological base, grew out of the CATV industry. This communications community has 30 years' experience in CATV/broadband component development and implementation. Broadband communications uses the same basic components and design aspects as well-established CATV.

Two factors must be considered in broadband network design: the network components and the network configuration. The design standards are the same for all manufacturers. As a result, all broadband components are interchangeable, making the components universal. Even the connectors and amplifiers have been standardized. Thus standards involved with network design and component selection are well known.

Broadband networks, because of their flexibility, can be designed for most applications. In fact, the tree topology of a broadband network allows for simple

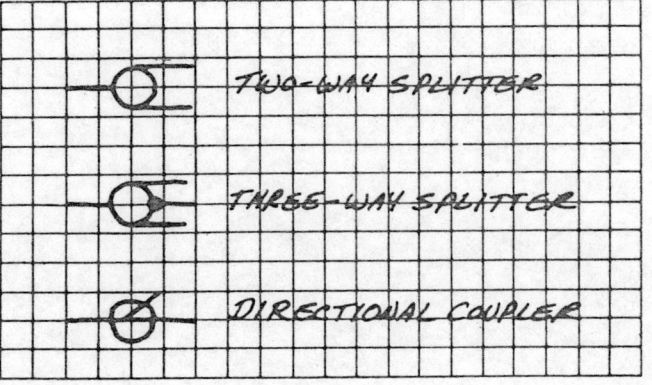

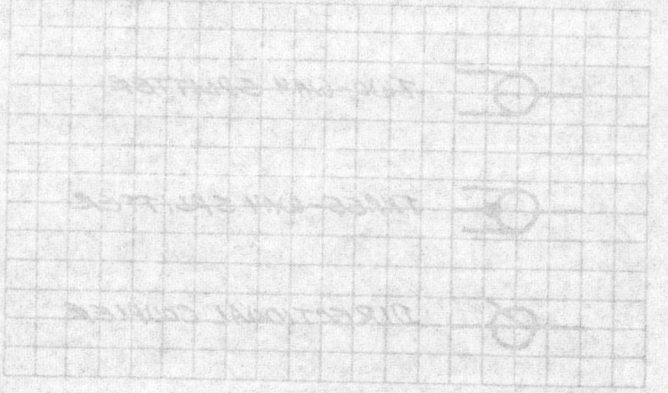

implementations of the technology.

Since 1978, the cable television industry has grown from $227.8 million to $1.8 billion in 1981. Projections indicate subscriber growth to 57.8 million in 1990, or 61 percent of the households throughout the United States.

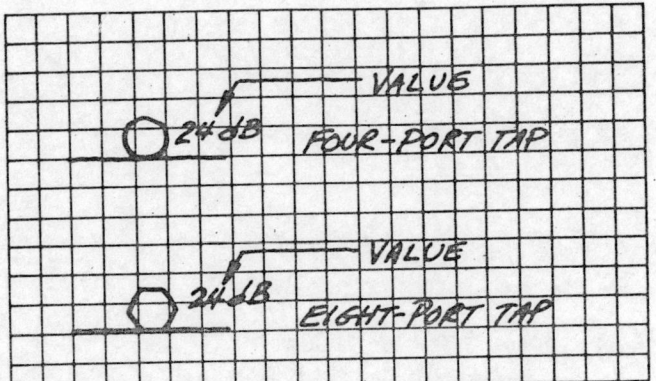

3 Must broadband be designed around a particular operating system?

Broadband is transparent to all operating systems. Once the network is designed, any RF service can be added. The network becomes transparent because of its ability to let systems operate with different signal levels and independent multiple channels. A broadband network is open-ended and allows multiple services on the network simultaneously.

4 How often do broadband components fail?

During the three decades of CATV networks, estimated mean time between failure (MTBF) of broadband components has been exceptionally high. A 30- to 40-year MTBF has been established for broadband's directional coupler tap and all other passive components. In addition, amplifiers used on broadband have an 18-year MTBF rating. Thus an average network MTBF is 25 years.

Because the cost of the cable taps is only around $20, a minimum initial capital investment exists for a basic cable network that will operate trouble-free for years. To illustrate this point, one Fortune 500 company has been operating a large broadband network (covering 5.6 million square feet) for five and a half years without a major broadband component failure.

This network is composed of 11 amplifiers, 400 taps, 20 miles of cable, and a sufficient number of outlets to allow anyone in the facility to connect to the network at any location in the plant. The network has no redundant cables, fancy switching schemes, or tandem amplifiers. Moreover, it uses off-the-shelf broadband components and amplifiers. Only at the head end are redundant data translators, switch-over units for the power supplies, and redundant CPUs used.

5 Does a broadband network's architecture limit its cable-run flexibility?

The CATV industry had to have a communications network that could be designed to meet a number of demanding specifications. The network had to be simple to install, easy to reconfigure, expandable, easily multidropped, user isolated, operational in every climate throughout the United States, and flexible enough to meet any physical requirements. A typical CATV network must be able to deliver up to 56 channels of video at no lower than a 44-dB carrier-to-noise ratio (the difference between the desired signal level and the noise activity on the cable). In addition, the network must operate with a tolerance of + or − 1.5 dB.

Because broadband local networks use the same off-the-shelf components as the CATV industry does, they also have the same performance characteristics. The branching-tree architecture of the broadband network permits a flexible scheme that can be made up of several cable lengths. Drop lengths can be up to 100 feet, with no special considerations in the backbone network's design. Consider that in a CATV environment, cable drops can be 100 to 500 feet long with additional splitters to provide cable connections to more than one TV set. Broadband local networks can be approached in the same manner, but normally each cable drop connects to only one device. That device, however, can support as many as eight RS-232-C units for data applications.

6 Does the FCC have to make periodic checks such as sweep tests on broadband networks?

Broadband networks are owned and controlled by their users, not the FCC. A typical broadband network usually is adjusted during installation. Sweep testing (to examine physical condition and set equalization and to adjust signal amplitude) of the cable is performed by the user to ensure the cable has not been damaged during installation. Once done, no further sweeping is required. This quality-performance checkout is the same for any other coaxial-based setup.

7 What basic test equipment is required to monitor a broadband local network?

In general, three items are recommended: a field-

strength meter, a spectrum analyzer calibrated for dBmV (decibels per millivolt) and 75 ohms, and a sweep and signal generator. An option is also recommended: a radiation leakage "sniffer." Of course, a datascope is handy for any data communications network as well.

8 Do broadband networks always need amplifiers?

Amplifiers are only used in broadband networks as required to meet performance standards. Because of the branching and splitting characteristics of the broadband network, signals can be distributed efficiently without amplification. Unlike networks that must be looped around, broadband can be split and directed to each area where it is required. Networks that use

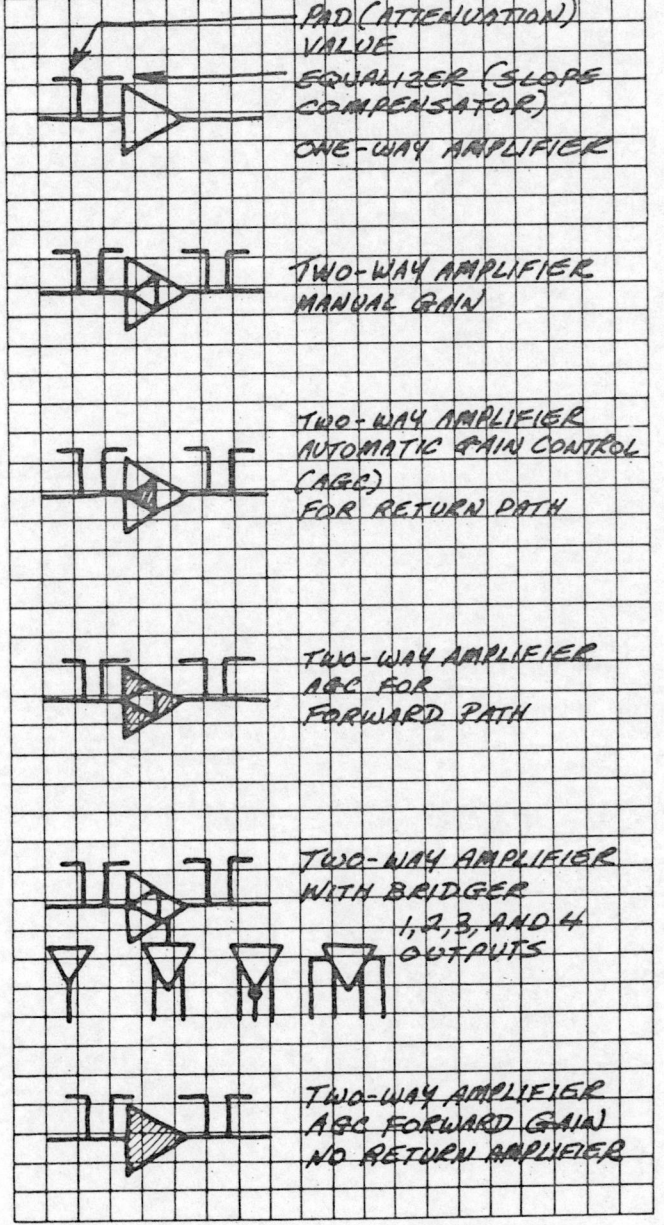

the looping technique tend to waste cable because it cannot be branched in this configuration.

For example, a 10-story building that was recently designed for broadband communications had a backbone network that could support 500 offices throughout the entire structure. The design called for no amplifiers and provided the user with long-term expansion capabilities without having to reconfigure the existing broadband setup. A broadband network of this type costs approximately $30,000, which includes both material and installation.

In another case, a large broadband network spanning several miles has over 3,000 connections throughout six buildings, each with two floors of distribution. Only six amplifiers were required to supply an RF connection anywhere in the facility within 20 feet of the main cable. If each RF outlet had an 8-port RF multiplexer connected to it, then 24,000 RS-232-C connections could be used.

9 How are adverse environmental conditions such as fluctuating temperatures handled?

Amplifiers are used to compensate for the cable's tilt (slope) in both the send and receive directions. This is done by equalizers installed in the amplifiers. Temperature variations that change the attenuation and tilt characteristics of the cable are handled in two ways. One is through thermal compensators built into the manual-gain amplifiers. Another uses a constant pilot tone generated from the head end. This pilot tone, which is transparent to the user, is detected and controlled by the automatic-gain amplifiers. Some RF modems employ pilot tones of their own, providing additional insurance that the units will operate under adverse temperature conditions. These modems use a standard sideband detection mechanism to maintain a constant signal level.

In supplying gain, the amplifier must contribute a minimum of noise injection. This noise figure directly relates to the amplifier's quality: the lower the figure, the better the amplifier. Through the use of highly efficient circuitry, amplifiers can do this job and still be in direct "cascade" alignment (amplifiers in line with each other). Up to 25 amplifiers can be used. Noise is readily calculated, with the general rule being that each time the number of amplifiers is doubled, the noise contribution goes up 3 dB. The average cost of each amplifier is less than $1,500.

Several major CATV operators have contracted with independent agencies to test radio-frequency modems over a multiple-amplifier cascade, in which the cascade ambient temperatures were changed from 0 to 100 degrees Fahrenheit. The test laboratories have up to 16 bidirectional amplifiers in environmentally controlled rooms. Data is collected on the results, which indicate that the RF modem meets the performance standards

41

for the cable television applications.

A standard broadband network would not generally be used in, say, a nuclear power plant or in certain sections of a chemical-manufacturing plant without special cable shielding.

10 Is broadband cable available with different coatings such as Teflon?

Yes. For the past 10 years, broadband CATV networks have been installed in spaces that require the use of nontoxic jacketed cables. Because CATV/broadband cables come in over 150 varieties, a cable can be selected that meets any building code standard in the United States. Unjacketed aluminum cable can be purchased that meets most state fire codes. Thus the coaxial cable becomes its own conduit through its basic construction. But the flexible drop cable also can be purchased with a Teflon coating. Four manufacturers carry and offer Teflon 75-ohm drop cables: Belden Cable, Berk-Tek, High Temp Wire, and Signa/Clad. Each manufacturer of CATV cable can provide assistance to anyone wishing to obtain Teflon coatings on their cables.

In addition, General Cable has developed a fused-disk coaxial cable that meets the most stringent fire tunnel tests that Underwriters Laboratories performs.

11 Are broadband network taps the same as those used with baseband?

Baseband networks use resistive pressure taps. These taps are installed and operate quite differently from the directional coupler taps used in broadband networks. Resistive pressure taps interface by coring the cable at the installation site. Once this is done, the taps fit around the outside of the cable, so each tap must be selected based on the cable size and the resistive value required. During the 1950s, the CATV industry used resistive taps in a few locations. It found, however, that the taps radiated at levels beyond FCC regulations. In addition, the taps allowed water to penetrate the cable, thus causing damage. As the number of channels increased on CATV networks, the resistive tap caused reflections because of its non-directivity. As a result, the directional coupler was designed.

The directional coupler has three operating parameters: isolation, directivity, and insertion loss. Isolation was an important development the resistive tap lacked. Users of the network have to be isolated from the main cable to prevent complications that could bring down the entire network.

These include isolating the user from the 60 VAC used to power amplifiers and preventing users' television sets from injecting 110 VAC into the cable. RF isolation is also needed between each user as well as

from each branch into the network. Directivity allows a more effective way of handling reflections—along with isolation—and ensures that all RF signals are directed to and from the head end.

Insertion loss is the amount of flat loss (equal loss across the entire RF spectrum) associated with each tap value. Insertion loss, which ranges from 4 dB to 2.6 dB, is generally lower for higher-value taps than for lower-value taps. All broadband taps have the same interface standards, allowing connectors from different vendors to be used.

12 What are the basic differences between broadband and baseband?

Although comparing broadband and baseband is a little like comparing apples and oranges, broadband is basically an RF-based, multiple-channel medium; baseband is a single-channel medium using digitized waveforms. The baseband medium is capable of handling up to 30 Mbit/s, while the broadband medium is capable of handling 10 times as much.

Both technologies evolved differently. Broadband was developed to meet the CATV industry's needs and was later adapted for use in the data communications field. Baseband was developed to transport digitized signals for shorter distances.

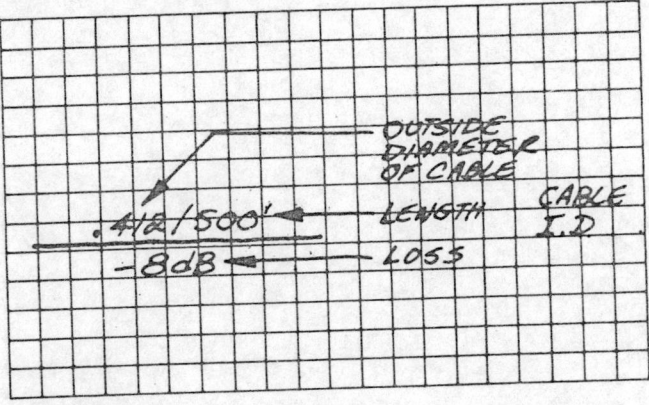

13 Is the broadband price per connection higher than baseband?

The price per connection is generally the same. A typical broadband installation with 500 drops would cost about $800 per connection.

This breaks down as follows: $50 per connection for the backbone network, including cable, taps, other components, and labor; and $750 per RF modem for each outlet.

The major benefit of broadband technology is usually considered to be its ability to allow simultaneous data, voice, and video transmission via different radio-frequency channels. ■

How fiber optics reduces a private net's growing pains

Richard C. McCaskill, Canoga Data Systems, Canoga Park, Calif.

The fiber-optic link has a much greater capacity for growth than other carriers. And fiber-optic parts now can be purchased for cost-effective network implementations.

As major corporations find more and more data communications applications, network managers are hard-pressed to interconnect their private networks cost-effectively. One method, the lightwave approach, has been used by telephone companies for some time. But glass fiber has only recently become a commercial product for data transmission networks, and businesses that experience rapid network expansion—banks, insurance companies, and brokerage houses—are discovering its benefits. In fact, optical fiber promises to be a major supplement to both twisted-pair and coaxial-cable private networks in the 1980s.

Fiber's most important electrical characteristic is its exceptional bandwidth. This can range from 400 MHz to 1 GHz—orders of magnitude more than twisted pair or coaxial cable. As a result, the multiple cables in private networks can be replaced by a single fiber.

But the wide bandwidth has an advantage more important than cable replacement. Fiber can not only provide an expandable high-capacity data network, it allows multiple channel services such as video and audio telephone to co-reside on the same fiber as pure data communications. Fiber-optic asynchronous and synchronous modems, multimegabyte data links, time-division multiplexers, and optical bus extenders (devices that convert parallel data streams to serial) are commercially available to do this job.

Even if system capacity is not considered very important, when the weight and size of twisted-pair and co-axial cables are compared with that of fiber-optic ca-

ble, fiber is still more cost-effective to install in data networks. For example, a two-fiber optic cable is the size of a lamp cord, and about 10 fiber-optic cables equal the size of one coaxial cable. Moreover, fiber-optic cable is 15 to 20 times lighter than its wire counterpart. This can mean substantial savings in both cable costs and installation costs.

Perhaps the best feature of the lightwave approach is that it can provide the network planner with a built-in capacity for growth. Until recently, network planners did not pay much attention to the long-term effects of an expanding data communications network. As new computers were needed, they installed new cables. Anticipated growth was not considered, since it was difficult to sell management on future services.

Now, at many sites, network growth is awesome. Facilities have sagging ceilings, and cable trays are at the point of collapse because of overload. And underground ducts are filled to the bursting point. As a result, streets have to be excavated for expensive duct work just to house the new cables required for growth. Such physical limitations of coaxial cable and fiber-optic's large bandwidth and small size have combined to make fiber-optic technology a more viable way of providing for network expansion.

Originally it was thought that most of the growth that fiber could satisfy would be based on modem-controlled point-to-point data links. As users became more familiar with fiber optics, they realized that the channel capacity of a fiber-optic modem was much larger than

43

that of conventional twisted-pair-based modems. With the increased bandwidth, they could more efficiently use statistical and time-division multiplexers in the network by implementing fiber-optic modems with high channel capacity (up to 56 kbit/s) to multiplex many lower-speed channels onto one fiber-optic cable.

For example, the original network might be a point-to-point link connecting a computer through a fiber-optic modem to a remote terminal. If expansion requires more terminals at the remote location, the network designer need only locate a remote terminal controller at the terminal location. This can expand the configuration to, say, 32 terminal ports connected through the same original fiber-optic modem link. Further terminal expansion can be achieved using multi-channel statistical multiplexers.

Private networks

Technology has developed to the point that both the fiber and all necessary electronic components are available for fiber-optic cabling of private networks in a variety of configurations. For example, if the computer center, located in one building, is connected to multiple terminals and printers in another building, fiber-optic cables can be supplied for aerial installation on telephone poles. Or they can be buried between buildings with rodent-proofing protection.

Regardless of which configuration is used, the availability of fiber-optic time-division multiplexers from companies such as Canoga Data Systems and Harris Corporation makes it possible to multiplex many terminals onto one single-fiber optic cable. A time-division multiplexer in each building requires only a single duplex fiber-optic cable that handles anywhere from 4 to 2,000 terminals.

Some fiber-optic time-division multiplexer manufacturers have used the cable's high bandwidth to multiplex several high-speed channels onto one fiber. For example, the Canoga Data Systems CMX-100 multiplexer can multiplex sixteen 56-kbit/s synchronous lines. Also, this unit can effectively remotely locate the electrical interface on individual multiplexer channels, since up to 3 kilometers of fiber cable can be used on each synchronous line. This eliminates any electrical interference or noise on individual channels.

Thus, the network planner does not have to locate the multiplexer near his terminal points and has greater freedom to pick convenient sites. He is not restricted by the hardware's requirements. As a bonus, those applications for which terminals and other data communications equipment are located far from the multiplexer are now possible if the multiplexer is used as a data concentrator.

An operating system developed around the remote multiplexer concept was recently installed by a midwestern computer manufacturer. (Remote, in this case, means not colocated at the data center.) This company's computer center is in one building, and its software-development center is in another. The staff had previously solved its data communications problem by installing sixteen 9,600-baud* circuits, using the local telephone company's leased lines. This arrangement was not expandable and cost $2,700 per month.

After reviewing the capabilities of fiber optics, the company elected to install the configuration illustrated in Figure 1. It placed a 16-channel multiplexer both in

*Normally the baud rate is equal to the bit rate and is expressed in bits per second. However, in some circumstances, depending on the coding or the modulation scheme used in the communications device, the baud rate and bit rate can differ.

1. Expanded multiplexing network. *A computer center in one building may be hooked up to another building's software facility with an aerial fiber-optic cable. All the* optical multiplexers and modems needed are now commercially available. The one cable has enough bandwidth for all anticipated growth.

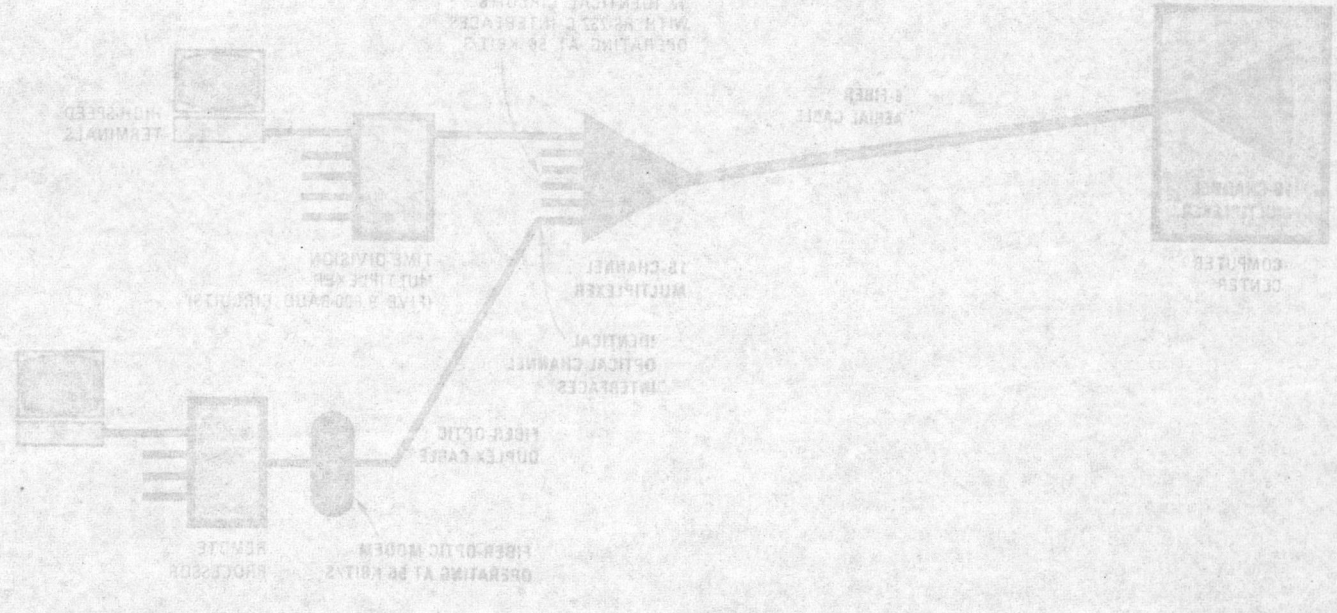

2. Internetworking. *Fiber-based modems and multiplexers enable a local network to hook up to remote local networks through satellite communications facilities. Other* *network capabilities may be used, and even international data communications may be established. Fiber bandwidth is never a problem.*

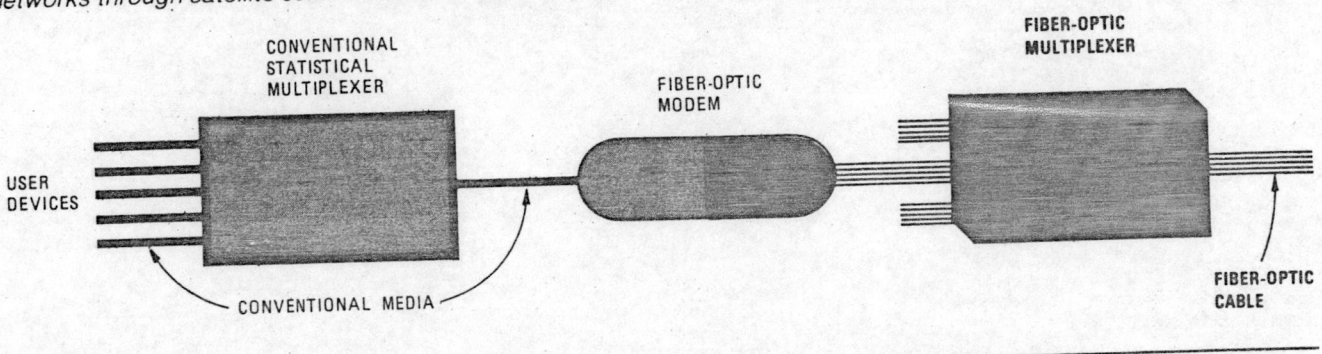

CONVENTIONAL
STATISTICAL
MULTIPLEXER

FIBER-OPTIC
MODEM

FIBER-OPTIC
MULTIPLEXER

USER
DEVICES

CONVENTIONAL MEDIA

FIBER-OPTIC
CABLE

the computer center and in the software facility. A 56-kbit/s data rate was available on all channels. To interconnect the multiplexers, the company installed a fiber-optic cable on existing telephone poles. Only two of the six fibers in the cable were needed, with four geared for expansion.

The software had to meet two requirements. On the one hand, it had to accommodate as many 9,600-baud lines as possible with no interaction of any channel to any other channel. On the other hand, it had to connect four remote processing stations (operating at a channel rate of 56 kbit/s). To satisfy these demands, the vendor added 12 RS-232-C channels, each connected to 12 Infotron time-division multiplexers. These provided five 9,600-baud lines each. The complete network thus provided sixty 9,600-baud channels.

Then, every remote processor was connected to a multiplexer through an optical channel to a synchronous fiber-optic modem. This interconnect method not only provided the high-speed lines required by the remote processors, but also eliminated the modem normally required at the multiplexer location.

The complete fiber-optic private network now serves a total of 400 users for an installed cost under $32,000. And it provides five to six times more capacity than the leased-circuit approach. Calculations based on the monthly lease price show that the expanded fiber-optic approach had a payback in less than one year.

Making it broadband

The midwestern manufacturer's fiber-optic private network can be further expanded into a broadband local network, interconnecting many buildings within a city or major industrial complex. The capabilities of fiber-optic time-division multiplexers make such networks realistic (Fig. 2). Because each channel of the time-division multiplexer can act as a remote site and handle 56-kbit/s synchronous data, it is possible to have a network in which a single fiber-optic channel extends from the network hub to a remote building. A multiplexer connected to the fiber-optic modem at the remote end of the fiber-optic link can be used to concentrate multiple terminals (from 4 to 250) onto one 56-kbit/s channel. At the same time, remote processors can use the 56-kbit/s channels to perform remote down-line

processing to the computing center.

Such fiber-optic networks with multiplexers allow users to connect directly from the computing center to the 56-kbit/s channels that are provided by RCA's service, American Satellite Corporation's services, and AT&T's Dataphone Digital Service, among others. In this way, a worldwide network can be established through one common fiber-optic network.

Distributing data

With twisted pair or coaxial cable, the network planner finds it difficult to achieve megabit-per-second rates when setting up a distributed data network in which one central computer addresses remote processing centers. In these networks, there is usually a computing center that handles the processing and data storage.

3. Distributed data. *Fiber-optic bus extenders make possible an intrabuilding distributed data network. They convert computer parallel data formats to serial formats.*

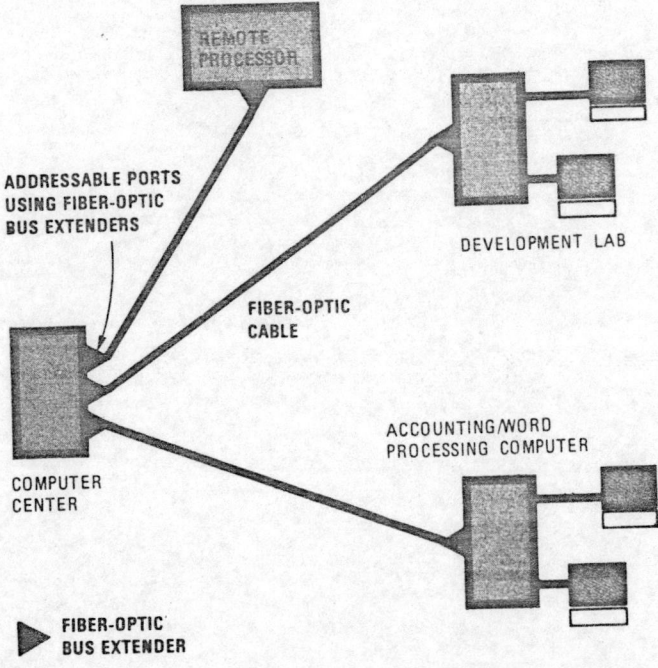

REMOTE
PROCESSOR

ADDRESSABLE PORTS
USING FIBER-OPTIC
BUS EXTENDERS

FIBER-OPTIC
CABLE

DEVELOPMENT LAB

COMPUTER
CENTER

ACCOUNTING/WORD
PROCESSING COMPUTER

FIBER-OPTIC
BUS EXTENDER

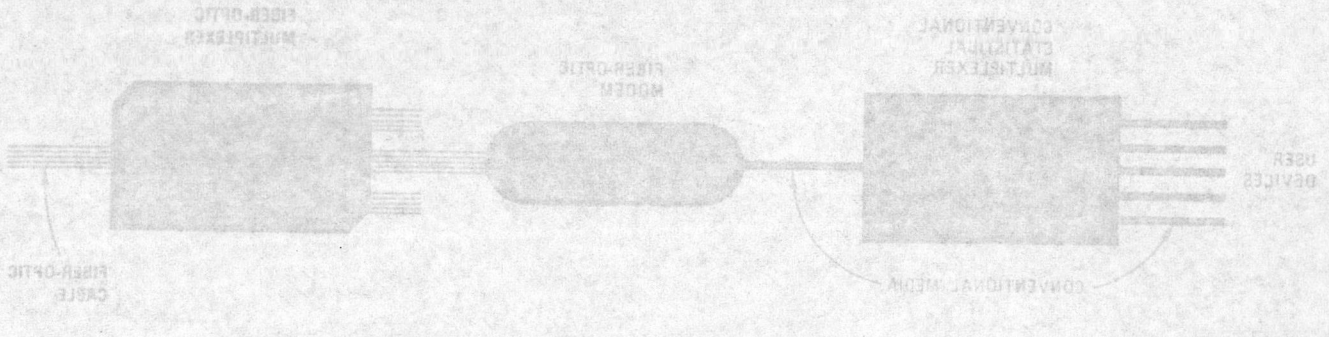

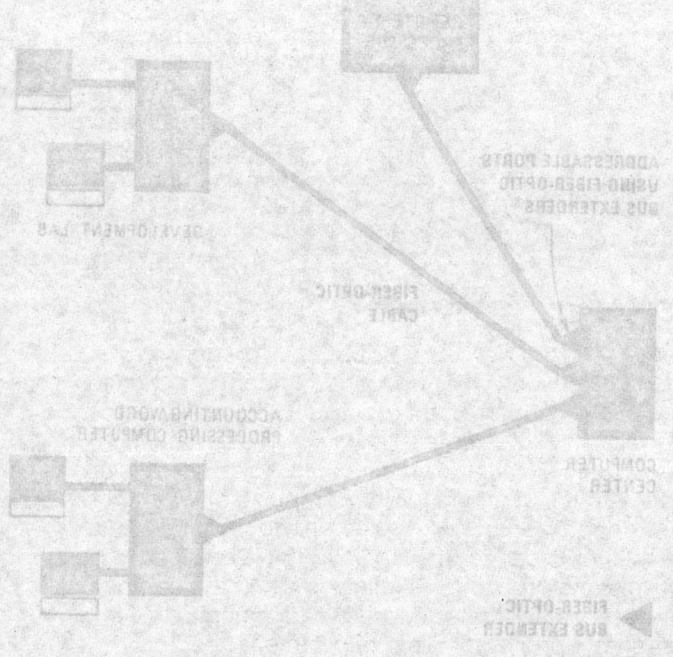

4. The same but different. *An optical bus network similar to Ethernet has hooked up terminals in a Japanese steel mill. It handles both digital and analog data transmissions,* *and defective stations are automatically bypassed. Because the fiber cable is immune to electrical noise, its data transmission is virtually error-free.*

COMMUNICATIONS EQUIPMENT

NETWORK ADAPTER

TERMINAL DISPLAY STATIONS

SINGLE-FIBER-OPTIC CABLE

OPTICAL SWITCH

Such networks are popular in corporations, college laboratories, and research and development facilities. In fact, this approach was the main data processing method in large corporations until recently when distributed data processing took hold.

Unlike in a central processing network, in a distributed data processing network, remote processors (with less capacity than the computing center) are located at various sites within the complex. In this setup, users who want to access the computing facility need not work with the slow batch processing commonly associated with computing centers.

Although remote processing is not subject to the speed limitations of batch processing, network planners realized that users of remote processors did not have the ability to tap into the large memory banks and processing capabilities of the main computer center. So these remote processing centers were hooked up to the computing center. But no high-speed communications ports were available that could communicate over twisted-pair or coaxial-type cable. The maximum data rates that could be employed in these networks was thus limited to about 1 Mbit/s serial. This is equivalent to a 50-kiloword-per-second data rate—too slow for transferring large amounts of data.

The slow data transfer problem has been overcome with recent advancements in fiber-optic high-speed parallel-to-serial bus extenders, such as those made by Canoga Data Systems and Harris Corporation. These bus extenders provide the network planner with the ability to transmit 16-bit words between processors with data speeds in the range of one-quarter million word transfers per second, thus increasing five-fold

the data transmission capacity between processors.

With such products, high-speed distributed data networks, such as that in Figure 3, can be realized. Remote processing centers, development labs, and accounting and word-processing computing centers can now all be tied into one central network connected to the main computing center. They can utilize its enormous memory capacity and computational capabilities.

For example, a large corporation has a corporate computer center based on a Digital Equipment Corporation VAX computer. In each major corporate department, there are minicomputers such as the PDP-11. All computers can be connected into one network using a 16-bit fiber-optic parallel bus extender. On each computer, the bus extender connects to a parallel 16-bit port. Each remote processor is then linked point-to-point to the computer center.

The network is controlled by the corporate computer center. This approach reduces the software required at the remote processors, since each device need communicate only with the central processor. All data is stored on disk and is accessible to all processors.

In this network, if the accounting department needs data stored in the central processor, the central processor collects the data, places it in the central high-speed memory bank, and executes a simple transfer routine to the accounting file. Complex software routines at each remote processor are not required, and the memory needed at every location is reduced.

The same procedure is followed when the company's development laboratory wants to communicate with the remote processor. That department need only transmit its data file to the central processor. This is

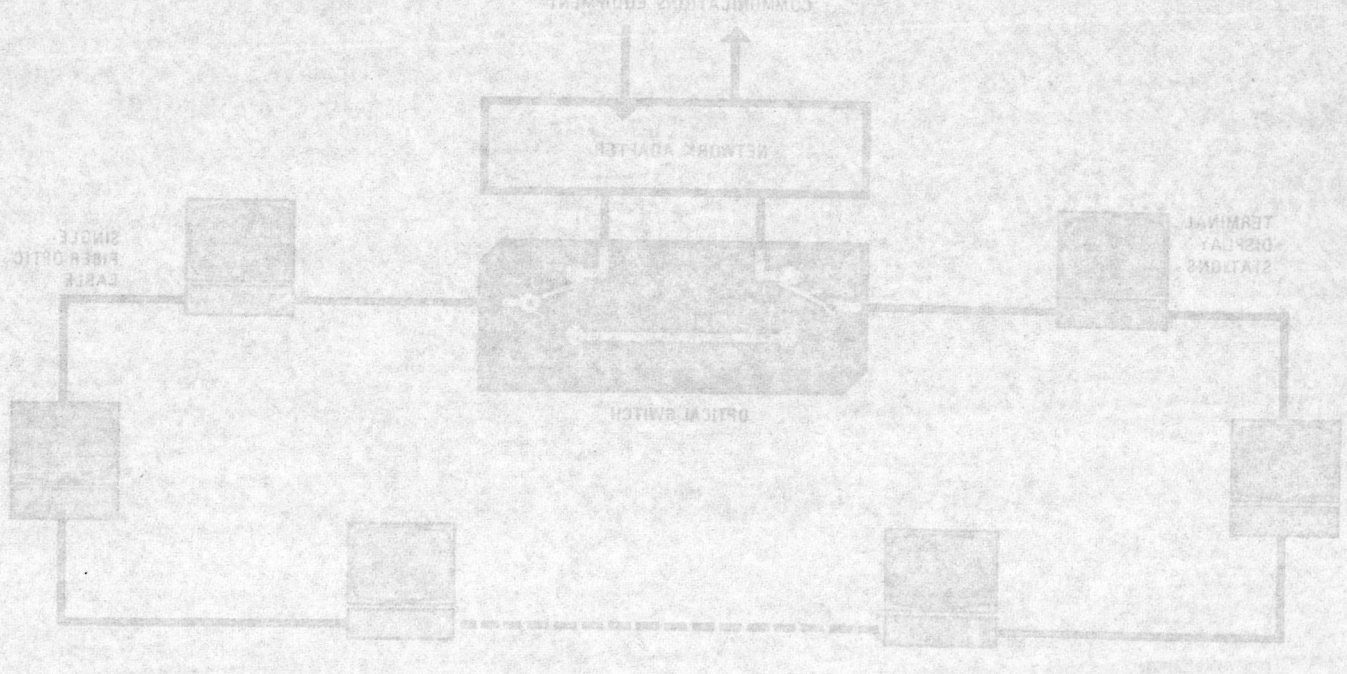

again stored in the central high-speed memory. For the last part of the procedure, the central processor notifies the remote processor that data is available and transfers the file to it.

Such a corporate communications network can be expanded even further. The high bandwidth of the fiber-optic cable allows the network to include voice (by the use of digital pulse-code-modulation channel banks with fiber-optic front ends), digital PBX (private branch exchange) devices, facsimile, and video teleconferencing. In the future, when multiple-wavelength fiber technology becomes available, network capacity will be increased even further—still with one fiber.

Not for all
Despite its advantages, fiber optics is not the ultimate networking solution. There is much discussion in the industry about establishing bus networks similar to the Ethernet and Hyperchannel approaches (see "Local networks' consensus: High speed," DATA COMMUNICATIONS, December 1980, p. 56). Fiber optics, at present, does not lend itself easily to bus networks like these. Optical tees and stars, that is, optical coupling networks, are available for use in constructing a bus configuration, but their cost and the high attenuation of signals through these couplers make this unfeasible. Fiber optics is just not yet practical in a multi-tap-off bus network.

The attenuation problem is not being ignored. There is a great deal of research going into the development of low-loss taps and tees. In fact, even with existing attenuation, in certain cases it may be advantageous to build an Ethernet-like fiber system. The enormous bandwidth, the possible elimination of radio frequency interference, and the security fiber cable provides can combine to make an irresistible private local network. This must be decided case by case.

Optical bus networks similar to Ethernet have been constructed in Japan. One (Fig. 4) is presently operating in a steel factory. It supports 34 telephones, 50 terminal display stations, and 37 sensors or indicators. The network operates at a bus data rate of 12.352 Mbit/s—enough to support 2,000 circuits over a 9-kilometer line. Both digital transmission of asynchronous data up to 6 kbit/s and synchronous data up to 64 kbit/s are provided, as is analog transmission from 300 to 3.4K Hz. This analog transmission is not provided by the U.S. Ethernet concept.

The Japanese loop operates in a passive mode wherein data is passed through each terminal data station. If any terminal display station fails, optical switches bypass the fault. The cost at each tap point is significantly more than that of the coaxial tap approach, but the single-fiber cable is considerably less expensive. The electrical noise of the machinery in the steel plant does not affect the fiber cable, and this makes the technique cost-effective for the Japanese. For applications not threatened by electrical interference, cost-effectiveness awaits the time when the cost of the optical taps and switches are lower. Then fiber optics will be an answer to the local network problem even for bus architectures. ∎

C. Kenneth Miller and David M. Thompson,
Concord Data Systems Inc., Lexington, Mass.

Making a case for token passing in local networks

This complex technique will be the ultimate standard access method because of its technical superiority and versatility, the authors contend.

Bus-based local networks have usually been implemented with the carrier-sense multiple-access/collision detection (CSMA/CD) access algorithms pioneered by Xerox's Ethernet. Recently, however, a more complex access method, token passing, has proved more versatile with fewer limitations than CSMA/CD and has been selected as the alternative access method in the proposed IEEE 802 standard (see "IEEE 802 update").

CSMA/CD has the advantage of simplicity, an essential attribute when Ethernet was first being developed, but of less importance today with the availability of high-speed advanced microprocessors.

The token passing technique was first used on ring-topology local networks. ["The ring method," DATA COMMUNICATIONS, December 1981, p. 67–68.] In such networks, each node passes a "token" to the next node on the physical ring. In bus-type architectures, where all nodes "hear" all transmissions, "logical rings" may be created (Fig. 1).

In the logical ring, the token bears the address of the next node in a logical sequence. The token passes from node to node—in a sequence established at network-implementation time—without requiring nodes to be physically adjacent as in a physical-ring topology. The node with the token has the right to transmit. If it does not have anything to communicate, it passes the token to the next node in the logical ring.

Access is deterministic, not contention-based. Therefore, response time is predictable for varying loads, and the maximum message length for one token pass is known. The maximum time for one complete circulation of the token (in the absence of token errors) is determined readily by

$$T = N\tau + \sum_{n=1}^{N} \Delta t_n$$

where n = node number

N = number of nodes

τ = maximum holding time of token by any node

and Δt_n = the propagation time between logical nodes.

The maximum time between successive accesses by node N is then

$$T_N = (N-1)\tau + \sum_{n=1}^{N} \Delta t_n$$

τ and N are network parameters that may be tailored to a particular application. Thus token-passing networks may be applied in real-time applications where fixed bounded response times are required and where CSMA/CD is unsuitable due to the statistical characteristics of contention access with no firm upper limit to access time.

Token passing was not applied to bus local networks until recently because the extension of the token concepts to bus topologies added many complexities that needed to be resolved. For example, noise may cause a token to get lost, a node in the logical ring may fail, or a new node may be activated on the logical ring. Additionally, an initialization procedure is needed to set up the logical ring at power-up time. By itself each problem is fairly simple and readily resolved. (For example, lost tokens and failed nodes are detected by means of a timeout on carrier sense, after which time the logical ring is broken and a ring repair procedure is performed.) The difficulty is in providing an economical means for solving all the problems in real time. This was difficult to accomplish economically until the advent of powerful high-speed microprocessors.

The techniques used in token-passing procedures

1. Sequencing the logical ring. Unlike the case of the physical ring, the nodes of the logical ring are not constrained to pass the token to a physically adjacent node. The token is actually a data frame, and each node stores the next node's address in that frame. The sequence is established at network implementation time.

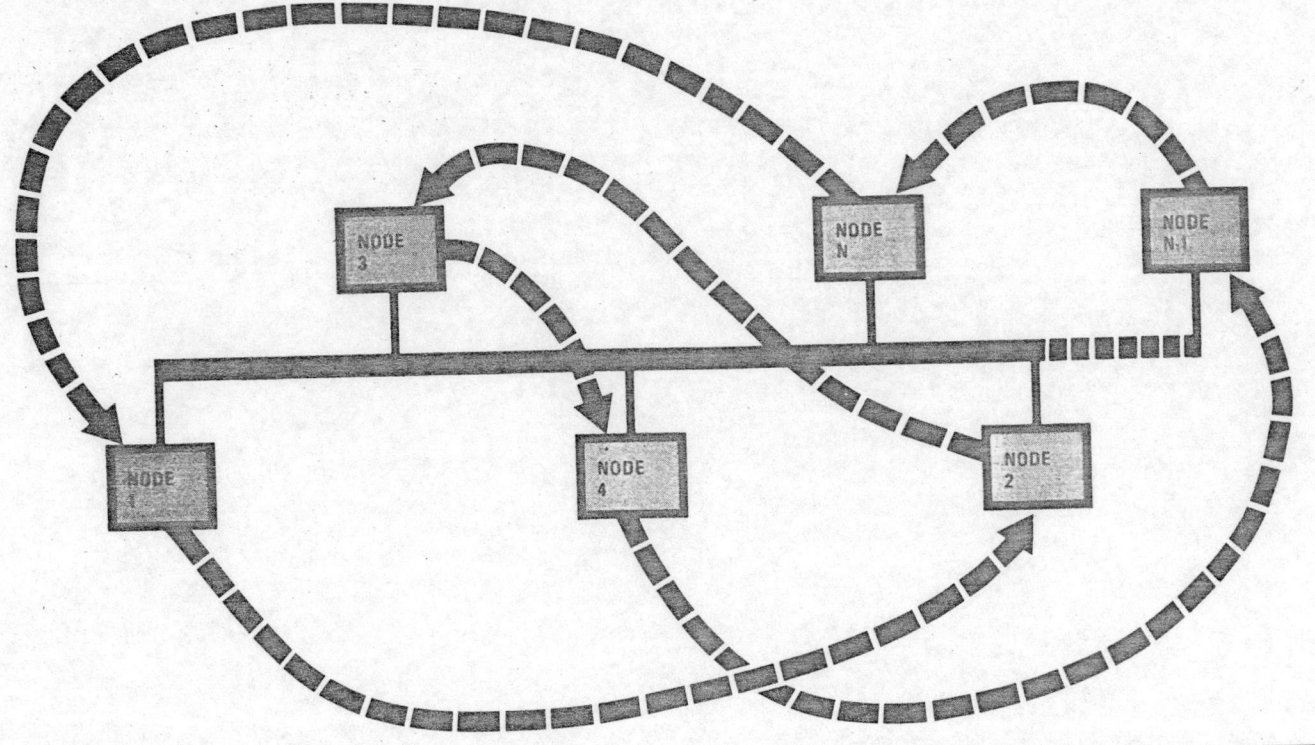

are controlled by a set of algorithms. These algorithms specify intra- and inter-node operation. The algorithms described herein are proposed for the emerging IEEE 802 bus standard.

The token is actually a frame passed from node to node. Each node stores the address of the next node to receive the token. A node holding the token may transmit data packets on the logical-ring bus for a specified maximum token-hold time. When this time expires (and the current transmission is completed), or the node has no data packets to send, the token is passed to the next node. Controlled contention mechanisms are used to initialize, repair, and modify the logical ring to maintain each node's linkage to the next node in the sequence.

Sequencing the logical ring

The token is passed in descending order of node address, with wraparound from the lowest to the highest. Addresses are in the form of binary fractions (most significant bit first). The distributed-configuration algorithms make use of this higher-to-lower characteristic to determine linkages through controlled contention. As with most distributed-access-control methods, all events on the bus are synchronized to a "slot" time equal to twice the maximum bus propagation delay plus the node's internal response time.

Individual linkages are adjusted for the addition of new nodes, or repaired for a garbled token pass or failure of the recipient node, through the use of "de-

mand windows," which are opened periodically for new node admission. Alternatively, when token-pass failure is detected (by nodes sensing a timeout on the bus), demand windows are opened to reestablish the linkage. To open demand windows, the token is transmitted followed by carrier-free time slots. In these "quiet" windows, nodes that wish to be active may demand "membership." A demand consists of the transmission of a "set-next-node" frame to set the linkage of the token holder to point to the demander. Both the token holder and the intended recipient monitor the bus during the window periods. If one or more demands are detected, the token pass is aborted in favor of admission of the new member.

If a valid set-next-node frame is received, the token holder sets its linkage accordingly and passes the token to the demander. The demander then uses the token to transmit data and establishes its own linkage via the demand process, using its own address for the source of the token frame.

Resolving contention

If only unrecognizable energy (noise) is received during the window period, it is assumed that there are multiple demanders. The resulting conflict is resolved by an address-based contention scheme. The token holder transmits a special "resolve-demanders" frame followed by four demand windows. Each demander observes the bus for a number of slots determined by the value of the first two bits of its own address. A value

49

of 0, 1, 2, or 3 corresponds to an observation time of 3, 2, 1, or 0 slots, respectively. If carrier is not detected during that period, the set-next-node frame is transmitted. If carrier is detected, the demand is dropped.

If the token holder still does not receive a valid set-next-node frame, it repeats the broadcast of the resolve-demanders frame. The remaining demanders again observe the bus, this time using their next two address bits. This process is repeated until either a valid set-next-node frame is received, no energy is detected, or a maximum retry count is exceeded. To help resolve duplicate-address problems, the demanders use two random bits for the last attempt.

Separate demand windows are used for nodes having addresses with values less than the token source and greater than the token destination. The lower window is always open. The higher window is opened only if the holder is currently the lowest address in the logical ring. The total number of demanders is always restricted to those demanders whose address value is between the source and destination addresses of the token frame. In the low-to-high wraparound case, this includes nodes with address values less than the token source (in the lower window) and greater than the destination (in the higher window). If the linkage is unknown, the source and destination of the token are considered equal, causing all nodes to respond. The lower window is always checked first, preserving the linkage address ordering.

Contending for ownership

If the token does not exist (such as at network start-up) or was lost due to failure of the token holder, all active nodes contend (controlled contention) for token ownership by broadcasting token-claim frames. At all times, all active nodes observe the bus. If carrier is not sensed for more than a specified timeout period, the token is considered lost. The ring must then be initialized; that is, the token must be claimed.

Multiple claims are resolved in an address-based contention scheme similar to that used for resolving demanders. The claim-token frame is padded with arbitrary data to a length determined from the value of bit-pairs of the node's address. The pad length is 0, 2, 4, or 6 slot times for bit-pair values of 0, 1, 2, or 3, respectively. When token loss is detected, the detecting node broadcasts a claim frame with padding determined by the value of the first two address bits. After transmission, the node pauses for one slot interval and then listens for carrier. If carrier is sensed, the claim is dropped. If carrier is not sensed, the transmit-listen sequence is repeated using the next two address bits. The last sequence uses a pair of random bits to assist the resolution of duplicate node addresses. If all address bits and the random bits have been used and carrier has not been detected, the node considers itself the token holder. In the event of duplicate addresses (including random bits), the token pass will either fail due to collision or fail because at least one node will detect the multiple ownership.

The ring is built (or rebuilt) starting with the new token holder using the linkage-establishment process

previously described. If a node desires to be removed, it can "gracefully" do so when it holds the token. The address of the previous token holder is known from the source field of the received token. A "set-next-node" frame is sent to change the linkage of the previous node to point to the successor of the node that is removing itself. The node has removed itself when it passes the token to its own successor.

It should be noted that these contention processes resolve very rapidly even in the worst cases due to the low propagation delays and efficiency of the algorithms. Additionally, such mechanisms are only used for initialization and error recovery, both infrequent operations in a local network.

The medium and the message

What effect the transmission medium has on network operation is an important consideration. Ethernet and CSMA/CD bus networks in general are designed for operation on baseband (passive) coaxial cable over limited distances. Both the basic CSMA algorithm and the requirement for collision detection cause limitations associated with the medium and the overall physical topology. These limitations do not exist with the token-access algorithms.

CSMA/CD is a contention mechanism, and its performance is statistical. Access is based on detection of no energy on the transmission medium. Propagation delay causes an "uncertainty" time window for a node to detect the no-energy condition. Often energy may be present on the medium but has not yet propagated to the node. As illustrated in Figure 2A, Δt equals the propagation delay for a transmission from node A to node B. This delay represents a time window during which the transmission energy is on the medium but is not yet detected by any other node.

The undetected-energy characteristic increases the probability of collision as the length of the cable and the data rate increase. This results in a severe speed/distance limitation: Increasing the network data rate for a given cable length increases the number of bits included within the uncertainty propagation time window and thus increases the probability of collision for a given packet length. Likewise for a given data rate, increasing the cable length increases the propagation delay and thus the number of bits in the uncertainty time window.

Double delay

This factor is further compounded when operating over active coaxial cable (CATV) where all node transmissions pass through a "headend" before reception, thereby effectively doubling the cable length for each transmission. As illustrated in Figure 2B, propagation time is worst when both nodes A and B are far from the headend. Energy propagates from A to the headend to B. The total delay is therefore $\Delta t_1 + \Delta t_2$, or twice the worst-case time of passive coax (Fig. 2A) for a given cable length. This discussion assumes that the headend is at one end of the installed network, as is probable in a single building. An upper bound on the uncertainty window for a given CSMA/CD network is

2. CSMA/CD problems. In the passive coax network example (A), Δt equals the propagation delay from node A to node B. Reception is undetected during this time "window." In the active (CATV) coax network example (B), the propagation delay from node A to node B is twice the worst case time of the passive network example.

(A)

NODE A TRANSMITS

NODE A ENERGY PROPAGATES TO
NODE B AND IS HEARD AT B

NODE A

NODE B

|← Δt →|

(B)

HEAD-END

NODE A TRANSMITS

NODE A ENERGY RECEIVED AT HEAD-END
AND RETRANSMITTED

RETRANSMITTED ENERGY
RECEIVED AT NODE B

NODE A

NODE B

|← Δt₁ →|← Δt₂ →|

the network slot time.

These delay effects do not occur in token-access networks under normal operating conditions, after initialization. The throughput increases predictably in these networks as the data rate increases, and the severe degradation of the CSMA/CD network, as the transmission medium's physical length increases, does not occur in the token-bus type. Because access is deterministic in the latter, response time has a firm maximum bound as load increases.

Collision-detection requirements

The need for collision detection places special requirements on the transmission medium and the modems. Ethernet currently detects collisions by adding a d.c. component to the a.c. signal. Ethernet receivers determine collisions by detecting d.c. components on the cable greater than would be expected from a single transmitter. This mechanism is quick and reliable, but creates the following problems:

■ It necessitates the use of active taps into the trunk cable to d.c.-couple the transmit signal to the center conductor and to detect the d.c. collision signal. This active tap consists of a transceiver that interfaces the DTE through four twisted-pair wires. The requirement for an active tap tied to a non-branched trunk cable limits allowable topologies to that of unbranched tree types, a serious limitation in many applications. For example, in a large building, the cable would have to be looped to each connected device, instead of estab-

lishing branch circuits for device groups.

■ Reliable detection of collisions is not simple in media other than passive coaxial cable. Broadband active coax configurations do not pass signals below 5 MHz, so the d.c. collision-detection scheme would not work. The common method used for collision detection on broadband networks is a bit-by-bit comparison of transmitted data with received data by the transmitting node. Differences in signal level during collision will likely result in the larger-signal-node not detecting the collision due to a "capture" effect—the smaller signal would be interpreted as noise and would be ignored. Meanwhile, the low-signal node would constantly detect a collision and defer transmission. Thus, over broadband networks, performance of CSMA/CD degrades due both to the doubling of the effective length described earlier and to the inability to detect collisions in a timely and accurate manner.

Less problems with token

In contrast, token-access networks require no collision detection and therefore do not have the accompanying problems. Passive taps are used on passive coax networks so that tree-cable topologies may be arranged very much like CATV configurations. By avoiding the requirements for collision detection, the token-access method operates on all transmission media and topologies, whereas CSMA/CD is oriented to one medium and a single topology. Besides limitations of the CSMA/CD method, the actual implementation chosen

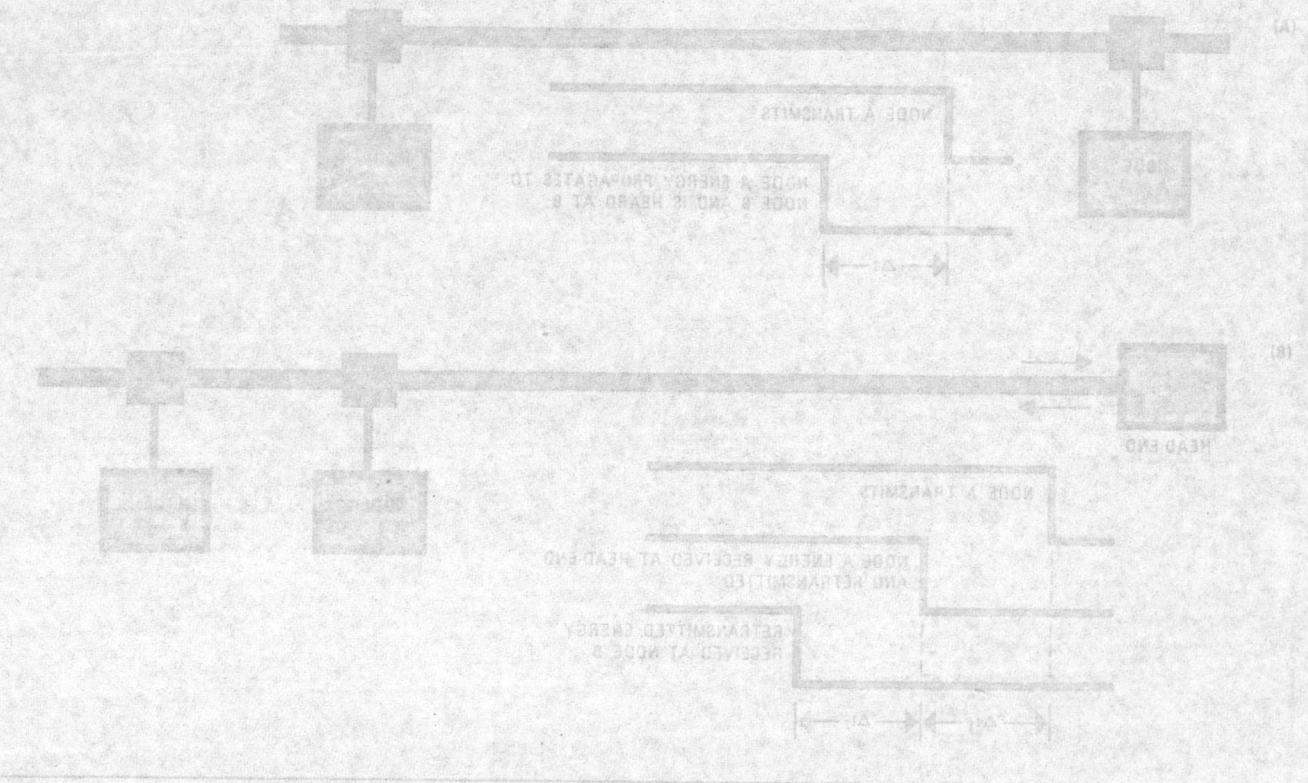

Ethernet cable

A special 50-ohm cable was developed for use with Ethernet. The Ethernet designers apparently felt that standard cables were not adequate. Following are some of the features of Ethernet cable:

■ High propagation velocity—about .77C, where C is the velocity of light in a vacuum. Most standard cable has a propagation velocity of about .65C. The improvement is accomplished by using a foam-type dielectric to minimize the propagation-delay portion of the slot time.

■ Low transfer impedance—this is needed both to prevent unwanted signals (from radio stations, for example) and to keep signals on the cable from radiating outside the cable. This is accomplished with double-braided and double-foil shielding.

■ Flexibility—not the semi-rigid, solid-aluminum-sheathed cable used in the CATV industry. Thus this cable can be readily pierced by "vampire" taps.

■ Marking and impedance—the outer jacket is striped to indicate acceptable tap-in points to prevent cable mismatch at these points. Taps into the cable are not matched but produce a high-impedance bridge, with resistance greater than 50,000 ohms and capacitance (excluding stray) of less than 2 pf. The capacitance portion is predominant and was the reason for not using 75-ohm cable; a given capacitance causes less mismatch at the lower (50-ohm) characteristic impedance.

for the latest version of Ethernet also has limitations adversely affecting the transmission medium.

The Ethernet network data rate selected is 10 Mbit/s. This choice apparently was based on a maximum demand in an office environment of 3 Mbit/s, as determined by Digital Equipment Corporation, Intel Corporation, and Xerox. Because average loading for Ethernet needs to be less than 40 percent to maintain stability (based on IEEE simulations), this requirement led to the 10-Mbit/s data rate. This rate, when coupled with the use of Manchester baseband signal encoding, which is a wide-bandwidth technique, approaches the upper bandwidth limit for transmission over passive coax when using bridged (non-matched) taps. This possible problem led to the specification of special 50-ohm cable for Ethernet use. [For more detail on Manchester encoding, see "Local networks' consensus: High speed," DATA COMMUNICATIONS, December 1980, p. 56.] Fifty-ohm cable was selected over standard 75-ohm CATV-style cable because the degrading effects of each tap are reduced at the lower impedance value (see "Ethernet cable").

Earthing Ethernet

Since Ethernet uses a baseband modulation technique, low-frequency components exist below about 2—3 MHz that must be passed. This does not allow each tap to be grounded to earth as is standard CATV practice, but rather requires the cable to be earthed in one location only. This practice creates a potential shock

Table 1 10-node comparison

ITEM	ETHERNET		TOKEN	
	UNIT COST	TOTAL COST	UNIT COST	TOTAL COST
TRUNK CABLE, 2.5 KM (1.55 MI) (ETHERNET USES 50-OHM CABLE @ $2.25/METER; TOKEN USES 75-OHM .412-IN. CATV CABLE @ $0.60/METER)	$5,625.00	$5,625.00	$1,500.00	$1,500.00
CABLE TAP (ETHERNET USES A TRANSCEIVER, WITH COST BASED ON 3COM QUOTE; TOKEN USES PASSIVE TAP)	400.00	4,000.00	25.00	250.00
DROP CABLE (25 METERS) (ETHERNET USES FOUR TWISTED-PAIR WIRES @ $2.25/METER; TOKEN USES RG-6 @ $0.25/METER)	56.25	562.50	6.25	62.50
NODE (FOUR RS-232-C/V.24 PORTS)	ABOUT 3,000.00	ABOUT 30,000.00	ABOUT 3,200.00	ABOUT 32,000.00
INSTALLATION	SEE TEXT		SEE TEXT	
TOTALS (EXCLUDING INSTALLATION)		$40,187.50		$33,812.50

TOKEN IS 16 PERCENT LESS EXPENSIVE.

Table 2 200-node comparison

ITEM	ETHERNET	TOKEN
	TOTAL COST	TOTAL COST
TRUNK CABLE	$5,625.00	$ 1,500.00
CABLE TAP	80,000.00	5,000.00
DROP CABLE	11,250.00	1,250.00
NODE	ABOUT 600,000.00	ABOUT 640,000.00
INSTALLATION	SEE TEXT	SEE TEXT
TOTALS (EXCLUDING INSTALLATION)	$696,875.00	$647,750.00

TOKEN IS 7 PERCENT LESS EXPENSIVE.

IEEE 802 update

The preliminary IEEE 802 standard went out for ballot for the first time in October 1981. There were great variations in the completeness of each section, which was recognized by the 802 committee. However, it was decided to release it for ballot to get written comments, which could then be factored into the next draft. These comments were discussed at the December meeting and resulted in a major restructuring of the document and change in emphasis in the media portion. Following are characteristics of the standard at this point:

1. Two access methods will be supported: CSMA/CD and token passing.

2. Both bus and ring physical topologies are supported—bus with either CSMA/CD or token access; ring with token access.

3. In ISO Level 2 (data-link), protocols are the same for all access methods and topologies.

4. Below the access sublayer of Level 2, at Level 1, there are different sets of physical layers: CSMA/CD bus, token bus, and token ring. Although there will be similarities in the physical media in all three categories, the emphasis is in optimizing the media to the access method and topology, with commonality a secondary priority. Each category will have multiple media (for example, CSMA/CD and token bus will have baseband and broadband coaxial media, and token ring will have twisted pair, coaxial, and lightwave media).

The standard will consist of five sections:

1. Introduction
2. Common parts of Level 2 (logical link control)
3. CSMA/CD
4. Token bus
5. Token ring

Shortly after this month's meeting, the 802 committee intends to complete sections 1 and 2, and to agree on at least one medium each for sections 3, 4, and 5.

The modulation method proposed for token baseband coax networks is a form of frequency-shift keying (FSK) that retains the self-clocking feature of Manchester coding, has an easily integrated implementation, has minimal spectral occupancy at frequencies below a few megahertz, and allows the trunk cable to be grounded to earth in multiple locations.

Two token-bus passive-coax topologies are being considered for the standard, and it is likely both will be sanctioned by the committee. The first is very much like broadband but uses non-directional, passive matching circuits for the taps rather than the directional taps used in broadband CATV networks. It is this topology that is used for a model in this article.

A second bus topology uses no taps or drop cables at all but rather extends the trunk cable to each modem directly. Each modem is bridged across the trunk cable in much the same way as Ethernet transceivers are, except all the active electronic circuitry is encompassed in one physical unit instead of being separated into two units (transceiver and DTE) as in Ethernet. This topology has been used extensively at 1-Mbit/s data rates with FSK modems by Computrol and has the advantage of requiring only modest dynamic ranges (30 dB) for quite large expanses of cable (such as 30,000 feet). The first topology, in contrast, requires a dynamic range of about 60 dB to overcome the insertion loss of the passive taps as well as the cable.

hazard. Unfortunately, it also prevents the common CATV practice of allowing the cable to be its own conduit. Additionally, an unearthed coaxial cable could appear as an antenna and be responsible for excessive electromagnetic radiation.

The constraints placed on the media by both the CSMA/CD method and the specific Ethernet implementation not only make for awkward topological constraints (such as non-earthed taps) but also lead to a cost higher than for a comparable token-bus network. For comparison's sake, let us assume four hypothetical networks, two Ethernet-based and two token-bus-based. Two different-sized network pairs are compared: a small one of 10 nodes and a large one of 200 nodes. The networks are assumed to operate on passive coaxial cable—50-ohm Ethernet cable for the Ethernet networks and .412-inch semi-rigid 75-ohm CATV coaxial cable for the token-based networks. 2.5 km of cable are assumed in all cases. Taps are passive in the case of token, and are active transceivers in the case of Ethernet. Drop cables from the tap are RG-6 coax for token, and four twisted pairs from the transceiver for Ethernet. Each node is assumed to include four RS-232-C/V.24 DTE-DCE ports similar to devices commercially available today, so that the network may support multiple DTE vendors.

The token-node device is assumed to be slightly more expensive than the Ethernet-node device, due primarily to the increased complexity of the token-node modem and access method used. A network throughput of 3 Mbit/s is assumed, resulting in network data rates of 10 Mbit/s for Ethernet (30 percent stable network loading) and 5 Mbit/s for the token network (60 percent network loading).

Table 1 compares costs for the 10-node networks and Table 2 for the 200-node networks. The token-based network is always less expensive despite somewhat higher node costs. This is due primarily to the less-expensive 75-ohm cable and the use of passive taps. Installation costs are not included and may turn out to be comparable, because token networks can use standard CATV practices such as earthing all taps and using the cable as its own conduit. CSMA/CD networks can use cable-piercing "vampire" taps, which are installed without cutting the cable. Note that since the token configuration may use standard CATV cable, a passive-cable installation may be upgraded at a later date to broadband—gaining a greater number of transmission channels—without the need to install new cable. ∎

Richard H. Sherman, Melvin G. Gable, and Anthony Chung,
Ford Motor Company, Dearborn, Mich.

Overcoming local and long-haul incompatibility

After the higher layers
of the OSI models are defined,
then what? Ford researchers
discuss the trials and tribulations
of developing end-to-end control.

There are long-distance data networks—composed of switched or leased facilities, point-to-point, or multipoint connections—and now there are local networks. Most agree that the two will have to interconnect, and some progress is being made in this area. But it remains unclear how this can be done while retaining end-to-end network efficiency, reliability, connectivity, and cost-effectiveness.

A network protocol layer is needed that can adapt to the evolution, operation, and interconnection of such diverse networks. The network should accommodate computers that implement different network protocols, and the network components, such as interfaces and computers, should be as easy to install as modems—without requiring communications or computer specialists. Some modems, for example, can now sense the data rate and modulation scheme and automatically adapt. Whole networks should be able to merge with or separate from other networks as easily as individual network components are added and removed.

In view of this, an experimental network has been developed at Ford in an attempt to implement these evolutionary and operational objectives. Different types of networks were interconnected using a uniform network protocol layer developed to perform measurement and control functions.

The Ford experimental network combines a unique local network architecture with a store-and-forward network called Distributed Computer Network, or DCNet. The local network architecture, using packet-switching technology, is a high-bandwidth (1-Mbit/s) multiaccess contention network. The contention technique is called feedback carrier-sense multiple access with collision detection (FB/CSMA/CD). The medium is standard coaxial cable. The network technology is packet switching, with each packet broadcast to all

local interface locations. Local network interfaces (LNIs)—microprocessor-based communications interfaces—implement an interprocess communications and synchronization (IPC) function that actually connects the computer or terminal equipment with the network services.

Local network applications are often simply an economical replacement of point-to-point wiring using a single coaxial cable. A terminal-emulation module in the Ford LNI is used to implement a direct device connection. This application requires short delays and features fast recovery from error conditions. The LNI also provides various connection modes that accommodate terminals, programmable controllers, and microprocessor-based equipment.

There are three different types of access methods to an LNI which are selected using LNI commands. An access method is a protocol between a host (DTE) and an LNI (DCE). The LNI commands can be entered by the attached host DTE or from any other host in the network. The characteristics of the LNI for each type of access method are shown in Figure 1. They are:

1. The terminal emulation mode, wherein the LNI provides a reliable transport service, including flow and error control, between two processes. This mode emulates point-to-point-type links. The LNI permits data transmission ranging from character-at-a-time to more efficient block data transfers.

2. The virtual-circuit mode provides the same service, but the host DTE is involved in multiplexing the circuits. A process may employ commands to create a new virtual circuit, and the LNI provides connection-control services in this case. Moreover, a connection requires that the local-network packet address and sequence numbers match.

3. In the datagram mode, the LNI provides reliable

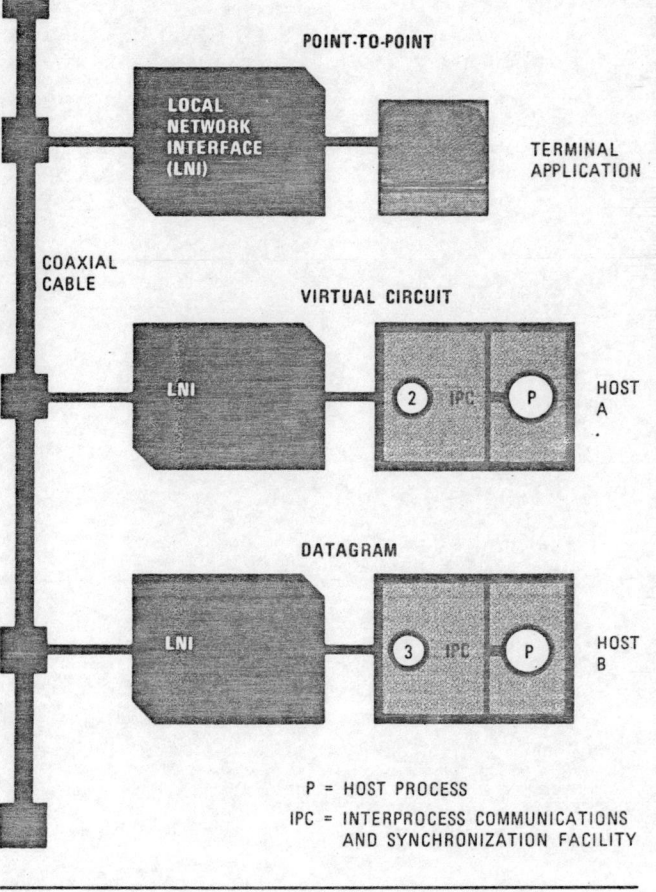

1. Triple interface. *Local network interface (LNI) handles point-to-point circuits, virtual circuits, and datagrams. IPC links host processes (P) with network services.*

P = HOST PROCESS
IPC = INTERPROCESS COMMUNICATIONS AND SYNCHRONIZATION FACILITY

transport of packets, but no connection-control service. Each packet can be individually addressed, and capabilities exist for both broadcast and selective group addressing. With datagrams, different reliability and delay behavior (under noisy or congested conditions) is possible by adjusting an upper limit on the number of retransmissions.

The Distributed Computer Network, DCNet, is a datagram packet-switched network based on the federal government Department of Defense internetwork protocol (IP). The DCNet supports several host services including virtual terminal, file transfer, and electronic mail. DCNet hosts are connected with point-to-point dedicated or switched links. DCNet employs a uniform operating environment with a naming scheme for all hosts, networks, and services. Names are symbolic representations of logical addresses. In DCNet, each host performs a store-and-forward routing function.

The Ford local network architecture is integrated into DCNet by using datagram access to the LNI for the transport of internetwork packets. The IP provides a uniform packet format that allows the transport of packets across the networks. Further, the transport layer consists of either a reliable end-to-end protocol, known as TCP, or a datagram protocol called UDP.

Both are implementations of the IPs developed by the Defense Department.

Comparison with OSI

The functional layering of the ISO model for open systems interconnection (OSI) can be used to illustrate the host organization in this experimental network (Fig. 2). A process corresponds to the application, presentation, and session layers. Each process has a unique name, which is a symbolic representation of the process port identification. The IPC facility contains the transport, network, and link layers.

The transport layer provides primitives (command statements) for sending and receiving messages on either a character-by-character basis or on an individual message basis. Synchronization occurs for the establishment of connections and for handling urgent requests. Buffer management is provided in this layer so that processes do not require communications buffers. In addition, end-to-end flow control, connection establishment, and error conditions are performed by the transport layer.

The link layer contains drivers for controlling the physical links between hosts and local networks. On the link level, not all hosts can be reached over the same link. For example, in Figure 3, host C cannot be reached from host A on link 1. A table in each host contains the necessary connectivity information.

The network layer dynamically probes the underlying network to determine the network's properties. These properties include host connectivity, network delay, data rate, and time synchronization information. Although these properties may be known at any given time, changing network conditions and host locations make a fixed configuration unacceptable. The determination and measurement of these properties provides a means for network control of disturbances (see Glossary). Based on this information, resultant actions are taken, such as decisions on routes, linked delays, clock updates, device resets, and host resets.

The network layer accommodates networks with a wide range of interconnection properties. For example, a point-to-point link of 2.4 kbit/s can have the same delay properties as a 1-Mbit/s satellite channel, although the maximum data rate (throughput) is much different. From a link-control point of view, there are three types of ports:

1. A point-to-point port provides the ability for a driver process to send to only one other driver process. From a user point of view, however, this port can provide access to several hosts in a store-and-forward network. Note that a permanent virtual circuit qualifies as a point-to-point port since intermediate processing units, if any, only retransmit messages, including acknowledgments used in error control.

2. A switched port allows connections with multiple driver processes. However, only one particular driver process is addressed at a time. Again, at the user level, this port may appear simultaneously to access multiple hosts. On the link level, however, the selection time can vary depending on the underlying network (for example, on the dialing procedure over the telephone

2. Layered architecture. *Network-control features in the Ford experimental network are compared with the ISO model for open systems interconnection (OSI). Network and transport layer functions are performed by the Ford interprocess communications and synchronization (IPC) facility, which includes several different protocols.*

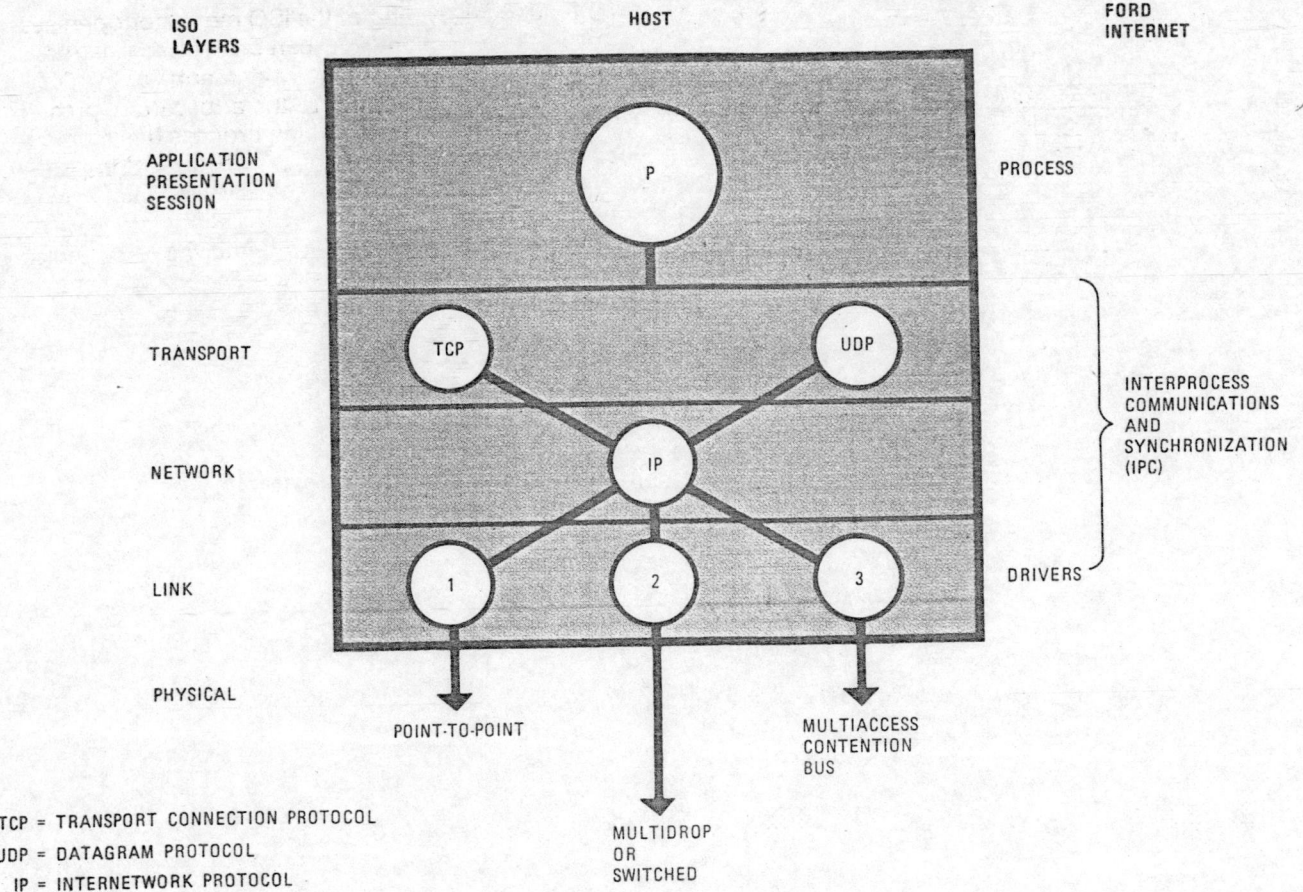

TCP = TRANSPORT CONNECTION PROTOCOL
UDP = DATAGRAM PROTOCOL
 IP = INTERNETWORK PROTOCOL

network or the call-request procedure on X.25 packet-switching networks).

3. A multiple-access port provides the ability for the driver process to send messages to a number of other host driver processes at any time; for example, an HDLC primary station sending messages to a secondary station. The host with a secondary station port, however, views connections as point-to-point since it can only address the host that is the primary station.

Since these port types have been defined abstractly, one must be careful to consider the appropriate protocol layer when applying the definitions. For example, a datagram access layer can be implemented on top of a virtual-circuit network; the switching is performed on each message or else several open connections are maintained simultaneously.

A further distinction in multiple-access ports is required when one considers addressing capability. Two types of broadcast are possible:

1. Broadcast messages can be sent by explicitly addressing all hosts reachable via the port.

2. Broadcast messages with a group, or all-party, address may be sent, with response messages returned by each individual host.

Response time can be measured through the use of broadcast messages, which requires a further distinction in the type of port. The broadcast-message delay to a shared-bus local network would probably be identical for all hosts. Otherwise, message delay could be a function of specific host locations, such as in a ring local network.

If the broadcast messages arrive at different times at the destination hosts, the response-time calculation requires a copy of time-stamp values provided by the remote hosts. In a multiaccess contention bus, the response time can be calculated as the sum of two local-port delays.

Small network, fast broadcast

The broadcast mechanism is also used to perform tasks such as the readdressing of all hosts on the network. In this way, the addresses of all hosts on one network can be changed to another network. In the Ford local setup, several different local networks can reside on the same multiaccess contention bus.

The speed at which measurements are made and controls are performed depends directly on the time it takes to perform a network broadcast. In general, assuming a constant host broadcast overhead, the smaller the network the faster the broadcast and the

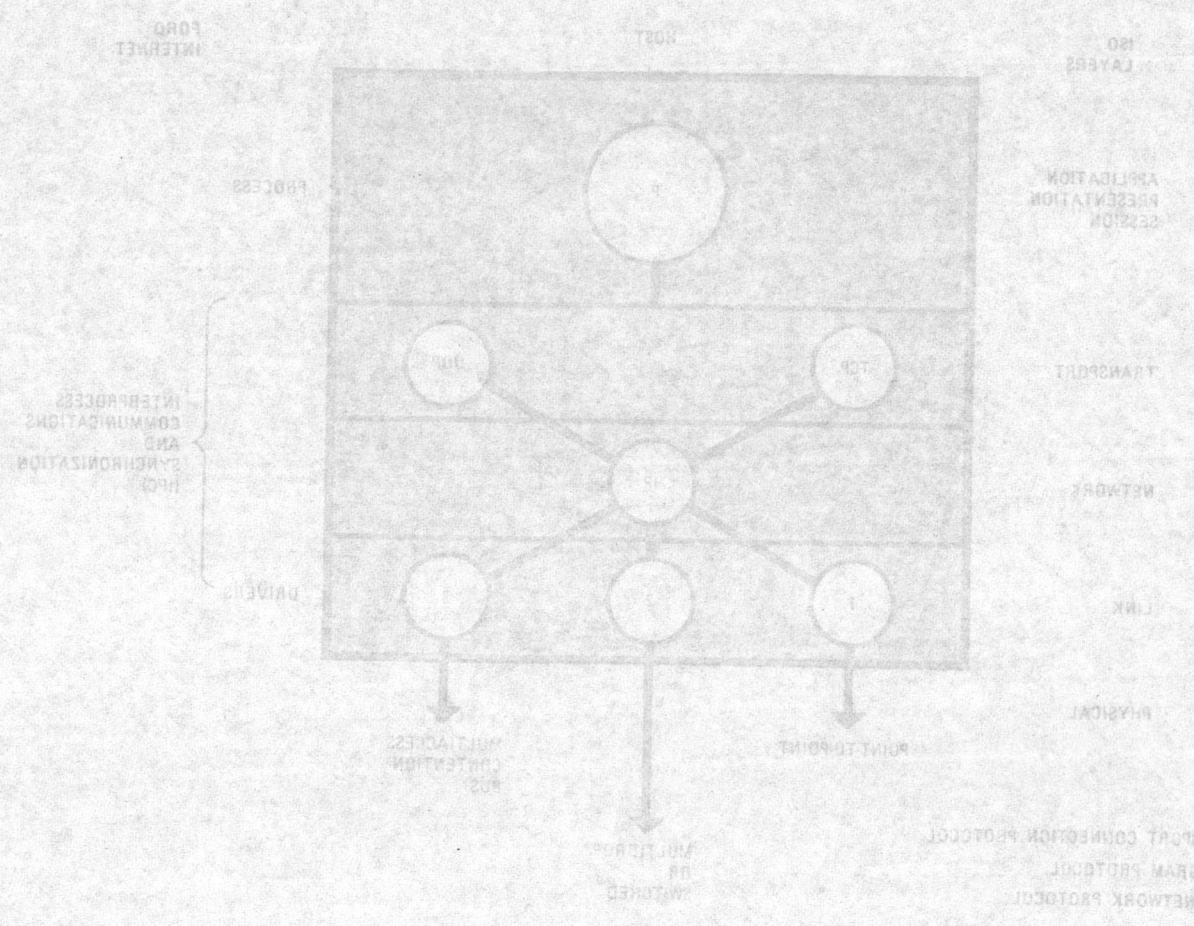

2. Layered architecture. *Network-control features in the Ford experimental network are compared with the ISO model for open systems interconnection (OSI). Network and transport layer functions are performed by the Ford interprocess communications and synchronization (IPC) facility, which includes several different protocols.*

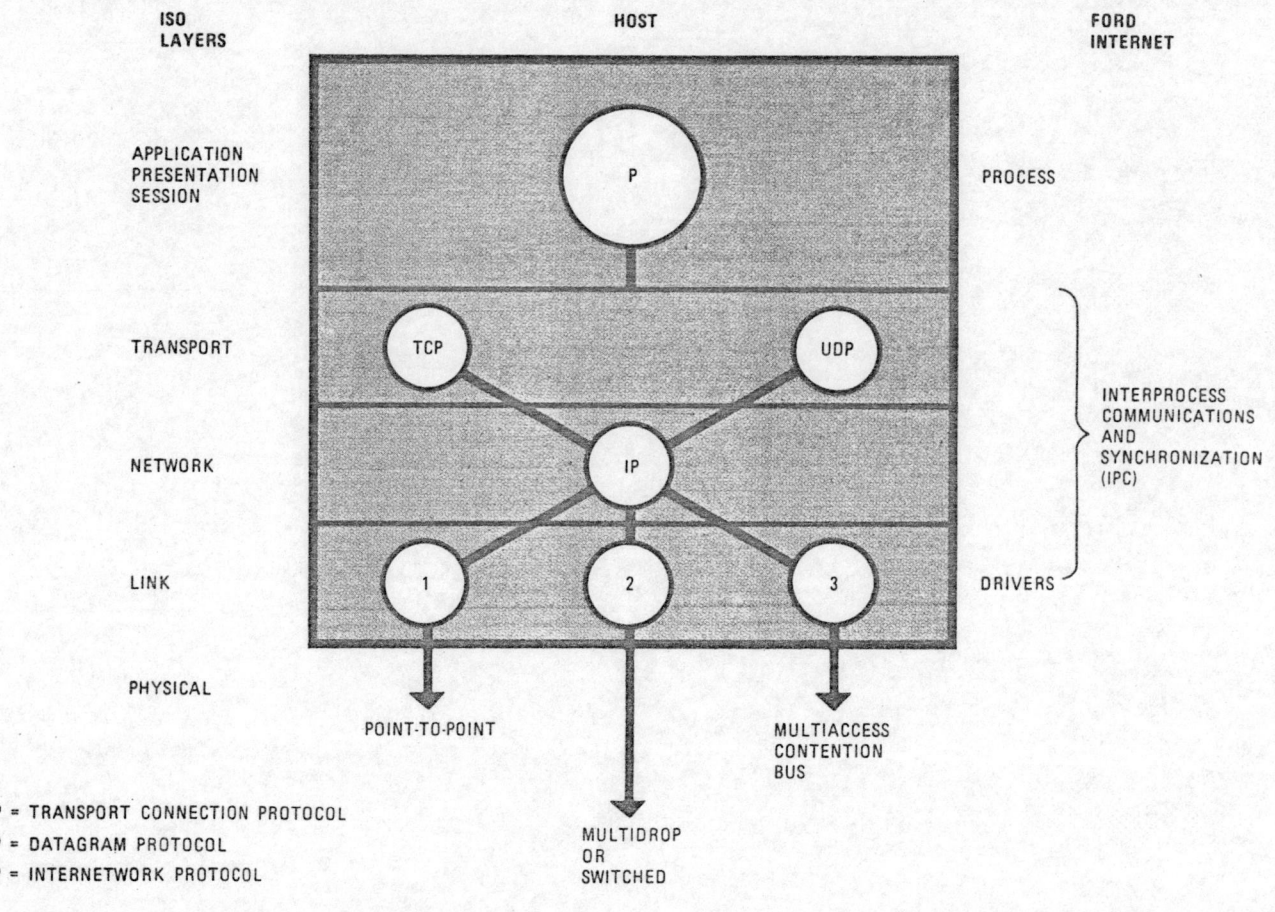

TCP = TRANSPORT CONNECTION PROTOCOL
UDP = DATAGRAM PROTOCOL
 IP = INTERNETWORK PROTOCOL

network or the call-request procedure on X.25 packet-switching networks).

3. A multiple-access port provides the ability for the driver process to send messages to a number of other host driver processes at any time; for example, an HDLC primary station sending messages to a secondary station. The host with a secondary station port, however, views connections as point-to-point since it can only address the host that is the primary station.

Since these port types have been defined abstractly, one must be careful to consider the appropriate protocol layer when applying the definitions. For example, a datagram access layer can be implemented on top of a virtual-circuit network; the switching is performed on each message or else several open connections are maintained simultaneously.

A further distinction in multiple-access ports is required when one considers addressing capability. Two types of broadcast are possible:

1. Broadcast messages can be sent by explicitly addressing all hosts reachable via the port.

2. Broadcast messages with a group, or all-party, address may be sent, with response messages returned by each individual host.

Response time can be measured through the use of broadcast messages, which requires a further distinction in the type of port. The broadcast-message delay to a shared-bus local network would probably be identical for all hosts. Otherwise, message delay could be a function of specific host locations, such as in a ring local network.

If the broadcast messages arrive at different times at the destination hosts, the response-time calculation requires a copy of time-stamp values provided by the remote hosts. In a multiaccess contention bus, the response time can be calculated as the sum of two local-port delays.

Small network, fast broadcast
The broadcast mechanism is also used to perform tasks such as the readdressing of all hosts on the network. In this way, the addresses of all hosts on one network can be changed to another network. In the Ford local setup, several different local networks can reside on the same multiaccess contention bus.

The speed at which measurements are made and controls are performed depends directly on the time it takes to perform a network broadcast. In general, assuming a constant host broadcast overhead, the smaller the network the faster the broadcast and the

each individual host until all network hosts have received this information.

Faulty processors are assumed not to pass on any bad information. This assumption is made because of two design factors. First, the broadcast uses the same table-lookup mechanism as the data packets. Therefore, failures in forwarding data packets can also be sensed as failures to forward a network broadcast packet. Second, individual broadcast packets are often responses to earlier broadcasts. The feedback of public information on broadcasts, therefore, can be used to check consistency and to protect against the propagation of bad information.

Delay measurement

The procedure for measuring delay involves the port type. The delay measurement for point-to-point ports is performed by exchanging hello packets and measuring round-trip delay. For store-and-forward networks, this procedure is repeated at each intermediate host. For switched or virtual-circuit links and multiaccess ports (without broadcast), the procedure is repeated for each host in succession.

The delay between hosts depends on the specific communications facilities employed in the network. Consider, for example, two communications facilities: a local-network point-to-point port and a direct-wire point-to-point port. Even though the local network employs a high-bandwidth medium, there is still a measurable delay between hosts accessing the local network. This is because the transfer rate of a packet between the host and the LNI is dependent on both the serial-data rate and the host operating-system performance for asynchronous parallel access. Also, the transmission between the source and destination LNIs may experience a contention delay depending on the utilization level of the local network. Finally, the transfer into the destination host depends on its interface rate. The result is that a local network represents more delay than a direct-wire connection with corresponding throughput (data rate).

For the local network, the objective is to measure the delay of the link port and add this delay to the delay each host encounters on the link port. A broadcast hello is sent with a time stamp to the port. After that, all network hosts, including the originating host, receive this hello packet. Finally, when the hello is received from the local-network medium, the calculation of port delay is then made.

Network delay also includes the contention delay inherent in local networks, along with buffer delay in the host-to-LNI interface. After receiving a hello message, other hosts respond with broadcast hellos containing their respective port delays. The round-trip delay, therefore, is the sum of the originator link delay and the remote-host port delay.

A reduction in overhead is achieved by only sending hellos on startup for hosts with only a single network port. These are called nonbridge hosts. A bridge host is defined as a host with more than one port. Nonbridge hosts receive broadcasts from bridge hosts to keep network status rapidly updated. When a non-bridge host comes up, a single hello can be sent that measures the port delay and informs the other hosts of its state.

Time synchronization is achieved throughout the internetwork by comparing the absolute clock values. The interaction of hello packets is used continually to feed back clock information. This is particularly fast on a multiple-access network because the same hello packet is received by all hosts within microseconds.

Names and addresses

A naming scheme exists for use in referencing local networks, hosts, processes, and data files and records. A name process resides in several hosts and is used to translate symbolic names to addresses. The name-table search is hierarchical. If a name is not found in the local context, the global context is searched. When multiple addresses exist for the same name, other qualifiers must be used to designate a unique name.

Internetwork addresses are composed of four bytes, each referring to a specific network, subnetwork, host, and subhost. Process names are identified with generic service-port numbers that are used consistently throughout the network, in conjunction with specific local-port numbers.

The local network behaves like an associative look-up table when a local-network address is received by the destination LNI or group of LNIs. The address mapping is shown in Figure 4. The Net-ID byte is used to locate the network, the subnet byte is used to locate the subnetwork, and the Host-ID byte is used to locate the host. In addition, a host port indicator defines the route to a logical host. If a port is connected to a local network, the host table is used to determine the local network address.

For addresses derived from a network, an inverse address map is made. A hello arriving at a host port results in the updating of mapping tables. The logical port is then recorded in the host table, and the local network address is derived from the source internetwork-packet address.

The address-mapping procedure is adequate when hosts are using the same interprocess communications and synchronization (IPC) procedures. A complication in addressing occurs when different types of driver ports are using the same LNI—say, when LNI address changes for datagram applications have to be tracked by point-to-point or virtual-circuit connections. One solution is to use separate LNIs for each type of application, but this involves a proportionate increase in network component cost. Another approach is to include the local-address header with all data packets, with an additional expense in host overhead. The local address can be used to identify the packet source and could also be included in the address map.

Determining the path

Routing is accomplished with the use of logical host address tables. Each host table contains several other host names, the associated port number, the round-trip delay to that host, and a status of when the last update was received. This information is used in the store-and-

4. Addressing scheme. *A consistent addressing scheme is the key to the interconnection of multiple, diverse networks. Addressing is hierarchical; the first address byte designates the destination network, the next denotes the subnetwork, and so on. Local-network addressing is easier, and uses an abbreviated procedure.*

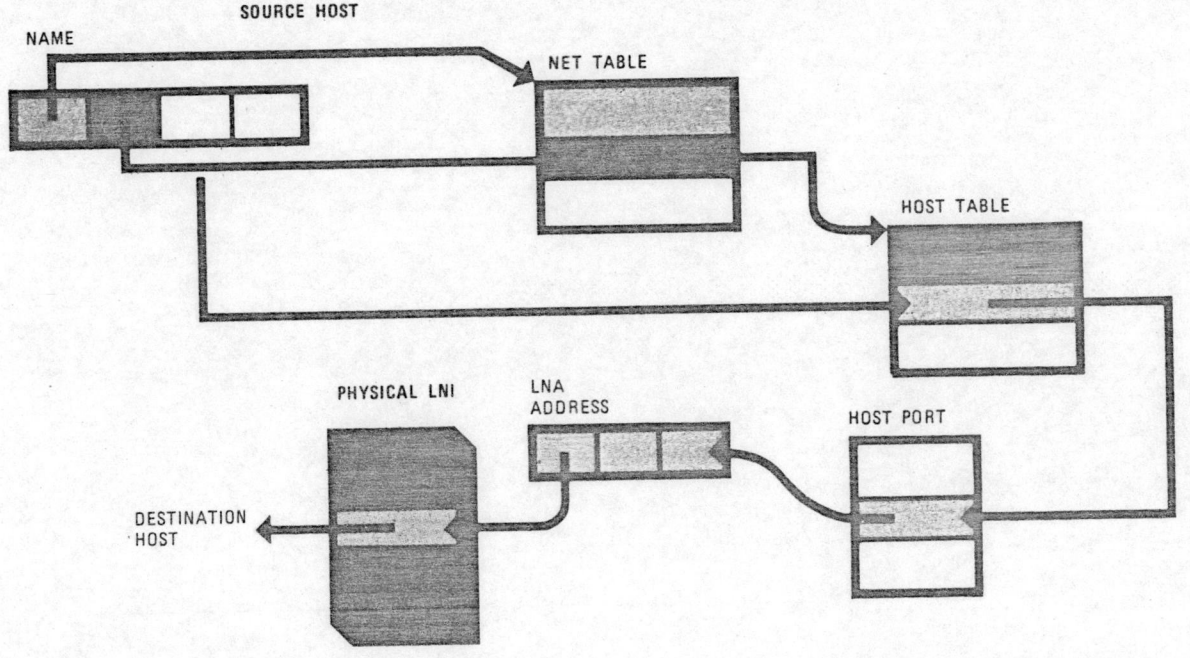

forward routing of data packets in the network.

Routing is direct on the local network. LNI and link interface faults, however, can be bypassed with the use of delay measurements. For example, if two local network hosts cannot communicate because of attenuation problems, but a host in between the two hosts can still communicate to both hosts, then a path is established. Unfortunately, a store-and-forward host also hears collisions that are undetected by other hosts, and the contention scheme loses some degree of performance.

Broadcasts are implemented using a reverse path-forwarding technique. A host forwards a broadcast packet it has received on each port except the incoming port. When a broadcast packet is sent to a local network, a broadcast destination address is used.

A "selective" broadcast can be implemented through an address-filter function in the LNI. The local network destination address contains the "all-parties" broadcast address (defined in HDLC), which has a standard representation. The address filter is then used to discriminate on this or any other portion of the address. The LNI port address represents the LNI on the shared local-network medium, while a segment address byte is used to designate the particular virtual network or network application.

Convenient network tools are desirable in measuring performance and tracking individual component problems. Such measurements are particularly important at Ford, considering the complexity of large data networks. Special-purpose instruments, such as oscilloscopes and data analyzers, do exist for specific diagnostic purposes, but these have not yet been inte-

grated into a general diagnostic setting.

Some valuable diagnostic tools include the network statistics gathered during network operation experiments. These can be used in examining selected network components. Since a virtual-terminal service can be used remotely to obtain access to a host, delay measurements can be retrieved and viewed at a remote site. When certain conditions are sensed, such as an increase in delay between a host and the local network, statistics on the host's local-network driver can be gathered and displayed. Host-interface hardware faults, as well as buffer overrun conditions, can also be identified in this manner.

The host local-network driver program collects statistics gathered by the LNI during the course of its operation. These include hardware errors, buffer-overrun conditions, and a packet-retry summary based on the last 100 packets sent.

For collecting network statistics, there are several procedures that can be performed. The controlled data loops that can be examined are:

- Internal loopback within one host computer.
- Host-generated loopback to its attached LNI.
- Host-generated loopback to its attached LNI, which in turn loops back externally through the shared local-network medium.
- Host loopback over the local network to a remote LNI on the local network. Data is looped back through the remote LNI without disturbing data flow to the remote host attached.
- Host-generated loopback to a remote host.

Data-delay statistics can be collected and displayed in a graph of delay versus frequency. A typical delay

Glossary

Internetworking involves the identification of network properties and the isolation of applications from network operation. This is done through the use of virtual host and network concepts. Considering the present variety of communications technology and practices, network terms need to be clarified. The following glossary is provided to aid the reader in understanding the concepts and principles discussed in this article.

disturbances network changes due to failures in either communications or computer facilities. Operators can cause disturbances as a result of their autonomous control actions.

driver a communications process associated with a physical I/O device. Multiplexing of messages through a driver, for example, is made possible by supervisor synchronizing commands, or primitives, which permit several sender processes to send messages to a single-receiver process port associated with the driver.

end user an application process or a person interacting with processes through a human interface.

gateways hosts used to interconnect networks. Two fundamental types of gateways may exist:

1. gateway has capability to perform routing functions when interconnected networks have a consistent message format.

2. gateway may have to translate services between interconnected networks when hosts use dissimilar message formats. In this case, the internetwork can only support services that can be mapped between the two dissimilar networks. End-to-end flow control is lost with this type of gateway.

host an abstraction of an operating environment wherein a set of processes interacts with a supervisor. The supervisor contains system processes and manages the operating environment, which includes input/output (I/O) devices, directories, and file systems. A host is a convenient boundary for containing specific resources desired by other hosts. A host is virtual, and several hosts may reside on the same computer.

internetwork a collection of networks with an IPC facility such that hosts on any network appear immediately accessible to hosts on any other network. Externally, an internetwork appears as a single network, with hosts on interconnected networks appearing as interconnected hosts. Internally, an internetwork is composed of heterogeneous networks with different message formats and protocols.

IPC for interprocess communications and synchronization facility; provides the capability for transmitting variable-length messages from any process in a host to any other process in the same or different hosts.

local network a network which is geographically local, such as in a plant or office. Examples include local loops and multidrop and multiaccess contention buses.

message consists of header and data; is an informational unit sent by a process to a named interface, such as a port.

network a collection of hosts and an IPC such that any host in the network appears immediately accessible to any other host. One requirement of a network is that there exist a consistent message format with a uniform addressing scheme for the hosts present (actually or potentially) in the network. Network functions may include data-flow control, error control, connection control, and routing.

network-layer process handles disturbances in topology and variations in data transfer rates.

port interface between a process and a communications connection. A process has at least one port used by the supervisor to identify the process.

process a single activity containing procedure code, data storage, and an interface for communication with other processes.

routing the process of finding a path to a host. To route, a host must decide on which of several ports to send a message. Routing is hierarchical in an internetwork. A host in an internetwork must know which port to use, and whether to send messages to another host or a gateway. For example, host P knows the direction to host Q when P and Q are on the same network. Otherwise, host P knows that gateway G knows the direction to host Q when P and Q are on different networks. The use of gateway G to denote the address of host P is an indirect reference which permits autonomy and efficiency in internetworking.

histogram on a local-network host-to-host loopback contains frequency peaks corresponding to the local-network retransmission cycle. There is another characteristic delay that occurs when hellos are being processed because of the multiplexing of packets through one host port.

The Ford internetwork experiments have resulted in some very definite conclusions. The control and measurement features used in the Ford test have been invaluable in evaluating internetwork efficiency and in performing system diagnostics. Such capabilities, it is believed, will have to be incorporated into commercially available internetworking products. Another feature found to be both useful and implementable is the use of alternative data paths in the design and operation of local networks.

The local network architecture has fit remarkably well into this internetworking scheme, primarily because of dynamic, hierarchical addresses and a link protocol that adapts to various host requirements including point-to-point links, virtual circuits, and datagrams. The local-network packet format is efficiently used in point-to-point link applications and is flexible enough to support the internetwork communications and synchronization required for the maintenance of virtual hosts and networks. ∎

Section 2

Local Network
Software
Software
Software
Software
Software
Software
Software
Software
Software
Software
Software
Software
Software

Dynamic reconfiguration by a local network's operating system

Robert Coyne, University of Houston at Clear Lake City, Tex.

This network operating system automatically reconfigures hardware and software resources to minimize downtime and loss of data and tasks and to adapt to different job needs.

In recent years, the amount of information stored, accessed, and processed on computer networks has greatly increased. Consequently, data communications users need safeguards to prevent damage resulting from failed components, loss of tasks and data, and jobs that cannot meet turnaround-time requirements.

To provide these safeguards for its network, the Uni-

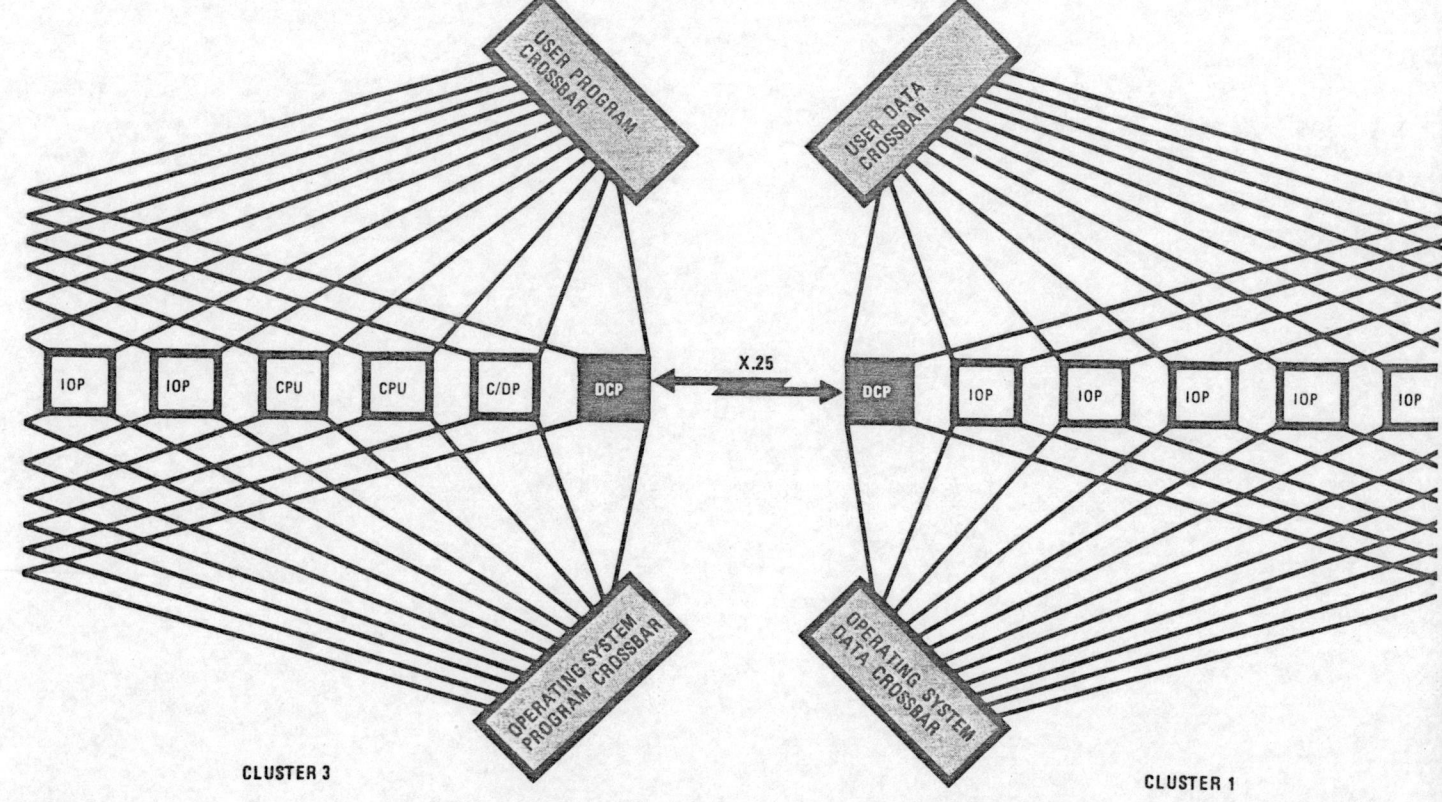

versity of Houston at Clear Lake City (UH/CLC), Texas, has designed an innovative, loosely coupled (containing autonomous but cooperative processors), locally distributed network of reconfigurable microcomputers. This network handles a mixture of real-time transaction processing, timesharing, and batch jobs.

During normal transaction processing, the autonomous, work-seeking microcomputer nodes cooperatively manage network resources. However, the presence of real-time jobs within the network sometimes dictates the need for other configuration-management capabilities. Under these conditions, the UH/CLC network, unlike most other local networks, can dynami-

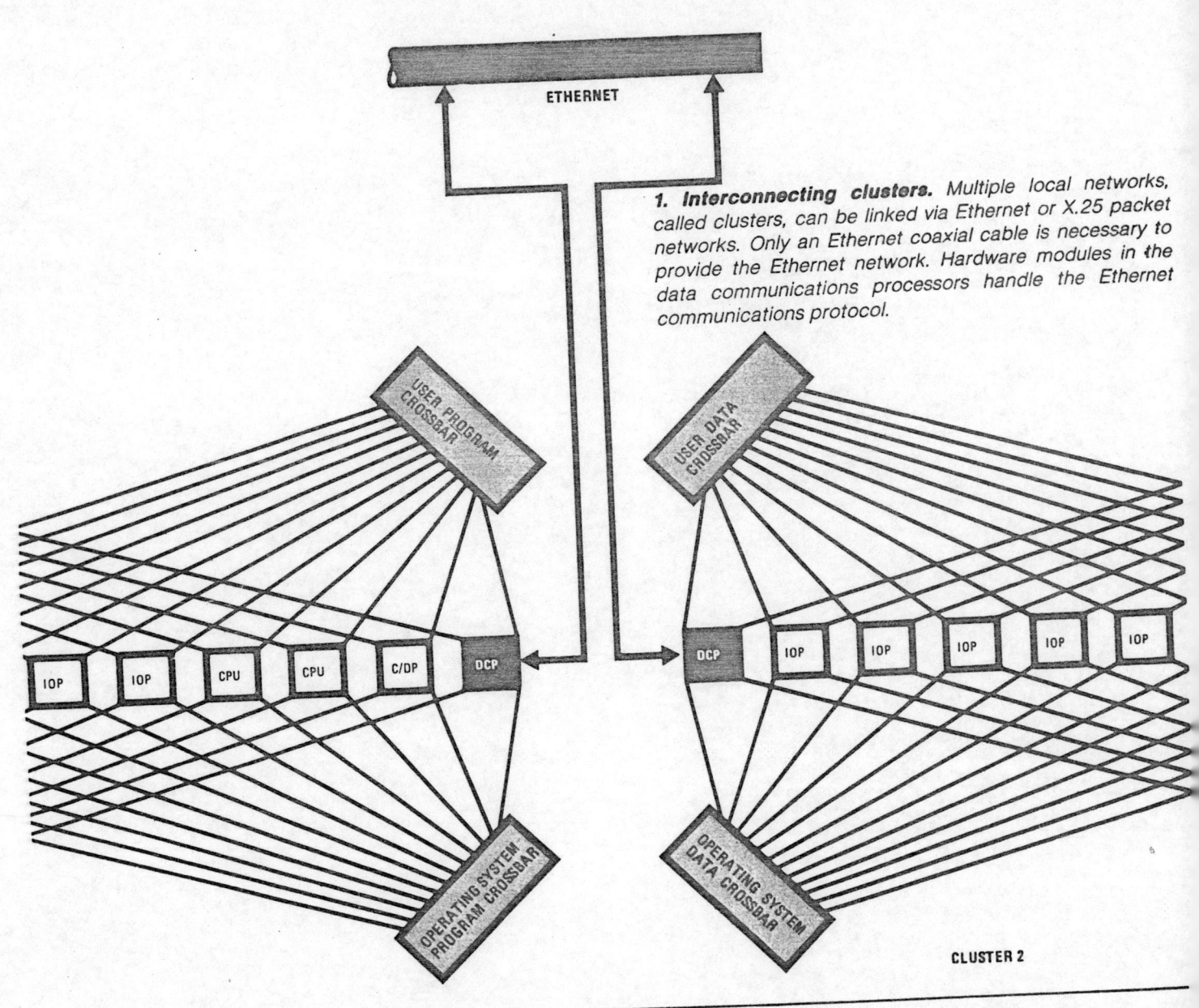

1. Interconnecting clusters. Multiple local networks, called clusters, can be linked via Ethernet or X.25 packet networks. Only an Ethernet coaxial cable is necessary to provide the Ethernet network. Hardware modules in the data communications processors handle the Ethernet communications protocol.

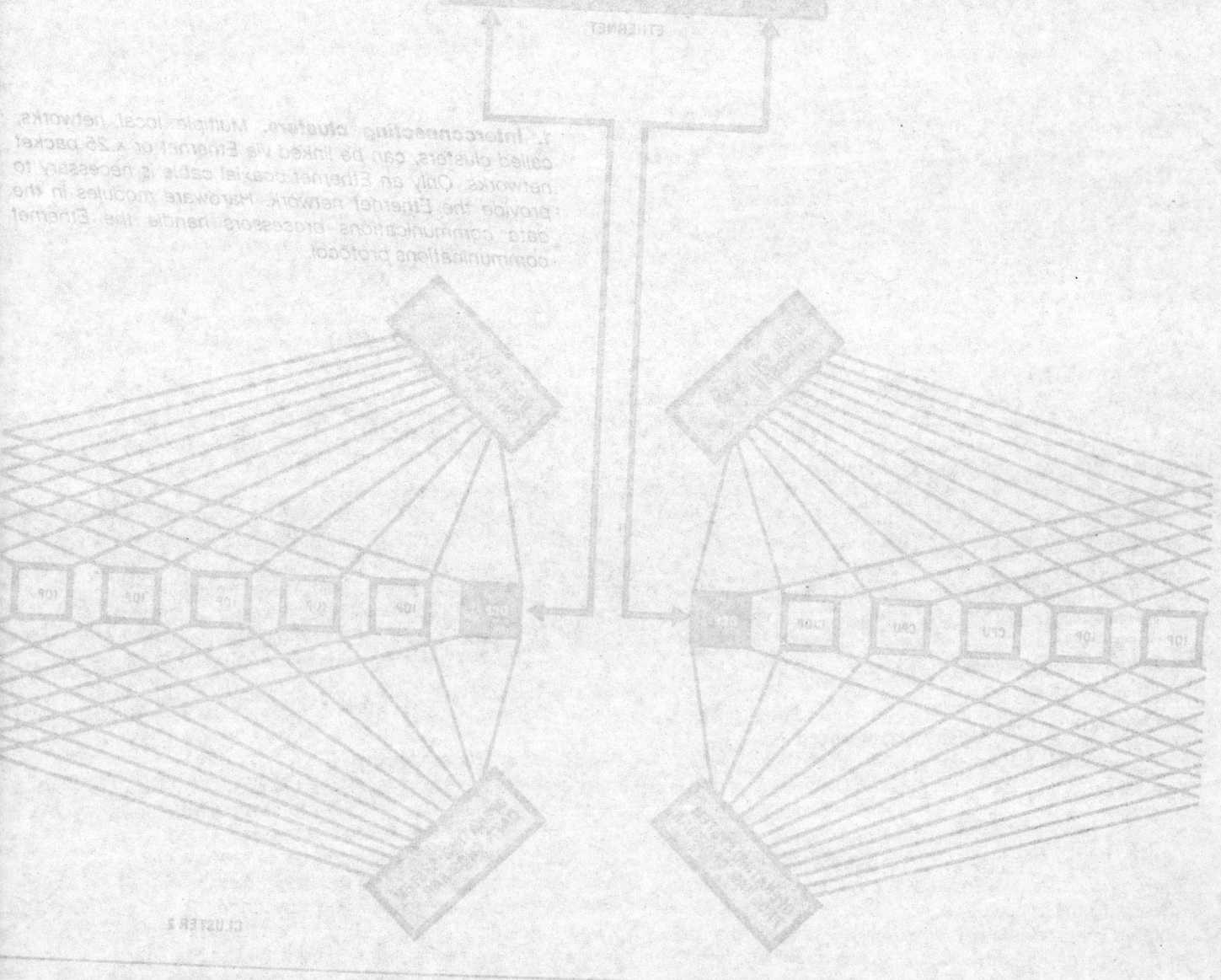

cally reconfigure its resources to meet the stringent time constraints imposed by real-time jobs. In particular, the network services real-time jobs in such a way that the potential for simultaneous task execution is maximized. This leads to faster job execution without increased data rates.

This dynamic-reconfiguration capability is also responsible for the UH/CLC network's fault tolerance. In other words, if any hardware or software component fails during job execution, its resources are automatically reconfigured, its workload and data are redistributed, and the job continues processing (see "Universities are setting trends in data communications nets," DATA COMMUNICATIONS, October, p. 69).

Other attributes of this network include multitasking (distributing a task over several processors for simultaneous processing), resource and task sharing, dynamic load balancing, and modularity. These attributes, as well as the dynamic-reconfiguration capability, are a function of both the network's architecture and its logically distributed operating system. The architecture and operating system were designed by hardware and software developers after they cooperatively defined the network's goals and evaluated the interdependencies of its hardware and software.

The UH/CLC network developers designed a local network that supports up to 256 microcomputer nodes with multiple parallel bus access to crossbar switches. There are four types of microcomputer nodes: central processing units (CPUs), input/output processors (IOPs), data communications processors (DCPs), and configuration/diagnostics processors (C/DPs). Multiple local networks, called clusters, can be serially interconnected via the Ethernet network cable and protocols and can also participate in networking activities with remotely located clusters via, say, X.25 packet networks (Fig. 1). The UH/CLC network also supports distribution of data and computation among microcomputer resources participating in local and remote clusters. The data communications processor in each cluster manages the data links with other clusters in the overall network.

The clusters are constructed so that all processors are work-seeking (always actively examining files and looking for work). Although all processors perform the activities for which they are specialized and operate with maximum independence and autonomy, they also cooperatively interact to maximize simultaneous processing of the workload.

No single point of failure in either software or hardware can stop an entire network cluster. In fact, at worst, a single network-resource failure causes automatic restart or migration of some jobs, tasks (independent program segments), or shared resources to another node or cluster.

The UH/CLC network is designed to help users identify the cause of any job or task that is lost or aborted. Every processor makes its best effort to provide a full account of all activities related to any job or task for which it is responsible. It does this by collecting status and performance statistics furnished by monitoring programs that are part of each local operating system

and its interface to the network operating system.

The network operating system, which manages and integrates the processors and resources, consists of software, hardware, and firmware modules distributed among the network processors. Some operating-system code is common to all types of processors; other codes, such as the intracluster device-management code, comprise a small portion of a CPU's local operating system program but a major portion of an IOP's.

Managing the network

Since CPUs are expected to execute compute-bound tasks optimally, they are not connected to any peripheral devices. To a large extent, traditional CPU supervisory functions, such as I/O interrupt handling, device handling, virtual memory management, data management, I/O recovery and restart, and file management, have been relegated to the IOPs. In addition, the IOPs manage peripheral devices such as printers, disks, and terminals. Intracluster device connectivity is illustrated in Figure 2.

The UH/CLC network operating system is arranged in layers of processes (Fig. 3). Although layers are not strictly hierarchical or even totally ordered, they closely correspond to the order of layers of the local operating-system code for each processor.

The operating-system layers for each type of processor interact. For example, if a user's task local to a cluster requests a record to be read from a data file stored within that same cluster, the "call" from the task goes directly to the intracluster information-management subsystem, bypassing the other layers (Fig. 3). If the requested record already exists in main memory, there is no call for device-management services.

If a user's task in one cluster requests a record residing in a remote cluster, the call from the task goes from the intercluster remote-communications-management subsystem of the first cluster to the same layer in the remote cluster. The call may then go directly to the intracluster information-management subsystem of the remote cluster, bypassing interaction with unneeded layers. If the requested record resides on disk, then a further call is made to the device-management-subsystem layer. The DCP, in Figure 2, connected to the X.25 interface module, would have the cluster's intercluster remote-communications-management code as a major portion of its local operating system. Similarly, the DCP connected to the Ethernet interface module would have the cluster's intercluster local-communications-management code as a major portion of its local operating system.

Feedback and evaluation

All operating-system layers must interface with the feedback monitor (Fig. 3). This monitor collects and analyzes empirical data about both network performance and the progress of each user or system job or task. This information is fed back to the nodes for dynamically improving network performance.

Feedback can take the form of "advisories" about job and resource information sent from the configuration/diagnostic processor to other nodes; dynamically

2. Intracluster device connectivity. *The input/output processors (IOPs) are connected to peripheral devices. The central processing units (CPUs) are connected only to the crossbar switch matrix. The data communications processors (DCPs) are connected to hardware and software modules for intercluster communications.*

altered priorities of jobs or tasks in the workload; or, in an emergency, such as a failed node, a temporary imposition of tight coupling among two or more nodes. The tight coupling makes the nodes less autonomous but allows them to respond to reconfiguration directions to cope with the emergency.

A major use of the feedback monitoring services is to analyze the behavior of the network while processing a benchmark workload. Programmers can then make changes in network-resource management (for exam-

ple, through a scheduling algorithm) and can study the effects of operating conditions on processing that workload. In this way, network managers can decide, in advance, how to best manage growth and network configuration under different situations.

Since the overhead imposed by data collection, analysis, and reporting requirements is high, the level of monitoring services in any layer can be user-selected by a software "key" provided with each request for operating-system services. In other words, the moni-

65

3. Operating-system layers. *The network operating system in each processor contains layers of processes. The layers in different processor types, in the same or different clusters, interact. All layers interface with the feedback monitor that both collects and analyzes job, task, and performance information.*

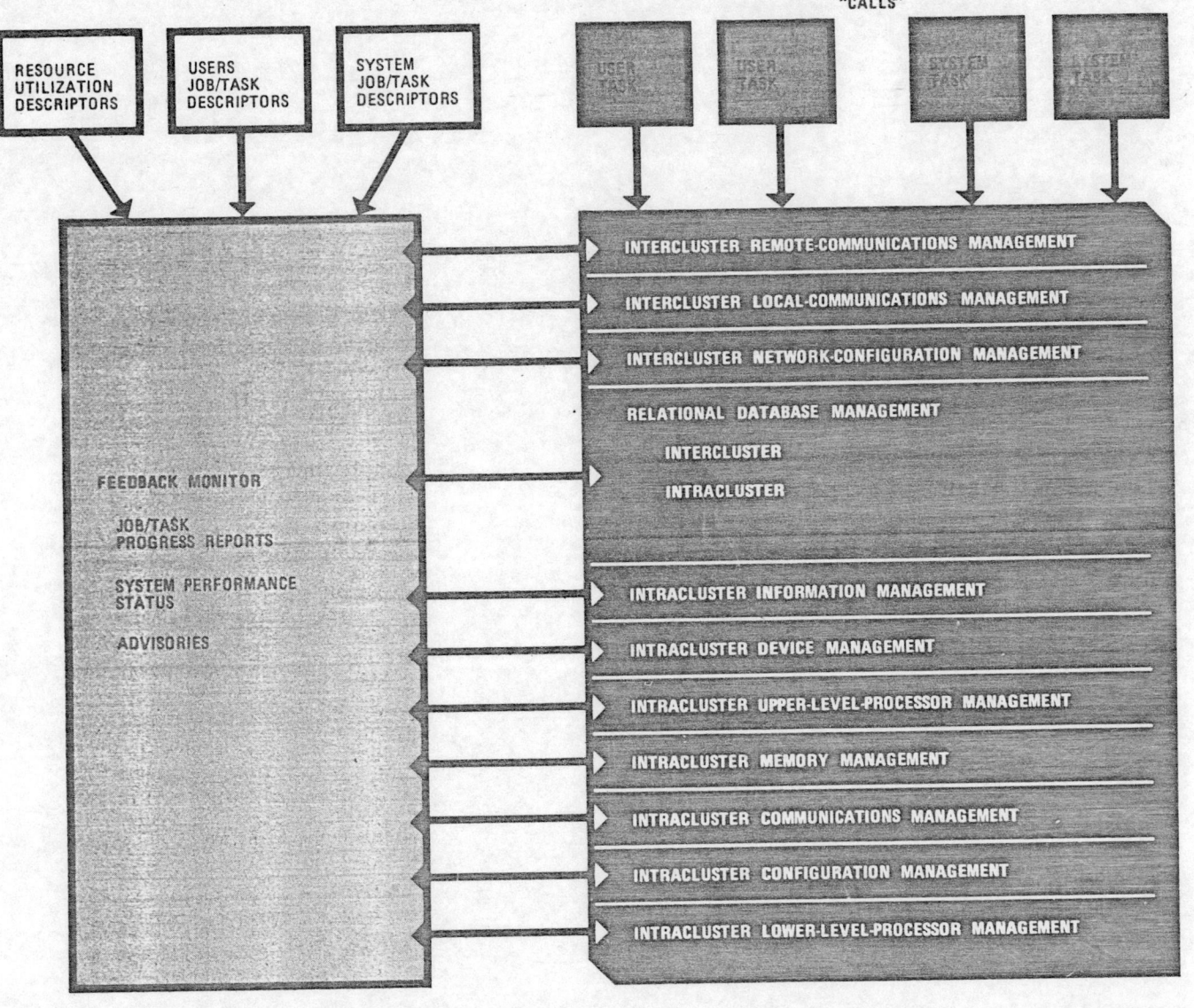

toring services in a layer contain keys that range from "maximum services with minimum throughput" to "minimum services with maximum throughput." The latter can be dynamically invoked by the operating system under emergency conditions—say, if a critical job is in danger of not being completed on time.

The feedback monitor evaluates network attributes, such as performance (throughput, operating-system overhead), modularity (ease and cost of adding or modifying hardware or software resources), and the effects of failure on network components. It can be used to investigate and evaluate techniques of problem representation, algorithm design and distributed solution alternatives, and protection (security and data integrity). In addition, the feedback monitor is regularly scheduled to predict the effects of potential reconfigurations in case of various failures. At the same time,

it keeps a job and network history so users can evaluate the ease and costs of network maintenance.

Cluster architecture

The network cluster uses a combination of multiple, parallel bus structures and shared access to portions of primary memory to facilitate both simultaneous and concurrent operations. Locally distributed physical resources are accessed in mutual exclusion, by processors or direct-memory-access devices, through the bus structures connected to a crossbar switch matrix (Fig. 4). The crossbar switch matrix implemented at UH/CLC is a modular hardware multibus switch arrangement of up to 256 shared-slot modules (hardware modules with slots for plugging in physical resources) and related switching circuitry. All of the crossbar-switching decision logic is contained in the processors.

Under processor control, the crossbar matrices permit the sharing of devices, programs, program data, files, task information, and memory resources within the cluster. Shared-slot resources may exist on any set of four crossbar switch matrices, each of which has its own data path.

These crossbar switch matrices facilitate distribution of executable code and data. A processor may be connected to four unique crossbars via four primary data paths, where each crossbar switch matrix is dedicated to user programs, user data, operating-system programs, or operating-system data (Fig. 4). The processor with exclusive read-write access to a shared-slot module is responsible for status checking, allocation, and deallocation procedures.

Each autonomous processor within a cluster shares physical and logical resources connected to the crossbars by a UH/CLC-defined set of communications protocols transmitted through a panel of registers, called a memory address register set (MARS) panel.

---

4. The crossbar switch matrix. Locally distributed physical resources are accessed through multiple parallel bus structures connected to a crossbar switch matrix. Four data paths connect a processor to four unique crossbars. Each crossbar is dedicated to user programs, user data, system programs, or system data.

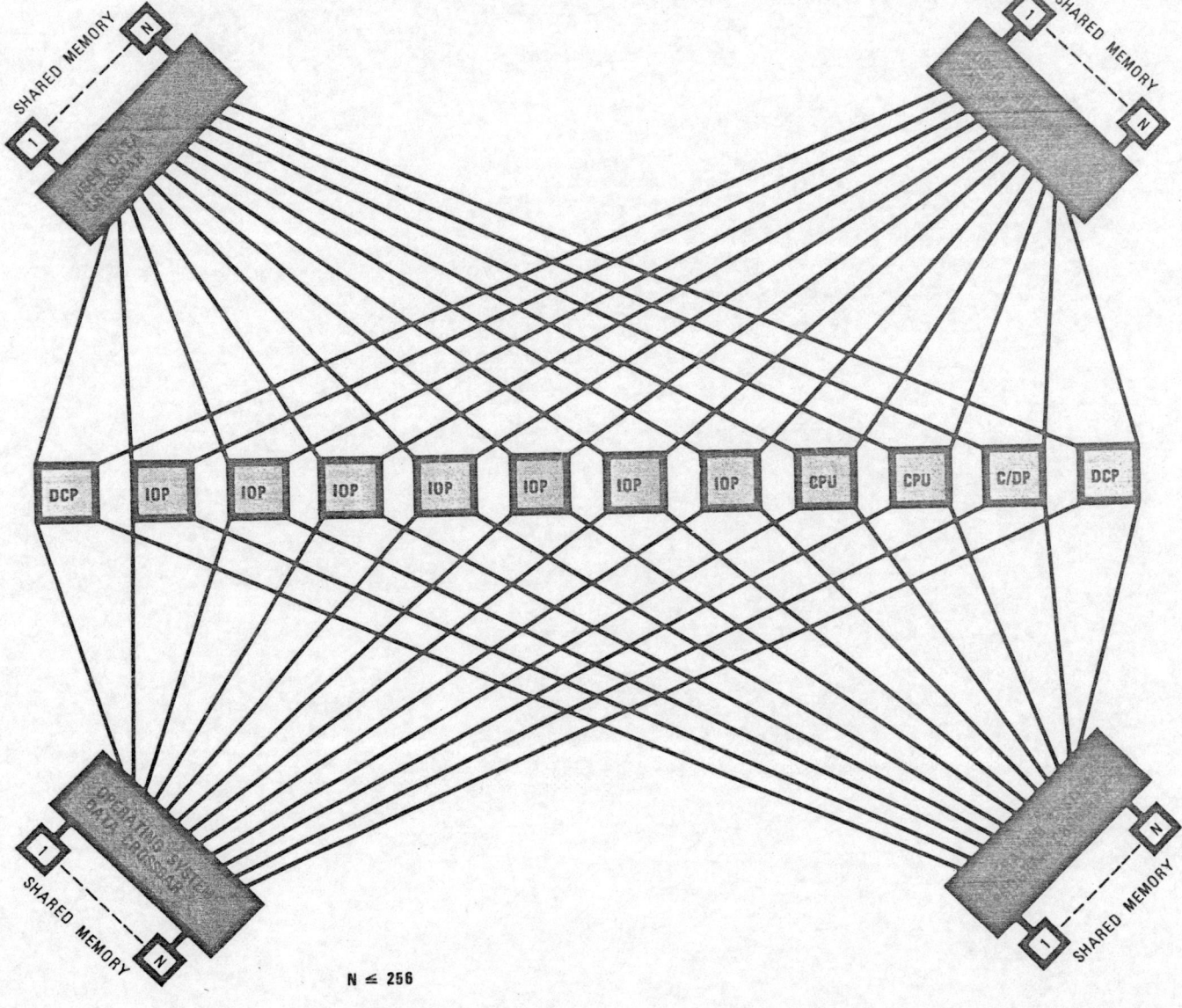

MARS panels in the microcomputer nodes permit simultaneous read-only access for all processors in the locally distributed network, and read-write access for the owner of the registers. Interprocessor communications and synchronization takes place through common but mutually exclusive access to memories connected to crossbars, interrupt-request signals, and the externally visible data in the MARS panels.

Processors within a cluster can also communicate directly using the MARS registers. A processor originating a dialogue exchange with another processor places the appropriate protocol-request structure in the MARS registers. It then directs an interrupt request to the node(s) it designates as the receiving processor(s). The autonomous receiving processor(s) may choose to accept the interrupt request, grant the request, or queue the request for later consideration. Figure 5 illustrates the interconnectivity of the protocol modules and MARS panels located within a cluster. Each interconnecting line in Figure 5 represents interrupt-request lines from each node's MARS panel, as well as the read-only-data buses from each node's protocol modules, to every other node's MARS panel.

The crossbar switch hardware (the shared-slot module) is not overly complex in terms of switching-control logic, since arbitration for exclusive access to a shared-slot resource is handled by the processors via protocols passed through their MARS panels. Figure 4 shows that each memory module is connected to a crossbar switch matrix that contains as many shared-slot modules as there are memory modules. Contention for these shared memory modules is reduced by including local memory in each processor. This use of local memory decreases the number of references to shared memory and speeds up execution. The reliability of the crossbar switch is enhanced by electronically isolating the shared-slot modules within the crossbar switch so there exists no single point of failure.

Types of processors
In the UC/CLC network, the Hickok K68000 microcomputer (a 16-bit-based microcomputer) functions as a central processing unit for processing compute-bound tasks within the network (Fig. 6). It contains the switching-decision logic that communicates information to the crossbars, as well as local memory and a MARS panel. Half of the MARS panel is used for UH/CLC protocol exchanges and half for checkpoint and restart information. The probes are interrupt-request signals that transmit information from other nodes to the CPU's MARS panel. The protocol modules read the MARS panel. Information then goes out to other nodes or devices on read-only lines.

Another node, also containing a K68000, but with specialized software, serves as a consultant to the network—the configuration/diagnostics processor. It is responsible for cluster and network-level "progress reports," advice on load balancing, and cluster and network-level diagnostics. It also performs cluster and network-level behavior analysis and projections based on job monitoring and knowledge of the workload and the network resources.

Other microcomputers, based on the Hickok K6800 (which uses an 8-bit microprocessor), function as autonomous, cooperative, and intelligent input/output processing nodes. CPU nodes request data from IOPs on a file, record, and data-block basis. In addition to having the traditional CPU supervisory functions, the IOPs perform such data processing functions as key searching, data blocking and chaining, data encryption, and file sorting.

The data communications processors, which will be installed within the year, will facilitate intercluster local and remote networking activities. The currently implemented intracluster communications techniques, which use processors with multiple bus structures and access to portions of shared memory, rely on 16-bit bus lines and parallel interfaces for speed. However, intercluster communications are transmitted and received bit-serially and are therefore inherently slower. The DCPs are actually CPUs with additional hardware that adapts them for this kind of communications.

Monitoring performance and resources
The configuration-management layer of the operating system and the feedback monitor implement a collection of operation policies and software functions that facilitate a suitable resource environment for the current network workload. A portion of all processors' local operating-system code is dedicated to configuration management. The local operating system's configuration-management layer communicates with the feedback monitor, allowing emergency reconfiguration calls to pass directly from the feedback monitor to the configuration-management software layer in the processors participating in the reconfiguration.

The feedback monitor and configuration-manage-

---

5. Intracluster communications. *Each line represents interrupt-request lines from each node's MARS panel and the read-only data buses from the protocol modules.*

ment function make up the major portion of the local operating-system code for the C/DP. The C/DP has three major responsibilities: workload configuration, failure detection and recovery, and performance monitoring. Workload configuration involves examining the workload at each processor node and advising the processors about suspending or reassigning activity where it best suits the total network's needs. Failure detection and recovery involves monitoring of network resources to determine when a failure occurs and initiating the proper action to recover from the failure with minimum impact to the work in progress.

The small amount of the configuration-management code that is part of each processor's local operating-system code communicates information to the C/DP. This software communicates status information and monitors the condition of locally dedicated components and devices (both hardware and software). In certain instances, the local operating system in all processors contains logic responsible for periodically checking the C/DP. Any CPU may function as a C/DP, thus protecting the part of the network that is providing fault detection and recovery capabilities by eliminating a single point of failure for C/DP processing.

Reconfiguring jobs

Workload configuration, or dynamic load balancing, means distributing the workload over the set of available processors to increase the performance of the network as a whole. Since all processors are work-seeking, jobs and tasks will normally tend to distribute evenly across the network. However, the introduction of a large real-time task in the network, the failure of a node or device, or the concentration of tasks around a node that contains a particular resource may require the direct intervention of the feedback monitor and configuration-management code within the configuration/diagnostics processor.

For real-time jobs or other high-priority activities, the C/DP configuration diagnostics processor provides continuous support to guarantee that the job is undertaken in the best possible resource environment and that the job will be completed within the allotted time. This support involves not only a look-ahead capability as the job prepares to enter the network, but a continuous monitoring of the job's progress—a feature called "feedback-coupled resource management."

The look-ahead capability provides preventative maintenance so that there will be no need to suspend or reassign tasks when the high-priority job enters the network. It involves comparing the job requirements against the resources currently available. The consultant function may be able to free needed resources by modifying the priority of active jobs and restricting some processors from accepting new work until the high-priority job is complete.

When the high-priority job has begun to execute, the feedback process comes into play to ensure its timely completion. This capability depends on the compilers and/or programmers providing information about the expected execution characteristics of the job. Where possible, this information is merged with historical data on actual run-time behavior recorded by the network feedback monitor during previous executions of the same job. This provides a reasonably accurate profile of the upcoming job in terms of resource utilization, run-time estimates, and requirements for intertask communications among simultaneously executing tasks within that job.

The job profile that results from the merging of user/compiler-supplied information and historical data is decomposed in to a set of milestones for the job and the times each milestone should occur. Failure to meet a milestone in the prescribed time invokes the consultant functions to investigate the cause and suggest remedies based on its knowledge of the status of all network resources. If possible, the required milestone time is met by reconfiguration of network resources. In some cases, failure to meet the milestone is caused by a component failure where the real-time job or a portion of that job resides. The C/DP must then restart the tasks affected by the failure.

For some real-time jobs, completion of the job within a prescribed time is critical, and failure of a network module or component cannot be tolerated. In these cases, a provision is made for duplication of files, tasks, and processing at different nodes, with the C/DP managing this redundant capability. The C/DP also facilitates execution of the real-time task by anticipating module or component failures at certain critical points in the processing. For each possible failure, the C/DP prepares, in advance, a reconfiguration plan that provides the most efficient recovery from the failure.

In spite of the C/DP functions during workload reconfiguration, the consultant functions are principally those of monitoring and advising. This includes monitoring the health of the many network components (for errors or spurious interrupts), as well as the activity relating to a particular job or task and the various work queues. Advisories are then posted at the beginning of the work-to-do files. Active intervention of the C/DP is seen as an exceptional condition. It is the duty of the activities scheduler of the work-seeking processors to consider the advisories in their efforts to maintain the network at near-maximum efficiency.

Failure detection and recovery

One of the primary justifications for distributed data processing is that the failure of any element within the network can be tolerated with minimal impact on the network. Therefore, one design constraint is that successive failures of the network elements should cause at worst a graceful degradation of network performance. It is the responsibility of the operating configuration management layer and the feedback monitor to detect existing faults in the network, and to then reconfigure the remaining elements in the network with the least possible effect on network performance.

The configuration/diagnostics processor is particularly concerned with failures that may exist at the hardware-module level, such as node failures, shared-slot resources, or specific devices. Failures at the component level are normally detected locally. The information is passed from the local node to the feedback

69

6. K68000 CPU node. *The node contains the switching logic that communicates information to the crossbars, local memory, a MARS panel, and higher-level protocol modules. Probes connect different nodes with the MARS panel. The protocol modules read the MARS panel. Data is then transmitted to nodes via the read-only lines.*

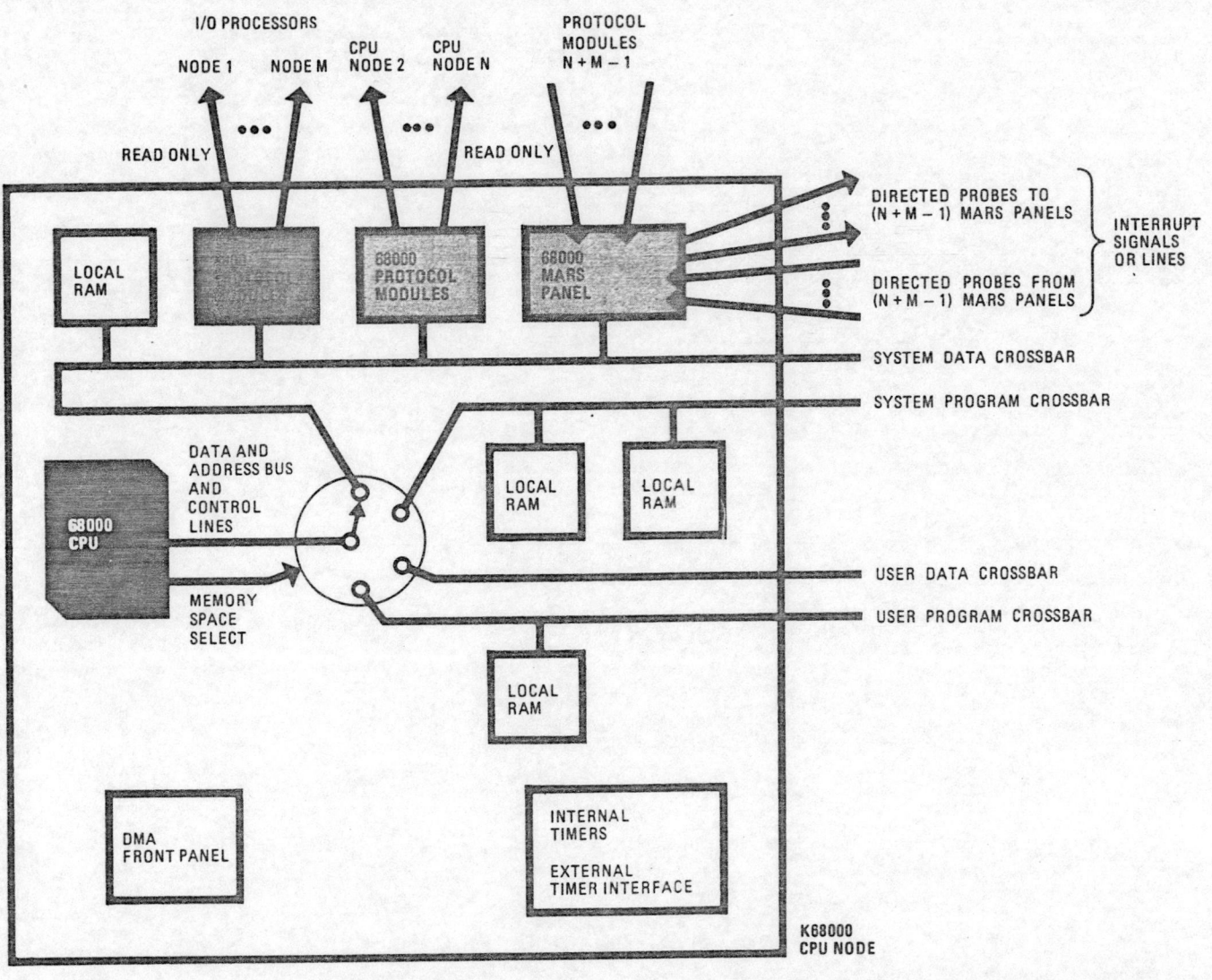

monitor in the configuration/diagnostics processor. However, if the failure of a specific component causes failure of the entire module that contains that component, the node suspecting this failure notifies the C/DP, which then investigates.

Failure detection within the network includes some redundancy. The configuration/diagnostics processor monitors the health of the nodes and the shared slots. For nodes, this may mean the issuance of status requests with the expectation of receiving a response within a given time. For shared slots, their status registers are examined to determine if a failure exists. In addition to this periodic checking, the individual nodes may detect failures in other nodes, in shared slots, or in locally dedicated devices. This information is then passed to the C/DP, which confirms or denies that an error condition exists. Since the possibility exists that the error was in the reporting node, the C/DP will also recheck the informer.

The confirmed failure of a node means that jobs and tasks currently assigned to that node must be aborted and requeued for processing elsewhere. Communicating tasks that exist on other nodes must similarly be restarted. The configuration manager will also take control of the shared-slot resources that had been assigned to the failed node, with the intention of yielding them to the first healthy node that requests them. The failed node may also have been in control of dedicated devices. Where hardware connections allow, the C/DP reassigns these devices to other nodes.

Failure of a shared-slot resource jeopardizes all jobs and tasks that were using the shared slot at the time of failure. These jobs and tasks may be migrated, requeued, and restarted. Failure of specific dedicated devices may be handled by the local node when redundancy exists. In other cases, the C/DP must reassign devices from other nodes to the affected node, based on existing hardware connections. ■

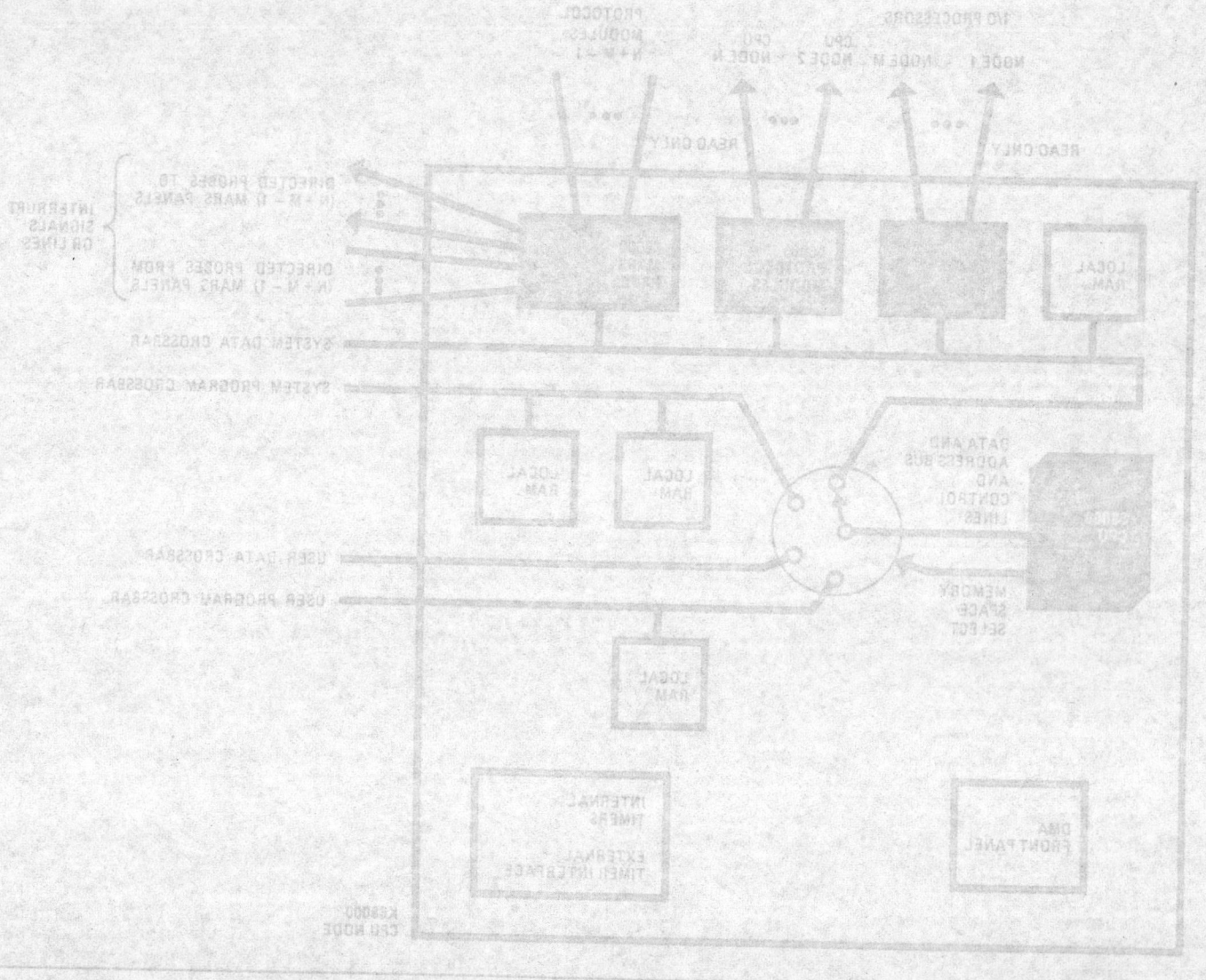

Unix: An operating system that means business

Wendy Rauch-Hindin, Data Communications

Small and friendly, Unix is at home in the automated office. It runs on many vendors' equipment and has commands for building Unix-to-Unix communications.

More than just a computer operating system, Unix is being developed as a prime contender to control the local networks of the future. It is portable and easy to use by both nonprogrammers in an office environment and programmers for program development. Moreover, its most recent versions incorporate a collection of primitive (fundamental) communications commands. Data communications users can readily connect these primitive commands to build their own Unix-to-Unix communications programs independent of the particular application at hand.

The most common Unix functions have been directly programmed into a single-chip, 32-bit microprocessor, the Belmac-32. Introduced by Bell Laboratories in February 1981, this hardware support of functions such as process context switching and system calls—previously implemented by large numbers of software instructions that consumed a great deal of execution time—gives Unix real-time capabilities. Thus, it is readily adapted for networking.

Says John M. Scanlon, executive director of processor and common software systems at Bell Laboratories, in Naperville, Ill.: "Unix is very applicable to the office of the future. Since it is small and does not require a lot of memory, it can be installed on the small machines that will be prevalent in local networks. It is also portable over a wide range of computers. And, programmers can easily build a high-level user-interface that can be readily understood and used by nonprogrammers."

Scanlon speaks from experience working with Bell Labs machines that can talk to any others located at Bell or at Western Electric—most of which are based on Unix—via some kind of network. Some of the machines are loosely coupled, meaning they are connected by the telephone system across geographical distances; others are tied into intra- or interbuilding local networks (see "Bell Labs's local networks").

At Bell Labs, Unix supports a variety of applications. For example, it is used for software development, for word processing and document preparation, and for support of compilers, assemblers, and test systems. It also handles applications involving large databases (megabytes of data), including administrative programs of telephone company trunks and lines, traffic measurements, and office record-keeping. Bell Labs development groups have also added communications capabilities to the basic operating system so that it can be used in their local networks.

Although Unix in software does not provide the real-time responses needed for telephone switching systems, it incorporates several features that give it some of these capabilities. As a result, Unix is applied to process control inside Western Electric's factories. For this application, the number of real-time events that an operating system must handle is much smaller than that in a telephone switching environment, which sees millions of signals per minute.

Unix has grown so popular in the Bell System that the current demand for Unix capacity is insatiable. Consequently, it has been transported from a Digital Equipment Corporation (DEC) PDP-11, on which it ran

71

Bell Labs' local networks

Within project areas in the same building, many Bell Laboratories machines running Unix are interconnected in tightly coupled networks. Each network has from 6 to 18 machines linked by an interface to a high-speed, time-division-multiplexed bus. Network arbitration is by contention.

Network Systems Corporation (NSC) provides its Hyperchannel network, which operates in the range of 50 Mbit/s. "However," Bell Labs's John M. Scanlon explains, "no machine in the minicomputer class can drive that. When you look at software protocols and transmissions together, you are actually exchanging at about 0.5 Mbyte/s."

In addition to using Hyperchannel, Bell connects many of its machines using Datakit—a Bell Labs hardware design for a tightly coupled packet network. Datakit is a packet switch that accommodates a mixture of distributed and centralized control. Its protocol and contention are distributed, but its maintenance is centralized.

"The Datakit approach to tightly coupled networks is still being researched at Bell," says Scanlon. "Among the differences between Datakit and NSC's Hyperchannel is that Datakit supports lower data rates of only 8 Mbit/s. However, it has the capability to interconnect many more machines."

All machines employ a user-level protocol, called UUCP (Unix-to-Unix copy procedure), except for those using a project-developed protocol that handles special requirements. For example, projects requiring a lot of file exchanging have special protocols for that application.

At the low level, most machines support BX.25, which is Bell's version of the X.25 protocol. However, some machines use an NSC protocol, others use CU (call up)—a low-level protocol invented for Unix—and, depending on the application intended, still others use all three low-level protocols.

---

originally, to the Perkin-Elmer 832, IBM 370 series, Amdahl 470, DEC's VAX 750 and 780, Intel Corporation 8086, Zilog 8000, Honeywell Level 6, IBM Series/1, Univac 1100, Bolt, Beranek, and Newman (BBN) C/70, and IBM 4300s up to the 3033s. This portability over a wide range of computers is unique to Unix and stems from two characteristics: It is a small system (100 kbytes) and is written in "C," a high-level programming language, instead of machine language. In comparison, most operating systems are written for specific hardware and, to be moved to a new machine, must be completely rewritten. Even worse, application programs must then be rewritten to be compatible with the new operating system.

Why is Unix unique?

Unix is a general-purpose, interactive, timesharing operating system (see "What is Unix?"). Its distinguishing characteristic, according to its inventor, Ken Thompson, of Bell Labs, Murray Hill, N.J., is its file sys-

tem. He explains that to Unix a file is simply a collection of bytes with no special format. This makes it easy for users to create a Unix file. The simple command *ls>x* will create a file named "x."

In contrast, in most other operating systems, such as IBM's and DEC's, users must write a program to create a file. The program must contain information about the physical characteristics of the file (binary or binary-coded decimal, logical record length, block size, fixed or variable length, and file format). It must also specify the type and name of the device the file will use, the disposition (for example, whether the file is old, new, or shared; temporary or permanent; and what to do if the job terminates abnormally), and primary and secondary space allocated for the file.

Although it is easy to create Unix files, it is not without problems. "The price paid for files with a general structure," says Thompson, "is difficulty getting a high input/output (I/O) throughput in bytes per second compared to formatted files." A significant advantage of Unix is that it is device-independent, which means the programmer does not have to write program commands specifying where information is coming from or going to. This advantage occurs because each I/O device is associated with a Unix file. These files are accessed as any other, except that the access itself activates the device to handle any transferred data.

Walter Zintz, executive director of Uniops, a Unix users' group, explains that "a programmer writing a program to execute under Unix merely says that his information comes from source 1 and goes to source 2. Only when the program is ready to execute does he specify whether sources 1 and 2 are terminals, files, or another program.

"However," Zintz continues, "in most other languages and operating systems, programmers must specify their input and output devices in the program. To change one of these devices, the programmer must go through pages of the program and change every specification written for it—and, in a long program, this may mean 500 changes."

In addition to the usual communicating of information to and from devices such as terminals, disks, and printers, the output of a program executing under Unix can be used directly as the input to another program. This information is transferred through software channels called pipes. Output data can also go to two other programs simultaneously through a special kind of pipe, called a "tee." Similarly, programs can receive their input from more than one file.

An extension of pipes and tees is a Unix feature known as a filter. A filter can selectively extract information from one file, modify it, and send the result as output to another file or into a pipe (Fig. 1). Douglas Parsons, communications product analyst for Cambridge, Mass.-based Bolt, Beranek, and Newman, says filters are helpful to a data communications user who is monitoring data from several nodes, such as in an X.25, SNA, or local network, and sending it to an analyzer program for processing (Fig. 2). If the program needs a certain kind of information, such as host-overload data or all data from a particular host, a filter can

What is Unix?

The Unix operating system, developed at Bell Laboratories, is made up of a kernel, a shell, and a group of utility programs that have been added to the basic system. The kernel is a large program that runs input/output devices and resources; supervises process context switching, scheduling, and synchronization; and allocates memory. The shell is a high-level programming and command language that allows the user to address the operating system directly. It contains constructs such as flow-control statements (if-then-else and do-while), variables, and subroutines. Users enter shell commands to read and write files, direct and redirect input and output, and invoke processes that communicate through software channels, or pipes. Users can also string together combinations of shell commands to build new programs to perform various jobs.

Unix utility programs include programs for editing and formatting texts, setting mathematical equations in type, interactive graphics, electronic mail, and phototypesetting. In addition, the system contains programs for designing wire-wrap boards and integrated circuits and for updating databases. A number of other programs, known collectively as Programmer's Workbench (PWB/Unix), have been added to Unix to serve as software-development tools. These tools keep track of program changes, recreate earlier versions of programs, collect specifications for jobs, and maintain records of dependencies between program parts. Programmers use these software-tool capabilities in developing new programs and modifying old ones.

Unix is written in "C," a high-level programming language somewhere between assembly language and a higher-level language (see "High-level language for easy X.25 updates," Data Communications, September, p. 65). "C" provides good flow-control and methods of structuring data. It is high-level enough to allow a programmer to refer to data by symbolic names (allows data abstractions) instead of by addresses and bit positions. In addition, its modular structure makes it easy to modify or add new features to the operating system. At the same time, it is low-level enough to allow the user to address memory directly, without resorting to assembler code.

The "C" language, written for Unix by Bell scientist Dennis Ritchie, is an updated form of the "B" language. Says Ritchie, "there never was an "A" language. The "B" language, which is like "C" except that it does not provide data types (like integer, floating point, and binary), was named for Bonnie Thompson, the wife of the inventor of Unix.

Unix is built up of a collection of components, called primitives, that represent single statements or subroutines. Examples of primitives are ls (list), sort (sort), cp (copy a file), and mv (move). Programmers simply connect these primitives to build new functions. For example, users employing Unix for word processing applications should be able to edit a document, proofread it, mail it to an address on an address list, and file a copy for themselves. Rather than write a monolithic program that does each task uniquely, they can build a macro function that does all tasks in response to primitive commands such as FORMAT EDITOR, SORT, and SPELL. The latter is a program that gives the user access to Webster's *New Collegiate Dictionary*.

For Unix-to-Unix communications, specific primitives are available. For example, multiplexing primitives combine data streams within one machine onto a single link. There are also retry and encryption primitives. Users can piece these together to build their communications capability. In this way, they can send messages, data, or programs to other users on other machines in the same or different networks.

Bell Labs's Scanlon claims that "other operating systems have message-sending capabilities, but none have as many communications features for fully interconnecting machines as Unix. Directories in the machines are used to set up connections, and the operating system also handles acknowledgments, information transfer, and error checking. However, as far as the user is concerned, commands to send information to others on either the same or different machines all look the same."

Monitoring networks with Unix

Unix files are organized into sets known as directories. Each user, network, or node has its own file directory. The file directories are hierarchically organized in a tree structure having one root and many levels of branches. With this architecture, all files can be found by tracing a path through the tree.

Unix's hierarchical file structure allows file directories that contain network programs, I/O devices, and network nodes to be set up so they resemble the actual network's topology. This, in turn, makes centralized monitoring of any number of networks particularly easy. It also allows data communications managers to add more nodes, hosts, devices, or networks to their existing network without greatly increasing the complexity of the monitoring program. For example, explains BBN's Parsons, one network-services program running on Unix can be used to monitor two independent networks called net 3 and net 4 (Fig. 3). Net 3 has three nodes, and each node has two hosts. Net 4 has four nodes and two hosts per node. In the same way, any number of networks can be added to the tree and monitored by the same network-services program.

In the Unix directory structure in Figure 3, general programs that relate to any of the networks are subdirectories under the main directory, or root. At the same level are the net 3 and net 4 subdirectories. General programs and files that relate to net 3 and net 4 are stored in subdirectories under net 3 and net 4, respec-

be used to exclude all information that does not satisfy the analyzer program's criteria. The path that the I/O data takes is programmer-defined. Such a filter makes it unnecessary for a programmer to modify the analyzer program as its criteria change.

73

1. Pipes and filters. *Unix programs may be linked by pipes and filters. The X.25 filter program changes the X.25 data to the format needed for the analyzer program. Its output is the input to the host-overload filter program, which filters out only the host-overload information and sends it to the analyzer program.*

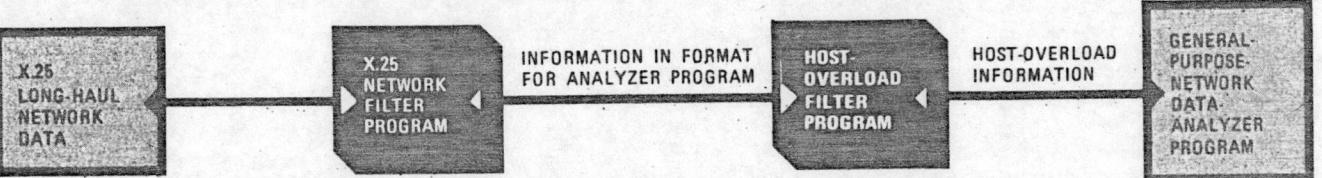

tively. In addition, net 3 and net 4 have separate sub-directories for each of their nodes. Each node directory contains its own subdirectories of programs and files, as well as subdirectories for each host. More levels of directories can be created, if desired, for files and information relating to each host.

The programmer names a host or node by specifying its path. This eliminates confusion in keeping track of hosts and nodes for monitoring or expanding the network. For example, net 3/node 1/host 2 is distinguishable from net 4/node 1/host 2 because they have different path names.

With non-Unix operating systems, hosts and nodes are given numbers—either absolute numbers or numbers relative to another host or node. In either case, since all network files are intermingled in one large directory, a data communications user wishing to add or remove a node or host first needs a map telling him

where that node is located relative to the others. Moreover, to make the operating system aware of every addition or deletion, the programmer must modify the programs that deal with the added or removed node or host. However, with the Unix directory's hierarchical structure, each added host simply becomes a subdirectory in a node directory.

Parsons claims that the Unix tree-structured directories also make it easy to investigate problems. For example, occasionally two identical programs execute on two identical hosts, but one program fails. This causes the networking software to take a memory dump of the problem host. The dump eventually becomes the output of the network-services program.

Under Unix, a file is created called net 3/node 3/host 2/dump/date/time so a programmer knows instantly which host had the problem. Other networks, such as the U.S. Department of Defense's Arpanet,

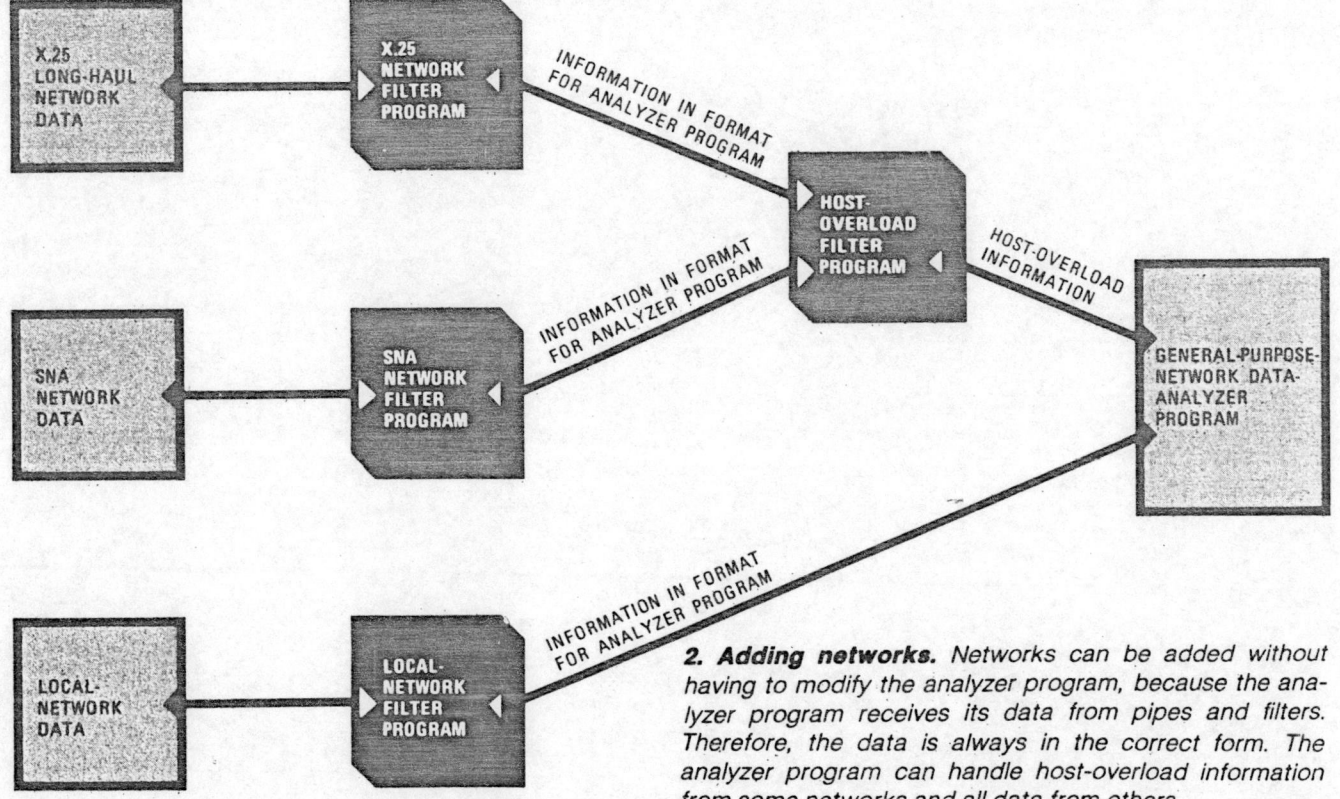

2. Adding networks. *Networks can be added without having to modify the analyzer program, because the analyzer program receives its data from pipes and filters. Therefore, the data is always in the correct form. The analyzer program can handle host-overload information from some networks and all data from others.*

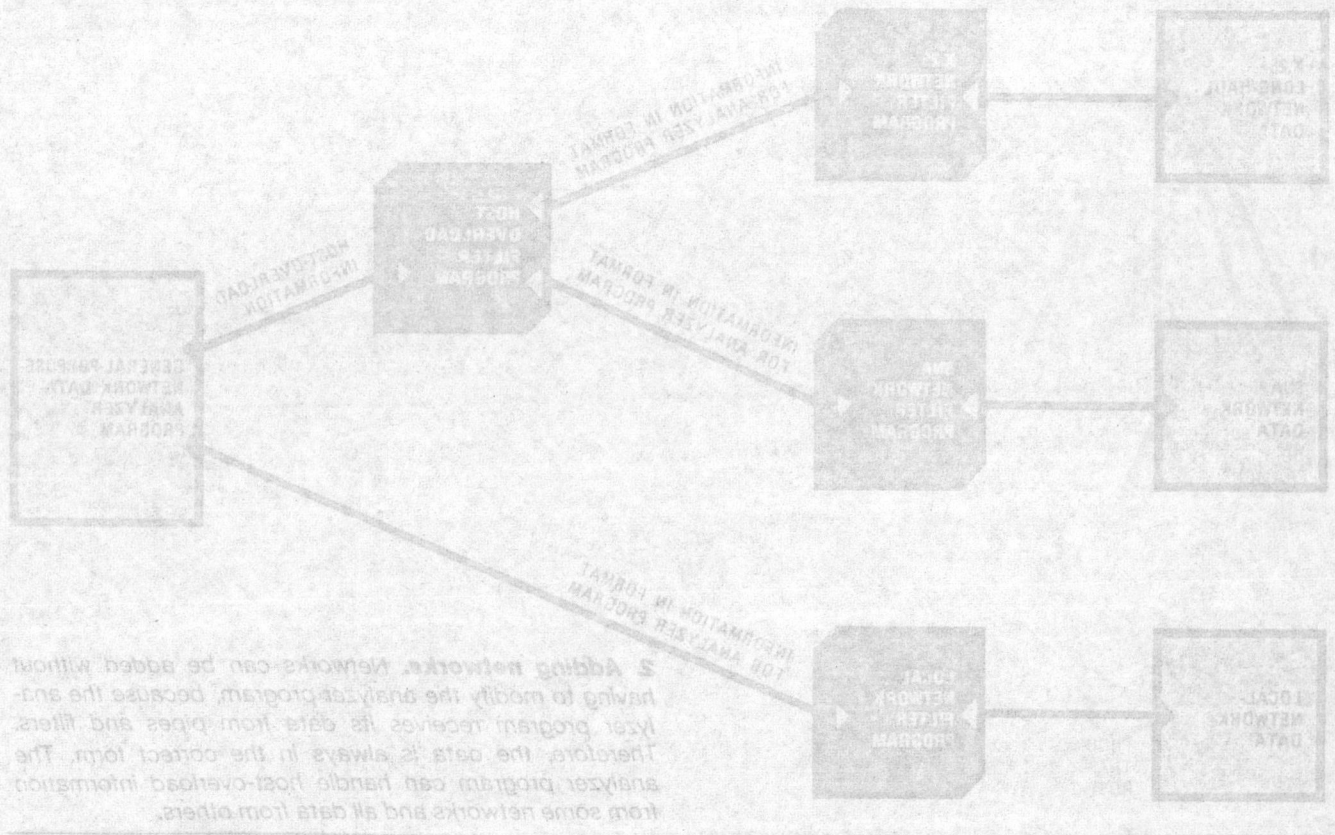

3. The Unix tree. *Unix file directories are organized in a tree structure with one root and many levels of branches. The programmer names directories by specifying their* *paths. Newly added hosts become subdirectories in their node directories. This allows network files to be set up to resemble the actual network topology.*

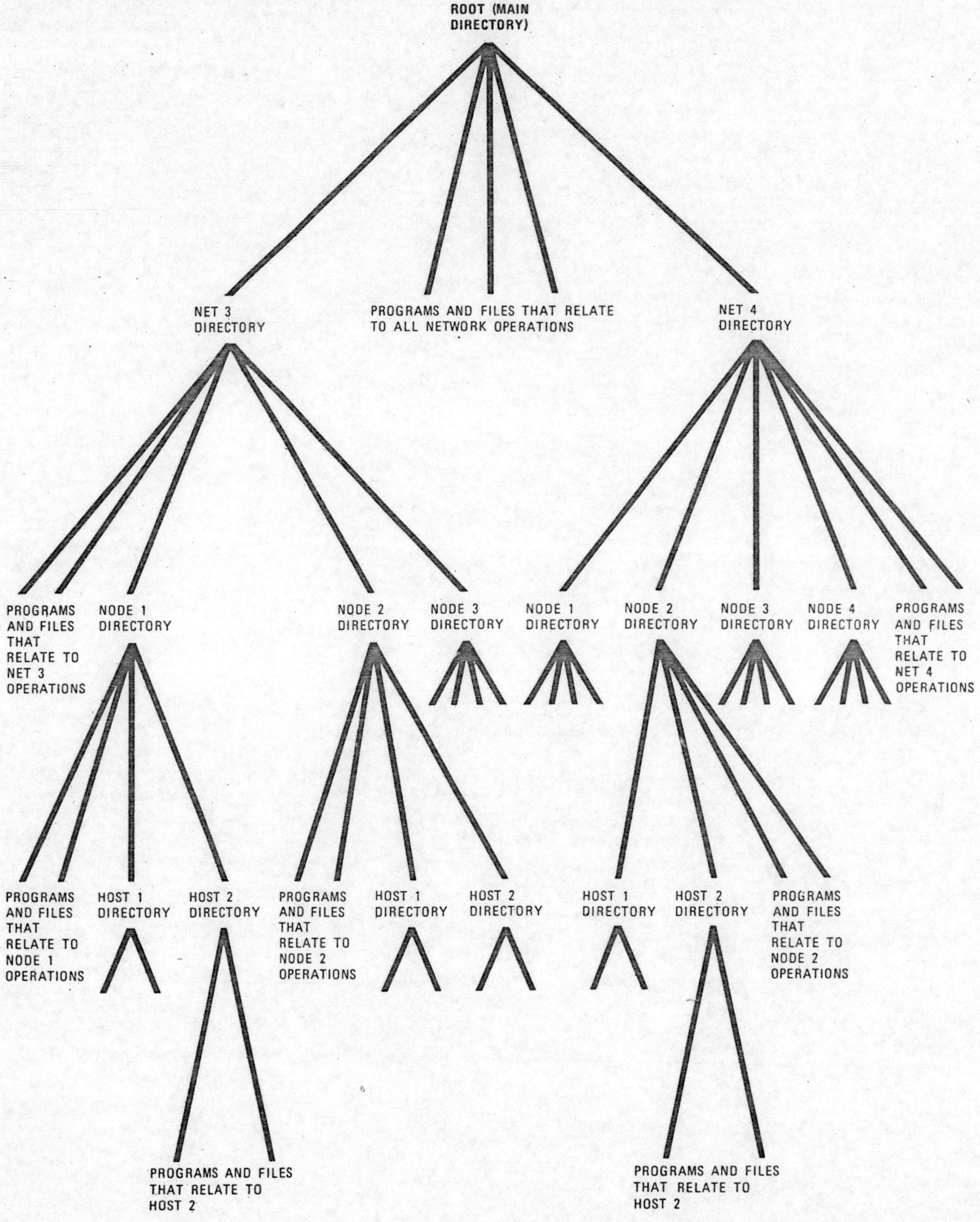

ROOT (MAIN DIRECTORY)

NET 3 DIRECTORY

PROGRAMS AND FILES THAT RELATE TO ALL NETWORK OPERATIONS

NET 4 DIRECTORY

PROGRAMS AND FILES THAT RELATE TO NET 3 OPERATIONS

NODE 1 DIRECTORY

NODE 2 DIRECTORY

NODE 3 DIRECTORY

NODE 1 DIRECTORY

NODE 2 DIRECTORY

NODE 3 DIRECTORY

NODE 4 DIRECTORY

PROGRAMS AND FILES THAT RELATE TO NET 4 OPERATIONS

PROGRAMS AND FILES THAT RELATE TO NODE 1 OPERATIONS

HOST 1 DIRECTORY

HOST 2 DIRECTORY

PROGRAMS AND FILES THAT RELATE TO NODE 2 OPERATIONS

HOST 1 DIRECTORY

HOST 2 DIRECTORY

HOST 1 DIRECTORY

HOST 2 DIRECTORY

PROGRAMS AND FILES THAT RELATE TO NODE 2 OPERATIONS

PROGRAMS AND FILES THAT RELATE TO HOST 2

PROGRAMS AND FILES THAT RELATE TO HOST 2

3. The Unix tree. Unix file directories are organized in a tree structure with one root and many levels of branches. The programmer names directories by specifying their paths. Newly added hosts become subdirectories in their node directories. This allows network files to be set up to resemble the actual network topology.

number every host relative to every node. Since a path name is not specified under the Arpanet computer's operating system, a programmer would have to figure out if host 2 belonged to node 1, node 2, or node 15. "It could be done," says Parsons, "but it is not as simple as with Unix, because the operating system files are not topologically similar to the network."

"Under Unix, monitoring one network is just as simple as monitoring 10 networks," Parsons claims. "In fact," he continues, "most computer tools are either simple to use initially and become unworkable as things get complicated or they are hopelessly complicated now but become easier as the network grows. But Unix is simple to work with when the network to be monitored is simple. In addition, as the network grows in complexity, Unix is still simple to work with because whenever another network is connected, the programmer only has to add one directory."

Adding hardware
It is easy to add device drivers and I/O devices to Unix. Since each I/O device is associated with a Unix file, adding a device merely entails making a new file in a device directory. Major and minor device numbers are assigned, and a few tables must be updated. However, unlike other operating systems, Unix need not be reassembled each time new hardware is added.

"In contrast," says Michael Davis, systems programmer at Matrix Electronics, Yaphank, N.Y., "adding equipment to the DEC RSX-11 operating system is an all-day job." He explains that in RSX-11 it is necessary to go through the "Sysgen procedure," during which the user specifies what hardware he is adding and any desired options. Options include type of job scheduling (round-robin, time-slice), memory-management support, time allocated to each job, type of output (fancy print, capable print, or limited print), and even 50- versus 60-Hz clock. The Sysgen procedure is similar to that used with the IBM/370 for adding hardware.

After specifications are made and options are selected, the operating system must be changed. The executive portion of the system, which provides I/O control, must be reassembled and then the entire operating system link-edited (linked to the rest of the operating system and new memory addresses calculated).

"But," says Davis, "among the reasons adding hardware to Unix takes less time is that Unix does not provide options that RSX-11 offers. RSX-11, on the other hand, is a real-time system that must be tailored to an individual's specific requirements."

Unix on a chip
The easy part of networking is interconnecting the medium and hardware. The difficult part is handling the protocols that enable machines to talk to each other. And the worst part about protocols is not inventing them but putting them together so that, after machines have finished their protocol functions, they still have enough real-time left over to do their work.

Says Bell Labs's Scanlon: "Unfortunately, it is not unusual for 25 percent of a machine's capacity to be used up just handling communications protocols. In other words, over a long period, like a day, 25 percent of a machine's cycles is spent on protocols. This is particularly true for tightly coupled networks and is unacceptable in many applications."

Scanlon claims that the 25 percent figure holds regardless of the operating system. He adds: "In the future, the ability to afford machine-to-machine communications is going to be determined by how many CPU (central processing unit) cycles you throw away to do it. And the only way to provide efficient protocols is to design the CPU, the operating system, and the protocols as a single system and provide silicon support for the software."

A good deal of the design of the Belmac-32 single-chip, 32-bit microprocessor is directed toward this capability. This chip was optimized to support both Unix and the "C" language used to write it. Chip designers investigated which functions were most important to the operating system, which most improved performance, and which used the most overhead. They then implemented the most heavily used software functions on the chip.

One of these software functions, process context switching (switching from process to process), is fundamental to operating systems and to the message-based environments that occur in networking. It consumes a large amount of overhead because the operating system must save the information about the first process before switching to the next, so it can later return to the first process. Implementing this function onto the chip increases the processing speed three times and requires only one-third of the instructions needed for a software implementation.

A large number of instructions and a large overhead are also needed for a system call in Unix. A system call is a call to Unix to perform a task such as reading a file or input/output. Implementation of system calls on the Belmac-32 increases processing speed four times and uses only one-fourth of the instructions.

Because "C" is the Unix language, its important, heavily used functions were studied in depth. In any high-level language, such as "C," there are frequent subroutine calls. Whenever a subroutine is called, the operating system must save all the registers and pointers, as well as the address of the calling routine, so it can return there. At the conclusion of the subroutine, the registers and pointers must be restored so execution of the calling routine can continue. A good deal of the subroutine-calling overhead is now done in the Belmac-32 chip, improving performance by 2:1.

In addition, popular string-manipulation (sequence of characters) instructions, such as COPY, generate a fair amount of assembly language code. About half of that code is now on the chip itself, and the processing speed is twice as fast.

"Software support by silicon," Scanlon says, "is the fundamental direction for people who want to design microprocessors. Microprocessors' hardware parameters, such as clock speed, number of transistors, and power dissipation, are only secondary."

Scanlon predicts that data communications users will see more operating systems in hardware. However,

of which will be determined by user demand and part by regulatory events In Washington, D.C. ("AT&T's offspring ends business as usual," DATA COMMUNICATIONS, March, page 44).

"Whether or not Western Electric will decide to sell components," Scanlon adds, "it sells both hardware and full systems outside the Bell System. Therefore, as the Belmac-32 is incorporated in hardware and systems, users might have use of this microprocessor. However, it is still too early to forecast."

Dissenting opinions

Unix is designed so that users can easily share files. Although this is an advantage for program developers, Fred Jenkins, manager of computer service at Bell Northern Research and president of the IBM virtual memory (VM) operating-system users' group Share, says: "If a user's aim is security, sharing and security do not go well together. In contrast, each VM user has his own file system."

However, Uniops Executive Director Walter Zintz says: "To use Unix in an environment where security is important, the systems programmer need only aod security features. It is very easy to add features to Unix; even the pipes and filters were added after Unix was written. In contrast, after most operating systems are finished, it is difficult, if not impossible, to add anything. And, a systems programmer takes his life in his hands if he tries to tamper with most operating systems."

Jenkins claims that although Unix has the reputation of being "easy to use," he finds the command environment very disconcerting. "Because the Unix commands are usually very brief—one or two characters only—it is difficult to deduce from the abbreviations what functions you are performing." For example, he explains, "w" means WRITE, but "q" means QUIT THE EDITOR MODE. In VM, guessing the meaning of a command is easier. Since the command PRINT means print, users can deduce that a read command might be called READ. As a worst case, Jenkins compares VM's command EDIT, meaning to edit a file, with Unix's command NROFF for the same function. "It just makes the system more difficult to use," he says. "In addition," he adds, "Unix has few fault diagnostics and error-recording capabilities. Consequently, if a problem arises, a company's operations staff cannot do much. Instead, systems programmers must be brought in to isolate and correct malfunctions."

Systems programmer Davis of Matrix Electronics puts it all in perspective, saying: "Preference for an operating system depends on what you are doing with it. If you want a real-time system, pick one like DEC's RSX-11. Its constructs allow you to do all the things associated with real time. For example, if you want to schedule tasks to run at specific times, you can program the operating system to execute a task at every tick of the clock. However, for a general-purpose, in-house system, pick Unix. It is more user-oriented. For payroll purposes, you need a good file system. In that case, also pick Unix because it has a superior file system. But," Davis adds, "if price is an object, pick RSX-11, because Unix is more expensive." ◾

A programming language for networks

Paul A. D. de Maine, Pennsylvania State University, University Park, Pa.

Researchers have built a truly transportable language. Programs written in it execute on any computer, and the compiler can make any language transportable.

Contrary to what many software vendors say, there is no portable programming language. Moreover, the word "portable" is used irresponsibly by both vendors and users. Users assume a portable program is one that will compile and execute on different computers. Actually, such "portable" programs may compile on different machines, but if they execute at all, they may do so incorrectly. A close look at available portable software shows that it is portable only after the user purchases a software-conversion package for his machine. Another common marketing term is "very nearly portable" software, which means a user must know intimately both the program and the executing machine to make the proper code changes.

Even programs in a language such as Cobol, which is more standardized than most, will not execute properly from one machine to the next. The reasons are that the machines may differ in size and architecture and each vendor implements the Cobol compiler differently.

Confusion arises, then, when users or vendors use terms such as "portability," "transferability," and "transportability" interchangeably. The difference is that a transportable program can compile and execute without error and without change over a range of small to large machines, while portable and transferable programs either compile but do not execute or cannot specify their environment well enough to execute correctly. Since high-level languages make assumptions about machine-dependent characteristics, such as word and byte size, programs written in those languages cannot be transportable.

But all is not lost. Researchers at Pennsylvania State University have built a prototype of a high-level transportable programming language (TPL) and a compiler coded in that language. This language and compiler allow the same programs to be correctly executed on all machines in any heterogeneous network.

The key to a language's transportability lies in its ability to respond to programmer-specified information such as a particular machine's word and byte size, orientation (byte or word), and maximum amount of core memory. Furthermore, any language can be standardized if its compiler is transportable.

A compiler is a program that translates an input program, called the source program, into an output program, known as the object program, or object code. The object code can be machine language, assembler language, or a high-level language that is closer to machine language than the source program language. Although compilers are not usually transportable, the TPL-coded compiler operates over a range of machines.

The TPL compiler takes any TPL program and produces Fortran, a language available on most computers. Fortran for different computers is not the same; however, since the TPL-coded compiler understands the machine-dependent characteristics specified by the programmer, the Fortran it produces is the Fortran for that particular machine.

TPL compilers can also be written to translate other high-level languages to TPL. They can also translate a nonportable compiler program, coded in Fortran instead of TPL (but eventually coded in any language), into a transportable one. To do this, the user's nontransportable compiler is fed twice into the TPL compiler. The first time, the TPL compiler flags nontransportable statements and advises changes; the second time, it takes the altered compiler and the specified machine characteristics and produces the user's original compiler coded in the Fortran for the user's machine.

Some vendors sell a "preprocessor" to make their software transportable. A preprocessor functions similarly to the TPL compiler, which is a sophisticated preprocessor. The major difference is that a preprocessor is not transportable. The TPL compiler, which recognizes dynamically specified machine-dependent characteristics for a range of machines, is transportable and needs to be coded only once.   — WR-H

Until recently, there has been no portable software language for data communications users' programs. Every language touted as transportable from one machine to another has actually needed a software-conversion package to make it operate correctly. But now, the prototypes for a new transportable programming language (TPL) and its compiler, both developed at Pennsylvania State University, promise to deliver real transportability.

TPL is transportable because it responds to programmer-supplied information such as word and byte size and the amount of core memory for a particular machine. Once the machine characteristics are specified, the TPL compiler can convert a TPL program into

the Fortran designed for a user's machine.

To understand TPL, it is necessary to understand the nature of a transportable language, how its compiler is organized, and how the language adapts to a computer's architecture. Then the data communications user will be able to decide what degree of transportability he needs in his application and whether or not a vendor's offerings are useful to him.

A programming language for writing operating systems and user software that will execute on any machine needs efficient, flexible, easy-to-use numerics and nonnumerics. In particular, the language's numerical computations must be independent of computer word size and hardware instruction sets, and its character manipulation must be independent of hardware character sets and machine-addressing modes.

These capabilities require that the language allow variable-precision arithmetic (different machines compute to a different number of decimal places) and contain a machine-independent character-variable type. A programming language with these two features is said to be machine-independent.

The language must also compensate for changes in

ticularly Fortran, are the most transferable. However, transferability does not mean a program will execute on a range of machines. Frequently programs will compile on several machines with different architectures but will either not execute or execute incorrectly.

The second factor, portability, is a measure of the control a language can exert over its environment during execution and compilation. This includes the ability to reserve memory space, to specify word or byte instructions, and to control the machine's registers. Assembler languages are the most portable, but they are also the least transferable. To be transportable, a language must be both transferable and portable.

Transportability can be achieved in one of two ways: the new-language approach or the extended-language approach. Pennsylvania State University's TPL is an example of the latter.

The new-language approach decrees transportability by requiring that any language and compiler be built according to standardized specifications (see "Failed attempts at standardization"). The goals of this method are desirable but unrealistic. All attempts to come up with a standard for language transportability

---

1. Software chain. *The user's high-level language program is the source code for its compiler that is coded in TPL. The Fortran object code outputted by the TPL compiler is the source code for the vendor-supplied Fortran compiler. This Fortran compiler generates optimized machine-dependent code for the user's machine.*

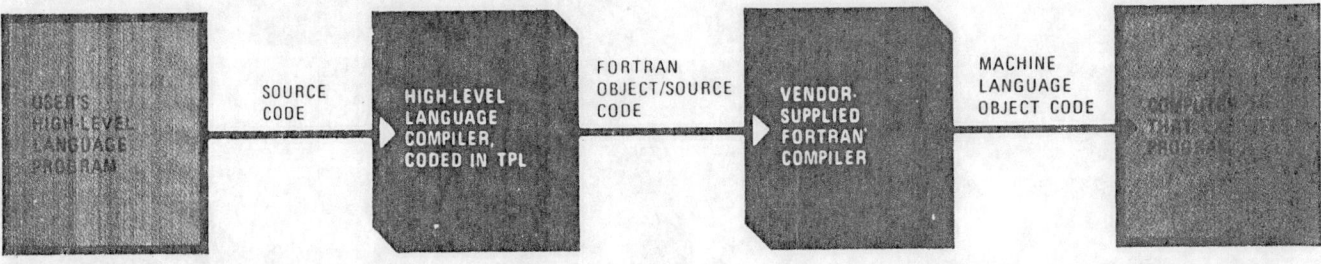

---

the amount of primary memory available to a program through some form of virtual memory so that the same program can be implemented on both small and large computers. Virtual-memory software contains instructions for swapping information stored in primary memory with information stored on a disk. As a result, large programs, which contain more information than can be accommodated in a computer's primary memory, can still execute on that computer. A programming language with this characteristic is said to be configuration-independent.

Finally, to be transportable across the range of computers in a heterogeneous network, the language must be easily learned and easily used. Programs coded in the language must also be efficient with respect to the execution time and the use of computer resources.

Two factors determine whether a language is transportable: transferability and portability. The first factor, transferability, is simply a measure of the compilability of a program by different machines' compilers. In other words, it indicates the degree of syntactic standardization of the programming language and the support provided for its compilers. High-level languages, par-

in the past 20 years have failed, even though large organizations, such as the Department of Defense and IBM, have supported them.

The second approach for creating a transportable programming language, the extended-language approach, has great potential for success, as evidenced by TPL. This transportable language is an open-ended, natural extension of a parent high-level language already implemented in a particular range of machines. The compiler must be coded in the transportable new language. Its source code is the parent high-level language for which a vendor-supplied optimizing compiler geared to the user's machine already exists.

For example, suppose a machine already has a compiler for a particular Fortran dialect. The transportable compiler can translate the code the programmer is writing into that computer's version of Fortran. This compiler's Fortran output program is the source code for the vendor-supplied Fortran compiler that both translates the Fortran code to machine or assembler language and optimizes the program to produce fast, efficient code for execution.

Researchers at Pennsylvania State wanted to begin

2. Conversion. *The user's nontransportable compiler is the source code for the TPL compiler. The TPL compiler flags all nontransportable code, which the user changes to TPL code. The TPL-coded compiler is fed again into the TPL compiler after the machine's characteristics have been specified. The output is the machine's Fortran.*

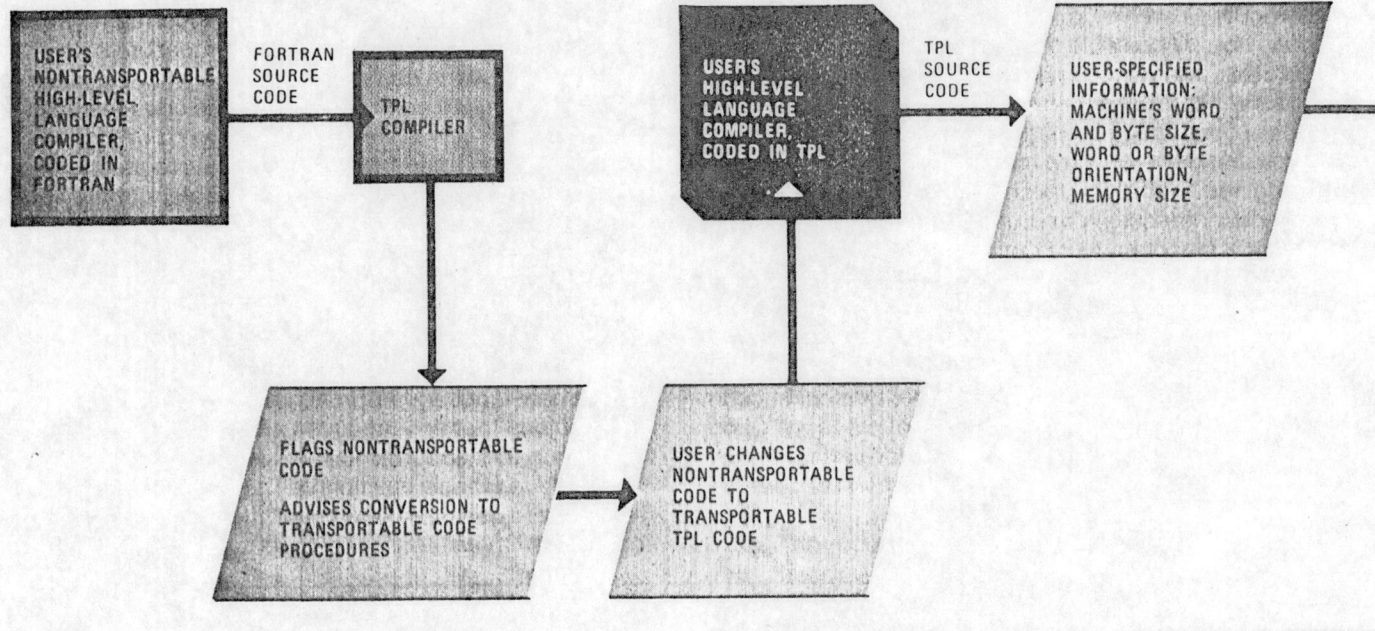

with a language that could run on the greatest possible number of computers. So, they chose the ubiquitous Fortran as the parent language for TPL. Fortran differs from computer to computer; however, since the TPL-coded compiler understands the machine-dependent characteristics specified by the programmer, it produces the Fortran for that particular machine, such as the IBM 370/3033 at the university.

Features of the language
TPL consists of a subset of declarative and executable Fortran instructions that are fully transportable for a desired range of machines. In addition, it contains new declarative and executable instructions that either replace nontransportable Fortran instructions or provide a special capability not present in most Fortrans.

Since TPL has been designed to appear as a simple and natural variant of Fortran, a large part of the TPL syntax has been obtained directly from Fortran. Moreover, TPL features have been designed, whenever possible, as natural extensions or generalizations of conventional Fortran instructions.

TPL's Fortran subset was obtained from a comparative study of seven versions of Fortran: ANSI-standard (American National Standards Institute) Fortran IV, IBM 360/370 Fortran G and H, Control Data Corporation (CDC) 6000 series Fortran IV, Univac 1108 Fortran IV, Digital Equipment Corporation (DEC) PDP-11 Fortran IV, DS Sigma 5/7 Fortran IV, and Honeywell Information Systems 6000 series Fortran. Fortran instructions were classified as to transferability and portability. Only transportable instructions are included in TPL.

However, information about transferable instructions that are not portable is used by the TPL compiler for testing and converting nontransportable statements to transportable ones. The replacements for nontransportable instructions were obtained by reconfiguring input/output and I/O-related instructions so that both the simplest and the most sophisticated options appear as natural variants. All extensions of ANSI-standard Fortran particular to a vendor's version of Fortran were eliminated, and constraints were imposed to scale down various features of different versions of Fortran to a common level.

The salient features of TPL are a virtual-array capability, variable-precision numerics, variable-size kernels for working with strings, flexible I/O capabilities, data compression/decompression capabilities during I/O operations, and several modular control structures to make the language more like Algol and PL/1. Some of these control structures have been added to Fortran 77. However, Fortran 77 is not transportable.

The virtual-array capability
Array are considered virtual if they have more than three dimensions (as may occur in an inventory program) or if the amount of primary memory is insufficient to contain all elements of the array. Every virtual array must be specified by a special nonexecutable statement. Also, the data type (real or integer) and the dimensional structure and total size of the virtual array must be specified. These are dynamic quantities that are set by the programmer during program execution.

A virtual array is referenced in the same way as conventional arrays. All executable TPL instructions that allow conventional-array references also allow virtual-array references.

Flexibility of the virtual-array capability is enhanced since the programmer can redefine an array without destroying information stored in it. Programmers can

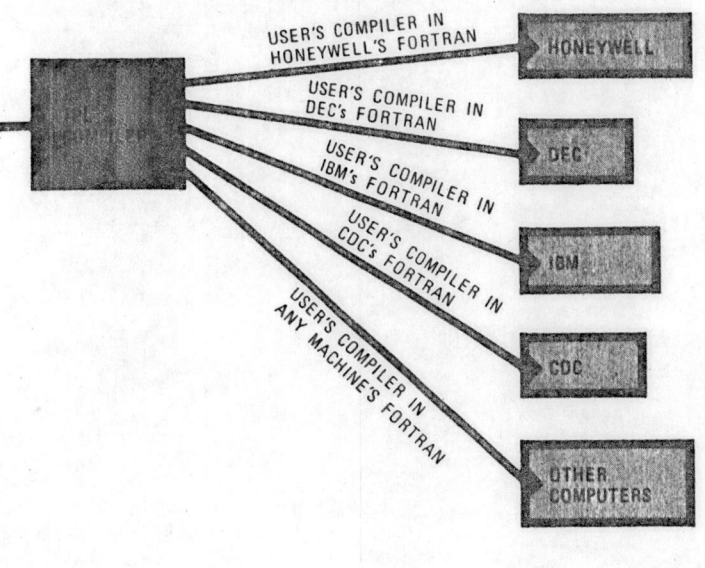

USER'S COMPILER IN HONEYWELL'S FORTRAN — HONEYWELL

USER'S COMPILER IN DEC's FORTRAN — DEC

USER'S COMPILER IN IBM's FORTRAN — IBM

USER'S COMPILER IN CDC's FORTRAN — CDC

USER'S COMPILER IN ANY MACHINE'S FORTRAN — OTHER COMPUTERS

Failed attempts at standardization

The new-language approach has not been successful in the past because the ANSI committees and major user groups, such as the Department of Defense (DOD), have found that it is impossible to impose rigid specifications for a language and a compiler. This method ignores the fact that programmers are not prepared to learn a new language when a familiar language is "nearly adequate."

In addition, the new-language approach does not take into account the many programs in widely used languages that will ultimately have to be translated to the new language. This means that, to be successful, the new language must be capable of facilitating the translation of these programs.

For these reasons, the several attempts to market new languages, such as IBM's PL/1, have not succeeded. In fact, with the possible exception of Cobol, which at best has been only partially successful — and then only because of its primary user, the DOD — all attempts to specify standards for high-level languages have failed.

The current work on the Ada language is yet another effort to instantaneously create a widely used transportable programming language. The DOD plans to standardize the language, by imposing strict specifications, and the compilers, by testing them for validity. It will meet the wide support problem by providing support tools and service programs. An extensive educational program will convince prospective users of the desirability of using the new language. However, the DOD is ignoring the difficulty of recoding existing programs.

also specify the way an array is stored (for example, by column or by row) and whether it is to be retained after program execution.

Variable precision

Since the word or byte size may vary from machine to machine, if a language makes assumptions about the word or byte size, it cannot be transportable. To make the language machine-independent, TPL contains two numeric variable types not found in conventional Fortran: variable-precision real and variable-precision integer. Any variable in a TPL program can be defined as variable-precision. The degree of precision may be set during program execution.

Conventional or virtual variables and subscripted or simple variables can be variable-precision and used like real variables. For example, they can be used in I/O statements or passed as subprogram arguments, which eliminates the need for programmers to work directly with local, machine-dependent packages.

For character and string manipulation, TPL contains a nonnumeric variable called the kernel. Like numeric variables, kernel variables must be defined by a specification statement. The kernel size, which is the actual number of bits making up one kernel, can be specified by the number of bits per kernel or by English-like characters or words. This variable-size capability eliminates dependency on machine architecture (such as character or word sizes).

Although kernel arrays, either conventional or virtual, must be defined before they are referenced, the number of dimensions, subscript ranges, total array size, and kernel size can be defined or altered during program execution. Kernel arrays are referenced in the same way as conventional arrays.

Input/output

The I/O in TPL is a generalized form of that found in most conventional Fortran dialects but with new features. For example, TPL allows three ways, instead of the normal one way, of specifying I/O, storage, or communications devices. Users can implement I/O by specifying the I/O task number, the device-type number, or the device-unit number.

The I/O task number indicates the type of I/O task to be performed. Each of six different tasks is assigned a number from 1 to 6. The tasks include read/received operations from the input device specified for system use, the same operation with the input device specified for user's use, a write/transmit operation with the output device specified for computer use, and the same operation with the output device specified for user use. Other task numbers specify read or write operations to be performed on a direct-access storage device, either permanently allocated or temporarily assigned for TPL. Information on permanent direct-access devices is saved at the end of each program.

I/O can also be specified by assigning numbers to all devices of a particular type that are similarly accessed. For example, all card readers are assigned one device-type number, and all disks with the same characteristics are assigned another. So far, TPL iden-

81

tifies about 20 types of devices.

The unit number, assigned to a particular device, is still another way to specify I/O. For example, a certain card reader might be assigned the number 18.

Initialization information supplied to TPL contains formats, error messages, and both the device type and the unit numbers for devices assigned for use with every value of I/O task. Other TPL I/O features that make TPL more efficient at execution time, more user friendly, and machine-independent include block transfer of data with or without format control to or from conventional and virtual arrays, and format-specification codes to allow for I/O of variable-precision variables and kernels. Moreover, data compression/decompression and operations such as encode/decode and stream-oriented I/O are provided in TPL, as is a conversion of hardware character codes into a special machine-independent character code set.

Besides the computational and control instructions derived from the TPL's Fortran subset, generalized control structures such as WHILE, UNTIL, FOR, and CASE are supported. A BEGIN-END type of statement, analogous to that in Algol and Pascal, can be used. These structures make the language more modular, which makes it easier to write and debug programs.

The compiler and transportability

To make programs transportable, the compiler must be given five parameters for any local machine on which a program is to execute:

■ The maximum size of a program module, exclusive of the storage needed for arrays
■ The maximum amount of core memory available for executing a program
■ Two parameters that together specify both the sizes of bytes (or characters) and words and the orientation (byte or word) of the machine
■ The kernel size, which is either an integral fraction or a multiple of the basic data unit (byte or word)

The maximum program-module size has been arbitrarily set equal to 5,000 bytes or, for small machines, to 2,500 sixteen-bit words. The other four parameters are set by the user when TPL is installed.

The compiler operates in two modes: transportability testing and compilation. To transport Fortran programs from one machine to another, the compiler, operating in the transportability test mode, checks the source program to find out what size word or byte it is geared to. At compilation time, the compiler uses this information to convert that source program to an object program with the word and byte length necessary for a user's machine. This requires only a minimum of special procedures, functions, or subroutines.

The compiler can also aid in translating existing programs in other languages to transportable versions for a user's machines. For example, a user might have a program written in Ada or in Cobol for an IBM computer but want to add a Honeywell, a DEC, and a CDC computer to his network. Since he wants the program to execute on all these computers, he needs a transportable compiler, such as TPL's.

Suppose this user's compiler is coded in Fortran,

3. Troubleshooter. The TPL compiler flags statements 5, 6, 7, 8, 9, 16, 18, and 20 to 22 with advisory messages so the programmer can convert them to transportable form.

```
C       Program I.                                              1
C       This program reads up to ulimit double precision        2
C       numbers, two at a time, then computes and prints        3
C       both the average and the standard deviation.            4
        INTEGER ULIMIT/1000000/, COUNT/0/                        5
        REAL*8 VALUES (1000000), AVERAGE/0D0/, STDDEV/0D0/       6
        DO 100 I=1, ULIMIT, 2                                    7
        READ (5,1000, END=200) VALUES (I), VALUES (I+1)          8
1000    FORMAT (2D25.16)                                         9
        COUNT = COUNT + 2                                       10
        AVERAGE = AVERAGE + VALUES (I) + VALUES (I+1)           11
100     CONTINUE                                                12
C                                                               13
200     IF (COUNT.LE.1) GO TO 400                               14
        AVERAGE = AVERAGE/COUNT                                 15
        DO 300 I=1, COUNT                                       16
300     STDDEV = STDDEV + (VALUES (I) - AVERAGE)**2             17
        STDDEV = DSQRT(STDDEV/COUNT-1) )                        18
C                                                               19
400     PRINT 2000, COUNT, AVERAGE, STDDEV                      20
2000    FORMAT ('0', 5X, 'NO OF VALUES =',I8, ' AVERAGE=',      21
        1D25.16,' AND STANDARD DEVIATION =', D25.16)            22
        STOP                                                    23
        END                                                     24
```

C INDICATES COMMENT.
NUMBERS ON LEFT ARE PROGRAM LABEL NUMBERS.
NUMBERS ON RIGHT ARE READER REFERENCE NUMBERS.

which is not transportable. Therefore, as shown in Figure 2, the user feeds his Fortran compiler through the TPL compiler, which flags all nontransportable code and informs the user how to convert it to transportable code. The nontransportable statements are then changed to TPL statements. As a result, the Ada or Cobol compiler is coded in transportable TPL.

To allow the program to execute on the Honeywell machine, the user now specifies Honeywell machine characteristics, such as the word size and byte orientation, to his TPL compiler. Once again, the Ada or Cobol compiler, now coded in TPL, is fed through the TPL compiler. The TPL compiler produces as object code the Ada or Cobol compiler in the Fortran geared to the Honeywell machine. The user employs the compiler to compile all his Ada and Cobol programs for that computer.

To produce compilers and execute programs for the DEC and CDC computers, the user follows the same procedures, setting the word and byte sizes for those machines. The TPL compiler then produces the user's high-level language compiler in Fortran suitable for the DEC or CDC machines. Thus, one software package can be used over all machines in a network. This capability allows programmers to continue using their favorite nontransportable languages while developing new

fully transportable programs.

The TPL compiler is table-driven (information necessary for operation is in parameter tables), and three of its key tables are the transportable code table, the transferable code table, and the I/O device table. The transportable code table comprises the entire instruction set for the TPL language, which includes the fully transportable subset of Fortran instructions. The transferable code table contains all nontransportable Fortran instructions that are transferable. The I/O device table contains information about the unit, device type, and I/O task numbers for a local installation.

Transportability testing mode

Parameters such as maximum amount of core memory, byte and word size, machine orientation, and kernel size, as well as the I/O device table, are affected by changes in a local installation. The local managers must update these parameters whenever the configuration or machine is changed.

The TPL compiler uses the maximum value of the program-module size and the information in the transportable code table to flag all nontransportable instructions and advise how to convert them to transportable ones. The programmer then alters all the flagged statements. Figure 3 shows an IBM-Fortran-coded program that reads data and computes average and standard deviations. The TPL compiler can convert this program into its transportable form. In this case, statements 5, 6, 7, 8, 9, 16, 18, and 20 to 22 will be flagged with appropriate messages. Figure 4 shows the programmer-produced transportable version.

In the transportable version, the precision of the integer (IIP) and real (IRP) variables must be set either before compilation or when the program is executed. Otherwise, they will default to a precision of 6 and 7 figures, respectively. The ALLOCATE statement stipulates that the real variable-precision virtual-array "values" have one dimension and length, Ulimit. The read and print operations are performed with the default devices allocated for user use (I/O task = 3 and 4). RPSQRT is the variable-precision equivalent of the real square-root routine. In the format statements, skip = 1 means skip a line; RP19.10 is a real variable-precision field of width 19 and with 10 significant figures; and IP8 is a variable-precision-integer field of width 8.

Because the conversion of Fortran to TPL is mechanical, the transportability testing mode of the TPL compiler can eventually be fully automated.

Compilation mode

In the compilation mode, the TPL compiler uses the values for the computer parameters and the information in the transportable code, transferable code, and I/O device tables to produce Fortran versions of TPL programs that are optimal for a local installation. A primary goal of the compiler is to minimize calls to the special routines in the TPL library by using, whenever possible, transferable Fortran code in place of the unique TPL instructions. For example, for the program in Figure 4, if IIP = 8 and IRP = 10 and there is sufficient core memory, then the TPL compiler will convert the TPL program in a way particular to a machine. For IBM machines with 21-bit words, variables will be defined as in the original program and the virtual array will be changed to the conventional double-precision array. For CDC machines with 48-bit words, single-precision variables will be used and the virtual array will be eliminated.

This means that the run-time efficiency of a TPL program is ultimately determined by the efficiency of the vendor-supplied Fortran compiler. Thus, a TPL program can never be less efficient than the parent Fortran program specifically altered for a particular machine.

The compilation mode of the TPL compiler has three major functions:

1. Translating the unique TPL syntax into Fortran instructions. In the best-case situation, where there is sufficient core memory and no need for special routines in the TPL system library, only transferable instructions are used and the translation is straightforward. In the worst case, a single TPL instruction is replaced by several Fortran instructions, additional variables are created and initialized, and calls to one or more routines in the TPL library are issued.

2. Processing the Fortran subset of TPL instructions. In the best case, such instructions are not changed. In the worst case, which occurs when calls are issued to the TPL library, certain instructions might be replaced by several instructions. For example, if virtual arrays are used, references to them must be followed by the computation of the actual in-core location and, if necessary, by the paging of information from secondary storage such as disks.

3. Performing selected types of reconfigurations of the object program to produce a more efficient Fortran version of the input TPL program. Such modification includes substitution of conventional memory-resident

---

Software terms

Compiler. A program that translates a high-level language input program into machine language, assembler language, or another high-level language that is closer to machine language.

Source code. The input program to be processed by a compiler.

Object code. The processed output code from a compiler.

Interpret. To decode a program and execute it statement by statement.

Compile. To decode a program as one logical unit before executing it.

Preprocessor. A nontransportable program that converts a high-level language program to a format accepted by a compiler.

Virtual memory. The appearance of more memory than actually exists. This concept is implemented by storing some information in primary memory and some in secondary storage, such as a disk. During program execution, data addresses are calculated and recalculated so information can be exchanged between primary and secondary storage.

4. Corrected program. *The IBM Fortran nontransportable program is converted to its transportable form by both the TPL compiler and the programmer.*

```
C       Program I.                                                      1
C       This program reads up to ulimit (precision IIP≤8)              2
C       real numbers (precision ≤10), two at a time, then             3
C       computes and prints both the average and standard            4
C       deviation. If IIP and IRP are not set via a                   5
C       constant statement the compiler will use the                  6
C       defaults for integer(=6) and real(=7) precision.             7
        INTEGER*IIP ULIMIT/1000000/, COUNT/0/,I                       8
        VIRTUAL VALUES                                                9
        REAL*IRP VALUES AVERAGE/0/,STDDEV/0/                          10
        ALLOCATE VALUES AS DIMEN = (ULIMIT)                           11
        DO 100 I=1 TO ULIMIT BY 2                                     12
        READ(IOTASK=3,FMT=1000,END=200)VALUES(I),VALUES(I+1)         13
1000    FORMAT (2RP25.16)                                            14
        AVERAGE = AVERAGE + VALUES(I) + VALUES(I+1)                  15
        COUNT = COUNT + 2                                            16
100     CONTINUE                                                     17
C                                                                    18
200     IF (COUNT.LE.1) GO TO 400                                    19
        AVERAGE = AVERAGE/COUNT                                      20
        DO 300 I=1 TO COUNT                                          21
300     STDDEV = STDDEV + (VALUES(I) - AVERAGE)**2                   22
        STDDEV = RPSQRT (STDDEV/(COUNT-1) )                          23
C                                                                    24
400     PRINT (IOTASK=4,FMT=2000) COUNT, AVERAGE, STDDEV             25
2000    FORMAT (SKIP=1,5X,'NUMBER OF VALUES=', IP8,'                  26
        1AVERAGE=',RP19.10,'AND STANDARD DEVIATION=',                27
        2RP19.10)                                                    28
        STOP                                                         29
        END                                                          30

C INDICATES COMMENT.
NUMBERS ON LEFT ARE PROGRAM LABEL NUMBERS.
NUMBERS ON RIGHT ARE READER REFERENCE NUMBERS.
```

arrays for selected virtual arrays and restructuring of DO loops (loops beginning with the statement DO) and I/O statements to increase their efficiency, particularly if TPL library routines are called. Various forms of execution-time error checking may also be introduced.

Other TPL components

In addition to the TPL language and compiler, a TPL package includes a TPL library that supplements the local operating-system library of routines with functions and services not normally available to all machines. The library is coded in TPL, and its Fortran-coded version for each different machine is generated at local network installations by the Fortran-coded version of the compiler.

Also part of the TPL software is a small machine-support package that permits programs designed for large computers to execute on computers with smaller amounts of primary memory. Chief among these pro-

grams is an "overlay" monitoring routine that contains instructions for moving different parts of a program in and out of main memory whenever the entire program cannot reside in core.

Most of this package is coded in TPL. However, some parts must be coded in assembler language and recoded for machines with different assemblers.

Development of a library is a conventional method of increasing program transportability by extending a high-level language with a package of special routines. However, this approach is usually only partially successful at best, because the complex procedures for calling many of the special routines tend to discourage even the most dedicated programmers from using them. In addition, to achieve wide transportability, the programs must be coded for the worst-case (least-core-memory) machine. However, since optimizing such programs with respect to their run-time efficiency is determined by the amount of core memory, kinds of peripherals, and architecture of each local machine, the optimization of programs for each local installation is inefficient and time-consuming.

Installation of TPL

The minimum hardware needed to install TPL on any computer is at least 10,000 bytes of core memory that can be used to execute TPL programs. In addition, sufficient direct-access storage for load modules for the TPL compiler, for the TPL library, for the small-machine support package, for TPL programs, and for virtual arrays is needed. Storage for the I/O devices for communicating with the machine is required as well.

The software needed to install TPL is a noninterpretative Fortran compiler. In other words, the Fortran compiler resident on the computer must be one that decodes the program for execution as one logical unit instead of decoding and executing each statement in turn. The usual loaders that prepare the machine-language program for execution and other system resource routines are also necessary.

To install a TPL package, users select the system parameters—maximum program module size, maximum amount of core memory for a program, byte and word size, orientation (byte or word) of the machine, and kernel size—then describe the I/O device table. The installer then uses the manufacturer-supplied compiler to compile a "primitive" TPL compiler. This primitive compiler, which produces nonoptimum Fortran code for a minimal machine, without using the small-machine support package, generates optimum Fortran code for the TPL compiler, the TPL library, and the small-machine support package.

This optimum Fortran code is tailored for a particular installation. Compiling the primitive compiler might involve the literal translation of, at most, two I/O instructions in the TPL library to the local Fortran dialect.

If the small-machine support package is used, the parts coded in assembler language must be recoded for the particular installation. If an installation is reconfigured, values for the computer parameters will have to be reset, the I/O device table reconstructed, and some modules recompiled. ▣

Section 3

Local Network Equipment

Section 3

Local Network Equipment

Minicomputers' network roles

Edwin E. Mier, Data Communications

The minicomputer is still envisioned by many as a small—and typically stand-alone—applications processor. But its face is changing. The traditional minicomputer is now being employed in a variety of communicating roles ranging, for example, from front-end processor to distributed system. Its implementations have become so diverse, in fact, that relatively few vendors still market their machines as generic minicomputers.

The 1960s saw the birth of the minicomputer as a cost-effective mainframe alternative. Today, an increasing number of configurations employ minicomputers to supplement, rather than replace, central processing units (CPUs).

With recent technological advances, the minicomputer's "bang-for-the-buck" ratio has improved tremendously. Minicomputers, as well as mainframes, are becoming less costly, doing more, and coming in smaller packages. In addition, computing power is being continually miniaturized (via large-scale integration, or LSI), and sophisticated microprocessor-based components are enabling the economical augmentation of functions, such as communica-

tions, on even the smallest processors.

These and other developments are causing a merger between the minicomputer and data communications. The days of viewing communications between remote devices as an ancillary function or a necessary evil of data processing are gone. Communications has become an integral part of virtually every computing system, and in some areas (such as electronic mail), it can be viewed as the application itself.

Several trends in recent years have been instrumental in binding together these two product groups:

1. The cost of communications facilities has not decreased nearly as much, or as fast, as the cost of computers. While the declining cost of machines has prompted users to increase both the size and the number of their computers, the cost of communications has encouraged the distribution of this computing power to remote facilities. Despite the physical separation, however, a strong need for communications between these remote, or distributed, processors and a central location has remained. For example, management's need for comprehensive corporate information has mandated that regional data centers constantly update centralized files. Also, the increasing cost of program development and expensive disk peripherals has kept centralized certain applications that are accessed from remote sites, such as database-management systems.

2. Many simple communications protocols, although originally designed as proprietary communications schemes between machines of the same vendor, have become de facto industry standards. This has made it possible for one vendor to "emulate" a popular device of another, in order to provide users greater flexibility in equipment selection.

3. Higher-level communications processing, in response to user demands for increased functional sophistication, has become more and more complex. Many vendors now offer proprietary network architectures that, while providing enhanced functions, are increasingly difficult for competitors to interface with or to emulate. In some cases, communications handling, which used to require only hardwired logic, is now being done almost completely in software. To make matters worse, some vendors have embedded this communications software into their operating systems and database managers, instead of consolidating it in a single, easily accessible software module.

4. A new wave of high-level bit-oriented protocols has evolved, partly from international standards efforts and partly from network architecture developments. Unlike their simpler predecessors, these protocols address developing requirements such as machine independence, higher transmission speeds, increased communications reliability, and sequencing of messages for large blocks, or files, of data. They also, unlike their predecessors, require a considerable degree of processing and memory storage for their implementation. For communications applications, this has all but obsoleted many conventional devices such as dumb terminals and hardwired cluster controllers.

So, as data processing continues to adapt more and more communications functions, communications is by necessity involving more and more data (or applications) processing. For example, while electronic mail applications use conventional data processing machines as their backbone, inputted messages are not "processed" in the traditional sense, since their content is not changed. The end product is actually communications—sending a block of textual data to a remote location without changing its form. All the processing performed is communications-oriented. Routines are invoked to handle conversion of the message from one character set to another, perform table searches for network routing, handle file storage and retrieval of messages, and perform error checking to ensure message integrity.

Recognizing these trends and developments, users have concluded that the modern data communications network requires a truly intelligent processor at virtually every termination point (node). And because users' needs are changing more rapidly than ever before, the versatile and programmable minicomputer seems to be the ideal choice.

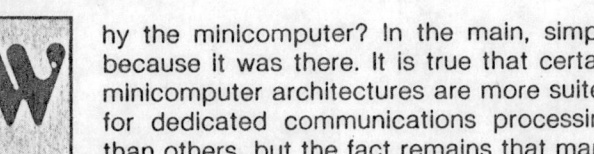hy the minicomputer? In the main, simply because it was there. It is true that certain minicomputer architectures are more suited for dedicated communications processing than others, but the fact remains that many large computer vendors had been marketing a wide range of minicomputers for years. As the need for a special-purpose processor arose, one of their minicomputers, appropriately configured with the right amount of computing power, memory, and peripherals, was selected. Also, most vendors had a choice between several proven operating systems and could select the one best suited for the particular application.

As Figure 1 illustrates, the different requirements imposed on these specialized processors has caused their configurations to vary significantly. As a result, the communications-oriented minicomputer can generally be regarded as either (1) a terminal cluster controller, (2) a standalone switching node, (3) a front-end processor, or (4) a distributed processor.

Functionally, the minicomputer cluster controller coordinates the transmissions of two or more terminal devices. Very little applications processing is required, except in cases where a number of different terminals, with different terminal protocols, are being controlled. The processor typically handles terminal polling, protocol conversions (if necessary), and data concentration, or multiplexing. A typical cluster-controlling minicomputer would include support for several low-speed remote lines (to terminals), several locally attached terminals (via coaxial cable or twisted pairs), and one or two high-speed remote lines (to a host or other network nodes). Such a configuration would require few, if any, peripherals and only a small amount of main memory (primarily for buffering), but would need a considerable number of I/O interfaces (depending on the number of controlled devices).

As a standalone switching node, the minicomputer handles high-speed inputs and high-speed outputs. It

87

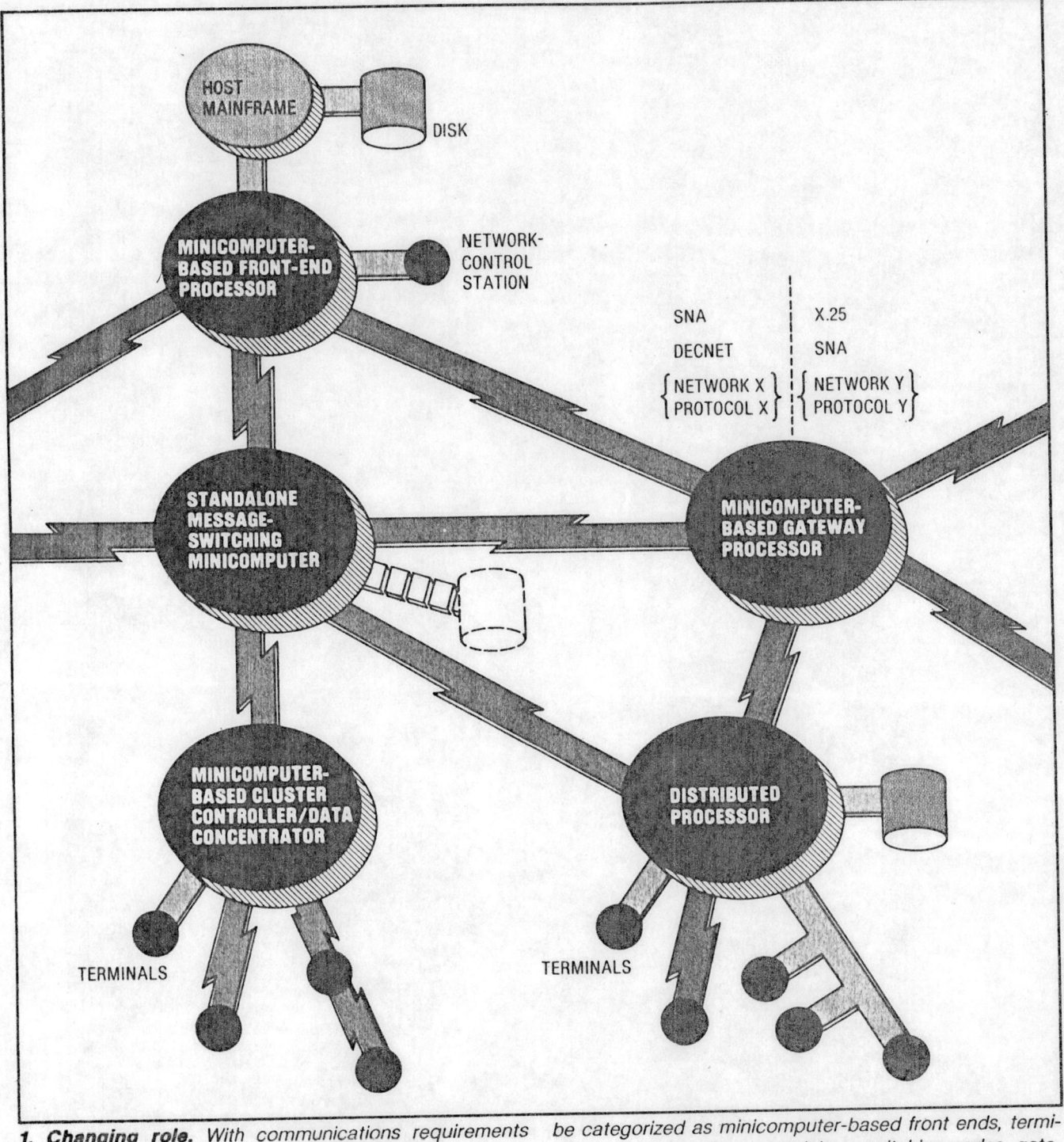

1. Changing role. With communications requirements increasing in all areas, use of the minicomputer in networking roles has become ubiquitous. Configurations can be categorized as minicomputer-based front ends, terminal cluster controllers, standalone switching nodes, gateway processors, and distributed processors.

also controls the transmission routing between terminals and hosts, between nodes, or between hosts. In its simplest form, processor software needs to handle routing algorithms (table searches), but the programmable nature of a minicomputer permits the addition of more-elaborate software functions such as flow control, least-cost routing, ordering transmission priorities, and alternate routing.

If a switching minicomputer operates in a circuit-switched network, it essentially becomes a computer-

ized branch exchange (CBX). In this capacity, its software reads the call-establishment information and acts appropriately. If, on the other hand, it is used in a store-and-forward environment, the software (or firmware) must handle additional tasks such as checking for errors, sequencing messages, performing acknowledgments, and serving retransmission requests. In very sophisticated situations, the switching node may spool copies of messages onto disks, but this is done only if an audit trail of processed messages is required, as in

the case of electronic funds transfer.

Therefore, the degree of software sophistication required for a switching minicomputer varies, depending on the machine's mode of operation and functions. The switching minicomputer may require a significant amount of main memory for both processing and buffering and because its high-speed lines are usually running one or more high-level, bit-oriented protocols. Mass storage peripherals may be employed, but if copies of processed messages must be sent to storage, the additional processing load tends to significantly degrade switching speed and throughput. (Electronic funds audit trails, however, are required by law.) Most switching operations, for efficiency and speed, are performed wholly in main memory. Even store-and-forward switchers do not routinely use disk memory for message storage because of the additional input/output cycles and time that would be consumed.

An even more specialized switching node—the gateway processor—has appeared in recent years in response to variations in proprietary network architectures, as well as to differing implementations of the evolving international standards protocols. A minicomputer employed in this capacity is essentially a large-scale protocol converter, but it functions at a higher level and usually with much higher throughput. The gateway processor takes multiple high-speed inputs of protocol X, strips the overhead, and outputs the user data on a single (or multiple) high-speed line using protocol Y (Fig. 2). The processor has all the software necessary to appear as a node to network X and at the same time appear to network Y as a compatible node. Because of the nature of the networks it connects, it frequently handles several high-level protocols and their conversions from one to another at the same time.

n many customized networks, users have found that they can employ a channel-attached minicomputer as an extremely versatile and user-programmable front-end processor. Vendors that market both minicomputers and mainframes have apparently reached the same conclusion, and many now market specially configured models of their minicomputers as front ends to their mainframes. The architectural differences between traditional front ends and minicomputer-based front ends is discussed later, but, in general, minicomputers offer more-flexible programming, a richer instruction set (and therefore more versatility), and, compared to many traditional front ends, more host-independent operation.

The problem with a minicomputer-based front-end processor is that the channel-attachment hardware and software to drive it in that capacity are very complex and expensive to produce. For this reason, vendors have typically limited their channel interfaces to those that work with their own mainframes, although some provide channel-attachment hardware for other vendors' mainframes (mostly IBM's) but not software support. Many systems houses, however, buy from original equipment manufacturers (OEMs) and resell the channel-attachment hardware and the minicomputer loaded with their own specialized front-end software.

A front-end processor offloads many or all communications processing chores from the mainframe. At least a portion of the front end's software must drive it in emulation of a standard channel-attached peripheral to the mainframe. The programming effort for this software, according to many vendors, is beyond the capability of most end users and best left to the OEM systems houses. Other than this mainframe interface, however, software can be written so that the minicomputer handles virtually any function including, for example, overall network control, multipoint terminal handling, and protocol conversions.

The front end generally needs a significant amount of main memory for the required buffering, queuing, and processing. A mass-storage peripheral may be implemented, but generally only for maintaining network statistics (should that be one of its software-driven functions). As with conventional front ends, a local "control" terminal may be employed for developing programs, changing routing tables, and configuring lines. Besides the channel-attachment hardware, a number of remote line interfaces are also needed.

Virtually every major vendor supports some configuration in which its minicomputer functions as a distributed processor. In this role, the minicomputer handles both applications and communications (usually to a remote host). Vendors who supply both mainframes and minicomputers generally offer a complete "distributed system" that is optimized for use with their own mainframes. In some cases, for example, vendors offer database packages for the minicomputer that are compatible with (but not distributed portions of) the mainframe's database-management system.

The distributed system can perform as a standalone applications processor—a feature that typically distinguishes it from, say, a terminal cluster controller. The added communications capability permits it, when necessary, to access the remote processor(s) and send or receive data in a format familiar to the remote machine. Depending on user requirements, the frequency and volume of communications with the remote host will determine whether the minicomputer is a tightly coupled or loosely coupled distributed system. A tightly coupled system requires access to a remote application for almost every transaction, while the loosely coupled system's communications requirements are much more infrequent.

A distributed system can incorporate virtually any size processor. A desktop computer with 32 kbytes of main memory and a single communications interface, for example, might satisfy one user, while another may need a machine with 2 Mbytes of memory (approaching the low-end mainframe class), several hundred megabytes of disk storage, and dozens of communications interfaces. User needs will also dictate the communications sophistication of the distributed processor.

Several communications-oriented factors are key in the user's selection of both a minicomputer vendor and a specific distributed processor. These include:

▪ *Processor support for line speed.* The user must delicately balance the frequency and volume of remote

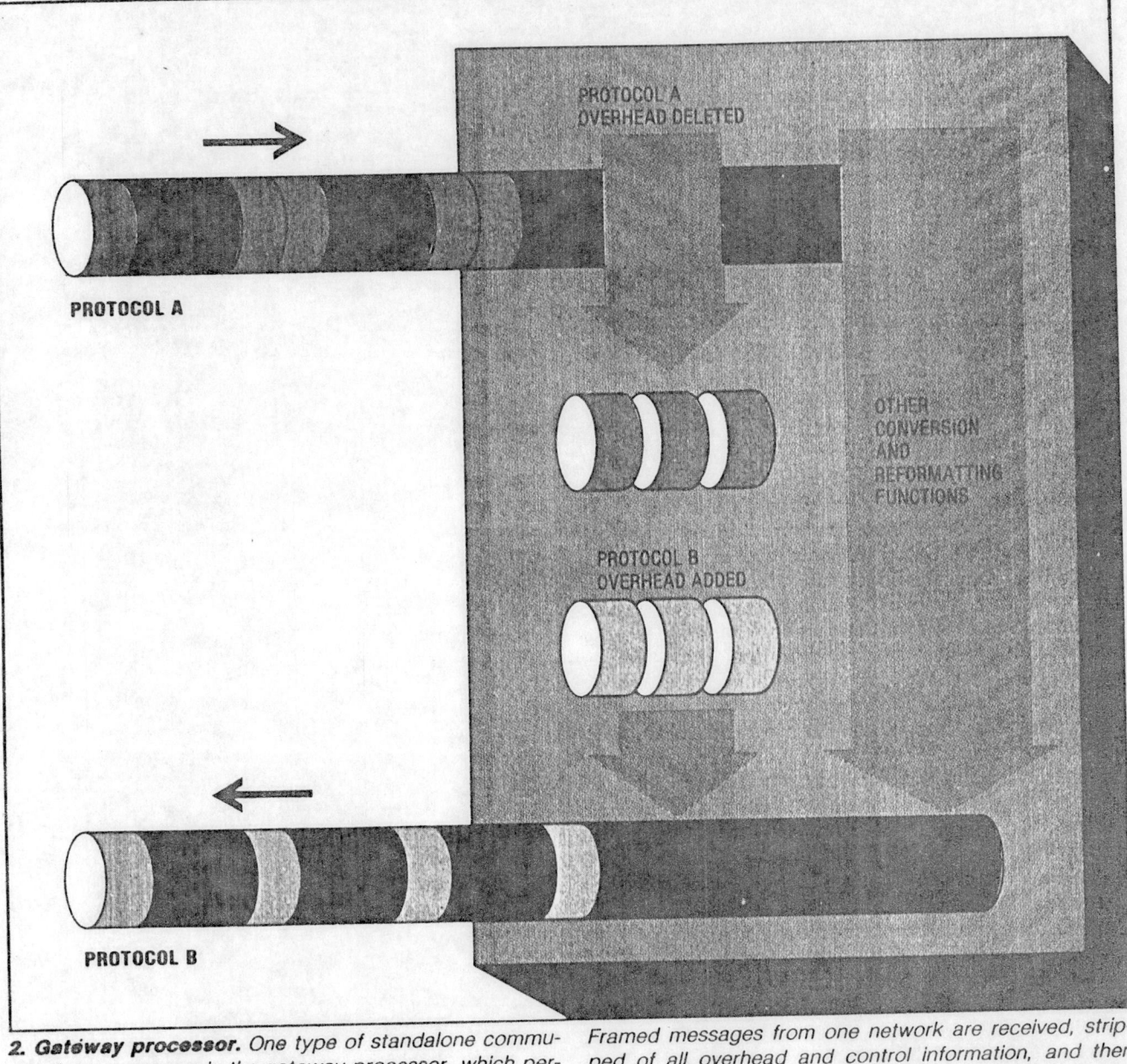

2. Gateway processor. *One type of standalone communications processor is the gateway processor, which permits the user to interconnect two different networks.* *Framed messages from one network are received, stripped of all overhead and control information, and then reformatted in the protocol required for the other network.*

communications with the cost of transmission facilities. For low-volume, infrequent usage, a single voice-grade dial-up line (up to 9.6 kbit/s) will probably suffice. However, for high-volume requirements, and particularly for interactive access to the remote host, a leased voice-grade or wideband line (up to or exceeding 56 kbit/s) may be cost-justifiable.

■ *Support for terminal emulations and protocols.* This criterion pertains both to the distributed machine's support of local and remote terminals and to communications with a remote host. In some cases, users choose a minicomputer that supports a certain terminal type (such as interactive CRTs, card readers, graphics terminals, teleprinters), or they may select a distributed minicomputer with communications support for a remote host. A user is normally constrained to a particular mainframe vendor, and, therefore, compatibility

with the mainframe is prerequisite. (Of all installations, about 60 percent are IBM-based.)

■ *Support for special communications features.* Many users have special communications requirements in a distributed environment, some of which are supported by relatively few vendors. These may include communications support for two or more different hosts from the same minicomputer, multiple (or parallel) lines to the same host, electronic mail software, or interface support to packet-switched networks. In addition, more and more users are becoming aware of the advantages of local networking—transmission schemes that support high-speed interconnection of multiple processors that are typically, but not necessarily, from the same vendor. While this may not yet be an overriding factor in the selection of a distributed minicomputer, several vendors are now developing, or already offer, local

90

networking products.

■ *Networking architectures.* This criterion pertains more to a new network installation than to one with many existing processors. In the latter, the user is already constrained to a particular vendor's mainframes, terminals, or both. Vendors' networking architectures can offer the user high-level communications functions, but, at present, the user generally becomes locked into that particular vendor's products as well. The capabilities vary from architecture to architecture but include functions like remote file access/transfer, down-line loading of applications and initial program loads (IPLs), resource and load sharing, and a bevy of networking features such as centrally controlled diagnostics, alternate routing, optimized route selection, and assignment of transmission priorities.

ust how do minicomputers differ? One way is in word length and in the width of most of the internal data paths (to memory, I/O, and so on). Take, for example, the never-ending discussion on the performance trade-offs of an 8-bit, 16-bit, or 32-bit machine. Theoretically, a 32-bit machine should have about double the throughput of a 16-bit machine for communications processing, but this is not always so.

"This can generally be said to be true," says Richard Sterry, data communications product manager for Prime Computer, in Wellesley, Mass., "but the manner in which each machine handles interrupts can completely negate this added throughput." (An interrupt is a signal to the main processor that incoming data has arrived.) Sterry points out that interrupt handling can make or break a minicomputer's communications capability. If, for example, the minicomputer handles interrupts on an individualized, or character, basis, the processor overhead could, with a large number of communications lines, completely consume the processor's capacity, leaving none for any other applications processing. The alternative, now generally implemented for communications-oriented machines, is direct memory access (DMA), which places incoming data directly into processor memory, thereby reducing the number of processor cycles required for interrupt handling (Fig. 3).

According to John Adams, distributed systems manager for Digital Equipment Corporation (DEC), in Maynard, Mass. (which pioneered the minicomputer), 32-bit machines are not really suited for communications processing as a dedicated function. "They contain large instructions and are optimized for memory and storage addressing," he says. "These qualities are not really important to communications processing."

Adams explains that for communications processing, "you don't need a very rich instruction set." Large instructions, he says, take a lot of processor cycles and increase what he refers to as "interrupt latency," or the time delay between the interrupt and the acknowledgment of it. "Small, clean instructions," he says, "have a low interrupt latency."

Adams points out that the instruction set for communications handling "should be geared toward 'string-and-bit' handling, as opposed to arithmetic operation." He says that most communications and protocol handling today is "simple bit manipulation." Even the cyclic redundancy check (CRC) polynomial for bit-oriented protocols is bit manipulation, he says, and not an arithmetic calculation (Fig. 4).

In benchmark testing on DEC machines, shifting from character interrupts to DMA cut processor overhead almost in half, according to the company. In distributed processing networks, however, a great deal of applications processing is done in addition to communications handling, so the larger instructions of the 32-bit machine may benefit the user.

"The large instructions," Adams says, "facilitate use of high-level languages and high-level compilers." He says that communications programming, on the other hand, is typically handled by assembly language-type programmers who are "adept at writing efficient code." These are not, he says, end users.

And DEC is not alone. Robert Arsenault, Level 6 product support manager for Honeywell, in Waltham, Mass., agrees. "Communications programming would typically be done by us (Honeywell)," he says, "and not by the end user." Arsenault says that he would expect a 32-bit machine to have better data-handling capability than a 16-bit or 8-bit, "but this is not a linear relationship."

He points out that the type of usage varies so much between machines, that "there are very few constants." As for Honeywell's Level 6 minicomputer (a 16-bit machine), Arsenault says that adding communications to a Level 6 that is otherwise dedicated to application processing "will degrade the processor's performance, but again, not in a linear manner."

nother recurring question in minicomputer design is which communications applications to put in microcode and which to keep in RAM (random access memory). The relative advantages? Microcoded applications are permanently etched in ROM (read-only memory) but execute more quickly than software resident in RAM (the "main memory" for CPUs and microprocessors). Software that runs in RAM, however, can be readily changed, while ROM software (also called firmware) requires "burning" a new ROM or PROM (programmable read-only memory). There are now also EPROMs (for erasable PROMs), but even their programming cannot be changed without removal from the processor.

Vendors have been bouncing communications programming between microcoding and main memory for some time. Many have gone toward the "soft" implementation of communications programs, because even the smallest error on microcode prevents it from being debugged. However, software-based programs must be continually reloaded every time the processor is powered-up, while microcode is nonvolatile. DEC's Adams claims that the company will never put even simple protocols like bisync in ROM.

"We know of 50 different implementations of bisync," he says, "and each varies slightly, particularly

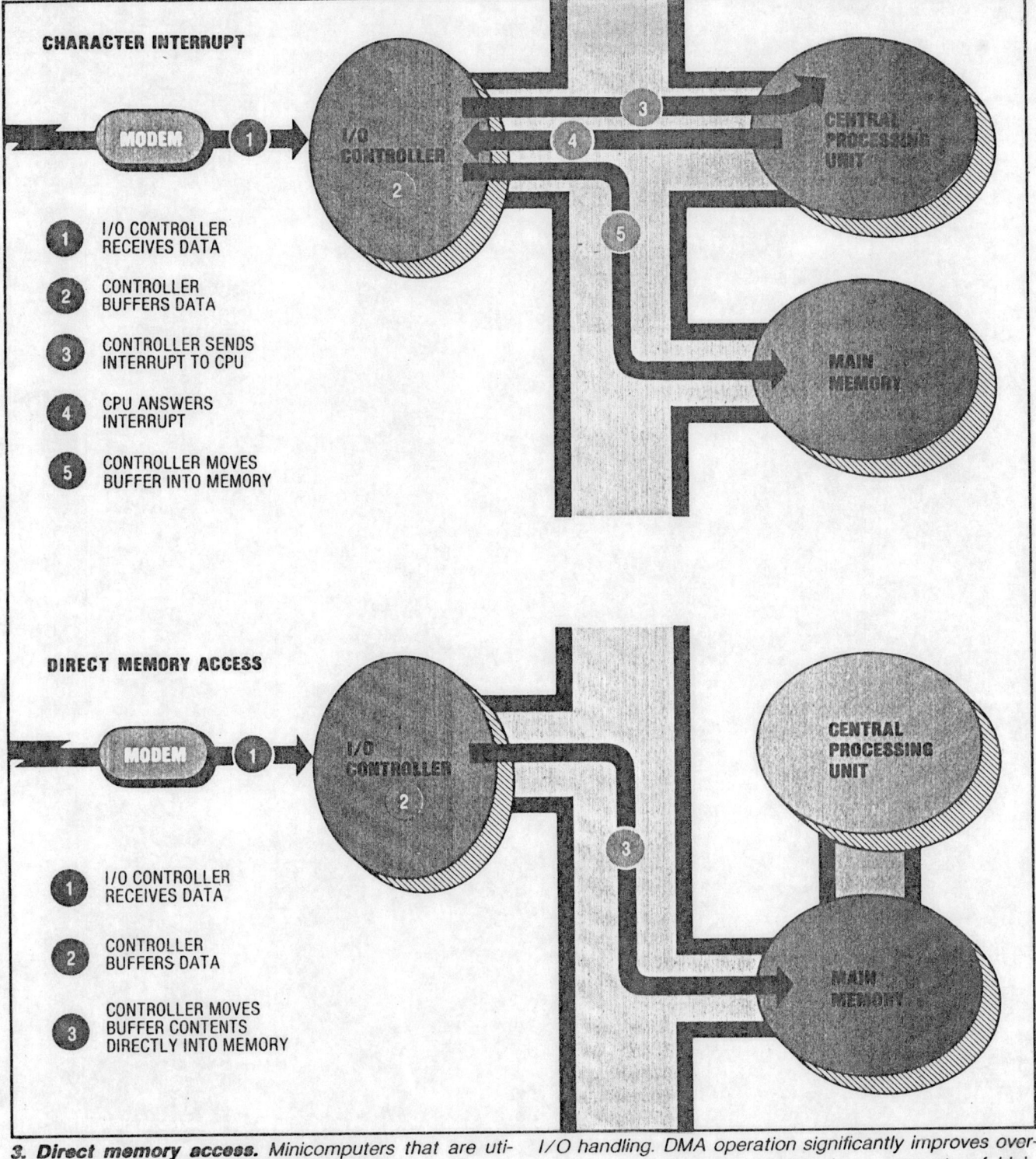

3. Direct memory access. *Minicomputers that are utilized in dedicated communications applications will typically employ the direct memory access (DMA) method for I/O handling. DMA operation significantly improves overall processor throughput when large amounts of high-speed communications processing are required.*

in timeouts and block lengths." Others at DEC go a bit further. "To put anything above the data link level of X.25 in microcode," another DEC manager says, "would be suicidal at this point."

An opposite view is held by DEC's competitor, Data General in Westboro, Mass. Barbara Babcock, Data General's marketing manager for Eclipse systems, says, "Software will never match the efficiency of microcode, no matter how efficient the programming is." Babcock does recognize that some high-level protocols are constantly being changed but claims that "as these newer protocols stabilize, more can, and will, be put into firmware."

Honeywell's Bob Arsenault agrees, saying that most simple protocols are best handled by microprocessor modules and microcode. "But," he warns, "the new

92

bit-oriented protocols, such as the X Series, are concerned with more than physical control of the transmission media." For this reason, he says, "they require, at least at present, an interactive handling between microcode and main processor software."

This raises the question of where, optimally, communications control should be placed in the minicomputer. Many vendors today offer microprocessor-based terminal handlers, or line controllers, which function more or less autonomously from the main processor (except, of course, to pass in data for processing and retrieve the results for output).

Honeywell's Arsenault explains that the centralization of communications control "will become less true as semiconductor manufacturers are able to pack more smarts on a single (microprocessor) chip." He maintains that a single microprocessor chip capable of handling X.25 Levels I, II, and III "will be out by the end of the year."

The open systems interconnection (OSI) model, now under development in Europe, is a different story, he says. Because of the proposed high-level functions that "go way beyond traditional communications processing, the optimal location of communications control for protocols such as OSI will be split between microcode and the main processor and gradually move toward the main processor."

At Prime, James Jackson, another communications program manager, agrees that microprocessors are being used more and more to offload communications handling from the minicomputer's main processor, a trend he says will continue. He sees X.25 Levels I, II, and III being placed on a single chip "easily within the next three years."

Data General's Babcock says that a single X.25 chip containing Levels I, II, and III of the protocol "presents a good opportunity for the semiconductor industry" and that it should be forthcoming "if not in six months, certainly within a year." She maintains that there is a tendency toward moving communications control into intelligent controllers and that the future communications-oriented minicomputer will consist of a myriad microprocessor modules.

According to DEC's John Adams, in a routing network (like Decnet), it is especially important to implement communications processing away from the main processor, via microprocessors, so that the main processor does not get cluttered by rerouting traffic not destined for it. He also says that whenever possible, a single microprocessor should handle concentration of incoming traffic to the main processor. For synchronization reasons, this can significantly offload the main processor. But this savings is lost when two or more communications microprocessors are used with a single main processor.

The minicomputer, therefore, is composed of a main processor (with main memory and arithmetic-logic unit, or ALU), perhaps one or more microprocessor-based controllers to "distribute" specialized functions away from the main processor, and possibly some micro-

coded programming (Fig. 5). These components are tied together on a high-speed system bus.

How, then, does this structure vary from, say, a conventional front-end processor? As previously mentioned, the instruction set required for communications processing is very simple. The minicomputer's instruction set is typically much more sophisticated because it is serving the end user, whereas the front end's software is transparent to the user. Because of this fundamental difference, many functions that are variable on a minicomputer are fixed on the front end. Scanning of line modules, for example, is done at a fixed rate on the front end, while this is determined by software in the minicomputer.

Front ends are usually geared for handling a larger number of lines and do not operate on an individualized interrupt basis, as many minicomputers still do. One minicomputer product manager says, "The main difference is in perception. There's no reason at all why you couldn't run applications on a front end or even a computerized branch exchange (CBX)." Interestingly, Rolm Corporation's CBX is actually based on a Data General Nova minicomputer.

According to William Kuntz, data communications product manager for Perkin-Elmer, the biggest drawback in utilizing the minicomputer as a front end, especially a 32-bit machine, is cost. "A 16-bit machine is quite sufficient," he says. Perkin-Elmer is one firm that offers an IBM channel interface but not the software to drive it as a front end. Kuntz points out, "We have done it on a customized basis, but for generalized applications, we leave it up to system houses."

Kuntz says that there are two ways of approaching the programming problem with a mini-based front end, but both require "an intimate knowledge of the host computer's access methods." In the first case, the programmer makes the minicomputer emulate a common peripheral to the host, such as a 270X controller or a local 3270 controller to an IBM mainframe. "Emulation," he says, "best supports the user who already has an extensive set of IBM software applications." However, he agrees that this would not be a job for most end users. "It would frighten the heck out of a Cobol programmer," he says.

Then there is the IBM documentation problem. While documentation from IBM is usually voluminous, that is not the case in this area. IBM's access methods, also, are changing all the time. A new release may subtly change the way the host treats the peripheral controller, and it may take months to identify the change and reprogram a front-end minicomputer.

An alternative to emulation is to write one's own specialized IBM access method. Kuntz points out that IBM macro instructions support this, but it would still require "an extremely sophisticated programmer." He says that most of the Perkin-Elmer front-end system house customers do this, however, because it permits them to optimize both the host and the minicomputer for certain applications.

This procedure, Kuntz explains, "is very good for

93

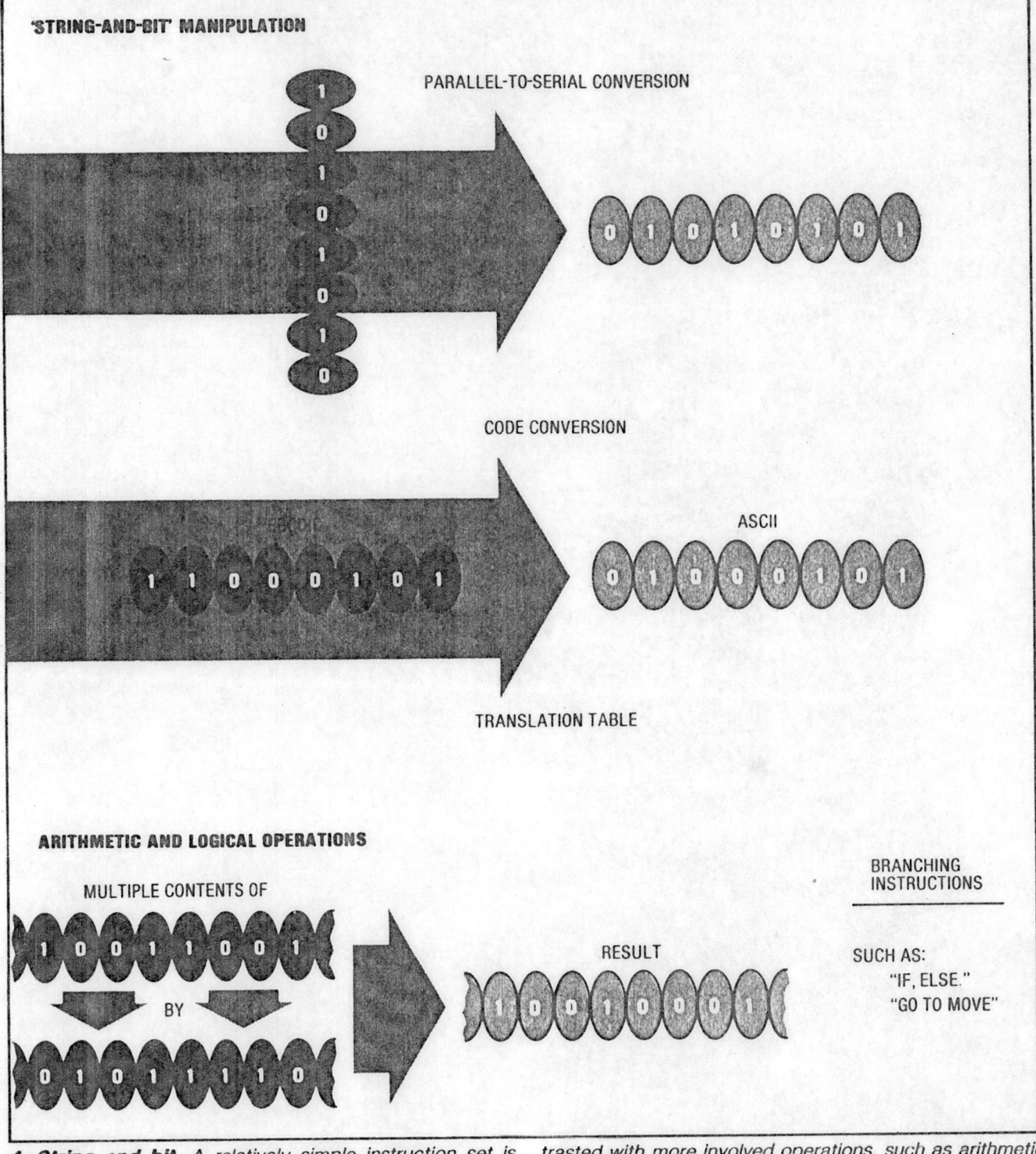

4. String and bit. *A relatively simple instruction set is used for most communications processing. This type of processing, called string-and-bit manipulation, is con-* *trasted with more involved operations, such as arithmetic calculations and logical operations, which also require many more processor cycles.*

efficiency, because you don't have to ramble through a lot of IBM access methods." This might be done, for example, if the user needed a channel-attached mini-computer to control a network of only IBM 3600 retail terminals. "It would not," he says, "be good for the user who wants to run all conventional IBM applications, however."

Several larger minicomputers today operate with

"virtual memory." In essence, these machines, such as IBM's new System/38 and Wang's VS series, use mass storage (disk) to supplement main memory. This operation is transparent to the user and, in fact, gives the user the perception of having unlimited main memory. The processor in a virtual memory environment actually uses a virtual address translator (as IBM calls it) to spool in and out portions of programs and files from

94

mass storage, when required, and then return them after the processing task is completed.

Most vendors agree that virtual machines, because of this additional overhead, are useless as dedicated communications processors. According to DEC's John Adams, virtual machines are geared for high-level languages and user-written applications "that may be inefficiently large." Communications processing, he says, has an immediacy that requires it be handled in real main memory, and while virtual machines facilitate user programming, they may wreak havoc on communications throughput and response times.

Of all minicomputer vendors, the big 10, examined below, represent about 75 pecent of the current installed base. The vendors' current offerings and plans for the future are crucial to any customer who intends to use minicomputers with communications.

Foremost in the minicomputer industry is Digital Equipment Corporation. The DEC product line represents an estimated 40 percent of the minicomputers installed to date. DEC's success has been based on the versatile PDP-11, which is available today in over a dozen models. (There are an estimated 100,000 PDP-11s currently installed.)

DEC is certainly keeping pace with user requirements in the communications area and last year saw many years of communications product development finally come to fruition. With its release of Decnet Phase III software, its digital network architecture (DNA) can at last be viewed as a viable multinodal networking architecture. Phases I and II offered questionable capabilities and met with limited user acceptance.

The last year has also seen DEC moving more in the direction of communications compatibility with IBM. Concurrent with the Decnet release, the firm announced a software product offering full SNA compatibility on most of its minicomputers (emulating an IBM 3790). Some work apparently needs to be done, though, in integrating such features with Decnet and DNA software. The SNA software cannot, for example, operate on a minicomputer that is also functioning as a Phase III Decnet node. DEC's most current communications product, an X.25 software module, reportedly will permit two DEC machines (PDP-11s, at present) to communicate over public packet-switched networks. This module is also not an integrated feature of Decnet, but it can run on a Decnet node.

Decnet now offers sophisticated routing features, including route optimization and alternate routing (see DATA COMMUNICATIONS, February, p. 24, and March, p. 85). Its users can also employ an X.25 option to interface the public packet-switched networks, but with some loss of the high-level features of Decnet software such as remote-file access, down-line program and IPL loading, and resource sharing.

DEC recently announced the discontinuation of support for its IBM channel interface (DX-11), although it never offered over-the-counter software that supported channel-attachment to IBM mainframes. (A number of system resellers did, however.) DEC remains mum

when questioned about whether it is developing a new microprocessor-based replacement. The firm also presently offers specially configured PDP-11s that serve as front ends to its Decsystem-10 and -20 mainframes. In most non-DNA cases, DEC seems satisfied to sell the hardware and let either the user or a systems house do the specialized software development.

DEC is a leader, rather than a follower, in the communications area. Several months ago, it announced a joint effort with Intel and Xerox to develop local-networking specifications (Ethernet-like) that it hopes will become an industry standard. This will probably come to pass, if the interface specifications are published soon enough. If DEC waits too long, the proliferation of local networking products elsewhere in the industry may negate this standardization effort.

Cupertino, Calif.-based Hewlett-Packard (HP) holds the number two position in the minicomputer industry and is somewhat of a johnny-come-lately in the communications arena. With an estimated market penetration of 15 percent, Hewlett-Packard has users that have traditionally been specialized, rather than general business customers. It is changing this reputation, however. HP's announcement last month of its new Distributed Systems Network (DSN) software was its first significant new communications release since it unveiled an IBM 3270 software package for its HP 3000 machines earlier this year.

HP's remote communications have up until now been limited to the IBM-compatible sector, although the company is apparently deviating from this path. Instead of offering an SNA-compatible package (which would seem to be the next logical step from its current IBM remote batch and interactive emulators), it is offering an X.25-based interprocessing package. The latest networking software for its HP 1000 line uses an X.25-based HDLC for interprocessor links (instead of the bisync-based protocol still used between HP 3000s). It appears as if the HP 3000 line is being groomed for customers desiring IBM-compatibility, while the HP 1000 is destined to become the HP-to-HP standard-bearer. It also seems that HP has decided to make its contribution toward universal interconnectability via the HP 1000, with X.25 support.

Hewlett-Packard has not indicated any serious efforts toward developing a proprietary local networking product, which might indicate that (1) its customers have not shown a strong interest in this area or (2) HP is sitting back, waiting to see what develops elsewhere. One HP source said that present HP point-to-point capabilities for local connections have more or less satisfied most customer requirements.

Data General Corporation holds an estimated 12 percent of the minicomputer market. Many of its machines, like DEC's, are sold in quantities to OEM systems houses, but a large percentage are still marketed to end users. One systems builder, Data Communications Corporation, of Memphis, Tenn., loads Data General

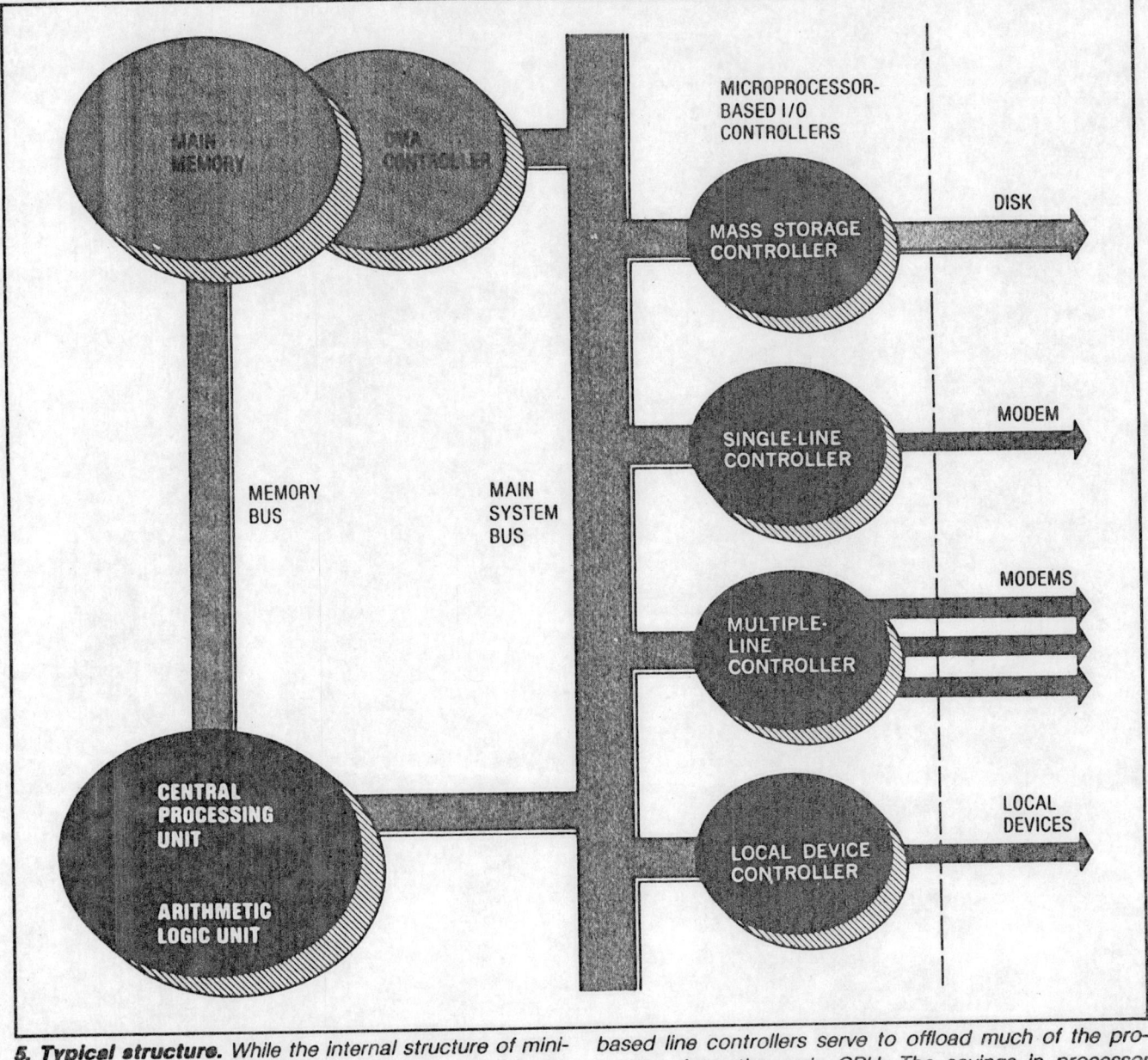

5. Typical structure. *While the internal structure of mini-computers varies somewhat from vendor to vendor, the basic components are common to each. Microprocessor-based line controllers serve to offload much of the processing from the main CPU. The savings in processor cycles significantly increases throughput.*

machines with software that supports a wide range of communications functions. The firm claims to offer its own networking architecture, electronic mail, and even IBM-SNA compatibility (via IBM 3270 emulation).

The communications features offered by Data General on its two major minicomputer lines, the Nova and the Eclipse, are akin to those supported by HP on its 1000 and 3000 series. For example, the smaller Nova (at present) supports only remote batch communications with IBM hosts (2780/3780 protocol), while the Eclipse supports that plus an IBM interactive capability (IBM 3270 emulation).

One Data General source said that it is the corporate strategy "to always offer DG-to-DG and IBM compatibility." This seems to capsulize DG's present communications support, except for its recently announced, X.25-based interprocessor architecture, Xodiac.

Will future Data General support include an IBM-SNA compatibility package? Possibly, but one source says that the company is convinced that IBM "will soon be forced to offer an X.25 alternative to its customers domestically." Data General will be waiting for this, even though the source says the IBM's X.25 "will not be very well integrated in its (IBM's) products."

At present, Xodiac's higher-level functions (including remote-file access/transfer and program-to-program communications) are limited to the Eclipse systems, but both the Nova and Eclipse machines can utilize the X.25 module for link-level communications. High-level Xodiac support for Nova systems will probably be forthcoming from DG as well.

Data General has stayed away from supplying front-end configurations, at least to end users, but it does offer a limited-distance local networking product that it

says "is used by virtually every Xodiac customer." The product has two versions: one with adapters for a ring type of local network and one with adapters for star topologies. Up to 15 processors can be attached locally, and transmission between machines is parallel at up to 2 Mbit/s.

Data General seems to be showing a growing interest in the word processing and electronic mail areas. Its recently announced AZ-Text package permits users to run word processing applications on the Eclipse systems. A similar package for the Nova, along with support for interprocessor message transmission (probably as a subset of Xodiac), is also anticipated.

The Level 6 minicomputer is Honeywell Information Systems' offering to the minicomputer world. It, like DEC's PDP-11, is very modular, enjoys a long development history, and comes in many different packages. Its communications options, however, are limited. According to one source, most Level 6s are sold to end users, but many are purchased by OEMs that repackage it. Its end-user clientele consists mainly of very large corporations with customized implementations.

The Level 6 is a particularly strong distributed system when used with Honeywell's Level 66 mainframes. Honeywell has strived to maintain a high degree of compatibility in the operating software of the two systems. For example, the Level 6's GCOS 6 operating system and the IDS-II database manager are both compatible subsets of similar packages that run on the Level 66 mainframes.

Honeywell reportedly obtained certification on an X.25 package from Telenet last June, but a company source said that it would be offered to end users "only on a customized basis," because it resulted from a special job that Honeywell had done for one client.

The Honeywell source said that the firm is moving toward general industry interconnection by supporting X.25 and "not through specific compatibilities like SNA." At present, Honeywell offers both batch and interactive compatibilities with IBM hosts, but both use the older bisync communications protocol. Honeywell will probably not offer SNA compatibility.

The Level 6 is not marketed as a dedicated communications processor, except for a specially modified version that serves as a front end to certain Honeywell mainframes. Honeywell points out that this front end uses "Level 6 technology but is not an off-the-shelf Level 6." The vendor is apparently not concerned by its lack of communications-oriented packages for its minicomputer. One Level 6 product manager says, "We are not in competition with the common carriers."

From a communications point of view, Honeywell will probably let its systems house customers and large users worry about specific implementations, except for the occasional and lucrative customized job. The Level 6 is nevertheless finding its way into communications applications. Metropolitan Life Insurance Company, for example, announced recently that it is implementing Level 6s as satellite link controllers, where they handle high-speed interface to the satellite transmission gear,

error detection and recovery, and compensation for the satellite propagation delay. In another recent announcement, New York-based Advanced Computer Techniques said that it would market specially loaded Level 6s as general-purpose network nodes handling functions such as cluster control, data concentration, and message switching.

Based on 1979 market figures, IBM would probably be considered about number five in the minicomputer arena. However, last year's sales on its newer machines (like the Series/1 and 8100) might have nudged it up slightly in the standings. Most of IBM's minicomputers come out of Atlanta's General Systems Division (System/3, 32, 34, 38, and Series/1), but the 8100 Information System, IBM's major distributed processor, belongs to the New York-based Data Processing Division. Regardless of division, most IBM communications, at present, fall under the SNA umbrella. (Even the word processing Displaywriter introduced this past summer, for example, communicates as an SNA device.) It may be surprising to note that most IBM terminals and devices emulated by other minicomputer vendors are not even supported as SNA devices by IBM but are typically accommodated through "patches" in the SNA structure.

One controversial topic in data communications today is whether or not SNA is catching on, either for IBM users or for vendors that market emulation devices for IBM users. There is no doubt that the number of 3705s running NCP instead of 270X emulation is increasing, but this number is still far from a majority. While the merits and shortcomings of SNA have been the basis for literally volumes of articles and books, the fact that IBM continually prods its users toward SNA seems indisputable. One of its latest minicomputer offerings, the System/38, for example, supports only SNA/SDLC communications.

IBM's thrust into distributed processing is manifested primarily in the 8100. The 8100 supports most IBM terminals (old and new) as standard options and even TTY-compatible machines (including IBM's 3101 asynchronous terminal). In addition, numerous software packages support the 8100 in communications with remote 370 mainframes. The reported success of 8100 sales will no doubt serve as a springboard for further IBM ventures in DDP.

The General Systems Division's Series/1 is also making headway and offers a rich array of communications options—including hardware for channel attachment to IBM mainframes. IBM has not yet supplied software using this feature to make the Series/1 a channel-attached SNA communications controller, but this might well be under development. Several systems houses are also buying the Series/1 in OEM quantities, including one that has developed software that lets the machine handle the X.25 protocol, in addition to the standard battery of bisync and SNA devices.

IBM will be forced by its U.S. customers to support X.25 (and public packet networks), and it is reportedly testing one such implementation on Canada's Data-

pac. The big question, however, is when, and how, it will offer this support domestically. Users can expect IBM to announce some kind of X.25 compatibility in 1981, with product delivery before 1983. IBM marketing managers, not technical staff, are currently wrestling with means to accomplish that. Insomuch as X.25 can effectively replace the lower layers of SNA, its most efficient implementation would be as a replacement for SDLC, with the balance of SNA functions remaining essentially unchanged in software. But despite the tremendous push that such a move would give the worldwide standardization efforts, one source points out that this would make it too easy to mix IBM and non-IBM machines. For this reason, IBM's implementation of X.25 will probably be irretrievably entangled in IBM's hardware and software peculiarities.

Careful not to turn its back on users of older processors, IBM has enhanced communications features for the System/34. Several special utilities and field-developed programs now offer System/34 users considerable interprocessor networking capabilities. These address both bisync and SDLC communications, as well as interconnection with other System/34s, System/3s, and remote 370 hosts. Because of IBM's hold on the mainframe world and because distributed processing is gaining in momentum, any move that IBM makes in the area of communications will have a worldwide impact.

rime Computer has become one of the leading minicomputer vendors. Because of its orientation toward the end user, the firm has itself had to develop the special features, including communications, that make minicomputers sell. Although it does not offer SNA compatibility, Prime has impressive communications features. It offers a rich library of terminal emulators (for five vendors' mainframes), a local networking scheme, X.25 packet-network support throughout the U.S., Canada, and Europe, and a sophisticated interprocessor networking architecture.

Its Primenet networking strategy addresses both X.25 support and local networking—two areas that most vendors regard as being at opposite ends of the communications spectrum. Prime takes the approach that when communications is required, it should be transparent to the user whether the remote machine is 1,000 feet away or 1,000 miles. Indeed, its software is structured to allow users access in either case with equal facility and efficiency.

Prime minicomputers are respected for communications-oriented applications. In fact, its machines support the base of the Telenet network (which probably explains Prime's preference for X.25 to a specific compatibility like IBM's SNA). The Prime local networking product, however, is based on an evolution of the Cambridge Ring—an entirely different structure from that used in the Ethernet-type of local network. If the local-network specifications being developed by DEC (and Intel and Xerox) do become networking standards, Prime may be forced to rethink its position.

Is Prime providing all the necessary communications

features? Certainly not, admit several of its communications product managers. Prime may not get into the front-end business (although one Prime manager said, "It is something we talk about from time to time"), but it will most likely push harder in the future office environment, possibly integrating control into a single minicomputer for data, word processing, electronic mail, facsimile, and maybe even digitized voice transmission. Prime already offers word processing and electronic message packages.

Prime is thinking ahead. One company source says that with the proliferation of networks, "the user tends to forget where he's at and goes to remote locations for data that may be found locally." The source predicted that, within the next couple of decades, "the network will be able to keep track of remote applications usage and automatically move applications to areas where it is frequently accessed."

erkin-Elmer, the Oceanport, N.J.-based firm, is also gaining ground in the minicomputer industry. From a communications viewpoint, it might be perceived as a jack-of-all-trades but master of none. It markets a powerful line of machines that support both 16- and 32-bit operation, but its communications offerings are somewhat shallow. Perkin-Elmer offers, for example, the usual support for IBM bisync terminals (including the interactive 3270) but no SNA. It provides X.25 compatibility, but only for the link-level (HDLC), and has not therefore sought certification by any public packet networks. It offers an IBM mainframe channel attachment but no software to support it.

Perkin-Elmer counts on systems houses (such as Intecom, the communications processor "affiliate" of Exxon) for the fine-tuning of these communications-oriented implementations. In so doing, however, it cannot offer sophisticated communications features directly to the user.

exas Instruments in Austin, Tex., has found a lucrative market in distributed processing. The reason for its success in this area is not completely clear, although many of its customers are very large users who seem to be sold on the company for product reliability, technical support, and service. Texas Instruments' strength lies in its lower end of minicomputer products, and a significant portion of its revenue comes from personal computers, microprocessors, and semiconductors.

As for communications capabilities, Texas Instruments has taken its intelligent terminal expertise and magnified it considerably in the distributed processing marketplace. Its Series 700 and DS 990 family of distributed systems are not particularly suited for dedicated communications applications (or as terminal cluster controllers), but they do serve ideally as regional machines, performing applications processing for users, with the added capability of communications with remote IBM (and Burroughs) hosts.

Texas Instruments' market is small communicating systems, which could permit it to figure prominently in

the home computing and home information areas that promise to boom in the very near future.

lthough originally directed at the word processing community, Wang Laboratories, in Lowell, Mass., has grown considerably in the direction of data processing and office automation. It now stands in an excellent position to integrate the three. For its older 2200 series of processors, Wang runs a unique version of distributed processing. Word and text processing software is down-line loaded into workstations, where the user need not worry about response times until text preparation is complete. He then transmits, going through the control processor, to the remote host (IBM and Burroughs are currently supported).

The down-line loading of word processing software is not, however, supported on the VS line of minicomputers. The Wang philosophy is that it will soon be cheaper to place a WP controller at the remote location than to pay for the communications facilities required for remote on-line text development.

Wang presently offers a star type of local networking configuration, but only for its 2200 series processors. Numerous terminal protocols are supported, primarily IBM, but again mainly on the 2200 machines. Similar features will probably be forthcoming for its VS series of 32-bit minicomputers.

At present, the 2200 workstation series seems to be lacking communications integration with the newer Wang minicomputers. These will probably be brought more into line with each other through introduction of enhanced automated office capabilities.

San Antonio, Texas-based Datapoint Corporation can attribute at least some of its success to its communications orientation. Before such functions became marketable, Datapoint was developing impressive interprocessor communications functions between its 8-bit machines. This led to the Attached Resource Computer (ARC) system, a local network that supports up to 255 locally attached Datapoint machines.

With its Infoswitch communications line controllers (that operate on a circuit-switched basis and incorporate a Datapoint 6600 processor), Datapoint seems to have a promising future in data/voice integration. Besides an exceptionally wide selection of terminal emulators for its data processing machines, the company offers efficient word processing and electronic mail packages. More important, Datapoint has ensured that all these products are integrated.

For distributed processing configurations, Datapoint has chosen to support a varied number of mainframe vendors and has not yet embraced support for X.25 or interfaced to any public packet networks. Its IBM compatibilities, however, are noteworthy. Fully supported SNA packages are available for emulating both the IBM 3270 and the 3770 series of terminal devices.

These are not the only minicomputer vendors that offer substantial communications features or have a promising communications future.

What is terminal emulation?

Many data communications users still think that a processor that supports binary synchronous (bisync) communications can interconnect with most other IBM bisync devices. Nothing could be further from the truth. The actual line protocol (such as bisync, SDLC, or HDLC) is only a part of the communications control that makes up a terminal emulation module.

Terminal emulation implies that a processor capable of this emulation can appear as a terminal compatible with another remote processor. For example, a minicomputer capable of IBM 3270 bisync emulation would be able to communicate with a remote host as either a standalone 3275 workstation or as a 3271/4/6 remote cluster controller. In rare cases the emulating processor may also be capable of handling the attachment (local or remote) of 327X displays and/or 328X printers. Some vendors (Hewlett-Packard, for example) provide emulation software for their minicomputers to communicate with a remote IBM host (as a 3270) but still require that their own terminals be used.

The table shows the communications characteristics of 10 commonly emulated terminal devices. Note that in order to fully emulate a device, the communications control software must take into account many factors peculiar to the terminal besides line protocol. These include the line configurations and facilities required (point-to-point or multipoint, leased or dial-up lines), character code (ASCII, EBCDIC, and so on), output formatting (whether for printer or CRT), type of operation (interactive or batch), data blocking for transmission (usually a part of the line protocol), and error checking (generally also a part of the protocol).

These terminal characteristics are, in most cases, the specifications as published by the manufacturing vendor, but there are also variations. Terminal emulators for bisync devices, for example, may implement slightly different record lengths (in the case of 2780 and 3780 emulators) and frequently implement different timeout values (the predefined time that a device awaits an acknowledgment before taking other action).

When a user shops for a distributed system that involves terminal emulation, he should question the vendor to ensure that *full* emulation and compatibility are included. A vendor may, for instance, provide a microcoded module that handles only the line protocol, leaving the user to write the software for the rest of the

99

terminal-specific communications features.

The table also shows the approximate size of the software required for the device emulation. For simple terminals, such as the asynchronous teletype, 4 kbytes of memory is sufficient to handle the software and buffering for communications control, while up to 30 kbytes is needed for more-complex devices (such as SNA-compatible 3270 cluster controllers). Much of this additional memory requirement is due to the complicated software or microcode needed to handle the SDLC protocol and its inherent characteristics of error checking, message sequencing, and special bit-oriented control fields. Because of this disparity in memory requirements, it is frequently unfeasible to implement a complicated terminal emulator on a small distributed processor (of, say, 64 kbytes), since this would require that half of its memory be constantly consumed with communications control alone.

When the user needs to implement two or more terminal emulators in the same processor, the problem of communications control is amplified geometrically. This is because the software and processing required to simultaneously handle two very different protocols is larger than the sum of the software necessary to run each emulator individually. (This is reportedly one of the problems now being faced by AT&T's programmers working on software for the ACS network.)

For users whose distributed processors must be able to operate more than one terminal emulator from the same site, there are a number of alternatives. One is to off-load the communications software from the processor (which could even be an intelligent terminal) via a protocol converter, but this generally requires that an unsavory price be paid in terms of response time and throughput efficiency. Yet another method is to divide the emulator software into discrete modules so that the individual emulators can be spooled into the processor (say, from a diskette) one at a time as required. The drawback in this case is the start-up time for the terminal operator. It may take a few minutes to load or change protocols, but this can be viewed as a necessary trade-off in order to switch constantly between several different mainframes. ■

Terminal protocol characteristics

SOURCE: INDUSTRIAL COMPUTER CONTROLS INC., CAMBRIDGE, MASS.

TERMINAL TYPE	APPROXIMATE SOFTWARE MEMORY REQUIRED (BYTES)	LINE CONFIGURATION	CHARACTER FRAMING/ TIMING	CHARACTER CODE	TYPICAL USE	PRIMARY OUTPUT MEDIUM	FACILITIES	BLOCKING	ERROR CORRECTION
TELETYPE (MODEL 33)									
DEC VT52	4K	POINT TO POINT	BYTE/ ASYNC	ASCII	INTERACTIVE	PRINT	DIAL-UP	UNBLOCKED	CHARACTER PARITY
IBM 2741									
IBM 2780	9K	POINT TO POINT	BYTE/ SYNC	ASCII EBCDIC	BATCH	PRINT	DIAL-UP	SINGLE/DOUBLE RECORD OF 80/132 CHARACTERS	BLOCK ACK (BSC/CRC)
IBM 3780	9K	POINT TO POINT	BYTE/ SYNC	ASCII	BATCH				
BURROUGHS TC/TD SERIES— POLL/SELECT	12K	MULTIPOINT	BYTE/ ASYNC AND SYNC	ASCII	INTERACTIVE	CRT	LEASED	BLOCKED	BLOCK ACK (CRC)
IBM 3275 (BSC)	13K	POINT TO POINT	BYTE/ SYNC				DIAL-UP		
UNIVAC V100/200	18K	MULTIPOINT	BYTE/ SYNC	ASCII WITH SPECIAL CHARACTERS	INTERACTIVE	CRT	LEASED	UNBLOCKED	DELAYED ACK (CRC)
IBM 3271/4/5 (BSC)		MULTIPOINT	BYTE	ASCII	INTERACTIVE	CRT	LEASED	BLOCKED	
IBM 3270/4/6 SNA-SDLC	30K	MULTIPOINT, POINT TO POINT	BIT- ORIENTED	ASCII EBCDIC	INTERACTIVE	CRT	LEASED, DIAL-UP (IF POINT TO POINT)	BLOCKED	GO BACK N WHERE N IS UP TO 7 (BSC)

100

Finesse versus force in bolstering micros' capabilities

John Wharton and Lionel Smith, Intel Corporation, Santa Clara, Calif.

In some cases, optimized software—not an extra peripheral chip—can give a microprocessor all the power it needs.

So far in the history of the microprocessor, the technology has advanced in two directions: microcomputers' tasks have become steadily more difficult and their throughput has increased to meet demand. To date, microprocessors' performance has been able to keep up with users' requirements, because each new generation of microprocessors operates faster than the previous one. For example, Intel's 8085A-2 microprocessor can execute in 800 nanoseconds the same instructions that took the older-generation 8008 10 microseconds five years earlier.

The systems designers, besides increasing the microprocessor's speed, have enhanced its performance by taking more and more routine input and output (I/O) tasks away from the central processing unit (CPU) and assigning them to sophisticated special-purpose peripheral circuitry. Thus, such jobs as transferring large blocks of data, scanning keyboards, or counting external events are executed on special circuits designed for direct-memory-access controllers, keyboard/display scanners, and programmable event counters offered by a growing number of major semiconductor manufacturers. Since the peripheral circuitry (implemented on silicon "chips") handles I/O processes that are usually slow and repetitive, at rates limited by external hardware, the CPU is free to do the tasks it does best: processing data, making decisions, and implementing elaborate custom algorithms developed specifically for new applications.

However, it is important to note that in many cases these tasks can be, and at times have been, handled quite readily by the CPU itself. Adding a dedicated peripheral chip increases overall performance only if the microprocessor is able to work on something else while the peripheral does the chores assigned to it. If this is not the case—if time is not of the essence—systems designers can reduce overall microprocessor cost and complexity by replacing hardware with software. They can write programs and subroutines to handle the same tasks that an extra peripheral chip performs. In fact, this may yield additional flexibility, since the microprocessor CPU is more versatile than many peripheral chips and has access to the microcomputer's full facilities.

To examine how software can effectively replace a peripheral chip, consider the case of a universal synchronous/asynchronous receiver/transmitter—the common USART. In its customary operating mode, this device translates data (ASCII characters) from 8-bit bytes into a standard format for transmission through a serial channel, and vice versa. Serial transmission schemes are used for a variety of reasons, such as to reduce the number of interconnections and line terminators required in a network of distributed processors or to communicate with a wide variety of common data communications terminals, such as CRTs or teletypewriters.

While most microprocessors are specifically designed for the kinds of parallel operations required for internal data processing, they usually have basic serial bit-handling capabilities as well. With a few exceptions, all microprocessors can move bits one at a time

through a memory location—a process called rotating a register or accumulator—into a specific memory location. The microprocessor can then, based on a carry or link bit, return the state of the memory location to binary 0 or reverse the value of the bit by expressing it as its opposite (that is, clear or complement the bit), and perform a specific subsequent step based on the state of the bit (do conditional branching).

These capabilities are sufficient to implement a variety of data processing routines such as the parallel-to-serial conversion often relegated to USARTs. For example, consider this potential product intended for the computer hobbyist market: a low-cost machine that can play a variety of simple games with the user. Input and output is through a console provided by the user in the form of a teletypewriter, commercial CRT, or (more likely) a home-brew video terminal such as a television set adapted for communications.

These terminals use a standard convention for transmitting serial ASCII code. Each data byte is transmitted as a series of 10 or more bits. The uniform transmission time for each bit, referred to as bit-time, is determined by the data transmission rate. For example, if the transmission rate is to be 2.4 kbit/s, each bit-time must be 1 ÷ 2,400 bit/s or about 417 microseconds/bit. The standard 10-bit sequence consists of a binary 0 "start" bit, 8 data bits with the least significant bit first, and one or more "stop" bits—a binary 1. Two or more stop bits are required for 110-bit/s teletypewriters. The binary 1 level mandated by ASCII standard code for the stop bits continues until the start bit of the next byte to ensure that each 10-bit sequence is initiated with a one-to-zero transition. In the case of ASCII code, the most significant bit—the last data bit transmitted—is determined by the parity convention. This sequence is illustrated in Figure 1 for the ASCII "space" character (20_H in hexadecimal notation) and is obtained by striking the space bar on the keyboard.

The algorithm for receiving serial code involves sampling the incoming data at the middle of each bit-time. The eight sampled values are shifted into a serial byte corresponding to the data originally transmitted. The one-to-zero transition at the beginning of each byte makes it possible to synchronize the sampling points relative to the start of each data sequence or charac-

1. Bit sequencing. Under ASCII code, bits are arranged so that the parity convention dictates transmission order of serial data (that is, the most important bit last).

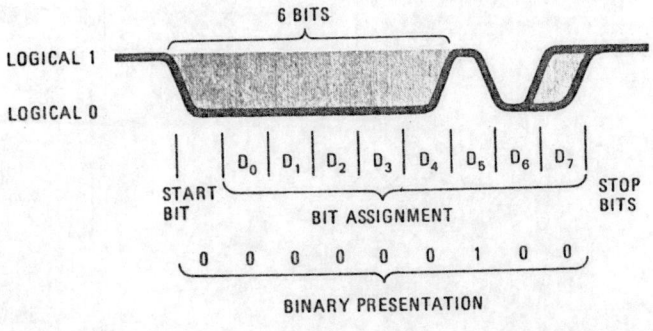

ter, which includes parity and start/stop bits.

The serial interface for the above-mentioned games computer must be able to operate at several different data rates to accommodate the customer's hardware. External switches let the user select from multiple rates. But since cost is critical, the number of components must be kept to a minimum.

Ideally, the machine would adjust automatically to the appropriate data rate. This would be convenient and would lower costs by eliminating the need for separate rate-selection switches and their associated input pins and connections.

Possible replacement

A likely candidate for the heart of this product would be a single-chip microcomputer. If, for example, the microcomputer combined a CPU, a read-only memory (ROM) capacity, random access memory (RAM), a timer/counter, interrupt handles, and I/O lines, it would not need a USART. The Intel MCS-48 is an example. The potential throughput increase a USART might provide is not relevant, since the games can progress no faster than the rate at which the user enters data. It makes no sense for the CPU to sit idle while the USART waits for a new character to arrive. The CPU might just as well be monitoring the serial channel.

Very seldom could the CPU be "thinking ahead" while the USART processes the most recently entered data. Most important, the added cost of a USART cannot be justified in a product for which the critical design factor is assumed to be the final sale price rather than throughput. In this extreme example, adding another peripheral chip would double the number of integrated circuits in the machine.

Instead, systems designers could substitute a set of subroutines for the USART; software could replace hardware. They could implement such a software package for microprocessors produced by many manufacturers. For instance, the collection of subroutines presented in this article could be the basis for a serial interface by any microcomputer in the Intel MCS-48 family.

In general, any serial communications system requires both hardware and software interfaces. The TTL-compatible (transitor-to-transistor-logic) MCS-48 output needs additional current and voltage buffering to be compatible with the digital interface standards used by most data communications terminals. A schematic for achieving this buffering is shown in Figure 2. The MC1488 and MC1489 output circuits interface positive binary TTL signals with the RS-232-C high-voltage, inverted binary levels, although discrete transistors could be substituted to accomplish this.

A software I/O

The software needed to drive the CRT interface is divided into three parts, or subroutines. All three use programmed timing and delay loops, with fixed and variable parameters, which can identify incoming signals and respond to them at rates from below 110 to over 2.4K bit/s.

When the CRT is turned on, or when it is reset, it calls the bit-rate-identification subroutine (BAUDID). This

2. Interfacing. Serial data communications systems require interfaces for both hardware and software. The TTL-compatible logic in this microcomputer family also needs buffering to make it compatible with RS-232-C interface standards. In this case, output circuits are used, but discrete transistors would serve the same purpose.

40-PIN MICROPROCESSOR   25-PIN RS-232-C INTERFACE CIRCUITRY   SERIAL TRANSMISSION

subroutine waits for the user to type an ASCII space character (20_H) on the console. As the CRT receives this special character, it computes a time parameter that corresponds to the bit-time of the transmission rate being used. Receiving any other character will result in an erroneous identification.

To output a character to the console, the CRT calls the second subroutine—CRTOUT. To accept a character from the keyboard, it calls the subroutine CRTIN. Since CRTOUT and CRTIN use time parameters computed by BAUDID, they function at the same rate as the space character that was initially inputted at the keyboard. Because of the software's characteristics, the rate does not depend on the CPU's internal cycle speed or clock frequency. This yields additional flexibility in the following respects:

1. The software need not be modified if the CPU's quartz crystal-based clock frequency is changed.

2. Since the processor-clock frequency is no longer critical, the quartz crystal that is its major component could be replaced by a less-expensive time base, provided the frequency does not drift by more than a few percent during a session. Any additional drift can be accommodated by the central processor's periodically recalling the BAUDID subroutine.

3. Communications is possible at nonstandard bit rates, which relaxes the constraints on the types of terminals used.

It should be noted, though, that slowing down the CPU clock will decrease the microprocessor's throughput proportionately. In addition, a slowed CPU clock will degrade the performance of internal delay mechanisms, with the result that the highest bit rates may no longer be achievable.

Often, programmers find that they must implement two or more similar tasks on one microprocessor. The most straightforward attack—writing slightly different subroutines for each case—is usually not the best approach for several reasons:

■ Much code space is wasted through duplication. This is an especially important consideration in single-chip computer applications, where the on-chip read-

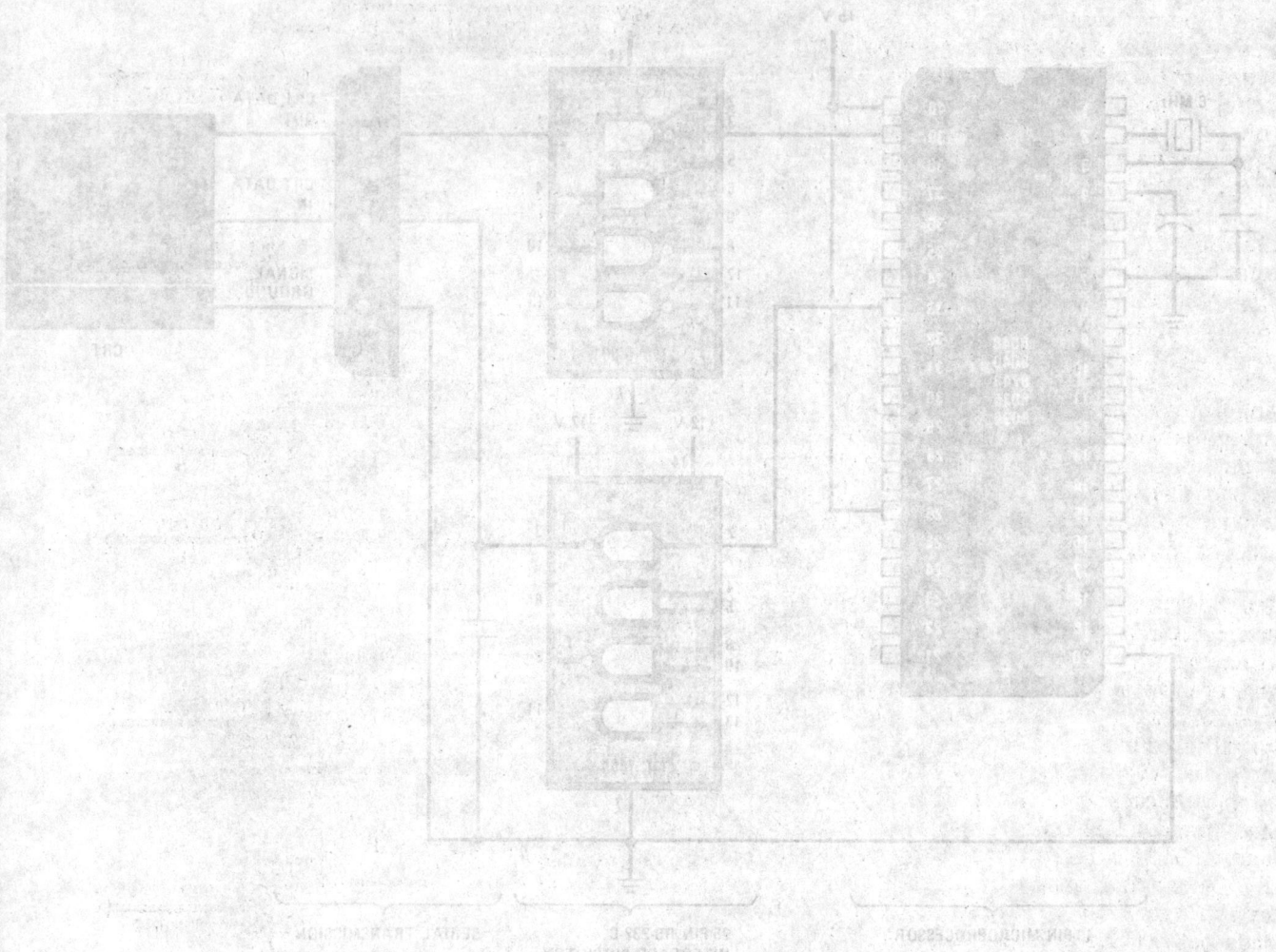

only memory must be conserved.
- Errors are much more frequent when blocks of code are entered repeatedly.
- Each section of code must be thoroughly checked out to verify proper operation.
- When there are errors in the logic or the program must be modified, it is both time-consuming and tedious to change multiple subsections.

More often, it is better to develop a single, slightly more elegant, algorithm that inherently handles all cases correctly. The following illustrates this technique.

Output routine

The "brute-force" method of outputting a character to the CRT would require the programmer to write three separate subroutines: one to output a start bit (0), one to loop eight times to output the data bits, and one to send the required stop bits (in this case, two 1s). Each subroutine would have its own delay and output modules, leading to unnecessary triplication of the code.

The code that implements a more efficient algorithm executes one main loop 11 times, with its bit-manipulation technique inherently forming the correct data

Some special microprocessing terms

Accumulator. A special-purpose register in most microcomputers through which data is placed into memory or brought into the processor from memory. It is also used to "accumulate" intermediate mathematical results.

Carry bit. An "extra" (usually ninth) bit associated with a register that indicates when a carry has resulted from a mathematical operation. It may also function, as in this article, as a "link" bit through which I/O operations are performed and monitored.

Machine cycle. An arbitrary amount of time that depends both on the processor's physical characteristics and on the processor's clock and signal timing. The length of time needed for a processor to execute any given instruction is measured in machine cycles.

Pseudo-register. Since almost all microprocessors have a finite number of registers available to the programmer, designers often define a memory location and treat it as if it were a register. To the processor, this is still an ordinary memory location.

Rotate. A register (not a pseudo-register) can be rotated to the right or left so that bit 0 becomes bit 1, bit 1 becomes bit 2, and so on. In such a case, the fate of bit 7 (or bit 0, depending on the direction of the rotation) depends on the exact instruction. Sometimes the last bit takes the place of the first; that is, bit 7 shifts into bit 0's former position. At other times the carry bit is used to receive the contents of bit 7, while its contents are placed into bit 0's old position.

Shift. Similar to a rotate instruction except that the last bit in the stream (bit 0, bit 7, or the carry bit, depending on the instruction) is usually lost. A "circular shift" refers to a register rotation instruction.

3. Rotation. *Efficient code creates a pseudo-register and moves bits through it one at a time via a carry-bit location to input and output data from the microprocessor's CPU.*

sequence of 0 through 10. The technique is simply to create a pseudo-register (see "Some special microprocessing terms") called CHAR. This 9-bit register, which contains 8 bits of data plus a carry bit, called CY, is implemented as the circular shift register with the carry bit initially set to 0. The algorithm, then, merely outputs the bit in the carry-bit location, waits 1 bit-time, sets the value of the carry bit to binary 1 (CY equals 1), and then circularly rotates the entire 9-bit pseudo-register 1 bit to the right (Fig. 3).

Initially, with the carry bit equal to binary 0 and the character to be sent contained in the pseudo-register CHAR, the algorithm outputs a 0 start bit, waits for the amount of time determined by the system's bit rate, sets the CY to 1, shifts the entire register 1 bit to the right, and then retransmits the carry bit. This time, the carry bit will be the least-significant bit of the transmitted character. By repeating this process 11 times, the algorithm will send a start bit, 8 data bits, and 2 stop bits. If the bit rate of the protocol required additional stop bits, they would be available in the pseudo-regis-

ter and could easily be sent by increasing the number of times the main loop is executed. This is the reason that CY is set to 1 each time a transmission has taken place and before the register is shifted.

Figure 4 is a flowchart depicting this CRTOUT algorithm. To demonstrate how the algorithm would be programmed in assembly language, Table 1 provides a partial listing of the USART software routine. The program depicted there is written in MCS-48 assembly language mnemonics.

Input routine

The character-input routine, CRTIN, operates similarly to CRTOUT, with, of course, some important and readily identifiable differences. One of the most obvious, visible in Figure 5, is that the input loop must only be executed nine times rather than the 11 times necessary for CRTOUT. This is because the input routine need only detect a transition from binary 1 to 0 to "know" that it is about to receive a character (recall that this is the purpose of sending stop bits). Once it receives the start bit, the input routine knows it must take the next 8 bits as data and then end its operations.

Another difference between CRTOUT and CRTIN is in the use of the half-bit delays. CRTOUT uses two such delays in succession. CRTIN, on the other hand, uses one delay immediately on detection of the one-to-zero transition indicating a start bit, and then uses two in succession while receiving the data byte. The first half-bit delay allows the system to synchronize itself with the middle of the bit-time, so that each subsequent delay of 1 full bit, achieved by calling the half-bit delay routine twice in succession, will also be positioned at the middle of the bit-time.

As each character bit is received, it is placed in the carry-bit position (CY) of the pseudo-register CHAR. Then, following a delay of 1 bit-time, the newly inputted character is shifted right into CHAR through the CY, and the algorithm returns to get the next bit being transmitted to it by the system output device. Ultimately, when all 8 character bits and the start bit have been received, the start bit is discarded into CY and the 8 bits contained in the pseudo-register CHAR are available to be read by the system's software.

Together, CRTIN and CRTOUT constitute a data-handling routine that places parallel data into the pseudo-register CHAR. The routine transmits data in the proper format (start bit/data bits/stop bits) to the I/O device and accepts serialized data from the I/O device, collecting all of it in a pseudo-register. Then it transmits data in parallel to the system. These are the classical functions of a USART. The only remaining problem is the "nicety" of enabling the software to determine the bit rate of the system's I/O device and the handling of subsequent data transactions at that rate. This is the function of the BAUDID subroutine.

Automatic rate identification

Table 1 (lines 21-26) shows a routine called HBWAIT (half-bit). Both CRTIN and CRTOUT call this routine to achieve the proper system timing. Note in line 21 that the routine's first action is to place an address called

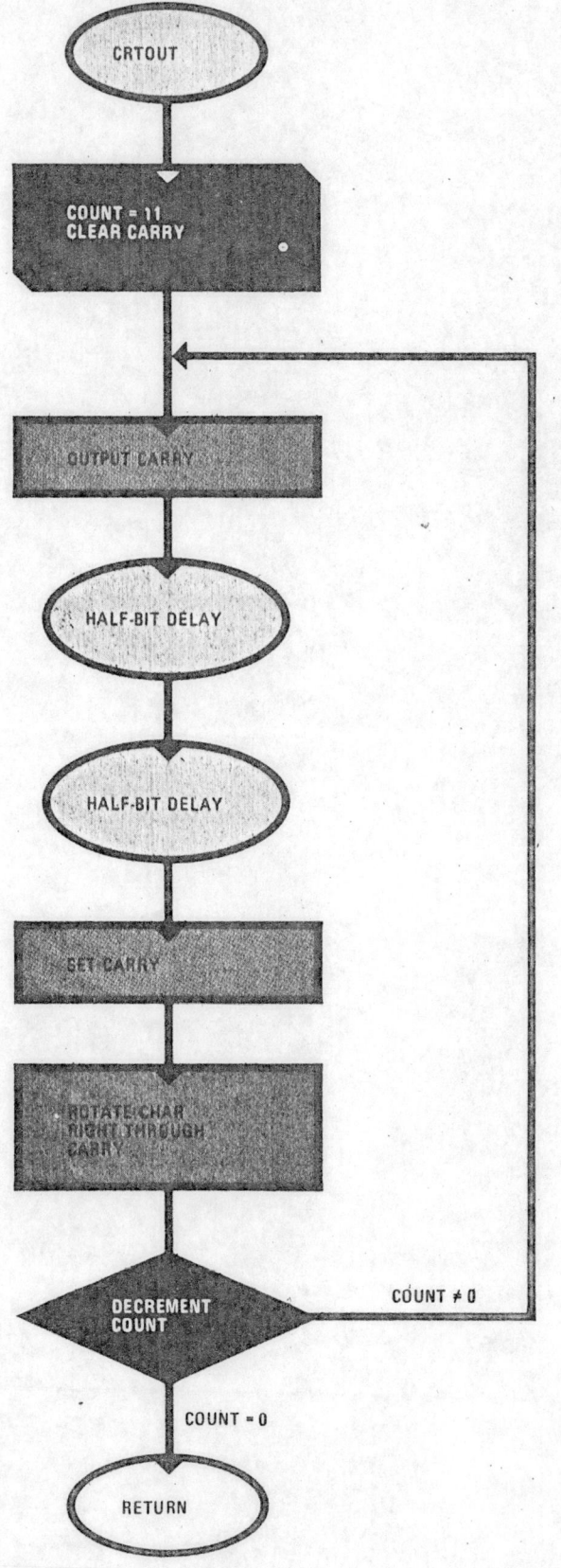

4. Character output. The entire CRTOUT algorithm can be depicted as a cycle in which the major software functions are repeated 11 times for each character.

Table 1 System timing

```
LOC  OBJ        LINE        SOURCE STATEMENT

                  1 $MACROFILE XREF
                  2 ;
0002              3 COUNT   EQU     R2
0003              4 CHAR    EQU     R3
0004              5 INDEX   EQU     R4
0005              6 DLAYHI  EQU     R5
0006              7 DLAYLO  EQU     R6
0020              8 TIMELO  EQU     20H     ;ADDRESS OF STORAGE FOR HALF BIT DELAY WORD
0021              9 TIMEHI  EQU     21H
0008             10 BITSO   EQU     11      ;DATA BITS PUT OUT (INCLUDING TWO STOP BITS)
0009             11 BITSI   EQU     9       ;DATA BITS TO BE RECEIVED (INCLUDING ONE STOP BIT)
                 12 ;
                 13 ;
0000             14         ORG     000H
                 15 ;
0000 0487        16         JMP     CRTTST
                 17 ;
                 18 ;
0020             19         ORG     20H
                 20 ;HBWAIT HALF-BIT TIME DELAY
0020 B920        21 HBWAIT: MOV     R1,#TIMELO
0022 F1          22         MOV     A,@R1
0023 AE          23         MOV     DLAYLO,A
0024 19          24         INC     R1
0025 F1          25         MOV     A,@R1
0026 AD          26         MOV     DLAYHI,A
0027 EE27        27 HBD1:   DJNZ    DLAYLO,HBD1
0027 ED27        28         DJNZ    DLAYHI,HBD1
0028 83          29         RET
                 30 ;
                 31 ;
                 32 ;CRTOUT CONSOLE OUTPUT SUBROUTINE
                 33 ;       WRITES THE CONTENTS OF THE ACC TO THE CRT DISPLAY SCREEN
002C AB          34 CRTOUT: MOV     CHAR,A
002D BA0B        35         MOV     COUNT,#BITSO    ;SET NUMBER OF BITS TO BE TRANSMITTED
002F 97          36         CLR     C               ;CLEAR CARRY
0030 F636        37 CO1:    JC      CO2
0032 993F        38         ANL     P1,#NOT 40H
0034 043A        39         JMP     CO3
0036 8940        40 CO2:    ORL     P1,#40H
0038 00          41         NOP                     ;NO OPS INSERTED TO EQUALIZE EXECUTION TIME
0039 00          42         NOP
003A 1420        43 CO3:    CALL    HBWAIT
003C 1420        44         CALL    HBWAIT
003E 97          45         CLR     C
003F A7          46         CPL     C               ;SET WHAT WILL EVENTUALLY BECOME A STOP BIT
0040 FB          47         MOV     A,CHAR          ;ROTATE CHARACTER RIGHT ONE BIT.
0041 67          48         RRC     A               ;\ MOVING NEXT DATA BIT INTO CARRY
0042 AB          49         MOV     CHAR,A
0043 EA30        50         DJNZ    COUNT,CO1       ;CHECK IF CHARACTER (AND STOP BIT(S)) DONE
0045 83          51         RET
                 52 ;
                 53 ;CRTIN  CONSOL INPUT SUBROUTINE WAITS FOR A KEYSTROKE AND
                 54 ;       RETURNS WITH 8 BITS IN THE ACCUMULATOR.
0046 BA09        55 CRTIN:  MOV     COUNT,#BITSI    ;DATA BITS TO BE READ (LAST RETURNED IN CY)
0048 5648        56 CI1:    JT1     CI1
004A 1420        57         CALL    HBWAIT
004C 5648        58         JT1     CI1             ;VERIFY INPUT LINE STILL LOW.
004E 97          59 CI2:    CLR     C
004F 4661        60         JNT1    CI4             ;CHECK INPUT SIGNAL LINE LEVEL
0051 A7          61         CPL     C               ;DATA BIT IN CY
0052 00          62         NOP                     ;EQUALIZE EXECUTION TIME.
0053 1420        63 CI3:    CALL    HBWAIT
0055 1420        64         CALL    HBWAIT
0057 FB          65         MOV     A,CHAR
0058 67          66         RRC     A
0059 AB          67         MOV     CHAR,A
005A 00          68         NOP                     ;NO-OPS NEEDED TO EQUALIZE EXECUTION TIME
005B 00          69         NOP                     ;\ OF INNER LOOP TO BE THE SAME AS THAT OF
005C 00          70         NOP                     ; \ SUBROUTINE CRTOUT.
005D EA4E        71         DJNZ    COUNT,CI2
005F FB          72         MOV     A,CHAR
0060 83          73         RET                     ;CHARACTER COMPLETE
                 74 ;
0061 0453        75 CI4:    JMP     CI3             ;JUMP CONSUMES SAME TIME AS 'CPL C; NOP' SEQUENCE.
                 76 ;
                 77 $EJECT
```

TIMELO (the "#" means TIMELO is treated as an address) into a register or memory location called R1. Next, the data stored at that address is moved to the accumulator (line 22) and from there into a memory location called DLAYLO. Register R1 is then made to point to the next memory location (line 24), and the process is repeated for a value that is now stored at DLAYHI. The result is that a 2-byte counter, DLAY (HI = high-order byte, LO = low-order byte), is now available as a counter to determine when the proper amount of time has elapsed.

The value of DLAY will determine the data's transmission rate. In a system where the configuration of I/O devices were known in advance, DLAYHI and DLAYLO would contain a 2-byte constant value stored in ROM for use each time a half-bit delay were needed. In the system described here, however, software written to replace hardware automatically determines what this value must be to communicate with the system's particular I/O device.

Two things affect bit duration. The first is the amount of time (in machine cycles, for this discussion) required to execute the primary loop in the CRTIN and CRTOUT subroutines. These routines, as shown in Table 1 (lines 41-42 and 68-70), are designed so that they require the same number of machine cycles to execute. (NOP—for "no operation"—instructions are frequently used to insert delays in loops such as these where timing is critical to proper performance.) Specifically, the CRTIN and CRTOUT subroutines require 17 machine cycles each to execute.

The second factor affecting the duration of each bit is the amount of time spent in the HBWAIT subroutine. This is a direct function of the value of DLAY. The HBWAIT subroutine, of course, has a certain amount of fixed overhead, so that even if DLAY were zero (an impossible situation for all practical purposes), it would still use 26 machine cycles to execute twice. This, combined with the 17 machine cycles of the particular character-handling subroutine (CRTIN or CRTOUT), yields a software overhead of 43 machine cycles. Each conditional jump taken by the routine as a result of the size of DLAY adds a total of four more machine cycles to the bit-time. This results in a total bit-time of 43 + 4N, where N is the value of DLAY.

It should be noted here that these values are valid only for the MCS-48 and the instructions in Table 1. Such factors are machine-dependent; the designer has to determine the number of machine cycles a specific subroutine will require for a particular microprocessor. At very slow data rates with large delays in DLAY, 4N becomes so large that the fixed overhead of 43 machine cycles is virtually negligible. The reverse is true for very fast data rates. The fixed overhead becomes sufficiently significant so that it must be taken into account. It can, in fact, limit the microprocessor's maximum transmission rate.

The algorithm for computing the time parameter detects when the processor receives the start-bit transition (from 1 to 0) for the identification character. It continues monitoring the serial-input signal while periodically incrementing a counter until the serial-input

5. Character input. *The CRTIN subroutine follows the same general rules as CRTOUT but differs in that the input loop need only be executed 9 rather than 11 times.*

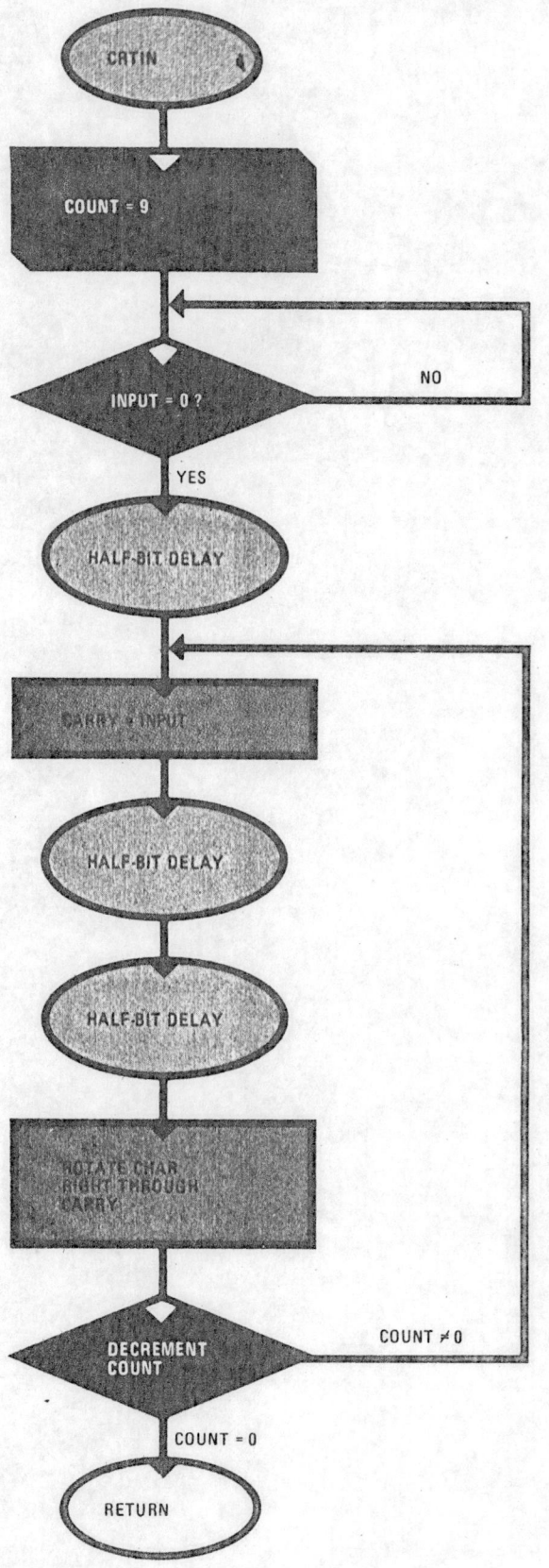

Table 2 Rate identification

```
LOC  OBJ        LINE        SOURCE STATEMENT

                 78 ;BAUDID BAUD RATE IDENTIFICATION SUBROUTINE
                 79 ;       EXPECTS A <SPACE> (ASCII 20H) TO BE RECEIVED FROM THE CONSOLE.
                 80 ;       THE LENGTH OF THE INITIAL ZERO LEVEL (SIX BITS WIDE) IS MEASURED
                 81 ;       IN ORDER TO DETERMINE THE DATA RATE FOR FUTURE COMMUNICATIONS.
0063 4663        82 BAUDID: JNT1     BAUDID   ;VERIFY THAT THE "ONE" LEVEL HAS BEEN ESTABLISHED
                 83                           ; \ AS THE CRT IS POWERING UP
0065 BE00        84         MOV      DLAYLO,#0
0067 BD00        85         MOV      DLAYHI,#0
0069 5669        86 BRI1:   JT1      BRI1     ;MONITOR SERIAL INPUT LINE UNTIL START BIT IS RECEIVED
006B 2356        87         MOV      A,#86
006D 07          88 BRI2:   DEC      A
006E 966D        89         JNZ      BRI2
0070 2305        90 BRI3:   MOV      A,#5
0072 07          91 BRI4:   DEC      A
0073 9672        92         JNZ      BRI4
0075 FE          93         MOV      A,DLAYLO
0076 17          94         INC      A
0077 AE          95         MOV      DLAYLO,A
0078 967B        96         JNZ      BRI5
007A 1D          97         INC      DLAYHI
007B 4670        98 BRI5:   JNT1     BRI3
                 99                           ;<DLAYHI>&<DLAYLO> NOW CORRESPONDS TO BIT TIME.
007D B920       100         MOV      R1,#TIMELO
007F FE         101         MOV      A,DLAYLO
0080 17         102         INC      A
0081 A1         103         MOV      @R1,A
0082 19         104         INC      R1
0083 FD         105         MOV      A,DLAYHI
0084 17         106         INC      A
0085 A1         107         MOV      @R1,A
0086 83         108         RET
                109 ;
                110 ;CRTTST CRT INTERFACE TEST.  WHEN CALLED, AWAITS THE SPACE BAR BEING PRESSED ON
                111 ;       THE SYSTEM CONSOLE, AND THEN RESPONDS WITH A DATA RATE VERIFICATION
                112 ;       MESSAGE.  THEREAFTER, CHARACTERS TYPED ON THE KEYBOARD ARE ECHOED
                113 ;       ON THE DISPLAY TUBE.  WHEN A BREAK KEY IS TYPED, THE ROUTINE IS
                114 ;       RE-STARTED, ALLOWING A DIFFERENT BAUD RATE TO BE SELECTED ON THE CRT.
0087 B940       115 CRTTST: ORL      P1,#40H           ;CRTPIN MUST BE HIGH BETWEEN CHARACTERS
0089 1463       116         CALL     BAUDID   ;IDENTIFY DATA RATE USED BY TERMINAL
008B 1495       117         CALL     SIGNON   ;OUTPUT SIGNON MESSAGE AT RATE DETECTED
008D 1446       118 ECHO:   CALL     CRTIN    ;READ NEXT KEYSTROKE INTO REGISTER C
                119                           ;CHECK IF CHARACTER WAS A <BREAK> (ASCII 00H)
008F C687       120         JZ       CRTTST   ;IF SO, RE-IDENTIFY DATA RATE
                121                           ;THIS ALLOWS ANOTHER RATE TO BE SELECTED ON CRT
0091 142C       122         CALL     CRTOUT   ;OTHERWISE COPY REGISTER C TO THE SCREEN
0093 048D       123         JMP      ECHO     ;CONTINUE INDEFINITELY (UNTIL BREAK)
                124 ;
                125 ;SIGNON WRITES A SIGN-ON MESSAGE TO THE CRT AT WHAT SHOULD BE THE CORRECT RATE.
                126 ;       IF THE MESSAGE IS UNINTELLIGIBLE. . . WELL, SO IT GOES.
0095 BCA1       127 SIGNON: MOV      INDEX,#STRNG   ;LOAD START OF SIGN-ON MESSAGE
0097 FC         128 S1:     MOV      A,INDEX  ;GET NEXT CHARACTER
0078 A3         129         MOVP     A,@A
0099 C6A0       130         JZ       SIGNRT   ;RETURN IF SIGN-ON COMPLETE
009B 142C       131         CALL     CRTOUT   ;ELSE OUTPUT CHARACTER TO CRT
009D 1C         132         INC      INDEX    ;INDEX POINTER
009E 0497       133         JMP      S1       ;ECHO NEXT CHARACTER
00A0 83         134 SIGNRT: RET
                135 ;
00A1            136 STRNG   EQU      LOW $
00A1 0D        137         DB       0DH,0AH  ;<CR><LF>
00A2 0A
00A3 4D43532D  138         DB       'MCS-48 SIGN-ON MESSAGE'
00A7 34382053
00AB 4947452D
00AF 4F4E204D
00B3 45535341
00B7 4745
00B9 0D        139         DB       0DH,0AH  ;<CR><LF>
00BA 0A
00BB 00        140         DB       00H      ;END-OF-STRING ESCAPE CODE
                141
                142         END
```

```
USER SYMBOLS
BAUDID 0063    BITSI 0009    BITSO 000B    BRI1  0069    BRI2  006D    BRI3  0070    BRI4  0072    BRI5  007B
CHAR   0003    CI1   0048    CI2   004E    CI3   0053    CI4   0061    CO1   0030    CO2   0036    CO3   003A
COUNT  0002    CRTIN 0046    CRTOUT 002C   CRTTST 0087   DLAYHI 0005   DLAYLO 0006   ECHO  008D    HBD1  0027
HBWAIT 0020    INDEX 0004    S1    0097    SIGNON 0095   SIGNRT 00A0   STRNG 00A1    TIMEHI 0021   TIMELO 0020

ASSEMBLY COMPLETE.   NO ERRORS
```

data returns to binary 1. When this happens, the counter holds the value of N (the number of conditional jumps taken in HBWAIT) corresponding to the data rate that would produce an initial 0 the same length as the one detected.

BAUDID (Table 2) first sets the variables DLAYHI and DLAYLO to 0 and then enters a wait loop until the user types a key on the console. By agreement, the first key typed must be the space bar, which produces an ASCII code of 20 hexadecimal. To the processor, this will appear as a single 0 start bit, 5 data-bit 0s, a 1, and another 0. This means that the first bits received will be 0s (remember that the start bit is defined as a 0). The subroutine BAUDID must treat the first information it receives as requiring 6 bit-times, since it has no way yet of knowing the processing time the 6 bits will actually need—individually or together. Since it is certain that these 6 bits require a minimum of 258 machine cycles (remember that there are 43 cycles per bit in overhead software), BAUDID now goes into a 258-machine-cycle loop.

At the end of that loop, the software checks to see if a binary 1 has been received. If the data is still low, TIMELO is incremented by one. As has already been shown, each increment of TIMELO causes four machine cycles to be added to the total bit time. If a TIMELO value of 1 were selected, the first 6 bits would re-quire 24 cycles in addition to the overhead. So, BAUDID is set up so that it increments TIMELO by one every 24 machine cycles until the data being received finally becomes a 1. If TIMELO exceeds the value of 255, it overflows into the variable TIMEHI, which will then contain the high-order byte of the total time delay needed, in addition to the overhead, to achieve the data rate of the specific I/O device being used.

There is one more step. CRTIN and CRTOUT use the HBWAIT subroutine to implement a half-bit wait. The subroutine (in Table 1, lines 21-29) illustrates how the software decrements a counter before making the test to see if time has expired. (This is the function of the DJNZ instruction, which means Decrement, Jump Not Zero.) Therefore, TIMELO/TIMEHI must be incremented by one before they are usable by the HBWAIT subroutine. This is handled by the code at lines 102 and 106 of Table 2.

The automatic bit-rate-identification capability shown here is not available from hardware alone. This task gives a prime example of software's utility as a replacement for hardware—especially when cost is a critical factor. On the other hand, in networks where performance is critical or where the CPU is heavily committed to numerous tasks, the systems designer would probably have to depend on peripheral chips to achieve acceptable system throughput. ▪

Microtalk's maxi applications could benefit companies

Frank J. Derfler, State of the Art, Herdon, Va.

The computer hobbyist, with a stake in the advance of information transfer, has made strides that could help corporate users save money.

This morning I dialed from my home-based terminal into my electronic mail box, collected a few messages, and dropped off some prerecorded notes that I had at home in ASCII disk files. Then I ran a program that was too big to run in my terminal's memory. Finally, I down-line loaded a Basic program from the host into my terminal for use later in the day.

These operations are usually attributed to large corporate networks, but in this case, the host was a microcomputer that cost its owner about $3,500 for all the hardware and software, and it cost the user nothing. The host is an Apple II, operated by an individual who can barely program and who thinks a register is something you keep cash in. Yet it is not a unique system. There are about 200 such operations running on microcomputers nationwide at this moment.

The small, independent operators are doing some big things with both message and program transfer. Creative corporate data communications specialists might benefit from a careful look at these inexpensive microcomputer options for their own dedicated information-transfer networks.

Microcomputer-based message systems can serve the needs of special sales and development teams, traveling executives and engineers, and small general business users. They can provide low-cost, quickly established, and private alternatives to more complex electronic mail or order-entry systems. Their ability to run and transfer programs can provide great flexibility without disrupting operations on larger equipment. A microcomputer message system might fulfill a big need in a company's data communications program.

Electronic mail systems were already sophisticated when the first microcomputer hit the market. Ironically, the developers of the first microcomputer-based message systems started almost from scratch. In the microcomputer field, Ward Christensen and Randy Suess are generally credited with instituting in Chicago the first dependable electronic mail system in early 1978. They called it the Computer Bulletin Board System (CBBS), because it was little more than the automation of an actual cork bulletin board at their local computer club. Individuals using any kind of ASCII terminal with a modem dialed into the CBBS and posted short messages. These messages could be read by anyone, although they might be addressed to an individual or special group or everyone (ALL).

The hardware consisted of an IEEE standard S-100 bus-type mainframe and various S-100 circuit cards from different manufacturers. An Intel 8080 microprocessor CPU card, an input/output card, 24 kbytes of 8-bit memory, a disk controller, an auto-answer modem, and a read-only memory (ROM) made up the host. A couple of 8-inch floppy disk drives provided the file space. Only one user at a time could access the host, but in spite of this, the number of users multiplied almost daily. As the word spread, the CBBS grew rapidly.

The CBBS software was designed to run under an operating system marketed by Digital Research called CP/M, but users of other systems wanted to set up the same sort of message service. Soon, software for the Apple, called ABBS (Apple Bulletin Board System),

and Forum-80 software for the Radio Shack TRS-80 computers appeared from different sources. The sophistication of this type of software has increased tremendously, but the price of a complete system-software package on disk has never exceeded $150.

Electronic message applications

Microcomputer-based systems now have many features that would be appreciated by any corporate electronic mail user. Frequent users can be notified if they have mail when they sign on. Experienced users can elect an "expert" mode that bypasses the operator instructions, while novice users can get extensive help from the machine. Programs can be run on the host, and the program listings can be up-line loaded into (or down-line loaded from) the host from the remote user's terminal, creating a software-exchange service despite the incompatibility of the various disk and tape formats. Messages can be protected by passwords, and public messages can be sorted and quickly scanned. The response time of these systems is relatively fast (less than 5 seconds), particularly to anyone used to the frequent delays in large timeshared networks.

These message-exchange, software-exchange, and bulletin board systems (most hobbyist networks have all of these services in varying degrees) exist only because of their operators' personal interests. Many systems are used by special-interest groups on a nationwide basis; for example, two networks support medical technology and medical training information, and one exists for individuals interested in photography. The number of special-interest hosts is growing quickly. Soon, any hobby or activity that can support several active newsletters may have its own microcomputer bulletin board message service.

As the number of available hosts and types of host software grows, so do the software and equipment to turn common microcomputers into very capable intelligent terminals for data communications. Such software already exists for NorthStar, Radio Shack, and Apple computers. Data and text can be formatted using powerful word processors, saved on disk, and transmitted through modem ports when appropriate. Incoming data can be saved either as operating programs or as various kinds of files.

Some microcomputers use compressed-data formats to speed throughput over long-distance lines. Since this software is usually written in machine-language code, it operates quickly and with little overhead, as opposed to programs written in such higher-level languages as Basic that use extensive operating systems like CP/M. Typical software prices range from $35 to $150 dollars. A complete two-disk data communications/word processing system can cost as little as $3,500. Part of this cost, about $750, allows a user to put a TRS-80 on-line as a terminal, capable of saving enormous quantities of received data on cassette tape at up to 1.2 kbit/s. Even at that low price, which includes the modem, this machine does not require an operator with special training.

Fallout

The use of communicating microcomputers has had a large impact on the modem market. Some bulletin systems have recorded over 20,000 users in under two years, indicating a strong demand for low-cost modems. This demand has been answered by a variety of large and small manufacturers, whose low-speed (0 to 300 bit/s), acoustically coupled, orginate/answer devices sell for less than $200. Directly connected modems are becoming more popular as prices drop.

More-sophisticated operators use modems configured on printed circuit cards for direct connection to their computer's data bus. These modem cards provide auto-answer and auto-dial capabilities plus full keyboard selection of the data rate, parity, word length, and originate/answer mode. Some devices, like the D.C. Hayes Micromodem designed for the Apple II computer, come with an on-board ROM to ensure the integration of modem and microcomputer without local software tailoring. The Micromodem is essentially a "plug-in-and-go" device. Others are less machine-specific, but they usually come with program listings for the more common computers to implement the modem's features. Prices for these sophisticated hardware-software combinations hover around $350.

Microcomputer smart terminal software

The following programs allow microcomputers to operate as intelligent terminals. The microcomputer communicates with a host, saves the received data, transmits files from disk, and allows keyboard selection of

transmission options such as speed, parity, and number of stop bits. Most packages include programs for file creation, reading, and editing. The suppliers, which are listed, offer various modem types (for example, those that connect to a data bus or are externally fed through an RS-232-C port).

The ASCII Express ($35) supports the Apple II microcomputer and is designed for interface to the D.C. Hayes Micromodem II, a bus-connected modem. (Bill Blue, Box 1318, Lakeside, Calif. 92040)

Telestar ($30) is made for the NorthStar Horizon computer. Allowing full service as an intelligent terminal, it also provides a remote user full access to the Horizon computer. (Leonard E. Garcia, 3517 Herschel Ave., Dallas, Tex. 75219)

Terminal Control Program ($30), a terminal program for the Radio Shack TRS-80, allows the user many options, such as how the programs are stored on disk and retrieved. Since it is modular, it can be called as a subroutine, run, and then dumped. This allows for easy integration into word processing or other communications programs. The software is available in disk form. (The Bottom Shelf Inc., P.O. Box 49014, Atlanta, Ga. 30359)

The ST80 Series ($25 to $150) is another group of programs for the TRS-80. This collection of programs includes packages for every level of user. An elementary ST80 program allows a very inexpensive TRS-80 to serve as a dumb terminal. The most sophisticated program (ST80 III) allows a TRS-80 to function as a terminal for the largest IBM and Harris mainframes that require very specific protocols. Most other programs described in this article will not work with IBM or Harris hardware. (Lance Micklus, 217 South Union St., Burlington, Vt. 05401)

Apple Bulletin Board Systems ($75), a complete software package written for the Apple II microcomputer, can transfer and run programs and control message passwords, among other functions. It is available on disk. (Bill Blue, Box 1318, Lakeside, Calif. 92040)

Forum-80 ($150 license fee) is a complete software package for the Radio Shack TRS-80 microcomputer. It has most features of the Apple Bulletin Board System and is available on disk. (Bill Abney, 7600 East 48th Terrace, Kansas City, Mo. 64129)

Remote Console ($30) is a series of programs designed for microcomputers using the NorthStar operating system or NorthStar disk drives and CP/M. The message system program is in Basic. This software, which is available on disk, has message handling and can run programs, but has limited program-transfer ability. (The Microstuf Company, P.O. Box 33337, Decatur, Ga. 30033)

Computer Bulletin Board System is the original microcomputer software program that runs under CP/M. (While this package is not a commercial enterprise, it is available through Randy Suess at 1930 Bradley, Chicago, Ill. 60613)

The new network roles of the statistical mux

Joseph Visvader, Timeplex Inc., Rochelle Park, N.J.

Part one of this report explores the effects of multiplexer enhancements in programming, monitoring, reconfiguration, and diagnostics. The second part introduces the multiplexer's newest talent—switching.

Statistical multiplexer technology has been dynamic. Since its inception, the multiplexer has evolved into one of the most versatile data communications building blocks, closely tracking the needs of growing networks to adapt to increased traffic and terminal types.

The most pronounced areas of multiplexer development have been monitoring, configuration programming, flow control, and the handling of data channels. However, reversing a recent trend, vendors are now de-emphasizing data compression in multiplexer operation because it has not proved as efficient as originally expected.

One of the most attractive features of the statistical multiplexer is its ability to concentrate data simultaneously from both asynchronous and synchronous terminals. Additionally, it can accommodate many line types, which may vary in channel speed, stop-bit combination (for asynchronous traffic), character code, and parity (odd, even, or none).

However, while the statistical multiplexer can serve different data terminals, changing the terminal mix has not always been easy. Until recently, each data channel had to be preprogrammed. Traffic from asynchronous terminals had to access data channels equipped with a special interface chip—the UART (universal asynchronous receive and transmit), while synchronous traffic required data channels configured with a USRT (universal synchronous receive and transmit) interface chip. Because of the difficulty in changing the channel interface chips, the statistical multiplexer was more or less limited to the mix of terminals present when the network first went into operation.

Within the past few years, however, the need for greater flexibility has been met by the USART (universal synchronous/asynchronous receive and transmit) chip, which has replaced the UART and USRT on each data channel. It allows each channel to carry either asynchronous or synchronous traffic. With the old UART/USRT, configuration programming generally allowed only one line type (picked from a relatively limited menu of 10 to 20) for each data channel. Increasing the size of the menu was possible, but often involved tedious additional programming. With the USART, users can select from a combination of 16 speeds, 3 stop-bit combinations, 4 character codes, and 3 parity selections—a total of 576 combinations.

In the past, adding data channels was also a complicated procedure. Although it was relatively simple to physically add channels, it was not as easy to add memory to counter the increase in input data feeding into the data link. Buffer pool memory was comparatively expensive, and there was little room on printed circuit boards to fit extra memory. As a result, upgrading the multiplexer came to mean that the amount of buffer pool memory per data channel decreased. The frequency with which the buffer pool experienced overloading correspondingly increased. This taxed the limited input flow control of the multiplexer.

Advances in LSI (large-scale integration) technology have since eliminated buffer contention as the price

113

1. Buffer overflow. *If all five users request extensive output simultaneously, the data surge overflows the multiplexer's buffer. Input flow control is needed.*

TERMINAL
1.2 KBIT/S

TERMINAL
1.2 KBIT/S

CRT
2.4 KBIT/S

CRT
4.8 KBIT/S

DATA
LINK
9.6
KBIT/S

CPU

MULTIPLEXER   MULTIPLEXER

RJE
9.6 KBIT/S

19.2 KBIT/S TOTAL

for increasing the number of data channels, and now an enormous amount of memory can be incorporated in the statistical multiplexer buffer pool at relatively low cost. For example, just four years ago, a typical buffer pool was 16 to 32 kbytes. Now, statistical multiplexers have about 4 kbytes per data channel—often with 100 kbytes of memory in the entire unit.

However, this increase in buffer memory has also increased the propagation delay of data through the statistical multiplexer. With more space on the queue feeding data into the channel, each data bit has to spend more time moving along this longer queue. But this is still preferable to having a data bit stuck in an external memory device waiting for an overloaded multiplexer buffer to clear.

Actually, the tremendous growth in statistical multiplexer memory has allowed these devices to become, effectively, peripheral memory for data terminals and the CPU. Consequently, terminal devices can more quickly free their own memory and devote it to computation rather than communications. This trend of placing more and more memory in statistical multiplexers

2. Input flow control. *Two methods are commonly employed to handle input flow control by the multiplexer. One is to drop the clear-to-send (CTS) signal—pin 5 of* the RS-232-C interface (A). The other involves in-band signaling between the multiplexer and the connected device (B). Here, the ASCII X-off signaling code is used.

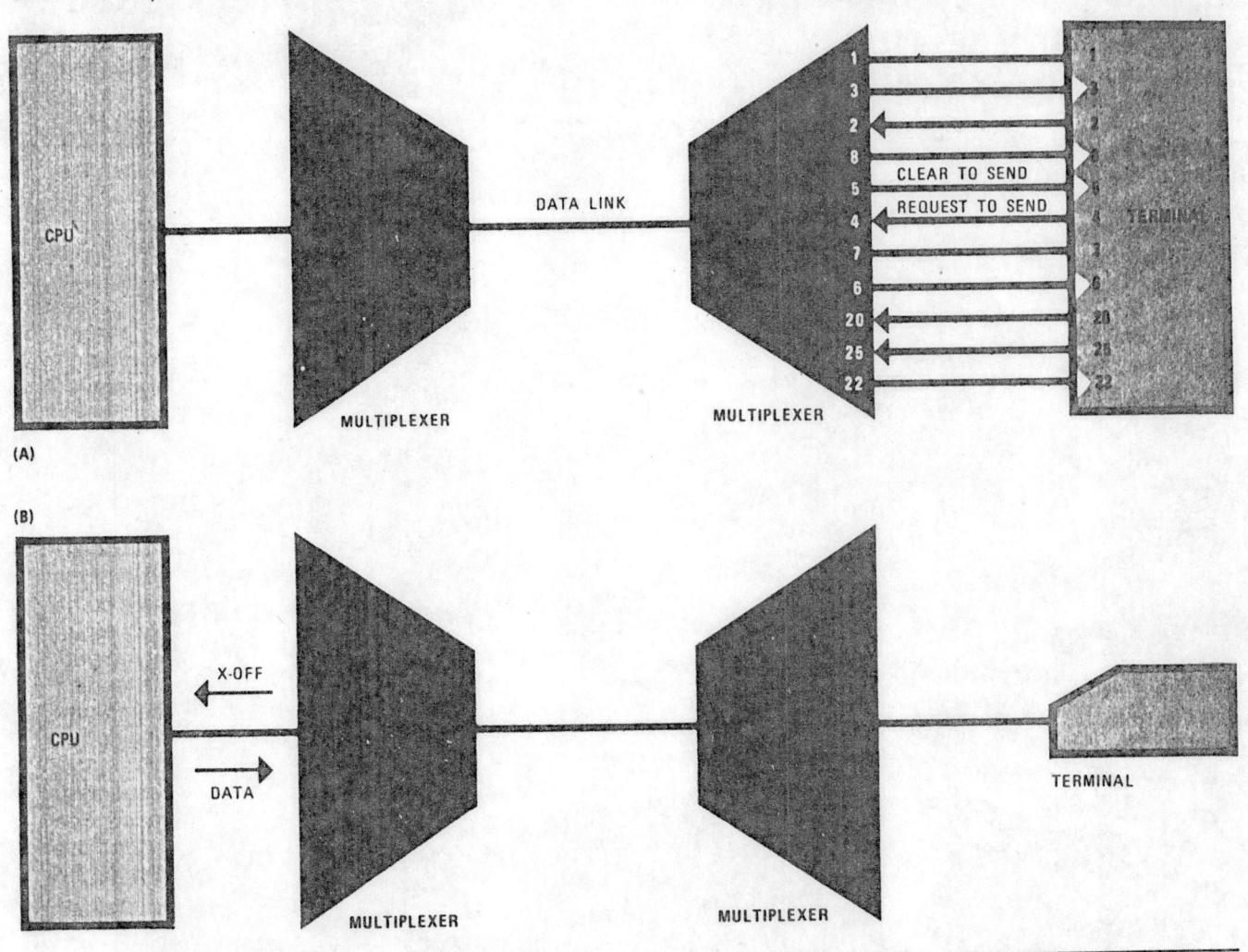

(A)

(B)

will most likely continue. As higher capacity data links (based, for example, on lightwave technology) become available, vendors will introduce more and more high-speed terminals to use them.

However, as the statistical multiplexer gains greater data storage capability, it also risks losing more data in the event of a failure. The true advantage of a larger buffer pool will be realized only if there is a corresponding improvement in multiplexer reliability.

Controlling data flow

Enhancements are being added to the statistical multiplexer that facilitate data traffic control and end-to-end message integrity. Even if communications links are performing according to specification, data can still be lost if transmission rates are improperly matched to the data rate of connected devices. Thus, the pacing and throttling of traffic is critical.

While statistical multiplexers typically do not manage network traffic, they are participating more and more in this function. To prevent data loss, the multiplexer must regulate traffic flow into and out of the network.

Input flow control requires that the multiplexer monitor an external device feeding it. All statistical multiplexers match incoming traffic to the data link rate by buffering. However, when the number of bits arriving during a fixed time period exceeds the number of bits that the link can transmit during this same period, the buffer pool can fill rapidly to capacity. The statistical multiplexer must regulate the incoming flow to stop data loss due to buffer overloading.

Figure 1 shows a typical situation requiring flow control. Here, five users at different terminals on a network simultaneously request long records from the CPU. The computer ports pump out data at the different terminal speeds, and the cumulative flow into the multiplexer is 19.2 kbit/s, double the data link rate. The buffer memory in the multiplexer at the CPU end will fill at a rate of 9.6 kbit/s and will, unless the incoming traffic is throttled, overflow.

Strange as it may seem, for a long time, many statistical multiplexers simply ignored the problem of input flow control. When there was a significantly large surge of input data, the buffer pool simply overflowed and data was lost. Subsequent data, arriving during an overflow condition, was also lost.

The economy achieved by omitting flow-control procedures was a false one. Without it, an end user would see "holes" in the data stream delivered to him. Statistical multiplexers that did address the problem of input flow control used one of two possible methods: a physical layer protocol (handshaking between the external data device and the multiplexer) and "in-band" signaling (intradevice communications over the same frequency used for transmitting data).

Figure 2A illustrates the first method. The various RS-232-C pins in one arrangement connect a statistical multiplexer and a terminal. Here, the multiplexer might wait until its buffer pool was filled to, say, 90 percent capacity and then drop the clear-to-send (CTS) flag, whereupon the terminal would halt its output. The input flow to the multiplexer would be effectively throttled.

The use of in-band signaling for the same task is shown in Figure 2B. When buffer use is high (because of a data surge from the central processing unit), the multiplexer sends back a character or a sequence of characters. The CPU recognizes this as a command to shut off. (Typically, the in-band signaling characters include the ASCII X-off.)

Both techniques accomplished input flow control, but they achieved it at the expense of network flexibility. The input flow-control procedure was a "box parameter"; that is, it was specified the same for all data channels and frozen in programming at the factory. The statistical multiplexer typically could not accommodate different input flow-control procedures on different data channels, and, as a result, the multiplexer was constrained to certain types of external data devices. If the data communications manager wanted to change the network and integrate devices not matched to the programmed flow-control procedure, he had to bring the entire network down (put out of service) and have it reprogrammed. Even with in-band signaling, anything beyond the ASCII command was often considered special order.

In today's statistical multiplexers, input flow control is no longer a box parameter—separate flow-control procedures can be programmed for the different data channels. As a result, the multiplexer configuration can accommodate many types of terminals (ASCII, EBCDIC, and even terminals on modem tail circuits). Also, the input flow-control procedure can be easily reprogrammed in the field while the network stays in operation. In fact, the individual data channel being reprogrammed generally need not be brought down.

Output control

Output flow control requires that an external data device monitor the traffic coming to it from the statistical multiplexer. For example, a programmer located at a buffered printer might run a program at the CPU. The CPU sends back a long report that may fill the printer's buffer before being completely printed. The external device, the printer, must regulate the CPU-generated traffic from the multiplexer to avoid an overflow of its own buffer.

Statistical multiplexers' handling of this problem has greatly improved in recent years. In the past, controlling the flow of traffic out of a multiplexer to such an external device was extremely difficult because of the "handshaking" required to initiate, maintain, and control such communications. When the CPU was ready to transmit its output to the printer, it raised the request-to-send (RTS) flag (a pin connection of the RS-232-C interface). The first multiplexer would respond with clear-to-send (CTS), after which the CPU would begin to transmit its data. If the printer's buffer became too full, the printer would transmit a halt signal. This could be a busy signal (pin 25 of the RS-232-C interface), the ASCII X-off, or an equivalent command. The multiplexer would return the halt signal through the CPU-based multiplexer to the CPU, which would respond by halting transmission.

This approach to output flow control has two defi-

ciencies. First, it is not a smooth throttling of data flow—traffic can be initiated and terminated, but the flow out of the terminal-end multiplexer cannot be matched with the variations in the printer's buffer availability. Second, this flow-control procedure often fails. Although data generated by the CPU is halted, there is typically enough data already in the multiplexers' buffer pools to cause the printer to overflow (while the halt signal is transmitting back to the CPU).

These weaknesses have since been corrected through the addition of microprocessor-based intelligence. Now when the printer generates a halt signal, the multiplexer's processor recognizes it and responds by halting its data flow to the printer. The intelligent processor then relays the halt signal to the central processor, which shuts off.

The multiplexer's ability to recognize a command from an external device and take the appropriate action is a major step toward improved flow control. That the transmitted data is no longer transparent to the multiplexer indicates a merging of functions between the statistical multiplexer and the terminal controller. This has been under way for some time.

A word of caution, however. A multiplexer that recognizes and acts on control commands may not, of itself, provide improved output flow control. Users need to carefully evaluate commercially available multiplexers to judge overall control performance. For example, the time taken by the multiplexer to recognize the halt signal and stop data flow is variable. This period should be brief (no longer than two to four character durations, which is typical of remaining buffer availability when overloading is sensed). This usually requires that the multiplexer process the halt signal at an intelligent interface, rather than place it in a queue into the centralized microprocessor.

Another variable is the procedure by which the multiplexer forwards the halt signal to the CPU. The CPU may not recognize the halt signal issued by the multiplexer. (For example, the multiplexer responds to a busy signal, while the CPU responds to X-off.) And if the CPU is not shut off, using the proper control signal, it will flood the buffer pools of both multiplexers. Some intelligent multiplexers can now translate their own halt signals to one recognized by the CPU before forwarding. Or they can restrict the access of the CPU to the buffer pool (through input flow control).

Multiplexer monitoring

Monitoring network activity is necessary to minimize network downtime. By taking advantage of the multiplexer's ability to sense and report abnormal conditions, network managers can take corrective action in time to avert possibly catastrophic failures.

Traditionally, the statistical multiplexer has been a center for two types of network monitoring: gathering statistics and diagnostic testing. It collects a number of statistical measurements, any one of which may indicate weakness in a network component. Its diagnostic tests, on the other hand, are aimed at locating the source of aberrant network behavior.

In early statistical multiplexers, monitoring was lim-

3. Loopback tests. The basic loopback tests performed by the multiplexer include the local data channel (A), the remote data channel (B), and the data link (C).

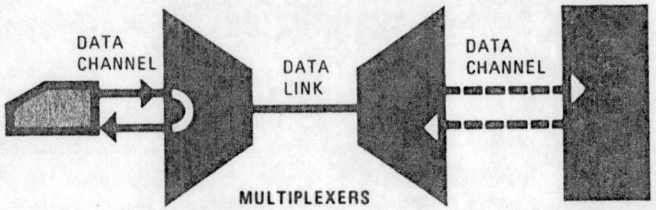

(A) LOCAL DATA CHANNEL LOOPBACK TEST

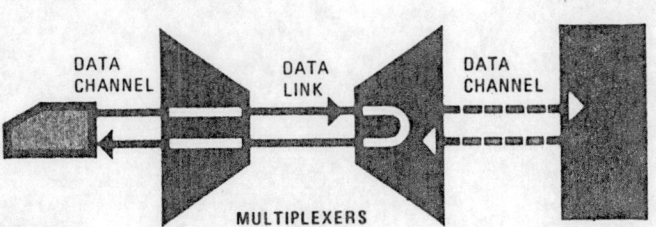

(B) REMOTE DATA CHANNEL LOOPBACK TEST

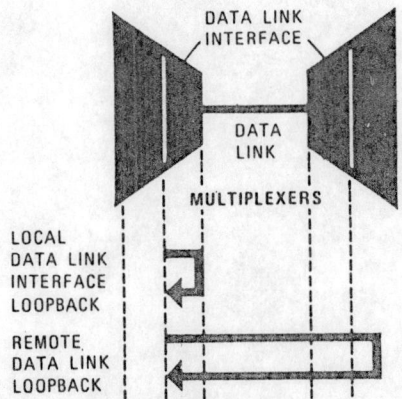

(C) DATA LINK LOOPBACK TEST

ited in scope. The preprogrammed routines could collect relatively few statistics, and most of these were related to data link integrity. Typical measurements were the number of line hits (errors) and retransmission attempts, outage durations, block error rates, and possibly, statistics about the multiplexer's buffer use.

Similarly, diagnostics were of the most basic type and usually probed line continuity, as shown by the loopback tests illustrated in Figure 3. The local data-channel loopback tested the interface between a data channel and the multiplexer to which it was connected. To execute it, a terminal generated a test message, and the results were compared with a received echo. In like manner, the remote data-channel loopback tested the interface between the multiplexer (remote to the terminal) and the central processing unit. The data-link loopbacks, similarly, tested the interfaces between the multiplexers and the data link. A test mes-

4. Improved diagnostics. *The testing of modem tail circuits is one of the new diagnostic capabilities found in statistical multiplexers. Signals from either the front panel or a supervisory terminal instruct the multiplexer to generate a test message, which is then looped back through the tail circuit and the device connected to it.*

sage was generated by the multiplexer, transmitted, and compared with the received echo. These monitoring activities were initiated by commands entered at the front panel of the multiplexer.

In order to obtain statistics from earlier multiplexers, data communications managers had to wade through much programming, key in codes, and hit buttons on the front panel. They had to memorize the many commands needed to obtain a statistic. Then, the measurements that were finally assembled came out one at a time. Furthermore, they were displayed only on the front panel, not summarized on hard copy. The loopback diagnostic tests initiated from the front panel allowed a degree of troubleshooting, but fault isolation was rather crude. If a test failed, there was no way of proceeding, via the front panel, to a more detailed level to locate the point of failure.

Data communications managers demanded better network-monitoring capabilities, so the statistical multiplexer was upgraded in this area. The number and scope of collectible statistics increased, including detailed multiplexer measurements of buffer and data-channel usage. The front panel remained the focal point of monitoring, but functions were enhanced through the addition of a "control port." This permitted the attachment of a receive-only terminal to a multiplexer data channel.

The statistical multiplexer could be preprogrammed to output certain statistics to the control port at specific times. And while the control port occupied a data channel, it allowed the multiplexer to provide an entire listing of measurements, all at once and on hard copy. Unfortunately, being a receive-only device, the control port could not provide statistics on command.

The control port has evolved into a more sophisticated supervisory port, capable of performing a wider variety of monitoring tasks. Frequently, the supervisory port now does not waste a data channel when connected to the multiplexer; it is linked by separate cable. More importantly, the supervisory port now supports interactive terminals that can receive output statistics automatically and input commands requesting specific statistics. In addition, the port can monitor the actual traffic on a given data channel.

These supervisory ports have also enhanced the multiplexer's diagnostic capability. The traditional loopback tests can still be initiated both from the front panel and through the supervisory port. In addition, when turned on, many multiplexers automatically perform a variety of testing procedures and continually examine interfaces and the integrity of programs controlling their operation. If any procedure fails, an alarm is typically activated on the front-panel display. The user can then, via the supervisory port, interrogate a multiplexer and determine the reason for failure. Commands issued through the supervisory port can often pinpoint failures down to the chip level.

Traditional loopback tests could not be performed effectively on terminals connected to a multiplexer from remote locations (on modem tail circuits), because they probed for continuity only through the multiplexer interfaces and often ignored faults on tail cir-

117

cuits. As Figure 4 illustrates, a supervisory port can now command the multiplexer to generate a test message and perform data-channel loopback tests on the tail circuits as well.

A common troublesome situation today is the presence of a variety of data equipment colocated in a data processing center and tied to a number of statistical multiplexers, each with its own supervisory port. Currently being developed to tie the operations of the different supervisory ports together is a supervisory port cluster controller. As envisioned, it will monitor and coordinate the different supervisory ports, allowing the multiplexers to gather, evaluate, and automatically store statistics. Evaluation reports and alarm indications, covering all connected devices, will also be issued automatically on the terminal connected to the cluster controller.

The multiplexer's front panel, the original focus of monitoring activity, has also been improved. It is now easier to read alphanumeric characters and to input commands. Rather than having to remember detailed instructions for specific statistics, the communications manager is prompted through a menu of possibilities displayed on the screen.

Data compression questions
In the development of any technology, some "advances" later appear to have had little impact. Just a few years ago, data compression, as one intelligent multiplexer feature, was believed to significantly increase the efficiency of data link operation. It supposedly removed the inherent redundancy in incoming data before it was put on the data link. With redundancy removed, it was expected that more link capacity would be available for "true" information transfer.

Two types of data compression were endorsed: redundant-character suppression and Huffman coding. Redundant-character suppression is a form of run-length coding. The multiplexer recognizes a stream of repeated characters and, rather than transmit the entire stream, sends only one character that indicates the stream's length. For Huffman coding, each incoming character is assigned a codeword, which is then transmitted on the data link. Codeword length, theoretically, is inversely proportional to the frequency of occurrence of the character; that is, frequently occurring characters have short codewords, and vice versa.

However, neither of these data-compression techniques achieved the advantage they initially promised. It is now generally held that compression of any kind can be done much more efficiently in the attached terminal or processor.

Experience has shown that redundant-character suppression improves data link efficiency only during periods of high traffic. (During such periods, there are enough characters in the multiplexer buffer pool to allow the recognition of a repeated-character stream.) In periods of low-to-moderate traffic, characters pass too quickly through the multiplexer for it to recognize a repetition. Intervals of high traffic simply do not occur often enough for character suppression to have any marked effect. Furthermore, as terminal intelligence

has grown, redundant-character suppression has often become a terminal-based capability.

Although redundant-character suppression may not help, it does not hurt communications efficiency. This is not true for Huffman coding. The improvement yielded with this technique is sensitive to the statistics of characters coming into the multiplexer. If there is a significant error between the actual character frequencies and those for which the Huffman coding algorithm is programmed, then data expansion, rather than compression, may result, leading to a loss in throughput. Suppose, for example, that Huffman coding is programmed in a multiplexer according to the statistics of ordinary English text. The character "Q," an infrequent character in this context, would receive a long codeword. However, say that a computer program inputted to the multiplexer denotes "Q" as a frequently occurring variable. As a result, a long codeword would be frequently transmitted on the data link, thereby degrading data throughput.

The sensitivity of Huffman coding to the actual character frequencies has been addressed in two ways: Either the multiplexer is constrained to only one type of traffic (such as newspaper English) or else it dynamically adapts to the actual statistics, trying to code characters based on real traffic. In the first case, communications managers are restricted to an inflexible configuration. In the second, a great deal of multiplexer processing overhead and time are devoted to the adaptation. These are hardly attractive trade-offs for obtaining marginally improved data link efficiency.

Configuration programming
Configuration programming was not easy in the early generations of statistical multiplexers. It was typically accomplished by DIP (dual in-line pin) switches, which had a fixed number of on/off positions. Each switch position could be coded as a binary 0 or 1. In most cases, there were eight positions per switch; thus, the DIP switch could be coded to represent a byte of data.

The switches were partitioned into groups, each corresponding to a given data channel. Every switch in a group corresponded to a data-channel parameter. In order to program or reprogram the multiplexer configuration, the network manager had to locate the appropriate DIP switch and then encode the new parameter value into the switch positions.

DIP switch programming accomplished its task, but it was cumbersome and required a great deal of expertise. Also, to reconfigure, the entire network had to be brought down; the mechanical switch had reliability problems; and there was no way of verifying that the multiplexer was interpreting the DIP switch code as the intended data-channel parameter.

Network managers subsequently used programmable read only memory/random access memory (PROM/RAM). They placed the initial configuration in PROM and then down-loaded it into a RAM. Programming in this manner lightened the burden on the data communications manager, particularly in making network changes. A routing table could be changed through the front panel merely by modifying the RAM

118

5. Tandem topology. *The tandem topology is one way to mix remote and local terminals at a single multiplexer. In this configuration, mux A assembles the inputs of muxes B and C and then transmits the combined data stream to mux 2. Mux 2 then segregates the traffic, sending the mux B input to mux 3 and the mux C input to mux 1.*

program, and the entire network did not have to be brought down to change a single channel parameter. Also, the memory available with the PROM/RAM cost less and occupied much less area. Consequently, many more data-channel parameters could be defined.

Although configuration programming with PROM did not suffer the mechanical failures associated with DIP switches, it was electrically unreliable. RAM is a volatile memory. Configuration changes made by reprogramming the RAM were typically erased if the statistical multiplexer lost power. Permanent changes to the configuration could be guaranteed only by creating a new PROM and replacing the one already in the statistical multiplexer.

Thus, ensuring reliability in the configuration program with PROMs resulted in the same physical inconvenience associated with DIP switches. (Putting in a new PROM also requires taking down the entire network.) Currently, the PROM/RAM has evolved into a RAM with battery backup. The PROM-based configuration has disappeared. The initial configuration programming, as well as subsequent modifications, now go directly into RAM, which is protected from erasure by the backup battery during a power outage.

Continuing cost and size reductions of LSI memory have allowed the definition of even more data-channel parameters. Less expensive memory has freed the data communications manager from having to remember the many individual commands associated with configuration programming. As with statistics gathering, either the front-panel display or the supervisory

port can prompt the manager through a menu of possibilities and help locate a given data channel, find out what channel parameter is to be set (or changed), and indicate the allowable values.

For some time, statistical multiplexers were used almost exclusively in point-to-point arrangements. As data communications managers began to understand the advantages of certain configurations, however, they employed more complex arrangements. There presently are a variety of topologies being implemented, including the tandem topology, the dual data-link topology, and several distributed topologies.

Topological variations

One of the more vexing issues in the point-to-point arrangement is the mixing of local data terminals (connected directly to the multiplexer) with those connected remotely via modem tail circuits. The tandem topology, shown in Figure 5, reduces the number of tail circuits (with their associated modem and line costs). In this case, the remote terminals are clustered and directly connected to a statistical multiplexer, mux B. Likewise, the local terminals are clustered and feed into another statistical multiplexer, mux A, via individual data channels, thus eliminating the modem tail circuits. At the central processor end, the traffic received at mux 2 is split into two streams. Traffic originating at mux B is routed to mux 3; traffic originating at mux C is routed to mux 1. The two traffic streams are then forwarded to the assigned central processor ports.

Under certain traffic conditions, the tandem topology

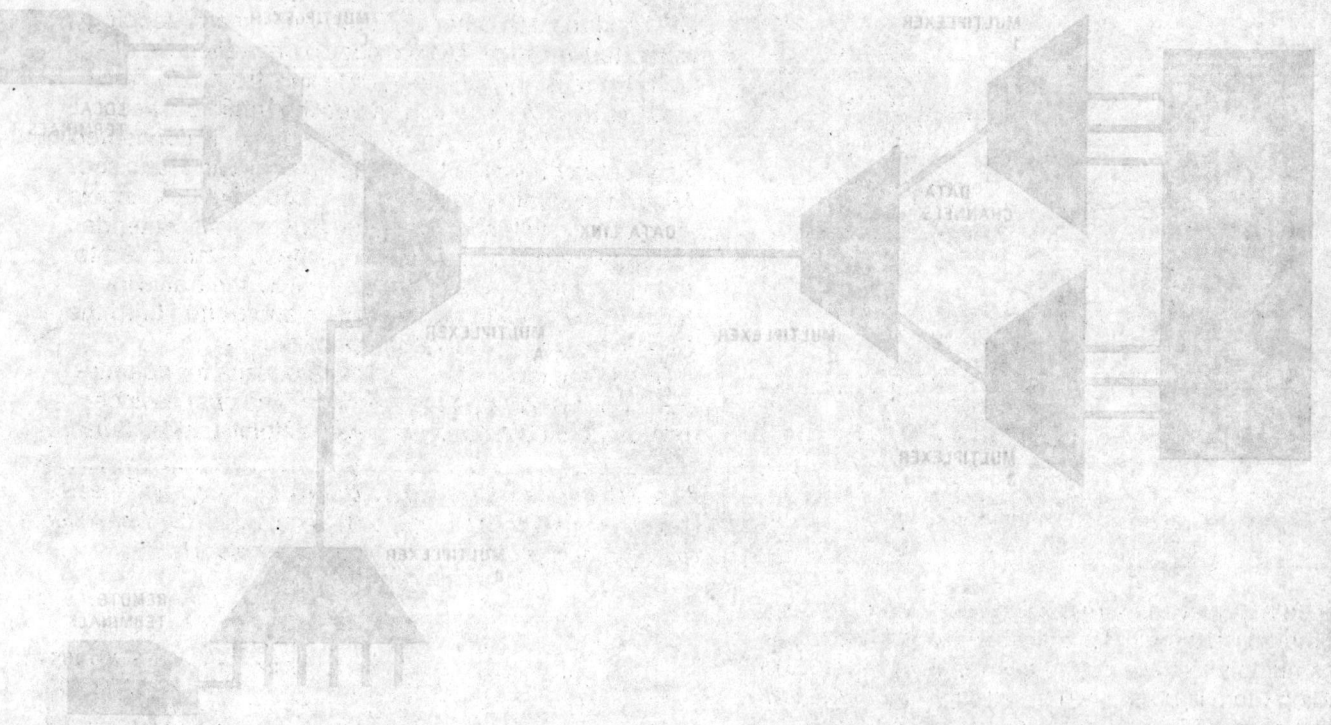

6. Dual data link. *In the dual data-link topology, the combined data streams of two remote multiplexers are demultiplexed by a single, CPU-based mux.*

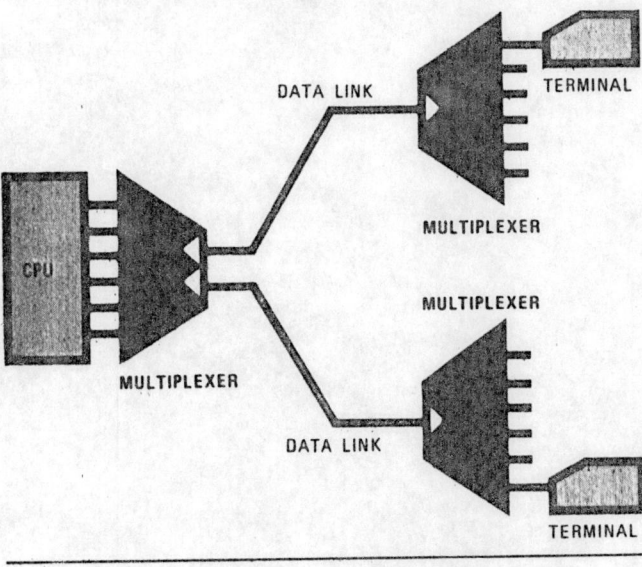

can be made even more cost-efficient through the use of time-division multiplexers. As a general rule, statistical multiplexers are more appropriate when the traffic feeding them is bursty, while the older time-division multiplexers (TDMs) are less expensive but are advantageous only for continuous traffic. In many situations, the traffic between statistical multiplexers is continuous—the type best suited for the TDM. In the configuration shown in Figure 5, mux A and mux 2 could be replaced effectively with time-division multiplexers. The result is a tandem configuration, where mux B and mux C essentially serve as data-concentration points for the terminal traffic.

The dual data-link topology is yet another approach for accommodating clusters of terminals at different locations. Such an arrangement is illustrated in Figure 6. There is one multiplexer at the CPU capable of supporting two separate data links, each connected to a multiplexer that services a cluster of terminals. The CPU-based multiplexer has two data link interfaces and two routing tables.

This topology needs fewer multiplexers but requires two data links. It reduces "nodal" costs by increasing transmission cost. If one data link is much shorter than the other, the transmission costs of the dual data-link topology will most likely be comparable to those of the tandem topology or even the point-to-point arrangement with modem tail circuits. However, the lower multiplexer costs make the dual data-link topology more attractive. On the other hand, if both data links are long and about the same length, the transmission costs of the tandem topology would probably be lower.

Distributed topologies
In centralized topologies, all communications is directed toward one point, a given CPU. However, if connection is required between terminal clusters and possibly several CPUs or between the terminal clusters

themselves, additional problems arise.

In Figure 7, there is a CPU in New York and two terminal clusters, one in Los Angeles and one in San Francisco. Both terminal clusters need connection to the CPU and to each other. A "drop-and-insert" topology, illustrated in Figure 7A, provides a cost-effective design. There is only one long data link, from San Francisco to New York, which serves the traffic between these cities. The Los Angeles multiplexer is connected via a data channel to the multiplexer in San Francisco. The traffic coming into San Francisco from Los Angeles is, in effect, switched. The Los Angeles traffic intended for San Francisco terminals is dropped—outputted to the appropriate data channels—while the traffic intended for New York is inserted in and routed onto the San Francisco-to-New York data link.

The dropping and inserting is the same for communications in the opposite direction. The cost savings over the dual data-link topology is significant because,

7. Distributed topologies. *Both the "drop-and-insert" topology (A) and the "bypass" topology (B) can offer savings in long-distance communications costs.*

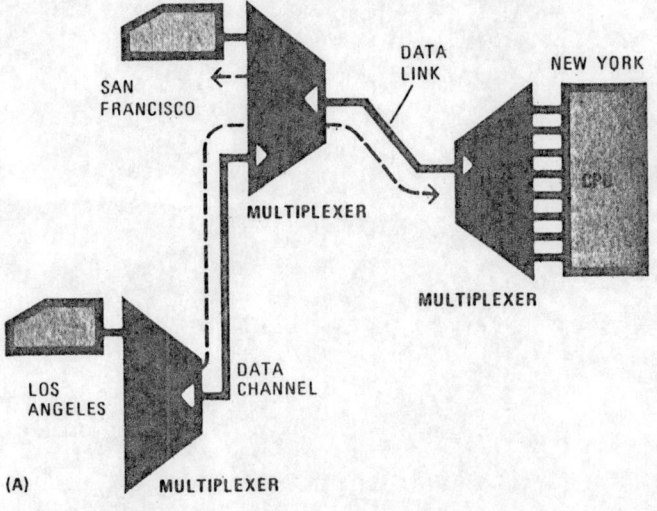

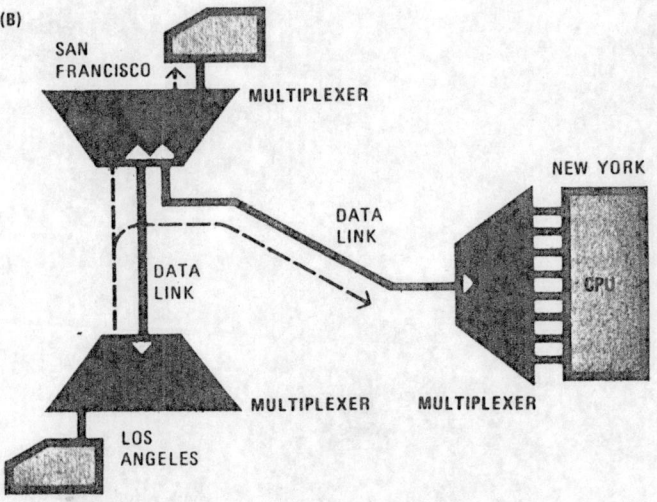

8. Multidropped muxes. *Like terminals, statistical multiplexers can handle the polling required to take advantage of the line sharing and cost savings of multidropping.*

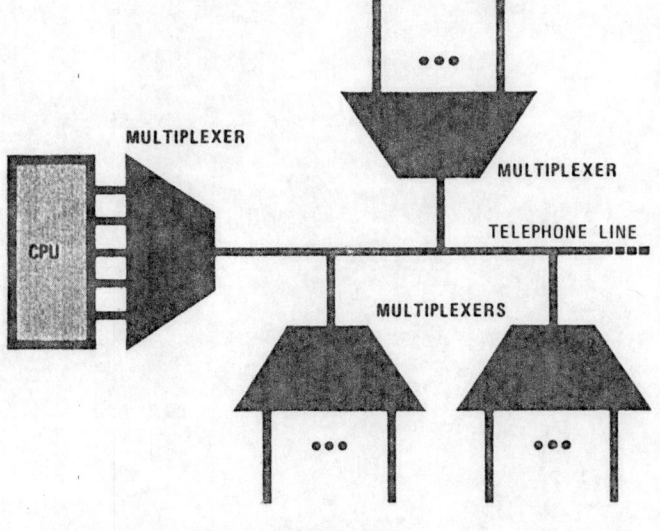

Instead of requiring two long data links (for a total of approximately 6,000 channel-miles), the drop-and-insert topology needs only one long link and a relatively short one—a total of about 3,400 channel-miles.

The bypass topology, shown in Figure 7B, represents an improvement even over the drop-and-insert topology. While offering the same cost advantages, its operation is more streamlined. Topologically, it is nearly the same as drop and insert, except that the Los Angeles multiplexer is tied to the San Francisco multiplexer by a data link rather than by a data channel. In turn, the San Francisco multiplexer connects with both New York and Los Angeles, using the dual data-link topology. As a result, traffic from Los Angeles to New York does not waste a data channel in the San Francisco

multiplexer, and there is less propagation delay in the San Francisco multiplexer.

Another alternative is multidropping. Multidropping is an arrangement that has long been used by terminals to share a single telephone line. Terminals access the line by one of several methods: contention (akin to the party line in voice communications), adhering to a polling discipline, or obeying a prearranged time-division multiple-access protocol.

This arrangement has also been applied lately to statistical multiplexers. Terminal clusters are then connected to the multiplexers, as illustrated in Figure 8. Data concentration and line sharing are provided by the multiplexers, which obey a polling discipline. The resultant cost savings, however, is countered by an increase in propagation caused by polling.

Another topological variation, the traffic-balancing configuration, uses two data links to connect multiplexers rather than one. The second data link provides the data communications manager with tremendous flexibility. If both links are active, the multiplexer can monitor traffic density on each and can reroute dynamically to balance traffic load. Throughput can be increased, even doubled, if both data links support the same speed. Some data channels can be dedicated to one link, while others are used, more or less, for unexpected traffic surges. This traffic balancing enables a priority structure (the dedicated data channels) as well as ameliorates buffer overloading and enhances reliability.

All traffic could initially be routed onto one data link, the primary, while the other serves as a hot standby, or fallback, link. Both links need not be the same type. The primary and fallback could be of different speeds, or the primary could be dedicated, and the fallback dial-up. For this arrangement, the data communications manager might also want to program the multiplexer to keep track of the number of times fallback occurs. Otherwise, he may never know how often, or if, the primary link fails. ∎

The new breed— Switching muxes

Thomas H. Scholl, Digital Communications Corporation, Germantown, Md.

These enhanced units are bringing economical switching to even the smallest networks.

The small-network manager has not been able to take advantage of the sophisticated switching technology that has evolved in the last five years—simply because of cost. In large computer networks, switching is performed by communications processors, or front ends, which can cost from $50,000 to $100,000 and up. Such a price tag is not acceptable to small networks,

which are based on the less-expensive minicomputer. (Actually, some communications processors are minicomputers that have been programmed with special switching software.)

Until recently, when the intelligence for switching was added to statistical multiplexers, the manager of a small data communications network had very few

switching alternatives. Essentially, his options were:
- Do without switching, thus either paying exorbitant line costs or maintaining in a single location multiple terminals, each dedicated to a different host
- Use a minicomputer vendor's networking package (such as Digital Equipment Corporation's Decnet or Data General Corporation's Xodiac), thereby limiting the network to that vendor's equipment
- Distribute the processing power geographically. Distributed data processing is a valid answer in many cases, but some organizations cannot tolerate, for example, the loss of centralized software development.

The modern switching multiplexer offers yet another alternative—and for little more than the cost of statistical time-division multiplexing equipment. Depending on the number of computer ports at each end of the network and on the terminal configuration, a communications manager can implement effective switching for less than $5,000 (assuming eight lines and not including modem or telephone line costs). A fully functional 64-line switching multiplexer network can be installed for about $15,000, depending on the vendor.

A switching multiplexer achieves the proper economy of scale because it combines the features of a statistical multiplexer, a port-contention unit, and a digital matrix switch. This unique combination of functions is possible because the fundamental hardware technology for all three products is comparable.

For example, each device typically consists of a microprocessor, read-only memory (ROM), random-access memory (RAM), and interface logic for input/output devices such as computer ports and terminals. The primary difference between these devices lies in the software that controls the microprocessors. And since software is the critical factor, the additional features in the switching multiplexer account for the incremental increase in cost over conventional, nonswitching multiplexing equipment.

Statistical multiplexers generally offer advantages over conventional time-division multiplexers (TDMs) by providing:
- Reduced telephone line costs
- Error protection of data exchanged between terminals and the CPU
- Other "value-added" features such as network diagnostics or statistics and automatic rate/code detection (see "What intelligent time-division multiplexers offer," DATA COMMUNICATIONS, July 1977, p. 29)

A conventional environment for multiplexing is shown in Figure 1. In this configuration, statistical multiplexers have been installed in a point-to-point topology between the host CPU (in building A) and its terminal users (in building B).

The manager of this network faces a tough problem if it becomes necessary to expand from one to two host computers. (For the purpose of simplification, we will assume that both computers reside next to one another in the same building.) This is an increasingly common situation in small- and medium-size companies where individual minicomputers are dedicated to specific data processing functions or to small groups of users with different interests. (Of course, the multi-

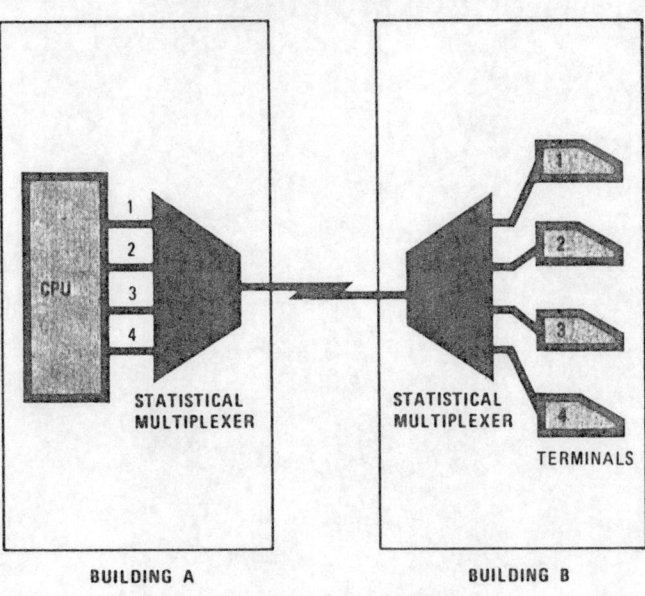

1. Point-to-point. In the classic multiplexing environment, several colocated terminals access a single computer over a shared, or multiplexed, communications link.

ple-host problem is amplified if the company grows and no single person is responsible for overall communications facilities.)

The network manager can provide communications to both CPUs either by expanding the number of ports on the multiplexers or by installing another pair of multiplexers. Both solutions are unsatisfactory because they require additional terminals, since each terminal is typically connected to only one computer port.

In Figure 2, this problem is addressed with switching

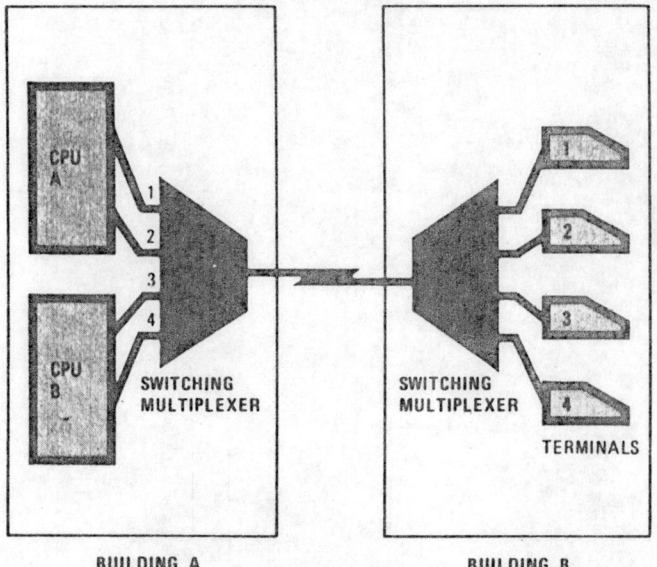

2. Switching muxes. With the addition of switching intelligence in the multiplexer, additional computer ports or communications links are unnecessary.

122

multiplexers. Figure 1's terminal user 1 must always be connected to computer port 1, but Figure 2's terminal user 1 may select any port connected to the remote (CPU) end of the network. Thus, multiple computer access from a single computer terminal is achieved. The switching multiplexer is especially economical if the user population that connects to host A consists of mostly the same users who need to access host B.

Demand port assignment

A statistical multiplexer assigns link bandwidth on a character-demand basis. Similarly, the switching multiplexer assigns computer ports on demand, therefore performing a second level of multiplexing. In some applications, depending on terminal usage, this feature may result in reduced communications line costs because lower-speed facilities can be used instead of more expensive high-speed lines. This concept of demand port assignment can be applied even in the simpler configuration illustrated in Figure 1.

Figure 3 shows switching multiplexers configured in an "unbalanced" point-to-point network. (In an unbalanced network, the number of terminals connected at one end differs from the number of computer ports connected at the other.) In this case, the primary advantage of the switching multiplexer is the cost savings realized by the reduction of multiplexer equipment and computer ports. For example, the network could be configured with an 8-line terminal multiplexer linked to a 4-line computer multiplexer, rather than following the conventional approach of using two 8-line multiplexers. Besides reducing the number of computer ports from 8 to 4, the user pays for 12 lines of multiplexer equipment instead of 16.

The switching multiplexer performs functions similar to those of a port-contention unit, or intelligent patch panel, although the latter also provides access to multiple CPU hosts and reduces the need to add computer ports when the terminal population increases (see "Controlling the mushrooming communications net," DATA COMMUNICATIONS, June 1980, p. 97). In fact, there are several applications for which it may be preferable to install contention, rather than multiplexer, equipment. Contention devices generally support more terminals and host ports than do multiplexers and, therefore, can often be configured for redundancy. But a user pays a considerable price for this expansion and redundant capability, regardless of the size of the network configuration supported.

If the computers are located remotely from the terminals, the data communications manager is still confronted with the problem of concentrating many lines into one. Unfortunately, port-contention units generally do not accommodate a trunk or multiplexer link interface, nor are they programmed to perform software demultiplexing.

Since most port-contention units require additional front-end multiplexing equipment in order to concentrate lines, even inexpensive ones may be too expensive (coupled with multiplexing gear) to achieve the desired economy. Furthermore, if both multiplexing and port contention are required in a network that has grown through several stages, it can be burdensome for the communications manager to deal with the many vendors involved (one for modems, another for multiplexers, and a third for the port-contention unit). By combining port-contention and port-selection capabilities within the multiplexer, the same functions can frequently be achieved without additional equipment cost—and the number of vendors is reduced to one.

Because switching multiplexers offer a line "class of service," the transparency associated with statistical

---

3. Unbalanced configuration. The switching multiplexer can address the problems associated with a disproportionate number of computer ports and terminals. In such cases, switching multiplexers handle the required line concentration as well as dynamic port assignment. Additional computer ports are therefore not required.

BUILDING A

BUILDING B

multiplexers need not be sacrificed. (Class of service is a term borrowed from the telephone industry that relates to the capabilities afforded various subscribers. For example, in a business telephone network, certain classes may be permitted to place conference calls or long-distance calls, while other classes of telephone users may not. This term, along with terms such as "call queuing" or "call forwarding," are now also being applied to data networks.)

Class of service

Each line of the switching multiplexer can be designated as either of two classes of service: dedicated (nonswitched, permanent) circuit and switched (virtual) circuit. If all lines are dedicated, the data is routed through the network in the same manner as with any statistical multiplexer. However, the ability to configure dedicated lines with switching multiplexers is important because of the security requirements of some users. Also, some computers require that CPU ports be accessed only by specific terminals, primarily because the port or terminal address is "hardwired" into the host-resident software.

On lines designated as switched circuits, users access computer ports by entering an English-like command specifying a port code or a group code (which represents a user-defined collection of ports). Computer ports therefore can be divided into groups so that if a user enters a command indicating a group code, the remote multiplexer automatically selects an available port. As with any contention switch, or PBX (private branch exchange), the user is informed via a "busy signal" if all ports in the group are busy. With a switching multiplexer, however, this busy signal is in fact an English-like response displayed at the user's terminal device.

Network supervision

Since it is often desirable to survey the status of any port, supervisory (operator) features are now generally provided to allow privileged users to obtain a directory listing of all ports. This directory, available on command, typically lists important information such as port or line number, connection status (for example, NOT CONNECTED, SIGNING ON, or CONNECTED TO LINE n), line speed, class of service, and other line characteristics (such as implementation of flow control).

Another useful feature typically implemented as a supervisory function is "third-party disconnect," which allows a third party (for example, a communications manager) to disconnect two other parties (a terminal user and a computer port) connected over a switched circuit. This ability guarantees that no user can tie up indefinitely a valuable computer port. Third-party disconnect facilitates maintenance on the network equipment by allowing all switched circuits to be cleared.

Supervisory features are typically accessible from any of the multiplexer's ports so that operators can obtain control information and statistics by entering commands at a terminal from either end of the multiplexing network. Because any port can be a supervisory port, an unlimited number of users can perform supervisory functions simultaneously.

In many applications, however, it is not desirable to allow all users to execute supervisory commands. As a rule, only one or two people are responsible for network operation, and only these people should be entitled to a privileged class of service. On the switching multiplexer, the supervisory class of service is typically engaged by entering a protected password in much the same manner that one signs on to a timesharing service: Users enter a nondisplayed password during the initial sign-on procedure to establish the appropriate class of service for the session.

Typically, the switching multiplexer attempts to find its switched users a computer port that matches the speed of the connecting terminal. However, in some cases, it may be possible to permit a user to connect to a port that operates at a faster or slower speed than the terminal. Then, the switching multiplexer usually notifies a terminal user of a speed mismatch by displaying SPEED CONVERSION at the user's terminal. This indicates, for example, that a 1.2-kbit/s terminal is currently connected to a 2.4-kbit/s computer port or vice versa. When the message appears, the user may choose to either proceed with the connection, if permitted to do so, or immediately disconnect.

The user may allow the speed mismatch if the faster device (either the terminal or computer port) can be flow-controlled. Flow control is a technique commonly used to prevent a statistical multiplexer from overflowing its buffers during long surges of input data. One of two flow-control techniques can be implemented (usually fixed when the multiplexer is first configured). First, a multiplexer can send to a line or port a sequence of X-off/X-on characters in-band. Alternately, it can switch on and off a modem-control signal such as clear-to-send (CTS).

In both cases, flow control is invoked automatically by the switching multiplexer based on its buffer capacity. The multiplexer monitors buffer use per line with respect to the total amount of buffer space available. Therefore, flow control can be invoked on individual lines without affecting other lines that may be operating within a normal buffer-use range.

Local and remote switching

Unlike port-contention units, the switching multiplexer offers all features symmetrically at both ends of the communications link. The capability to perform local, as well as remote, switching introduces the third functional product contained in the switching multiplexer — the digital matrix switch. Matrix switches are frequently provided by the telephone company to connect n incoming lines to m outgoing lines in any combination. Normally, n equals m.

With a switching multiplexer, the matrix switch is implemented electronically, rather than manually. Consequently, it is as simple to connect to a local port as it is to a remote port. Local ports can also be divided into groups similar to those of remote ports. Connections are established using the same English-like command/response language in both cases.

This matrix-switching capability is different from the

port-contention/selection capability. Normally, port-contention units are not symmetrical; that is, the unit is basically split between computer ports on one side (n) and terminals on the other (m). Generally, m is greater than n. It is generally not possible to connect from one "terminal" line to another because the electronics associated with the port side of the unit is different from the electronics associated with the terminal side. (Usually, a customer must specify how many port and terminal interfaces are required when buying the port-contention unit.) The matrix switch (and therefore the switching multiplexer) treat computer ports and terminal lines in the same fashion. There is no electronic difference.

Functional integration

Putting the three products together in the switching multiplexer provides a solution to the networking problem illustrated in Figure 4. Here, users in building A as well as users in building B need to access either CPU A or CPU B. This is a common situation in which data processing functions are performed locally during the day but at remote sites after normal working hours. From a user's point of view, the difference between accessing the local computer and the remote computer is imperceptible. With a switching multiplexer, either may be accessed with equal facility by entering a specific access code.

Using multiplexer equipment to facilitate intrafacility local networking is also possible with the advent of combined multiplexing and switching. Local networking can become an unwieldy problem if corporate management distributes computer terminals throughout employee offices (as opposed to centralizing terminals in a single user-designated area). In the past, this could not be done easily because there was no clear way to

interconnect multiple terminals to multiple hosts. However, with switching multiplexers implemented in intrafacility configurations, any terminal can connect with any other terminal. Besides enabling more flexible CPU-to-terminal communications, this allows easy implementation of applications such as electronic mail.

Yet another capability provided by the switching multiplexer is "peripheral contention," since any port or group of ports can be contention-based, regardless of the end of the link on which they reside. This resource sharing is useful in, say, a laboratory or distributed computing environment, where terminals (input/output devices) must serve a variety of applications; for example, several CRT terminal operators might need access to the same local printer.

Since switched ports are controlled by a single command/response language, it is also possible to write interpretative, nonprocedural programs (sometimes called command files) that, when executed under operator control, offer access to a peripheral device that is contended for on a demand-assignment basis. In this environment, the peripheral commonly serves as a slave device that can be accessed by multiple terminals or computers.

Although the savings vary depending on the network configuration, the switching multiplexer lowers overall communications costs by combining one or more of the following cost benefits:

▫ Line concentration through the statistical multiplexing technique. In some cases, additional line concentration may be achieved as a result of the demand port assignment.

▫ Fewer computer ports. The number of computer ports should be a function of the maximum number of terminal users who need to access the computer simultaneously, rather than the maximum number of terminals available to users.

▫ Fewer terminals. It is generally more economical to multiplex and switch data between terminals and multiple hosts, rather than to add dedicated terminals that speak to only one computer.

▫ Reduced multiplexing equipment. The switching multiplexer can be configured in an unbalanced network, which usually yields multiplexer port savings. ▪

---

4. Local and remote switching. Because of its internal architecture, the switching multiplexer does not distinguish between local and remote port connections.

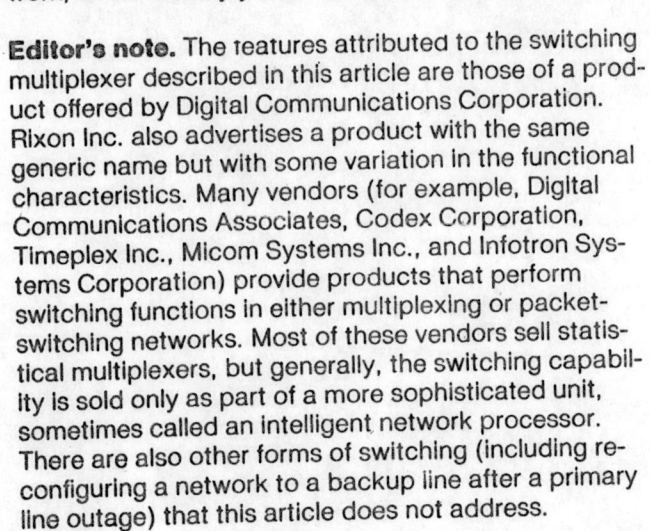
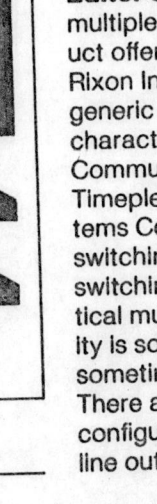
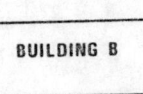
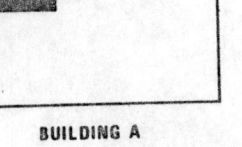

Editor's note. The features attributed to the switching multiplexer described in this article are those of a product offered by Digital Communications Corporation. Rixon Inc. also advertises a product with the same generic name but with some variation in the functional characteristics. Many vendors (for example, Digital Communications Associates, Codex Corporation, Timeplex Inc., Micom Systems Inc., and Infotron Systems Corporation) provide products that perform switching functions in either multiplexing or packet-switching networks. Most of these vendors sell statistical multiplexers, but generally, the switching capability is sold only as part of a more sophisticated unit, sometimes called an intelligent network processor. There are also other forms of switching (including reconfiguring a network to a backup line after a primary line outage) that this article does not address.

James H. Scharen-Guivel and A. A. Carlson, U.S. Senate, Washington, D.C.

A buyers guide to today's versatile statistical multiplexers

The authors teamed up to produce the most thorough research yet compiled for the purchaser of statistical multiplexer equipment.

Statistical multiplexers have been commercially available for barely five years, yet already there are more than 15 "stat mux" vendors offering products ranging in price from under $1,000 to over $100,000. Deciding which one to buy, the user may be somewhat bewildered by the different products, options, and various network topologies possible. And the problem is exacerbated by the rapid rate at which new offerings are made available.

But the buyer should be aware of the characteristic differences between statistical and frequency- and time-division multiplexers. Unlike TDMs and FDMs, statistical multiplexers provide efficient use of idle time between characters or transmission, error checks, and automatic retransmission.

The reason for employing any multiplexer is to share the cost of a data communications line. A statistical multiplexer does this by allocating available bandwidth dynamically. The goal is to maximize the loading of each line for economy. A statistical multiplexer stores input data in a buffer until an entire frame is present; after that it prepares and transmits the frame.

On the receive end, the communications terminate unless the receiver detects an error. If so, the multiplexer is signaled and it retransmits the frame. In all statistical multiplexers, the frame lengths vary in accordance with the input data.

Following are specific characteristics the buyer must measure to determine if the statistical multiplexer will operate effectively in his application:

- Low-speed data capabilities
- Aggregate data-link characteristics
- Internal multiplexer operation
- External multiplexer operation

These four areas are summarized for a number of statistical multiplexer vendors in the tables throughout this article. (Space does not permit every product or every vendor to be listed, but the selection represents a good cross-section of available units at the lower end of the product lines.)

Table I details the low-speed data characteristics. The number of ports determines the number of devices that can be simultaneously connected to a statistical multiplexer. A geographic distribution of terminal population determines the number of ports required for each user grouping.

Network modeling programs are available to determine the optimum locations and size of statistical multiplexers. Input to these programs include the locations of the accessing devices, the devices' traffic characteristics, the host computer locations, multiplexer costs for different numbers of ports, and the different types of communications lines and associated costs. Although network optimizing programs are available from several firms, care must be taken to ensure that a proper match of the optimization tool is made with the network being addressed. The areas of concern include topology, applicable common-carrier tariffs, number of terminals, circuits, and the like. The analysis could be more complicated if multipoint statistical multiplexers are considered. Multipoint models allow terminals in several different locations to be multidropped. Examples of these are Codex's 670 Series, General Datacomm's Pollkat, and Prentice's Multimux.

Additional factors must be taken into consideration. These include floor space and environmental needs for large statistical multiplexers, operational reliability, and the impact of a failure.

The majority of devices attached to statistical multiplexers, at present, are asynchronous start-stop terminals, although most statistical multiplexer manufacturers allow synchronous devices to be used as well. The

When satellite links or large networks are used the echoplex mode is a must.

transmission of isochronous data, like telemetry, is possible on some newer units.

Line speeds from 150 to 4.8K bit/s are supported universally, and many units handle a range from 50 to 9.6K bit/s. The 9.6-kbit/s limitation is usually adequate for today's terminal population.

Speed intermix

For most units specifying synchronous input, the data rate (in protocol-transparent mode) cannot exceed the speed of the output link. Some models, like Racal-Milgo's Omnimux, specify that the synchronous-input line speed cannot exceed half the output link speed. However, many units permit each input line to operate independently at any permissible rate. Because the character-input bit stream has to be intact, with no dead time between the bits of an individual character after passing through a statistical multiplexer, each port must be adjusted to recognize the attached device's character code. (With a continuous synchronous bit stream in a protocol transparent mode, there is no need to recognize and manipulate the character code.)

Nearly all statistical multiplexers surveyed accept any 5-to-8-level code (a code consisting of 5, 6, 7, or 8 data bits). In addition, ASCII and IBM's EBCDIC are usually supported. A smaller group of manufacturers support BCD (binary coded decimal), correspondence, and Baudot codes, as well as 9-bit graphics input.

Echoplexing

Many network terminals use an echoplex mode that requires a CPU to "echo" each character back to the terminal. This mode can cause a problem if a statistical multiplexer is used in such a circuit. Because of propagation delay, buffer queue, and data-frame assembly and disassembly (several tens of milliseconds or more, perhaps), the unit's keyboard may seem "spongy." The Compre Comm Data Express, for example, solves this problem with an "addressed character block" protocol. This makes the delay almost unnoticeable on terrestrial links.

When satellite links or very large networks are to be used, local echoplex operation is a must. In such cases, a local statistical multiplexer is set up to perform the echoing. This local echoplex function is available either as a standard or as an optional feature from many manufacturers. But some manufacturers, for packaging, engineering, or marketing reasons, require that the local echoplex circuit be installed in groups of lines (usually four). For example, with the Codex 6001, ei-

ther all ports or no ports in the group operate in local echoplex mode. If the local statistical multiplexer detects an error while in the local echoplex mode, an explicit garble character is sent to the terminal. The multiplexers save processing time by removing from the computer the responsibility for echoing characters, and the traffic on the network is reduced.

Flyback buffering delay is used on unbuffered terminals (like the Texas Instruments Silent 700) or printers. A delay is provided after a carriage-return character so that the electromechanical print head is ready on the next line. There are several statistical multiplexers that recognize the carriage-return character and automatically send a series of fill characters to provide the necessary flyback buffering delay. The buffering delay time can be specified for each port, and in some models the character, after which the delay is inserted, can be user specified.

ADRD

Automatic data rate detection (ADRD) is a useful capability that recognizes a terminal's speed from the first character. Some vendors provide ADRD as an option at speeds up to 1.2 kbit/s. With ADRD, one application may support terminals at one speed while another is supporting terminals at another speed without reconfiguring the statistical multiplexer ports. Such flexibility is also valuable with dial-up ports. The ADRD option can add $200 to the price of the statistical multiplexer. Note that although all manufacturers provide support for dial-up access, some (Com Design is one) emphasize that both ends of a pair of their statistical multiplexers can provide dial-up access.

All vendors provide ports that are configured as DCEs with RS-232-C/CCITT V.24 interfaces and a 20-mA current-loop interface is often provided as an option. DCA provides 20-mA current-loop interfaces as a no-cost option. Some provide even more interfaces: Infotron provides 60 mA; and Halcyon provides 20-, 40-, and 60-mA active or passive interfaces. Another useful interface—the MIL-STD 188 digital interface—is provided as an option on the Codex 6000 series and Timeplex Series II Microplexers. A separate MIL Spec unit, the TD-1344/FYC, based on the Supermux 480, is available from Infotron.

The Timeplex Series II Microplexer includes RS-422 balanced and RS-423 unbalanced interfaces, which are part of the EIA RS-449 standard. But few others make these available. EIA's 449 interface allows cabling lengths between terminals and the multiplexer to

Statistical multiplexer low-speed channel characteristics

	CODEX 6001	COM DESIGN TC-5 CONCENTRATOR	COMPRE COMM DE-4	DCA SYSTEM 105	DCC CM 9100	GANDALF S-MUX P/N 9103
MANUFACTURER AND MODEL						
NUMBER OF PORTS	4, 6	MIN 4, MAX 16	4	2, 8	MIN 4, INCREMENTS 4, MAX 32	MIN 4, INCREMENTS 8, MAX 32
TRANSMISSION MODE	ASYNC	ASYNC	ASYNC	ASYNC/SYNC	ASYNC/SYNC	ASYNC/SYNC
LINE SPEED (BIT/S)	50 TO 9.6K	50 TO 9.6K	134.5 TO 9.6K	75 TO 4.8K	50 TO 9.6K	50 TO 9.6K
LINE SPEED INTERMIX	ANY	ANY	ANY	ANY	ANY	ANY
CODES ACCEPTED	ANY 5 TO 8 LEVEL	ANY 5 TO 8 LEVEL	ANY 5 TO 8 LEVEL	ANY 5 TO 8 LEVEL	ANY 5 TO 8 LEVEL	ANY 5 TO 8 LEVEL
INTERFACE	RS-232-C/V.24 DCE	RS-232-C DCE OR DTE (20mA OPTION)	RS-232-C/V.24/V.28 DCE OR DTE	RS-232-C/V.24/V.28 DCE (2,000 FT. DRIVERS STANDARD)	RS-232-C/V.24/V.28 DTE OR DCE	RS-232-C/V.24 DTE OR DCE
AUTOMATIC DATA RATE	YES	YES	NO	YES	OPTIONAL	NO
FLOW CONTROL (SIGNALS)	NO (X-ON/X-OFF CTS, DSR/DTR)	YES (X-ON/X-OFF CTS, DSR/DTR)	NO (X-ON/X-OFF CTS)	YES (X-ON/X-OFF CTS)	YES (X-ON/X-OFF CTS)	YES (X-ON/X-OFF CTS)
LOCAL ECHOPLEX	NO	YES	NO	YES	NO	YES
FLYBACK BUFFERING DELAY	NO	NO	NO	YES	NO	NO
FULL-DUPLEX EIA CONTROL	5	4	1 (RTS PROPAGATED)	3	4	4
DIAL-UP SUPPORTED	YES	YES (EITHER END)	YES (CARRIER DETECT)	YES	YES	YES
SWITCHING OPTION FOR PORT SELECTION AND CONTENTION	NO	NO	NO	NO	NO (SM9200 YES)	NO
SERIAL DATA DISTORTION (% INPUT, % OUTPUT)	PROPRIETARY	PROPRIETARY	PROPRIETARY	PROPRIETARY	PROPRIETARY	<40, <1

	GDC MODEL TDM 1240	HALCYON 4200 NETWORK PROCESSOR	INFOTRON SUPERMUX 480	MICOM MICRO 800/2	PRENTICE SNP-1000	RACAL-MILGO OMNIMUX	RIXON DCX 815	TIMEPLEX SERIES II MICROPLEXER
		BLK 2, INCREMENTS 8, MAX 60	8	MIN 2, MAX 16	2, 4, 8	4, 8 (MODELS TO 32)	4, 8	4, 8 (MODELS TO 48)
	ASYNC	ASYNC/MAX 16 SYNC	ASYNC/MAX 2 SYNC PORTS (OPTION)	ASYNC/MAX 4 SYNC PORTS (OPTION)	ASYNC	ASYNC/MAX 8 SYNC (OPTION)	ASYNC	ASYNC/MAX 8 SYNC OR BISYNC (OPTION)
	50 TO 9.6K	50 TO 9.5K	50 TO 9.6K	50 TO 9.6K	110 TO 9.6K	ASYNC 50 TO 9.6K SYNC 1.2 K TO 9.6K	50 TO 9.6K	50 TO 9.6K INTERNAL OR EXTERNAL CLOCK
	ANY	ANY	ANY	ANY	ANY	ANY SYNC ≤0.5 LINE RATE	50 TO 9.6K	50 TO 9.6K
	ANY 5 TO 8 LEVEL	ANY 5 TO 8 LEVEL (PLUS SYNC. PROTOCOLS)	ANY 5 TO 8 LEVEL	ANY 5 TO 8 LEVEL	6 OR 7 BIT ASCII, IBM (OTHERS PRESET)	ANY 5 TO 8 LEVEL	ANY 5 TO 8 LEVEL	ANY 5 TO 8 LEVEL
	RS-232-C/V.24/V.28 DCE	RS-232-C/V.24/20, 20 AND 60MA DTC OR DCE	RS-232-C/V.24/V.28 DCE (20, 60MA OPTION)	RS-232-C/V.24/V.28 DCE (20MA OPTION)	RS-232-C/V.24/V.28 DTE OR DCE	RS-232-C/V.24/V.28 DTE OR DCE	RS-232-C/V.24 DCE	RS-232-C/V.24 DTE OR DCE
	OPTIONAL	YES	OPTIONAL	YES	OPTIONAL	OPTIONAL	YES	OPTIONAL
	NO (X-ON/X-OFF CTS)	YES (X-ON/X-OFF DTR, OTHERS IN PROM)	YES (X-ON/X-OFF CTS)	YES (X-ON/X-OFF CTS, DTR)	NO (X-ON/X-OFF CTS)	YES (X-ON/X-OFF CTS)	YES (X-ON/X-OFF CTS)	YES (X-ON/X-OFF CTS, EIA, OTHERS)
	NO	YES	YES	YES	NO	YES	NO	YES
	YES (FACTORY SET)	YES	NO	YES (FACTORY SET)	NO	YES	NO (SET PER UNIT)	YES
	4	4	4	4	4	4	4	4
	YES	YES	YES	YES	YES	YES	YES	YES
	NO	NO	NO	NO	NO	NO	NO	NO
	PROPRIETARY	<45, ≤2	<45, ≤1	NOT AVAILABLE	NOT AVAILABLE	<40, <1	<49, <2	<45, <1

129

be up to 1,000 feet without modems, compared to the 50 feet maximum of the EIA RS-232-C interfaces. With a dispersed terminal population in a building, the longer distances possible with the RS-422 or RS-423 interface can be a valuable alternative to using modems even considering the cost of these interfaces. It is expected that the RS-449 standard will be increasingly used at speeds over 1.2 kbit/s, say, for high-speed graphics terminals.

Some vendors that do not provide RS-449 interface capabilities do provide built-in line drivers so that cabling distances of up to 2,000 feet are possible.

Input rates

The characteristics of the UART, USRT, or USART chips widely employed in modern statistical multiplexers determine how much serial data distortion can be tolerated on the input side. However, pulse shaping and retiming limit the serial distortion to less than 1 or 2 percent at the output ports. The Timeplex Series II, Halcyon, and Infotron statistical multiplexers can tolerate up to 45 percent serial data distortion on the input ports. All manufacturers' input ports can be configured either as DTEs or DCEs by using external cables. Some vendors also provide the change more directly; for example, DCC uses a jumper block.

The EIA flow-control signals, which include DTR, DSR, CTS, and RTS for the RS-232-C interface, need to be propagated from a terminal connected to a statistical multiplexer port through the pair of statistical multiplexers all the way to the device at the other end. These signals must be converted into special signaling characters and propagated in the frames between the statistical multiplexers.

The signaling characters have to be recognized and appropriate EIA control signals generated. Except for the Compre Comm Data Express, which only propagates RTS as Data Carrier Detect (DCD), all manufacturers progagate at least three control signals and several send more. The Codex 6000 series supports DTR/DSR, BUSY/RI, RTS/DCD, CTS, and pin 14 (as data restraint). Halcyon's statistical multiplexers support DTR/DSR, RTS/DCD, CTS, RI, pin 11, and pin 25. The Racal-Milgo Omnimuxes support DTR/DSR, BUSY/RI, RTS/DCD, and CTS. Some firms provide support for the RS-232-C secondary data channels (for example, the Codex 6050). These extra capabilities may be very helpful to a user who needs extra control information to be passed for special devices.

For effective device control with minimum delays, EIA control signals have to be propagated rapidly. In the Timeplex Series II Microplexers, an effort is made in the software to insert the appropriate control signals in the very next block transmitted to the corresponding multiplexer.

With increasing use of the CCITT standard protocols, enhanced functionality and even better control capabilities will become available in the future. The X.3 PAD functions can be performed by a statistical multiplexer with the X.28 interface providing data-character control information and the X.29 interface providing data-packet control information so that enhanced and standardized end-to-end device-control functions can be performed. The extended inband signaling capabilities of the X.21 interface can be used effectively for interconnecting switched devices.

There are several other low-speed data capabilities, not detailed in Table I, that come up in statistical multiplexer shopping circles. These include the use or non-use of LEDs and the propagation of a break signal. To display the status and activity of the port and key EIA leads, many manufacturers provide several LEDs for each port. The Halcyon 4200 Network Processor has two indicators and red, green, or off states for the DTR, RTS, DSR, CTS, DCD, and RI leads of the RS-232-C interface for a selected port. The Com Design TC-5 has nine multifunction LEDs. When a statistical multiplexer is installed in a remote site, the LEDs are of no direct use, so several manufacturers provide statistical multiplexers without front-panel displays or controls for these cases.

Extensive network control and monitoring capabilities are provided by several manufacturers. These include the Racal-Milgo CMS system, the Timeplex Alpha-star, and the Infotron 790 Supermux. Extensive diagnostic and display facilities are available at a control console, and the need for a set of LEDs on each multiplexer front panel becomes less important.

Break

A terminal user may use the "break" or "attention" key to signal the CPU. Many computers require that the break be signaled for some minimum time. So, many statistical multiplexer manufacturers propagate the break for some time greater than 100 milliseconds. DCA's DCA105, for instance, signals the break for at least 300 milliseconds and Racal-Milgo's Omnimux uses a 200-millisecond signal. The Timeplex Microplexers use a minimum time of 150 milliseconds but continue to signal the break to the CPU until another char-

Extensive network control and monitoring capabilities are provided by several manufacturers.

acter is entered by the user. Some units, like the Prentice SNP-1000, can be set for break durations from 150 to 600 milliseconds, in increments of 150 milliseconds. The Codex 6050 passes break for a maximum of 500 milliseconds.

For the data links, all manufacturers provide RS-232-C/CCITT V.24 interfaces configured as DTEs, as shown in Table II. A few manufacturers do provide a RS-422 or RS-423 interface capability and others like Timeplex offer RS-423 as an option. Considerable savings in communications equipment and line costs can be realized because of the increased cabling distances provided by the newer standard interface. Such an application would be connecting several statistical multiplexers in a building to a single split-stream modem. Some manufacturers also provide V.35 and Bell 303 interfaces. All support a maximum link speed of at least 9.6 kbit/s synchronous with either internal or external clocks. Some, including DCA, Gandalf, the Micom Micro 800/2, and Racal-Milgo, provide synchronous outputs up to 19.2 kbit/s. Codex provides speeds up to 64 kbit/s and Infotron up to 72 kbit/s.

With high-speed data links, a simple and inexpensive network supporting hundreds of terminals can be set up to connect locations, either several miles apart using limited-distance modems or for longer distances using DDS or other common-carrier services. Most manufacturers provide asynchronous data links as an option at speeds of up to 9.6 kbit/s.

Larger statistical multiplexers often support two or more data links. Multiple links enable load sharing, fall-soft capabilities, and service restoration, creating a new link on the public switched telephone network. The DCC multiplexers use the second link for automatic fall-back, while Halcyon employs the link for dynamic load sharing and Timeplex for traffic balancing or to connect one multiplexer to two separate statistical multiplexers for a 3-point star network. The DCA 355 can have 62 links and the Infotron 790 Supermux can handle eight.

Multiporting

Using these large statistical multiplexers, networks with complex topologies are possible. They can provide traffic balancing and alternate-path routing. None of the statistical multiplexers, surveyed, however, provides automatic dial backup as an option. Auto-calling and other options available with modems will be incorporated into statistical multiplexers in the future. Some of the statistical multiplexers are available with built-in modems. This gives a very compact unit occupying no more room than a small box. This option is found, for example, in the Codex 6001, the Infotron Supermux 480, and the Micom Micro 800/2. A good number of statistical multiplexers studied operate with point-to-point data links. The new polling statistical multiplexers available include the Codex 670 series, the General Datacomm Polikat, and the Prentice Multimux. DCA has had a multipoint capability for several years with the DCA 355 Network Processor

MANUFACTURER AND MODEL	INTERFACE (DTE)	MAXIMUM NUMBER OF LINKS	MAXIMUM LINE SPEED (KBIT/S)	TRANSMISSION MODE	MULTIPOINT CAPABILITY	OPTIONAL BUILT-IN MODEM (SPEED IN KBIT/S)
CODEX 6001	RS-232-C/V.24	1	9.6	SYNC	NO (YES W/CODEX 6030, 6040, AND 6050)	YES (4.8 AND 9.6)
CODI DESIGN TC-5 CONCENTRATOR	RS-232-C	1	9.6	SYNC/ASYNC	NO	NO
COMPRE COMM DE-4	RS-232-C/V.24	1	9.6	SYNC/OPTIONAL ASYNC (NOT CHARACTER MODE)	NO	NO
DCA SYSTEM 105	RS-232-C/V.24/V.28	1	9.6	SYNC	YES (AS SLAVE TO DCA 355)	NO
DCC CM 9100	RS-232-C/V.24/V.20	2 (ONE ACTIVE, ONE STANDBY)	9.6	SYNC	NO	NO
GANDALF S-MUX PIN 9103	RS-232-C/V.24	1	19.2	SYNC	NO	NO

as the master and any mix of DCA 105 or 115 statistical multiplexers configured as slave processors.

Polling statistical multiplexers provide capabilities and economies in network costs with asynchronous start-stop terminals. Previously, these savings and functions could only be obtained with synchronous terminals on multipoint lines. If line costs are high and the terminal population is dispersed so that only small terminal clusters are possible, then polling statistical multiplexers can be very cost-effective. All the advantages of statistical multiplexing can be realized, including error protection. There are also savings in modem costs when compared to a network of several separate point-to-point lines required to support the same number of remote multiplexers. Unlike frequency-division multiplexers, polling statistical multiplexers, as master devices, have slave multiplexers that can transmit, when polled, using the full bandwidth. The traffic load from all the slave statistical multiplexers must not overload the multipoint line. Otherwise, response time to the users will be intolerably long. With a multipoint arrangement, because of polling, the round-trip delays are longer than with point-to-point lines. If the master polling multiplexer fails, or if there is a line failure, several users would be affected. With a set of separate point-to-point statistical multiplexers, a single failure would impact only the users on one line.

Unlike frequency- and time-division multiplexers, statistical multiplexers provide data integrity with redundancy checking on the lines. Table III reveals that all the manufacturers except Compre Comm provide an X.25 level 2 or DDCMP-type block with a 16-bit CRC. The receiving unit checks the CRC and in case of an error transmits a NAK. The transmitter then retransmits the block. The CCITT standard or CRC-16 polynomial is widely used. With the CRC—even in the case of communications lines with an average bit-error rate as bad as 1 in 10,000—only about 1 character in each trillion would be received with an undetected error. The Compre Comm Data Express, on the other hand, uses a checksum on each of its small addressed character blocks. As a rule, unless the errors are "bursty," (a number of bits in error followed by clear data, as opposed to single errors evenly distributed), the smaller the blocking size the greater the effective throughput for a given error rate. This ignores protocol overhead and assumes that end-to-end delays are insignificant.

Bit stuffing

Nearly all the manufacturers use an X.25 level 2 bit-oriented protocol. DCA uses the DDCMP protocol that employs a byte count on each block in addition to a CRC flag byte. Packets in DDCMP are separated by sync characters. DCA also offers X.25 level 3 communications interfaces on its System 355.

X.25 level 3 capabilities are also available from Memotex. The X.25 level-2-type frame, used by most manufacturers, consists typically of a flag byte, address byte, control-byte port address, and data for

133

MODEL							
GDC TDM 1240	HALCYON 4200 NETWORK PROCESSOR	INFOTRON SUPERMUX 490	MICOM MICRO 800/2	PRENTICE SNP-1000	RACAL-MILGO OMNIMUX	RIXON DCX 815	TIMEPLEX SERIES II MICROPLEXER
RS-232-C/V.24/V.28	RS-232-C/V.24	RS-232-C/V.24/V.28	RS-232-C/V.24	RS-232-C/V.24/V.28	RS-232-C/V.24/V.28	RS-232-C/V.24/V.28	RS-232-C/V.24 (RS-429 OPTION)
1	2 (LEASED)	1	1	1	1	1	2 (DYNAMIC LOAD BALANCING)
9.6 SYNC, 1.8 ASYNC	19.2 (9.6 FOR 2 LINKS)	9.6 SYNC, 1.8 ASYNC	19.2 SYNC, 9.6 ASYNC	9.6	19.2	9.6	9.6
SYNC OR CHARACTER ASYNC	SYNC	SYNC OR ASYNC	SYNC OPTIONAL ASYNC)	SYNC	SYNC	SYNC	SYNC (OPTIONAL ASYNC)
NO	NO	NO	NO	YES	NO	NO	NO
YES (2,4)	NO	YES (9,6)	YES (9,6)	NO	NO	NO	YES (2,4)

For switching statistical multiplexers the overhead is somewhat higher.

each port, followed by the 2-byte CRC and a flag byte. Bit stuffing is used to keep the bit pattern of the flag byte unique. If a consecutive string of five or more bits of ones occur in the data stream, extra zeroes are inserted in the data on transmission and removed from the data when received. It is important to point out that it is time consuming to perform framing, CRC generation and checking, bit stuffing, and deletion.

High-performance chips
Special chips are often used in statistical multiplexers on the data-link ends to perform these functions, relieving the microprocessor's load. The chips can also be extended to handle full protocol support including automatic repeat request (ARQ) for blocks in error. The microprocessor specifies a memory address for a block to be transmitted, notifies the protocol chip of the starting address and number of bits of data, and then proceeds with other processing. The chip handles framing and transmitting the data correctly, as well as notifying the microprocessor of completion.

Similar functions can be performed at the receiving end. Such high-performance chips then are actually performing functions of communications interfaces. Most commercial systems, at present, do not perform the full sophisticated functions of the X.25 protocol on a separate communications chip but merely provide a manufacturer's version of the protocol. Part of the link protocol is handled by microprocessor software. The protocol overhead (the number of bytes introduced because of the protocol) is about 8 (10 for DDCMP). For switching statistical multiplexers, the overhead is somewhat higher because of the possible extended addressing.

Length
When dealing with long frames, statistical multiplexers experience a delay since the whole frame has to be received and the CRC performed before the data can be passed on. The Compre Comm Data Express uses its addressed character block to eliminate this delay. The machine transmits an address and data (maximum 2 bytes) for a channel as an individual block and separates blocks with sync characters. The protocol overhead is 1 byte. The ARQ implemented is special and only explicit NAKs are sent.

For a Go-Back-N ARQ, if a frame received is found in error, it and all subsequent blocks must be retransmitted. In keeping with the most common X.25 level 2 implementations, statistical multiplexers allow a maximum of seven frames outstanding before acknowledgment is received. This minimizes the amount of buffer space to be allocated in the transmitting multiplexer.

Given the characteristics of the transmission medium, for a specified bit error rate and line speed, and a given Go-Back-N ARQ, an optimum frame length (in bits) can be calculated. Several manufacturers' data frames use a maximum 256 bytes. Another popular length is 128 bytes. Com Design uses a variable maximum frame length depending on the line speed, with a maximum of 64 bytes at 9.6 kbit/s. With Codex's statistical multiplexers, maximum frame lengths up to some 3,000 bytes are possible. Timeplex dynamically adjusts the maximum frame length transmitted depending on the number of eroded frames (line errors) encountered; the more errors the shorter the frame.

For a long terrestrial link between two multiplexers, the round-trip time—including transmission time, modem delay, and processing in the multiplexer to check the CRC and generate an ACK, if necessary—is barely sufficient to require two data frames outstanding waiting for the acknowledgment. But with a single-hop satellite link, with a one-way-trip delay of about 250 milliseconds, additional delays are incurred. This means that if no throughput degradation is to be encountered waiting for ACK, almost a full seven data frames must be outstanding at 9.6 kbit/s with 128-byte data frames. The X.25 level 2 protocol with extended frame numbering has to be used and provides for more than seven frames outstanding. The Codex 6001 can have a maximum of 127 data frames outstanding. The higher the speed of the data link for a given frame size, the more frames outstanding. With the DDCMP protocol, up to 255 frames can be outstanding; DCA typically uses a maximum of 20 frames.

In the case of satellite links, because of the extra time that buffers have to be held in the transmitting multiplexer awaiting acknowledgment from the receiver, more data buffer space is required. Some manufacturers—Timeplex is one—have sufficient memory so that no addition is required. Others supply a satellite-link capability as an optional package. Codex, DCA, DCC, Infotron, Micom, and Racal-Milgo are some. Not all yet provide a satellite link capability (for example, Com Design, Halcyon, the Prentice SNP-1000, and Rixon), although announcements are expected. A typical satellite-link option costs about $200 per multiplexer. Because of the unique protocol of the Compre Comm Data Express, it is not compatible with satellite-link operation; a new model is expected. Data bytes

are taken from the low-speed data ports, and frames are assembled and then transmitted on the high-speed data links. Data frames are held in memory until the receiving multiplexer signals that the data has been received. The receiver allocates buffers to receive frames. When a frame is received without error the data is moved, disassembled, and passed on to the appropriate data ports. In addition, supervisory frames are generated, received, and acted upon.

For these functions buffers are needed. Some manufacturers permanently allocate fixed-size receive buffers; 256-byte receive buffers are used by DCA, Infotron, and Racal-Milgo. Other manufacturers allocate the entire memory buffer for both transmit and receive. With increasing numbers of data ports, faster links, and terminals and with the long delays associated with satellite links, more and more buffer memory is needed. Timeplex has a buffer pool that is proportional to the number of data ports, allocating 4 kbytes of buffer per port. In the large Codex 6000 series processors it is possible to find 10 Mbytes of memory. Meanwhile, several manufacturers' figures for memory include that used for multiplexer operation, meaning that the actual buffer memory will be smaller than stated. DCC's CM9100 with 16K of memory has 6.5 kbytes of memory available for buffers. Compre Comm requires only 4 kbytes for an eight-channel Data Express unit. To determine whether sufficient buffer space is provided requires assessment of a number of factors. A direct comparison of advertised memory is not sufficient.

In the future it is expected that statistical multiplexers will use even more memory for buffer space. However, as the buffer memory increases to accommodate increased queues, a user's data will take a longer time to move through the queues at both ends. The delay can be reduced by using a faster microprocessor and additional logic or microprocessors to accomplish some functions in a parallel fashion.

Buffer priority

All vendors provide dynamic buffering on all channels. The statistical multiplexers effectively provide auxiliary memory to the devices. Because the buffers are shared there could be a need for buffer-use priorities. For example, digitized voice or a facsimile machine might be given a higher priority. Otherwise there might be intolerable pauses and in some cases even data loss. Some manufacturers provide buffer priorities on a per-port basis. Halcyon provides two levels of buffer priorities and Timeplex provides three. This means that the high-

er-priority ports can use a larger percentage of the buffer pool.

Besides buffer-use priorities there is a need for flow control. If a sending device transmits data too fast for the receiving device, data will be lost. The receiving device must somehow signal the transmitting device to slow down. These flow-control signals must be recognized and passed through by the statistical multiplexers. Also, the multiplexer buffers at either end may simply fill up. After the congestion is cleared, it is necessary to signal the transmitter to start again. All statistical multiplexers use an on-off flow-control mechanism. The ASCII X-on/X-off control characters are transmitted, or for the RS-232-C interface, the voltage on the RTS and CTS pins is changed. Usually the receiving data port may need a different flow-control protocol from the transmitting port; for example, the CPU port might recognize CTS/RTS while the terminal might recognize X-on/X-off. Most statistical multiplexer manufacturers provide the capability to configure the flow-control signals separately for each port.

The range of buffer usage at which flow control is invoked by a statistical multiplexer varies considerably with the manufacturer. For example, DCA bases flow control on character usage, DCC uses a range of 30 to 40 percent per channel and 60 to 80 percent global buffer-pool usage. The upper limit on flow control is typically in the 75 to 90 percent range. At the lower limit, however, there is considerable variation. Codex, Com Design, Compre Comm, and Racal-Milgo use the 25 to 33 percent range at which a device that was stopped can resume transmission. General Datacomm, Halcyon, Infotron, Micom, Prentice, and Rixon have a lower limit in the 50 to 67 percent range. Timeplex employs an upper limit of 90 percent and a lower limit of 87 percent global-buffer use. While a shorter range allows better throughput and tight control, oscillating feedback situations become possible. If too much statistical-multiplexer microprocessor overhead is involved, throughput suffers.

It is not yet clear how a comprehensive flow-control mechanism can be implemented with synchronous data. If the statistical multiplexer is to be transparent to the bit stream with a continuous synchronous data stream, no protocol intervention is possible. Synchronous data must pass at the highest priority, without benefit of flow control. Many manufacturers currently provide just this kind of support for synchronous data. In fact, in most cases the synchronous stream is passed through in a TDM fashion without CRC. This

Several manufacturers' figures for memory include that used for multiplexer operation.

In the future, bandwidth required for synchronous data will be allocated dynamically.

means that the synchronous data rate must be lower than the data-link speed. Infotron, Micom, and Racal-Milgo units do this. In the future, bandwidth required for synchronous data will be allocated dynamically—up to about 90 percent of the data-link speed. The remaining bandwidth will be available for asynchronous data. Such an arrangement is suitable for the transmission of digital facsimile.

A number of manufacturers, including Halcyon and Timeplex, pass the synchronous data as part of the data frames between multiplexers. The data, therefore, is included in the CRC checking. Questions of end-to-end clock synchronization and what happens in case of retransmissions because of errors on the line need to be addressed. In this case, a fast microprocessor is needed in the statistical multiplexers to perform in-frame synchronous-data pass-through.

The bulk of synchronous data transmissions, however, adhere to a protocol like bisync (2780, 3270, 3780) or HDLC/SDLC. These have internal error checking. For synchronous bit- or (especially) byte-oriented protocols, it is possible to respond actively to the protocol using the statistical multiplexers. Such intervention can be effective with polled bisync terminals on satellite links. The statistical multiplexers generate bisync protocol ACKs, NAKs, WACKs, EOTs, and the like, and appropriate alarm and delaying messages to the polling host and terminal. But considerable intelligence is required in the statistical multiplexers. Also, a rather complicated configuration definition is necessary for multihost applications. Several units either provide such capabilities or will in the future. Examples include Codex, DCA, DCC, Halcyon, Infotron, Micom, Rixon, and Timeplex.

Remote-job-entry applications for a wide variety of protocols, including IPARS, CDC UT200, Honeywell VIP, Univac, and IBM (2780/3780) are being used today. The use of statistical multiplexers in such applications is expected to grow, pointing the way to increased function, more memory, and more processing capabilities in the statistical multiplexers. Support for a variety of protocols brings statistical multiplexers in competition with some of the functions provided by the Paradyne Pixnet and communications processors like IBM's 3705, Burroughs' CP9400, NCR's Comten, Computer Communications Inc., and Honeywell's Datanet. Statistical multiplexers could also compete with the Tymnet II Engine with ISIS and the GTE Telenet TP4000 and TP3010.

With devices using a full-duplex packet protocol, like X.25 or SNA, however, little advantage is gained by using a statistical multiplexer. While the multiplexer performs well in an X.3 PAD function, it offers no bandwidth savings. In fact, throughput suffers since additional delays occur.

Intel 8273 and Motorola 6854 chips, which implement the SDLC/HDLC protocol, allow protocol functions to be packaged into statistical multiplexers. The Intel 8274 MSPC can already support async, bisync, and bit-synchronous protocols (SDLC/HDLC), as well as other user-specified protocols extending the functions of statistical multiplexers.

All statistical multiplexers use some form of data compression. With asynchronous terminals, the start and stop bits can be easily removed. More data compression can include replacing repeated characters by a count. This is especially effective for formatted text data, for example, where several consecutive blanks are possible. Extra processing is required in statistical multiplexers for this function. In fact, as microprocessors become an integral part of terminals, a portion of this function could be effectively incorporated in the terminals themselves.

Another technique is Huffman encoding. A variable-length coding scheme is used, replacing most common characters with short code words, and longer code words for the more infrequently occurring characters. If the data consists of many characters that give long code words, then the performance of the encoding scheme is quite poor. For efficient operation in this case, an adaptive encoding table is needed. Each port monitors the statistical-frequency distribution of characters and dynamically adjusts the code tables. The corresponding receiving port is notified of the code-table change. Such techniques are used, for example, by the high-end Codex 6000 series processors.

While data compression is effective when link traffic is heavy, many processor cycles are required to carry it off. Sophisticated data-compression techniques can in effect rob a processor of its needed cycles. Yet the scheme does afford some measure of data security without explicit encryption.

Another advantage of statistical multiplexers is saving ports on the host computer. For each communicating terminal, a virtual circuit and the host software perform the demultiplexing functions. Some statistical multiplexer manufacturers do not provide any support for this software demultiplexing. Others, like Codex and Prentice, do provide documentation permitting implementation by the user. Micom provides a sepa-

rate device, the Micro 200 Port Concentrator, to perform the cyclic redundancy checking and message assembly so that the software demultiplexing effort is considerably simplified. Significant price and performance advantages can be realized with direct host connections, for example, with Com Design and DCA devices for DEC systems. In addition, direct connection to a CPU channel is a useful feature, and connections to many different mainframes can be expected in the future. Also in the future, X.25 level 3 links will become widely available, and direct input to host or front-end computers will be practical. (DCA already provides this capability.) Considerable savings can be realized depending on the traffic loads, network topologies, and host and terminal distributions. Internetworking will also become possible with X.75 gateways provided by advanced multiplexers.

The average frame-synchronization time for statistical multiplexers is quite rapid compared with bit- or even character-interleaved multiplexers. The end-to-end character delay with a statistical multiplexer includes the data clocking time to output the data bits on a line, modem delays, and statistical multiplexer queuing and processing delays. With terrestrial links at 9.6 kbit/s, average end-to-end delay can be as high as 200 milliseconds.

The maximum input-data burst rate is dependent on how rapidly the microprocessors can move the data from input to make frames ready to transmit. Some multiplexers can take an instantaneous data rate of eight full 9.6-kbit/s inputs with only one 9.6-kbit/s output data link. Examples include the eight-port Infotron, Racal-Milgo Omnimux, and the Timeplex Series II Microplexer.

Most statistical multiplexers use 8-bit microprocessors like the Z80, TI 9900, Intel 8085, and the M6800. The DCC CM9100 statistical multiplexer and the SM9100 switching statistical multiplexer use the same 500-nanosecond 8-bit microprocessor as the Telenet TP4000. Some statistical multiplexers have a separate microprocessor for every four low-speed ports and another to handle the high-speed link (examples include Halcyon and Timeplex). Others have as many as 70 microprocessors.

DCC, Rixon, and Timeplex have announced switching statistical multiplexers, and others are expected. Switching statistical multiplexers connect n devices (terminals) to m ports. Since all terminals are not active all the time, n can be greater than m. Savings in host ports are possible, and the terminals contend for the host ports. The switched ports can also be grouped. In this way, a user can be connected to any one of a group of switched ports. Host port selection is also possible. The user specifies the multiplexer name and port number. Speed and code conversion can be performed by the multiplexers, resulting in a flexible method of accessing any host in a network. Some restrictions, like passwords, subnetworks, and closed user groups, can be enforced. One switching statistical multiplexer can be used to provide a simple local network with full connectivity and contention. In the future, switching and patching—now performed at network-control centers—can be effectively performed under software control with a switching statistical multiplexer.

Data security
The switching statistical multiplexer data frames must, in general, carry more information than the simple point-to-point statistical multiplexer data frames. Thus, for example, the formats of the Timeplex switching multiplexers and the Series II Microplexers are incompatible.

Data security becomes especially important with switching statistical multiplexers and dial-up access. The switched virtual circuit has to be taken down and all buffers flushed, for example, in case of a buffer overflow or if one side hangs up, before the particular ports can again be made available to another user.

The switching functions provided by a switching statistical multiplexer are quite similar to a data PBX. Large switching statistical multiplexers at present can have several hundred ports, making them competitors of the Develcon, Gandalf, and Infotron data switches. They begin, in fact, to take on some of the functional capabilities of the advanced PBXs from Intecom, Datapoint, Mitel, Rolm, NEC, and Northern Telecom. However, the per-port price of advanced PBXs are still about three times the cost of a statistical multiplexer port. So, for data-only applications, switching statistical multiplexers are quite competitive with integrated voice and data PBXs.

Operational characteristics
Remote statistical multiplexers are often located far from individuals who can troubleshoot them. This means there is a need to perform diagnostics and problem determination remotely from a network-control center. It is advantageous in large statistical multiplexer networks to have the multiplexers at the net-

With terrestrial links at 9.6 kbit/s, average end-to-end delay can be as high as 200 milliseconds.

statistical multiplexer comparison characteristics

MANUFACTURER AND MODEL	CODEX 6001	COM DESIGN TC-5 CONCENTRATOR	COMPRE COMM DE-4	DCA SYSTEM 105	DCC CM 9100	GANDALF S-MUX P/N 9103
CONFIGURATION SETTING	DIP SWITCHES	DIP SWITCHES	PROGRAM	DIP SWITCHES	FROM OR DOWN-LINE LOAD	OPERATOR CONSOLE INTERFACE
DOWN-LINE LOAD SLAVE UNIT	YES (AUTOMATIC)	YES (AUTOMATIC)	YES (UP LINE AND DOWN LINE)	NO	YES (AUTOMATIC)	YES (AUTOMATIC)
DISPLAY LOCAL AND REMOTE CHANNELS AND LINK PARAMETERS	YES	YES	NO	YES	NO	YES (OPERATOR CONSOLE)
STATUS MONITORING	YES (LED)	YES (LED AND ALPHA DISPLAY)	YES (LED)	YES (LED)	YES (LED)	YES (LED)
DIAGNOSTICS (INTERNAL SELF TESTS, LOCAL AND REMOTE LOOPBACK TESTS OF CHANNELS AND LINKS)	YES	YES	NO (LOCAL LOOPBACKS ONLY)	NO (LOCAL AND COMPOSITE LOOPBACKS ONLY)	NO	YES
CONTINUOUS BACKGROUND DIAGNOSTICS	YES	NO	NO	NO	NO	NO
INTERNAL TEST MESSAGE GENERATOR (FOX MESSAGE)	YES	NO (ASCII SET)	NO	NO	NO	NO
BROADCAST SUPERVISORY MESSAGES TO ANY TERMINAL	YES	NO	NO	NO	NO	YES
BUFFER OVERFLOW SENT TO AFFECTED TERMINALS	YES	YES	NO	NO	YES	YES
AUTOMATIC RESTART	YES (POWER FAILURE, WATCHDOG TIME OUT)	YES (POWER FAILURE)	YES (POWER FAILURE)	YES (POWER FAILURE)	YES (POWER FAILURE)	YES (POWER FAILURE)
CONFIGURATION STORED	EAROM	EAROM	DIP SWITCHES	EAROM	EAROM	BATTERY BACKUP
STATISTICS	NO	NO	NO	NO	NO	YES (OPERATOR CONSOLE)
SERVICE LOCATIONS	NATIONWIDE	CALIF.	CHAMPAIGN, ILL.	NATIONWIDE	MD. OR ALANTHUS NATIONWIDE	9 LOCATIONS

	60C MODEL TDM 1240	HALCYON 4200 NETWORK PROCESSOR	INFOTRON SUPERMUX 480	NICOM MICRO 800/2	PRENTICE SNP-1000	RACAL-MILGO OMNIMUX	RIXON DCX 815	TIMEPLEX, SERIES H MICROPLEXER
	?SWITCHES	PROCESSOR FROM KEYPAD PROGRAM, OR CONTROL TERMINAL	DIP SWITCHES	DIP SWITCHES	PROGRAM, DIP SWITCHES	PROGRAM, DIP SWITCHES	DIP SWITCHES	PROGRAM, THUMBWHEEL, DIP SWITCHES
	YES (AUTOMATIC)	YES (AUTOMATIC; ALSO UP LINE)	YES (AUTOMATIC)	YES (AUTOMATIC)	YES (AUTOMATIC)	YES (AUTOMATIC)	YES (AUTOMATIC)	YES (AUTOMATIC)
	?	YES	YES	NO	YES	YES	NO	YES
	NO	YES (LED AND AUDIO ALARMS)	YES (LED)	YES (LED)	YES (LED)	YES (LED)	YES (LED)	NO (FAULT LED ONLY)
	?	YES (EXTENSIVE)	YES	YES	YES	YES	YES	YES
	YES (SELF-TEST)	YES	NO	NO	NO	YES	NO	YES
	NO	YES	YES	NO	NO	YES	NO	YES
	NO	YES	YES	NO	YES	YES	NO	YES
	NO	YES	YES	YES	NO	YES	YES	YES
	YES (POWER FAILURE)	YES (POWER FAILURE)	YES (POWER FAILURE)	YES (POWER FAILURE, WATCHDOG TIMEOUT)	YES (POWER FAILURE)	YES (POWER FAILURE)	YES (POWER FAILURE)	YES (POWER FAILURE)
	EAROM	FROM OTHER UNIT OR EXTERNAL	EAROM	EAROM	BATTERY BACKUP	EAROM	DIP SWITCHES	BATTERY BACKUP
	NO	YES	YES	NO	LIMITED	YES	NO	YES
	NATIONWIDE	NATIONWIDE	3RD PARTY NATIONWIDE	CALIF, PA	SUNNYVALE, CALIF	NATIONWIDE	6 LOCATIONS	NATIONWIDE

IV Statistical multiplexer internal characteristics

MANUFACTURER AND MODEL	CODEX 6001	COM DESIGN TC-5 CONCENTRATOR	COMPRE COMM DE-4	DCA SYSTEM 105	DCC CM 9100	GANDALF S-MUX P/N 9103
MICROPROCESSOR	6800	9900	8085A	Z80A	6502A	Z80A PLUS SERIAL I/O PROCESSOR (SPECIAL ORDER)
MAXIMUM INPUT DATA BURST RATE (KBIT/S)	38.4	24	19.2	19.2	19.2	38.4
AVERAGE SYNCHRONIZATION TIME (FRAMES)	2	1.1	1.1	4	1.1	2
END-TO-END CHARACTER DELAY	80 MILLISEC	100 MILLISEC	1.5 CHARACTER TIMES	15 CHARACTER TIMES	24 MILLISEC PLUS DATA CLOCKING TIME	50 MILLISEC PLUS DATA CLOCKING TIME
PROTOCOL OVERHEAD IN A DATA FRAME (BYTES)	8	8	1	10	8	8
MAX LENGTH OF DATA FRAME (BYTES)	3000	VARIABLE, 64 AT 9.6 KBIT/S	2	255	255	133
WINDOW SIZE WITH GO-BACK-N ARQ	127	7	SPECIAL, ONLY NAKS SENT	20 (MAX 255 POSSIBLE)	7	4
DATA-LINK PROTOCOL	X.25 LEVEL 2	X.25 LEVEL 2	SPECIAL BISYNC LIKE	DEC DDCMP	X.25 LEVEL 2	X.25 LEVEL 2
REDUNDANCY CHECK	CRC 16	CRC 16	SPECIAL	CRC 16	CRC 16	CRC 16
DATA COMPRESSION ON LINK	YES (START AND STOP BITS)	YES (START AND STOP BITS)	YES (START AND STOP BITS)	YES (START AND STOP BITS, REPEATED CHARACTERS)	YES (START AND STOP BITS)	YES (START AND STOP BITS, REDUNDANT PATTERNS, PARITY IF 8 BIT PLUS PARITY)
SOFTWARE DEMULTIPLEXING SUPPORT	YES (DOCUMENTATION)	NO	NO	NO	YES	NO
DATA BUFFER (BYTES)	16K	4.5K WITH 8K MEMORY	1K	2K TRANSMIT PLUS 256 RECEIVE	6.5K WITH 16K MEMORY	12K TRANSMIT PLUS 128 CHARACTER RECEIVE
SATELLITE LINK COMPATIBILITY	YES	NO	(TO BE ANNOUNCED)	YES	YES	UNKNOWN
DYNAMIC BUFFERING ON ALL DATA CHANNELS	YES	YES	YES	YES	YES	YES
BUFFER USE PRIORITIES	NO	NO	NO	NO	YES FIXED	NO
DATA RESTRAINT PER CHANNEL X-ON/X-OFF USAGE RANGE (%)	25, 75 GLOBAL	33, 67 GLOBAL	25, NEARLY FULL GLOBAL	SPECIAL (BASED ON CHARACTER USAGE 256 BYTES MAX)	30, 40 PER CHANNEL 60, 80 GLOBAL	12.5, 50 (INPUT STRING PER CHANNEL)

	GDC MODEL TDM 1240	HALCYON 4200 NETWORK PROCESSOR 480	INFOTRON SUPERMUX 480	MICOM MICRO 800/2	PRENTICE SNP-1000	RACAL-MILGO OMNIMUX	RIXON DCX 815	TIMEPLEX SERIES II MICROPLEXER
	SPECIAL	2 6800s	6502B	Z80	8085	2 8085As	9900	2 6809s
	19.2	38.4	76.8	9.6 (OPTIONS TO 76.8)	19.2	307 (32 PORT MODEL)	9600	76.8
	2	5	1.5	1.1	1.1	1.5	1.1	1.5
	1.5 CHARACTER TIMES	200 MILLISEC	60 MILLISEC (AT 2.4 KBIT/S PLUS 2 CHARACTER TIMES)	2 CHARACTER TIMES PLUS 50 MILLISEC (AT 1.2 KBIT/S)	2 CHARACTER TIMES	3 CHARACTER TIMES	3 CHARACTER TIMES	3 CHARACTER TIMES
	PROPRIETARY	8	8	8	8	5	8	8
	PROPRIETARY	1000 BITS	128	PROPRIETARY	128	256	128	120
	1	1	1	PROPRIETARY	1	VARIABLE	1	1
	MODIFIED HDLC	X.25 LEVEL 2	SPECIAL X.25 LEVEL 2 LIKE	MICOM	X.25 LEVEL 2	MODIFIED X.25 LEVEL 2	MODIFIED X.25	X.25 LEVEL 2
	CRC 16	CRC 16	CRC 16	CRC 16	CRC 16	CRC 16	CRC 16	CRC 16
	YES (START AND STOP BITS)	YES (START AND STOP BITS, REPEATED CHARACTERS)	YES (START AND STOP BITS)	YES (START AND STOP BITS)	YES (START AND STOP BITS)	YES (START AND STOP BITS)	YES (START AND STOP BITS)	YES (START AND STOP BITS)
	NO	YES	YES	YES WITH MICRO 220	YES (DOCUMENTATION)	NEGOTIABLE	YES (DOCUMENTATION)	YES
	2K	32K	12K BYTES TRANSMIT PLUS 256 BYTES RECEIVE	2.6K (MAX 15K)	7.6K TRANSMIT PLUS 8 BYTES/PORT RECEIVE	4K TRANSMIT PLUS 256 BYTES/CHANNEL RECEIVE	5.5K	16K FOR EACH 4 PORTS
	NO	NO	YES	OPTIONAL	NO	YES (WITH ADDITIONAL 4K TRANSMIT BUFFER)	NO	YES
	YES	YES	YES	YES	YES	YES	YES	YES
	NO	YES 4 LEVELS	NO	NO	NO	NO	NO	YES 3 LEVELS
	62, 87 GLOBAL	67, 87 GLOBAL	60, 80 GLOBAL	63, 87 GLOBAL	60, 80 GLOBAL	30, 80 GLOBAL	50, 75 GLOBAL	87, 90 GLOBAL

Statistical multiplexers have virtually taken over the FDM market.

work-control center as a master and the remote multiplexer configured as a slave. Then in case of any errors, the slave-unit data ports and line configurations can be down-line loaded automatically. As shown in Table IV, Com Design provides both up-line and down-line loading. Compre Comm has both units as masters and only local loopback tests can be performed. Local and remote loopback tests that can be performed by a network-control center, for both the data link and the low-speed data ports, enable a thorough check of the various interfaces. It is desirable to be able to loop the data from any low-speed port to any other port for monitoring. A built-in test-character generator using the "fox" test message is commonly used. One exception is Com Design's unit, which uses a full ASCII set.

It should be possible to display the configuration of any port in the statistical multiplexer network. This becomes more important as the number of programmable options for each port increases.

Comprehensive diagnostic capabilities and extensive alarm features are available with most units, including Codex, Com Design, DCA, DCC, Halcyon, Infotron, Micom, Racal-Milgo, Rixon, and Timeplex.

Statistical data about traffic, link errors, buffer use, and response times are vital for network management and planning. Today most statistical multiplexers provide a control or supervisory port. On the Racal-Milgo Omnimux, an asynchronous data port can be dedicated to the supervisory and monitor functions. These monitoring, control, and diagnostic functions can be extensive when integrated with the Racal-Milgo Communications Management System (CMS 1000 or 2000). On some systems, a separate supervisory port is provided. Timeplex has the Alphastar to monitor up to 16 master statistical multiplexers, gather and display statistics, display configurations of each data port, and simplify the configuration programming.

Comprehensive network-management and problem-determination tools are provided with operator consoles on the larger units like Codex's 6040 and 6050, DCA's 355, Infotron's 790, and Rixon's 850. In fact, with large networks of these kinds of statistical multiplexers, tools are available for each subnetwork and can be accessed from a control console.

In simple statistical multiplexers the configuration can be stored by setting DIP switches.

Some statistical multiplexers use battery backup to store the programmed configuration in case of power failure. Examples of these are the Gandalf S-Mux PIN 9103, the Prentice SNP-1000, and the Timeplex Series II Microplexer. Other manufacturers use EAROM and do not need battery back up.

In a large statistical multiplexer network, it may be necessary to have some units on standby at critical nodes. In case of a failure the data in the buffers is lost, and for large memories the effect of the loss has an impact on several users. So, many statistical multiplexers provide capabilities to broadcast "data lost" and other supervisory messages, to the ports.

Additional remote diagnostics, alarm capabilities, network-statistics gathering, reconfiguration, and management capabilities are expected soon. Full integration of these functions, many of which will be automated at network-control centers, will take place.

What's next

From the preceding it is seen that some functions performed by statistical multiplexers overlap the functions of PBXs, front-end processors, concentrators, packet-switching nodes, protocol converters, and even satellite-delay compensators. Statistical multiplexers have virtually taken over the FDM market and made serious inroads in the pure-TDM market. And further inroads are expected. On the other hand, a statistical multiplexer cannot seriously compete with a standalone packet-switched node, especially in the international marketplace where the PTT tariffs limit competition. In the case of local networks, if the user owns the transmission medium, the statistical multiplexer is again not seriously cost-competitive. It is in long-haul networks that statistical multiplexers offer strong competition. But the intelligence and storage required for electronic-mail functions is better handled separately, rather than as an extension of the terminal-to-terminal connection capability provided by a statistical multiplexer.

For many statistical multiplexer manufacturers, more than 75 percent of revenue is derived from products introduced after 1978. Therefore, even more new product announcements will be forthcoming providing new features, increased functionality, and low cost.

Provision of different statistical multiplexer functions in separate devices, and the integration of functions in different ways, will give rise to products that are completely different in character. Presently available devices include CRC generation and checking devices, local-network interfaces, terminal concentrators with efficient host port interfaces, and synchronous/asynchronous buffers and convertors. ◼

This article will be presented at Interface '82, this month in Dallas.

How to keep terminal users honest

Alan Berman, Citibank, N.A., New York City

Locks and keys are a nuisance. Lip prints are messy. Perhaps the best method is a new software approach—virtual passwords.

Successful terminal security—being able to identify a user and control his or her activity—involves more than hardware and software. It requires knowing what security equipment will best fit into the user's data processing environment. Especially difficult is setting up a security system for on-line configurations that have multiple applications and several operators on any given terminal during a normal working day.

There are two basic means to identify terminals and their operators: physical devices and software devices (passwords). In security circles these methods are generally referred to as "something you have" and "something you know," respectively.

Physical devices take on several forms. The most common is the key-operated terminal. A key is required to turn on the terminal and keep it on. Remove the key and the terminal is inoperative. It is easy to identify those terminals equipped with key "protection"; the key is in the terminal 24 hours a day, 7 days a week.

From keys we progress to magnetic-strip readable cards. By inserting the card in the attached reader, the user can access the network based on some preset control restrictions. If the card is lost, somebody else can use the terminal as he pleases.

Chaos reigns when a key or card is lost or stolen. The card must be invalidated and replaced, locks removed, and new keys issued. Obviously, these security devices are not very sophisticated.

A new product introduced by Intelsec Corporation of Santa Fe, N. Mex., has brought computer technolo-

gy to terminal security. The device, TAC II, consists of a control unit placed in a secure location up to 1,000 feet from the terminal and connected to a remote unit at the terminal. The remote unit is cabled either to enable or to block serial data transmission from the terminal. The control unit generates a random challenge word to the remote unit, which returns an authentication as long as the terminal-access-control (TAC) printed-circuit card is inserted in the remote unit. The authentication is then compared with the control unit's own answer: if there is no match, the control unit interrupts the terminal's transmission.

This challenge-response pattern continues at a rate of approximately once a second. Should the terminal operator remove the card from the remote unit, the connection is broken. An optional alarm can be installed to warn if the card is removed from the premises. When a card is either lost or stolen, the matching-pattern section of the card is removed from the control unit, and a different pattern segment and access card are substituted.

But physical security is not limited to the use of removable devices. Fingerprint identification, used for data center access control, is now being tested for

terminal identification. In addition, other parts of the anatomy have been tested for that purpose. Lip prints were considered, but it was feared that kissing a terminal every morning would foster a love-hate relationship. Several operators donned helmets connected to terminals to investigate the possible use of phrenology to identify users.

The major problems with physical security are the expense of additional equipment and the need for stringent controls of physically removable devices, such as cards and keys. Many organizations find these requirements too complicated and too expensive, so they opt to use passwords.

Passwords are cheap and easy to produce. Anyone can create a password identification system, and almost everyone does. But there are problems inherent in this approach. First, conventional passwords exist on a file and are relatively easy to compromise. Depending on the degree of security at a site, anyone from the mail clerk to the systems programmer may have access to any and all passwords. This situation does not promote an attitude of responsibility for protecting user identifications and passwords.

Additionally, changing conventional passwords is cumbersome and often ties up the data processing area and its personnel when updates, recompilations, and reloads are necessary. The end product of all this activity is a password system that may have been compromised at any of several levels and requires data processing support for maintenance.

An alternative to conventional passwords is a new approach called virtual passwords. Virtual passwords are not contained in any files and are created at the time the user identifies himself to the system. Implementing a virtual password identification system requires an authorized on-line user file, which contains such identifying items as name, employee number, social security number, and department number. One additional field should be set aside for the password-generation number. This number determines the starting point from which to calculate a user password and may have any value from 1 on.

Generating the password

For the sake of this discussion, let us examine a unique five-digit employee number and a nine-digit social security or equivalent number. The 14 digits are arranged in a predetermined sequential pattern of columns, resulting in a number table of single digits:

E1	S6	S3	S2
S9	E3	S2	E2
S8	S5	E5	E3
E2	S4	S1	S7
S7	E4	E1	S4, etc.

where En = digit of employee number
Sn = digit of social security number

Consider employee number 57598 and social security number 014-97-6247. Thus, $E1 = 5$ (the first digit of the employee number), and $S9 = 7$ (the ninth digit of the social security number). This pattern can be arranged as desired.

After deciding on a pattern for the numbers, we select a pattern for the alphabetic characters. Two sample tables, one for consonants and the other for vowels, are shown below.

CONSONANT TABLE			VOWEL TABLE
X	Q	J	E
Z	M	P	I
B	C	K	U
F	N	S	O
Y	H	R	A
L	D	W	
V	G	T	

145

Three-character passwords are recommended because they are short enough to remember and, hence, do not have to be written on terminals, on desks, or on pieces of paper taped to the bottoms of desk drawers. Even easier to remember are consonant-vowel-consonant constructions that make up short, pronounceable passwords.

We then consider the algorithms necessary to generate a number that will point to an entry in the consonant-vowel tables. This number is referred to as an offset, subscript, or displacement, depending on the preferred programming language. If possible, three separate programs or subroutines should be written by three different programmers and then linked together for execution. Additionally, the numbers table and letters table should be kept separate to provide a greater degree of security through independent software components.

Here is an example of the use of three algorithms. Each yields a quotient and a remainder.

Algorithm 1: $\dfrac{N + (N + 1) + (N + 2)^2}{21}$

The remainder + 1 = the pointer to the first letter in the consonant table.

Algorithm 2: $\dfrac{N + (N + 2)}{5}$

The remainder + 1 = the pointer to the second letter in the vowel table.

Algorithm 3: $\dfrac{N^2 + (N + 2)^2}{21}$

The remainder + 1 = the pointer to the third letter in the consonant table.

N, the start position of the number table, is the generation number. The contents of the number table indexed by N is substituted into each algorithm.

Using the above information, we can construct a password. Assume that the generation number is 1. Thus, N points to the first position of the number table (E1, the first digit of the employee number), which in our example is 5. Therefore, N + 1 points to the second position of the number table (S9, the ninth digit of the social security number), which is 7. And N + 2 points to the third position of the number table (S8, the eighth digit of the social security number), which is 4. So, substituting the actual numbers from the number table, the results of the three algorithms are:

Algorithm 1: $\dfrac{5 + 7 + 4^2}{21}$

Adding 1 to the remainder gives us 8. (A 1 is added to forestall a meaningless remainder of zero.) The offset (subscript, displacement) into the consonant table is 8. This yields a first letter, "Q."

Algorithm 2: $\dfrac{5 + 4}{5}$

Adding 1 to the remainder gives us 5. This offset into the vowel table yields a second letter, "A."

Algorithm 3: $\dfrac{25 + 16}{21}$

Adding 1 to this remainder gives us 21. This offset into the consonant table yields a third letter, "T."

We can then issue a first generation password of QAT for employee 57598. This method of deriving passwords is simple and straightforward, which is reason enough to install such a system. But there is another advantage to this approach.

In most environments, passwords are changed periodically or on request, but there is no reference kept of previously issued passwords. This may not be very important in batch systems, but in on-line systems reference to previous passwords provides a tool to identify an unauthorized user.

Illegal entry
The following scenario illustrates this point. Employee A (whose employee number and social security number are those in the previous example) feels his password has been compromised. He notifies his supervisor, who in turn notifies the data security officer (DSO), who decides that a new password should be issued to employee A. The DSO uses his on-line terminal to request an operator-profile update on his screen, and he updates the password by simply placing a "Y" in the appropriate field (see figure).

Internally, the generation number is incremented by 1, and the newly generated password is compared to the prior one. If they are the same, the generation number is again incremented until a unique password emerges. Externally, the DSO does not know the password, and there is no intervention by data processing staff members or operations personnel. The update occurs instantly without anyone's knowledge.

Now the data security officer requests that the employee sign on in a secure area, so that no one else may observe the new password. (This is usually done under the DSO's direct supervision or while in telephone contact with him.) When employee A signs on, he sees his new password, which, based on our tables and algorithms, is "RAJ." This password will not be displayed again.

The scenario is complete when employee B (who has compromised employee A's password) attempts to sign on using A's identification and password. When employee B enters the password QAT (in a nondisplayable mode), the system recognizes that this is not the current password. However, instead of rejecting it and issuing an error message, which is the common procedure, the system internally reduces the current generation number (2) by 1 and generates the user's previous password. If the previously issued password matches the one entered, a message to the DSO's on-line printer informs him of the violation and the terminal's location. The system then allows the unauthorized operator to sign on but restricts him to nonsensitive inquiry-only information. This gives security personnel time to confront the unauthorized user while he is still at the terminal.

For a security system to work this well requires a

146

knowledgeable and conscientious data security officer. This individual is generally responsible for monitoring terminal activity, issuing new passwords, and assigning employee identification. The DSO usually has an on-line terminal station to execute his various duties. It is relatively easy for him to monitor the direct-line local terminals and even the leased-line remote ones (which are in actuality extensions of direct-line terminals). There is a logical address associated with each one of these terminals, and this can be translated into a physical location, such as a building, a floor, a department, a group, and a position.

Security with dial-ups

However, a different problem is associated with location of dial-up terminals. All dial-up terminals should be equipped with an answerback capability (generally an option) to let them send precoded identifiers with data transmissions—even automatically when the modem's carrier-detector signal is first received. Even though the precoded identifier may not pinpoint the location of the terminal, the equipment is identified for future investigation.

In addition to deciding on password methodologies

Screened employee. To update a password, the data security officer requests the operator's profile on his on-line terminal and places a "Y" in the proper field.

and physical devices, the user must decide whether to control the terminal operator or the terminal itself. Are certain transactions allowed only from terminal XYZ or only by employee Jo Doe? This is not an easy question to resolve.

Restricting the entry of transactions to predetermined terminals works if the environment involves low-volume, highly sensitive transactions, but it may require the additional expense of backup terminals to ensure continuous processing. By tightly constraining terminal use, the network planner risks designing a terminal security system that will directly conflict with the move toward the "universal" terminal. This approach also jeopardizes a terminal operator's productivity by forc-

ing him to move to the appropriate terminal to accomplish a task. But even so, some staff members will feel secure only in this type of environment.

The alternative to the secured terminal is to control the operators and allow them to use any terminal that is convenient and available. This method is feasible, but it requires, above all else, a belief that the security system—whether physical, password, or a combination of both—can identify a terminal user with a high degree of accuracy.

It is important that management define every operator's job responsibility and authority. This information can then be made a part of the operator's profile, which is retained on the same file that is used to control passwords. There should also be a mechanism to continually update the profile on-line.

Degrees of control

This operator-control approach supports the universal-terminal concept, reduces the need for backup equipment, and lends itself to greater flexibility and productivity. Even with these positive points, there may still be a real need to have some highly secure terminals. How is this apparent dilemma resolved?

The solution is to combine both approaches for maximum benefit. That means, for very sensitive transactions, requiring entry from selected terminals and restricting the entries to certain individuals, and, for high-volume, less sensitive transactions, allowing other operators to input data from any available terminal.

There are additional programming requirements. A terminal-restriction file must be available on-line, and the file entry associated with a particular terminal must be combined with the profile of the operator (from the operator file) who is using the terminal on the premises.

A proper evaluation of the user environment is necessary before designing a security system. If terminal security directly interferes with a production area, personnel will naturally resist it. On the other hand, if a system has minimal impact upon productivity, the staff will show little or no opposition. ☐

147

Section 4

Local Network
Implementation
Implementation
Implementation
Implementation
Implementation
Implementation
Implementation
Implementation
Implementation
Implementation
Implementation
Implementation
Implementation

Implementing Ethernet from soup to nuts

Jeffrey Mason and Gregory Shaw, 3Com Corporation, Mountain View, Calif.

Off-the-shelf hardware and software for constructing an Ethernet local network is now available from one vendor.

Promoted by Xerox Corporation, Digital Equipment Corporation, and Intel Corporation, Ethernet consists of a single coaxial cable that connects up to 100 computers and other devices and permits 10-Mbit/s transmission between any two stations. Building a complete Ethernet network requires a combination of hardware and software components that fits into the layers of the International Standards Organization's (ISO's) open systems interconnection model (see "How Ethernet/Unix conforms to OSI").

The physical layer consists of Ethernet transceivers connected to one another by a 50-ohm coaxial cable. Each transceiver is positioned wherever network access is required. A length of interface cable joins each transceiver to an Ethernet controller, which plugs into a computer backplane. This controller, together with software, implements the data link layer of the open systems interconnection model. Communications protocol software implements the higher levels of the ISO model, completing the network (see "The Ethernet local-network approach").

So far, only one vendor, 3Com Corporation, of Mountain View, Calif., provides off-the-shelf hardware and software components for a complete Ethernet solution based on Bell Systems' Unix operating system and Digital Equipment Corporation's (DEC's) LSI-11, PDP-11, and VAX-11 machines. It supplies the 3C100 Ethernet transceiver, the 3C200 LSI-11 Ethernet controller, and the high-level communications software called Unet (see "The missing link to full Ethernet compatibility is high-level software," DATA COMMUNICATIONS,

October, p. 50). A (DEC) Unibus controller for PDP-11s and VAX-11s will be available shortly. Other manufacturers provide Ethernet equipment, but only 3Com also provides a total Ethernet solution, including the higher-level software in prepackaged form.

3Com's decision to build the initial Ethernet components for the DEC computers and the Unix operating system was deliberate. Currently, DEC has shipped over 300,000 minicomputers worldwide, making it the largest distributor of machines of this size. Over 130,000 of these computers belong to the LSI-11/Q-bus family. In addition to their popularity, the DEC computers provide a hardware environment for the Unix operating system. Unix is an emerging standard operating system for 16-bit computers. It is an extremely lean and adaptable operating system, which has been implemented in several different hardware environments (see "Unix: An operating system that means business," DATA COMMUNICATIONS, October, p. 101). The combination of a family of compatible computers, a portable, standard operating system, communications software, and Ethernet hardware form a high-performance, flexible local network. Techniques also exist for linking non-DEC computers into the Ethernet/Unet-based network.

The subsystems necessary to implement the DEC/Unix/Ethernet connection are the coaxial cables, a transceiver, a controller, and the higher-level software necessary for communications between stations. The 50-ohm coaxial cable is a nonstandard type, and, at present, Belden Corporation is the only manufacturer

150

How Ethernet/Unix conforms to OSI

The International Standards Organization has been developing an open systems interconnection (OSI) model since 1977 for a universal data communications network architecture (see "A long-awaited standard for heterogeneous nets," DATA COMMUNICATIONS, January, p. 63). This model describes seven distinct layers of service ranging from the physical interface to the application. The network communications answer offered by 3Com adheres to this model (see figure).

The physical and data link layers are represented by the Ethernet transmission system and the Ethernet data link specification. The network and transport layers are implemented by the IP (Internet Protocol) and the TCP (Transmission Control Protocol), respectively.

Above these, Unet completes several pieces of the model. The session layer is unimplemented. File Transfer (Unet File Transfer Program—UFTP) and Virtual Terminal (Unet Virtual Terminal Program—UVTP) services are provided as presentation layer components. The UFTP and the UVTP user interfaces, together with mail transfer (Unet Mail Transfer Program—UMTP), are available at the application layer. Unet is flexible and allows a programmer access to all layers.

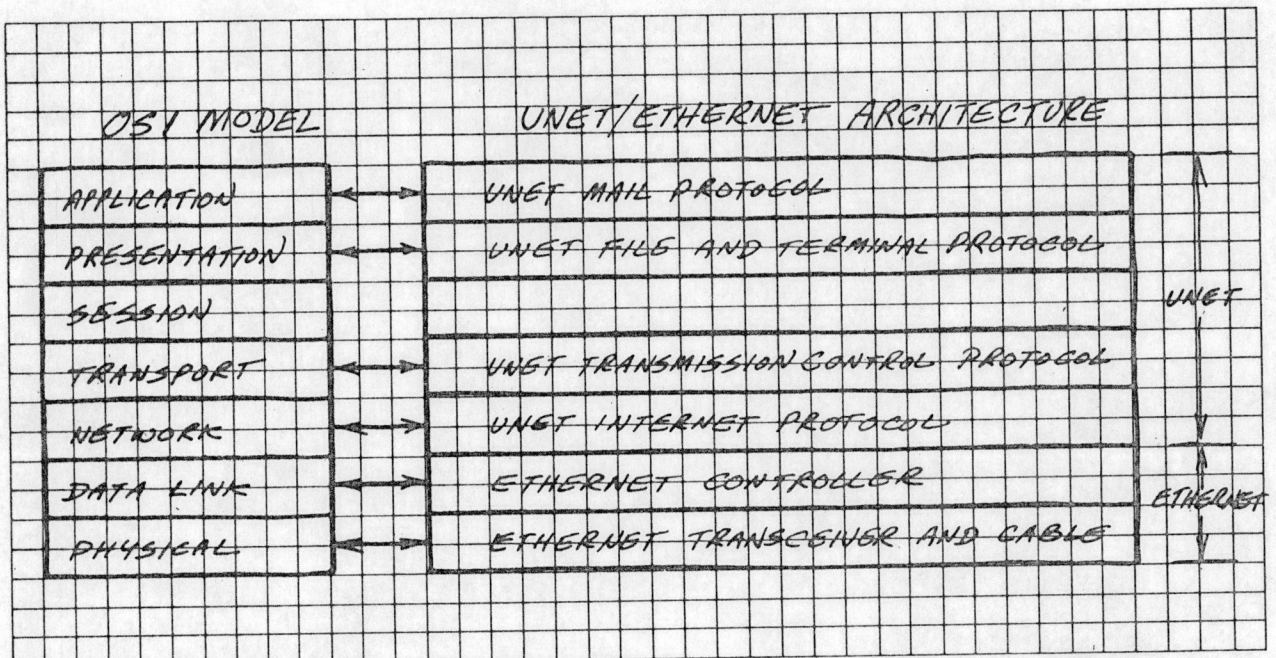

that makes it to Ethernet specifications.

Any one Ethernet cable is limited to a maximum length of 500 meters. The coaxial cable is laid along a path near the stations that are to be interconnected. Individual Ethernet segments may be joined by active repeaters and gateways to form larger networks. Segments that are connected by repeaters appear as one continuous local Ethernet; however, the total network end-to-end length is limited to 2,500 meters. Any two stations can be separated by no more than two repeaters. Gateways connect Ethernet and non-Ethernet communications networks.

Transceiving signals

The 3Com 3C100 Ethernet transceiver provides a high-impedance connection to the coaxial cable (greater than 50,000 ohms resistance and less than 4-picofarad capacitance). It can transmit and receive 10-Mbit/s serial bit streams and detect collisions.

Three signals, in addition to power, are carried by an interface cable between the transceiver and a controller located in the computer backplane, shown in Figure 1. These signals, each on a separate twisted pair, are transmit, receive, and collision detect. The transmit signal traveling from the controller passes through an isolation stage in the transceiver before being injected into the coaxial cable. The receiver circuits continually monitor signals on the coaxial cable with similar isolation. After leaving the cable, the receive signal undergoes conditioning (an equalization process to correct for distortion that is introduced when the signal travels through the line) before driving the receive twisted pair in the interface cable back to the controller. The collision-detect signal, a 10-MHz waveform, becomes active either when one transceiver begins transmitting and another unit attempts to transmit soon after or when two or more transceivers attempt to transmit simultaneously.

The transceiver accepts input voltages of from 9 to 15 volts and electrically isolates the interface cable from the coaxial cable. Faults in the coaxial line may be detected by specialized maintenance electronics to implement time-domain reflectometry. This is a radar-like method of studying reflected pulses on a line to determine if faults are present. The 3Com transceiver connects directly to the coaxial cable with conven-

tional N-series connectors. Installation consists of nothing more than connecting the transceiver to the coaxial cable; no adjustments are necessary.

A D-series 15-pin connector joins the transceiver to the controller with an interface cable consisting of four twisted-pair conductors, as well as an overall shield and an insulating jacket. The characteristic impedance of all signal pairs is 78 ohms ±5 ohms, and the signal attenuation of any pair cannot exceed 3 dB measured at 10 MHz.

Transceivers that are physically attached to the cable have no impact on Ethernet communications if left unpowered by an associated controller. This facilitates the future connecting and disconnecting of different vendors' network-compatible devices. The 3Com Ethernet transceiver conforms to the published Ethernet specification, version 1.0.

Individual transceivers may be placed arbitrarily along the coaxial cable provided they are spaced at least 2.5 meters apart (Fig. 2). Computers may be connected up to 50 meters from their transceivers using the special transceiver interface cable.

Implementing the data link layer

The 3Com Ethernet controller is a link-level controller that interfaces a host computer to the Ethernet transceiver. Sixteen 2,048-byte buffers of dual-ported memory (accessible from two places—in this case from the CPU and the controller) allow 10-Mbit/s Ethernet transfers without using the CPU bus. Independent transmit and receive queues, together with interrupt signals, implement the capability to transmit and receive back-to-back Ethernet packets.

Data packets to be transmitted are placed into the buffer memory, and the buffer identifier is then written into the controller's transmit-control register by the host processor. When the coaxial cable is quiescent, the controller hardware extracts the data from the buffer, serializes the data, and sends it to the transceiver with an Ethernet preamble and cyclic redundancy check (CRC) field attached. If multiple buffer identifiers are written into the transmit-control register, the indicated packets will be sent in the order submitted, separated by the required 9.6-microsecond gap.

To receive packets, the buffer identifier of an available receive buffer is written into the receive-control register by the host processor. When carrier is sensed on the coaxial cable, the controller hardware receives each bit from the transceiver, assembles consecutive bytes, and stores them in the indicated data buffer, verifying the attached CRC field. If multiple buffer identifiers are stored in the receive-control register, back-to-back packets will be properly received into the specified buffers. The host processor may then read the received packets from the buffer memory. Host packet processing and controller transactions are independent and may take place concurrently, if desired.

The address recognition of incoming packets and the binary exponential backoff algorithm used to calculate the retransmission of packets are implemented in software and are provided with the controller.

Ethernet alone is insufficient to provide a meaningful

The Ethernet local-network approach

A convenient method of connecting computers over short distances is the Ethernet local computer network. In fact, Ethernet has now been recognized by more than a dozen manufacturers as the de facto standard for local computer communications.

The 10-Mbit/s, packet-switching network is designed to interconnect hundreds of high-function computers or workstations within 2.5 kilometers of each other. Ethernet uses a passive, equitable, highly efficient statistical method known as carrier-sense multiple-access with collision detection (CSMA/CD) that enables stations on the network to share access to the coaxial cable transmission medium.

Carrier-sense means that each station "listens" to the cable before transmitting a packet; if some other station is already transmitting, the first station senses the presence of the carrier and defers transmitting its own packet until the cable is quiescent. Multiple-access means that all stations tap into and share the same coaxial cable. Every transmitted packet is "heard" by all stations on the Ethernet. The intended recipients detect incoming packets by recognizing their addresses embedded in the packets; other packets are discarded.

If two or more stations transmit packets at the same time, their signals will be intermixed on the coaxial cable. This is known as a collision. By listening while transmitting and comparing what is heard on the cable with the data being transmitted, each station can detect collisions and back off by waiting a random time interval before attempting to retransmit the packet. The efficiency of the network remains high even under conditions of heavy load, because the mean of the random backoff interval increases each time a collision occurs.

communications service. Higher-level protocols, corresponding to layers 3 through 7 of the open systems interconnection model, are essential. 3Com Corporation has developed networking software that maps well into these layers. Called Unet, it provides networking services to Unix users.

Network and transport layers

At the lowest level, Unet implements data link drivers for the physical network, in this case, the Ethernet controller. Above that are the Internet Protocol (IP) and the Transmission Control Protocol (TCP). Both protocols are standards approved by the U.S. Department of Defense.

The IP layer implements a lower-level datagram facility. Two simple interface procedures are available to the "clients" (higher software layers that use the services provided by a lower one) of IP (such as TCP):

Send	Sends a datagram (single-packet message) to a remote host.
Receive	Receives a datagram from a remote host.

1. Sending signals. *Receive, transmit, and collision-detect signals, as well as power, are carried by an interface cable. Signals travel through an isolation stage between the controller and the coaxial cable. The receive signal also undergoes conditioning when traveling from the coaxial cable to the controller.*

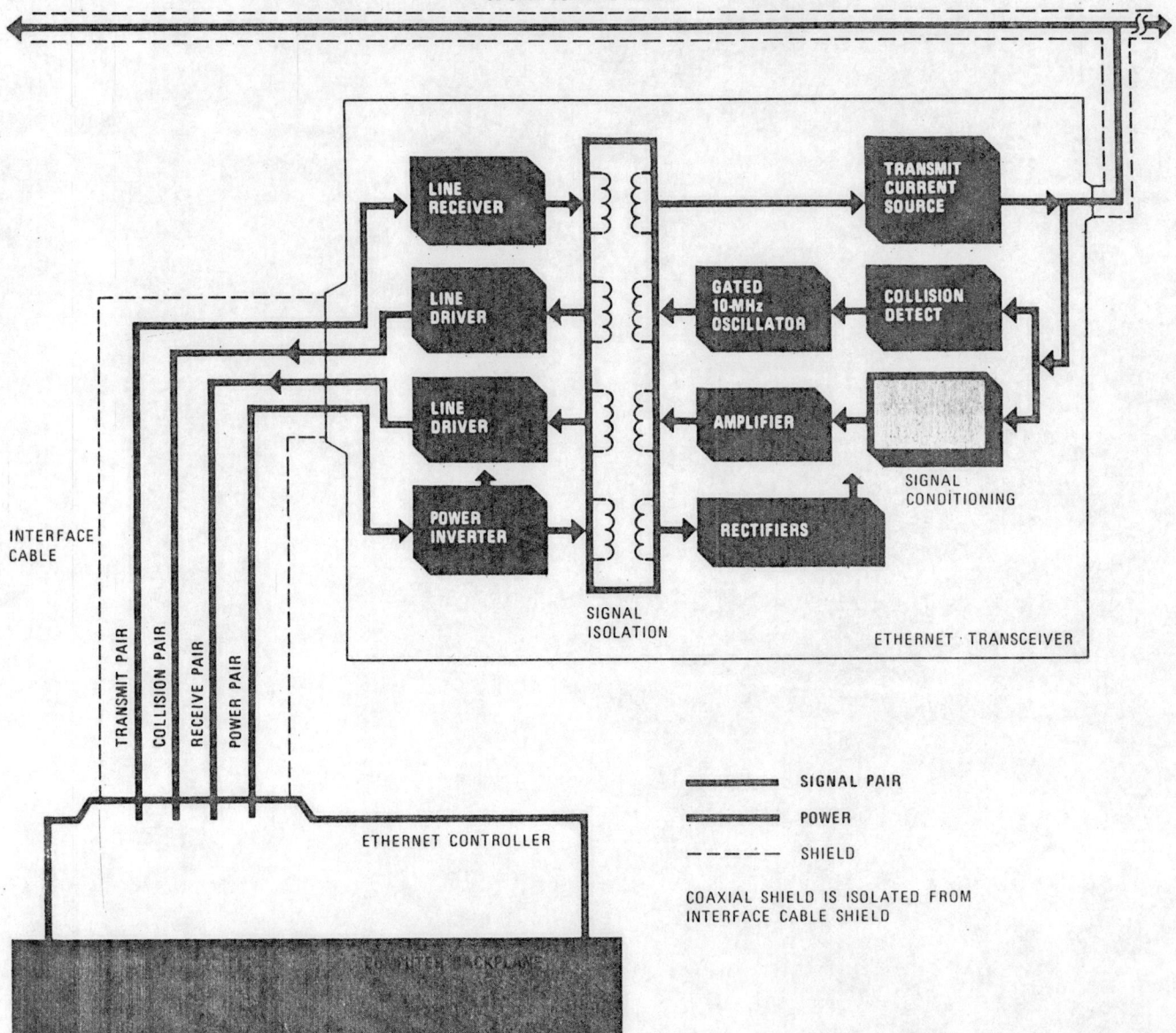

Datagrams are tagged by the client with a destination host address. IP attaches a source address to the datagram, decides how the datagram should be routed based on the destination address, and hands it to the appropriate data link driver. If the datagram is too large for the selected data link, the IP fragments the datagram into smaller packets, and the IP at the remote host reassembles the packets transparently.

The TCP layer uses the datagram services of the IP layer to provide secure, reliable connections between software processes via bidirectional byte streams, called virtual circuits. From 4 to 64 configurable virtual circuits, each corresponding to a separate interprocess dialogue, can be established at once. The interface functions provided to clients are:

Open	Establishes a virtual circuit to a specified process on a remote host.
Send	Sends some data over a specified virtual circuit.
Receive	Receives some data from a specified virtual circuit.
Abort	Abruptly terminates a virtual circuit.
Close	Closes down a virtual circuit gracefully (in contrast to closing down abruptly).

Providing such a general-purpose facility requires a number of processing steps that are internal to TCP. For example, the continuous byte stream supplied by the TCP client is broken up into datagrams for shipment to IP. To avoid sending data faster than the other host is prepared to receive it, a windowing facility (a mechanism for indicating the amount of data that the host can receive) is used to control the bidirectional flow of datagrams.

A checksum is attached to each datagram and verified by the remote TCP for added reliability. Successful delivery of all datagrams transmitted is ensured by a positive-acknowledgment scheme. Data that is lost, damaged, or delivered out of order causes a retransmission of the corrupted datagram. The TCP is designed so that it is not confused by unreliable data link facilities, system failures, or an incorrect protocol. If error-free, in-sequence, timely data cannot be delivered, the virtual circuit is terminated and the clients at both ends are informed by error messages.

Above the communications protocols, Unet offers three end-user application programs.

The upper layer

In the upper layer, the Unet File Transfer Program (UFTP) transfers Unix files between different host machines on the network. When invoked, an interactive connection is established to the remote host and a log in is then performed, setting up the directory environment and access rights on the remote host. The following commands are then available:

Get	Retrieves a remote file from the local host.
Put	Stores a local file onto the remote host.
Mget	Retrieves multiple files from the remote host.
Mput	Stores multiple files onto the remote host.
Rename	Changes the name of a file on the remote host.

2. Typical Ethernet configuration. A single local Ethernet network consists of 500-meter segments of coaxial cable, connected with repeaters. Individual transceivers may be placed arbitrarily along the cable but spaced at least 2.5 meters apart. Computers may be connected up to 50 meters from their transceivers.

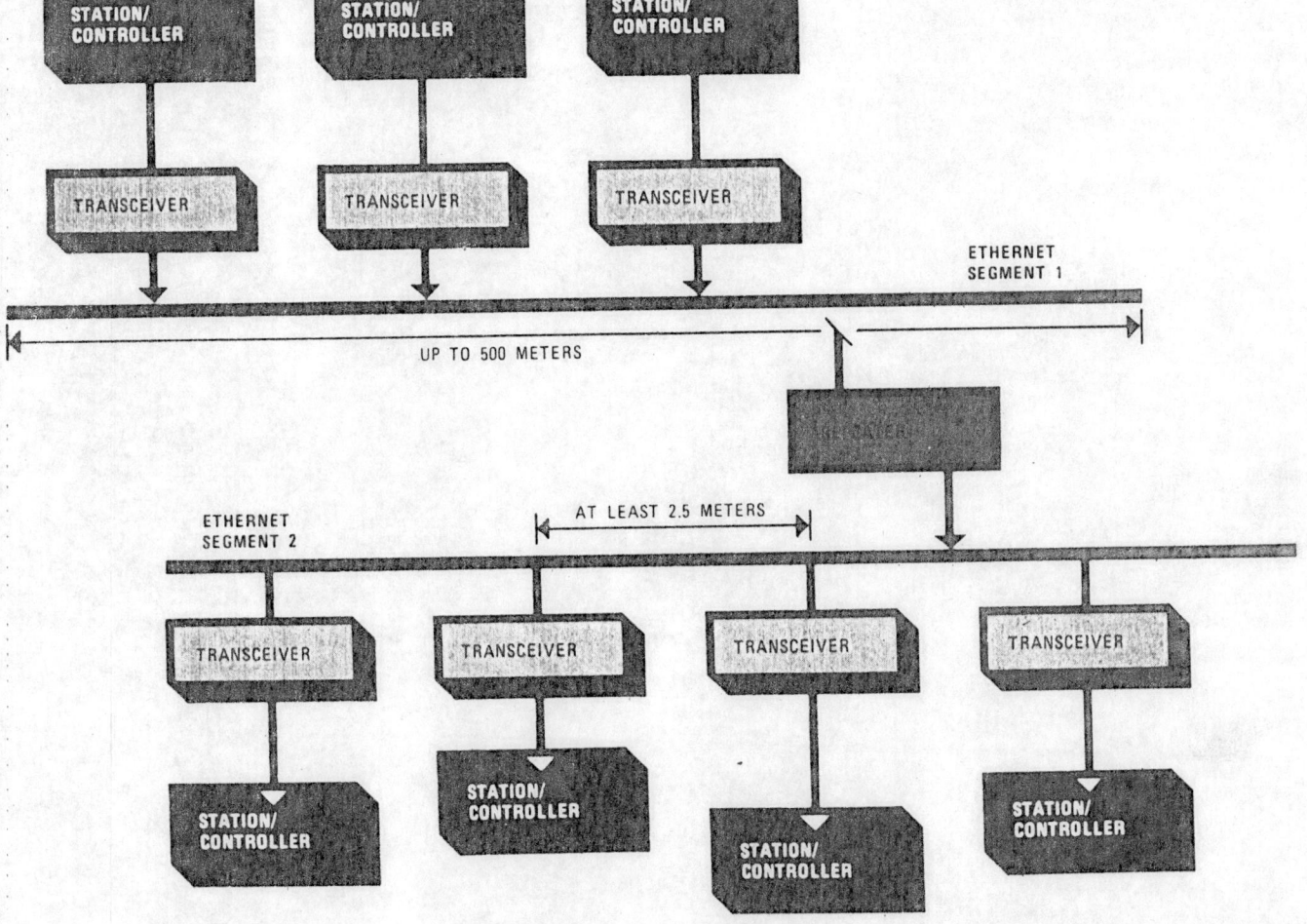

Delete	Removes a file on the remote host computer.		

	content
Body	The main message text

The Unet Mail Transfer Program (UMTP) uses the file-transfer protocol to distribute Unix electronic mail among network hosts. An electronic-mail message can be sent to a list of "mailboxes" located on any host accessible via Unet. Mail is sent immediately, if possible, or queued for later delivery if the destination host is not responding. And queued mail that cannot be sent after three days is returned to the sender with an explanatory message. A UMTP message contains the following fields:

To	A list of message recipients
From	The originator of the message
Cc	A list of additional mailboxes to receive the message for information only
Subject	A brief statement of the message

The Unet Virtual Terminal Program (UVTP) allows a user who is sitting at a terminal on one computer to log in to a remote computer and then perform various operations as if the terminal were connected directly to that machine. When invoked, a connection is established to the remote machine, and the initial login prompt from that remote machine appears on the user's screen. From that point on, characters to and from the local terminal are ferried between the remote system and the terminal. An escape sequence may be typed by the user to temporarily execute commands on the local system or to terminate the connection (see "A sample data flow").

Direct access to Unet protocols
In addition to the services provided by the upper layers, the user may directly access the datagram (IP) and

A sample data flow
A text file is transferred from one machine to another using Unet's File Transfer Program (UFTP). The user executes the UFTP from the terminal, connects to the remote host, and specifies the file to be transferred. The UFTP then processes the characters and maps the character set of the local host into a machine-independent virtual character set.

The mapped character stream is then passed to a virtual circuit set up between the local and remote hosts. The Transmission Control Protocol (TCP) breaks up the stream into packets for transmission, retransmits corrupted packets to ensure reliability, limits the data-flow rate to avoid overruns, and provides multiplexing to support multiple simultaneous virtual circuits.

The TCP packets are passed to the Internet Protocol (IP), which contains the multiplexing facilities to interconnect multiple network types. The IP notices that the TCP packets are destined for a particular host on the Ethernet network, and therefore it passes the packet on to the Ethernet driver.

The Ethernet driver selects an unused Ethernet controller buffer, copies the packet into it, and tells the controller to transmit the packet. The controller waits until the Ethernet transceiver indicates that the coaxial cable is not in use, then sends the packet to the transceiver 1 bit at a time.

The Ethernet transceiver receives the bit stream from the controller and injects it onto the attached coaxial cable, listening all the while for collisions. If a collision is detected, the controller is informed so that the packet can be retransmitted.

At the remote station, the reverse occurs. Bits are received by the transceiver, stored by the controller in a receive buffer, and passed by the IP to the TCP. The TCP assembles the packets into a continuous byte stream and passes this stream to the UFTP, which maps characters back into the character set of the remote host. The result is stored in a remote file.

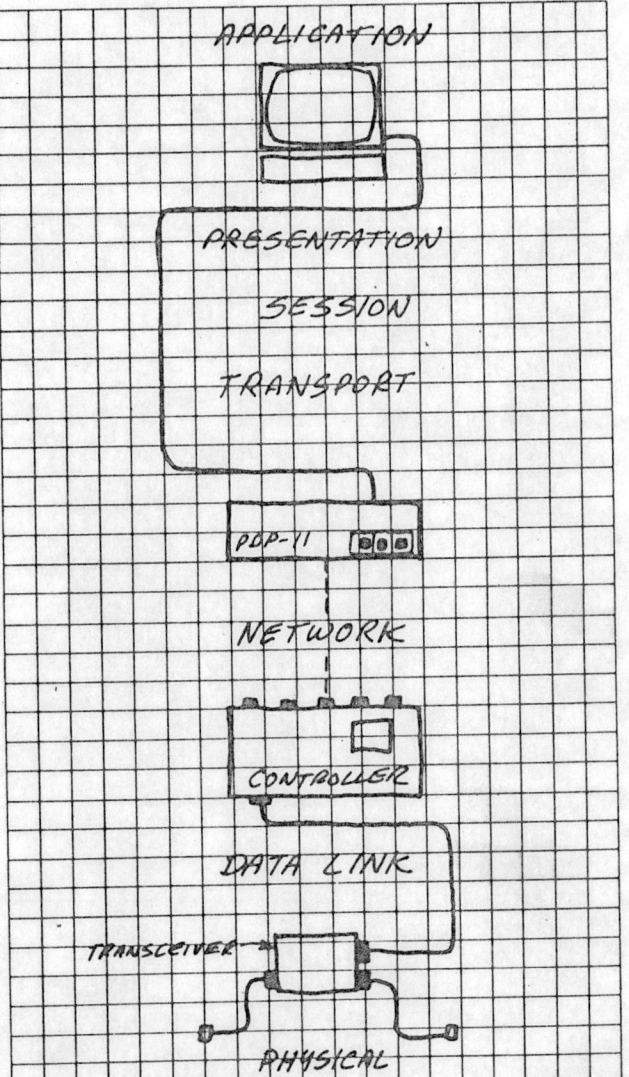

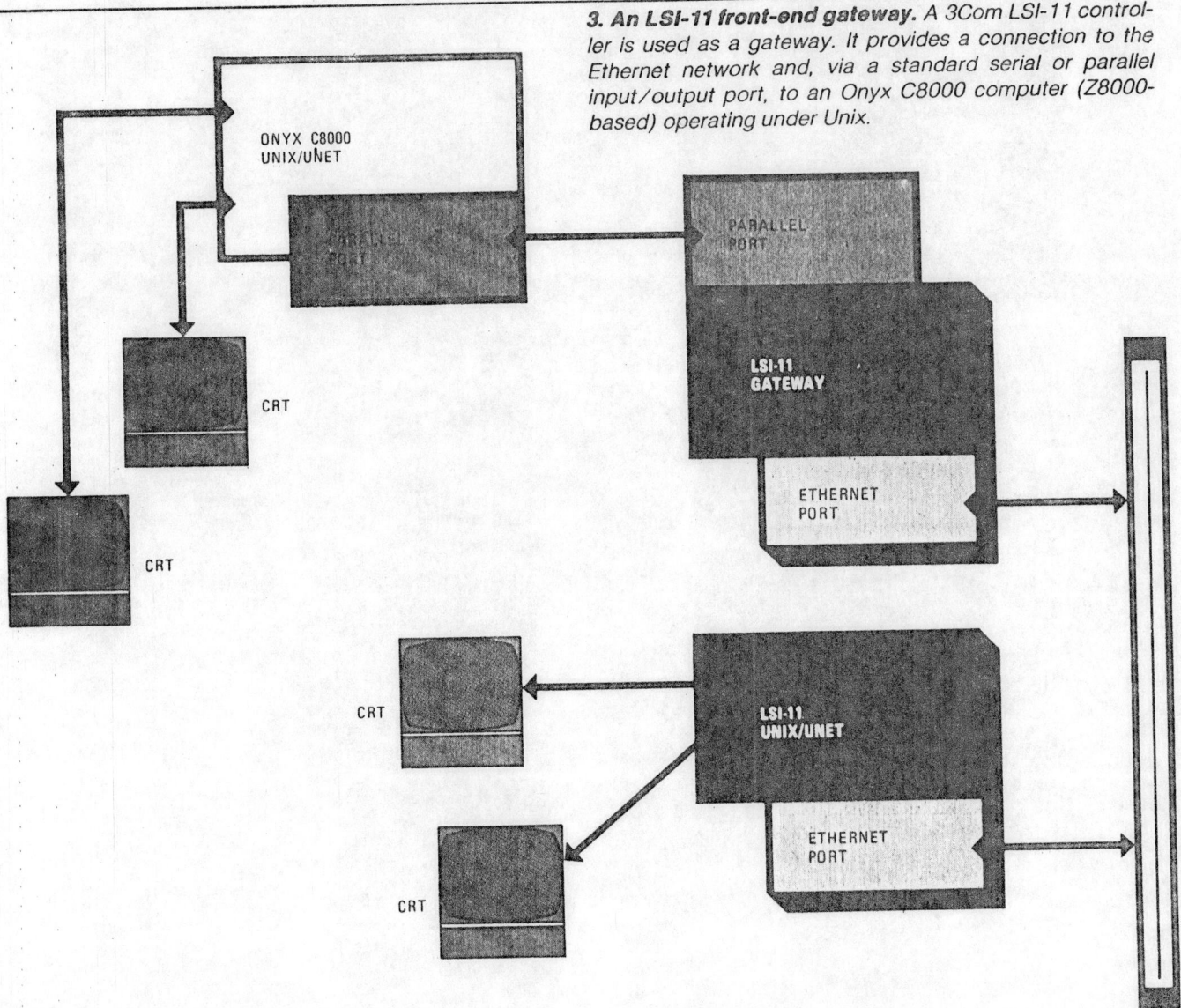

3. An LSI-11 front-end gateway. *A 3Com LSI-11 controller is used as a gateway. It provides a connection to the Ethernet network and, via a standard serial or parallel input/output port, to an Onyx C8000 computer (Z8000-based) operating under Unix.*

virtual-circuit (TCP) facilities of Unet. This feature is useful in custom-fitting specialized Ethernet applications. For example, several stations on the network might not require software multiplexing (maintaining multiple virtual circuits simultaneously) or even the reliable delivery of packets provided by TCP. These stations could be factory control or sampling units, each dedicated to a single operation. If the sampled information that these stations generate is averaged, the receipt of every piece might not be critical. A trade-off is then available for faster processing by not acknowledging each packet.

Ethernet/Unet for other computers
This Ethernet/Unet solution can also be used for non-DEC computers. The approach employs the LSI-11 computer as a front-end gateway. A 3Com LSI-11 communications controller provides a connection to Ethernet, while a standard serial or parallel I/O port links to the non-DEC, Unix-based host computer. The

Unix-based computer then uses Unet to exchange Internet Protocol packets with the LSI-11 gateway. This is possible because Unet is designed to be independent of the underlying transmission scheme. Unet drivers for serial, parallel, and Network Systems Corporation's Hyperchannel interfaces are supported. The user-supplied gateway software shuttles packets between the two computers, associating IP addresses with Ethernet addresses through a table lookup.

Such a configuration, shown in Figure 3, has been implemented to interface an Onyx C8000 (Z8000-based) computer with an Ethernet network for communicating with other Unix/Unet-based computers. Moreover, non-Ethernet-compatible peripheral devices can be linked to the network if they are operated by a host computer that is interfaced to such an LSI-11 gateway. Thus, an Ethernet transceiver, controller, interconnect cables, and Unet software provide local computer networking not only for DEC computers but also for any Unix-based computer. ▪

The first all-in-one local network

Didier S. Castueil, Domenic L. Giovachino, and Dennis L. Lengyel,
Amecom Division, Litton Industries, College Park, Md.

**This all-digital local network, with very high speeds
and a simple protocol, integrates data, voice, and
video, supports any vendor's equipment, and promises
additional protocol/speed-conversion capabilities.**

Network planners are justifiably concerned that today's
local networks may become obsolete in the near future.
This is particularly true of the baseband, Ethernet-like,
coaxial networks, which lack the throughput or bandwidth needed for the addition of digitized voice or video
and, in some cases, the capability of moving large
blocks of data quickly as required for file transfer or
document retrieval.

Today's commercially available local networks offer
distributed communications links, or paths, in a bus
topology, which support standard data communications functions. And since most of these local networks
are designed to replace more commonly used point-
to-point data connections, they usually add no significant capabilities in themselves. They do not offer an
integrated real-time voice capability, nor do they provide for network-control functions, which typically must
be performed by the host computers or other user
devices connected to the network. Additionally, many
of these products interconnect only one vendor's
equipment or computers.

Network planners need to achieve local networking
by interconnecting existing devices. They also need
the flexibility to add equipment from a variety of vendors. Because users are likely to have a mixture of
equipment manufactured by various companies, usually with a variety of incompatible interfaces, planners
must now modify existing software or purchase a variety of protocol-conversion devices to create a network.
In many cases, equipment such as simple terminals

do not have the capability to perform network-control
functions, while more-intelligent devices lack the resources to develop new software. Real-time voice, at
present, is handled separately and typically requires
an additional set of wires.

The Amecom Division of Litton Industries addressed
these problems by developing a unique local network
architecture, which resulted from a project aimed at
military command, control, and communications (C^3)
applications. The universal bus information transfer
system (Ubits), developed at Amecom, consists of one
or more high-speed local networks interconnected via
point-to-point serial links that may use cable, optical
fiber, microwave, or satellite facilities.

In Ubits, digitized voice, video, and data are integrated in a single, high-speed digital communications
network. It enables secure, real-time communications
that is essential in a C^3 environment. Ubits's unique
features are its high speed and real-time voice capability; it also provides transport and connectivity for a
wide variety of devices. Ubits is not tailored to a specific vendor's equipment but offers generalized network-control functions such as end-to-end flow control,
error control, and a virtual-circuit capability. It provides
for the error-free delivery of sequenced data packets.

Because considerable intelligence is built into the
user interface, the network provides other value-added
services such as code, speed, and protocol conversion.
This significant development allows dissimilar equipment (ranging from large computers to simple asyn-

1. Interconnected local networks. The Ubits architecture consists of multiple high-speed local buses, interconnected by high-speed point-to-point links. Although the link between global interface units (GIUs) is designed to operate at 45 Mbit/s, T1-capacity (1.544-Mbit/s) facilities can be used, but with load limitations.

chronous terminals) to interface with the network.

In Ubits, point-to-point links are established between specialized nodes, called global interface units (GIUs), which reside on local buses (Fig. 1). These links operate at data transmission rates up to 45 Mbit/s, and since transmission delays across these links are negligible (measured in tens of microseconds), real-time voice communications is practical.

Network architecture

As a node on the local bus, the GIU listens to all local traffic. However, it is programmed to receive only those messages addressed to it and transmit only those packets destined for nodes across the channel. At the remote end, the other GIU delivers these packets to the local bus, where they can be received by the des-

tination node. The GIU performs no other processing except parallel-to-serial conversion and temporary data buffering.

The same node-to-node protocol operates across the remote link as on the local bus. Thus, the entire network appears like a single logical bus. The network can be expanded without the changes to nodal software or the significant delays that are experienced with other store-and-forward techniques.

A GIU contending for its local bus uses the same protocol as any other node. However, there is no contention across the point-to-point links. As a result, the distance between GIUs in no way affects end-to-end network throughput. Therefore, GIUs, connected via terrestrial or satellite links, function as gateways to interconnect local-bus networks that may be physically

2. NMU structure. *Vendor transparency in this local network scheme is achieved through software modules in the network management units (NMUs). Programmable interface modules (PIMs) handle the formatting of all traffic— data, voice, or video—into simple packets. Data PIMs can also handle code, speed, and protocol conversion.*

HIGH-SPEED BUS

NETWORK-ORIENTED MODULES

NMU CONTROLLER (REDUNDANT INTEL 8086-BASED CPUs)

HIGH-SPEED BUS I/O (HSBIO)

SHARED MEMORY

NMU COMMON BUS

USER-ORIENTED MODULES

VOICE PIM

DATA PIM

VIDEO PIM

HOST

SYNCHRONOUS TERMINAL

ASYNCHRONOUS TERMINAL

DIGITAL VOICE SWITCH

TV CAMERA

---

separated by large distances.

A high-speed (160-Mbit/s) bus interconnects devices locally—within a command center, computer room, or one floor of a building, for example. User devices access this local network through intelligent, high-throughput nodes, called network management units (NMUs), which are connected in a bus topology by a high-speed broadcast transmission medium (currently a multiple-twisted-pair parallel cable). The NMUs employ a decentralized, carrier-sense multiple-access (CSMA) contention scheme to access the bus.

Short packets

All information—data, digitized voice, facsimile, and even video—is assembled into packets. Each packet consists of a four-word header (2 bytes per header)

and up to a 60-word information field. These relatively short packets are desirable for communicating real-time, delay-sensitive information such as digitized voice. Large blocks of data, subsequently, are transmitted in a series of short packets.

Bus efficiency is maintained by the small header size relative to the information-field size. This results in minimum overhead per packet. The small header size, coupled with wide bus bandwidth, results in almost instantaneous access to the bus (approximately 6 microseconds). To make effective use of the high-speed transmission, the NMU is designed for a throughput of 10,000 packets per second.

The NMUs in the Ubits network are microprocessor-based and can support up to 127 logical hosts or terminals. Functionally, an NMU accepts data from a host,

separated by large distances.

A high-speed (180-Mbit/s) bus interconnects devices locally — within a command center, computer
room, or one floor of a building, for example. User devices access this local network through intelligent, high-
throughput nodes, called network management units
(NMUs), which are connected in a bus topology by a
high-speed broadcast transmission medium (currently
a multiple-twisted-pair parallel cable). The NMUs employ a decentralized carrier-sense multiple-access
(CSMA) contention scheme to access the bus.

Short packets

All information — data, digitized voice, facsimile, and
even video — is assembled into packets. Each packet
consists of a four-word header (2 bytes per header)

and up to a 60-word information field. These relatively
short packets are desirable for a communicating real-
time, delay-sensitive information such as digitized
voice. Large blocks of data, subsequently, are na-
...ted in a series of short packets.

This efficiency is maintained by the small header size
relative to the information-field size. This results in minimum overhead per packet. The small packet size,
coupled with wide bus bandwidth, results in almost
instantaneous access to the bus (approximately 6 microseconds). To make effective use of the high-speed
transmission, the NMU is designed for a throughput of
10,000 packets per second.

The NMUs in the UDLS network are microprocessor-
based and can support up to 127 logical hosts or terminals. Functionally, an NMU accepts data from a host

assembles packets (appends the appropriate header information), and delivers them to the high-speed bus. It also monitors the bus, accepts any packets that are addressed to it, disassembles these packets, and delivers the data to the appropriate attached device.

The NMU functions can be separated into two types: network-oriented and user-oriented. Network-oriented functions, such as packet assembly/disassembly (PAD), flow control, and error control, are performed by hardware and software that is independent of the type of device being supported by the node. These functions are performed identically throughout the network in each NMU. User-oriented hardware/software components are referred to as programmable interface modules (PIMs) and are application-dependent. A PIM interfaces with the network-oriented hardware via shared memory on a common-access bus (Fig. 2).

Network administration

Decentralized control and distributed access are inherent to a bus-oriented network, but certain network-management functions are best performed by a single controlling device: In the Ubits network, one NMU is designated as a "task director." The task director provides two management functions: network control, including system direction and administration, and quality control, which includes monitoring and diagnostic analyses.

The task director sends messages that initialize the other NMUs, request NMU status, and down-load specified protocols into PIMs. It also monitors network health and status by gathering statistical information on bus utilization, monitoring the number of retransmissions, and analyzing fault indicators. If the controller encounters a problem, it runs diagnostic tests and displays the results on a CRT (Fig. 1). In addition, it functions as a repository for all network-configuration information and maintains a central database for network directories and files.

Reconfiguration

Changes to network operation or configuration, such as the movement of user equipment, changes in priorities, or changes to user identifications, are initiated by the task director. The user or application program does not need to know the physical location or unique network address of any other device. Through the use of logical identifiers, the task director handles all routing and addressing.

Ubits developers constructed a network consisting of three NMUs interconnected via a 160-Mbit/s bus to evaluate the network architecture, control functions, and transport protocols. This model is currently being operated as a test bed for PIM evaluation and for the development of additional services such as code, speed, and protocol conversion. The table summarizes the performance, functions, and features currently provided by the Ubits components.

In real-time communications networks, reliability is a critical factor. Consequently, this has been emphasized in the Ubits development effort. The twisted-pair cable used as the transmission medium between NMUs

Ubits network components

NETWORK COMPONENT	CHARACTERISTICS	FUNCTION	PERFORMANCE	APPLICATION
GLOBAL INTERFACE UNIT (GIU)	HARDWIRED DESIGN	HIGH-SPEED SERIAL	UP TO 45 MBIT/S	POINT-TO-POINT LINKS FOR PRIVATE NETWORKS
NETWORK MANAGEMENT UNIT (NMU)	16-BIT, MICROPROCESSOR-CONTROLLED (REDUNDANT), COMMON BUS ARCHITECTURE	HIGH-SPEED PARALLEL INTERFACE TO OTHER NMUs CONTENTION, ERROR, AND FLOW CONTROL PROVIDED	160-MBIT/S PARALLEL INTERFACE 10-MBIT/S THROUGHPUT	REAL-TIME, INTEGRATED VOICE, VIDEO, AND DATA COMMUNICATIONS NETWORKS
VOICE PIM	HARDWIRED DESIGN MULTIBUS-COMPATIBLE	MUX/DEMUX T1 CARRIER SYSTEM	24 CHANNELS AT 64 KBIT/S 3-MBIT/S THROUGHPUT	VOICE-SWITCHING INTERFACE TO DIGITAL SERVICE
VIDEO PIM	HARDWIRED DESIGN MULTIBUS-COMPATIBLE	A/D, D/A CONVERSIONS CCTV CAMERA, TV MONITOR INTERFACES	2 FRAMES PER SECOND 1-MBIT/S THROUGHPUT	VIDEO CONFERENCING SECURITY SYSTEMS
DATA PIM	16-BIT MICROPROCESSOR-BASED MULTIBUS-COMPATIBLE DMA CAPABILITY SOFTWARE RECONFIGURABLE OPTIONAL I/O PROCESSOR	PACKET ASSEMBLY/DISASSEMBLY (PAD) FOR NONPACKET DEVICES EXECUTES PIM-TO-PIM PROTOCOL EXECUTES ASYNCHRONOUS AND SYNCHRONOUS (SDLC, HDLC) LINK PROTOCOLS	SINGLE-PROCESSOR CONFIGURATION: 220 KBIT/S MAXIMUM THROUGHPUT FOR SINGLE DEVICE UP TO 16 HALF-DUPLEX, 9.6-KBIT/S PORTS PARALLEL I/O PROCESSOR: 1.5 MBIT/S MAXIMUM THROUGHPUT FOR SINGLE PORT UP TO 48 HALF-DUPLEX, 9.6-KBIT/S PORTS	TERMINAL HANDLER ASYNC/SYNC PORTS PUBLIC NETWORK GATEWAY PROTOCOL CONVERSION DATA CONCENTRATION STATISTICAL MULTIPLEXING

3. Programmable interface module. *Functional components of a data PIM (programmable interface module) are shown. Code, speed, and protocol conversion, if necessary, are performed first on incoming data streams. Processed data is then assembled into packets and passed on to the NMU bus for subsequent transmission.*

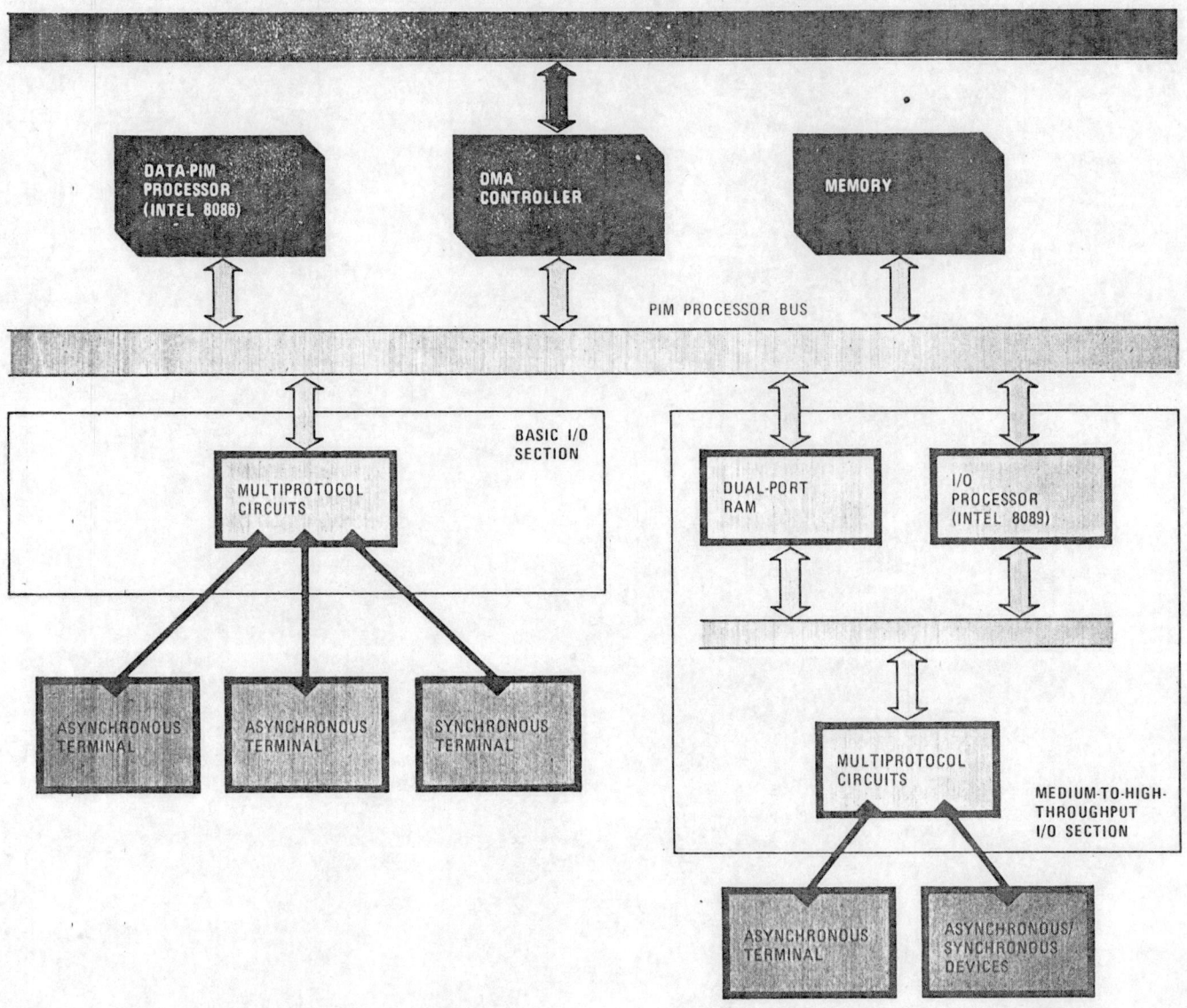

is inherently reliable because of its simplicity and its straightforward interface requirements. However, the processor portion of the NMU is a possible point of failure for all user devices connected to the NMU. Therefore, a redundant CPU design was implemented: A hot standby processor takes over control of the NMU operation without disrupting communications.

Also emphasized in the Ubits design were performance capabilities. The NMU offers a throughput of 10 Mbit/s and a modular construction (Fig. 2). All operational modules, including input/output (I/O), shared CPU memory, and the PIMs, are interconnected via a common NMU bus. The advantage to this is that any NMU function can be expanded when necessary.

The data PIM provides the digital-data interface to Ubits. It is microprocessor-based and supports multiple

I/O ports, as shown in Figure 3. Because of the addition of intelligence at this point in the architecture, Ubits is transparent to any connected device. It supports a variety of protocols.

A real-time multitasking operating system was written to run on both the network and the data-PIM processors. In the data PIM, this operating system runs tasks that perform the PAD function as described in CCITT Recommendation X.3. In this mode, the PIM functions like a terminal driver in a computer network. The interaction between an asynchronous terminal and the PIM follows the specification in CCITT Recommendation X.28. A prime application of the PIM, therefore, is to convert asynchronous traffic to synchronous, allowing its use in existing computer networks.

For data-PIM applications requiring a small number

4. Ubits and OSI. *The high-speed-bus I/O (HSBIO) performs the functions defined in the OSI model's Level 1. The NMU handles the link- and network-level tasks.*

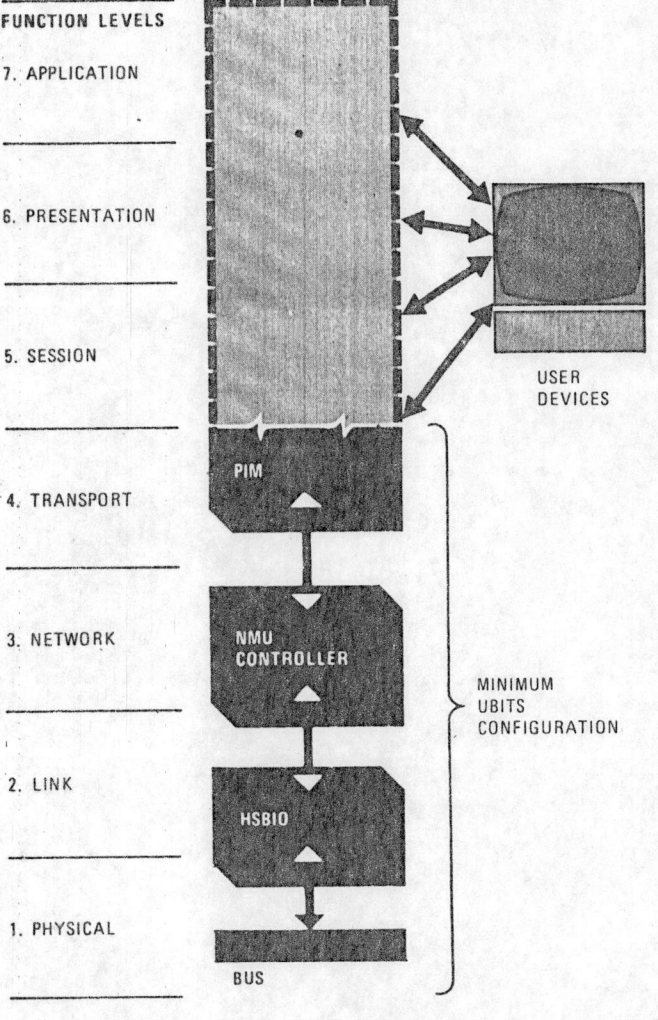

verts the digital information to a composite video signal for display on a standard TV monitor. In this way, rapidly updated still frames are transmitted at a rate of two complete frames per second, equal to a PIM-to-PIM transfer rate of approximately 1 Mbit/s.

T1-compatible

The digital-voice PIM supports 24 simultaneous full-duplex voice conversations. The T1-carrier format is used, offering an aggregate throughput of 1.544 Mbit/s in each direction. This transfer rate requires the NMU to process 3,000 packets per second. The digital-voice PIM was designed specifically for T1 compatibility and uses PCM/TDM (pulse-code modulated/time-division multiplexed) 64-kbit/s digital-voice circuits. In addition, it supports an interface to standard telephone equipment.

In applications that require few connections (such as an intercom function), the digital-voice PIM can handle digitized voice at a reduced rate of 32 kbit/s. Its traffic may then be processed through a data PIM— thus allowing the data PIM to serve a dual function.

To support real-time communications, the Ubits network protocol had to minimize the software overhead required to perform the various network functions. Major design criteria were:

---

5. Bus access scheme. *In addition to 16 synchronized, parallel data streams, separate lines indicate carrier usage, denote parity, and provide for clocking.*

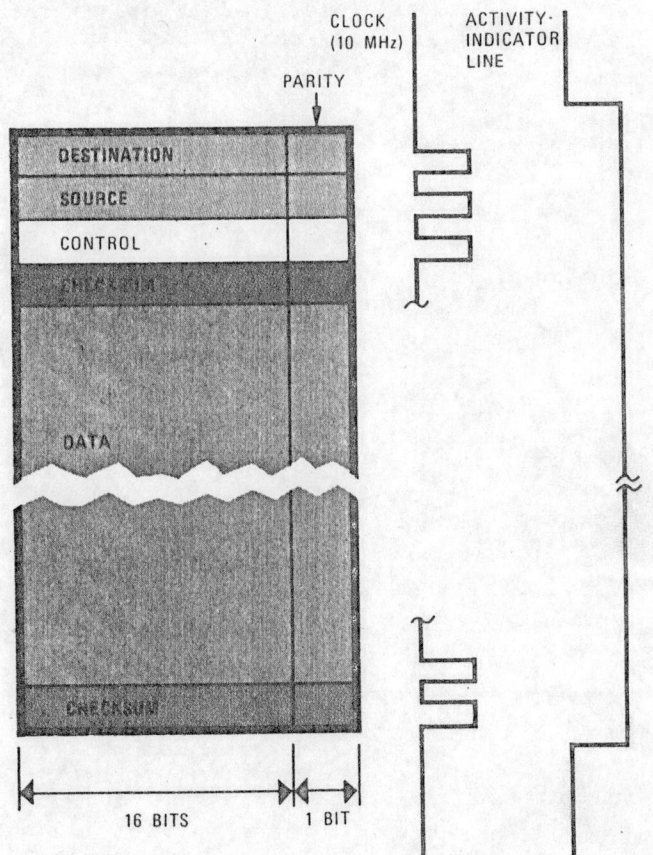

---

of low-speed (9.6-kbit/s and slower) ports, a single processor is used to support up to 16 devices, which may be running a variety of protocols. In medium-to-high-throughput applications (over 9.6 kbit/s), an I/O processor is added, which operates in parallel with the data-PIM processor and supports up to 48 devices. For any application, the total PIM throughput is a function of the speed, the number of ports, and the complexity of the protocols implemented. The PIM achieves a maximum throughput of 1.5 Mbit/s when processing a simple, serial bit stream.

Voice and video

The real-time features of the Ubits network are embodied in the video and digital-voice PIMs. The video PIM interfaces a standard closed-circuit television (CCTV) camera and TV monitor to the network, thus providing a video-teleconferencing capability. Composite video from a standard black-and-white CCTV camera is accepted and digitized by the transmitting video PIM. The digital image is sent to a receiving PIM, which con-

■ High throughput, to support 10 Mbit/s at each NMU
■ Low delay, to support interactive real-time voice
■ Multimode capability, to support the integration of voice, video, and data

To ensure application flexibility and compatibility with other equipment and networks, the Ubits architecture is layered similarly to the open systems interconnection (OSI) model (Fig. 4).

Level 1 involves physical connection to the high-speed bus, which consists of 16 data lines, a parity line, an activity-indicator line, and a clock line (Fig. 5). The 10-MHz clock is generated by the transmitting NMU to provide a timing reference for the receiving NMU. Each high-speed-bus I/O (HSBIO) interface contains independent transmit and receive sections that operate simultaneously. Therefore, each node "listens" to its own transmission. Furthermore, simultaneous operation ensures that packets arriving during what would normally be the turnaround time in modem-based networks are not missed.

Level 2 employs CSMA for bus access and uses the activity-indicator line for framing. When this line is active, a packet is being transmitted. Thus, no preamble (or flag) is required, which reduces the overhead and increases bus utilization. For synchronization, a clock pulse is associated with each word of every packet.

Also, for each 16-bit word, a parity bit is generated and transmitted.

The receive portion of the HSBIO verifies the parity before delivering a received packet to the NMU controller. A checksum (16-bit binary field) is calculated and verified by the NMU for the control information of each packet. Packets received in error are simply discarded (either by the HSBIO or by the NMU controller) at the link level. The HSBIO hardware also checks the packet addresses and accepts only packets intended for its NMU. In this manner, the NMU software is not burdened with processing unnecessary packets.

For voice applications, the Level 2 hardware ignores the parity bits in the information portion of the packet. However, parity bits in the header of every packet are always checked.

Level 3 of the Ubits protocol uses a simple packet format consisting of a four-word fixed header and an information section varying from 12 to 60 words (Fig. 6). The first 16-bit word is the destination identification. Two of these bits inform the HSBIO Level 2 error-detection function of the packet type (data, voice, video, or control). The other 14 bits identify the NMU and the port number within an NMU. Any combination is possible, providing for a maximum of 16,383 network ports. An NMU destination identification of zero is used

---

6. Frame format. *Ubits uses very simple, short frame formats. A checksum is always employed for the header information of each packet (data, voice, and video) but* *not for the information fields of voice or video packets. Use of the checksum for data packets is optional, depending on the grade of service required.*

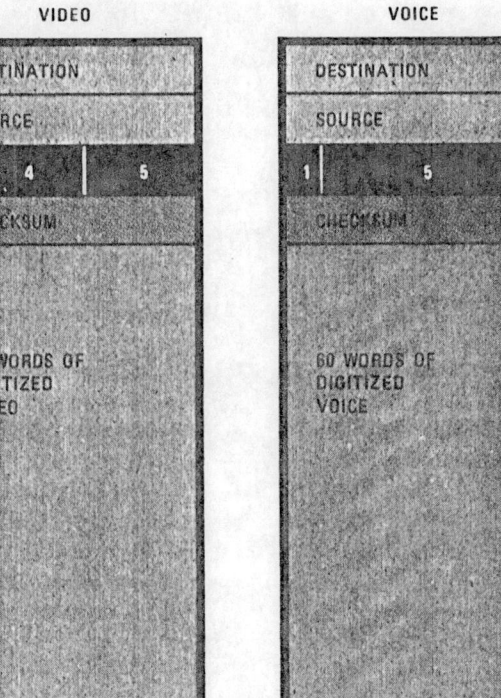

CONTROL

1. PACKET TYPE–2 BITS
2. LENGTH (WORDS)–6 BITS
3. CONTROL CODES–8 BITS

CHECKSUM FOR ENTIRE PACKET

DATA

1. PACKET TYPE–2 BITS
2. LENGTH (BYTES)–7 BITS
4. SEQUENCE NUMBER–7 BITS

SEPARATE CHECKSUMS FOR HEADER AND DATA

VIDEO

1. PACKET TYPE–2 BITS
4. SEQUENCE NUMBER–7 BITS
5. UNUSED–7 BITS

CHECKSUM FOR HEADER ONLY

VOICE

1. PACKET TYPE–2 BITS
5. UNUSED–14 BITS

CHECKSUM FOR HEADER ONLY

for broadcasting, and a port address of zero denotes network-administration functions such as traffic-data reporting, diagnostics, and configuration functions.

The second word in the header is the source identification, which has the same types of information and format as the destination word, except for two reserved bits. These bits indicate either a datagram service or a virtual-circuit service.

The third word in the header is a control word that contains the packet type, control type, byte count, and sequence number. A header checksum forms the fourth word, which is always used, regardless of packet type. A checksum for the data section of the packet can be added as an option, depending on the grade of service required.

High-level control
The NMU controller also manages packet buffers and indicates to other NMUs when buffer space is limited. End-to-end control of information flow between two data ports is handled at the transport level by the data PIM. A data PIM performs packet assembly and disassembly and uses the X.25 control-packet exchange sequence for call setup and tear-down.

Flow control is implemented using a "window" of sequence numbers. This is a high-level function whereby a receiving device, because of limited buffer space, will reduce the number of packets that the transmitting device may send to it. Packet-sequence numbers up to 127 are used, with a variable window width between 1 and 22 packets. The sequence numbers are then used to properly reassemble a user message consisting of more than one Ubits packet.

The data PIM performs several functions at Level 4. It may interface with a host operating under its own Level 4 protocol (thereby accepting frames already formatted) or it may perform this framing function as a service for the host. It can also be programmed to accept data in an asynchronous, ASCII format for a terminal, provide terminal-oriented call-setup and PAD functions, or accept data from synchronous terminals using bisync (IBM's binary synchronous communications) or SDLC (synchronous data link control) protocols. In addition, the data PIM can interface directly with a Level 4 protocol [such as the Department of Defense (DOD) standard TCP4], or it can be programmed to act as a gateway to other networks using protocols such as X.25 or the DOD's internet protocol.

Protocol functions at Levels 5, 6, and 7 can also be implemented in Ubits, when required. Functions such as a virtual-terminal protocol handler and code conversion can be implemented within a data PIM, and specialized functions such as file management, database management, distributed data processing, and electronic mail are also possible.

The simplicity of the internal Ubits protocol and the intelligence provided in each NMU results in high throughput, low delays, and network transparency. The network may be accessed at any level in the protocol hierarchy and therefore offers a variety of services that can be tailored to satisfy virtually all interface requirements—including real-time voice. ▫

Small controllers, small costs

LSI devices control loop-mode SDLC data links

John Beaston, Intel Corp., Santa Clara, Calif.

SDLC, specified for loop-mode configurations, offers a low-cost alternative for many users; the new LSI data communications devices promise to keep these costs down

Besides specifying a protocol for point-to-point and multidrop networks, IBM's synchronous data link control (SDLC) also details a loop-mode protocol for networks with multiple users in a small geographical area. In these networks, protocol control can often be handled by a single large-scale integrated circuit.

An LSI implementation of data link controls allows on-chip inclusion of all the essential SDLC loop-mode features, drastically reducing hardware and software requirements. To fully grasp the impact of these new data link controllers, it is necessary first to "return to the basics" of loop-mode operation.

The greatest advantage of loop-mode SDLC is its low-cost implementation. There are two reasons for this. First, because loop-mode SDLC is the simplest form of the protocol, a loop-mode SDLC station (node) requires less intelligence than a station on a multipoint or a point-to-point network. Second, loop mode offers a lower interconnect cost. The basic loop network shown in Figure 1 consists of a controller station and one or more secondary down-loop nodes.

As indicated by Figure 1, only a single cable assembly—coaxial, fiber optic, etc.—is required to connect all loop nodes. Since no discrete data timing information is passed between the nodes, each station derives its timing from the received data stream. This data

clock recovery procedure is usually accomplished with a phase-lock loop. In addition to handling the station's timing chores, each station also repowers the loop signal to move the data to other addresses.

Communications on the loop rely on the fact that secondary stations operate in a repeater mode. In this mode, stations retransmit incoming data with one bit time of delay. The one-bit delay allows a secondary to capture the loop and insert its message.

Loop SDLC's frame structure, shown in Figure 2, is identical to normal SDLC (multipoint or point-to-point). The opening and closing flags form the frame boundaries and all fields within the frame are positionally related to these flags. Within the frame boundaries, SDLC is code transparent. That is, the content and format of the data between the flags may take any form and be from any source. This, of course, implies that a flag character pattern must never occur within the frame. If so, this inadvertent flag would be interpreted as a closing flag and invalidate the frame. This chance happening is eliminated by the technique of zero-bit insertion. Zero-bit insertion specifies that the transmitter will insert a binary 0 after any string of five contigious binary 1s (between the flags). Thus, no inadvertent flag character could occur within the frame.

The receiver performs the inverse operation by re-

165

1 Basic loop

One way. In a loop network, secondary stations cannot communicate with each other directly; all data conversations are initiated by the network's loop controller station.

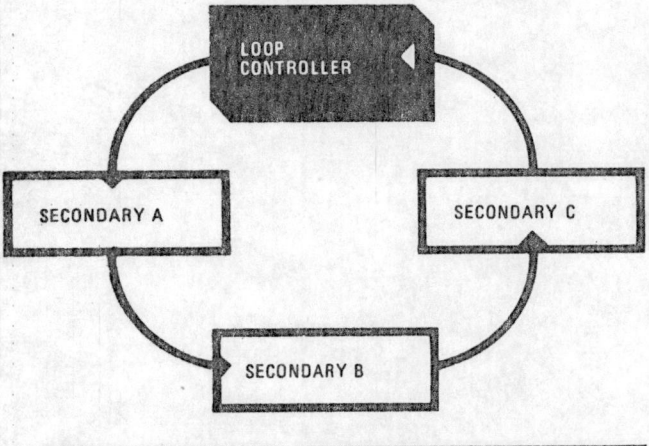

moving any 0 following five 1s. Besides the advantage of code transparency, zero bit insertion helps provide transitions on the loop for phase locking the loop.

To aid in a station's phase-lock loop capture, a non-return-to-zero-inverted (NRZI) data encoding and decoding format is employed. NRZI is a modified form of non-return-to-zero (NRZ) data encoding in which the state of the transmission medium changes when the information changes from a 1 to a 0. NRZI coding specifies that the signal condition does not change for a transmitted binary 1, while a binary 0 does cause a change of state. Using NRZI and zero-bit insertion, an active line is guaranteed to undergo a transition at least every five bit times; long strings of zeroes cause the line to undergo a transition every bit time, while long strings of ones are broken up by zero-bit insertion.

Half-duplex operation

Communication on the loop is instigated by the loop controller. A secondary station must be polled by the controller before the station can respond. Thus, the loop operation is half-duplex. Also, contiguous frames may not be transmitted. Each station may only transmit one frame per poll or response.

The eight bits immediately following the opening flag form the frame's address field (see Fig. 2). The address field has the same function, whether in loop or normal SDLC. Each secondary station is assigned a unique eight-bit address. When the controller wishes to direct a message to a specific secondary, it places the secondary's address in the frame's address field. The secondaries examine each frame for its particular address. If a match occurs, the secondary transfers that frame to memory for analysis.

When responding to a poll, the secondary uses its own address in the response frame's address field. This ensures that the controller knows which secondary originated the response.

For general polls, an "all-parties" address field is

used (typically eight 1s). Thus, secondaries must recognize both their own addresses plus the all-parties address. An all-parties poll allows each secondary, in turn, to place a message on the loop. Even when responding to an all-parties poll, the secondary uses its own address in the response frame.

The control field is formed by the eight bits following the address field. Although the control field embodies the same functions for both loop and normal SDLC, some commands are different. A discussion of these differences is not important for the project at hand, since single-device controllers do not utilize the control field in any way other than just passing it to the station's processor for analysis.

End-of-poll

One character defined in SDLC loop mode which is not found in normal SDLC is an end-of-poll (EOP) character. EOP contains a binary 0 followed by seven binary 1s. The EOP character controls loop activity.

Remember that secondaries normally operate in the repeater mode, retransmitting received data with one bit time of delay. When the loop is idle, the controller transmits flag characters. This keeps transitions on the line for the down-loop phase-lock loop.

When the controller has a frame to transmit, it starts transmission on a flag boundary. If the frame specifies a poll, the controller transmits all 1s after the frame's closing flag with no zero-bit insertion. The final zero of the closing flag plus the first seven 1s form an EOP character. While repeating, the secondaries monitor their incoming line for an EOP.

When an EOP is received, the secondary checks to see if it has a response for the controller. If it does, it changes the seventh EOP 1 into a 0 (the one bit time of delay allows time for this) and repeats it, forming an opening flag for the other down-loop stations. After this flag is transmitted, the secondary terminates its repeater function and, switching to transmit mode, inserts its response frame.

After the closing flag of the response, the secondary re-enters its one-bit delay repeater function. Notice that the final zero of the response frame's closing flag plus the repeated 1s from the controller form a new EOP for the next down-loop secondary. This new EOP allows the next secondary to insert a response if it desires. If the secondary has no response for the controller, it simply does not capture the loop. Any response must then wait for the next EOP.

After the controller has transmitted the poll and begins transmitting continuous 1s, it waits until it receives an EOP. Receiving the EOP informs the controller that the original poll has propagated around the loop and that it is followed by any responses inserted by down-loop secondaries. At this point, the controller may either send flags to idle the loop or transmit the next frame.

Obviously the importance of the controller in a loop network cannot be overstated, and this has not gone unnoticed by LSI manufacturers. Recently several of these vendors introduced devices which can generally be categorized as single-chip protocol controllers. These circuits, for the most part, are intended to aid

2 Frame format

Boundaries. In loop-mode SDLC, the flags form the boundaries for all other fields. The flags are used for frame synchronization and can be used for line-fill between frames. There is no intraframe timefill requirement in SDLC as there is in bisync. The information field can be any length, but it's usually made up of a multiple of eight bits.

OPENING FLAG	ADDRESS FIELD (A)	CONTROL FIELD (C)	INFORMATION FIELD (I)	FRAME CHECK SEQUENCE (B)	CLOSING FLAG
01111110	8 BITS	8 BITS	0 TO n BITS	16 BITS	01111110

in the implementation of SDLC. But, in some cases, multi-protocol support, including bisync and async, is contained on a single chip. LSI controllers are the latest in a line of integrated circuits which are aimed at combining several related operations on a single integrated circuit (in this case, the devices are aimed specifically at data communications protocol control).

As a comparison of these circuits (see Table 1) points out, numerous features are available from competing manufacturers. For exclusive SDLC loop-mode operation in a single network, some of these features are not as important as others. Multi-protocol support, for instance, is an attractive feature for multidrop and point-to-point networks, but it offers little in a fully SDLC loop-mode configuration.

Device "wish list"

Table 1 assumes that all the controllers perform the basic SDLC functions of zero-bit insertion/deletion and cyclic redundancy checking. Also the listing assumes TTL (transistor-transistor-logic) compatibility which all currently available SDLC controllers meet.

The features listed in the left-most column of Table 1 actually represent a "wish list" of all possible functions necessary for loop-mode SDLC control, including:
- Speed—Like mom and apple pie, high speed is always good, but it is usually not as important for loop operation as it is for some SDLC applications. Typical loop speeds are 9.6 kbit/s.
- Selective receive—For loop mode, the SDLC controller should have the capability to receive (transfer to memory) only those frames having an address field matching a preprogrammed address byte.
- All-parties address—Since a secondary station needs to recognize an all-parties address in addition to its own address, this function is advantageous.
- General receive—the loop controller must be able to receive any frame regardless of the frame's address field. Thus, loop controllers need this ability, and all have it.
- NRZI—NRZI encoding/decoding is needed to provide the necessary line transitions to keep clock recovery circuitry in synchronization.
- Internal PLL—Having the clock recovery circuitry on-chip is desirable, but not essential.
- Flag stream/idle—Since the loop controller must switch between transmitting flags and idles (all 1s), this feature should be programmable.

- EOP detect—The loop controller station needs this feature to know when all frames have been received after a poll.
- Preframe sync—With the loop being basically asynchronous, and with clock recovery circuitry involved, it is often required that the loop controller preface all frames with preframe sync characters. These characters supply transitions to ensure that the clock recovery circuitry is in sync by the time the opening flag is received.
- Loop pickup—When a secondary station is coming on-loop, it must use caution when it begins inserting its one-bit delay. Clearly, if it inserted its delay during a frame, the frame's contents would be altered. The secondary must wait for an EOP. At this point, it switches in the one-bit delay. Since the frame is already down-loop and 1s are coming from up-loop, no loop disturbance results. At the next EOP, the station informs the controller of its presence.
- Multiprotocol—While SDLC is used exclusively for loop, the capability of other protocols such as bisync or async may or may not be an important feature.
- Variable character length—Although SDLC almost exclusively uses an eight-bit character, it may be desirable to vary the character length in some applications.

The full impact of LSI's role in controlling SDLC loop protocol can be assessed by a detailed examination of one of these devices—Intel's 8273. The 8273, as indicated in Table 1, is unique in that it contains an on-chip digital phase-lock loop. In addition, the 8273 incorporates a frame level command structure which allows frames to be transmitted and received with macro-like (high-level) commands. The load on the station processor is thus reduced.

Uncovering the device

Internally, the 8273 comprises a dual processor architecture. A high-speed bit processor handles the serial data manipulations and character recognition. A lower speed byte processor implements the frame level commands by managing the data channels.

The internal registers provide the command and result interface between the 8273 and the station processor as shown in Figure 3. They are addressed by a combination of the address 1 (A1), address 0 (A0), read (R0), write (WR), and chip select (CS) pins. These registers are key to the 8273 operation:
- Command—8273 operations are initiated by writing

167

Table 1 Chip controllers compared

	WESTERN DIGITAL 1933	SIGNETICS 2652	STANDARD MICROSYSTEMS CORP. 5025	INTEL 8273	MOTOROLA 6854
SPEED (BIT/S)	1.5M	1M/2M	2M	64K	1M
SELECTIVE RECEIVE	●	●	●	●	
ALL PARTIES		●	●	●	●
GENERAL RECEIVE	●	●	●	●	
NRZI	●			●	●
INTERNAL PLL				●	
FLAG STREAM/IDLE	●	●	●	●	●
EOP DETECT	●	●	●	●	●
PREFRAME SYNC				●	
LOOP PICKUP				●	●
MULTIPROTOCOL		●	●		
VARIABLE CHARACTER LENGTH	●	●	●		●

the appropriate command byte into this register.

■ Parameter—Many commands require more information than that found in the command itself. This additional information is provided by way of the parameter register.

■ Immediate result—The completion information for commands which execute immediately are provided by this register.

■ Transmit interrupt result—Results of transmit operations are passed to the processor in this register.

■ Receiver interrupt result—Receive operation results are passed to the processor via this register.

■ Status—The general status of the 8273 is reflected in this register. The status register supplies the handshaking necessary during various phases of operation.

■ Test mode—This register provides a software reset function for the device.

Each 8273 operation consists of three sequential phases: command, execution, and result. During the command phase, the station processor issues commands to the 8273 by way of the command register. For some commands, when the 8273 needs more information than is contained in the command byte itself, the parameter register provides the input. Typical parameters are the frame length desired for transmission and the size of the allocated buffer memory for reception. Once the command is issued and all parameters are given, the execution phase is entered.

As the name implies, it is during the execution phase that the actual command is executed. Assume for a moment that the command specified a frame transmission. At this point, the 8273 would transmit the frame. If DMA (direct memory access) is being used, no processor intervention is needed, since the DMA controller and the device would coordinate data transfers. If DMA is not used, the processor would supply the data transfers in response to either transmitter data request interrupts, or by polling the status register. The actual transfer mode is programmable. In either case, the 8273 does all the byte counting and ceases DMA requests or data request interrupts once the number of bytes specified by the command parameter has been transmitted. Of course, the opening and closing flags plus the frame check sequence are automatically formatted.

When the execution is complete, the result phase is entered by interrupting the processor (the processor can also poll the 8273 for this, if interrupts are not used). In response to the interrupt, the processor reads the associated interrupt result register (TxI/R for transmitter interrupts or RxI/R for receiver interrupts). The interrupt result register contains the result of the operation plus any additional information required, such as received frame length. Once all results are read, the operation is complete.

Locking the loop

While this frame level command structure helps decrease the software processing load of the station processor, it is the digital phase-lock loop which makes for easy loop station hardware design. To use the DPLL, a clock at 32 times the desired data rate must be supplied to the 32XCLK pin. This clock provides

the timing interval at which the DPLL samples the received data. The DPLL uses the 32 times clock and the received data to generate an output pulse at the DPLL pin. This DPLL pulse is positioned at the nominal center of the received data bit cell. Thus, the DPLL output may be wired to RxCLK (receiver clock) and/or TxCLK (transmitter clock) to supply the data timing. The exact position of the pulse is varied, depending on the line noise and bit distortion of the received data. The adjustment of the DPLL position is determined according to the rules outlined in Figure 4.

Adjustments of the sample phase of DPLL with respect to the received data are made in discrete increments. Referring to Figure 4, following the occurrence of DPLL pulse A, the DPLL counts thirty-two 32XCLK

pulses and examines the received data for a data edge. Should no edge be detected in 32 pulses, the DPLL positions the next DPLL pulse, B, at 32 clock pulses from pulse A. Since no new phase information is contained in the data stream, the sample phase is assumed to be at a nominal one times the data rate.

Now, assume that a data edge occurs after DPLL pulse B. The distance from B to the next pulse, C, is influenced according to which quadrant (A1, B1, B2, or A2) the data edge falls in. Each quadrant represents eight 32XCLK pulses.

For example, if the edge is detected in quadrant A1, it is apparent that pulse B was too close to the data edge and the time to the next pulse must be shortened. The adjustment for quadrant A1 is specified as −2;

3 Chip block diagram

Construction. *Intel Corp.'s 8273 protocol controller consists of two interfaces: CPU and modem. The dash over some pin inputs (i.e. $\overline{RD}$, $\overline{WR}$, $\overline{CS}$, etc.) indicates a* *low state (binary 0) is used to enable the pin. Once the device receives a command and executes it, the results of the command go to read/write/control logic circuits.*

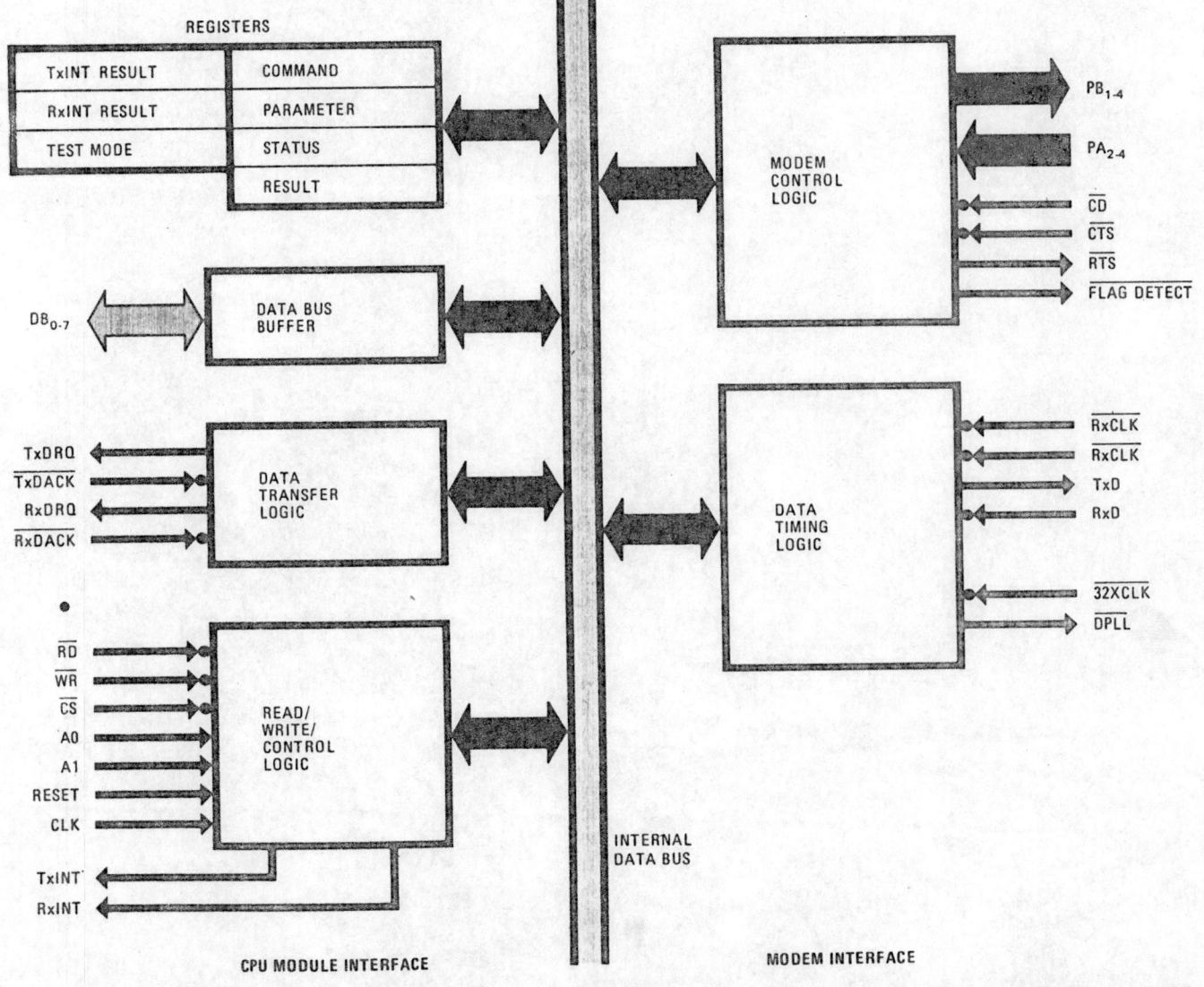

4 DPLL timing

Clocking. *The digital phase-lock loop (DPLL) provides a means of clock recovery from the received data stream. This allows the chip to interface without external synch-* *ronization to low-cost async modems which do not usually supply clocks. To use the DPLL, a clock at 32 times the data rate must be supplied to the device's 32XCLK pin.*

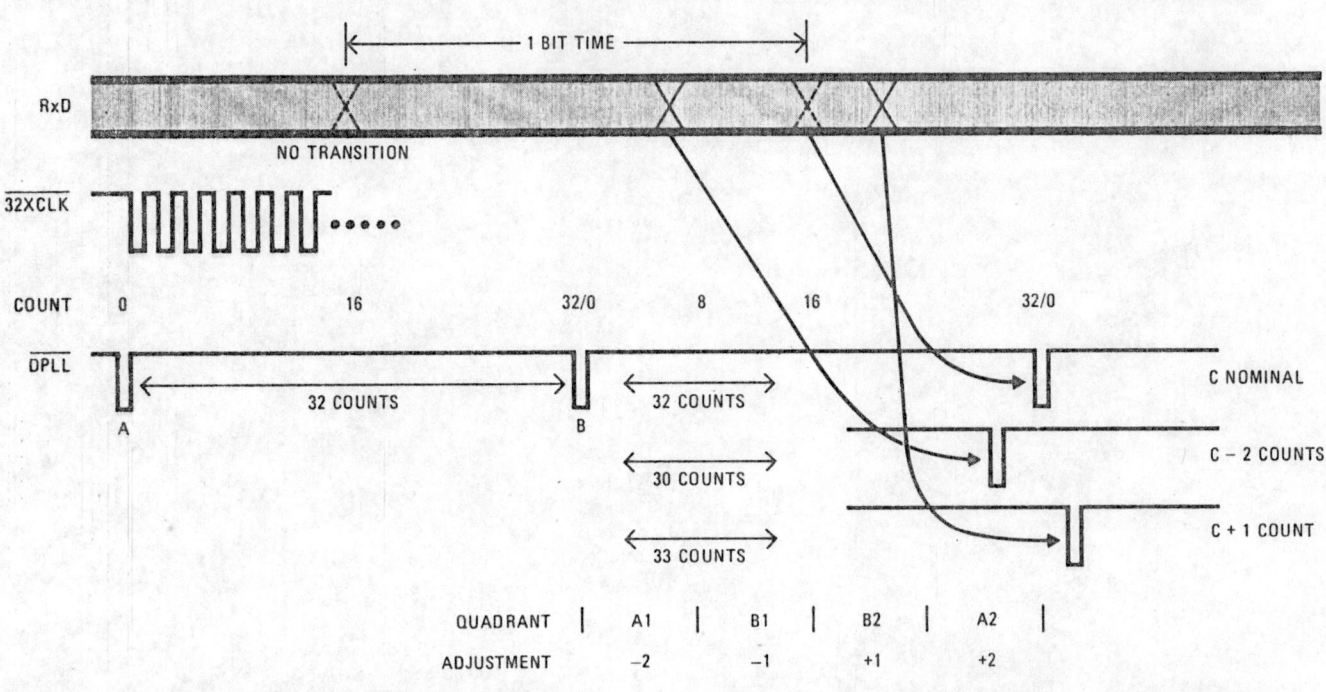

thus, the next DPLL pulse, pulse C, is positioned 32 minus two or thirty 32XCLK pulses following DPLL pulse B. This adjustment moves pulse C closer to the nominal bit center of the next received data cell.

A data edge occurring in quadrant B2 would have caused the adjustment to be small, namely 32 plus one or thirty-three 32XCLK pulses. Using this technique, in the worst case, the DPLL pulse converges to the nominal bit center within 12 data transitions. This is equal to four bit times adjusting through quadrant A1 or A2 and eight bit times through B1 or B2.

When the receive data stream goes idle, DPLL pulses are generated at 32 pulse intervals of the 32X clock. This allows the DPLL pulses to be used as both transmitter and receiver clocks.

Link data flow

Figure 5 details the controller command sequence. The controller is initialized with commands which specify that the NRZI, preframe sync, flag stream, and EOP interrupt modes are set. Thus, the controller encodes and decodes all data using NRZI format. Preframe Sync mode specifies that all transmitted frames be prefaced with 16 line transitions. This ensures that the minimum of 12 transitions needed by the DPLLs to lock after an all 1s line have occurred by the time the secondary sees a frame's opening flag. Setting the flag stream mode starts the transmitter to send flags. This idles the loop. The EOP interrupt mode specifies that the controller processor will be interrupted whenever the receiver sees an EOP, indicating the completion of a

poll cycle. When the controller wishes to transmit a non-polling frame, it simply executes a frame transmit command. Since the flag stream mode is set, no EOP is formed after the closing flag. When a polling frame is to be transmitted; a general receive command is executed first. This enables the receiver and allows reception of the original polling frame plus any response frames inserted by the secondaries. After the general receive command, the frame is transmitted with a frame transmit command. When the frame is complete, a transmitter interrupt is generated. The loop-controller processor uses this interrupt to reset the flag stream mode. This causes the transmitter to start sending all 1s. An EOP is formed by the final zero of the last flag and the first seven 1s. This completes the loop controller transmit sequence.

At any time following the start of the polling frame transmission, the loop-controller receiver will start receiving the frame. (The exact time difference depends, of course, on the number of down-loop secondaries.) The first received frame is simply the original polling frame. However, any additional frames are those inserted by the secondaries. The loop-controller processor knows that all frames have been received when it sees an EOP interrupt. This interrupt is generated by the 8273 since its EOP interrupt mode was set during initialization. At this point, the transmitter may be commanded either to enter the flag stream mode, idling the loop, or to transmit the next frame.

Figure 6 illustrates the secondary command sequence. The secondaries are initialized with the NRZI

170

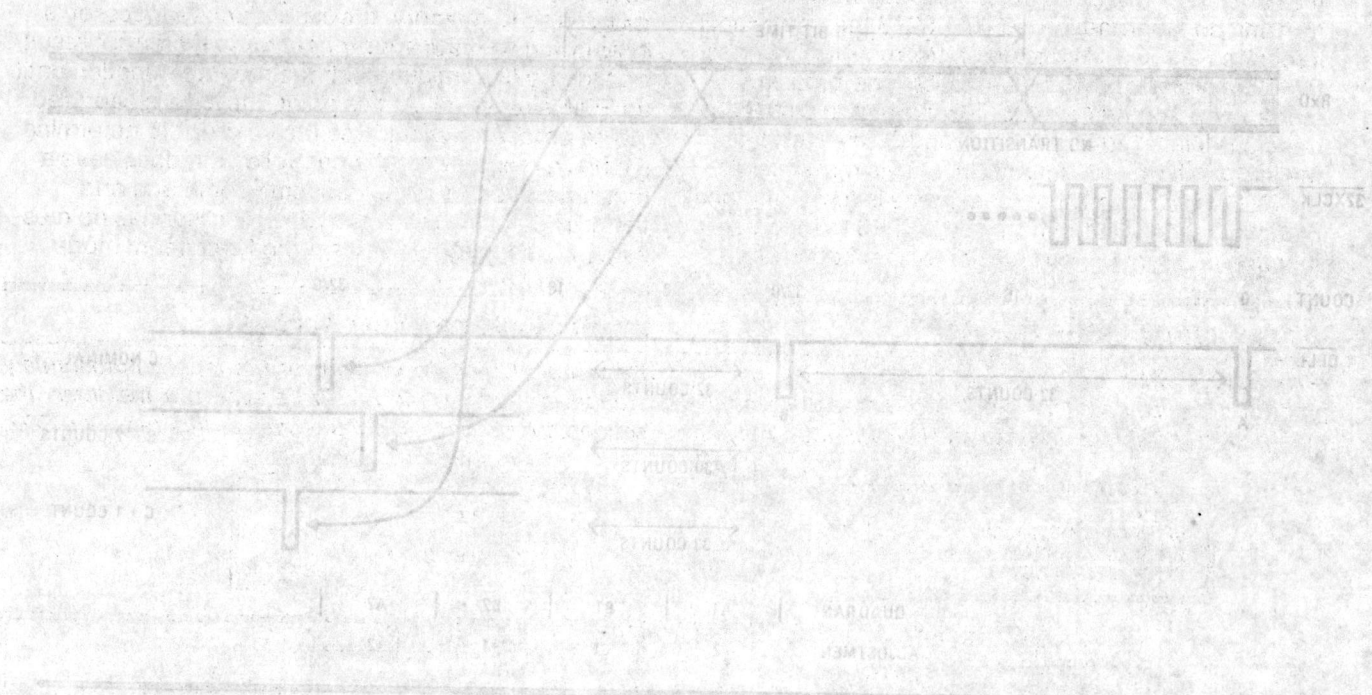

and one-bit delay modes set. This puts the 8273 into the repeater mode with the transmitter repeating the received data with one bit time of delay. Since a loop station cannot transmit until it sees an EOP character, the 8273 queues all transmitter commands. Whenever the secondary wishes to transmit a response, a loop-transmit command is issued. The 8273 then waits until it receives an EOP. At this point, the receiver changes the EOP into a flag, repeats it, resets one-bit delay mode (stopping the repeater function), and sets the transmitter into the flag stream mode. This captures the loop. The transmitter now inserts its message. At the closing flag, the flag stream mode is reset, and one-bit delay mode is set, returning the 8273 to repeater function and forming an EOP for the next down-loop

station. These actions happen automatically after a loop transmit command is issued.

When the secondary wants its receiver enabled, a selective loop-receive command is issued. The receiver then looks for a frame having a match in the address field. Once such a frame is received, repeated, and transferred to memory, the secondary's processor is interrupted with the appropriate match-interrupt result and the 8273 continues with the repeater function until an EOP is received. At this point, the loop is captured.

The processor should use the interrupt to determine if it has a message for the controller. If it does have a message, it issues a loop-transmit command and things progress as above. If the processor has no message, the software must reset the flag stream mode

5 Controller flow chart

Procedure. Once all initial conditions are met, the loop controller transmits either a poll or a non-poll frame. For non-poll, the frame is transmitted into the loop network.

6 Secondary flow chart

Repeater. Normal operation for the loop net secondary station is repeater mode. To become a transmitter, the secondary issues a loop transmit and awaits an EOP.

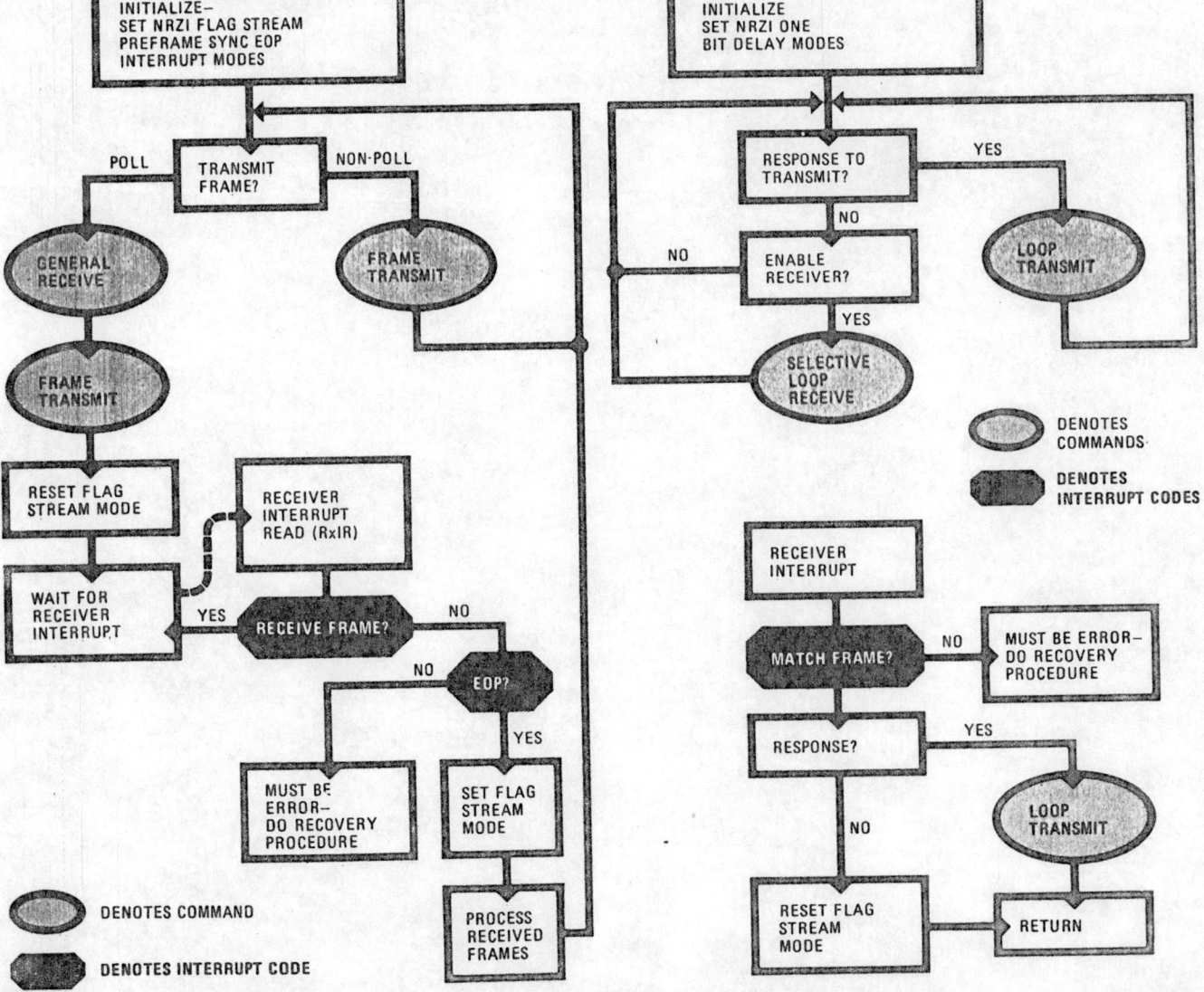

171

Glossary

All parties address—general address to all stations on the loop.

Chip controller—LSI implementation of a protocol controller.

Controller station—node controlling communications on a loop network.

Data clock recovery—retrieving data timing information from a received data stream.

Data edge—leading or trailing edge of a bit.

Down-loop (or up-loop)—location reference to a node's position on a loop network.

Idle loop—no transmissions on the loop network.

Loop capture—a station or node controls the network's transmission medium for a period of time required for a data transmission (no other station may transmit during the capture time).

Loop network—a network configuration in which all nodes are connected in a ring.

Repeater mode—in a loop network, a station retransmits received data after it inserts a one-bit delay.

Secondary station—a station which relies on a loop controller for initiating its communications.

Poll—interrogating a station for a message.

Zero bit insertion/deletion—a bit-stuffing technique used to maintain data integrity.

A0—address zero.

A1—address one.

An—address n.

CD—carrier detect.

CLK—clock.

CRC—cyclic redundancy check.

CS—chip select.

CTS—clear to send.

D—data.

DACK—direct memory access acknowledge.

DB—database.

DMA—direct memory access.

DPLL—digital phase-lock loop.

DRQ—direct memory access request.

EOP—end of poll.

FCS—frame check sequence.

INT—interrupt.

NRZ—non-return to zero.

NRZI—non-return to zero inverted.

PA—modem control input ports (2 through 4).

PB—modem control output ports (1 through 4).

PLL—phase-lock loop.

RD—read.

RTS—request to send.

Rx—receiver.

RxI/R—receiver interrupt result.

TTL-transistor-to-transistor logic.

Tx—transmitter.

TxI/R—transmitter interrupt result.

WR—write.

1—high state.

0—low state.

32×CLK—32 times the clock.

7 Pickup interface logic

Logic. The loop pickup interface logic diagram includes two AND gates feeding an OR gate. The gate symbol in the port line indicates a NOT gate or inverted logic function.

PORT HIGH — OFF-LINE
LOW — ON-LINE

bit in the operating mode register. This will inhibit the 8273 from capturing the loop at the EOP. (The match frame and the EOP may be separated in time by several frames, depending on how many up-loop stations inserted messages of their own.)

If the timing is such that the receiver has already captured the loop when the flag stream mode bit is reset, the mode is exited on a flag boundary and the frame appears to have extra closing flags before the EOP. Notice that the 8273 handles the queuing of the transmit commands and the setting and resetting of the mode bits automatically.

Coming on-line

When an off-line secondary wishes to come on-line, it must do so in a manner which does not disturb data on the loop. Figure 7 shows a typical hardware interface. The line labeled port could be one of the 8273's port B outputs and is assumed to be high (1) initially. Thus up-loop data is simply passed down-loop with no delay. However, the receiver may still monitor data on the loop.

To come on-line, the secondary is initialized with only the EOP interrupt mode set. The up-loop data is then monitored until an EOP occurs. At this point, the secondary's CPU is interrupted with an EOP interrupt. This signals the CPU to set one-bit delay mode in the 8273 and then to set the port low (active). These actions switch the secondary's one-bit delay into the loop. Since after the EOP only 1s are traversing the loop, no loop disturbance occurs. The secondary now waits for the next EOP, captures the loop, and inserts a new on-line message. This signals the controller that a new secondary exists and must be acknowledged. After the secondary receives its acknowledgement from the controller, the normal command flow sequence is re-established. ◘

Section 5

Local Network
Applications
Applications
Applications
Applications
Applications
Applications
Applications
Applications
Applications
Applications
Applications
Applications
Applications

Special report:

Data communications in the office

Office automation is clearly in the hands of the data communications user. The drive for office automation is increased office productivity, which has been fueled, up to now, by the replacement of discrete office equipment with electronic counterparts. This has allowed individual users to do perhaps a few tasks easier. But significant, overall improvements in office productivity have not resulted from these one-to-one equipment substitutions.

Still largely missing in the digitized office is

resource sharing. With the new office networks, however, users will soon be able to achieve this. Although still in the infant stage, a well-designed local network in conjunction with digital data gatherers and disseminators can have a positive effect on office productivity. The following two-feature special report examines the technology behind the data communications office network and details the different types of tools available for the user.

— GRD

The so-called "office of the future" is technologically possible today. In fact, much of the equipment that will compose this automated, or "paperless," office has been available in some form for years. What is new is that equipment designers and vendors have begun to tailor data processing systems and communications products to the office environment.

Virtually every existing manual office operation has the potential for automation, and scores of vendors, recognizing this, have jumped on the bandwagon. In

bled in virtually all cases" through the use of available automated office equipment. Landau cites the rapidly decreasing cost of computing power as the primary reason for this new product direction.

"Not too many years ago," he says, "the cost for connect time to a computer was about $10 per hour. It is now close to $5 an hour, and in a couple of years it will approach $1 an hour or even less."

As do other industry observers, Landau foresees rapid growth in the number of offices migrating toward

Tying together telephones and typewriters

By Edwin E. Mier, Data Communications

a recent survey conducted by the Yankee Group, a data communications consultant firm in Cambridge, Mass., the majority of office managers and executives reported a need for a multifunction, automated office-type workstation. The survey revealed that the most sought-after features of this workstation are:
- An ability to communicate with other devices
- Easy access to multiple databases
- Easy attachment of peripheral devices
- A standalone processing capability

Consonant with these findings, the current direction in product development is toward integration — combining previously segregated functions and devices via data communications. Although a new family of office workstations has emerged over the past few years, it represents only the tip of the iceberg. In several office-related areas — especially data communications — development is under way which will result in products that not only combine functions but also support local and remote interdevice networking.

The concept of the automated office entails the extension of computer and communications technology to the office environment. Considering the range of office applications, this new frontier is apt to be huge.

Figure 1 illustrates the effects of computerization on many manual office tasks. Several of the automated functions, such as word and text processing, are already widely used today. Others, such as integrated communications and the interconnection of incompatible devices, are still being developed.

The overwhelming motivation toward office automation for vendors and users alike is the potential for increased productivity — at a cost equal to or less than that of existing manual office procedures. According to Robert Landau, a director of Micronet Inc., a Washington, D.C-based consulting firm specializing in office automation, current productivity "can be at least dou-

automation. "It's a pretty good return on investment," he says, "to add two or three thousand dollars in equipment per office worker and reap a 100 percent increase in productivity."

Office automation will mean new and more-efficient ways of performing the four principal office functions: information generation and preparation, computation, dissemination, and storage. In a typical office, these functions include the following tasks:
- Preparation — creating business letters, schedules, interoffice memoranda, and reports
- Computation — compiling data to complete forms, generating graphics, management charts
- Dissemination — distributing the above, manually or electronically
- Storage — storing and retrieving documents, maintaining mailing lists

Computer technology has for years had its greatest impact on the first of these, generation and preparation, although to some degree all four have been affected by the computer.

The computerization of information preparation first appeared with word processing. At one point, storing correspondence locally on magnetic media (cassette tapes, magnetic cards) was found to facilitate repetitive typing tasks and error correction.

As processor and intelligence prices dropped, the text-editing terminal, which added operator functions and increased storage capacity, came into being. The logic that supported these applications was initially placed in the terminal itself (generally not more than 16K bytes of memory), but later, shared-logic configurations (a central intelligent controller with mass storage) became popular.

Communications for these configurations was limited to within the cluster, and while it involved only point-to-point coaxial cable connections, it was a first step

toward facilitating dissemination tasks.

It became clear that all four office functions could be better served if the text or word processing requirements were considered along with data processing. Hence, product systems were unveiled that permitted word and data processing from the same workstation. Many manufacturers of data terminal equipment, such as Datapoint and Wang, saw a natural migration in this direction. Both presently offer combined word and data processing configurations.

This merging of capabilities was not a trivial achievement, according to the vendors. The logic requirements for data applications (processor and memory) could not be met in a terminal designed for word processing only. This meant that for users to upgrade their word processing terminals to include data processing, a highly intelligent and expensive controller (typically a minicomputer) was necessary. Also, a new problem arose: the simultaneous handling, in the same processor and over the same communications link, of both data and text traffic.

To address this, Wang Laboratories charged a single communications engineering group with developing compatible protocols for both. According to Tony Mallia, communications product manager for Wang, this group devised a protocol "similar to IBM's binary synchronous," which handles transmission for both. He explains that Wang's communications software driver is structured to keep the peculiar qualities of the word processing traffic intact. These peculiarities include special control characters that are not required for the transmission of data traffic.

Other vendors, however, did not have the benefit of concurrent data and text communications development. For example, Raytheon's Data Systems Division, headquartered in Mansfield, Mass., entered the office arena two years ago through its acquisition of Lexitron, a word processing company. Lexitron is now engaged in an engineering effort to interconnect its word processing terminals—the VT line—with the Raytheon PTS data terminals. The firm offers an interim capability that enables Lexitron's VTs to locally access the Raytheon PTS 1200, but this requires that a two-board processing unit be added to the VT and that special software be loaded in the PTS 1200. Stan Bour, project manager for Lexitron, says that the development of standalone data processing and remote communications (IBM 3270 emulation) for the Lexitron word processor line is being given top priority.

Target: Post office

As a result of this development, processors began to treat word and text messages as data. This merging paved the way for the electronic mail and electronic message services that are now evolving. With electronic mail, text messages are manipulated by applications software, filed on mass-storage devices, and transmitted along with normal data files.

According to the Yankee Group, the desire for electronic mail is still relatively low on the list of automated office needs. Although industry observers differ in their explanations of this, a consensus indicates that com-

puter-based message systems will nevertheless become an integral part of the modern office.

The capability for electronic mail is available to customers right now in many different forms. As Figure 1 shows, this capability can be viewed as the computerized replacement for interoffice mail and memoranda and, sometime in the future, for the postal system. A message is keyed on a terminal and transmitted to a central "post office" processor where it is forwarded to the destination terminal or, in the case of a lengthy message, stored until the destination terminal checks for messages. Any electronic message system involves a disk-based processor, a CRT- or a hard-copy terminal for each user, and, most important, communica-

---

1. Computerization. *Most manual office operations can be replaced or enhanced by computer-based systems that may be local, or accessible via communications.*

INFORMATION PROCESSING	MANUAL TASKS	AUTOMATED OFFICE FUNCTIONS
PREPARATION	ADDRESSING ENVELOPES TYPING LETTERS PREPARING TEXT	WORD AND TEXT PROCESSING
	TYPING MEMOS INTEROFFICE MAIL	
DISSEMINATION	POSTAGE AND MAILING	ELECTRONIC MAIL
	PHOTOCOPYING FOR LOCAL DISTRIBUTION	
	PHOTOCOPYING FOR MAIL	FACSIMILE
	PHOTOCOPYING FOR FILE	
STORAGE	STORING DOCUMENTS	ELECTRONIC FILING (DBMS STORAGE)
	MAINTAINING MAILING LISTS RETRIEVING DOCUMENTS	
COMPUTATION	FORMS COMPLETION GENERATING MANAGEMENT REPORTS PREPARING GRAPHICS	DATA PROCESSING

tions control for addressing and switching.

The cost for such a configuration is apparently the stumbling block to ubiquitous acceptance of the electronic mail concept. Proprietary systems are being implemented only by very large corporations, and still mainly on a test basis.

Recognizing this, several remote computing services and value-added carriers are providing alternatives. The timesharing firms, including Toronto-based I.P. Sharpe and Scientific Time Sharing Corporation (STSC) of Bethesda, Md., now offer complete electronic message packages. The user needs only a terminal at his site and does not require the expensive computers, software, mass-storage systems, or communications control that handle the network.

Other versions are offered by some specialized carriers, including Tymnet, Telenet, and Western Union. These services—Tymnet's OnTyme, Telenet's recently announced Telemail, and Western Union's Infomaster—are electronic mail networks that, like the timesharing companies, use the carrier's computers, peripherals, and communications equipment for the storage and distribution of electronic mail messages.

Unlike word and text processing, electronic mail is viewed as a productivity enhancement for the executive. According to Dale Kutnick, director of research with the Yankee Group, electronic mail is a subset of distributed processing that is designed for high-level management, because its primary advantage is in time saving. Although information still must be manually keyed, savings in travel and in time lost establishing phone conversations can be significant, Kutnick says.

While users are not exactly standing in line to buy full-blown electronic message systems, many seem concerned with being prepared for such future expansion. Approximately 90 percent of all word processing terminals now being delivered have a communications-interface-upgrade capability. About a third of these are being factory-equipped with a remote communications adapter, and another 10 to 15 percent will have this capability added in the near future.

Storing with fax, OCR
It is estimated that a single double-sided, double-density magnetic disk can hold a volume of information equivalent to a full three-drawer filing cabinet. In view of this, the application of computer technology to manual document storage is readily apparent. But while the advantage in space saving is undeniable, some question remains as to the efficiency of the means of input and output. It is impractical to have a secretary rekey a document so that it can be recorded on disk. This would invariably be a duplication of effort. Two other, more efficient means of input may be applied— digital facsimile and optical character recognition.

Digital facsimile, which encodes an entire page of information into a series of bits, has both pros and cons in this application. Because of the facsimile's scanning procedures, a page of information (text, picture, or graphics) translates to almost a million bits of information when digitized. This can be reduced with compression techniques (eliminating white areas, for example) to several hundred thousand bits. This is still a lot of information to store. However, digital facsimile is transparent to the actual content of the information on the page.

Since approximately 80 percent of all office documents filed or copied are in text form, optical character recognition (OCR) is an attractive means of inputting such information into a computerized "filing cabinet." Products from vendors such as Scan-Data are designed to read whole pages of text and require much less storage space per page than digital facsimile. Such products, however, have only limited applicability for digitally storing graphics.

Once a page of information resides within the mass-storage peripheral of a computer, it can be easily transmitted to any device—a printer, a CRT screen, or even on microfilm (a relatively expensive process, but necessary when a space-saving hard copy of information is required for, say, archival storage).

Presently, cost prohibits many users from adopting such storage systems. Besides the cost of input and output terminals, a computer with expensive disk peripherals is required, as well as a database management system. According to Micronet's Robert Landau, office information today is about 95 percent resident on paper, with no more than 5 percent in digital form. He predicts, however, that by 1982 about 20 percent will be digital. For such growth to occur, the cost of converting information from paper to computer will need to drop. Digital facsimile is by far the cheaper means of the two. A fax terminal costs about $5,000, compared with almost $30,000 for a quality OCR page-reading device. Moreover, digital fax has already become a standard office product, but primarily in communications applications—not for data storage.

Facts about fax
Facsimile machines have been employed for years to transmit document information between remote locations. The majority of these machines installed to date, however, use analog transmission, although the newer and faster facsimile terminals use digital. Digitizing page information permits it to be easily transmitted, manipulated by processors, and then accurately reconstructed into its original form. In a digital form (unlike in analog form), facsimile information can be stored, encrypted, merged with other digital information on the same communications facilities and equipment, and converted from one format to another. This conversion of format or protocol is a key feature of the communications technology for the automated office.

The CCITT has established three standard groups of facsimile machines. Groups 1 and 2 include analog machines that transmit a page of information in 2 to 6 minutes. Group 3 covers digital machines that transmit a page of information in less than a minute. It seems clear that the subminute, digital fax machine will prevail over analog models in the automated office. However, some industry observers believe that facsimile, whether analog or digital, may be too inefficient to "pay its way" as a dedicated device. Eventually facsimile will be replaced by more-efficient devices such as graphics

terminals, page readers, and the like, according to Landau. He says that the decline of the fax machine will not begin for several years, and until then, its use will continue to flourish.

Today, most facsimile machines operate over dial-up, point-to-point communications links with other, compatible fax machines. However, communications controllers are being developed that permit facsimile transmission to be stored, switched, and converted to other formats. One such product is available now from Compression Labs Inc. (CLI). CLI markets a store-and-forward facsimile-switching controller (the CLI-441), which, at present, handles a variety of analog fax inputs, as well as ASCII terminal data. The analog fax is converted to digital within the controller, compressed, and appended with address and other control characters. The ASCII terminal input that the controller accepts (including TTY and Telex) can be switched or converted for output on facsimile machines.

According to Cloyd Marvin, CLI marketing vice president, the CLI-441, which costs about $10,000, will soon be upgraded to support digital facsimile input. Marvin points out that until recently there was no standardization of digital fax machines and that variations in coding and signaling methods have made communications among incompatible machines impossible. Marvin says that although the standards set by the CCITT for the Group 3 digital facsimile machines were initially not supported by major vendors, they have since been "tacitly accepted," which should result in compatibility between some vendors' fax machines.

The CLI-441, originally designed to perform analog facsimile compression, has since mutated into a communications controller that begins to address the unique problems of integrating communications for the automated office. The four-channel controller can accept a mixture of facsimile and ASCII data input, as well as handle the individualized storage, addressing, and forwarding of both. In addition, it allows a number of format and protocol conversions: ASCII to fax (but not vice versa), fax A to fax B, TTY to Telex, asynchronous ASCII to synchronous BSC, and so on. Marvin points out that, as customers demand additional functions, further enhancements will be made (such as support for the Group 3 digital facsimile machines).

Incompatibilities

Wang's Mallia points out that one factor of the automated office that has not been sufficiently addressed is human interaction, or what he calls the "soft problems" of product development. Mallia admits that although Wang is not sure just what degree of integration is needed, simplicity of operation will certainly be a prerequisite. Indeed, it is hardly cost effective to expect that a user company acquiring an integrated, automated office will replace each secretary with a combination programmer, computer operator, and communications technician. The multifunction terminals for the automated office, above all else, need to be easy to operate. In addition, the complex communications handling needed to tie this automated office together must be transparent to the end user.

The biggest challenge to be faced in automated office development is incompatibility—a two-fold problem. It exists between the automated office machines and the user on the one hand, and among the machines themselves on the other.

The multifunction workstations of the automated office will be operated by relatively unsophisticated users. According to Landau, a problem of "command language" is evolving, since each vendor is developing a unique proprietary instruction set for machine operation. While Landau advocates "a standard set of commands for standard functions," he sees no hope for such standardization. Should this be the case (and history has regrettably shown it to be true), then the office secretary of the future will certainly be a specialized technician. Experience gained on an IBM office system, for example, will probably be of little value if a company converts to Wang or Datapoint equipment.

The other facet of incompatibility—communications—is more complex. Although CCITT has made some progress in standardizing digital facsimile machines, the word and data processing products of different vendors remain basically incompatible. Incompatibilities include differences in transmission block length, transmission mode (asynchronous or synchronous, half- or full-duplex), character codes, control characters, polling/response sequences, and protocols. These are the very differences that have existed for years between data terminals and processors.

However, as the communications industry has discovered, one common denominator provides at least a starting point for solving this problem. The commonality lies in the digital nature of computer output. It is fairly well established that the automated office communications controller will be digital, computer-driven, and will handle mixed inputs of digitized text, data, facsimile, and even voice traffic. Most industry observers claim that this is the key to integrated office communications control.

Voice integration

To fully derive the advantages of the digital office network, voice, too, must be included. While integrating voice into the same network will not increase an office worker's productivity, using the same facilities, local and remote, for all transmission traffic would certainly be cost effective.

There are no technical problems that prevent the manufacturers from integrating voice into the automated office network, but opinions vary on how it will be accomplished. According to Yankee Group's Dale Kutnick, there will be a slow migration from the existing analog voice environment to one of digitized voice. This, he says, will not be limited to users of data processing and automated office systems. He predicts that combined voice and data systems will "be just beginning in 1985, but will be considerably more widespread in the late 1980s."

Other authorities, however, feel that digital voice will be integrated only in a high-volume data environment and that the analog voice environment will remain essentially unchanged. Some insist that digitized voice

may indeed evolve, but to a limited degree, and exclusive of computerization.

The key to digitized voice integration, most authorities agree, lies in an all-digital computerized private branch exchange (CBX). There are digital CBXs available today, some of which handle a mixture of voice and data traffic, but the nature of CBXs will change rapidly over the next decade. Users will begin to install digital CBXs even in existing analog voice networks. These CBXs would use present wiring but would require that analog voice traffic be digitized before being switched by the CBX. The digitization could be done either at each phone site or, more likely, at the CBX.

To complete the picture, an all-digital telephone, which would eliminate the need for analog-to-digital conversion (at least on the user side of the CBX) will have to become generally available. To succeed it should probably cost less than $100 per unit.

As already stated, when voice is digitized it can be readily merged with data, text, and facsimile. This means that essentially the same communications control equipment and facilities can be used for all transmission. For security applications, digitized voice is easily encoded and decoded because the digitized voice stream is already in a form that can be manipulated by processors. The same is true for equipment and applications that include voice response and voice recognition. These applications could also become a part of a truly sophisticated automated office.

Difficulties in digitizing

Some problems remain in digital voice, however. When analog voice is digitized with today's relatively inexpensive processors, a considerably wide bandwidth is required for transmission. Each voice conversation consumes about 64 kbit/s of bandwidth with the digitization method that is commonly used, and any less bandwidth would adversely affect the quality of the conversation. In the automated office, if digitized voice required this kind of bandwidth, voice transmission would be more or less limited to the local environment. Coaxial and CATV cable can easily support 64-kbit/s transmission (as can twisted pairs, but with a distance limitation). However, for remote communications, a wideband medium, such as microwave, satellite, or expensive wideband leased lines, would be required. This presumes, of course, that a wide bandwidth is necessary. Recent technology has produced several methods of digitizing a voice conversation which permit it to be carried on a much smaller bandwidth (see "Vocalizing data streams," parts 1 and 2, DATA COMMUNICATIONS, March, April 1978).

One company that manufactures such a voice digitizer is Time and Space Processing (TSP), which uses a linear predictive coding technique that can transmit a voice conversation at 2.4 kbit/s. This technique requires relatively expensive processors (about $10,000 each) at both ends of a voice link. According to Howard Strachman, TSP president, the processors extract key parameters from the voice track, synthesize the speech by encoding those parameters, and then reconstruct the voice track at the other end. The reconstructed voice, according to some sources, is not nearly the quality that most people are accustomed to, but it is understandable. The significant achievement is that a single voice-grade phone line can carry multiple voice conversations or, more important to the needs of the automated office, a voice conversation *and* data, text, or facsimile transmission.

The super CBX

The automated office network will revolve around the computerized private branch exchange, although the nature and capabilities of that CBX are still undetermined. Several companies, such as Rolm and Northern Telecom, market digital CBXs that handle voice and data, but their devices (Rolm's CBX and Northern Telecom's SL-1) were designed for a predominance of voice, with data handling later added on. Digital voice/data CBXs that will more equitably distribute voice and data are said to be forthcoming from companies such as Time and Space Processing, Intecom, Datapoint, and even IBM. In addition, similar products are reportedly under development by Anderson-Jacobson and the Bell Labs branch of AT&T.

According to Tom Aschenbrenner, marketing vice president of Intecom (an Exxon affiliate), the forthcoming CBXs will correct some problems of mixed traffic integration and interface with a variety of carriers. Aschenbrenner says that existing mixed-mode digital CBXs carry about 5 to 12 percent data and the rest voice. Data messages are characterized by either very short or very long connect- and data-holding times, unlike voice. The forthcoming CBXs, Aschenbrenner predicts, will have to be more efficient and reliable to handle the additional data load and will be "virtually insensitive to the type of traffic."

Gerald Tomanek, a group product manager with Rolm, says that there is no need yet for a high-data-volume CBX. He estimates that data transmission constitutes about 7 percent of present traffic requirements, and predicts that by 1985 it will reach about 35 percent. This rate of increase, he says, can be supported by Rolm's CBX. Tomanek acknowledges, however, that data traffic has to be handled differently by the CBX, because it requires different processor "supervision" and involves different kinds of signaling. He agrees with most others that migration to an all-digital environment is forthcoming, and he foresees that by 1982 user demand for digital communications controllers will be "profuse."

Apparently CBX manufacturers feel that interface with the "outside world" will, for some time to come, require a digital-to-analog conversion, primarily because AT&T has dedicated too much of its installed equipment base to analog transmission. According to Yankee Group's Kutnick, AT&T could expand on its digital offerings (including the Dataphone Digital Service, DDS, and the Dataphone Switched Digital Service, DSDS) and even convert the existing switched network to digital. But, he says, "they won't." With the exception of on-site satellite and microwave facilities (which may not be cost effective for a remote automated office branch), users will probably still have to access

AT&T's analog telephone network.

The proposed offerings of Xerox's XTEN, Satellite Business Systems' services, and GTE/Telenet's new services will ease but not eliminate AT&T's hold on the data transmission market. With SBS, for instance, a user will apparently still need to access at least a local telephone loop. While XTEN would place an antenna on each user's rooftop, Xerox has not revealed how it will carry that off at affordable prices.

However, as the number of carrier alternatives increases, so must the complexity of the CBX. According to Intecom's Tom Aschenbrenner, as processor costs continue to drop and user demand increases, additional functions will be added to the CBX. These include, he says, least-cost routing, code and protocol conversions, and security encryptions. Aschenbrenner maintains that as public networks proliferate, problems with synchronization timing in the CBX will surface. "Even GTE and AT&T cannot agree on switched-network timing," he says, "so imagine the confusion when a single node (CBX) must also interface with XTEN, SBS, GTE/Telenet, and whatever."

The digital CBX will need an "elastic" buffer and the capability to automatically adjust to the various synchronization timings of the different public networks. But the CBX that supports these multiple interfaces may no longer be cost competitive.

The traditional CBX, like its forerunner the PBX, is a circuit-switched controller; that is, it establishes an end-to-end circuit for the originating device (based on signaling information received) before any user information is transmitted. This is an ideal procedure for time-sensitive transmissions, such as voice, but undesirable when the accuracy of every bit is critical, as with data messages.

Store-and-forward CBXs

In a paper presented at the Computer Networking Symposium in Washington this past December, Osama Mowafi and William Kelly, of Computer Science Corporation, concluded that the ideal communications controller for digital voice and data would need the characteristics of both a circuit-switched device and a store-and-forward node.

A digitized voice message in a real-time environment cannot afford the delay associated with store-and-forward processing, because the continuity of the conversation would significantly deteriorate. By the same token, if a poor-quality transmission link connects two data processing devices, they may get no further than requesting retransmission of the same data block from each other. Facsimile messages, like voice, can afford several bit errors in transmission, but data cannot. According to both Tomanek and Aschenbrenner, the

---

2. Split operation. In order to truly integrate communications into a single controller, two types of traffic need to be handled separately. Time-dependent traffic, such as digital voice, will invariably need to be circuit-switched, while time-insensitive transmissions, including data, word, and text, will ideally be stored and forwarded.

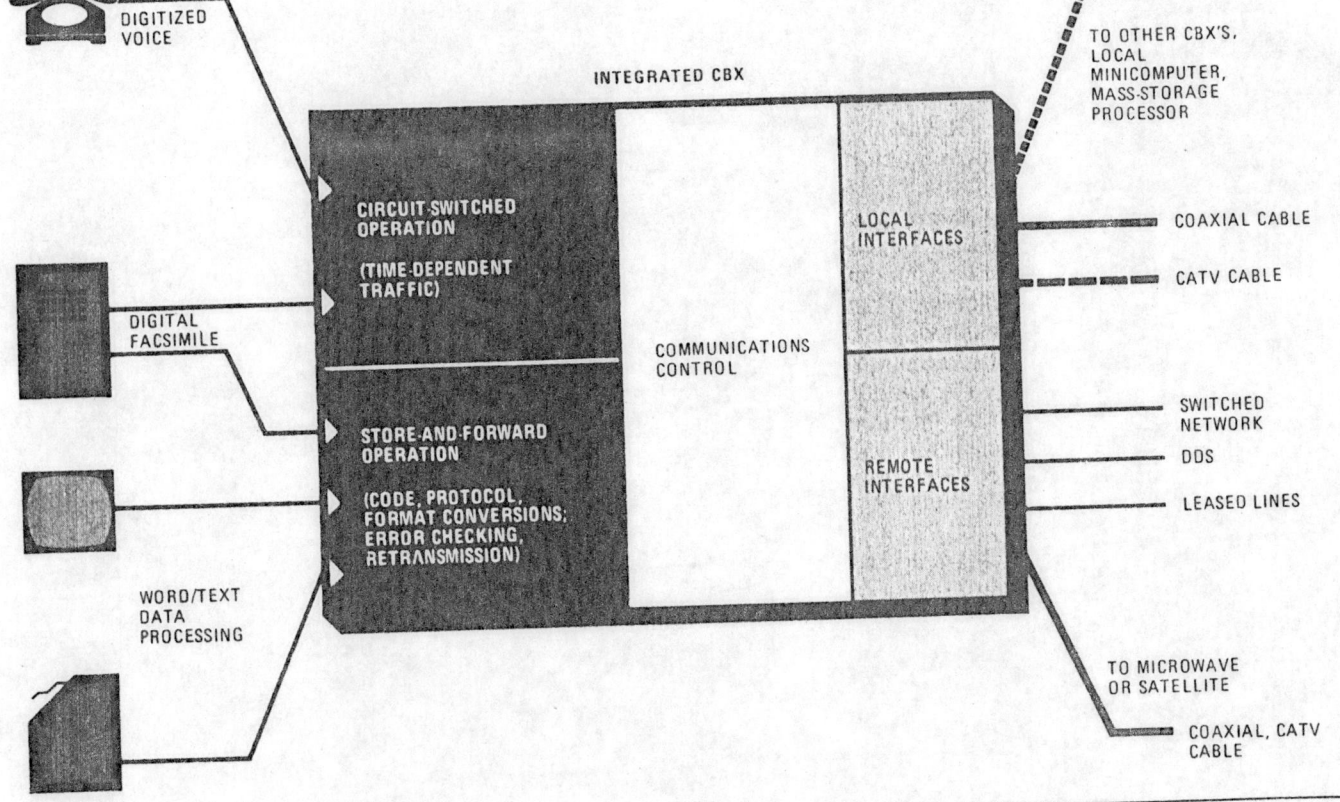

combined CBX that offers both circuit-switching and packet-switching capabilities is viable and marketable, but no such product presently exists.

Most others agree that the CBX of the automated office will have to offer a store-and-forward capability in order to perform any additional data-manipulation functions. According to CLI's Cloyd Marvin, adding real-time digitized voice to the CLI-441 store-and-forward processor is "a nice thing to think about," but he would not project when, if ever, this capability would be added to their product line.

There is no technological reason why both capabilities cannot be offered in the same automated office controller (Fig. 2). It might require, however, dedicating certain groups of lines to either voice (real-time) or data (time-independent). There would not even be a problem if, say, time-division multiplexing were added to the controller, as long as inputs and outputs were segregated by the time-sensitivity of their content.

Local networks

The office communications controller will not only interface the branch office with public carrier networks but also manage the local office network. Figure 3 suggests some variations in local automated office networks. The volume and mix of transmissions will depend greatly on the degree of sophistication and integration required in the specific office. Certain functions, such as word processing and text editing, will involve only local communications. Others, such as voice, facsimile, and electronic mail, will require remote communications almost exclusively. Most data processing will require local communications and, to a lesser degree, remote communications. Accommodating these varying transmissions may well result in a hierarchical network of communications controllers.

A typical automated office network will assume a star topology, with user devices radiating from the communications controller (digital CBX) via coaxial cable and twisted-pair links. As local networks grow, another network connecting the communications controllers will most likely evolve. It will use a higher-speed medium such as fiber-optic or CATV cable (Fig. 4.).

It is possible that in many applications a local minicomputer may serve as both the destination device for, say, word, text, and data processing terminals, and as the communications controller (local node) for fax, voice, and electronic mail transmissions to be routed remotely. Both the Wang and Datapoint offerings lean in this direction, but functional integration now includes only word and data processing and electronic mail.

According to Wang's Tony Mallia, including digitized voice in the company's systems communications is

---

3. Star topology. The automated office network will probably be configured in a star, with all-digital devices radiating from the communications controller (CBX) on twisted-pair and coaxial cable links. Switching, whether within the local network or over remote links, will be handled by common controller logic and be transparent to the user.

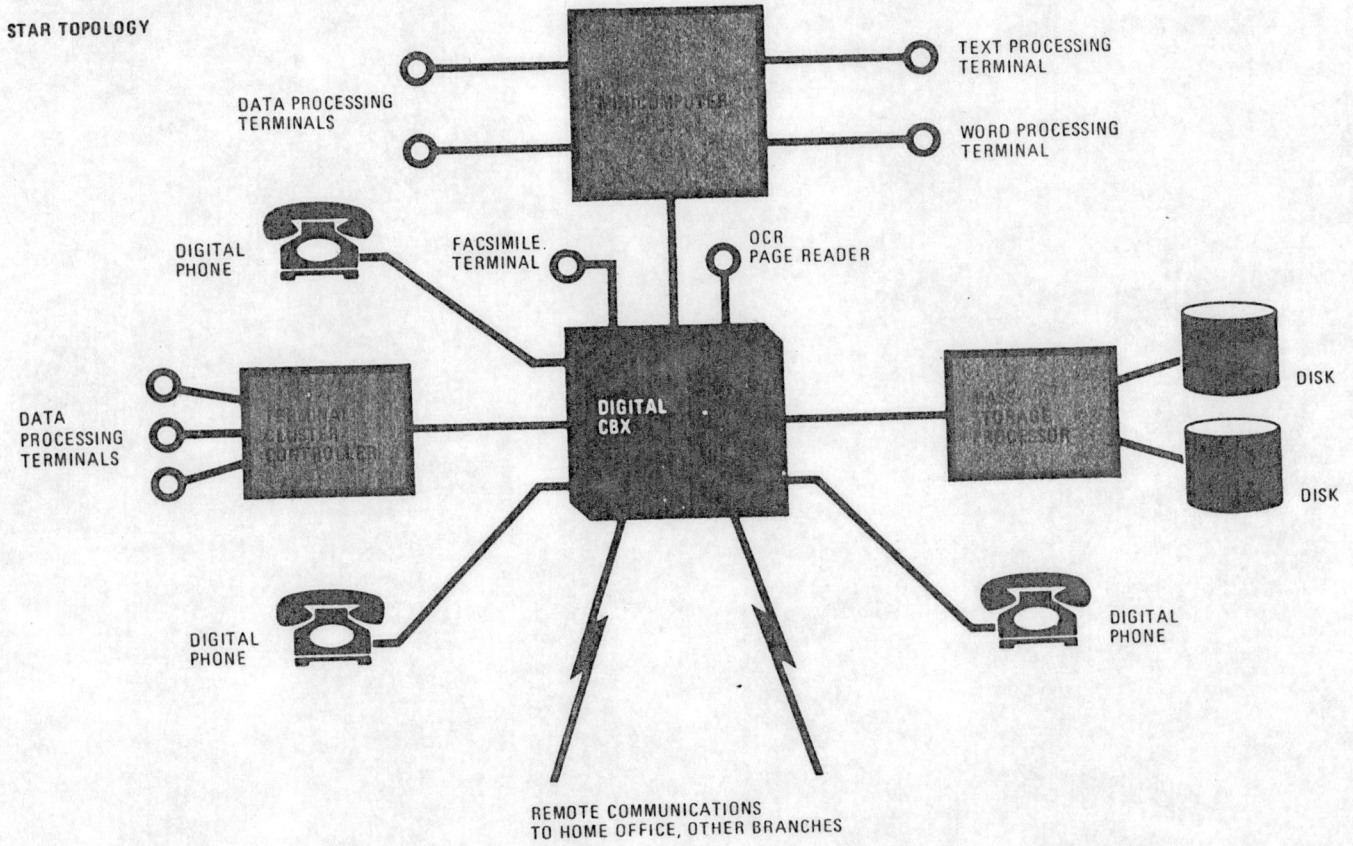

"something that we are very concerned about, but we have made no commitment in this direction." He points out that Wang products are primarily data-oriented and not designed to handle "real-time telephone traffic" that, he says, "requires a CBX-type of machine." Wang, however, recently acquired Comex, a firm that manufactures voice-digitization equipment. Mallia says that Wang's new direction could possibly include a digitized-voice-message capability, but it would not be time-dependent and would use store-and-forward communications.

Since it is not clear just which functions will be included in the automated office, there is an even cloudier picture of what the local networking structure will

look like. One Government agency, for example, recently endorsed broadband (CATV) cable as the desired medium for local integrated office networking. While this technology is particularly attractive to mixed-mode transmissions, the number of RF modems required for the inordinate amount of digital-to-RF-to-digital conversion would probably be cost-prohibitive to anyone but the Government.

Other areas of application, such as voice response/recognition and video teleconferencing, will follow the first wave of office systems. Voice-response and voice-recognition systems are both expensive and limited in application. Video teleconferencing, because of the bandwidth and equipment needed, make its

---

4. Hierarchical communications. As integrated office communications grows, multiple local networks may evolve. Each CBX would handle multiplexing and switch-ing for a subarea of multiple-function devices, and interface with a high-capacity local network connecting the CBXs to each other and to remote communications links.

CC = CLUSTER CONTROLLER
M = MINICOMPUTER
T = TERMINAL
P = PHONE
TDM = TIME-DIVISION MULTIPLEXER

application to the general office questionable.

The truly integrated office will not evolve overnight. While the desire for integrated functions does exist, new functions will probably be added, one at a time, to already marketed products. Problems of further integration and communications need to be solved.

Vendors are preparing now for this new frontier primarily through acquisitions and combined-subsidiary product development. Data processing vendors, for example, are branching into word processing and com-

munications. Giants like IBM are pooling the resources of their specialized office products, systems communications, and general systems divisions. Even Exxon is directing joint-product development between its word processing, facsimile, and communications "affiliates."

The first battery of products for the automated office is already available, and user reaction will determine how future equipment develops. As the product offerings grow, so will the demand for integrated communications to permit their interconnection. ■

The hierarchy of office components

By J. Peter Schmader, Data Communications

The ballyhoo over electronically beefed-up office equipment causes needless confusion. Part of the muddle stems from changes in the marketplace as well as in the technology. Other influences include the self-interested sales and marketing methods of manufacturers and distributors; the incompatibility of equipment and lack of standards; users' varying needs and degrees of acceptance and application of the technology; and even the nomenclature.

Nonetheless, there are clear, orderly ways of examining the equipment. Stripped of their promotional trappings, the devices designed for automating office work fall into categories that mirror what users do: prepare material for their own or another's use. Some preparation is routine and lends itself readily to automation. Some requires cumbersome handling and revision that is distressingly time-consuming; it, too, lends itself to automation. And some demands analysis and judgment, which even super-intelligent gear cannot provide.

In every office, however, the steps for the preparation of material are constant: office workers prepare, compute, disseminate, and store material for future preparation. Most equipment that office workers use, from the manual typewriter to terminals tied to mainframe computers in a distributed processing network, aid in performing those functions to some degree.

For those organizations whose offices require sophisticated equipment to facilitate their employees' day-to-day tasks, one element is inconspicuous but can play a vital role: a communications link. On this link — whether it runs through one building, an office complex, or throughout a company and its branches — travels each piece of material produced by the equipment used for gathering, preparing, revising, producing, distributing, and storing.

The key link to office networking is the digital private branch exchange. Through this digital communications

spinal cord run the elements designed for automating office work: information from data processing terminals, word processors, data entry devices, intelligent printers, electronic message systems, facsimile machines, computers, and telephones. With its multiplexing technique, the digital PBX joins and carries, on a three-pair cable, the digital signals those devices emit. Data rates of more than 100 Mbit/s through coaxial and fiber-optic cables are possible. Such data communications capability should not be out of reach to most medium- and large-size companies.

At the low end, both in price and in technical sophistication, the processing devices usually comprise a keyboard, typing heads, and memory. As the machines move up the scale of electronic sophistication, their elements become increasingly specialized. Whereas an electronic typewriter having memory and storage is a self-contained unit, the equipment at the higher end has separate and interactive components that perform specific jobs.

An equipment presentation follows, which covers a wide range of sophistication and capacity from self-contained units to systems consisting, to a greater or lesser extent, of the bolstered components of those self-contained units.

Self-contained devices

As indicated by equipment orders, the business world seems ready to pay $2,000 and more for a typewriter that uses a combination of mechanical elements and electronic circuitry.

The IBM 75, housing large-scale integrated circuits on a microprocessor chip, lets a typist store, retrieve, and revise words, phrases, and pages for limited repetitive-letter production. It as yet has no communications capability. A 36-kbit random-access-memory chip provides storage for 7,500 characters, with an option

183

IBM 75

Qyx

for another 8,000 characters. The chip, about a quarter of an inch square, receives signals from the keyboard and directs an electronic impulse to the electromagnets that control the typing element. The microprocessor contains the equivalent of 1,200 logic circuits and is mounted on a board with two read-only storage components for the microprocessor's programs. The logic board also holds two high-density silicon and aluminum semiconductor chips that contain the 36 kbits of storage for documents, phrases, and tab and margin settings. A second logic board, containing 1,000 circuits, controls instructions activated by 19 of the 26 alphabetic keys. This board also contains the instructions for phrase storage, number alignment, and paper insertion activated by numeric keys. Any alphabetic key can be used to identify stored material.

Components as systems

The Qyx line of electronic typewriters, also microprocessor-based, has communications capability. A Qyx Level 5, for instance, can communicate with another Qyx, a Vydec text processor, or a teletypewriter terminal for access to a computer database. In a Qyx-to-Qyx communications tie-in, the machines' memories interact through a data-link-control protocol and ASCII-modified code, at one page every 20 seconds. The Qyx Level 5, the top of the line, has dual minidiskettes of 60,000 characters each. Such capacity and communications options give users the beginnings of network capability. The typewriter becomes a terminal.

Keyboards, displays, intelligence, memory, printers, and communications capability are the hallmarks of components as systems. Vendors offer them as packages: IBM Office System/6, IBM 5520 Administrative System, Xerox 860 Information Processing System, Datapoint 3800, and so on. A generic system would have a cathode-ray-tube terminal with display screen, a full keyboard with an additional key pad for special instructions, processing power (residing either in a local minicomputer or in a remote mainframe computer), and a high-speed printer. These packages are capable of performing the functions of specific office jobs, such as records processing, data processing, text processing, and the like.

The Office System/6, for instance, has a display, diskette storage, a magnetic card reader and recorder, a 96-character keyboard, an ink-jet printer, and an automatic paper and envelope feeder and stacker. It transmits over telephone lines at up to 2.4 kbit/s. The OS/6 also communicates with suitably programmed computers, allowing the merging of databases with material stored on diskettes. OS/6 diskettes store up to 274,000 characters, or about 130 pages of text.

The IBM 5520 is composed of similar elements. The differences appear in the processing power, the storage capacity, and the sophistication of the output device. The 5520 includes a display, a daisywheel printer, and a central processing unit with 29 Mbytes of disk storage and 1 Mbyte of on-line diskette storage. There is also optional storage capacity of up to 130 Mbytes

Honeywell Level 68/DPS Wordpro

Datapoint 3800

IBM OS/6

on the disk and 23 Mbytes on-line. The 5520 communicates over switched lines at 4.8 Mbit/s or over non-switched links at 9.6 Mbit/s, and in either of two IBM protocols, binary synchronous communications or syncronous data link control (SDLC). The OS/6 and the IBM 6670 Information Distributor, as point-to-point devices, can interconnect with the 5520, thereby increasing storage capacity and network capability. The enhanced disk capacity of 130 Mbytes will store the program that allows the 5520 to act as a store-and-forward device. This capability will be available later this year, according to IBM.

The Xerox 860 combines text, data, and records processing. Operators at full-page display units share a printer and a controller housing operating and text-processing software. The 860 can also operate on Xerox's local network, Ethernet (the 860 is currently the only product that can do so). The controller includes a microprocessor; two single-sided floppy disks, each storing 300,000 characters; and 96K of random-access memory, expandable to 128K. Programs are loaded from a systems software disk, which is eventually removed. Communications are point-to-point for the 860s. There is emulation of the IBM 2770 communications controller for interfacing the OS/6, of the IBM 2780 data transmission terminal for batch communications, and for teletype communications.

Whereas microprocessors and minicomputers drive these and other similar systems, large-scale mainframe computers provide the processing force for such high-

capacity gear as Wang's Virtual Storage 100 Interactive Processor and Honeywell's Level 68/Distributed Processing System. But even at this level, the components—say, a Ramtek or Datapoint terminal—perform specific, yet integrated, functions. And the processing unit, because of its capacity, performs many other jobs in addition to text, data, or records processing. The VS 100 has up to 2 Mbytes of main memory, a 32-kbyte cache memory, and a true 32-bit architecture. It also supports up to 4.6 gbytes (10^9 bytes) of disk storage and 128 terminals, which spans the capacity of, say, an IBM 370/158. Such text and data processing interactivity allows the user to add statistics, for instance, to a management report, or explanatory text to a data printout.

Printers

Combinations of technologies are helping to change the face of office printers. Computer, laser, and xerographic technologies are printing data and text directly from digital information, in the integrated fashion of, say, a Wang Intelligent Image Printer. The functional units of the Xerox 9700 Electronic Printing System, to use another example, include a xerographic printer, an image generator, an output module, a system controller, and a CRT console.

The controller provides data handling, formatting, buffering, operator control, and communications. It contains a computer with up to 128 kbytes of core memory, a 2.6-Mbyte disk drive, a character dispatch-

Datapoint 8200

Tektronix 4014-1

Ramtek 8210

Lexitron VT 1303 and VT 1000

er, the output-device controller, and the CRT. In addition, the controller accepts information on-line from IBM System 360s and 370s. Off-line, it accepts any 1.6-kbit-per-inch nine-track magnetic tape, in ANSI-approved or other suitable formats used by IBM, Burroughs, Honeywell, and Univac. Incoming information is preprocessed, then buffered on the disk. The buffer stores up to 800 pages of information from tape or computer.

In on-line use for most jobs, the mainframe can resume processing as soon as data transfer to the 9700's disk is completed, without retransmission. In off-line use, it is not necessary to rewind the tape for additional copies on a typical job because the information can be replayed from the disk. Further, a user can mount new tape while the previous job is being run.

The 9700 prints on plain 8½- by 11-inch paper, at a rate of two pages per second, or up to 18,000 lines per minute, depending on type size and data format.

Facsimile and electronic message

Two approaches to distributing material produced in offices—facsimile transmission and electronic message dissemination—provide unusual examples of technological sophistication that are presently somewhat limited by lack of user acceptance.

There are thousands of analog facsimile-machine installations across the country. There are many makes and models. A service offered by ITT, called Faxpak, takes care of converting one analog facsimile maker's code to another, so that users can send material to most other facsmimile users over telephone lines.

Digital facsimile machines, which transmit pages at speeds under a minute (most analog devices are upwards of 3 to 6 minutes), possess the binary coding that data communications users would be happy to see in more office equipment. Applying digital applications to facsimile technology is so new that only a relative few users have latched on to the machines. Burroughs and 3M are two of the handful of digital facsimile vendors, and their digital facsimile machines are incompatible. Neither Faxpak, nor any other facsimile service carrier, is convinced that there are enough digital facsimile users to warrant a digital facsimile network that includes machine-to-machine conversion. And so the digital facsimile machines, functionally designed to be among the most communicative devices in the office world, are unique, and purchased mostly by large companies with extensive dedicated facsimile installations. Many Burroughs Dex 5100s can talk to many other 5100s. The 3M 9600s can only talk among themselves as well.

With electronic message schemes there are both advantages and drawbacks. Some of the confusion over the advanced office equipment scene is moving fast into the electronic message arena. Users are trying to determine if vendors are offering message or mail systems. If mail, then how do these products or services fit into the Postal Service's efforts toward a nationwide electronic mail network? And if it's electronic

Burroughs DEX 5100

Xerox 9700

IBM 5520

Wang Intelligent Image Printer

message, then how do users determine the kind of message to allow on the system? In what cases, for instance, does an electronic message become more efficient than a handwritten note that does not use costly memory and can be tossed quickly into a waste basket? For valid messages like memos, meeting schedules, and directives for immediate action, users who voice concern over postage costs and telephone privacy might employ electronic message systems. Regardless of the pros and cons, the market is preparing users for electronic message systems.

Wang's Mailway, one available message system, is fine for Wang users. It carries messages from one piece of Wang equipment to another, using existing Wang telecommunications protocols.

Datapoint's Electronic Message System is also designed to complement existing Datapoint products, including its Word Processing System and Attached Resource Computer. The Datapoint message approach, however, possesses interconnection capability to the company's Infoswitch/Long Distance Control System, which is capable of transmitting voice, message, and data traffic. The Long Distance Control System (LDCS) sends messages in between voice calls going out on WATS lines. The LDCS host can determine whether voice or message has first access to flat-rate, long-distance facilities. Voice calls may be allowed to go through before message calls. This ensures that the transmission of messages falls into a valley between peak-usage traffic periods. The LDCS host

also recognizes voice build-up and overflow on direct-dial lines. It may then interrupt a message transmission to allow the voice call to proceed. An interrupted message is then requeued within the electronic message system and retransmitted when the line is free. To avoid confusion, the partially transmitted message is erased at the receiving end.

Storage

While cassettes and cassette drives, floppy disks and floppy-disk drives are familiar storage media on the office scene, special-function terminals like electronic mailboxes have begun to draw user attention as well, especially for tasks such as order processing and for reducing communications costs.

Electronic mailboxes are attached to users' terminals through an RS-232-C connection. Predefined commands for data communications and file management simplify data entry and transmission. Driven by single or dual floppy disks ranging from 4 to 40 kbytes of user-programmable memory, the mailboxes almost always work with their own intelligence, provided in their microprocessors. Such power supports forms-data entry, validation, diskette storage, and data transmission, as well as local sorting.

Electronic mailboxes cut communications costs by editing material locally and sending only the data necessary to complete a transaction. Operating at up to 9.6 kbit/s on leased lines and up to 1.2 kbit/s on switched lines, they generally feature full-duplex com-

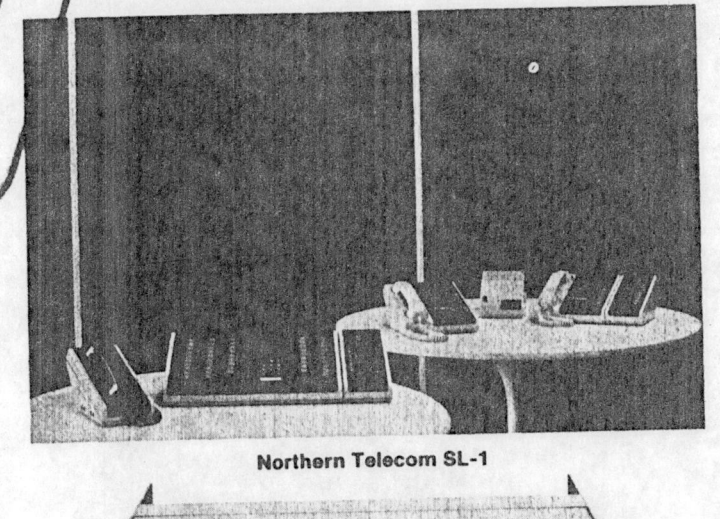

Northern Telecom SL-1

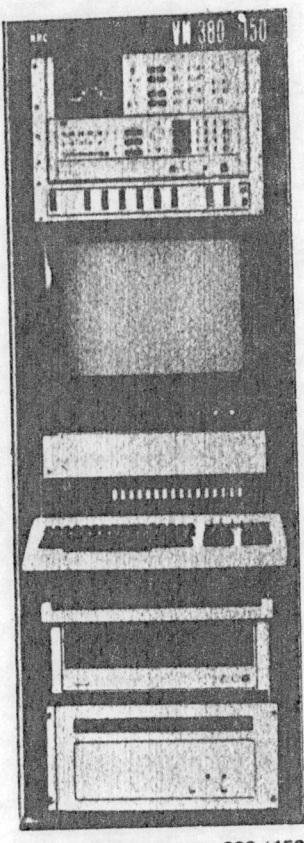

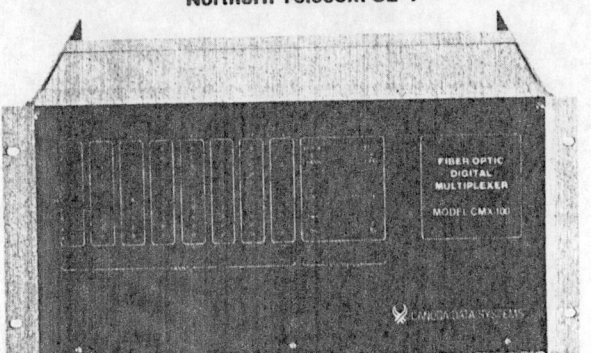

Canoga CMX-100

Network Resources 380/150

munications and standard modem, protocol, and code compatibility, including ASCII and EBCDIC.

Data communications products are now available that, to some degree, support linking the products used in automated office work. However, equipment is being developed that will permit further interconnection of previously incompatible devices.

Xerox's Ethernet, for instance, provides a ring-structured, contention-access, coaxial network that transfers information at up to 3 Mbit/s. It is, though, limited at present to Xerox equipment. A Xerox 860 interconnection to Ethernet provides local networking capability for functional distribution, electronic messages, file management, and electronic printing.

The communications link

Coaxial cable is by no means the only transmission medium for local-office networking, though it is certainly one of the most developed products available. Two other transmission media—broadband CATV and fiber-optic cable—are bound to find their place in the automated office network, primarily because of their wider bandwidths.

Products such as the CMX-100 Fiber Optic Digital Multiplexer from Canoga Data Systems are beginning to emerge. The CMX-100, like any other multiplexer, permits multiple devices to share a common transmission medium, which, in this case, is fiber-optic cable. It accepts up to 16 channels of digital input, each up to 56 kbit/s. This input may be from twisted pairs,

coaxial cable, or whatever, as long as transmission is bit-serial digital and the interface conforms to any supported common standards (including RS-232-C and CCITT V.35). The company boasts a bit error rate of less than in 1 in 10^9, and communications links can be as long as 3,000 feet.

The Canoga multiplexer is essentially transparent to the type of traffic it handles, because it connects the intelligent devices that perform high-level functions such as protocol and error checking. However, office communications control should perform far more extensive duties than the transparent connection of point A to point B. Control should include reformatting of bit streams, switching, least-cost routing, and so on.

The computer-controlled Private Branch Exchange, the CBX, will be required for any sophisticated office network. Companies such as Rolm and Northern Telecom, forerunners in this area, delivered an all-digital CBX designed to handle bit streams of data, facsimile, text, or even voice. Northern Telecom's offering, the SL-1, supports configurations of as little as 100 lines, and up to several thousand. Intelligence in the SL-1 even supports least-cost routing, which connects a user with the least-expensive network, whether it be WATS, tie-lines, or DDD.

Systems that fully integrate the automation of office work are not available today from a single vendor. The products in this section, nevertheless, represent the efforts of various manufacturers to link components to support office tasks. ■

Wendy Rauch-Hindin, Data Communications

Which technology will rule the automated office?

It is uncertain whether the automated office will be based on timesharing systems or local networks, 8- or 16-bit microprocessors, and driven by customized or off-the-shelf software. Controversy abounds.

Within the next several years, vendors of office-automation products and services will vie for data communications managers' attention. They will represent the competing technologies in this multibillion-dollar industry: timesharing versus local networks, 8- versus 16-bit microprocessors, and packaged versus customized applications software.

Ultimately, users will determine the prevailing techniques for controlling automated office functions. But first, they must evaluate each office-automation method in terms of its file-transfer speed, equipment's ease of use, and ability to accept additional hardware and software. Other important factors are information-storage capacity, security, owned but not-yet-amortized equipment, and even equipment aesthetics.

Unfortunately, the information a user obtains depends on the bias of the vendor, the consultant, or another user. For example, proponents of automating offices with mainframe-based timesharing systems insist that only mainframe computers can maintain and manage the very large databases used in the information processing industry. On the other hand, proponents of local networks claim that processing in a timesharing environment is excessively expensive because users must be on-line all the time. Moreover, file-transfer speeds between a centralized computer and its attached terminals are very slow (300 bit/s is common), resulting in lowered productivity.

Many timesharing devotees circumvent these problems by using intelligent instead of dumb terminals. Intelligent terminals allow users to preprocess much data locally. Then they can use their timesharing systems to access the large, complex programs or databases not available on their smaller machines. Still oth-

er users espouse a minicomputer-based timesharing system because, unlike local networks, minicomputers are already available with multiuser capability. In addition, users claim, it is easy to obtain service, and resale value is high.

Personal-computer advocates say that timesharing advantages are counterbalanced by the chaos that ensues when all office work must halt because a centralized computer fails. Yet another viewpoint urges users to choose a system based on whatever office and data processing equipment they already own; any other choice means junking hardware and software not yet amortized and starting from scratch.

The overall architecture of an office-automation system is only one of many decisions a data communications manager must make. Just as important are questions such as whether or not an automated office should contain one or many vendors' equipment, who will write the software tailored to a company's needs, and who will use the computing resources.

Vendors and consultants agree that whatever office-automation system users choose, it must have sufficient information-storage capacity. They disagree on how much is enough.

The greatest controversy is about floppy disks. Charles Grant, president of North Star Computer Corporation, says: "The automated office must be able to accommodate applications such as financial management, mailing lists, word processing, and data processing. For these applications, a minimum of 700 kbytes of disk storage is necessary." He adds, "IBM's new personal computer has only 160 kbytes of storage on one drive. This is not enough."

Grant explains that although it is possible to add

disk drives to any computer, this means more dollars. For IBM's part, the company acknowledges that a problem may exist under certain circumstances. Les Szabo, of IBM's Information Systems Division in Boca Raton, Fla., admitted, "One hundred sixty kbytes of disk storage is not enough for many applications." However, he refused to elaborate on why IBM chose that figure for its disk storage.

An unexpected companion problem to the storage issue is the equipment's appearance and the status it lends to an office. Edward Currie, marketing and new business development manager at Lifeboat Associates Software Company, in New York City, says: "A machine like the Xerox 820 sells very well in the plush office environments where people would not feel comfortable having equipment labeled Radio Shack on their desks. Yet, the 820 has a capacity of only 80 kbytes of floppy storage. Contrast that with the TRS-80 Model 2, which has 600 kbytes of disk storage."

But Xerox Corporation's view, according to Gayle Tinsley, manager of the Program Office for the Office Products Division, is that "neither high speeds nor large storage capacity are absolute requirements." He explains: "Xerox offers disk storage capacity for its 860 computer, ranging from 160 kbytes (two disk drives) to 240 kbytes, and plans still more capabilities. So customers with different applications can fit the products to their needs, instead of vice versa."

What about software?

Office-automation equipment is driven by software. The problem with software, however, is that a shortage exists, especially for 16-bit computers.

North Star's Grant claims that "the abundant software available at a low cost for 8-bit microprocessor-based computers is the reason that the automated office will start its lifespan using 8-bit machines. It will take some time before sufficient 16-bit-based software is written so that the personal-computer field can gravitate to more powerful computers."

However, Ronald Sander, president of Sander Consulting Group in Severna Park, Md., argues: "Personal computers are relatively new, and their large software base has only appeared on the market in the last three years. It will not take any longer to write the software for 16-bit machines. The same people who wrote the software for 8-bit machines will jump at the opportunity to write it for the 16-bit ones. In fact," he says, "vendors will take popular existing software and modify it for the more powerful machines."

Lifeboat's Currie disagrees. He explains that most designers who write software for the popular 8-bit computers will not write for the 16-bit ones. The reason involves standard business sense. They do not know if the 16-bit machines will be popular and consider writing software for them a speculative business. Worse yet, software people who want to try writing 16-bit-based software do not have access to the machines

because they are not widely distributed.

However, Currie adds that IBM's recent announcement of its 16-bit personal computer will most likely accelerate the development of 16-bit-based software by providing a reason for writing it. He explains that many people will buy the IBM computer because they are comfortable with the IBM name. Knowing this, software companies and developers will convert their 8-bit software to make it compatible with the IBM offering.

IBM has made its machine readily available to its software designers who can write 16-bit software. Says an IBM employee who prefers anonymity: "It's no accident that IBM is offering substantial discounts to their employees who buy their personal computers. And IBM software developers, who love to spend their time hacking out software, can't wait to get their hands on these machines. The combination of the discounts, the available hardware, and IBM's remunerative offers to freelance software writers adds up to the formation of a large potential base of software writers for the 16-bit IBM machine."

Keep it safe

Large centralized networks in which everyone shares databases do not easily lend themselves to security. Notwithstanding the techniques available for locking out unauthorized users, operators with unlimited access to files, programmers who know how to find operating-system flaws and thus become privileged users, and former employees with knowledge of a company's computers and files can read, change, and destroy sensitive data.

A much greater measure of security is provided by interconnected personal computers. Their design does not allow easy unauthorized access. For example, personal computers have local storage controllable by the user. Even if another user figured out how to access one machine from another, he would be just as likely to find that the machine he was accessing was turned off or that the disk containing the desired information was locked in a drawer.

In the 1980s, a generation of users with little exposure to or knowledge of computers will work with another generation that has grown up with computers. Data communications users should take this into account when designing their automated offices.

Fear of automation

Although managers are aware that automating the office increases productivity, they are hindered by computer anxiety. They want a terminal on their desk—but as a status symbol not a productivity aid.

In one survey, 98 percent of the 400 managers and executives questioned said they would use an advanced workstation if they had one. "But," says George Colony, a senior analyst with the Boston-based Yankee Group that conducted the survey, "when these managers and executives were asked to choose a real workstation, they balked. Then they expressed distrust of computers and declared they would consider using a workstation in two to three years—not now—and only after the automated office had proven its worth

among secretarial workers."

Colony explains that objections to using a workstation ranged from the rational to the emotional. Objections included such statements as, "I don't like to look at screens," "I need my secretary," "I won't touch any input device," "It's too dehumanizing," and even, "I don't want that thing on my desk."

For Barry Abrams, assistant vice president and data communications manager of Republic National Bank of New York, it is not clear that managers really need workstations. "They do not care who does the typing."

Abrams adds that computers must be made very easy for managers and executives to use. He explains that these people bring their own tested methods to their jobs and have neither the time nor the inclination to learn new, unproved ones. In addition, many older executives were never exposed to computers in school.

"The time and exposure problems are compounded by job pressures," says Abrams. "Managers want to know enough about computers to understand what their secretaries and office staff are doing. However, learning to use the computers may mean competition with their secretaries who are more proficient because they use the computers constantly. This creates status problems for many managers."

Abrams contrasts the attitude of these managers with that of clerical workers who are more amenable to learning to operate a computer. The reason is partly because they are used to doing what they are told and partly because many of them are younger and have been exposed to computers.

Diana de Jesus, a secretary at McGraw-Hill, in New York City, confirms this pliable attitude of office workers but sees a maintenance problem arising. She says, "It is easy to open a typewriter and fix it when minor problems occur. With computers, we are more likely to be out of action, waiting for expert service people."

Lifeboat Associates' Currie doubts that the computerized office will come as fast or be as pervasive as people think. He says: "Computers will increase the throughput of clerical workers and even automate less-interesting aspects of their jobs, such as checking spelling. Unfortunately, they also correct people unceremoniously, and the less friendly ones are even rude. Many managers do not want to cope with their word not being law. They also do not like the feeling of losing control of their environment when their computer goes off and crunches numbers.

"Worse yet," continues Currie, "a factor inhibiting computers from permeating industry is the intuitive feel that managers have developed for their businesses. They have no desire to ignore their intuition in favor of some prognostication or recommendation based on computer-generated reports."

Many vendors, for their parts, are accelerating the acceptance of automated-office systems by simplifying user interfaces. The friendly interfaces they are creating provide users with special-function keys, menus for selecting commands, help symbols, and self-teaching programs. Xerox Corporation has carried its concept of a friendly user interface a step further by providing a menu, for its Star computer, consisting of pictorial

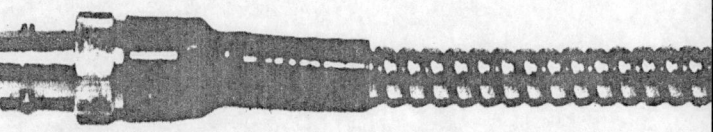

symbols called icons (Fig. 1). Icons look like the office objects that they represent, such as printers, file drawers, in- and out-baskets, documents, workstations, and communications units. Users can move a pointer to a file-drawer icon to find and read a document within it and then move the pointer to a printer icon to obtain a hard-copy printout.

The proving ground

The automated office is still more a vision than a reality, as evidenced by the absence of existing electronic office systems. Says the Yankee Group's George Colony: "Most office-automation systems today are basically word processing systems. However, true automated offices consist of five levels: communications processors, utility processors (machines for developing, storing, and distributing software), advanced peripheral devices, a local network, and user processors (advanced workstations). Success of these office systems will hinge on tailored software."

A pilot project to assess the effects of such an electronic office has been conducted at Bell Northern Research (BNR), in Toronto, Ontario. There, 20 people—executives, managers, professionals, administrators, and clerical employees—were given workstations that were part of an integrated office-automation network. The network provided asynchronous and synchronous communications facilities, administrative tools, text processing, databases and information retrieval, and computing and analytical tools. The workers' attitudes, time use, and communications patterns were compared with those of a control group of 26 people in an office without automation.

The BNR automated office is based on a Digital Equipment Corporation (DEC) PDP-11/70 with a Unix operating system and DEC VT-100 terminals with ad-

1. Menu of icons. Users move a pointer to an icon to obtain automatic services. Other menu selections, such as width and style, are made by depressing a key.

vanced video features (Fig. 2). The software was developed at BNR. The people using the system were part of BNR's Office Information Communications Systems Group, which is helping Bell Canada set up automated offices and is also assessing the impact of products for Northern Telecom. The study results are somewhat skewed because the pilot group consisted partly of people whose job is studying office automation and of psychologists—not the typical office staff.

Data collected during the pilot study indicated that the communications and the text-processing facilities were the most commonly used features, while information-handling and administrative-handling facilities were the least used. Although managers in the study group keyed in their own text instead of relying on clerical persons, the BNR study team observed that executives further up in the organizational hierarchy were less likely to use the computers.

The study group also found that it took personnel several months to learn to use the electronic office equipment—a great deal longer than originally antici-

pated. It concluded that people who operate computers in the office need a very friendly user interface that understands the natural English language. The study team therefore redesigned its interface to include a series of menus instead of the original coded commands keyed in by the operator.

According to Morley Greenberg, manager of Office Information Communications Systems' research at BNR, "The BNR system was operational 98 percent of the time, but this did not turn out to be good enough. In the initial stages of adjustment, if the computerized-office system failed, the office staff reverted to manual methods of performing work functions. Later, however, the users became so dependent on the automated system that downtime caused strange behavior, including the staff moping around the office looking for something to do."

Overall, attitudes toward the BNR electronic office were positive. Only one person refused to use the system initially, but he eventually changed his mind.

At the Rome Air Development Center (RADC) at Griffiths Air Force Base in Rome, N.Y., where a fully distributed office-automation network is operational, managers' hostility toward the electronic equipment lasted six months and then petered out. The RADC

2. BNR's office network. A DEC PDP-11/70 computer is connected to tape and disk storage devices by a 32-bit-wide Massbus; the Unibus connects it to all other devices. Users access the network through terminals hardwired to multiplexers. Outside users gain access through a Datapac line linked to a peripheral PDP-11/03.

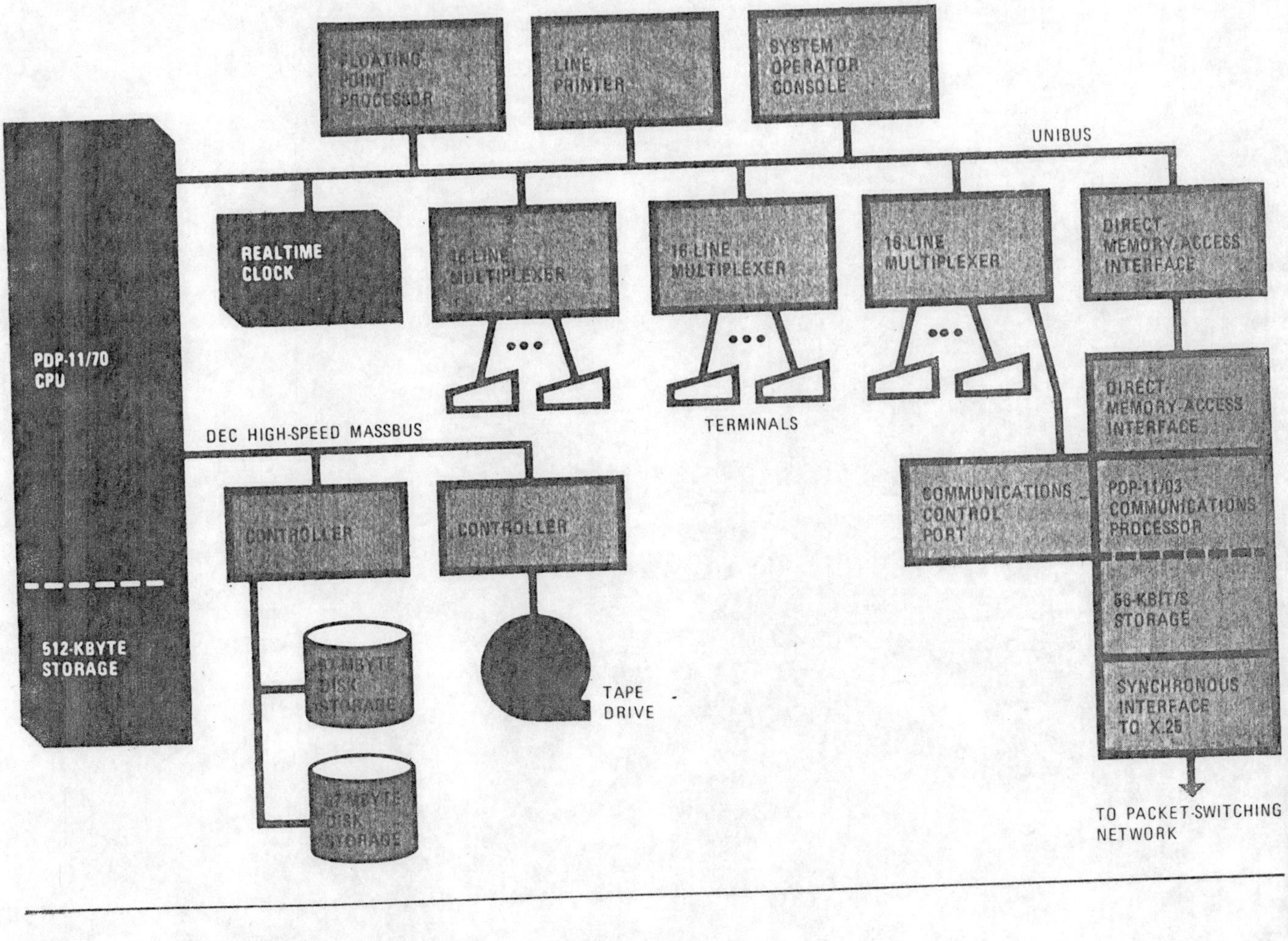

system, which is Unix-based and incorporates distributed databases, was installed by Westlake Village, Calif.'s Bunker Ramo Corporation last year and was integrated this spring. It consists of 10 DEC PDP-11/44s and 10 DEC PDP-11/23s, coupled to a DEC PDP-11/70 and to dumb terminals (Fig. 3). Half the software is custom-developed, and half is packaged.

RADC's automated-office system provides the basic office tools such as word processing, information retrieval, communications, computing, and administrative functions. The targeted users were mainly contract managers, who did not believe the electronic office system would be installed, work, or be useful. Typical initial reactions were to refuse to be high-paid typists—then it was pointed out that they were already high-paid scribes. Only after secretaries proved the system's worth by increased productivity did middle management's resistance break down. Then the system became quickly accepted, particularly for information retrieval, document review, and conferencing.

Many in RADC's top management are still resisting the system. In general, this level of management wants output but does not want to input information and is interested in having voice-activated commands.

"The key to office-automation systems like RADC's"

says Kenneth Larson, a Bunker Ramo systems engineer, "is cost. While the cost of computers is decreasing, software costs are skyrocketing. The way around that is commercial development of standard software packages for office-automation functions. Then costs would be distributed over a wide market base, and individual software costs would decrease to an affordable level for users."

Price/productivity trade-offs

But software, or any equipment costs, are only a part of the office-automation picture. Users deciding about implementing an electronic office system must perform a cost-benefit analysis and evaluate the trade-offs in the costs of initial purchase and installation of equipment versus increased productivity. However, there is little agreement among vendors, users, or consultants on how to measure productivity.

"Measure productivity by metrics such as bottom line, return on assets, or return on investments," says Duncan B. Sutherland, Jr., director of Advanced Sys-

3. *Typical Bunker Ramo system.* *An integrated local/wide-area network implements office automation. Twisted-pair and telephone lines connect different buildings. Computers in each building service various numbers of workstations. Two backup PDP-11/70s store documents that are accessible from anywhere in the network.*

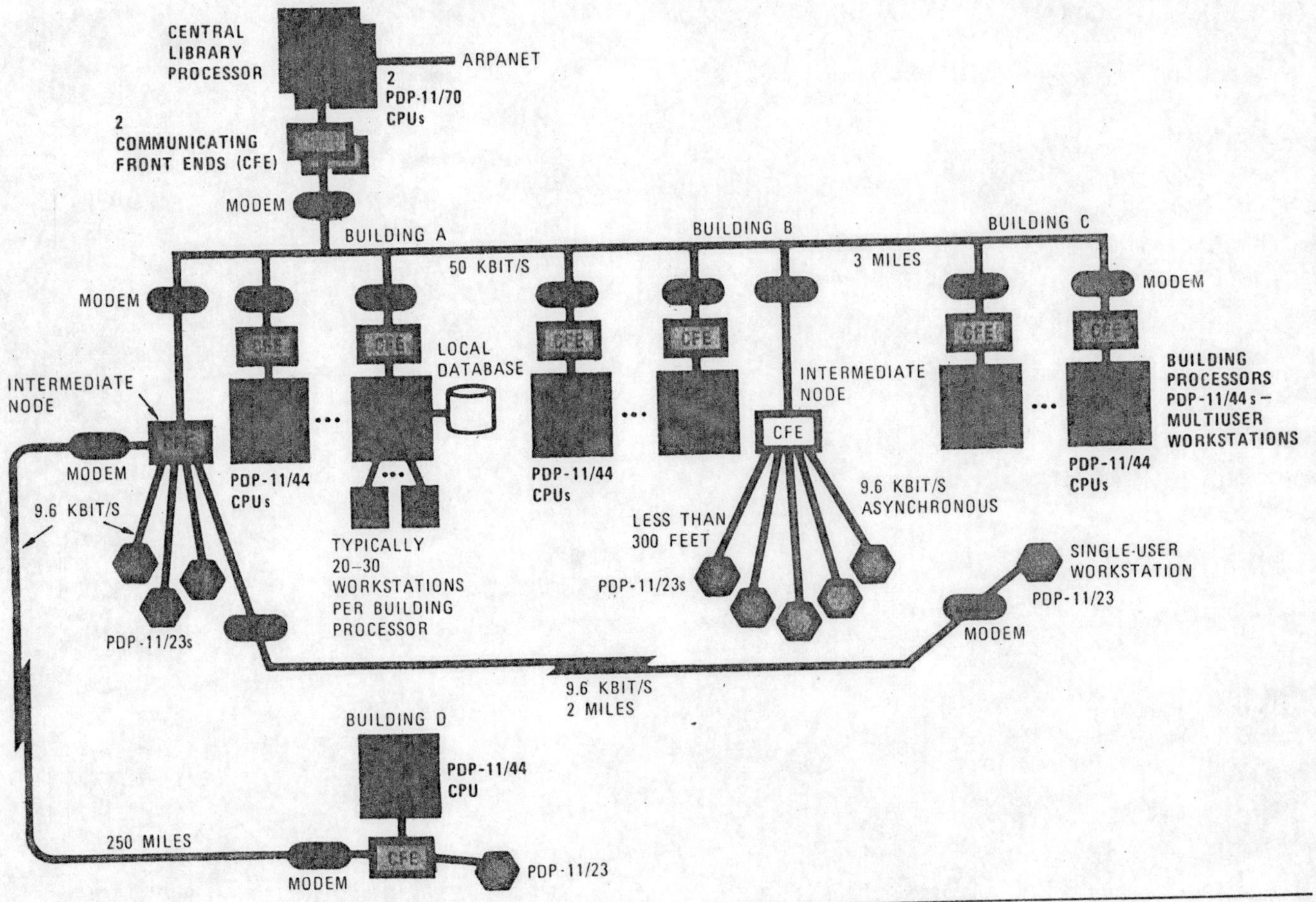

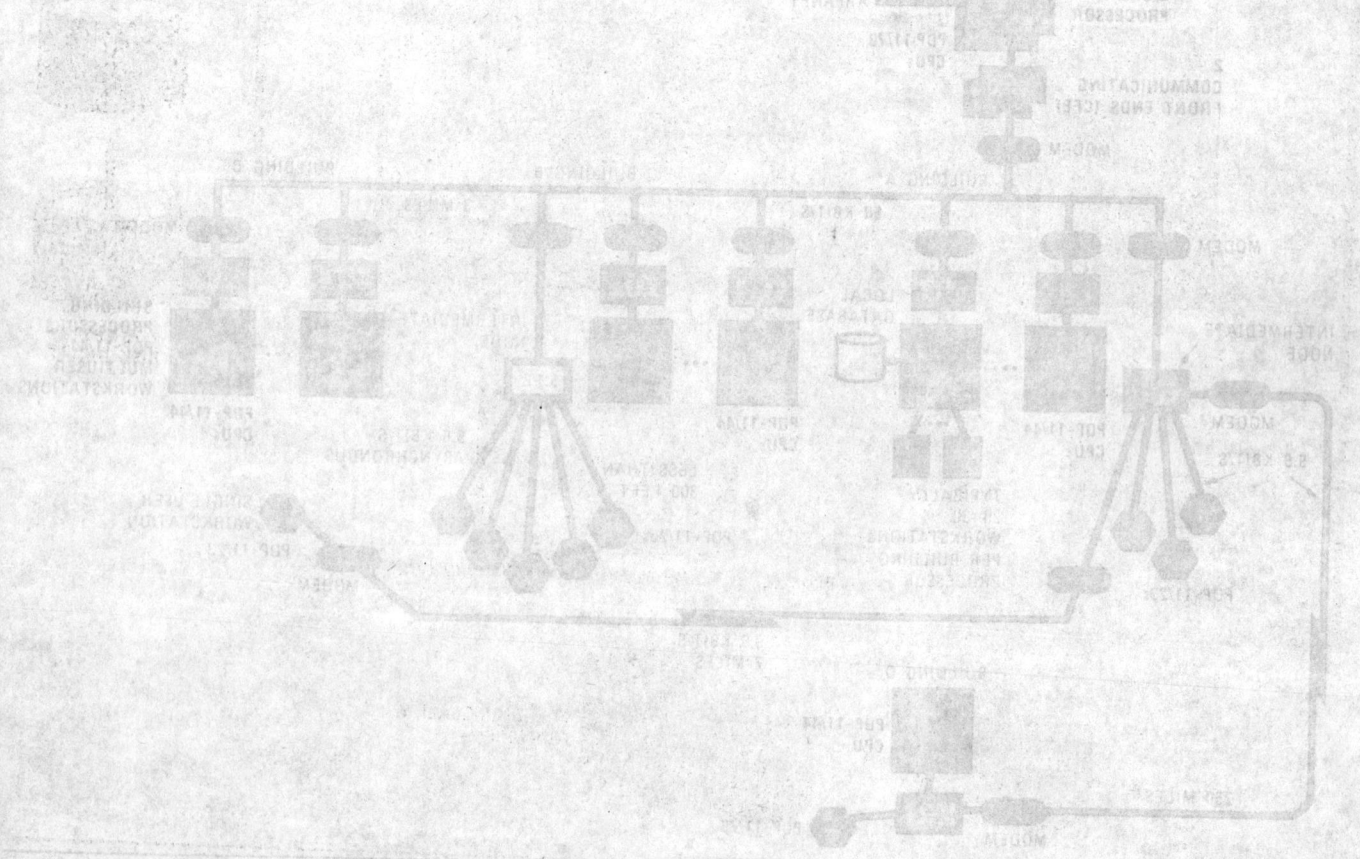

tem Laboratory Development at Wang Laboratories Inc., in Lowell, Mass. He explains that to get a good return, however, it is necessary to do more than buy and learn to use electronic equipment. "Users need to understand their organization, what it is doing, and how it works, and perhaps redesign job functions. Users who merely automate an inefficient organization get an automated inefficient organization. And part of the increased return on assets should arise from displacing labor as a result of increased productivity."

But the Air Force Office of Scientific Research (AFOSR) at Bolling Air Force Base, in Washington, D.C., has a two-year-old office-automation system that, says Major Richard Kopka, "increased productivity but hasn't saved jobs." The AFOSR system contains 26 workstations, 14 printers, 1 high-speed line printer, and two 75-Mbyte disk packs—Wang equipment linked by coaxial cable (Fig. 4). Software is custom-developed by Booz, Allen, and Hamilton.

This automated office is primarily geared to secretaries who are preparing purchase-request packages.

Although the system provides all the subsystem functions that the Yankee Group and RADC consider necessary, word processing, information retrieval, and financial record-keeping based on user-built databases are the major functions used. The primary benefits are time-saving as a result of ease of report preparation and lack of need to perform redundantly many routine bookkeeping and administrative functions.

Because time is saved, secretaries are freed to do other work that they previously had no time to do. "But the cost benefits must be carefully weighed," says Kopka, "because part of the time saved is used to train people to use the office-automation equipment. And, in an area where people are constantly switching jobs or departments, training programs are ongoing and occupy a sizeable amount of time."

Opinions on implementation

It is partly the scarcity of specific information on techniques for implementing office automation and their consequences for users, in addition to the high costs and lack of standard protocols, that is delaying the widespread adoption of this new technology for increasing office productivity. Potential users need to gain a better understanding of what each implementa-

---

4. Office automation at Bolling Air Force Base. The Office of Scientific Research implements office automation with all Wang equipment including CPUs, operator consoles, combination word processors/workstations, disk drives, printers, high-speed printers, and input/output processors. Software is custom-developed.

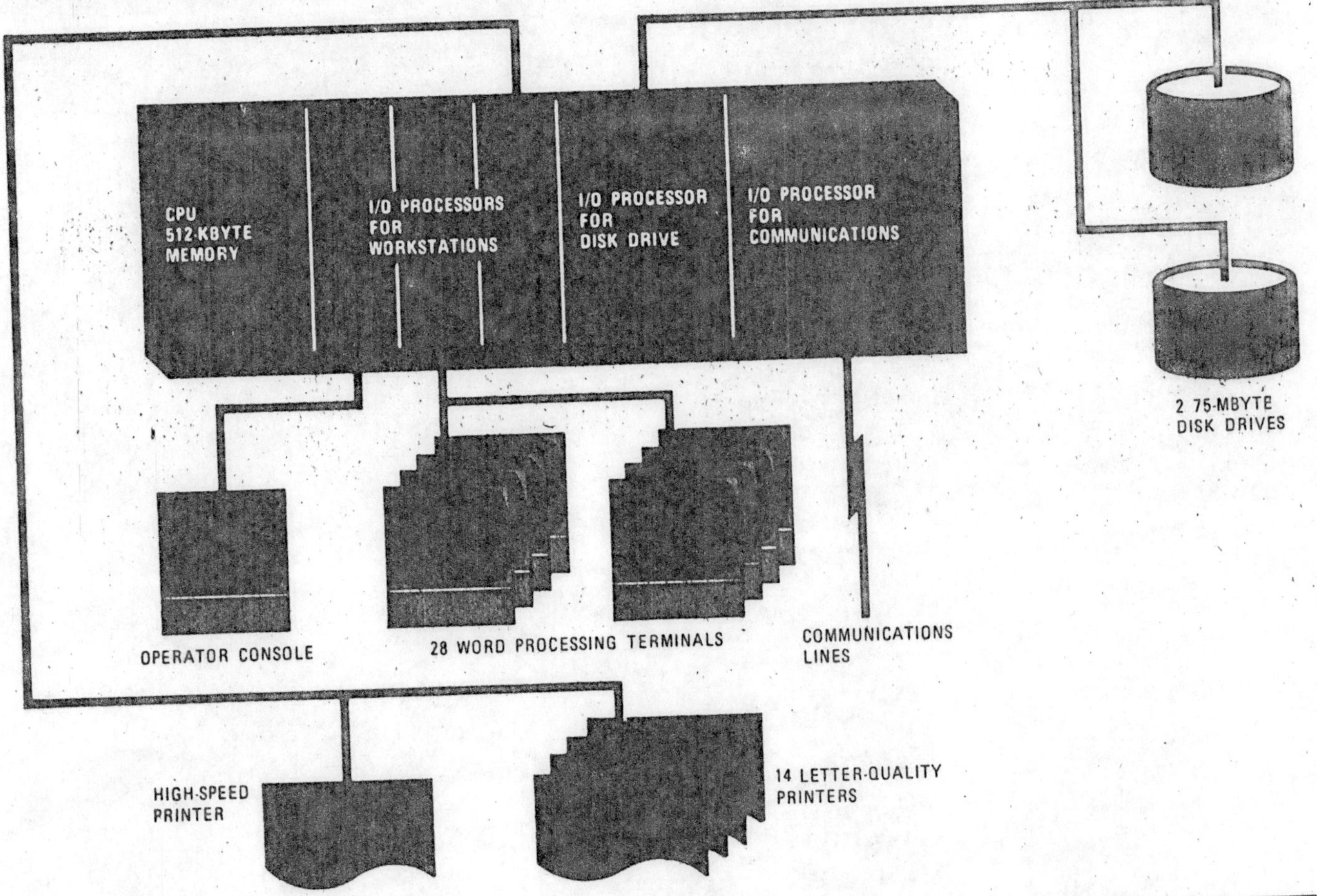

tion method can accomplish for them and what issues and trade-offs are involved before they spend large sums of money for equipment that will change their style of doing business.

The following nine articles are intended to remedy this situation by presenting office-automation implementation methods and their ramifications from different points of view. All are written by either hardware vendors, software vendors, or consultants and detail the reasons for and the implications of the different techniques. Vendors' articles express the reasons for their companies' marketing strategies.

No definitive technique
Burt Bralliar, Peachtree Software, Atlanta, Ga.

Without doubt, office-automation technology will spread not only among the Fortune 1000 companies, but also among the thousands of smaller companies not yet computerized. In the next few years, these smaller companies will either buy their own computers or arrange for shared time on larger systems to automate such currently paper-choked activities as payrolls, inventories, and accounting processes. Larger companies will install office-automation systems that will enable them to bypass the bottlenecks that exist because of separate data processing departments.

Word processing is a major aspect of office-automation systems. Until now, many companies that needed the speed and accuracy of automated typing and text creation bought standalone word processing systems such as those offered by Wang and Lanier. But the question that will face many businesses in the next few years, when considering automated word processing, is this: Instead of spending $5,000 or $10,000 on a word processing system, why not spend the same amount on a microcomputer with word processing capability—and also the ability to handle payroll, keep track of inventory, and figure salesmen's commissions? Moreover, microcomputers can be linked together or to larger computers, and users can either build their own databases on the small computer or access the databases on the large computer. Additionally, users can gather information in the field with a microcomputer and send it to a company's big computer, thus giving top management instantaneous field feedback.

As managers realize the tremendous computer power within their grasp with the spread of microcomputers, they must simultaneously focus on the intelligence controlling the computers—software. Increasingly in the industry, hardware is being advertised and sold on the basis of what the software can make it do and with what software it is compatible. A major attraction of the Apple II is the sheer volume of software being produced for it, and when IBM announced its own long-awaited personal computer in August, it did so with compatible software packages, such as the Visicalc financial-planning package.

The real root of the office-automation revolution is that managers must analyze and determine what is best for their particular situation and then find the equipment to fill their needs rather than rushing out to buy whatever "nifty" equipment other users are buying or salesmen recommend. Users may not find what they need on the market because the market is still young. Since electronic office systems will change job definitions and business styles, users will gain the greatest benefit over the long term by waiting until the equipment best suited to their needs is available.

Trends will emerge, and some brand names and lines of equipment will prosper while others fade. But managers implementing the automated office have the best chance of installing a system that does not quickly become outmoded if they remember that the computer is not really a tool to solve office problems. Instead, it is a tool that can be used to create a variety of other tools to handle those problems.

Burt Bralliar is marketing communications director of Peachtree Software Inc., a division of the software firm Management Science America. He has worked with computer-typesetting and word processing applications since 1978.

Mainframe-based is best
Philip J. Berg, Applied Data Research Inc., Princeton, N.J.

The automated office, with its electronic mailboxes, requires that message retrieval, routing, and broadcasting be electronic. For data communications users, a mainframe-based network for those functions means that the necessary hardware—including terminals, teleprinters, and CRTs—is already installed as part of other data processing operations. Thus, the transition to new office technology is achieved at a quicker pace and a smaller price. In fact, the start-up cost is limited to the cost of the software, with little need for special hardware, floor space, or operations personnel.

Electronic file cabinets for on-line text and information retrieval, as well as extensive facilities for correspondence archives, are necessary in an automated office. With this comes demand for storage space that only a mainframe-based system can handle. Not only do mainframe computers have access to large magnetic storage, (larger than the total storage capacity of interconnected small computers), but they can also manage and control information with a greater efficiency than any network of small computers.

Word processing, another integral function in the automated office, means different things to different

people. To some, it means letters and memos; to others, large manuals, documents, and books. In practice, it is usually some combination of these. Only a mainframe-based automated office can accommodate the extremes of different requirements. For example, there are no limits to the size and complexity of a document, and a mainframe has worksavers like automatic tables of contents, indexes, and page or section numbering. Moreover, it enables access to large reserves of existing data—data that is already in place in support of data processing operations but is also common to various word processing applications. This ready access to files and databases, containing names, addresses, and product and order information, reduces workers' efforts and thus increases productivity. Small computer networks cannot take full advantage of either the commonality or the availability of the needed data.

Productivity can be further increased by automating many applications that, on small computers, require operator involvement. For example, mass mailings are particularly amenable to automation, as are form letters, variable substitution, text selection, and compilations of special mailing lists. Even if an application cannot be fully computerized, the mainframe computer offers capabilities for predefined formats, paragraphs, and whole letters. If typical correspondence is repetitive, why not take advantage of the commonality to reduce data entry and increase office productivity?

However, data communications users must remember that not all mainframe-based processors are equal. They differ in the features they offer and in their functional designs. Some are designed for data processing professionals—not for clerical personnel; others try to combine unrelated functions, such as remote job entry, program development, and word processing, and end up short-changing the word processing user. Potential office-automation users must choose a system that can satisfy their present, as well as future, applications.

Philip J. Berg is vice president of Applied Data Research Inc., a software firm. He is responsible for all of ADR's word processing and office-automation products and has been involved in software development for 15 years.

One for multivendor local nets
Ronald Yara, Intel Corporation,
Santa Clara, Calif.

Even though 16-bit microprocessors have greater capabilities than their 8-bit counterparts, the automat-

ed office of the future will contain a mixture of 8-, 16-, and 32-bit equipment, interconnected in vendor-independent local networks.

The selection of 16-bit microprocessors for some equipment and 8-bit processors for others will depend on the intended applications. For example, since the 16-bit microprocessor supports a much larger (2^{16}) directly addressable memory space than the 8-bit one (2^8), it will be used to execute much larger programs. In addition, modern 16-bit microprocessors have more-powerful instructions and greater performance characteristics. As a result, most new systems designed to meet the needs of multiuser, multifunction workstations are being built with 16-bit chips.

Other workstations, however, that are either more limited in function or designed as part of a distributed processing network, are still being designed with 8-bit microprocessors.

The lack of software has often hampered the penetration of computer-based products into the marketplace. However, the growth of a third-party software industry is helping to fill the need for special- and general-purpose applications programs. In other words, a large cottage industry is writing software for other vendors' products, and a segment of this new industry has targeted hardware-dependent system-software needs.

As automated offices begin to proliferate and microcomputer-based equipment flourishes, these third-party software houses will provide a large choice of operating systems and compatible applications programs, available off-the-shelf, for both manufacturers and users. In addition, these programs will be easy to write and inexpensive because of the use of common operating systems such as CP/M (for 8-bit machines), Unix (for 16-bit machines), and RMX (for 8-bit or 16-bit Intel Corporation equipment).

Microprocessor manufacturers are helping to ease the software problem by offering tools for converting programs written for their 8-bit products into formats used in their 16-bit products. Intel has gone further by offering two 16-bit microprocessors—the 8088 with an 8-bit data bus and the 8086 with a 16-bit data bus—that have identical instruction sets. As a result, the same software may be used on both chips. Since the 8088 is compatible with all 8-bit peripheral controller chips (like an 8-bit CRT controller), 8088 users have 16-bit address space and fast internal performance for their applications. Unfortunately, they also have large loss in I/O throughput, but they are compensated by not needing to pay for 8-bit I/O buffering. (IBM's personal computer is one example of a desktop machine based on the 8088.)

Sharing either an 8-bit or a 16-bit central processing unit among several terminals and floppy-disk drives creates a noticeable drop in performance. However, most equipment makers see no benefit in sharing a processor among low-cost, low-performance peripherals. Instead, new methods are being designed to share high-performance mass-storage and printer peripherals with workstations. And the workstations are often "intelligent" and capable of local processing. Thus, by

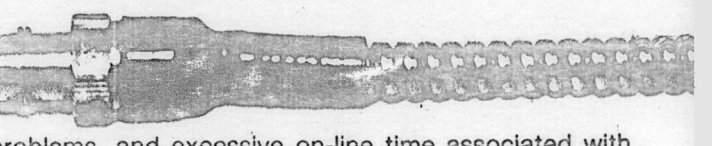

balancing the processing load among intelligent workstations and expensive, high-performance peripherals, there will be no data communications bottlenecks regardless of whether the equipment has 8- or 16-bit microprocessors.

These resource-sharing schemes are emerging in local-area networks. Some, like Datapoint's ARC, are vendor-dependent and interconnect a particular vendor's equipment. Others, like Ethernet, are vendor-independent. When they become well-supported with very-large-scale-integration (VLSI) products, they will connect many vendors' equipment for sharing information, resources, and tasks.

Unlike most large companies' data processing departments, which traditionally have been single-vendor locations, offices are not homogeneously equipped. Typically, in most offices the typewriters are from one manufacturer, the copiers are from another, and the word processors from a third.

Although several large manufacturers are attempting to convince prospective buyers that they can fulfill all of a customer's office-equipment needs, most users believe that a selection of equipment from several vendors is the best approach. Thus, no one vendor is likely to dominate the automated-office market. And competing vendors will be not only traditional office-products manufacturers but also manufacturers of personal computers, such as Radio Shack and Apple.

The appeal of a well-known nameplate on a machine may pale if other manufacturers can show better productivity coupled with lower prices. Therefore, the automated office could be a truly open market for those who can deliver products with office-automation capabilities at the right time. The establishment of vendor-independent local-area network specifications will permit the end user to select the optimum product/vendor mix to meet his particular requirements.

Ronald Yara is the strategic marketing manager for peripheral controller products at Intel Corporation, where he has worked for seven years. Previously, he was a design and an applications engineer.

Eight-bit is best
Edward Currie, Lifeboat Associates,
New York, N.Y.

Vendors of 16- and 32-bit microcomputers claim that the "paperless" office will be based on local networks built from such machines. They cite, as reasons, the high performance of the 16/32-bit microcomputers that, when interconnected, can provide office capabilities while overcoming slow file-transfer rates, security

problems, and excessive on-line time associated with mainframe timesharing systems.

Unfortunately, these claims ignore practical considerations such as lack of available software, lead time to write software, and bottlenecks in peripheral equipment. Theoretically, only a local network based on 16/32-bit machines would enable users to efficiently share resources such as large disks, high-speed printers, and other office equipment. Such a network would also increase the variety of jobs that can be automated, such as financial planning, report writing, accounting, and statistical analysis. But 16/32-bit local networks have several problems that must be resolved before they can become cost-effective.

The major problem is that the software needed to support the new 16- and 32-bit machines is not yet available. It will take years before sufficient software is written to make these machines commonplace in offices. Moreover, most computer operations, especially in an office, are input/output bound, instead of compute-bound. Although an extensive body of data can be processed in microseconds, transferring files to mass-storage devices and printing the actual results take much longer.

This bottleneck in peripheral equipment, which cancels many advantages of 16/32-bit computers, occurs because most office copiers, printers, and Telexes have only 8-bit data paths and are also inherently slow devices. For example, a formed-character printer may print only 45 to 65 characters per second. The slowdown occurs partly because more than one transfer is necessary to transmit 16- or 32-bit information to or from an 8-bit device. In addition, these peripherals have nonstandard protocols and are just not designed for use in 16/32-bit networking.

Data communications users who expect to benefit from the new 16/32-bit hardware must first survey the present state of both software and computer technology. Eight-bit microprocessors, like the 8080/8085/Z80s, are well known, stable, and regarded as "friendly." They are already supported by a large base of end users, software programmers, manufacturers, and vendors, and are therefore not likely to be retired for a long time.

A large body of 8-bit applications software, operating systems, languages, and development tools is already available. As 16-bit machines have been developed, software vendors have tended to transport existing 8-bit software to the larger machines, rather than develop new 16-bit packages. This does not necessarily result in efficient programs for the new hardware environment or take advantage of all the new 16-bit hardware features, but it does eliminate the need for extensive and costly program rewriting.

The program-rewriting difficulty is made worse because the newer 16- and 32-bit architectures require considerably more complex programming than the 8-bit ones. And this problem is compounded by the

scarcity of good, widely used operating systems, languages, and development tools.

In fact, state-of-the-art 8-bit software is so advanced that 8-bit microcomputers are now in wide use and well-entrenched. On the other hand, 16-bit microprocessors, like Intel's 8086 and Motorola's 68000, both announced four years ago, have been slow to find their places in the microcomputer industry.

It may take another decade before software for the 16/32-bit machines catches up with software for their 8-bit counterparts. Until then, the 16/32-bit microcomputers will be most suitable for either special applications or the scientific realms whose applications are mostly compute-bound.

Edward H. Currie is the marketing and business development manager for Lifeboat Associates, a software publisher. Previously, he was a product manager for Pertec Computer Corporation.

Homogeneity eases transition
John Molitor, Wang Laboratories Inc.,
Lowell, Mass.

The implementation of office automation should be based on the realization that the office is a dynamic place. People often work on several projects at once and are frequently interrupted by the phone, their superiors, or other workers who need information. Moreover, it is a place where information must be easily accessible and readily understandable. Office work is a mixture of repetitive, standardized, structured activities and spontaneous, unstructured activities that characterize the flow of information between employees.

Office automation is an evolving process—it is people using technology to manage and communicate information more effectively. To maximize productivity, all levels of a corporation's personnel, from the chief executive officer to the entry-level secretary, require access to the office-automation networks. But people learn and work at different rates. Moreover, they move from one department to another. Equipment training and retraining time and the negative effects on human resources can be minimized if the selected equipment is easy to use and has consistent user interfaces. And the most cost-effective, people-oriented method for providing access to automated capabilities, consistent user interfaces, and processing power is via a single vendor's local network that connects a corporation's individual departments.

Automation of individual departments must include the integration of data processing, word processing, video, and voice. With distributed data and word-processing capabilities at local sites, people with interrelated and interdependent jobs can benefit from sharing the same functions and resources. Different departments can be linked through local-area networks.

The key to office automation, therefore, is distributed information. Widespread distribution of local networks, based on 8- and 16-bit computers, does not entail the obsolescence of mainframe computers. On the contrary, mainframes are securely anchored in the Fortune 500 companies and will always be useful for projects such as corporate reporting. But the trend is toward local processing, which provides greater involvement in and use of local applications. Not only are the programs tailored for each site but the actual programming tasks are often easier. Also, mainframe vendors are encouraging local processing through the production of dumb terminals; but the cost saving predicted from using this approach does not take into account additional equipment purchases such as extra memory, disk capacity, line costs or processing degradation, and local autonomy.

For companies that use distributed information processing, 8- and 16-bit computers can serve as valuable resources for central processors. At the same time, the mainframe becomes one more interrelated resource for the distributed network. The delivery of enhanced processing power at the local level allows increased departmental autonomy, while communications capabilities permit the local system to link up with the mainframe when necessary.

In some cases, major reprogramming has partially, or even totally, made the mainframe's software obsolete during the upgrading process—an expensive proposition. Certainly, users of distributed systems also must expect added costs for equipment as their needs grow. However, maintenance costs for office networks are lower because their design allows users to build on existing systems, thus avoiding large software changes. Long-term gains and returns on investment are accrued through the system's evolution.

How long will it be before we see widespread implementation of electronic office capabilities? The key to this ongoing transition—from the central mainframe or the word processing center to fully distributed data and word processing systems and advanced networking—is user acceptance of existing technology.

John Molitor is vice president of marketing support at Wang Laboratories. He has 22 years of experience in domestic and international marketing for the computer industry.

Homogeneity eases transition
John Molitor, Wang Laboratories Inc.
Lowell, Mass.

Build on existing equipment

Kenneth J. Thurber, Architecture Technology
Corporation, Minneapolis, Minn.

The most important concerns in choosing an automated-office design are the user's purposes and the hardware and software investments he has already made. In comparison, issues such as whether to purchase an 8-, 16-, or 32-bit-based network, a mini- or mainframe system, and the software base available for future purchase are irrelevant.

Various manufacturers are touting their equipment as being best for the automated office. The four key groups of manufacturers are telephone/PBX manufacturers, mainframe manufacturers, office-equipment manufacturers, and independent local-network/office-products manufacturers. Each manufacturer insists that the best office-automation system is based on its equipment. This is ridiculous! Data communications users already have a phone system, a computer center, and various other equipment. They must integrate all of these into one system by looking at the overall system design—not just a set of its parts. Users must therefore ask themselves questions such as "How does my phone system relate to Manufacturer X's local network?" and "How does my computer center connect to Manufacturer X's office equipment?"

Office automation is more than just applying word processing technology. Productivity improvements will also stem from automation of management functions. Therefore, users must decide whether the executive workstation should be based on a PBX or on a local-computer network and whether it should connect to the company's existing computer center.

Local-network technology provides the means to interconnect the proliferation of nonhomogeneous equipment that exists in most businesses. In fact, most local-network manufacturers provide an RS-232-C interface so users' various equipment can connect and communicate. Unfortunately, this communications capability is a myth. The RS-232-C interface provides only a physical connection. After the physical connection is established, the user must generally solve his own software problems. And what vendor can the user call on to make the software written for one device communicate with other devices' software?

Many people claim that the big problem in setting up an office-automation system is picking the right word processor, personal computer, workstation, or microprocessor-based system to capture the large, commercially available software base. Actually, the more important problem for a data communications user is deciding what kind of network will allow him to continue using his current software base when his office systems are connected to his computer center. Other user considerations are the gateways between systems and the software strategy for a user interface (should a uniform user view of the entire system be required?), as well as mundane issues, such as wiring buildings to meet fire and building codes.

Instead of worrying about individual system parts,

users must decide on an overall strategy and implement test sites to prove design feasibility. They must assess the hardware and software facilities they already own and also take into account the speed with which technology is changing. In fact, technology is changing so rapidly that users should depreciate their equipment as soon as possible. Now is the time for users to try various equipment; however, now is not the time for them to lock themselves into a single vendor or hypothetical solutions with unproved benefits.

Kenneth J. Thurber is president of Architecture Technology Corporation, a consulting firm specializing in computer architecture, local networks, and office systems. His previous jobs were in hardware and in VLSI development at Sperry Univac.

The PBX will overcome

Walter Ulrich, Walter E. Ulrich Consulting,
Houston, Tex.

Private-branch-exchange technology is nearly as old as the telephone (which is 105 years old) and has been proven to be reliable. Interconnect-companies' products are accepted. Rolm Corporation, for example, has 7,000 PBXs installed in the field.

Anyone who suggests that the telephone will be replaced by data-message systems is dreaming. Data- and voice-message handling will not only coexist but will converge. Data messages will be forwarded with voice comments. Voice messages will refer to data.

Integrated voice/data PBXs are available for handling both voice (telephone) and data (terminal) communications. Rolm and Northern Telecom are the first to have products available. Datapoint and Intecom (Exxon Enterprises) will deliver new products this year. Additional product announcements have been made, and AT&T's Antelope can be expected for delivery in 1982 or 1983.

In contrast to the ease of telephone use, companies have experienced growing pains and problems with data processing. Regardless of the technical merits, most executives are not going to trust their telephone service to a data communications approach. For the next five years, the PBX will be preferred over local-area network choices for telephone communications.

Primary office-automation applications include message services and database access. Low-cost terminals (those priced under $700) will make it possible for the occasional user to access these services from his or

her desk. For this kind of user, the terminal is similar to the telephone and can be easily handled by the same system.

Initially implementing automated offices with PBXs has further advantages over other techniques because the transition can be gradual; many companies will simply add a few terminals at a time to an existing network. This means making many small decisions instead of a big one. Even if, in aggregate, alternate local-network technologies are more cost-effective, the psychological barrier to making a big decision (or a big commitment) favors the PBX and other traditional approaches.

To overcome this barrier, integrated terminal/telephone instruments are being developed. Northern Telecom has its Displayphone, and the French have the Matra terminal, among others. These terminals have a CRT screen, a low-volume keyboard, a telephone handset, an auto-dial capability, and they take up very little desk space. The Matra terminal will cost under $700 in the U.S.

Store-and-forward voice systems are still in their infancy but have attracted much favorable attention. PBX vendors will develop this capability. Imagine a PBX that can handle voice and data, has an integral voice- and data-message system, and interfaces to a small, attractive, integrated terminal/telephone. The pieces are available. It is now a matter of integration.

Finally, perhaps in this decade, a speech-processing miracle will occur. Computers and memory are getting cheaper, and advances are being made in speech recognition. Although no one can predict the exact products, speech processing will make it easy for everyone to use office automation. What is the likely vehicle for delivering this speech-processing function? The good old PBX.

Success of the PBX is not assured. It depends on the vendors' competence and their will in making the necessary marketing and development investments. Half-hearted efforts will fail.

Will the PBX be part of the office of 1986? You bet! The mainframe will still be the repository of corporate records. Other local-network technologies will serve local communities of interest. Personal computers will provide personal processing power. The PBX will be the hub of voice communications and provide the communications infrastructure for many terminal users.

Walter Ulrich is president of Walter E. Ulrich Consulting, a management and technology consulting firm. He is an expert in office automation and helped pioneer electronic mail.

Linking low-cost microcomputers
Harry J. Saal, Nestar Systems Inc.,
Palo Alto, Calif.

Currently, the two largest barriers to finding and installing an office-automation network are the cost and the lack of systems-integrated software. Investment houses, banks, and real estate and manufacturing offices seeking to maximize their productivity often do not need (and cannot afford) the high-performance, number-crunching capabilities of a mainframe or high-end minicomputer. Further, businesses are learning that they cannot tolerate total dependence on a single machine that halts all operations when it fails. Office managers need equipment and software that make data available for use, manipulation, and transfer by multiple users, who must also be able to communicate freely with each other and with remote locations.

Such needs have several consequences for office-automation-systems design. For example, electromechanical devices, such as disks, printers, terminals, and cables, generally cost more than an entire central processor. Since the cost of CPUs is no longer a dominant concern, many manufacturers build computing capabilities around distributed logic and shared peripherals. In this way, the individual needs of users are served, and information can be shared and exchanged as necessary, while equipment costs are minimized.

Intelligent desktop workstations, connected via a local network, provide an excellent vehicle for distributed computing. Together with the applications-level software, such a network offers computational, data-storage, and communications capabilities for the office. Connecting this local network to other local networks, to inexpensive dedicated processors, or to mainframes forms an extensive hierarchy of data processing solutions. And, most importantly, the low cost of microcomputers makes distributed logic, from a computational standpoint, the least expensive of the available high-flexibility networks. One such low-cost, microcomputer-based network is Nestar Systems' Cluster/One, which is built around the Apple II computer.

The prospective buyer of an office-automation system must understand, however, that software is the key to affordable implementation. Why is this so? In the office, data must flow freely between workstations. But, although lower-level interface protocols for computers and other devices have been standardized and implemented in hardware, high-level protocols will probably not be standardized in the near future. Because of the great variety and flux found in high-level protocols, most current office-automation-network applications are implemented in software rather than in hardware. Therefore, for any office system purchased, an integrafed software base must exist, and this base must include strong graphics- and text-processing facilities and modules that allow the sharing of peripherals, communications between user stations, and local and remote network connections.

This type of software must be transparent to high-level languages and operating systems. One tool used

200

to implement this transparency is programmed virtual I/O. For example, network-interface cards in each workstation may masquerade as disk controllers. The user, familiar with his own operating system, issues familiar I/O commands that manipulate mass-storage memory as if it were located in local peripherals.

Applications and communications programs can be implemented in the same way. From a familiar operating system, the user executes an electronic-mail program or printer-request program as if it were applications software on a minifloppy disk. In addition, departments can compute, store, and manipulate data and communicate over the network, unaware of the multiple protocol levels that lie beneath the applications layer. For example, Nestar's Cluster/One is transparent to operating systems and high-level languages and supports other vendors' programs.

Rounding out the automated office's integrated computing/communications environment are remote communications requirements. In low-cost, sophisticated, software office-automation systems, internetwork connections are accomplished by file-transfer and data-gateway programs running on dedicated CPUs, with remote hookups via modems. Such extended networks can transmit messages all over the globe, at rates under $1 per 250 words.

Harry Saal is the founder and president of Nestar Systems Inc. He has worked extensively in software design and implementation and in project management at IBM and with the Stanford University Linear Accelerator Center's Computation Group.

Stick to one vendor
Robert L. Puette, Hewlett-Packard Company, Cupertino, Calif.

In the next decade, the cost of the $100,000 computer will shrink to $5,000, and the computer, or a terminal linked to it, will be found on almost every desk in the office. That will throw a burden of responsibility on those who must select among the many available computers and peripheral equipment. They must ask several questions before making a purchase: Will the equipment communicate with larger computers? With one another? Will each machine's software be compatible with other electronic office equipment? Will documents written on one word processor be accessible from others? Will the overall system be affordable?

And, the best way for users to ensure an affirmative answer to these questions, and thereby maximize office productivity, is to implement office automation with personal computers, low-cost terminals, and shared peripherals, interconnected in local networks and

linked to a larger computer—all supplied by a single vendor. The personal computers and terminals allow office staff, from clerks to executives, to interact with information-processing hardware and software as easily as they now use their telephones and without having to call in a programmer. Personnel can use low-cost terminals for tasks such as simple forms of word processing, while saving the more expensive personal computers for sophisticated word processing applications and financial-planning packages.

The large computer, connected to the local network, stores and manages large databases that can be accessed by local machines and also processes large matrices that cannot be handled on smaller machines. And, if all the equipment is supplied by a single vendor, users can be assured of hardware and software compatibility, ongoing support, and reliable service.

Cases abound in which not even the vendor is certain if his peripherals or computers will operate properly with another vendor's equipment. Moreover, software packages executing on one computer may work differently on various kinds of peripherals. If this happens, who can fix, or even diagnose, the problem?

In contrast, a vendor not only knows which of his equipment works well together but also has the diagnostics to support his configuration and to pinpoint the problems. This kind of support is particularly difficult with multiple-vendor-supplied equipment because suitable diagnostic methods are generally not available.

Furthermore, users of single-vendor configurations can count on the vendors to verify that their equipment meets regulatory standards, such as FCC requirements for radiated radio-frequency interference (RFI). Fabricating or obtaining equipment to verify the various configurations of different kinds of hardware is a difficult task with multivendor equipment.

Some form of centralized control over the purchase of new office-automation equipment is necessary to ensure the best selection. This control must leave users free to choose what they need to do their jobs, but ensure management that volume-purchasing agreements are made for the best prices, that common needs are served, and that vital functions remain auditable. The way of the future is not to eliminate, or even to reduce, the role of central EDP, but instead to make EDP people the source of all the information needed locally to choose the equipment.

Robert L. Puette is general manager of Hewlett-Packard Company's General Systems Division. He joined HP in 1966 and has extensive experience in marketing and systems analysis.

Stick to one vendor

Robert L. Puette, Hewlett-Packard Company
Cupertino, Calif.

Wendy Rauch-Hindin, Data Communications

Universities are setting trends in data communications nets

New networking technologies are already in place at college campuses. Now coming along are developments in networking software and data communications training for nonscience majors.

If you want to know what is to come in data communications and information processing, go to the universities. Campus research and development efforts include advanced local networks, gateways between these networks, and dynamically reconfigurable and fault-tolerant networks, as well as the associated software. These technological developments at schools are an outgrowth of academia's recognition that every educated person today should have some knowledge of information processing in order to cope with our information-oriented society.

Because so many students need access to computers, university computer centers have become saturated with users. It is not unusual for a university to open a new computer science or computer engineering department and immediately have 1,000 registrants the first semester. Since it is not cost-effective to increase local processing power for these students, the trend at universities is toward local networking.

"To get more power from a mainframe computer in a centralized facility, it is necessary to add core memory, input/output devices, disks, terminals, processors, and communications ports," says Jack Heller, chairman of the Computer Science Department of the State University of New York at Stonybrook.

This, he continues, has disadvantages. "For example," he says, "as more people interact with the machine at the same time, there is a greater chance that some timing flaw that was not taken into account in the original design of the hardware and software will

cause the system to be unreliable and crash."

The adding of peripherals and processors to an already saturated machine is not only unreliable, it is also becoming prohibitively expensive. Officials at the New York State University system estimate that the rental price for hardware additions to its centralized facility is $250,000. An outright purchase could cost $1 million. Even if the money for the resources were available, the standalone system would not support all potential users, and the school would have to invest in yet another centralized facility.

However, several manufacturers sell midsize minicomputers, for about $250,000 each, that support up to 32 users each. User capacity can be further increased at a smaller cost by interconnecting several of these machines into a local network than by centralized facility expansion.

An example of the local-networking approach is seen at Stanford University, in Palo Alto, Calif. Stanford has a Decnet network (Digital Equipment Corporation), an Ethernet network (Xerox Corporation), and an Arpanet node (U.S. Department of Defense). Its Ethernet—a predecessor of the present Xerox—Intel Corporation—Digital Equipment Corporation (DEC) 10-MHz one—operates at 3 MHz. It connects Xerox Altos personal computers and DEC VAX 11/780s. Stanford plans to extend its Ethernet to include access to IBM 3033s, 2331s, Series 1s, and DECsystem 10s and 20s located in centralized facilities on campus. The university also intends to adopt the newer 10-MHz Ethernet

202

as soon as it becomes available.

However, Ethernet is limited in geographical range because of the attenuation in the coaxial cable. To make networks span larger distances, more local networks with gateways between them are needed.

Gateways already exist at Stanford to connect the Ethernet network to Arpanet, but the gateway machine involved is a DECsystem 10. Stanford is presently building network gateways using the Motorola 68000 processor instead—simply because of money.

"The DEC 10," says Stanford's director of computers, Ralph Gorin, "costs $1 million, while the 68000 costs $250. By the time we finish augmenting the 68000 with connecting parts, case, and power supply, we might be up to $2,000. Double that to account for underestimates, and it is clear that even though the DEC 10 performs other than gateway functions, it is hard to justify its purchase as a gateway."

The 68000 is a 16-bit microprocessor that is ubiquitous at universities because of its speed, size, and functionality. At Stanford, it will be used as a gateway to interconnect the 3-MHz Ethernet network, Decnet, Arpanet, and a yet-to-be-installed 10-MHz Ethernet. Plans are also in the offing to use the 68000 as the cornerstone for building a terminal interface processor to connect RS-232-C-based terminals to the networks. The processor will provide a terminal session to whatever central processing unit (CPU) the user selects.

Stanford's local networks resolve three complaints that Gorin continuously hears from both students and faculty. The first is, "My terminal isn't connected to the right computer." The second is, "My data isn't in the right place." This is often heard when data is gathered by a small computer that controls an experiment in one location, then sent to a large programming system with resident files for data reduction or statistical analysis. The third complaint is, "I want to send a message to another user, but he doesn't use the computer I do."

Mail controversy
The electronic mail question has caused some controversy among different schools. Although computers perform functions besides electronic mail, several schools have said that the electronic message system is a major benefit of their networks. A faculty member in one major university (who cannot be named), when asked if it was cheaper to hand-carry messages from one department to another, replied, "No, because then the school would need to hire messengers."

Dr. William Lewis, chairman of the Department of Computer Science at Arizona State University at Tempe [a school with a Tran network (Tran Telecommunications Corporation) and a Decnet network], says, "Electronic mail is convenient, especially for sending hard copy fast. But for college campuses it can be a very expensive messenger." Lewis suggests that it is cheaper to pick up the telephone than to send messages via networks or messengers.

"There are colleges," Lewis explains, "that need networks because of the number of students using their computer or because the college curricula warrant it. "However, for many schools installing networks, it would be more cost-effective to distribute the student load by distributing student accounts over various machines, to distribute classes at different sites near different machines, and to use floppy disks to transfer files." The Tempe-Arizona school is doing just that.

CRT blackboards
Brown University in Providence, R.I., is using local networking to provide improved computer science instruction. Local links are being installed in the computer science classrooms, and every pair of students has its own Apollo computer. The students' computers are linked to one another and to the instructor's CPU, in a network called Domain. This setup allows an instructor to display information on the computer screen instead of a blackboard.

To teach students program development in available class time, the instructor broadcasts a sample program or part of a program to students' computers. Each student can then work out his own variations of that program. Thus, students receive immediate feedback on their comprehension of course material and instant reinforcement of their understanding of the abstract concepts being taught.

Typing time for keying-in programs is kept to a minimum because the computer editor knows the major constructs of the programming language being used. Students need merely pick the constructs they need, like a DO LOOP, from a menu, fill in their variable names wherever necessary, perhaps add a statement of their own or pick another program construct, and then try to execute the program.

To get a concrete idea of what is happening in computer memory during program execution and as an aid in debugging programs, Brown uses a combination of high-resolution graphics and a "window manager," which partitions its terminal screens into windows, along with software developed at the university. The software allows students who write programs that manipulate a data structure to see their programs in one window on their screens and the data structure they are manipulating in another window.

During program execution, when the computer steps through the code at a preselected speed, the student can view the changes taking place in the data structure (Fig. 1). For example, a common program adds an item to a particular place in a list of items. To do this, a binary search algorithm is used to find out if the item is already part of the list, and, if not, the student's program provides instructions to decide where in the list the item belongs. As the program executes, students see pointers going through the data structure, showing which part of the structure they are looking at. Finally, when the right place is found, students see the item being placed in the data structure.

This technique gives students a concrete and intuitive grasp of data structures and algorithms, since they can see the structures, experiment with the algorithms, and stop the program at any stage to study the highlighted program statement and data structure. This method of debugging programs is faster and more reliable than are the usual methods, which are either

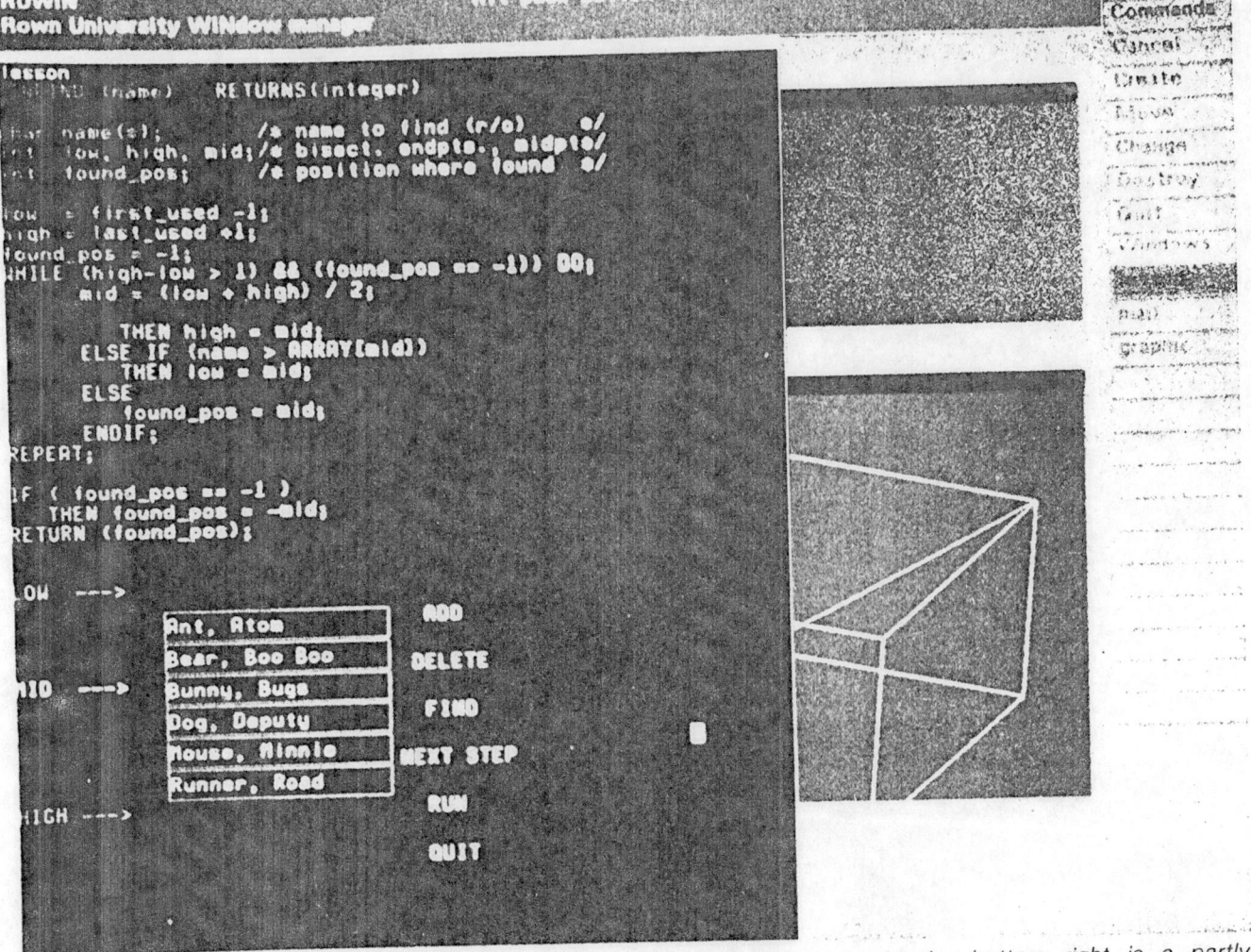

1. The window manager. *The big window contains a lesson on the binary search algorithm. The top half contains the code, and the bottom holds a representation of* the data structure. At the bottom right is a partly obscured picture of a cube that rotates in real time. The top right window displays the student's electronic mail.

trial and error or hacking away at a program until the error disappears.

Brown's Apollo Domain network uses the token-passing access scheme for network arbitration for this type of software development. This local network, however, is only one of many at the university. Each of 125 buildings on campus has its own local network. All local networks are connected to Brunet (Brown University Network), a campus-wide broadband path that interconnects the local networks and the university's large mainframe computers. Brunet is based on 300-MHz coaxial cable and Sytek Corporation hardware that supports channels for terminal traffic and computer-to-computer traffic, video channels for security monitoring and educational TV, as well as channels for controlling heating, ventilation, and air conditioning.

Domain networks are currently being installed and interfaced to other information processors on the campus through gateways to Brunet. For each Domain network, one Apollo computer functions as a gateway. The two 68000 microprocessors in each Apollo are sufficient to take care of all gateway functions, according to Brown's network scientist, professor Thomas W.

Doeppner, Jr., Xerox's Ethernet network is also a strong candidate for installation at Brown. It would use a Xerox star gateway.

Sharing research

Massachusetts Institute of Technology requires any faculty member or researcher to provide something akin to a telephone company's yellow pages before he connects to any one of that school's local networks. This directory information tells other users about his research and what the new user can offer, and it is stored in the network. All users receive a yellow pages directory that guides them in using the network for file sharing and accessing the work of others.

The MIT Computer Science Department networks include two ring networks (a 1-Mbit and a 10-Mbit network), an MIT-developed in-house network called Chaos, Decnet, and a 3 MHz-Ethernet, as well as connections to Arpanet. Each network has incorporated a potpourri of computers, including large machines, midsize computers, minicomputers, personal computers, and some unique peripheral devices such as high-speed, book-quality printers and high-

2. Multinetwork gateways. *A file must pass through a sequence of software packages and steps when an MIT Multics user directs the output of his word processing job from the Honeywell computer, through three gateways on different networks, to the Xerox Dover laser printer. This operation requires protocol translation at three levels.*

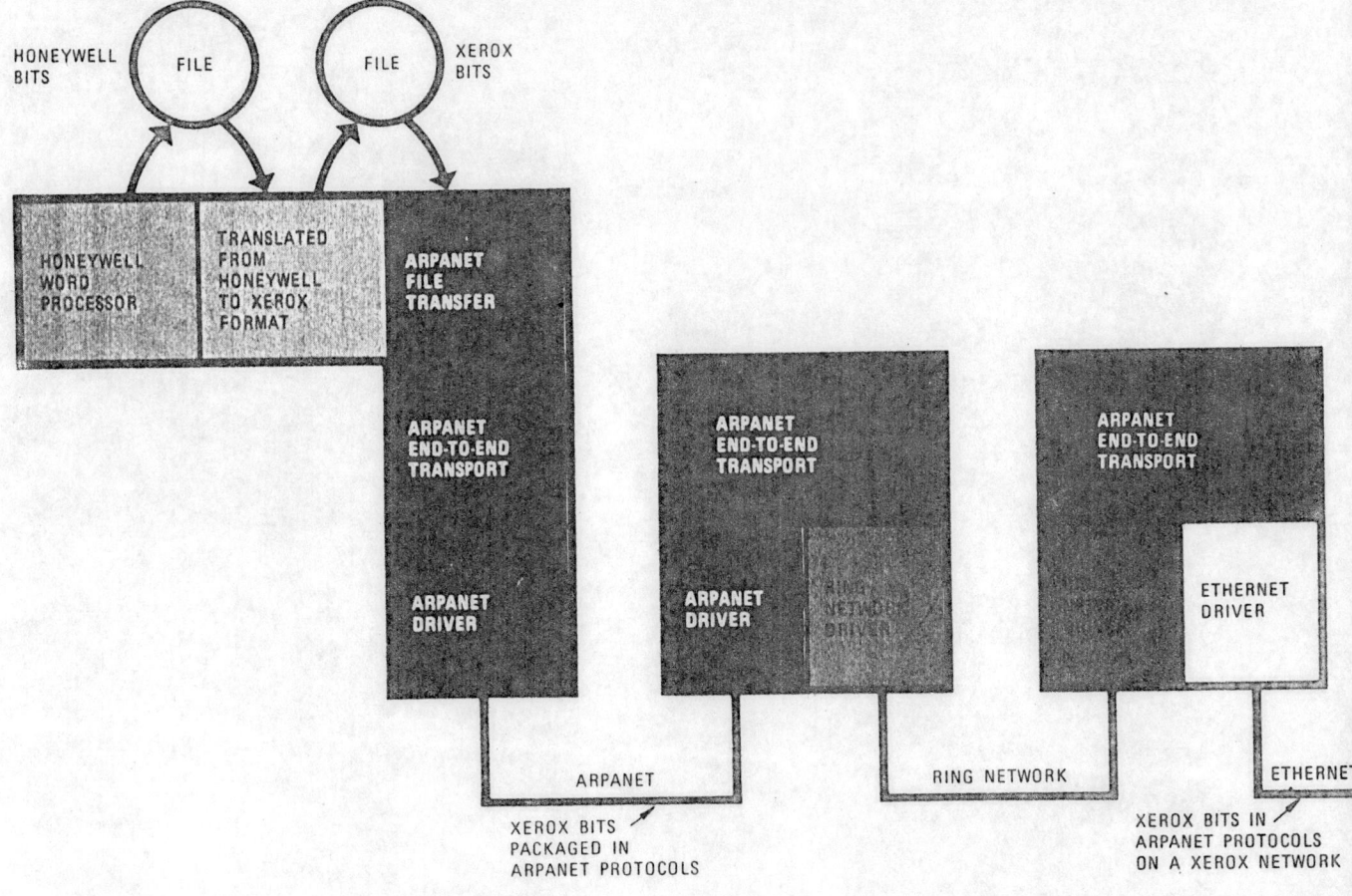

speed multifont printers, which are shared. The personal computers are designed by MIT, manufactured by Western Digital, and based on Motorola's 68000 microprocessor. Michael Dertouzos, MIT's Computer Science Department chairman, says "There are no Pet, Apple, or TRS-80 computers in the networks because they are not big or powerful enough, nor do they contain enough functions to allow capabilities such as high-resolution graphics, specialized keyboards, or high-speed interfaces."

Since MIT's local networks contain so many vendors' hardware, gateways that perform full conversion up through the network layer would require massive software. Therefore, protocol conversion is restricted to the link level only. At this low level, the gateways handle only the physical incompatibility between networks. For example, the actual packet format is converted if the hardware-specific formats on the networks are different. But the higher levels are not modified at all.

A common network path enables communications between machines in the same or different networks, as long as the machines speak the same protocols. In other words, hosts that both speak TCP or Xerox PUP can communicate, but a Xerox PUP machine cannot communicate with a TCP machine, even if they are on the same network. "These low-level gateways are important because scattered around MIT are numerous machines that speak protocols such as TCP or PUP or DDCMP [Decnet's link protocol]."

To allow machines that speak different protocols to communicate, special-purpose protocol converters are being written (Fig. 2). For example, specialized converters enable a TCP machine to access a laser xerographic printer. These converters do not convert TCP to Xerox protocols, in general. They do a simpler task: They convert from one specific set of protocols that could drive a printer to some other set of protocols used to drive a printer. Special-purpose protocol converters may also be written for functions such as the forwarding of mail, file transfer, or remote log-in. Although not trivial, special-purpose gateways are much simpler to write than gateways that perform conversions for a wide class of applications.

Beyond this, protocol conversion at MIT is done by modifying the host machine so that it contains one or more different sets of protocols. David Clark, MIT systems programmer, says that "modifying a Decnet machine so that it also speaks TCP is easier than building a third machine that speaks DDCMP on one side and TCP on the other."

A common problem plaguing university network managers is downtime. The traditional safeguard for this malady is redundant processors. But UH/CLC has designed a fault-tolerant network that contains unique, instead of redundant, processors. Not only does this prevent downtime, it also prevents the loss of tasks, and even data, if computers or other resources malfunction.

Charles McKay, director of technologies at UH/CLC, points out that fault tolerance is achieved by dynamic reconfiguration. If any processor in the network fails, its workload is automatically redistributed among other nodes. Other resources either migrate with the task for which they were allocated or are released to the network resource pool.

The reconfiguration occurs because of on-line diagnostics performed in part by every processor in the network and particularly by a processor known as the configuration-diagnostics processor. The configuration-diagnostics processor continuously collects reports on the status of all network components and feeds them back to the network operating system.

In this way, the operating system not only is knowledgeable about standard information such as task priorities and resources needed for each task being executed but also keeps performance statistics for the tasks. These include information such as how often a task has actually been executed, its results, whether any retries occurred, and, if so, what paths were used to which resources. Besides keeping status reports, the operating system maintains files of anticipated causes of failure in various network components and actions that the network should take if a component fails. By the time predetermined error thresholds have been noted, the operating system has already made reconfiguration and adjustment decisions that allow the network to continue processing jobs that have been submitted. Consequently, reconfiguration occurs before serious damage is done to any job in the network.

The UH/CLC network can tolerate failures of components such as processors, memory, carrier medium, crossbar switch matrices, and software modules. When a processor fails, the network hardware and software remove that node from the system, deallocate its resources, and reconfigure other hardware and software so the job can continue processing. The programmer specifies whether the task should restart at the beginning or at one of the extensive program- or data-restart checkpoints. As soon as the reconfiguration takes place, a new plan is made ready in case another processor fails. However, if several processors fail at once, reconfiguration efforts will slow down.

If some memory fails, the network can choose to transfer the data to another part of the memory module or to move it to another node. Or, if it has replicated the data elsewhere in the network or physically distributed the data (both services are provided), it can merely switch memories and continue processing. These options are preprogrammed, depending on the application being processed. The decisions are made dynamically by the network. The UH/CLC network can even lose an entire crossbar switch matrix (Fig. 3),

"However," he adds, "those that prefer to write something in a different machine are fearful of making the manufacturer mad at them for violating his software. This," Clark adds, "is not a problem at MIT."

In fact, the opposite is true. It is not unusual for Clark to discover that someone who wanted access to a particular resource, like the laser xerographic printer, wrote his own gateway. The gateway might be a specialized conversion machine on the network, or a modification of host software. "The nice thing about a common physical network," Clark says, "is that it gives everyone options."

Fault-tolerant

Robert Coyne, Jr., systems programmer for IBM's Federal Systems Division (FSD), in Houston, Tex., who is part of the team designing and installing a fault-tolerant network at the University of Houston in Clear Lake City (UH/CLC) claims that it is easier to use a general-purpose protocol converter at UH/CLC as a gateway than an intermediate technique like MIT's, since the entire network at UH/CLC is being implemented at once. The MIT approach lends itself more to real-world situations, since it is the rare university or company that can use a single vendor's equipment for very long.

3. One possible configuration. The crossbar switch matrices connects processors to four crossbars via four primary data paths. Each crossbar switch matrix is dedicated to either user programs, user data, system programs, or system data. All the crossbar-switching logic is in the CPU and the I/O processors.

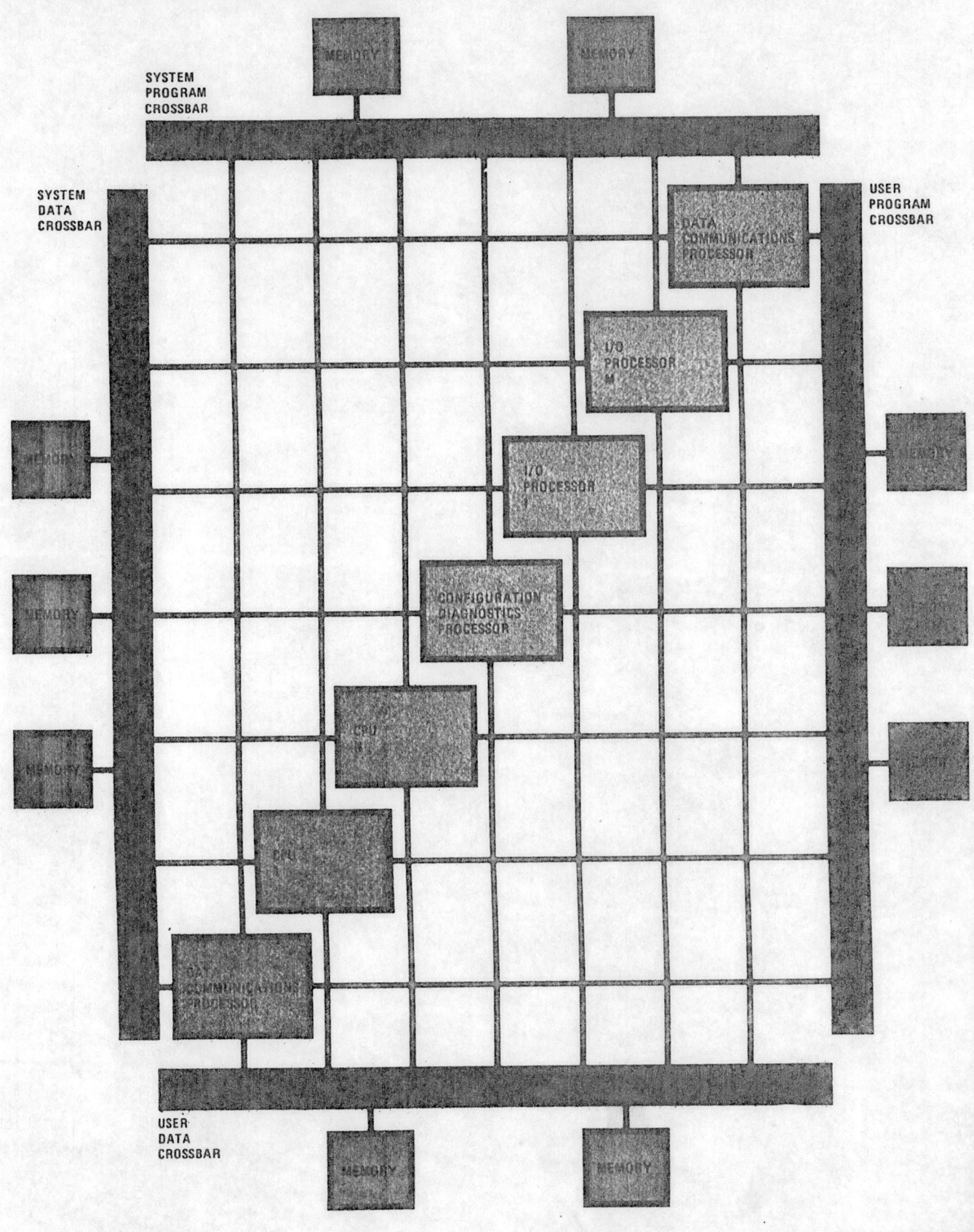

4. K68000 CPU node. The newer K68000 protocol modules expand the previously existing K6800 protocol modules. They can carry and pass data, thus avoiding much switching of memory. These modules talks to the new CPUs, such as the data communications processor and the diagnostics processors, and to the I/O processors.

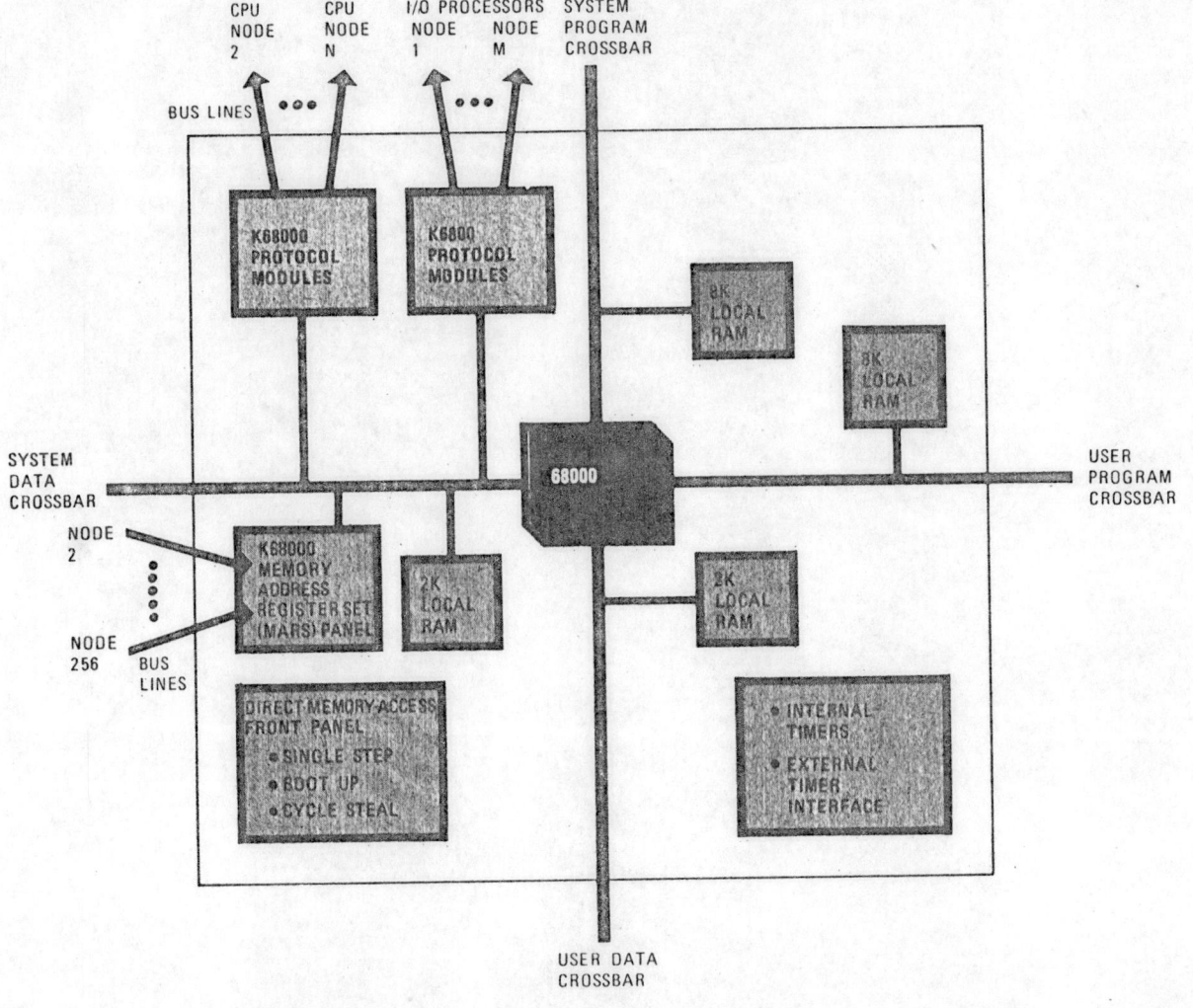

which switches memories back and forth between processors, and still function normally. [Experts in fault-tolerant computing have recommended this kind of dynamically reconfigurable communications network for the Columbia and other space shuttles (see Gallery, DATA COMMUNICATIONS, May, p. 48].

Multitasks, multiprograms

The UH/CLC network will eventually comprise 256 microcomputer nodes. The microcomputers, the K68000s sold by Hickok Electronics, are based on Motorola's 68000 microprocessor (Fig. 4). The microprocessors can be divided into four types: the CPU processors, the I/O processors that perform a lot of front-end network functions, and the configuration-diagnostics processor that is in charge of the diagnostics pertaining to fault tolerance and of the dynamic network reconfiguration. The fourth is a data communications microprocessor. It will be installed within the year and will allow the UH/CLC network to handle X.25, Ethernet, Arpanet, and SDLC. For performing remote distributed processing, the entire UH/CLC local network will act as a node to the remote networks such as Telenet or Arpanet.

A major aspect of the UH/CLC network is the multitasking environment in which it executes its programs. Multitasking means that many tasks can execute at one time because they are physically distributed on multiple processors. Multitasking is frequently confused with multiprogramming, which means multiple programs are executed by many programmers at one time. The difference is that multiprogramming involves programs operating on one CPU. Therefore, although a programmer may think his program is operating simultaneously with someone else's, it is not. A machine that has multitasking capabilities can achieve the processing power of a much larger computer because tasks execute simultaneously rather than faster. To do multitasking, not only must the computer have multitasking capabilities, but multidistributed tasking must also be built into the programming language and the compiler being used. For example, the Department of Defense's

How students crack computer security

There is no computer security on university campuses because too many students know too much about computers. And incidents of students' cracking computer security systems, such as have made recent newspaper headlines, are neither new nor uncommon.

Michael Dertouzos, chairman of the Computer Science Department at the Massachusetts Institute of Technology (MIT), cites 1964 as the first year a student broke into the MIT computer security system.

"At that time," he says, "computer access was based on a priority system, with the faculty having higher priority than the students."

This meant that a faculty member could preempt a student, who would suddenly find himself logged off the system. One outraged student, who had been logged off too many times, broke into the operating system and reversed the priority system. Pandemonium ensued when the faculty found themselves logged off because the students had preempted them.

Unfortunately, it is not difficult to crack a computer security system. Security is controlled by the CPU operating system. In addition to having regular users who need passwords and IDs to log in to their files, operating systems also incorporate the concept of a super-user or a privileged user or a systems-programmer-type of user. These special users have read-and-write access to any file in the entire computer.

The usual campus method of cracking the "system" is to become one of the super-users or privileged users or systems programmers users. For those in the know—and there are many such people on college campuses—this can be done with time and programming knowledge. Operating systems programs are long and complex. It is impossible for the designer to test for every possible flaw that can occur.

Therefore, some students with time on their hands study the operating system program long enough to find a program flaw that will allow them to log in to the computer as a special user. It is a challenge and gives students a feeling of power to have control over the computer. In some schools, among the class of computer students who sit at the computer day after day until their eyes are bulging, cracking the security system is an initiation rite that allows them to become part of some elite group of computer buffs. Encryption will prevent students from understanding the files they are reading, but it will not prevent them from tampering with those files.

There are two theories of how to prevent students from tampering with the operating system. One theory says, "After a while all the flaws will be found and plugged." The other viewpoint claims, "There are so many flaws that a creative student can always find one." This would make it almost impossible to have a really secure operating system.

Some security on the campuses is provided by maintaining accounts of who is logged in where and when. But these accounts are so long that most colleges provide their security by keeping administrative work and any sensitive material out of computers that students access. In some cases, this material is removed from the computers and kept elsewhere, on disks. In other cases, such material is kept on a different computer, and preferably a different kind of computer than the one the students use. This prevents students from becoming too familiar with the administration's computer and its operating system.

MIT's Dertouzos says that an advantage to the interconnected personal computers that the school is currently building and installing is that it eliminates the need for any supervisory computer. The systems programmer operates the network, but since each personal computer is self-contained, the network operating system does not know all the information in each computer. Hence, the systems programmer does not know it either, and user privacy is enhanced.

Data communications users should note that many of these computer science students will carry their skills—operating systems skills included—with them into the business world. — *Wendy Rauch-Hinden*

---

programming language, Ada, and its compiler, offer the ability to divide work among multiple processors. This results from a symbiotic relationship between the compiler, the operating system, and the hardware. The compiler allows the applications to command it, and the operating system allows the hardware to execute the applications. So the University of Houston is downline loading Ada object code into its network.

Ada commands such as TASK and BEGIN THIS TASK allow a task to create other tasks—a process called spawning. The task created can execute on another processor that can talk to the first processor. This feature, coupled with the yet-to-be-installed data communications gateway processor, will allow the UH/CLC network to distribute a single job so that part of it executes in Boston, part in Los Angeles, and part on the campus network.

Ada also has a feature called "rendezvous," which allows interprocess communications to take place synchronously. Synchronization between processes is achieved when one process issues an "entry" call and the other process accepts the call.

Once a match between the entry and accept statements is made, a rendezvous takes place. During this time, the process that asked to make the entry is suspended, while the other process executes the accept statement. Only when the second process has completed the acceptance is the entry process released. This is different from the usual method of interprocess communications, which is asynchronous and involves setting flags, locking data when a process begins, and unlocking the data afterwards.

The University of Houston is planning to use its network to investigate Ada's rendezvous, since, as Coyne says: "Little is known about the rendezvous function because the language is still so new. It does

not work very well unless memory is shared. However, it seems to be particularly useful in file-transfer operations and in local networking but not in remote data communications."

Teaching data communications

Among its other uses, the UH/CLC network provides students with the opportunity to do research in networking and distributed data processing. This application is beginning to catch on at many schools that want to give students real-world experience.

Atlanta's Georgia Institute of Technology's Philip Enslow, professor of computer science, says: "Computer science students need real-world, hands-on contact with computers themselves—not only experience writing and executing programs from terminals or card readers. Students who don't even know how to change a disk are graduating from universities with degrees in computer science."

During their undergraduate training, Georgia Tech computer science students learn to perform tasks such as loading the operating system into a machine that has no power. They go through the initial configuration, bring up the machine, and make it execute programs. This is a complicated procedure, especially if a student is doing it for the first time.

"Direct machine experience," Enslow says, "is more valuable than using a simulator, because a simulator is not realistic enough. To make the experience even more real-world, the documentation given to the students is just as it would be in the field—incomplete."

Most colleges and universities cannot afford to provide this kind of experience for the students because they do not have enough machines. Lack of sufficient machines at Georgia Tech was solved by installing local networks (Fig. 5). The school uses a Prime Computer Inc. ring consisting of five Prime computers, an IBM Series 1 ring, and an Ungerman Bass Net/One. All three connect to CSNET (computer science network), a new nationwide network sponsored by the National Science Foundation. The latter network is intended to connect computer science research establishments throughout the United States.

All networks can communicate with each other, since there is at least one computer in each network that acts as a gateway node. It either links to the network-interface unit or forms a point-to-point connection to a computer in another network. Georgia Tech is developing the software so the local network can be connected to the school computer center's Control Data Corporation (CDC) Cyber mainframe.

Teaching the networking art

Georgia Tech is planning uses for these networks in a joint graduate computer science and electrical engineering program, with emphasis on data communications, as well as in graduate and undergraduate courses in these subjects. For these programs, Enslow would like to see the school laboratories equipped with more data communications equipment, such as modems, test sets, multiplexers, and concentrators. He says, "Students could then get practical hands-on experience in testing this equipment and making it work under various conditions."

A local network located on a university campus can serve as a tool not only for teaching data communications to computer science or engineering students but for teaching data communications applications to humanities and business students. For example, the Business College at Arizona State, in Tempe, uses its network for a Computer Information Systems program. This program, which provides students with a business degree, requires all students to take from six to eight computer courses that teach them to use the computer in a problem-solving mode. The courses include programming in Cobol and Basic, simulations, and database structures. In the database courses, students do not create their own databases, but they learn how to apply some of the existing database systems, such as Cincorn's Total or one of the Codasyl or relational databases, to different businesses.

Brown University has also developed a computer culture program, which will be ready for implementation next year. This program, geared to humanities students, teaches students about data communications applications, such as electronics funds transfer and airline reservation systems, through simulation programs. For example, students use the Apollo computers in their Domain network to simulate a banking system. They sit at the computers and initiate funds transfers from one Apollo computer to another. In this way, they are able to experience how computers function in a banking system.

In a similar fashion, students learn about airline reservation systems by using computers to simulate a network of travel agents or ticket agents. Using the classroom as a laboratory, they work as travel agents, sell tickets and book flights, and discover the nitty-gritty of this data communications application.

The personal touch

Personal computer manufacturers have high hopes that their products will become the core of the school data communications networks. A move in this direction was launched with the installation of two Ethernet-like networks—Nestar's Cluster/One Model As, which consist of Apple computers. One of these networks is installed at the Monterey Institute of Technology in Monterey, Mexico and the other operates at the McDowell Intermediate High School in Erie, Pa.

At the Monterey Institute, the network accommodates a larger number of students than the school's IBM 370/158 timeshared computer at less cost. Unlike the standalone Apples originally considered, the Apples with networking capability allow many students and faculty members to access the same software package, share the same printers and database, and have computer power if one computer malfunctions.

McDowell's network comprises personal computers simple enough to be operated by people without strong computer backgrounds. Since a network manager, instead of students, handles the floppy disks, the disks are preserved. Even the manual at McDowell High is well written—not necessarily a typical situation.

5. Local networking for students. Georgia Tech provides computer experience for its students with four local networks and many vendors' equipment. The networks are a Prime ring, IBM Series 1 ring, Ungerman Bass Net/One, and CSNET. All networks communicate, since at least one computer per network acts as a gateway.

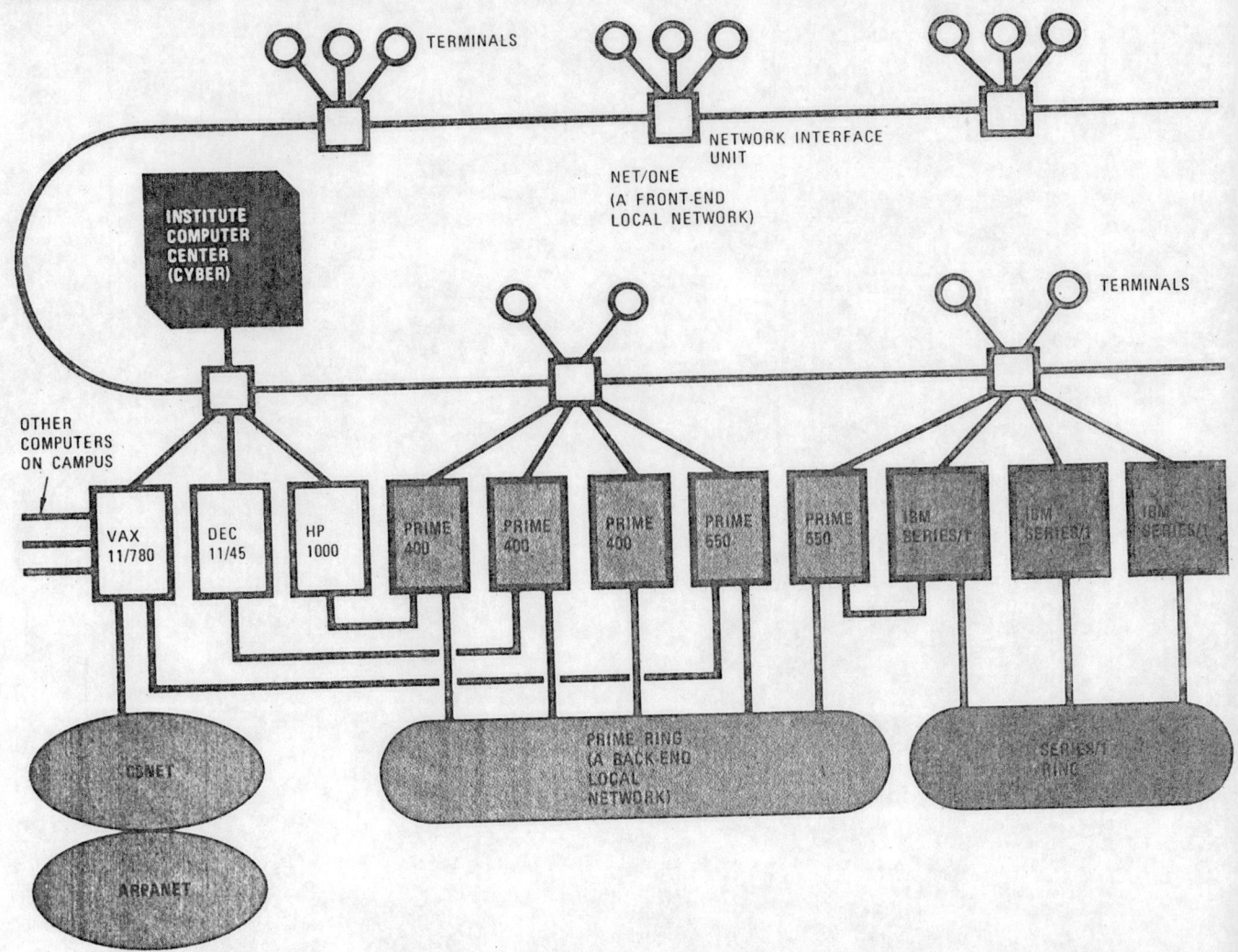

McDowell has 11 Apple II's linked to each other and to printers, an optical mark reader, telephone modems, and a music synthesizer. The workstations are daisy-chained with a Nestar network interface card and multi-wire cabling for distances up to 1,000 feet. One Apple acts as a network server, providing services such as shared disks, files, database management systems, printers, and modems to other stations. Network-access control is contention-based.

The Monterey Institute has 340 Apples in its inter-connected Nestar networks, plus a communications link between the Apples and its 370/158. The school has developed its own local protocol for communications, since the commercially available standards "are not particularly standard," according to the school.

Nestar is going to offer a communications facility between the networking Apples and the 370, and the Monterey Institute will install this facility by the January semester. Students will use this capability for preparing programs too large to fit on the Apples, as well as to access those programs available only on the 370. In addition, although the school's accounting and administration is done on the Nestar network, some of the final processing, such as post-registration processing, is transferred to the 370 for execution.

McDowell is using its Nestar network mostly for computer-aided instruction in all subjects, but it wants to diminish that role. Instead, it wants students to work with problem-solving activities such as "what-if" programs and simulation programs that emulate anything from historic events to dangerous chemical reactions.

Office-of-the-future applications

The seemingly trivial ability to revise and reorganize writing by giving commands through a text editor instead of by correcting and recopying the work has the not-so-trivial consequence of helping people to write better material in the first place. Not just applicable to students, this concept will affect both manager and clerical workers in automated offices.

A study of how and why text editors improve writing quality and, consequently, office productivity, is being

conducted at Teachers College at Columbia University, in New York City, where classes of adults and children are using computers and text editors to learn how to write better. These classes are part of a program to study how memory limits people's ability to write grammatically correct, complete sentences and why people—from secretaries to executives—have so much trouble revising their writing.

Programs to teach writing via computers are used at Teachers College, in selected New York City and Connecticut public and private schools, and in the United Nations school. Says Colette Daiute, assistant professor and research associate at Teachers College and administrator of the Computers in Writing research program: "One's ability to write grammatically correct sentences is partly influenced by two types of memory—short- and long-term. Things we hear or read, such as phone numbers, are entered in short-term memory, where they reside briefly. But unless we have practiced memorizing them so they are sent into long-term memory, we forget them."

Daiute explains that the same thing happens with understanding and producing sentences. As we hear a sentence, we process the exact words in our short-term memory. "But as soon as our minds have captured the first clause," she explains, "we throw the exact words out of our short-term memory and just store the meaning. The short-term memory is then free to work on the next clause."

"But," Daiute continues, "if people write very slowly, there is a tendency to forget the exact wording of a clause they are writing, even if they remember its gist. So, they will tend to make a grammatical error like 'The outbreak of riots are upsetting'—a very common type of error where the verb agrees with an adjacent noun but not with the first noun four or five words back. This error is made because the verb and adjacent noun are both remembered in short-term memory, while the first noun has been thrown out.

"People can write more quickly when they are using a text editor instead of an electric typewriter, and therefore they make fewer errors," Daiute adds. She explains that the ability to write faster with a text editor is related to most people's dislike of revising what they write. The reason is simple: Revising usually means also recopying, which is a tedious process. That is why, with a typewriter, people tend to correct their mistakes as they write. But immediate correction of mistakes slows down the writing process, and then the short-term memory, which contained the exact grammatical construction of a sentence, breaks down.

The consequences of making a mistake when using a computer are less severe because the revising process is easier. Daiute says, "Since texts can be reformatted and repaged, and paragraphs can be transposed, and errors corrected with simple commands, people write without correcting and are willing to revise later."

The revising process is further aided by text editors that help find errors in spelling, grammar, organization, and transitions. There are text editors being developed that will find mistakes in compositions, as well as in business letters. ∎

Interbranch banking

Bank finds proven methods lead to successful network

Frederick S. Haines, Rainier National Bank, Seattle

Rainier National Bank believes that sticking to basics is the best way to overcome the problems of building a new network

The conviction that computers and data communications are destined to play an increasingly important role in the way business will be conducted in the future has a direct relation to why on-line banking terminal networks have been on the rise in recent years. In fact, some of this country's most prominent bankers believe that the nation is on the threshold of an era in which electronic information and its rapid exchange will become the predominant currency of commerce.

With that in mind, plus a desire to improve customer service while controlling communications and personnel costs during a period a rapid expansion, Rainier National Bank, Seattle, began in 1974 to evaluate the available means of applying advanced electronic and data communications technology to the commercial banking business.

The first, and most obvious, answer at that time was the installation of automatic teller machines (ATMs) in key locations to allow customers to perform simple transactions after normal business hours and on weekends. It was soon discovered, however, that this required the establishment of a data communications network. In conducting the preliminary studies in this area, the bank's planners decided that installing ATMs first would be premature.

It was clear to them that if the bank was going to

invest the time, effort, and money to set up a dedicated data communications network for the operation of perhaps as little as 40 ATMs, it might be better to establish an on-line teller-terminal data communications network with a potential for immediate improvement in branch customer service and reduction in conventional branch communications costs, and later to piggyback the ATM terminals onto the network. By constructing a teller-terminal operation first, the bank management committed itself to a long-range, "horizontal" development program.

Although some may consider the horizontal, step-by-step approach a conservative one, Rainier believes that putting terminals and functions on line one at a time throughout the branch network is building a more solid foundation in on-line data communications and operations than the vertical "all-at-once" approach. Furthermore, Rainier also feels that initially concentrating on data communications network hardware and software integration provides the flexibility to take advantage of looming technological, legal, and legislative developments.

Flexibility to modify and improve the Rainier network to meet changing conditions was one of the principal criteria used in choosing the mini-computer branch-control units, applications software, and terminal

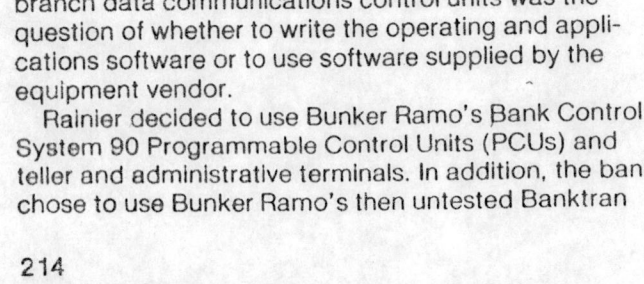

1. Teller terminals. *Drive-up windows, like all other teller stations, are equipped with CRT terminals that give basic account information in five seconds or less. All are* *equipped with 5-inch screens that can display up to 240 characters of information at one time—including blank forms that are used for computer-prompted data entry.*

equipment that was needed for the bank network.

Before making any network design or equipment decisions, however, it was first decided to build an internal staff of people with experience in on-line data communications network design and installation.

Deciding on design

The bank was faced with the task of designing the on-line network, choosing hardware and software vendors, and starting installation with only a handful of people who had any experience in data communications networks and transaction processing. Today, that staff has grown from 23 to more than 80 experienced, highly professional people.

One of the first decisions that had to be made was the choice of branch minicomputer controllers and other branch network hardware, such as teller and administrative terminals. Central to the choice of branch data communications control units was the question of whether to write the operating and applications software or to use software supplied by the equipment vendor.

Rainier decided to use Bunker Ramo's Bank Control System 90 Programmable Control Units (PCUs) and teller and administrative terminals. In addition, the bank chose to use Bunker Ramo's then untested Banktran

transaction-processing bank-application software package.

The first branch PCU and teller-terminal combination was installed in less than three months and installation of PCUs and teller terminals continued throughout the branch network until all 121 branches were tied together in November 1978—less than 20 months later. The toughest part of the entire design and installation process was the development of the data communications network to economically link all these terminals, plus future ones, to the host IBM 370/158 computer system.

Evaluations and decisions had to be made on terminal response time, number of terminals per line, line speeds, and terminal mixes. Operating, data communications, and applications software additions and modifications were also evaluated.

Watch and learn

Most of the early decisions about the network were based on visits to other network operations, or they were empirically concluded. For instance, it was determined that minimum acceptable response time at any teller terminal would be five seconds at least 90 percent of the time. This was decided by visiting similar on-line terminal installations in thrift banks, airline and

214

hotel reservation centers, insurance service centers, and other transaction-oriented operations, and talking to the people responsible for running them.

It was also decided to use 2.4-kbit/s, bisynchronous leased lines as the data communications medium, because that was what everyone else was using.

Rainier was fortunate enough to have recruited several people who had extensive experience designing and installing on-line networks. Therefore, time wasn't wasted trying to predict how often the tellers and supervisors would use their terminals to determine the number that could run on a single line.

The first series of teller terminals (Fig. 1) was set up in a branch only a few blocks from the host computer and hooked to the center through a single 2.4-kbit/s leased line with standard 201C AT&T and Codex modems interfacing with the Bunker Ramo PCU in the branch, and an IBM 3705 communications controller on the 370/158 central processor. (2.4-kbit/s, bisynchronous leased lines were chosen largely because that was what everyone else was using.) Two more nearby branches were set up in the same way and tied to the same data communications line.

Distributing 25 terminals in only these branches, on one 2.4-kbit/s line, might have appeared exorbitant, but the line charge was nominal because the branches were close to the computer center. The important thing was to be certain of maintaining the minimum five-second response time and to be close enough to the branches to assist them with any problems.

The actual traffic from the branches was carefully measured under normal working conditions. Then, using simulation software, a computer projected response times per terminal over a range of phone-circuit speeds. From this information, the maximum number of terminals that could be handled by a single 2.4-kbit/s line was calculated: it was estimated that each line could easily handle up to 55 terminals.

Network expansion

Once the initial installations and the resultant calculations were completed, the next step was to install the remaining terminals throughout Rainier's 121-branch network. This was done in stages. Alternate data communications strategies were explored to be certain that the network was operating both at minimum cost and with minimum risk.

Pacific Northwest Bell handled the connections with the 14 other telephone companies serving various parts of the State of Washington, and provided Rainier's development staff with data on rates for various lines, drops, and modem combinations.

Nevertheless, the trade-offs between combinations of intra- and inter-exchange lines are almost infinite. Calculation of the most cost-efficient combination of branches, when some branches have only two terminals and others can have as many as 17, was quite complicated. In addition, there was the question of whether to use line concentrators, and whether there was any advantage in going out of state and coming back in again at the extremes of the network to take advantage of lower interstate rates.

A good, hard look was taken at concentrators in eastern Washington because a single line from Seattle to Spokane costs more than $1,500 per month, and the bank has several lines of that length. But then a paper design was created in which those lines were multiplexed by a 9.6-kbit/s concentrator. The total cost of bringing the lines together at the proposed concentrator site, plus the cost of leasing the concentrator, was just $100 per month less than operating four separate lines. Because using the concentrator would have left the bank's entire eastern Washington operation dependent upon just one data communications line, Rainier felt that the savings fell far short of warranting the risk.

Similarly, in southern Washington, the possibility of running lines into Oregon and back again at several points to take advantage of interstate rates was investigated. Again, there was no advantage because the higher local line charges offset the interstate savings.

The bank hasn't given up analyzing and looking for new options, however. One important thing learned from all the early exercises is that there are, indeed, ways of keeping data communications costs to a minimum, but it takes time and manpower to find them.

Once the design of the branch network was completed in each geographic area, however, installation proceeded at a rapid pace. All 860 terminals and 121 PCUs in 121 branch offices went on line in a data communication network that stretches from the Pacific Ocean to the Oregon, Idaho, and Canadian borders. All these terminals were integrated with the host 370/158 computer at the Rainier data center.

Local control

The heart of the network's hardware is made up of PCUs. They are compact, minicomputer-based units that provide the control logic, memory, CRT display subsystem, communications control, and interface functions for all teller and administrative terminals in each branch and for the ATMs.

Each PCU has a comprehensive front maintenance panel, a power supply, a back panel for up to 15 circuit boards, a programmable read-only memory (PROM) bootstrap loader, a variable amount of random access memory (RAM), a real-time clock, and connectors for terminal and peripheral devices. The PCUs are organized around a single system bus with a throughput capability of more than 1.2 million characters/s, and an addressing capacity of 32 work stations, which is more than enough for any single Rainier bank branch now or in the foreseeable future. All non-display components—including the processor, up to 256K bytes of memory, and peripheral-device interfaces of either the programmed I/O or direct-memory access type—communicate via the PCU's single bus.

In addition, the PCUs are microprogrammed and modular in design for easy programming and field upgrading—a feature that proved useful when Rainier began adding ATMs to some key branches. Options that add to PCU flexibility include single- or dual-disk storage units that can simply be plugged in when the bank is ready to take advantage of the sophis-

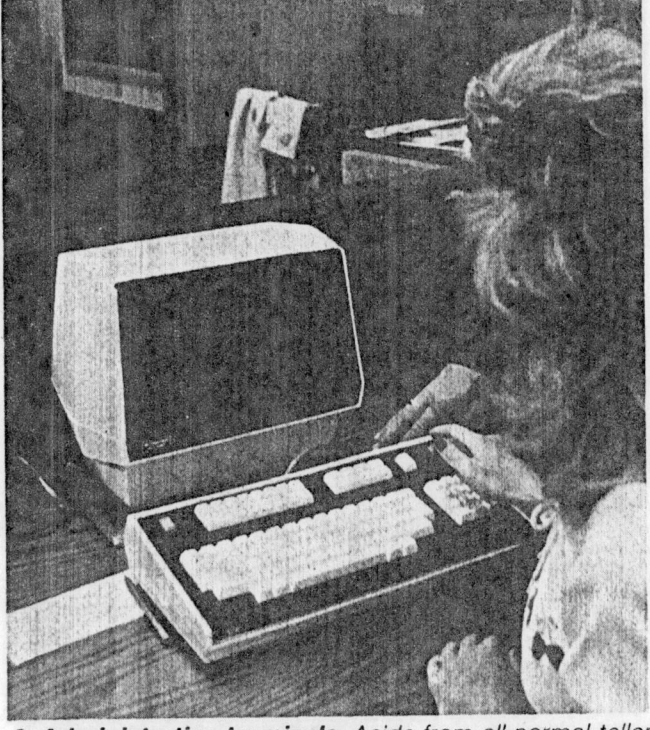

2. Administrative terminals. *Aside from all normal teller functions, the larger terminals used by management access more detailed information for solving problems.*

ticated programmable control unit architecture.

Because most banks operate either IBM or Burroughs equipment in their data processing centers, the PCUs are fully compatible with mainframes of either manufacturer. At Rainier, the PCUs are set up to appear to the host IBM 370/158 processor as IBM 3270 devices capable of operating under binary synchronous communications (BSC) or synchronous data link control (SDLC) line disciplines using standard IBM access methods.

User interface
The Bunker Ramo teller terminal (Fig. 1) is about the size of a desktop calculator. Equipped with a 5-inch CRT screen that can display up to 240 characters of information at one time, each terminal is operated by means of an 11-key numeric pad for entering account numbers and transaction amounts, plus 20 special function keys, four adding machine keys, and "clear" and "transmit" keys.

When transaction data is being entered, each terminal guides the teller through each process by means of "fill-in-the-blanks" displays in which all titles, instructions, and system responses are provided in English.

Rainier now has these small teller terminals at each branch teller station, and all of the bank's basic teller functions are performed exclusively through them. This includes deposit and withdrawal memo posting for more than 700,000 checking, regular savings, and 90-day savings accounts. It also includes account status inquiries, stop-payment orders, split-transaction calculations, multi-item transaction totals, currency conversion of Canadian and 10 other commonly used curren-

cies, certificate of deposit (CD) rate quotation, loan payment and annual percentage rate calculation, and other normal teller functions.

Currency and CD rates are changed daily—and more frequently when necessary—by bank management to meet changing money market conditions. Once the new rates are entered into the system, they go into effect immediately throughout the branch network.

Once installation of the on-line teller-terminal network was proceeding on schedule, attention was turned to the addition of administrative terminals (Fig. 2). They are used by platform and teller supervisory personnel in resolving the more complex problems that arise in the course of day-to-day banking.

Also provided by Bunker Ramo as part of its multi-faceted Bank Control System 90 package, these administrative terminals are capable of performing all teller functions, plus a variety of other bank functions that can only be handled by authorized supervisory personnel. The larger terminals, which are equipped with 9-inch screens capable of displaying up to 960 characters of information, are used for the retrieval of detailed account problems, and for reporting and system maintenance. The bank recently started using the administrative terminals to implement a new centralized account processing system that promises to reduce considerably check-handling costs when in full operation.

Automated check handling
Under this new central check-processing system, which is already in operation at 19 Rainier branches, all customer checks are processed at the central data processing facility and all customer statements are mailed from this one location, thus saving the cost of physically transporting checks to each branch for forwarding to customers, and allowing the bank to take greater advantage of automated check handling, statement preparation, and envelope-stuffing equipment in processing checks for more than 350,000 checking-account customers each month.

The one normal drawback to such a central check-processing system is that the local branch management is not physically available to assist in making sensitive account decisions, such as those involved in overdrawn accounts. However, the bank is utilizing the branch administrative terminals to solve that problem. As checks that exceed account balances arrive at the central data processing facility, the host computer separates them by branch. A list of the day's questionable checks by account name and number is transmitted to each branch manager's administrative terminal the following morning.

Using this list and the detailed account information that can be displayed on his terminal, plus whatever information about the individual customers the manager or other members of the branch staff have gained through personal contact, the branch manager can take whatever action is necessary. The results are then communicated back to the data center through the terminal, and the overdrawn checks are either paid or

3. ATM. The automatic teller machines prompted the original Rainier investigation into data communications, but were one of the last parts of the bank's network to go on line. A second-level network using a modem bypass and a protocol similar to that of an IBM 2260 terminal allows direct polling of the cash dispensers by the host.

returned. Thus, through use of the data communications network, Rainier has preserved the personal nature of branch banking, while taking advantage of modern check-handling procedures.

This is an example of the programmability feature of the PCU architecture. Although assisted by the vendor in putting this application on the system, the bank's own personnel put together the detailed programs for both the PCUs and the 370/158 that are enabling this new capability. With this experience under their belts, the data communications staff is now actively exploring a wide variety of other applications for the administrative terminals.

Because they are equipped with full 96-character ASCII alphanumeric keyboards and have larger screens, the administrative terminals' range of applications is far greater than that of the smaller teller terminals. In addition, because the administrative terminals can access much more detailed and confidential customer data than the teller terminals, they can be equipped with keylocks, alarms, and other physical security devices, as well as a multilevel personal name and identification number security system that prevents unauthorized use.

At the PCU end of the data communications network, the bank is utilizing Bunker Ramo's bank oper-

ating system (BOS) software and its Banktran retail-banking application package. Banktran software efficiently controls the total operation of teller and administrative terminals—and ATMs—and their interface with the data communications lines that connect them to the host mainframe.

Although this Bunker Ramo software contains all the basic function modules required for teller, branch, and supervisory functions, as well as for ATM operation, one has the option of making modifications to the basic software in a number of areas. They include transaction sequences, display mark formats, journal data formats, and input validation procedures to fit in with present or future operation procedures and requirements.

At the host computer, the bank is operating the entire on-line branch system under the communications modules of the IBM information management systems (IMS) software package. To date, everything is running smoothly.

Automated tellers

The third stage of expansion of the on-line network— the part that prompted the bank to consider data communications in the first place—went into gear in May 1977, when a Rainier team that had been studying

4. Network control. *In a banking environment, network control includes sending out teams to fill empty cash drawers and clearing ATMs of jammed paper as well as monitoring all leased data communications lines and modems. Repairs are normally carried out by in-house patching procedures or by phone-company service crews.*

competitive automatic teller machines for several years recommended the selection of Diebold's Tabs ATM unit (Fig. 3) to interface with the on-line network through the branch office PCUs. There are now 27 such automatic teller machines installed, and the bank expects to install close to 40 of them.

Using a special program written to eliminate the need for a separate data communications network for the ATMs, the branch PCUs poll their associated ATMs through a tributary, second-level network using a modem bypass and a protocol that simulates an IBM 2260 terminal. The host computer thinks the ATM is a teller terminal. The ATM thinks it is talking directly to the host. Meanwhile, the PCU is in the middle, transparent to both.

This polling technique is satisfactory for use with the ATMs, which receive their heaviest usage at night and on weekends, when branches are closed. However, in connecting the teller and administrative terminals to each branch's PCU, a parallel cable is used in order to help the bank achieve a five-second response time. This configuration is one of the most important factors in the responsiveness of the network.

When a key on any teller or administrative branch terminal is depressed, its data is transmitted directly to the PCU at channel speeds. Therefore, with the ex-

ception of the ATMs, all data bits from each terminal run in parallel, rather than serially. The only thing that can slow up transmission is line overload. This is an important point because in other branch systems that were considered, all terminals on the line were serially polled for message traffic, and slower terminals, such as 15- or 30-character/s, greatly slowed down response time for all other terminals on the line. This might be acceptable in many types of operatons, but is highly undesirable in a retail banking system where the customer is standing in front of the teller waiting for a transaction to be completed.

Network control

Now that most of Rainier's banking operations are almost totally dependent upon the proper functioning of branch terminals, PCUs, many thousands of miles of data communications lines, and dozens of modems, it is extremely important to have the capability to monitor the performance of the various elements in the network throughout the periods it is used the most.

In order to achieve this, the bank has established a six-person on-line control department at the Rainier data center (Fig. 4) that monitors the entire network from 6 a.m. to 10 p.m. on weekdays, and from 6 a.m. to midnight on weekends. In addition, there are service

teams that are on call during the hours that branches are not open. These teams service the ATMs when the monitoring system indicates they are out of money or have jammed paper-form dispensers, two of the most frequent problems associated with ATMs.

But the most important function of this system monitoring and control group is the monitoring of leased communications lines and modems. To aid them in this function, the bank installed a Spectron Datascope and a Spectron modem patch panel. The phone company provided another patch panel, in the basement of the data center.

Using the Datascope, carrier waves can be monitored visually on the unit's CRT display or through the use of an audio alarm system that is automatically activated if a carrier wave fails. That happens occasionally—most often in the mountainous parts of the state when a relay box or microwave station is damaged during a heavy winter storm. When a carrier wave fails, Rainier is normally the first to inform the phone-company repair department.

Monitoring of line transmissions can also be performed through one of the patch panels by means of audio speakers that will pick up static or other unusual sounds on a line. The primary function of one patch panel, however, is to allow the control department to temporarily replace failed master modems until the phone company can make permanent repairs. The principal function of the other patch panel is to permit the change of cable circuits from the host CPU to the replacement modem without needing physically to disconnect the cable and reconnect it to the new patch modem.

As can be readily understood, monitoring and maintenance of an on-line network is a never-ending task. Everything is happening interactively, so when something goes wrong, corrective action must come as close to real time as possible.

Assessing net worth

Right now, Rainier has a program of ATM installation, and a number of system groups studying new administrative terminal applications. In addition, long-range plans call for off-loading some of the processing that does not depend on time, such as name and address changes, from the central processor to each local branch. That will require the addition of storage capability and new applications software.

Also under serious consideration is the addition of on-line cash control to the teller-terminal functions. Present posting of checks, deposits, and withdrawals is on a memo basis, with actual cash accounting and control performed overnight in the bank's central processing unit.

As an example of how changes in one part of an on-line network can affect other elements of it, there appears to be a strong possibility that greatly increased administrative terminal traffic may cause loads on the 2.4-kbit/s lines that will violate the teller-terminal-response-time requirement of five seconds. Should that happen, the system may have to be upgraded to 4.8-kbit/s lines and modems. At that point, the whole

question of leasing modems vs purchasing them, and using concentrators, will have to be restudied by the venture and system development teams.

But that's all in the future. What about today? What benefits have Rainier Bank, its employees, and its customers derived from the enormous effort that has gone into the installation and operation of this on-line retail terminal system?

As noted earlier, short-term cost reductions and other immediate economic benefits were not the major reasons Rainier Bank entered the on-line world. The management of the bank wanted to achieve a level of system development and a communications capability that would enable it to use state-of-the-art technology to improve customer service and the overall efficiency of current bank operations, and at the same time provide the bank the flexibility to take advantage rapidly of changing technological and business conditions in the future.

Management believes it has succeeded in all of these areas, and those, then, are the basic benefits the on-line network has brought. To be a bit more specific, the following is a list of the more obvious benefits for the bank, its employees, and its customers.

Among the benefits to the bank:
- Development of a large trained and experienced internal technical staff of on-line network and data communications specialists.
- Development of a branch administrative and teller staff well versed in on-line terminal operation.
- Development of a functioning statewide data communications network.
- Installation and operation of a statewide network of highly flexible, state-of-the-art branch minicomputers.
- Reduction in teller errors.
- Faster handling of customer transactions, with a resultant lowering of branch staffing requirements.
- Significant reductions in the number of phone circuits and manually dialed calls at each branch.
- Increased teller confidence and job satisfaction.

Some of the benefits to employees are already cited above in that they also provide benefits to the bank. Other employee benefits:
- Immediate availability to tellers of the detailed account information required to answer most customer questions, handle routine problems, and make routine decisions.
- Elimination of the need for tellers to lock cash drawers and leave their stations to phone the central office for account information.
- Branch managers and supervisors also appreciate the immediate access to detailed account problems that their administrative terminals give them when trying to resolve customer problems.

And, finally, from the customer's point of view, there are two distinct benefits, both of which also benefit the bank and its branch employees:
- Customers get faster and better service.
- Customer transactions are handled more confidentially, because tellers no longer have to discuss the problems normally associated with an account with other branches or with their supervisors.

Section 6

Local Network
Selection
Selection
Selection
Selection
Selection
Selection
Selection
Selection
Selection
Selection
Selection
Selection

Section 6

Local Network
Selection

The many faces of local networking

Kenneth J. Thurber and Harvey A. Freeman,
Architecture Technology Corporation, Eden Prairie, Minn.

The authors explain the basic local-networking technologies and list, by category, the currently available local-network products.

There is still much debate about what exactly a local network is. In fact, the definitions are as diverse as the local-network products now available.

In general, local networks have the following basic properties:

1. They are owned by a single organization.
2. They are geographically limited; that is, a local network's backbone spans a distance on the order of only a few miles.
3. They contain some type of switching technology.
4. Their transmission rates are usually faster than those of networks covering a broad geographic area.

Local networks can be based on one of several technologies, such as PBX/CBX (private branch exchange/computerized private branch exchange), baseband, and broadband, and can incorporate architectures including centralized, bus, and loop.

Distributed networks and, in particular, local networks offer several advantages. They have the potential for resource sharing, which gives users access to special facilities without direct ownership. Since communications costs are a major factor in large networks, and interactive computation only increases this cost, economics is on the side of decentralization.

It has been said that microprocessors do not follow Grosch's Law: performance is proportional to cost squared. This tends to favor distributed data processing and local networks, which employ primarily microprocessors. However, the cost balance would change drastically if large centralized networks were to be built from such small processors (which are growing in complexity and functionality daily).

Distributed networks also exhibit promise for improved maintainability, availability, and reliability. Furthermore, it may be easier to update a distributed network piecemeal as technology improves. By linking such networks to others (say, connecting local networks via satellites and common-carrier facilities), a user could migrate from currently centralized configurations at separate locations to a single integrated one.

The development of local networks appears to be due to two types of users. The first is mainly those people who are reaching the limits of their current networking capabilities and are seeking ways to extend and improve them. Some networks in this group evolved either from attempts to interconnect several specific applications or from products built for this purpose. The resulting local network improves the performance of the existing, separate computers, and extends their useful life by allowing them to share mass-storage or communications devices. Such configurations are typified by Network Systems Corporation's (NSC's) Hyperchannel design.

The second group consists of users looking to distribute their data processing capabilities. Specialized functions (such as database or array processing), it was found, could be offloaded from a single host, developed as separate subsystems with optimized architectures, and used by other network nodes. Also in this category are devices that were not originally designed for, but can be effectively applied in, local networks. A classic example is the Rolm Corporation's

CBX at the center of a star-shaped "local" network.

Other CBX manufacturers have strategies similar to Rolm's. Datapoint Corporation's ISX can provide complete voice and data integration. The ISX, coupled with the ARC (Attached Resource Computer) network, could be a major market force. Another vendor to watch is Teltone Corporation, with its DCS-2B Data Carrier System. The DCS is designed to adapt a PBX to a local network. Lastly, a newly formed company, Ztel, is designing a PBX-based local network specifically for data and voice integration.

Then there are the baseband local networks, such as Xerox Corporation's Ethernet, NSC's Hyperchannel, and NSC's Cluster/One Model A, each with its special capabilities: Hyperchannel provides the highest throughput available today; Ethernet's medium throughput capabilities are useful in, say, automated-office environments; and Cluster/One Model A links personal computers. By comparing these networks with both the ring-structure and broadband implementations, users can better understand the development and future of local networks.

Ethernet, for example, started as a single local network and evolved into several local Ethernets connected via a set of gateways. One gateway connects to the U.S. Department of Defense's Arpanet and another into the DOD's Bay Area Packet Radio Network. In late 1979, Xerox introduced an Ethernet product, the 860 information processing system, which is shown in Figure 1 in a typical Ethernet contention configuration.

Physically, Ethernet can be viewed as a set of nodes connected onto a coaxial cable that is terminated at each end by its characteristic impedance. Each node

consists of a cable connector, a transceiver, a cable-to-processor interface, and the processor. Most processors on the Xerox Palo Alto Research Center (PARC) networks are Altos (Xerox's custom-designed minicomputers); however, Digital Equipment Corporation (DEC), Data General Corporation, and Hewlett-Packard Company processors have also been adapted. A typical Ethernet local-network design may have as many as 100 nodes.

A processor accesses the communications channel by contention. Each node monitors the state of the coaxial cable, and if the cable is not in use, the node then transmits. This monitoring is known as carrier sensing. If two nodes try to transmit at about the same time, a collision occurs. When this happens, the nodes go into a jamming procedure designed to ensure that all nodes see the collision. After the procedure, each processor involved in the collision determines the time at which it will again try to broadcast, by generating a start time within a particular interval. Each time a transmission attempt fails, this interval is doubled—a process known as a binary exponential backoff scheme. If the interval reaches a predetermined maximum size, an error routine is initiated.

No ensured reception

A node broadcasts a datagram, which is an individual, self-contained packet of information. A datagram interface between processors promises a "best-effort" transmission and thus does not guarantee delivery, order of delivery, time taken for delivery, existence of duplicates, or error-free delivery. If a datagram is not delivered, the appropriate acknowledgments will not

1. The archetype of the species. Physically, Ethernet can be viewed as a set of nodes connected onto a coaxial cable that is terminated at each end by its characteristic *impedance. Each node consists of a cable connector, a transceiver, a cable-to-processor interface, and the processor. A typical network may have up to 100 nodes.*

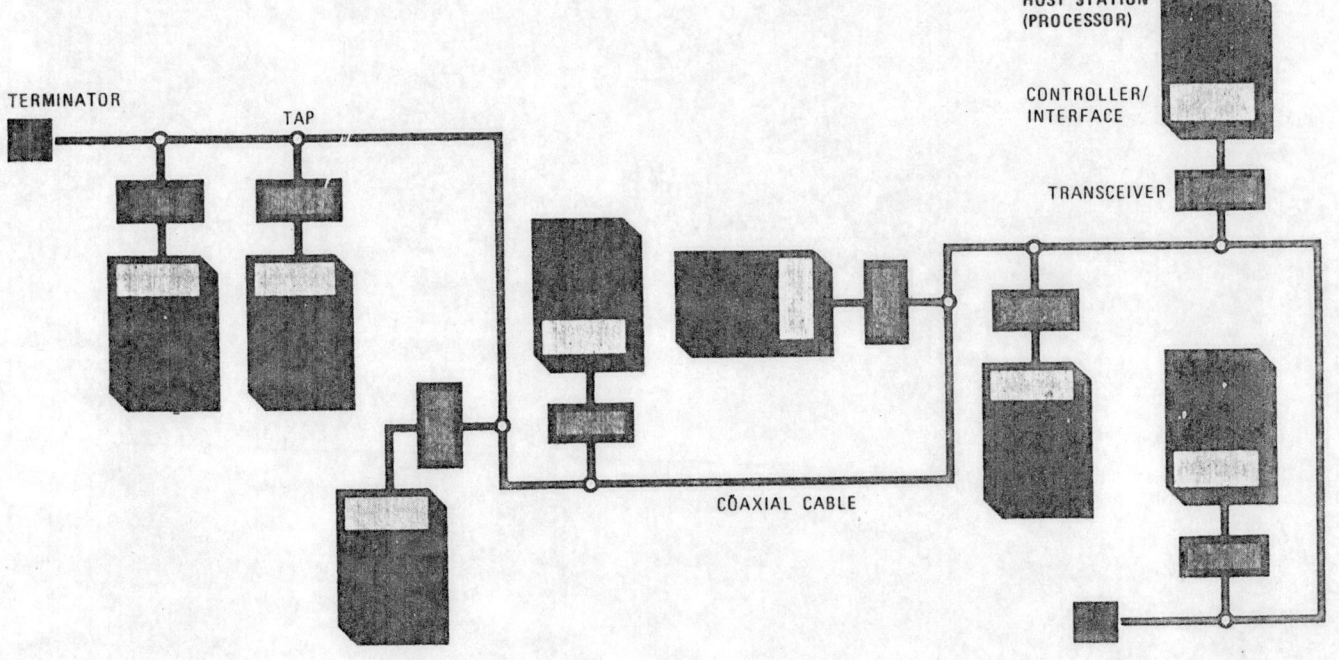

2. Encapsulating Ethernet's PUP. Ethernet's internetwork communications requires the datagram called PUP, for PARC universal packet. The basic PUP datagram encapsulates various internetwork transmissions in the forms shown. The otherwise "unreliable" datagram here uses higher-level protocol structures.

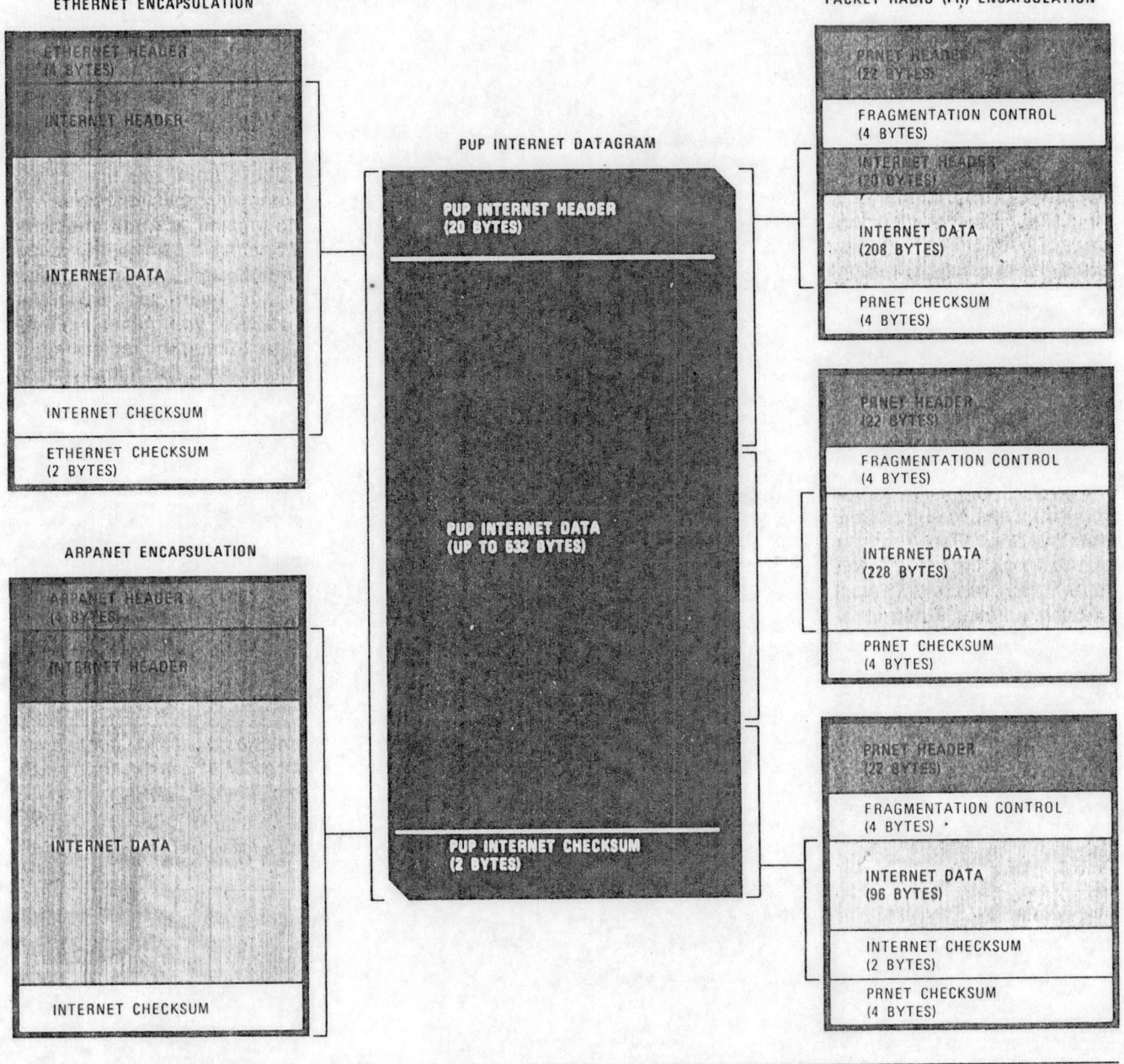

be received, and the datagram will be rebroadcast. A reliable communications mechanism, using higher-level protocol structures, is built on this "unreliable" datagram operation.

Ethernet's overall internetwork strategy calls for a special datagram called PUP, for PARC universal packet. The basic PUP datagram encapsulates various formats for transmission to Arpanet and packet-radio networks (Fig. 2). Routing is performed via a decentralized adaptive router, similar to that employed in the Arpanet design (Fig. 3).

Typical of Ethernet performance, at peak periods, single networks with about 130 nodes exhibit commu-

nications loads near 40 percent of capacity. Overall average loads, however, range from 2 to 3 percent. Xerox's measurements of the communications mechanism show that the combination of carrier sense for collision avoidance and exponential backoff provide stable linear communications. Other local networks without these control mechanisms become unstable during large loads.

Network Systems Corporation's Hyperchannel is a set of building blocks for both local computer networks and "backend" storage networks. Originally, the company's goal was to build backend storage networks for the "computer center of the future." However, be-

224

3. Transmitting between networks. Internetwork routing is performed via a decentralized adaptive router, similar to that employed in Arpanet. Peak-period Ethernet performance is typified by a 130-node network exhibiting communications loads near 40 percent of capacity. Average loads range from about 2 to 3 percent.

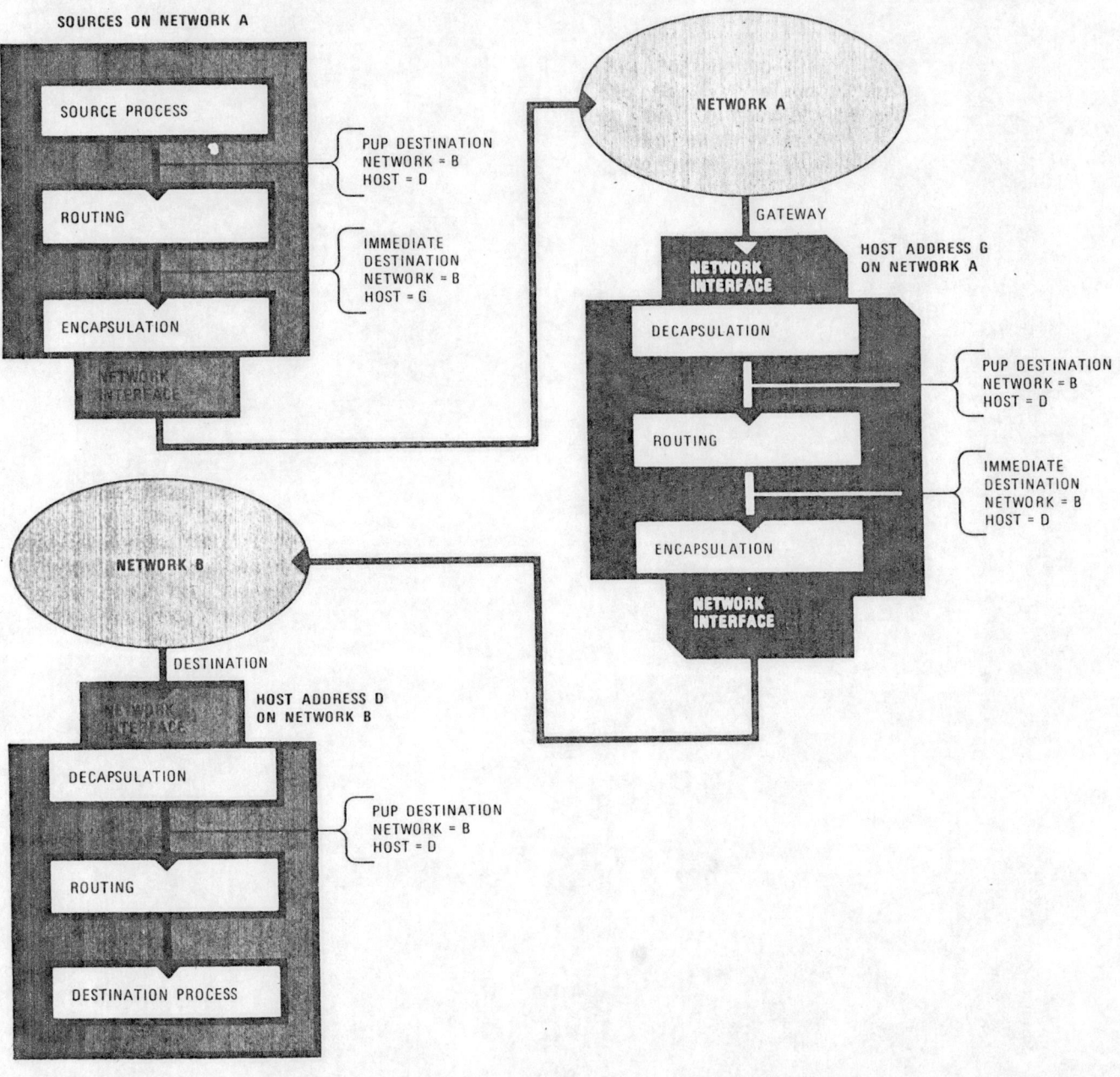

cause this project was too expensive, the products originally developed provided the communications mechanisms for a local network. Figure 4 summarizes the Hyperchannel concept.

The Hyperchannel network consists of a tapped coaxial cable capable of transmitting signals over distances of about 1,000 meters at rates of up to 50 Mbit/s. Connected to this cable are adapters, each consisting of a buffer-storage area and a micropro-grammed processor. The adapter interfaces to a communicating device and accepts and transmits data to another adapter, using a special format. Each adapter can connect to up to four coaxial cables in parallel,

and each is designed to interface with its particular device: Some connect to processors via I/O channels; others connect to memories via direct-memory-access (DMA) channels. Additional adapters are available for connection to a channel control unit (CU). This permits unit record equipment (punched-card-format machines) to be interfaced with the cable via an adapter connected to the equipment's channel control unit.

If the devices are separate from each other, the adapter connected to the processor desiring to use the unit record equipment will transfer the transmission-channel program to the equipment's adapter (which looks like the processor's adapter to the chan-

225

nel control unit). In some cases, the processor's operating system may be modified so that the channel program can reside on the remote adapter and be addressed from the processor.

Allocating by sensing

The Hyperchannel bus-allocation scheme is based on a carrier-sense-by-priority concept. Any device can access the bus if no device is transmitting; however, if a device is "locked out" from transmitting for an extended period of time, a priority change automatically occurs to ensure bus access. The carrier-sense concept is modified by a collision-detection scheme whereby the lack of a transmission acknowledgment, a negative acknowledgment (NAK), or a detected collision causes a transmission retry. Actual data transmission is bit-serial.

The Hypercache, a later offering from NSC, is a megabyte-range, high-speed buffer memory that connects to the Hyperchannel through a set of adapters. It is used primarily to buffer a transmission when a sender is ready but the destination is not. In addition, Hypercache can be used as a centralized store-and-forward buffer pool. Multiple Hypercaches could in this way be employed as packet switches distributed on the Hyperchannel. Still another application is for forming a back-end storage network, using the Hypercache as a temporary buffer. Another product developed around this concept is Masstor Corporation's Shared VSS (virtual storage system).

One complaint about Hyperchannel is its cost compared to that of a minicomputer network. Hyperchannel is more expensive because of the great expense of developing and building the high-speed hardware. However, it should be noted that on Hyperchannel, up to four minis (or hosts) can be multiplexed onto a single adapter. Also, NSC has a lower-speed local-network product, Hyperbus (see "Local networks' consensus: High speed," DATA COMMUNICATIONS, December 1980, p. 56).

Connecting personal computers

NSC's Cluster/One Model A network links Apple computers onto the network's backbone, the ClusterBus, a low-cost implementation of the techniques employed in such coaxial-cable-based local networks as Ethernet. (A Cluster/One connection costs about $400; Ethernet's is at least $1,000.) The bus-interface card plugs into an Apple II or III I/O card slot and provides access to the bus, based on a modified contention algorithm. Data is transmitted in a byte-parallel fashion (a unique feature of this network) over eight twisted pairs of wires at 30 kbyte/s—equivalent to 240 kbit/s in aggregate. There is a separate "busy," or "carrier," line, and synchronization is achieved through distinct "handshake" lines.

The network-interface cards contain a parallel 8-bit address recognizer, RAM (random-access-memory) buffers, and ROM (read-only-memory)-based packet protocols. The CPU of the personal computer—rather than a separate processor on the interface card—is used as the network processor. The network is topol-

---

4. Assembly materials. Network Systems' Hyperchannel is a set of building blocks for both local networks and "backend" storage networks. The tapped coaxial cable can transmit signals up to 50 Mbit/s over about 1,000 meters. The tapping adapters consist of a buffered storage area and a microprogrammed processor.

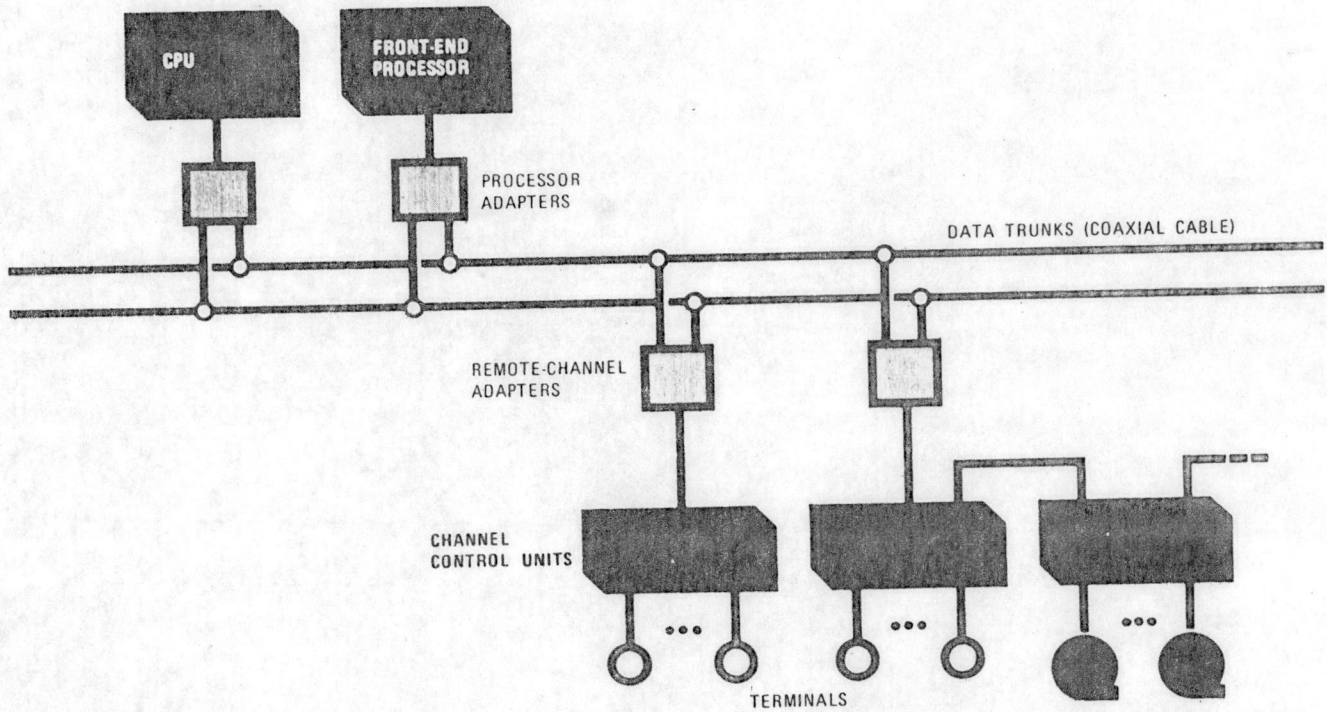

5. Getting personal. *Nestar Systems' Cluster/One Model A uses Apple II or III computers. The network's basis is the "ClusterBus," a comparatively low-cost implementation of* *Ethernet-like techniques. The bus-interface card plugs into an Apple card slot, providing access to the bus based on a modified contention algorithm.*

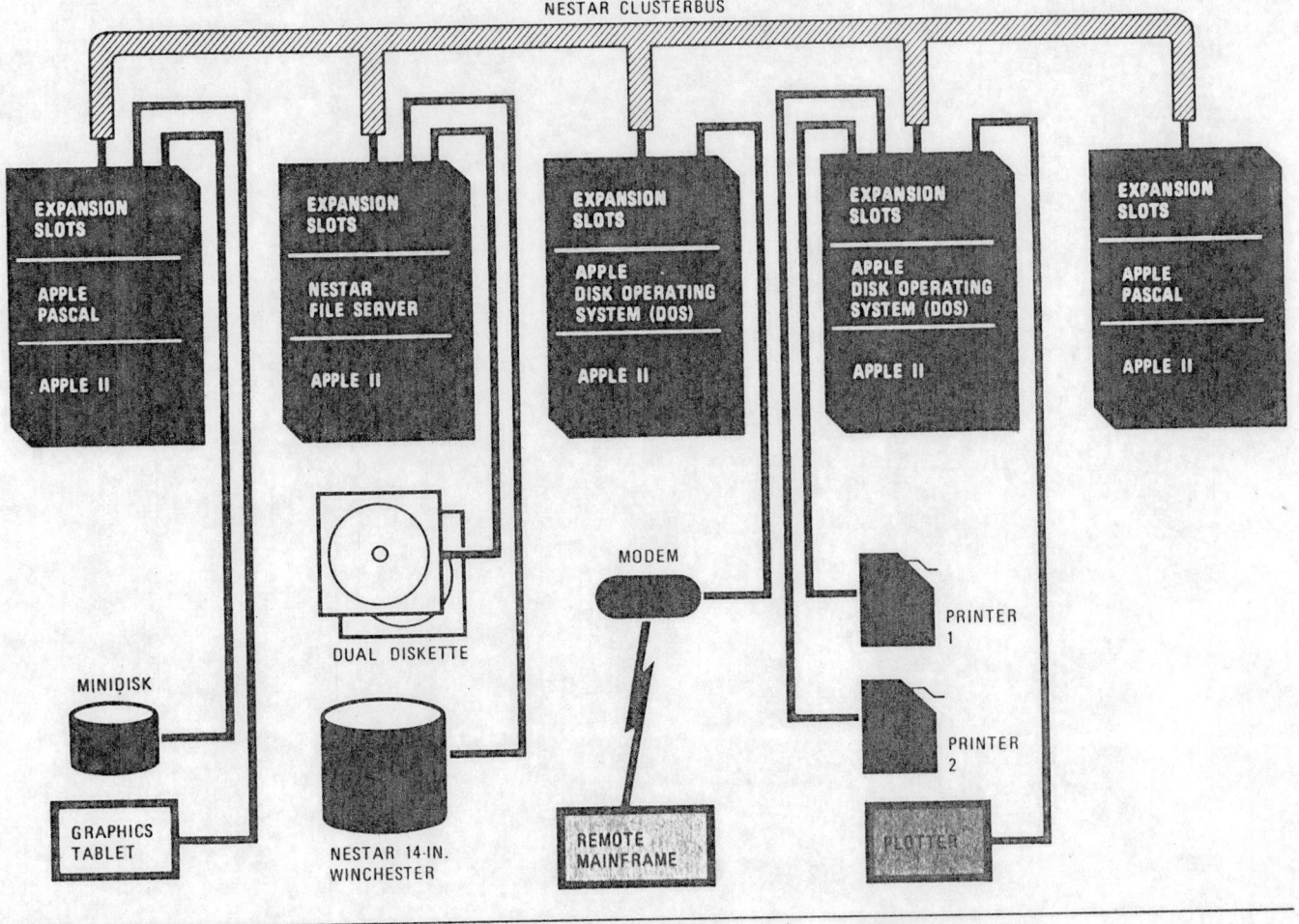

ogy-independent (not restricted to a particular network configuration) but is constrained to about 1,000 feet. Cabling can be twisted-pair or flat (ribbon) wire. The data rates are kept low (compared to coaxial-cable-based networks), so that impedance matching and reflection do not affect network transmission.

The Cluster/One is a general local network (Fig. 5) that can be specialized with the addition of software components to operate in environments such as elementary schools. There are presently several such installations in which elementary school children share peripherals, files, programs, and other network components. An immediate benefit realized in one installation was the elimination of diskettes used for program loading. The network's file server controls sharing of data and programs and thereby reduces or eliminates the need for individual loading of programs.

Personal-computer-based local networks must be easy to use to be attractive and cost-effective to small businesses such as realtors and consulting firms. In fact, Cluster/One software has already been developed by OEM system houses, creating specialized information-gathering networks for applications in real estate and other fields.

Staying within the price range of the personal computer marketplace imposes difficult design limitations on such local-network hardware as Nestar's. Consequently, the adapter card must fit into an I/O card slot of the Apple computer, draw its power from the computer, and be cost-competitive with other personal-computer options. With a cost of under $400 per adapter, the Nestar local-network hardware costs are considered acceptable.

The ring method

There is a wide variety of ring, or loop, networks available. One reason for their popularity is that they are relatively easy to implement. There are really two primary ring strategies: the Pierce Loop and the distributed-loop computer network (DLCN) Loop of Lui. Another variation, the Newell Loop, is an extension of the Pierce concept.

The Pierce Loop can be thought of as the cylinders of a revolver. Each message slot (cylinder) is well defined by a code indicating whether it is empty or full. If the slot is empty, a message may be placed in the slot, and the slot marked as full. If the slot is full, it may not be used. As the slots circulate (the cylinder spins),

each slot passing a processor is examined. Usually a processor is linked to the ring by a special ring interface, designed to perform this slot-access processing.

In the Pierce Loop configuration, the messages transmitted are of a fixed length. The data being circulated in a ring slot may actually be only part of a larger message. Thus, the ring interface requires software to reassemble the original message. The design of the ring protocol can be such that the ring acts either as a circuit switch (virtual circuit) or as a datagram-oriented network. There may be several messages in transit on the ring at a given time.

United Kingdom-based Logica VTS's Polynet is a commercial offering of the Cambridge ring, probably the best-known of the local networks based on the Pierce Loop approach. Polynet's node and cable transmission delays allow the circulation of up to 16 messages at 10 Mbit/s.

Passing the token
Newell Loops also accommodate variable-length messages but otherwise operate much like a Pierce Loop. Loop control is passed from processor to processor (commonly called token passing). When a processor has control of the loop and wishes to transmit a message, it does so and subsequently relinquishes control. When a processor — through its ring interface — detects a message for itself, it removes the message from the ring. There can be only one message on the Newell Loop at any time.

The strategy of Lui for the DLCN loops is commonly known as shift-register insertion. This concept requires two buffers in the ring interface: an output buffer and a delay buffer. Messages produced at the processor connected to the interface are placed in the output buffer. The delay buffer is used to buffer incoming messages. If a processor desires to transmit a message, it finds the end of an outgoing message and inserts its outbound message (from the output buffer) while delaying any incoming message in the delay buffer. Then the processor retransmits the accumulated messages in the delay buffer either to itself (if it is the destination) or to the next processor in the ring. This strategy allows multiple, variable-length messages to be handled but requires that the DLCN ring interfaces have a store-and-forward capability.

Other ring strategies vary as to message length, traffic flow — bidirectional or unidirectional, whether bidirectional traffic can occur simultaneously, and whether multiple rings are provided for reliability. Most configurations, however, are variations on either the Pierce, Newell, or Lui DLCN rings.

Today's performance levels
Currently, the major local-network activity is centered around the 3- to 10-Mbit/s performance range. In addition to the NSC's Hyperbus, another important offering in this range is the Sytek LocalNet. LocalNet is aimed at the RS-232-C market, but it uses broadband techniques compatible with CATV systems. Another broadband offering is Wang Laboratories' Wangnet, which provides three distinct communications bands:

Wang, interconnect, and utility (see "Broadband at base of Wang's far-reaching local network," DATA COMMUNICATIONS, July, p. 30).

The Ungermann-Bass Net/One is a baseband product that emphasizes modularity and flexibility. Net/One allows up to 16 RS-232-C terminals to connect to a single node and accommodates a large number of protocol variations.

The Datapoint ARC network has over 7,000 bus interfaces in more than 1,000 installations, making it probably one of the largest installed local networks. A significant feature is its ability to connect devices such as CBXs to the network via Datapoint's Infoswitch product. Datapoint's own CBX, the ISX, connects directly to the ARC bus. Similarly, Rolm and Intecom, with their data/voice CBX products, will also be formidable competitors in this market. But the use of the CBX as a gateway between local networks — as has been suggested by some "experts" — will not work as long as the throughput is limited by the CBX's maximum transmission speed of 56 kbit/s.

Local-net availability
How does one go about locating the right local-network vendor? Unfortunately, for all of the emphasis on this area of technology, the majority of networks are either experimental or custom-built and are therefore not commercially available. There are, however, many hardware choices. The key word, of course, is hardware. In general, the user must write his own software.

Local-network hardware exists at many levels and therefore is harder to classify than local networks themselves. Some local-network hardware, for example, is not available as a separate entity; it is embedded in the network. Hardware may also be deeply embedded in the application. For example, the Xerox 860 offering contains an embedded Ethernet interface.

There are firms that provide turnkey local networks incorporating specific mainframes or minicomputers. It is relatively easy to adapt an existing networking product to work in a geographically local environment. In fact, this may even simplify the network design. One such development is the ring-oriented structure that provides local-networking capabilities in the Primenet product of Prime Computer Corporation. Other concepts such as IBM's systems network architecture (SNA) and DEC's Decnet could be similarly modified for a local-network framework.

Local-net building blocks
With certain components, it may be possible to build a variety of local-network products. Hardware subsystems are now appearing.

One such subsystem, Masstor Corporation's Shared VSS, is a backend storage network. This subsystem is based on the NSC's Hyperchannel and Hypercache, in conjunction with the IBM 3850 mass storage system and IBM 4341 processor. Shared VSS provides for the on-line capability of sharing a backend storage network with several nonhomogeneous host computers. A large database is maintained in archival storage, and its movement into a host is handled by a control pro-

cessor. Files are moved to and from a Hypercache and, via the Hyperchannel, into the appropriate host.

The most challenging problem for local networking is interconnecting nonhomogeneous computers with the network. Since machines come from a variety of manufacturers, there is typically little or no software available from a computer vendor for this type of implementation. In fact, manufacturers probably try to discourage such interconnection for obvious reasons. Nevertheless, the majority of the available local-network hardware does fall into this category. Competition in this area of local-networking can be expected to increase unrelentingly.

To date, the most significant commercial-grade local-network hardware components (modules) are available from Network Systems Corporation. Almost 20 adapter types (each compatible with a different vendor's processor) are available for the Hyperchannel.

In addition, Control Data Corporation has shown signs of producing hardware competitive to NSC's adapters, and Sperry Univac has introduced military-oriented hardware to construct bus-oriented local networks using multiple vendors' processors.

Chip-level components

Chips and chip sets that may be used to support local network construction are also now becoming available. Western Digital is producing an X.25 chip, for example, and Harris Corporation is developing hybrid and single chips for military-bus interfaces. A number of other semiconductor manufacturers also plan to introduce local-network bus chips. In particular, Intel and DEC and Xerox have announced their intention to jointly develop a standard local-network interface chip based on the Ethernet concept. Zilog also announced that it will make this type of chip. ■

Sources for local-net products

Since a local network cannot be precisely defined, a survey of off-the-shelf components will probably not be all-inclusive. However, the following is a list of most of the available hardware in the current local-networking market. Products are categorized as application-embedded hardware, turnkey systems, subsystems building blocks, and chips and other components.

Application-embedded hardware

Datapoint's Attached Resource Computer (ARC) local network. Datapoint claims to have delivered over 7,000 local-network nodes.

Intecom's Integrated Business Exchange (IBX), a computerized branch exchange supporting RS-232-C-interfaced data terminals and designed for the mixed voice/data environment.

Rolm's Electronic Mail System (REMS), an electronic mail product built around the Rolm CBX, which also supports RS-232-C terminals.

Wang's Mailway, an electronic-mail product incorporating Wang word processors.

Xerox's 860 is basically a word processor with an Ethernet interface.

Turnkey systems

A. B. Dick's Magna III, a word processing package including a token-ring local network.

Apollo Computer's Domain, a local network of high-end personal computers.

Concord Data Systems, with a token-passing, bus- or ring-based local network reportedly modeled on the developing IEEE 802 standard.

Corvus' Omninet and *Constellation 2*, local networks for personal computers.

Digital Equipment Corporation's Digital Network Architecture (DNA), considered a local network, especially with Phase III Decnet software and when processors are placed in close proximity.

Digital Microsystems' HiNet, a local-network product for Z-80-based processors.

IBM's Series/1 Local Communications, a ring-based local network for up to 16 Series/1 minicomputers.

IBM's Systems Network Architecture (SNA), and the *IBM 8100 SDLC Ring*, again, assuming the processors and terminals are placed in close proximity.

Prime Computer's Primenet, a token-passing, ring-based network.

Proteon Associates, with a star-shaped, ring-based local network.

Three Rivers Computer's Packet Stream Network, a local network of personal computers.

Wang's Wangnet and *Wang Inter System Exchange (WISE)*. Wangnet is a broadband cable network; WISE, an older offering, supports star-shaped local connections of Wang equipment.

Zeda Computers International's Infinet, a low-speed, low-access-cost local network.

Zilog's Z-Net, a bus-based, Ethernet-technology local network used to interconnect Zilog's MCZ 2 computer workstations.

Subsystems building blocks

AMDAX's CableNet, a broadband local network.

Bolt, Beranek & Newman, Inc.'s Pluribus IMP, a multiprocessor interface message processor originally designed for Arpanet.

Burroughs's Inter-System Control (ISC), for connecting Burroughs mainframes.

Codex, a local network based on twisted pairs and modems.

Computrol's Megalink, a multidropped bus topology using direct memory access (DMA).

Control Data Corporation's Loosely Coupled Network (LCN), for connecting Cyber 205s.

Datapoint's ISX, a CBX that can work with the ARC local network.

Digital Communications Corporation's Cable Access Packet Communications system (CAPAC), a local network permitting RS-232-C devices to be interfaced with FSK (frequency-shift-keyed) modems and a lightwave multiplexer, the LM 9500.

Digital Equipment Corporation's various DEC interface cards (such as the PCL-11 and DR-11) that can be used in constructing local networks.

Electrosound Systems, a twisted-pair local network.

General Electric's Gemlink, the Model LSD-052A microwave link.

GTE's local network, PBX-based for the GTD-1000 and GTD-4600.

Harris, a PBX-based local network.

Hewlett-Packard's DS 1000, packet-switch connections for local networks.

IEEE's 488 Bus, a standard followed by various manufacturers, which can also be employed in local network designs.

Intecom's IBX, a CBX.

Interlan announced a series of local-network-interconnection devices.

Logica VTS's Polynet, based on the Cambridge ring experimental network.

Masstor's Shared VSS, a backend mass-storage network based on NSC's Hyperchannel and Hypercache network offerings.

Modular Technology's Laser Link.

Nestar Systems' Cluster/One Model A, a local network for use with personal computers.

Network Systems Corporation's Hyperchannel and *Hyperbus*, offering a large selection of adapters for high-speed local networks of communicating nonhomogeneous processors.

Nippon Electric's NEAX 22, also a PBX-based local network.

Personal Micro Computers's Downloader, a TRS-80-compatible local network.

Rolm's Release 7 local network and a *CBX*.

Sperry Univac's Shinpads (shipboard integrated dp system), a high-speed bus; *EPIC/DPS*, a ring-based local network; and *AN/USQ-67*, a militarized circuit switch for local networks.

Sytek's LocalNet, a broadband network for RS-232-C-interfaced devices.

T-Bar's Virtual Switch Matrix (VSM), a large circuit switch.

Teletone, equipment for a PBX-based local network.

3M's Advanced Local Area Network (ALAN), a broadband local network.

Ungermann-Bass's Net/One, a digital local network for RS-232-C devices, with special features for IBM 3270 protocols.

United Technologies Lexar's LBX, a CBX.

Ztel, a PBX-based local network.

Chips and other components

AMD, Ethernet chips.

Computer Energy, wiring products for IBM 3270-based local interconnections.

Harris's 1553, a standard military serial interface on a single chip.

Mostek, Ethernet chips.

3Com, Ethernet-compatible transceivers.

TLC, Ethernet transceivers.

Western Digital, chips incorporating the X.25 standard and token-ring local-network control.

Zilog, announced development of an Ethernet chip.

Build a local network on proven software

Dale Way, Zilog Inc., Campbell, Calif.

Unbundled local-network software changes the rules. Here is how to take advantage of it.

Any user with a good grasp of the application can buy local-network technology and build on top of it. This is possible today since the idea of unbundling hardware and software in local networks has surfaced. It remains to be seen, though, just how many manufacturers will make such an option available in the future, but for now at least, Zilog is offering unbundled hardware and software of its distributed commercial network, Z-Net.

Z-Net implements a subset of elements through the fifth, or session, level of the International Standards Organization's open systems interconnection model (see "A long-awaited standard for heterogeneous nets," DATA COMMUNICATIONS, January, p. 63), from which users can build their own integrated network.

It is implemented with a single-channel, packet-switching, common-bus, baseband architecture using the carrier-sense, multiple-access with collision detection (CSMA/CD) access method, based on the 8-bit LSI technology of the Z80 microprocessor and peripheral family. Each microcomputer-based node handles the functions of network access and data management so that remote-resource access is transparent.

Before delving into the implementation, a user must define a number of system requirements.

First, he should determine the level of desired functionality: Is the network expected simply to facilitate the sharing of resources, in which case simple file-

By building on available local-network backbones, you can save time and energy and concentrate on implementing functions.

transfer-type communications between stations will do? Or should it provide intimate cooperation among distributed tasks, which would require more complex interprocess communications? The current technological push is toward the latter, higher-level capability, in which large applications can be broken into individual cooperating parts and distributed among network nodes for increased functionality.

Second, the user must determine the performance range: What levels of throughput and response time are needed? In answering that question users must keep in mind that packet-per-second throughput is more meaningful than raw data-transfer rates, as the former takes into account the significance of packet-processing overhead.

Is concurrent compatibility with other networks systems and their elements and services desired? If so, the builder may want to reserve space to run alternative sets of high-level protocols or the appropriate protocol-translation program.

These requirements are affected by design and implementation choices such as how processing power and memory resources are distributed between the network-processing function and the host-processing function. A basic issue is whether to share the resources of a single central processing unit for both the host application and network functions or to use a separate CPU on a tightly coupled controller board for network functions.

If the emphasis is on local storage at each workstation node, the network may not have to be accessed as often. Thus, sharing a single CPU may be adequate. On the other hand, if the network will incorporate more shared resources, there may be a high level of traffic into and out of the node—perhaps more than a shared CPU can handle efficiently. Here the host can be offloaded by using a separate CPU-based controller. Likewise, if the designer envisions extending the network into a hybrid integrated/data-connection architecture (see "Classifying local networks"), the network could be used heavily. Again, a distinct CPU-based network controller will help offload the host.

This is essentially a cost-versus-performance issue. Although a separate controller costs more, it also provides a higher level of performance. But the choice is not a simple one, and other factors are involved:

■ *Processor interrupt latency.* If the host processor has a slow interrupt response time, or if interrupts must be disabled for any extended period of time (because of some of the other tasks managed by the host), incoming messages may be missed. This would force a choice in favor of intelligent controllers.

■ *Processing power.* Protocol processing can consume large amounts of processing power and can significantly slow down other applications controlled by the host.

■ *Processor type.* If the host processor is not a Z80 or Z80-compatible microcomputer, the protocol software will have to be translated to execute.

Separate processors
Once the decision to implement an intelligent controller for the network is made, several other choices must be faced. How much memory will the controller use? How will it be accessed? The options include private local memory versus dual-ported memory, CPU-controlled memory access versus direct-memory-access (DMA) controlled, and so on. This decision goes hand in hand with determining which network protocol layers to implement and how they should be distributed between the host and the network controller.

Next, a user must specify how the intelligent network controller will communicate with the host. Control, data, and synchronization should be considered.

Control information (such as a SEND PACKET command with its associated parameters) may be passed through specialized registers accessible from either the controller processor or the host processor. This method is an alternative to providing fully shared memory between the two processors.

Data information—such as the contents of a packet—must pass through the controller memory space when going to or coming from the network. Dual-port memory avoids the time-consuming message-copy operation. Alternatively, if the controller and host memory spaces are fully disjointed, data must be transferred back and forth by the two cooperating processors, or more elegantly, by a specialized DMA channel. The DMA could even be made intelligent enough to perform on-the-fly processing, such as packet-header stripping or filtering. Bus-acquisition latency may become a bottleneck during these copy operations. Considération should be given to using a high-speed private bus, rather than the system bus, between network controller memory and host memory.

Synchronization between the two processors may

Classifying local nets

There are several ways of categorizing local networks: by topology, access method, signaling techniques, and so on. The following looks at the local-network population from the integration level of the functions into the nodes.

Local networks can be classified into three types:
- Physical connection
- Data connection
- Integrated connection

Each is characterized by the way it partitions its communications functions.

The physical-connection approach, detailed in Figure 1, simply manages the physical link between network

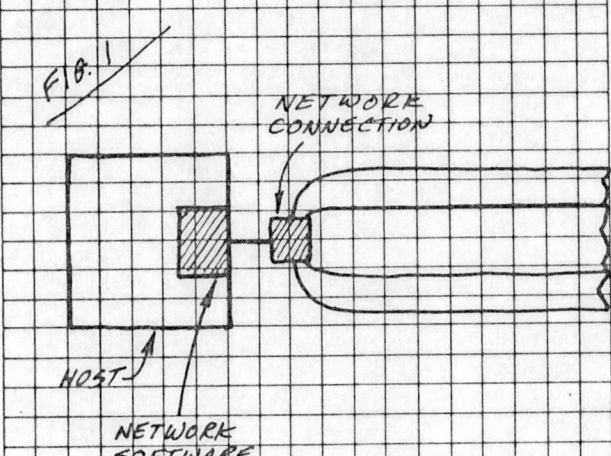

elements. Although a physical connection can be made, all software functions must be implemented within the devices themselves, while the network backbone has only a circuit-switching or routing role.

CBX data switches offered by Rolm Corporation and

Northern Telecom are examples of physical-connection types of local networks. Another is the Computrol baseband network. The planned interconnect Band of Wang's Wangnet also falls into this category. All physical-connection local networks can link components, but the real communications tasks are left to the attached devices. Their advantage is that they can support concurrent voice and data traffic.

Limited. However, physical-connection local networks are generally limited to data rates between 300 and 19.2K bit/s (speeds up to 56 or 64 kbit/s are possible only in special cases). Moreover, the implementor must design the necessary communications functions into the attached devices.

In the data-connection network (Fig. 2), lower-level protocols are typically offloaded from attached hosts into the network itself. The nodes of the data-connection network perform the functions of a communica-

require a mutual interrupt capability—say, command-present and command-completion interrupts.

Any of these alternatives may be valid under certain conditions. Cost, intended application, and various other constraints will be the determining factors.

Layering

Besides the hardware choices, there are significant decisions related to software—or spanning both hardware and software. A fundamental choice involves the levels of Z-Net protocol that need to be implemented. If a user has already developed some high-level protocols and wants to protect that investment, he may wish to use only the lower layers and isolate those on a separate board, while executing the proprietary high-level protocols on the host.

If, on the other hand, the user needs to implement all of Z-Net's protocol layers, he must decide on which machines these various protocols will run. If the system

is being designed from scratch, this is fundamentally a performance issue: Can the host afford the extra workload? If a system with some protocols is already developed, another consideration emerges. To what extent will the existing network design be disrupted by the addition of new protocols?

Protocol layering minimizes the extent of this disruption by providing well-defined interfaces and hiding lower-level control parameters from higher-level interfaces. However, the junction point between the Z-Net layers and the existing user-supplied layers will require some call translation, possible relocation of host components to leave room for the Z-Net software, and slowing down of other applications by the protocol-processing overhead. If these issues are of concern, the intelligent controller may be the wise choice.

Now the user has to integrate the network hardware into the host design. If the network interface must be integrated into the existing board-level hardware, por-

tions server. Each node can attach from one to eight host devices using serial ports. However, the higher-level protocol functions are still left to the host.

Ungermann-Bass's Net/One is a baseband example of a data-connection local net; the Sytek System 20/40 is a broadband implementation. Like the physical-connection network, the data-connection network is usually limited in speed, although efforts are under way to develop high-speed interfaces between hosts and communications servers and to integrate more high-level protocols into the communications servers. This means that network access is not transparent but is gained only through a communications server.

Today, data-connection networks are well suited for connecting multiple terminals to multiple hosts. Beyond that—when shared resources or distributed applications are desirable—more is needed. This gap is filled by the integrated-connection or integrated local net-

work, shown in Figure 3. In this architecture, the host devices are designed with their integral network role in mind. They serve as nodes. Hence, the hosts are immersed in the network, and the network is embedded in the hosts. User transparency is accomplished via a standard built-in interface—not through a separate interface layer.

The Datapoint ARC network, Xerox's planned Star-based network, and Zilog's DCS network are examples of integrated networks. The announced Wang Band of Wangnet will apparently develop into an integrated network.

In the integrated network, the physical link does not exist because the network protocols, operating system, and network-access interface are tightly coupled into a single system. This tight coupling allows higher access speeds to the network via a uniform single interface.

Hybrids. An advantage of the integrated network is that it can be extended, using communications servers developed outside of or on top of the basic network, to build a hybrid integrated/data-connection network that allows foreign host attachment. A purely integrated network is proprietary (although elements of it may not be), because the vendor that designs the network also designs the host devices to incorporate that network.

There are similarities between the physical-connection network with implemented communications functions and an integrated network. In fact, an integrated network could be built on top of a physical-connection network. But a major appeal of the physical network is the implied connectability of existing equipment. The development of those communications functions must take into account the architecture and individual requirements of heterogeneous machines. The resulting communications network will often lack the unity, flexibility, and overall potential achieved in an integrated local computer network where every node has the networking function at the heart of its design.

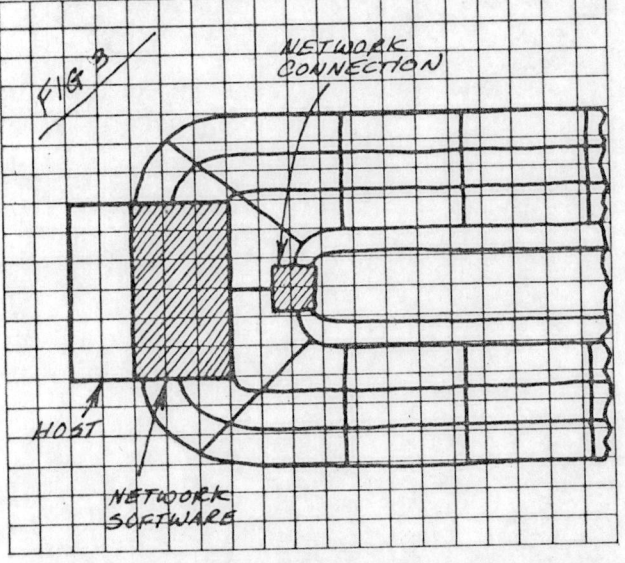

tions of the existing board need to be modified or redesigned. If a separate intelligent network controller has been chosen, the user must design an interface between the supplied Z-Net network interface and the bus structure, as well as the necessary circuits to support the host-to-network controller communications using one of the techniques noted earlier, after evaluating the various cost-to-performance trade-offs. The next step is developing the higher-level protocols (open systems interconnection model layers 6 and 7) or, if these already exist, developing an interface layer to the Z-Net protocols.

Takes time
These two steps—integrating the network hardware with the host design and developing or interfacing the high-level protocols—may take from one to three man-years, depending on the level of complexity chosen for the implementation. What is more significant, how-

ever, is what the user does not have to do. By using the existing network technology, he can save up to eight man-years of labor. He also avoids having to develop a new network architecture, specify network protocols from scratch, and design a network hardware interface. Further, he eliminates the coding tasks, documentation, and algorithm testing. Most important, the user avoids the essential fine-tuning of internal interlayer interfaces and data-manipulation algorithms for performance optimization—an extremely time- and resource-consuming procedure that is especially critical in the time-dependent lower protocol layers.

Clearly, if an integrated-network approach fits the application, a user gains significant benefits by purchasing the technology outside rather than by developing it himself. This new concept of licensing arrangements for network technology allows a broad range of opportunities to realize the potential competitive advantages that networking capabilities can bring. ▪

Inside Wang's local net architecture

Mark Stahlman, Wang Laboratories Inc., Lowell, Mass.

Wangnet uses a broadband technique based on a dual-cable, branching-tree topology to provide multiple services.

Local-networking concepts and technologies are not new. What is new is putting these technologies to work in addressing the overall needs in today's office environment. In taking this step, local networking takes on a product life of its own, independent of the specific applications or devices that use the network. From Wang's point of view this meant going back to the drawing board and examining the requirements for information interchange in the office.

As a result of this basic re-examination, Wangnet has been designed to meet two principle objectives: it must be able to handle the diverse forms of information in the office environment and it must handle these forms simultaneously. Broadband was chosen as the technology that satisfies these objectives.

There are a number of reasons for that choice. First, data in the office is by necessity highly diverse in form. This diversity is typically indicated listing key office automation technologies — word processing, data processing, audio processing, and image processing. People communicate through words, numbers, speech, and visual images. In the design review that preceded the decisions to build Wangnet, the expressed needs of a wide cross section of office automation users were weighted. This survey emphasized the present and future requirements for video and related image technologies, including graphics. A broadband design uniquely permits this wide variety of information forms.

Another dimension of this diversity is reflected by the proliferation of devices and their associated communications protocols in today's office. This protocol diversity is based not only in history but in utility. As any communications design engineer will say, there are significant performance and cost tradeoffs in matching protocols to their applications, and small details can make a large difference. For any office-automation user who wishes to install functionally integrated networks and true multifunction workstations, the market today offers powerful solutions. But any network that only supports one vendors' equipment is by its nature limited. The choice is not limited to functional integration or transmission integration because broadband designs allow for both.

Second, the flow of information in its many forms is simultaneous. Consider that protocols refer to the time domain; or, in other words, a specific protocol will typically employ a time-division multiplexing scheme to permit many devices to share a communications channel. The simultaneous character of information flow in the office cannot be practically solved by an extremely fast, very sophisticated time-division scheme. The traditional solution to this problem could be called the space-division multiplexing approach — a separate wire for each device or channel. Broadband solves this problem by replacing this jungle of cables and wires with a single medium. Unlike baseband networks, which are inherently limited to a single channel and therefore a single protocol, broadband employs one of the oldest communications techniques, frequency-division multiplexing (FDM).

Examples of frequency-division multiplexing to achieve multiple channels are very common, and it is

1. Standard. *Wangnet is designed around industry-standard protocol specifications using a packet format. The company plans to follow the Open Systems Interconnection model as the basis for its future software releases in the communications arena. Fully configured Wangnets are currently installed in a number of beta test sites.*

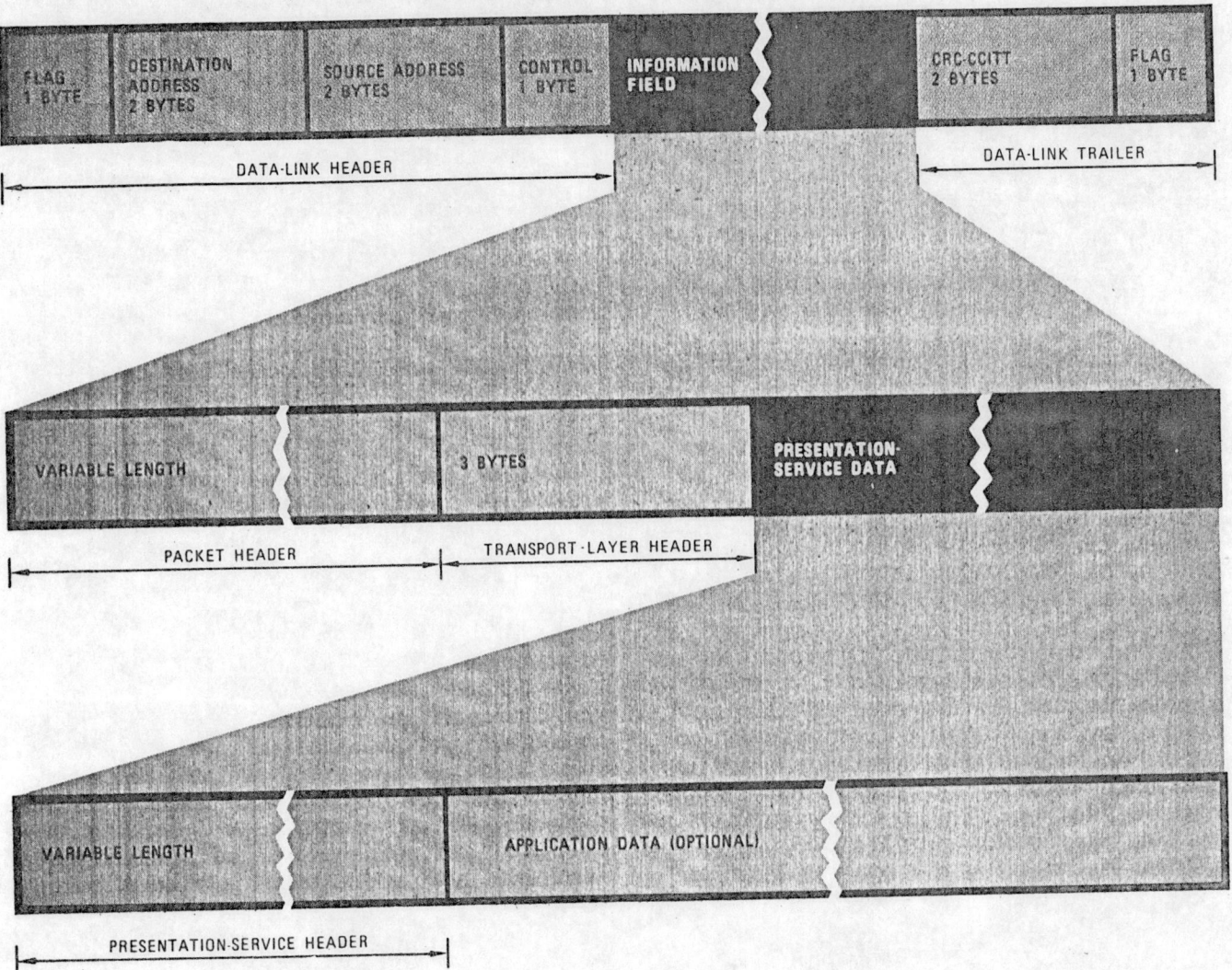

the development of frequency-division equipment on a large scale by the cable-TV industry that makes broadband particularly attractive. With more than 20 percent of United States households wired for cable today, significant economies of scale have been realized by cable and component manufacturers. Semiconductor makers have made a contribution to reducing parts' cost for radio frequency (RF) devices. Integrated circuits — many designed for television or radio — are being used extensively in modern RF modems. These modems are an important factor in the price per network connection for broadband networks. Contrary to the claim that broadband is more expensive on this account, at a price of $250 to $600 per user, the price per connection for broadband is currently below that for baseband networks.

When compared with the normally expected reliability of computer equipment, the use of CATV technology also brings with it higher reliability. Mean-time-between-failure figures in excess of 20 years are common for active components, and these typically refer to an outside plant installation considerably more hostile than the average office. The single most commonly cited cause of CATV failures is lightning strikes.

Outlet cost

Another advantage afforded by the use of CATV technology is the cost effectiveness of the true network outlet. It is attractive for information users to consider cabling an entire office complex with such outlets. The ongoing need to move equipment, as well as people, when added to the continuing introduction of new equipment can produce significant rewiring costs and intolerable delays. In order for this widely popularized network outlet notion to become a reality a few simple requirements must be met. The network outlet must have an installed cost that is about equal to the cost of wiring a facility for electrical power. Also, the outlet has to be there when and where its needed, without any need to get a building crew to rewire an office.

Finally, a network outlet has to be inexpensive enough to be left on the wall, unused, without worrying about underutilized capital.

Distance and topological restrictions often play havoc with plans to introduce local networks into offices. It is generally considered that bus topologies are superior to star or ring (often folded into a star-like pattern) arrangements. But all buses are not created equal. A segmented or repeatered bus, which places limits on the number of repeaters in a path between devices (one such design allows two repeaters), can put some major restrictions on the ability to grow new branches as the network expands. Wangnet is configured as a branching tree. This bus architecture permits the wiring of one floor or department or even a portion of a floor. Later, new branches can be installed as they are needed. Campus configurations of dozens of buildings are often connected together with such a topology. It is certainly cost effective, however, to begin small and expand as needed.

Inasmuch as Wangnet is a local network, it like any such network has distance limitations. This stems from two root causes. One cause is the propagation delay. Over even a couple of miles of cable, it can be a significant factor in protocol design, and therefore network performance. Using a 75-ohm CATV coaxial cable in Wangnet, a mile represents about 8 microseconds of propagation delay. In the carrier sense multiple access with collision detection (CSMA/CD) protocol, the minimum packet size is directly related to this delay. Given a maximum signal path distance of two miles for Wangnet, any signal which must propagate from one end of the cable to the other and back again will be delayed 32 microseconds in the round trip. At a signaling rate of 12 Mbit/s, 32 microseconds represents 384 bits or 48 bytes of information. There is no reason why a CSMA/CD protocol could not be employed over longer distances. For example, a 2,000-mile-long signal path would require a 48-kbyte minimum packet size. To demonstrate this more dramatically, consider a satellite in orbit 22,300 miles above the equator. For a round trip propagation delay of 540 milliseconds, CSMA/CD would require an 810-kbyte minimum packet size at a signaling rate of 12 Mbit/s.

The other source for distance limitations on local networks could generally be called signal quality. Broadband networks use amplifiers and baseband systems use repeaters, but the purpose of both is to extend the distance that a signal can be transmitted. It is a fact of transmission engineering that cables attenuate and distort signals. Moreover, these effects are not the same at all frequencies. In addition, noise from a variety of sources is also a constant concern. As a point of comparison, the probability of a bit being received in error is 1 out of every 1,000 for a dial-up telephone line, and 1 out of 100,000 for a conditioned leased line. Local-area networks are typically designed for errors rates in the range from 1 out of 100 million to 1 billion. Some interesting results emerge as signal quality declines. In general, video signals will visibly suffer first, with audio signals worsening next, and data signals being seriously affected only under considerably poorer conditions. The most sensitive of these, video, is routinely transmitted over tens of miles of metropolitan CATV networks.

The structure of the branching-tree topology is actually a Siamese twin of two parallel cables. Each is amplified in one direction only, so that one becomes the transmit and one becomes the receive cable. The cables are joined in a simple loop at the base of the tree.

A question of bandwidth

Wangnet offers an aggregate bandwidth of 340 MHz. This is an order of magnitude greater than anything else available. Why so much? Let's answer that by making some bandwidth calculations. Let's measure bandwidth in increments of 6 MHz since this is the bandwidth required by a television channel, and it is a convenient metric for high-speed data. Also let's assume that 5 Mbit/s occupies 6 MHz of spectrum. While all RF modems don't employ modulation techniques that show this efficiency, it is a reasonable standard for data rates at 5 Mbit/s and above. At rates below 5 Mbit/s, assume 2 Hz for every bit per second. So a 9.6-kbit/s modem might use about 20 kHz.

A 10- to 12-Mbit/s channel for system interconnection needs at least two 6-MHz increments. Each IBM 3270 control unit would need 6 MHz to attach its terminals. Wang's Office Information Systems (OIS) and Virtual Storage (VS) computers need about the same to attach workstations to their controllers or CPUs. Voice digitized at today's standard rates needs 64 kbit/s for each side of a conversation, or about 6 MHz for both sides of 24 conversations. A thousand slow-speed full-duplex devices might take six 6-MHz increments if each had its own frequency assignment.

It's not likely that two installations will have the same inventory of frequency needs. For the purpose of this example, let's take a perhaps not so typical corporate headquarters with about 3,500 people occupying 500,000 square feet of office space. Projecting a bit into the future we can foresee a density of office automation equipment that averages one device per 200 square feet, or approximately 2,500 devices. Let's assume that 1,000 of these are slow speed synchronous or asynchronous terminals (printers, etc). The other 1,500 of them are intelligent Wang workstations, IBM 3270s, or similiar equipment connected over the network to approximately 75 controllers. These in turn are connected to each other over a local channel. We need six television channels for video conferencing and other applications, and a distributed PBX uses sixteen TI-speed (1.544-Mbit/s) carrier links over the network. This adds up to approximately 97 pieces of 6-MHz bandwidth or more than even a full Wangnet could handle.

At this time it is appropriate to introduce a notion that addresses the problem posed by the numbers game above: hierarchical spectrum allocation. Just as any corporation is organized into smaller units—be they divisions, departments, and the like—a local-area networks can be divided into public and private frequency spectrums. In the example above, 75 of the 6-MHz increments were used for connecting worksta-

3. Interconnect Band. The Peripheral Service is not in itself a band, but rather a means of hooking peripherals to larger systems on the network. The Interconnect Band is for Wang as well as non-Wang devices and dedicated and switched channels. Any protocol common to both sending and receiving units is allowed.

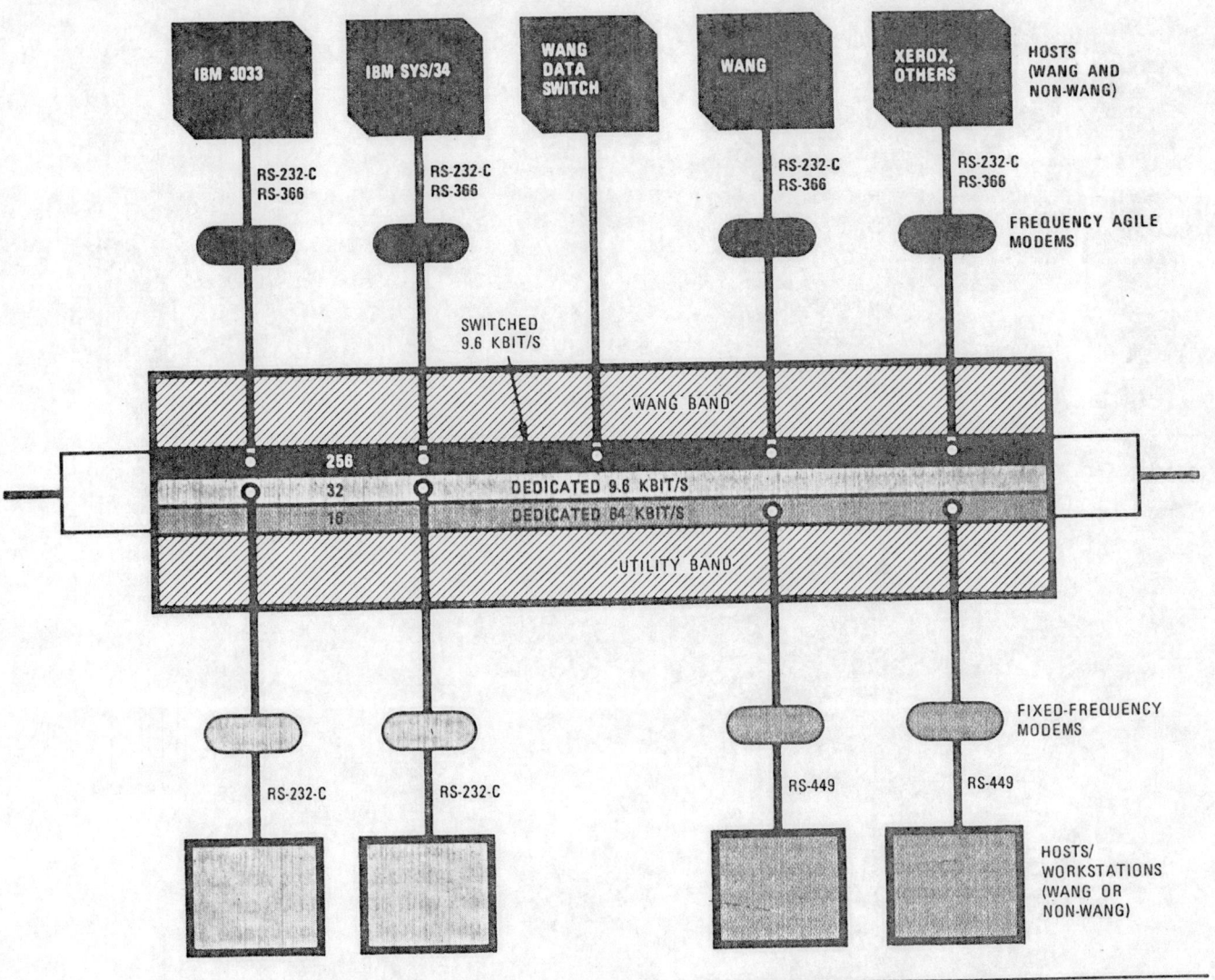

tions to their controllers or CPUs. In general, these controllers will be distributed at the departmental or divisional level and there is no reason to use a corporatewide public spectrum for what is clearly a private data requirement of a particular part of the organization. On the other hand, interconnection of these systems' controllers or CPUs, video conferencing, PBX functions, and mainframe-based terminal attachment will likely need to exist in the public-frequency spectrum because their use crosses departmental boundaries.

Since there is one public and many private spectrums, the total network capacity can be expanded almost indefinitely. Medium- to large-scale Wangnets will support 300 to 400 increments of 6 MHz when they are fully grown.

Service approach

Wangnet, as a broadband local network, consists of not one but a number of communications services.

These services are grouped into the Wang Band, the Interconnect Band, the Utility Band, and the Peripheral Attachment service. A good deal of the available frequency spectrum has been reserved for the future introduction of additional services.

The Wang Band—a 12-Mbit/s channel for the interconnection of systems—employs a CSMA/CD protocol to control contention and uses a variable length HDLC-derived packet format (see Fig. 1). Up to 16,384 devices can be attached to the Wang Band. A Cable Interface Unit (CIU) connects systems to the communications channel, as shown in Figure 2. The CIU is a generalized network processor built around the ISO's Open Systems Interconnection Reference Model concept. Wang's implementation of the lower five layers execute in the CIU. This allows the CIU to be used without change with each of the three otherwise quite distinct Wang systems, the OIS, the VS, and the 2200 product lines. The CIU also assumes the responsibility for extensive network diagnostic and network admin-

2. Wang Band. *Intended for connecting Wang products, Wang Band can facilitate Wang's Mailway service—an electronic-message distribution system for VS, OIS, and* *Wang 2200 systems. Other Wang Band applications include remote data processing for the VS systems, document editing on the OIS offering, and file transfers.*

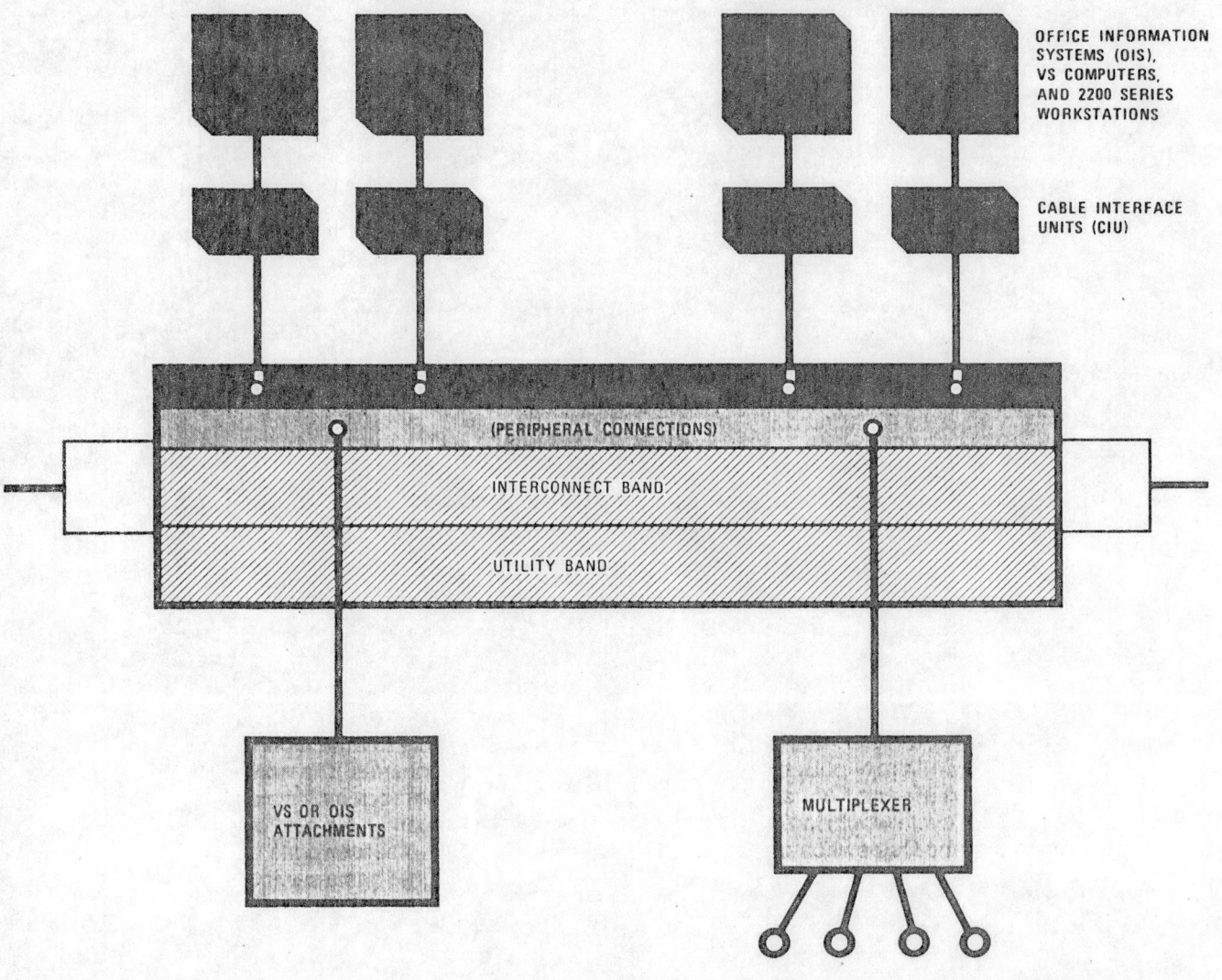

istrative functions.

The advantages of interconnecting between and among these systems families are considerable. While all of these product lines have already integrated word and data processing, they each have specific strengths and weaknesses. Particular applications, databases, interfaces, and peripherals can now be accessed from terminals attached to any of the systems. A multifunction workstation can now edit or even typeset documents at an OIS, run Cobol programs at a VS, or log-on through 3270 emulation to an IBM mainframe—all from the same workstation.

The CIU sells for $3,800. Since this is a system-level network interface, its cost is shared by all workstations attached to that system. Average configurations of VS or OIS systems might have 10 terminals, making the cost approximately $400 per user for each CIU network interface.

The Interconnect Band is divided into three separate services which are comparable to leased-line, wide-

band, and a special sort of circuit-switched channel. Each of these services are protocol independent, and therefore support equipment from virtually any manufacturer. As shown in Figure 3 the first service is made up of 32 dedicated full-duplex channels for handling data at speeds up to 9.6 kbit/s, sync or async, and point-to-point or multipoint. In the second, there are 16 channels with the same attributes but with maximum signaling rate of 64 kbit/s. The equipment to interface to these two sets of channels are known as fixed frequency modems (FFM). The 9.6 kbit/s FFM sells for $850, and the price of the 64 kbit/s FFM is $1,200.

In the third interconnect service, there are 256 switched channels operating at speeds up to 9.6 kbit/s, sync or async. The data stations for this portio of the Interconnect Band are known as frequency agile modems (FAM). The full FAM consists of a small enclosure and a desktop control unit. The enclosure has five data interfaces—two for the network (transmit and

4. Utility Band. *Each Utility Band channel is capable of handling one composite video-and-audio signal. The band has seven channels. Any approved cable-television head-* *end equipment is permitted. Interconnection is accomplished with the use of type F 75-ohm dual-captive manually terminated plug.*

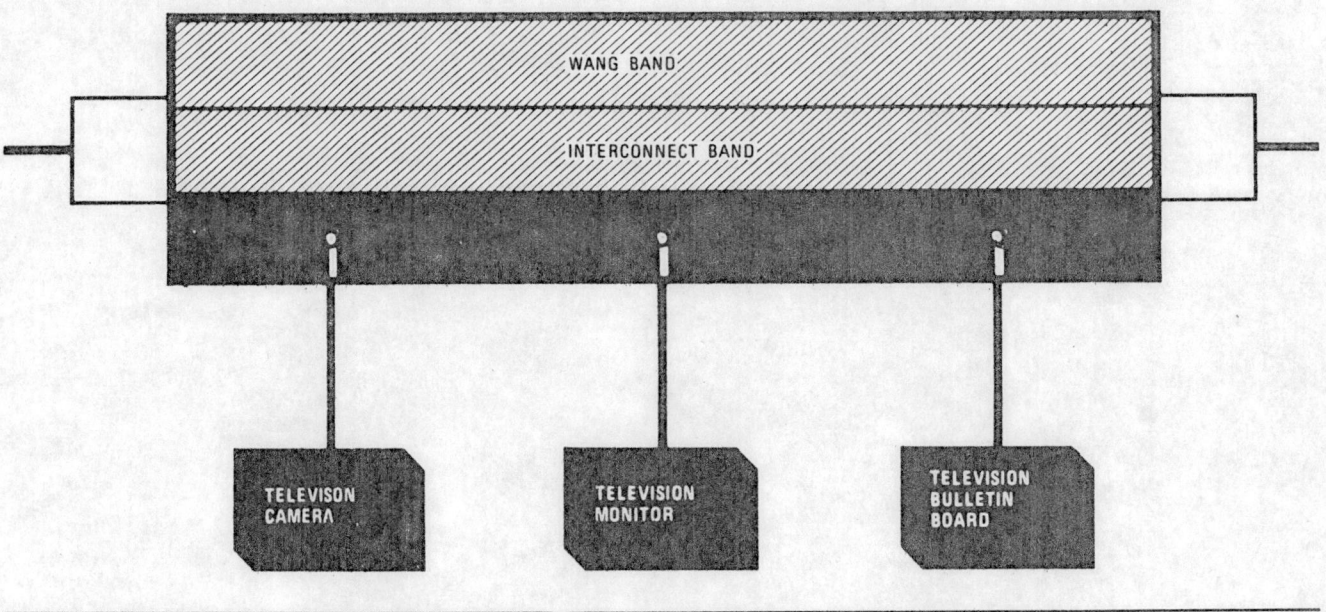

receive), an RS-232-C connector (DCE), an RS-366 connector (automatic dial), and an analog/data interface. The control unit has a numeric keypad for dialing and various indicators and buttons to control the data station.

In addition to the FAMs, a Dataswitch is required. This master controller continually polls the FAMs and keeps track of the status of each FAM and each channel. A typical operating cycle would look something like this: a FAM signals the Dataswitch over a control channel that it wishes to be connected across the network. After handshaking, the FAM tells the Dataswitch that it wants a connection to another FAM at number 2487, for instance. The FAM sends this data after either an operator has manually keyed it at the control unit or an attached DTE signals at the RS-366 interface. If this number is free or the start number of a hunt sequence, the Dataswitch will assign an unoccupied frequency to both FAMs and step out of the connection. At this time, data and control leads are connected between the two FAMs and the circuit looks like a long RS-232-C cable. Polling continues and the reverse process is invoked to disconnect a circuit. The FAM sells for $1,250, and the Dataswitch price is $12,000.

These Interconnect Band services can be used for Wang and non-Wang products alike. For instance, Wang 2200 terminals can attach to their CPUs over the Interconnect Band since they are interfaced using RS-232-C. A typical Interconnect Band configuration might have IBM remote 3270 control units multi-dropped using 9.6-kbit/s FFMs, two 3705 or similar units tied together at 56 kbit/s with the 64-kbit/s FFMs, and a hundred or more asynchronous terminals attached to a variety of minicomputers using the FAMs and a Dataswitch.

The Peripheral Attachment service is used to attach Wang OIS and VS workstations, printers, and other peripherals to their controllers or CPUs directly over Wangnet. Series 5300 and 5700 workstations for OIS or VS systems can be optioned to individually attach to Wangnet. Additionally, a four-port network multiplexer is available to attach printers and other workstations or peripherals. The workstation options sell for $600. The network multiplexer has a price of $1,050, which can give a cost of approximately $250 per workstation if all four ports are used.

Finally, Wangnet has a service called the Utility Band (see Fig. 4). This is a 42-MHz slice of the spectrum set aside for non-Wang RF devices. The frequencies correspond to VHF television channels 7 through 13. Video signals will often be carried by this band, but other RF devices that meet CATV power levels and frequency specifications can be used as well. While teleconferencing and video conferencing are best used across distances far beyond the reach of a local-area network, local distribution of video signals for this and other educational, security, or experimental purposes is growing in demand.

Office-automation vendors have long depended on local networking. Proprietary networks linking word processors and other intelligent devices are widespread in today's office. Over 20,000 such networks have been installed as the basis of Wang's OIS and VS products alone.

Wangnet is part of a new generation in local networks. Such networks are open to many vendors and multiple purposes. It is now practical to install network outlets to handle a range of information needs. Whether they are supporting an office complex or a handful of systems, such networks are the cornerstone of the future in office automation. ∎

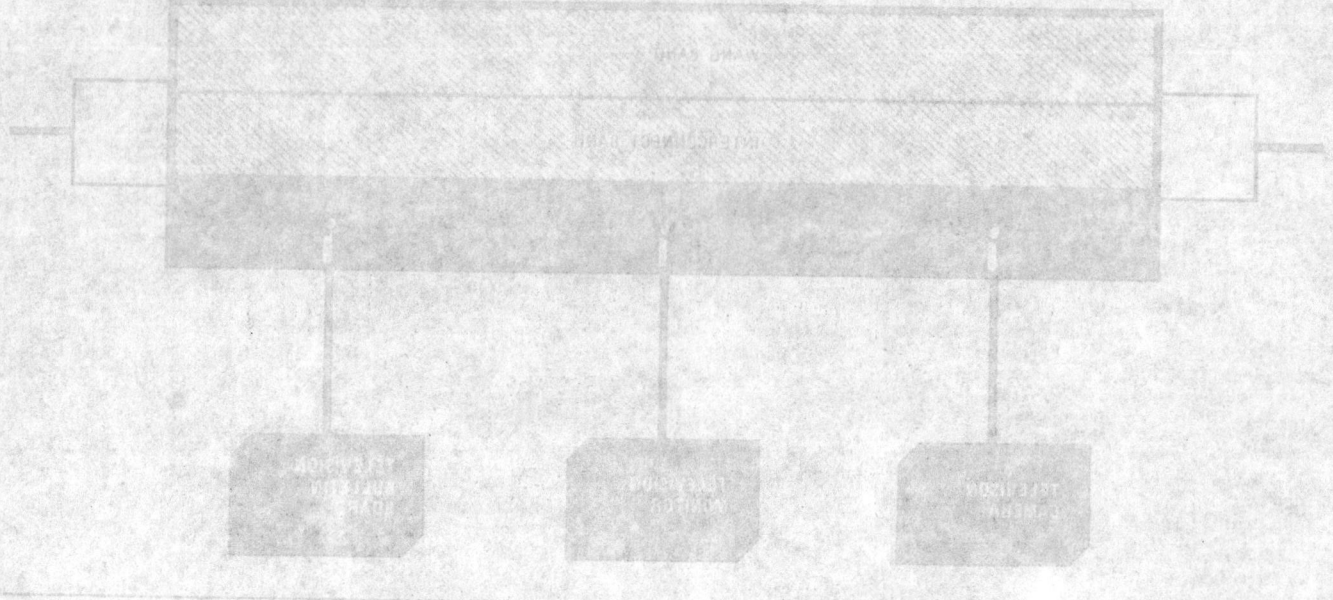

Ring nets: Passing the token in local network circles

Richard E. Sterry, Prime Computer Inc., Natick, Mass.

Sequential transmission has advantages over contention for office-of-the-future applications — among them, adaptability to growing data traffic.

Although Ethernet-like networks have gotten much publicity, practical hardware and software to connect data transmitting and receiving equipment to such local networks is not generally available. Also, users need a network with upward compatibility to handle voice and video signals. As designed, Ethernet, which requires users to contend for control of the network bus, is not readily adaptable to these functions.

While contention-type local networks provide a viable approach to local communications, there is another methodology that avoids the delays and sensitive retry algorithms associated with Ethernet message collisions. This approach is based on a ring-network topology. It uses a circulating token for the arbitration of messages on the network. Local data network products based on the ring structure have been commercially available from many vendors for several years and are a proven technology.

The advantages of ring-network structures are evident in Prime Computers Inc.'s Primenet local network. As is the case with the ring networks supplied by other vendors, in the future, Primenet will support even more vendors' hardware and software.

The Primenet concept is simple. A series of processors are interfaced to a continuous coaxial transmission path or ring. This ring provides a means for the processors to transmit data to both terminals and other processors at up to 8 Mbit/s. Primenet is designed to interconnect processors up to several hundred feet apart using commonly available coaxial transmission cable. Typically, the network achieves less than 1 sec-

ond total round-trip delay through all its software and hardware layers. The combination of high transmission speed and short delay times and the capability to handle multiple types of data allows ring networks to compete favorably with other local networks (see "Token or contention?").

For the data communications manager to be able to choose intelligently between token- or contention-based local networks, it is not sufficient that he understand the advantages and disadvantages of each concept. He must also be familiar with the details of a typical token-passing network, such as Primenet.

The Primenet hardware is configured to achieve a high degree of processor autonomy and decentralized control (Fig. 1). Each node has three parts. The first is the junction box, which provides the actual coaxial interface and the first level of network protection. An electronic relay inside the junction box can completely bypass the node itself. This allows for complete isolation from the node in the event of a power failure. The second component is the node controller. It interprets part of the packet coming in from the junction box and determines if it should interrupt the third component, the node itself. By design, these separate layers of hardware combine with the token-control mechanism to provide node autonomy. This is important because each node's user is then isolated from the problems that other nodes may have.

Network control is achieved by a special circulating bit pattern known as the token. There is only one token, and it arbitrates all the nodes in the network. The

Token or contention?

There is no single answer to the question of which local-network control scheme is best for the end user. Adding to the confusion, the IEEE's local-network standards committee has approved both token and contention buses. In fact, the two approaches do have a degree of commonality. For example, both use baseband techniques and the entire available bandwidth. However, neither has addressed the synchronization problem involved with transmitting over multiple bands to one node.

Both approaches are packet-oriented. This makes both relatively compatible with other types of networks. Token and contention schemes are also adaptable to almost any type of communications device on the network, from the dumbest teletypewriter to the smartest mainframe. Finally, both schemes are designed for local environments.

The differences between token and contention networks are numerous and profound. Although both are in use in a variety of environments, the key to the acceptance of either is adaptability to future environments. The difference between token and contention networks is particularly important for growing networks, since the techniques differ in their resilience to overload situations.

As more and more users gain access to a local network, more data begins to flow. With a contention scheme, there is then more chance for collision. This problem can be solved only partially by increasing the data rate, because the detection techniques must be changed also. On the other hand, the ring allows almost unlimited data rate increases because the token arbitrates the network.

There is also the question of resilience to hardware failures. The token-based ring requires a continuous ring for proper operation. If the ring is physically broken, the token gets lost. Without using some sophisticated techniques to loop back on the ring, the token network becomes inoperative until the break is repaired. In contrast, the collision-detection method broadcasts in all directions and, depending on the type of break, might ignore it.

The complexity and number of attached devices should also be considered. Both the token and the contention networks require a degree of intelligence at each attached device. This intelligence is different in each case, and proponents of both methods each think that theirs is less complex. For some network designers, the simplicity of the token-passing algorithm compared with the retry algorithm needed in a contention network (especially at high data rates) makes it more appealing for long-range growth. On the other hand, the active taps available on networks such as Ethernet allow more flexibility in terms of physical connection. The real problem, however, is the ability to place a connection on the coaxial cable without regard for its distance from another attached device. Neither method has come up with a sufficient solution.

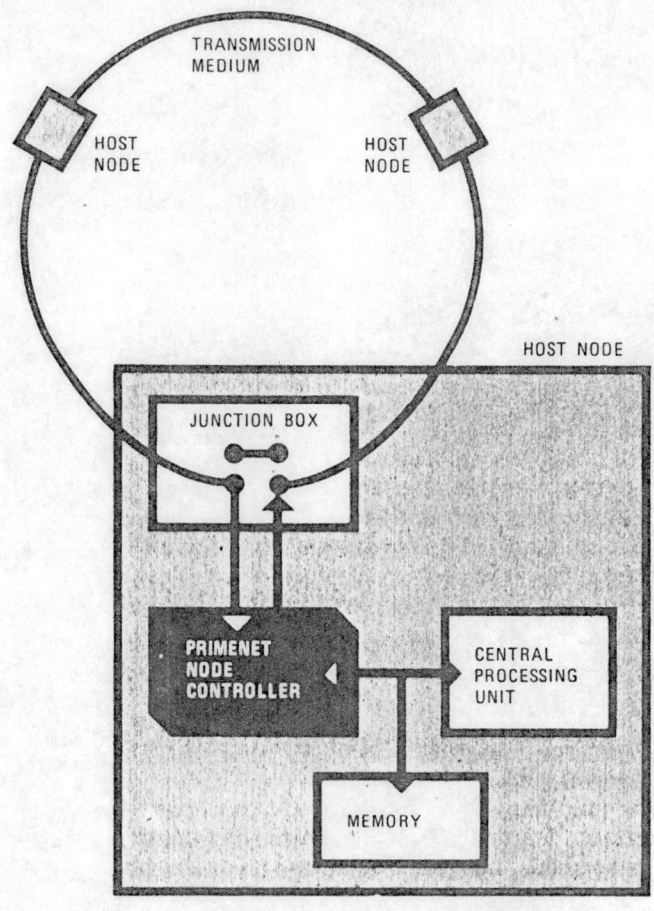

1. Typical setup. A Primenet node has a junction box that functions as the network interface. Its controller accepts packets addressed to the node.

rules for the token are simple. First, no node can put a message onto the network until it has the token. This means that only one node at a time actively puts data on the network. Second, only the node putting a message onto the network can remove the message. Every node, therefore, "sees" a message and has an opportunity to verify its integrity and its address. If a node is disassociated from the network (by the junction box or node controller), it simply does not see its message, and the sending node recognizes this because it does not receive a packet acknowledgment. Thus, the token provides decentralized control.

The token continually circles the ring network at 8 Mbit/s. A 0.35-microsecond delay at each node controller is caused by token and message regeneration. Each node controller transmits and receives every bit of every message and token. As part of this process, algorithms based on bit- and packet timing discover missing tokens or multiple tokens caused by malfunctioning hardware. These error conditions are automatically corrected in the node controller. Thus, they never interrupt user processing except when a node becomes completely inoperative.

Since a single token controls all the messages, data collision is impossible, eliminating the need for error-

Token or contention?

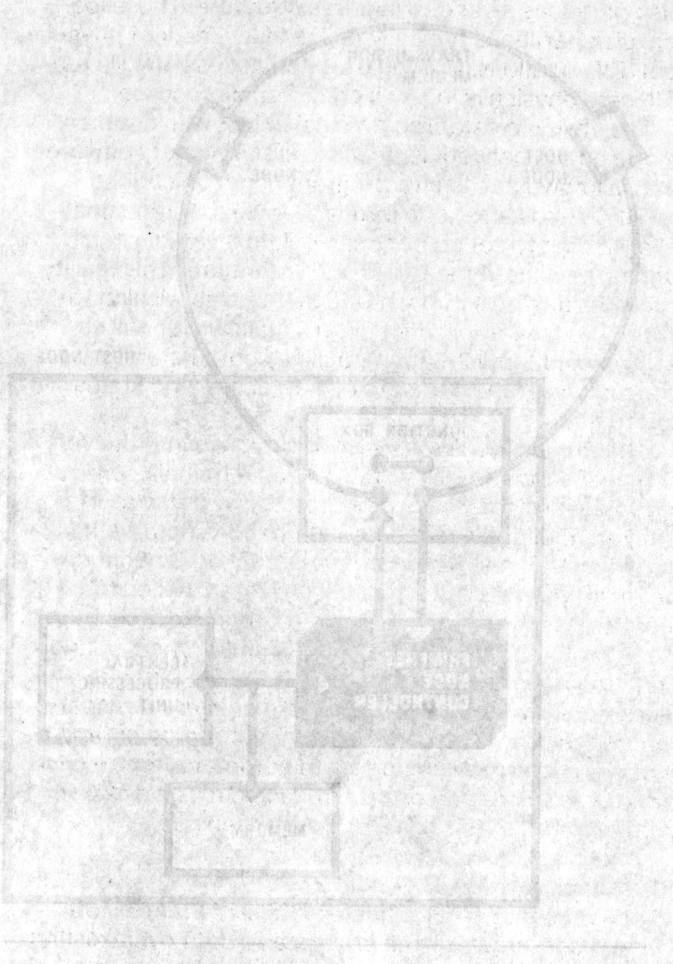

recovery procedures. Also, the ring network provides an environment in which individual nodes can be switched out of or into the network from both a logical (software) and a physical (junction box) standpoint. No major network modifications are needed.

Data travels on the ring in one direction after being formed into packets, using a frame structure similar to the CCITT's high-level data link control (HDLC) standard. Each message on the network is sent as one or more packets. A packet consists of a header, a data field, and a trailer, as shown in Figure 2, and varies in size from 4 bytes (header only) to 2,048 bytes. Only when the node controller has a packet ready for transmission and detects the token can it place its packet on the network.

Only part of the packet is actually presented to the host node. In this approach to ring-network design, part of the header and the entire trailer are managed by the node controller so there is no interruption to the host processor. This provides added efficiency and makes each node independent.

Although control of this network—which is called peer-coupled—is decentralized, each node can be configured by the network software to access the disks in any particular CPU operating on the ring. The level of sharing of these host files may be altered by the software as desired. This provides a network-security layer by limiting access to those users with authority to obtain restricted data.

Layered architecture

This local network's layered architecture, as illustrated in Figure 3, allows for a high degree of flexibility in both the type of software implemented and the variety of access to other network facilities. For example, the physical and data link layers, as well as the software services available in layers 3 and above of the International Standards Organization's open systems interconnection (OSI) standard (see "A long-awaited standard for heterogeneous nets," DATA COMMUNICATIONS, January, p. 63), combine to make Primenet transparent to the wide-area network capabilities of X.25 packet-switching networks, which are becoming increasingly popular among modern users.

As in other local networks, the software includes a transparent, remote-file facility or file-access manager. This program extends local functions of the primary

file to files residing on physical disks attached to other network nodes. It has the capability to establish distributed files within the ring network by utilizing logical disk partitions arranged in a tree structure. These logical disk partitions typically reside in a variety of physical disk locations. But the user can access any file as if it were physically located on his local processor.

The ability to establish a virtual circuit with another mode on the network is provided by Primenet software that is known as the interprogram communications facility. This is a set of subroutine-level programs that allow a user to set up and manipulate a virtual circuit under the rules in the CCITT X.25 standard. This facility provides an application interface for users wishing to distribute their application. Thus, it allows for call establishment, adjustment of facilities parameters, data transmission, and accumulation of usage and status information.

The Primenet software also includes an interactive terminal-support facility. This allows terminals connected to the ring to access other remote systems as if they were directly connected. It provides data paths for asynchronous terminals into a packet-network environment as well. The terminal services provided are easy to use since the only thing a user needs to know to log in to a system is the node's name. Once logged in to the node by means of the interactive terminal-support software, the layers of Primenet are transparent to the user, who can then concentrate on his application. This is most important in automated-office environments where personnel often have minimal skills in interacting with terminals or other machines.

Internetworking

Since Primenet is compatible with all of Prime's software, users can transmit and receive data over existing public data networks. This allows interconnection of any non-Prime processor operating on these networks. The Primenet series of remote-job-entry emulation packages allows communications with mainframes from a variety of vendors including Control Data Corporation, Honeywell, IBM, and Univac.

As local networks are more commonly used in computer installations, it will become critical to offer gateways to other types of networks. These other networks will undoubtedly include industry-standard and de facto-standard networks, servicing both wide and local

---

2. Inside the packet. Packets can vary in size from 4 to 2,048 bytes. Primenet packets, like those of other token-passing networks, contain header and trailer information straddling the data. The packet can be transmitted only from a node that has possession of the token. The token continually circulates around the network.

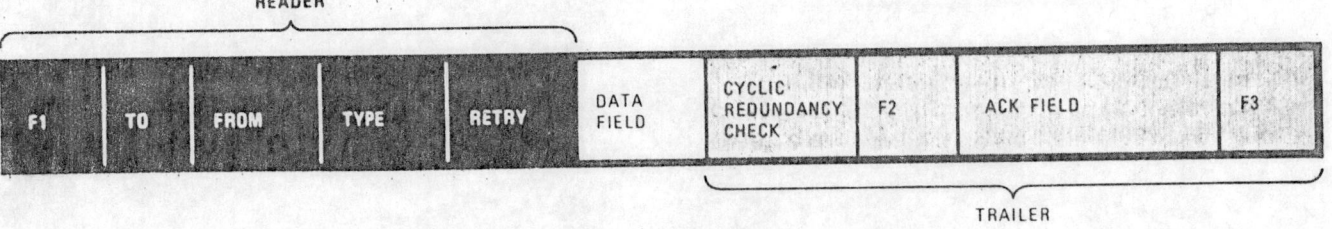

3. Layered architecture. *The hardware and software levels of the Primenet local network are modeled after the International Standards Organization's open systems interconnection standard. Thus, Primenet is compatible with X.25 packet-switching networks, and gateways can be established to other local networks when required.*

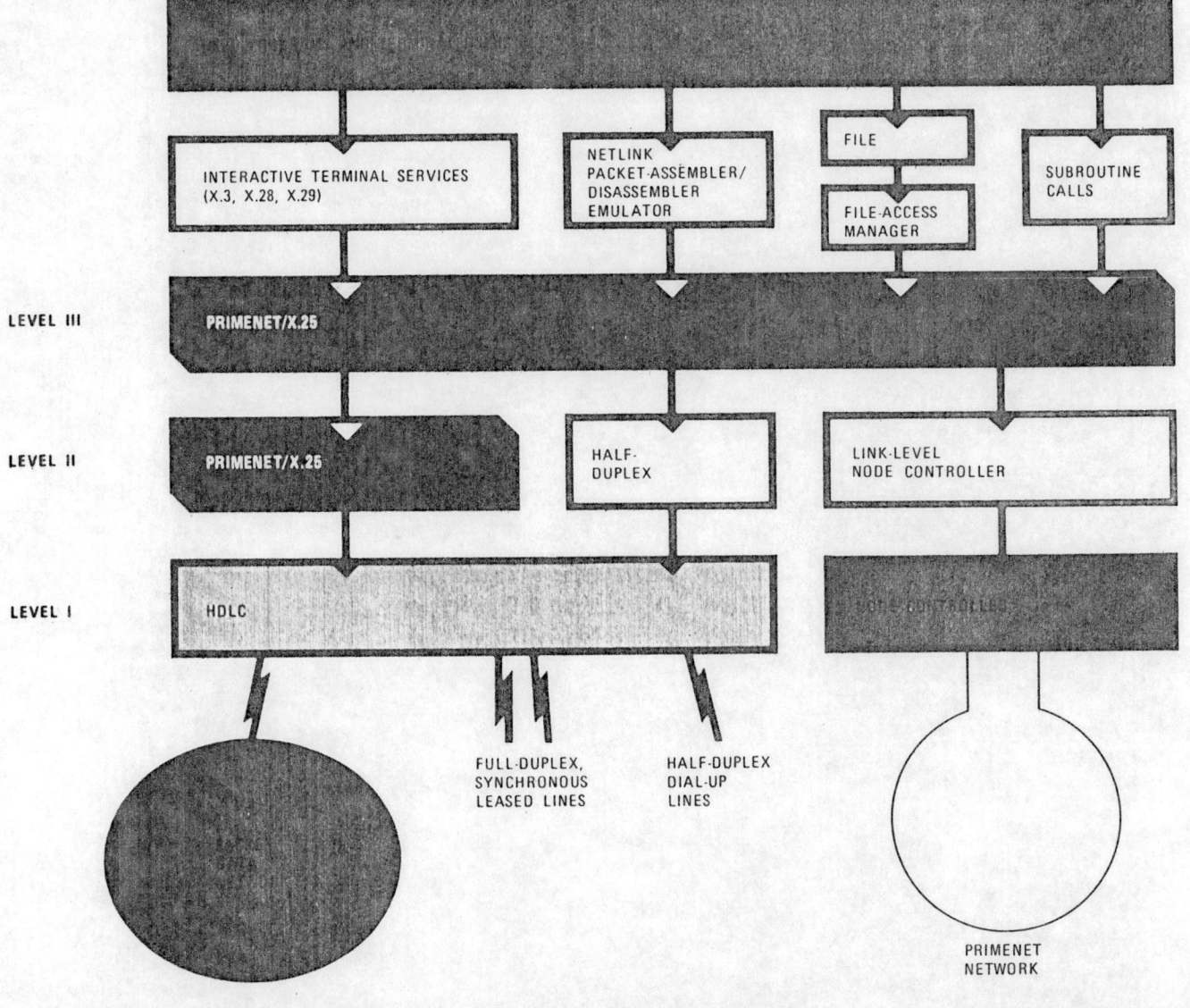

areas. As more and more networks become available for interconnection, the burden of handling the details in software will become too great, and some of the architectural layers will have to be handled in integrated hardware. Prime has already done this for Primenet, and other local-network manufacturers are increasing their use of integrated software.

An objection

One objection to ring networks is their sensitivity to distance and their complexity for interfacing. This is not an insurmountable problem. For example, the distance between active nodes on the Primenet can be 700 feet. And this can readily be extended. The easiest way is to place repeaters, which regenerate all signals on the coaxial cable, at the maximum distance points. The number of repeaters that can be placed between

active nodes depends primarily on the cable's electrical environment because repeaters amplify valid signals and noise without discrimination.

Another way to increase the distance between active nodes is to reduce the network data rate. This, of course, will affect overall network performance. Prime's experience has shown that several hundred feet can be gained at the cost of a few megabits in speed.

Finally, the ring distance can be increased by changing the transmission media used. Little has been done in this area because of the cost of components. But as the price of fiber-optic cable decreases, ring-based local networks may use this long-distance transmission technique. Many local-network manufacturers have begun experimenting with fiber to determine its capabilities for longer-distance, high-data-rate automated-office applications. ■

The microcomputer connection to local networks

Joe Malone, Nestar Systems Inc., Palo Alto, Calif.

Personal computers—as typified by the Apple—together with integrated software and a high-level language are the keystones of this 240-kbit/s local network.

High hardware costs and a lack of integrated software are two major barriers to widespread use of local networks in the business environment. By emphasizing low-cost hardware and a systems approach, some network manufacturers are breaking down these barriers without abandoning their original commitment to the development of flexible, high-function networks.

Sophistication in networking today is achieved through integrated-software development. In a network architecture, networking software is at the lowest level, high-level languages and the operating system are at the next-higher level, and the application software is at the highest level. Integrated software results in each level being transparent to all levels above and being able to embed in itself the next lower level. It makes all network resources available to application programs on a turnkey basis.

However, linking computers with integrated software in a network is no easy task. Communications software has inherent design problems. For example, although the Basic programming language is available for most microcomputers, a Basic program written to use a particular disk that runs on one microcomputer usually will not run on another. Microcomputer manufacturers implement different dialects of the Basic language, using interpreters specially designed for their particular machines. (Interpreters are programs that read other programs and carry out their instructions.) Consequently, application programs written for network use must be replicated or reworked to accommodate each type of computer that will use the network—at considerable cost in development time.

Network manufacturers are attempting to produce competitively priced components that can handle high-level languages and operating systems and can share mass storage and expensive peripherals. To some extent, this can be achieved using simple application programs. These networking programs are becoming common and, for some business applications, are all that is required for use on the network.

For some business users, in fact, the only "network" needed is a collection of communications peripherals or terminals sharing a printer and disk, or a timesharing minicomputer and a collection of dumb terminals. Other networks, like Nestar Systems Cluster/One Model A, are built for business applications that take advantage of an integrated computing/communications environment, with application programs written to fill specific needs.

Companies that want to add more and more applications to their networks must first make the choices that center around cost. Sophisticated software appropriate for the office environment does not necessarily require high-end hardware. In fact, much networking hardware today is wasted: The user will never need the speed available.

A network built around personal computers (typically 8-bit machines with 64 kbytes of memory) has a set of cost goals and decisions different from a larger computer network's. The network hardware and software

1. An Apple "tree." *Each personal computer in the Nestar local network is independent and can function as a standalone workstation. The operating system may be* *Apple DOS, Apple Pascal, or CP/M. Some of the microcomputers function as file- or print servers. Network topologies may be straight-line bus, star, tree, and daisy-chain.*

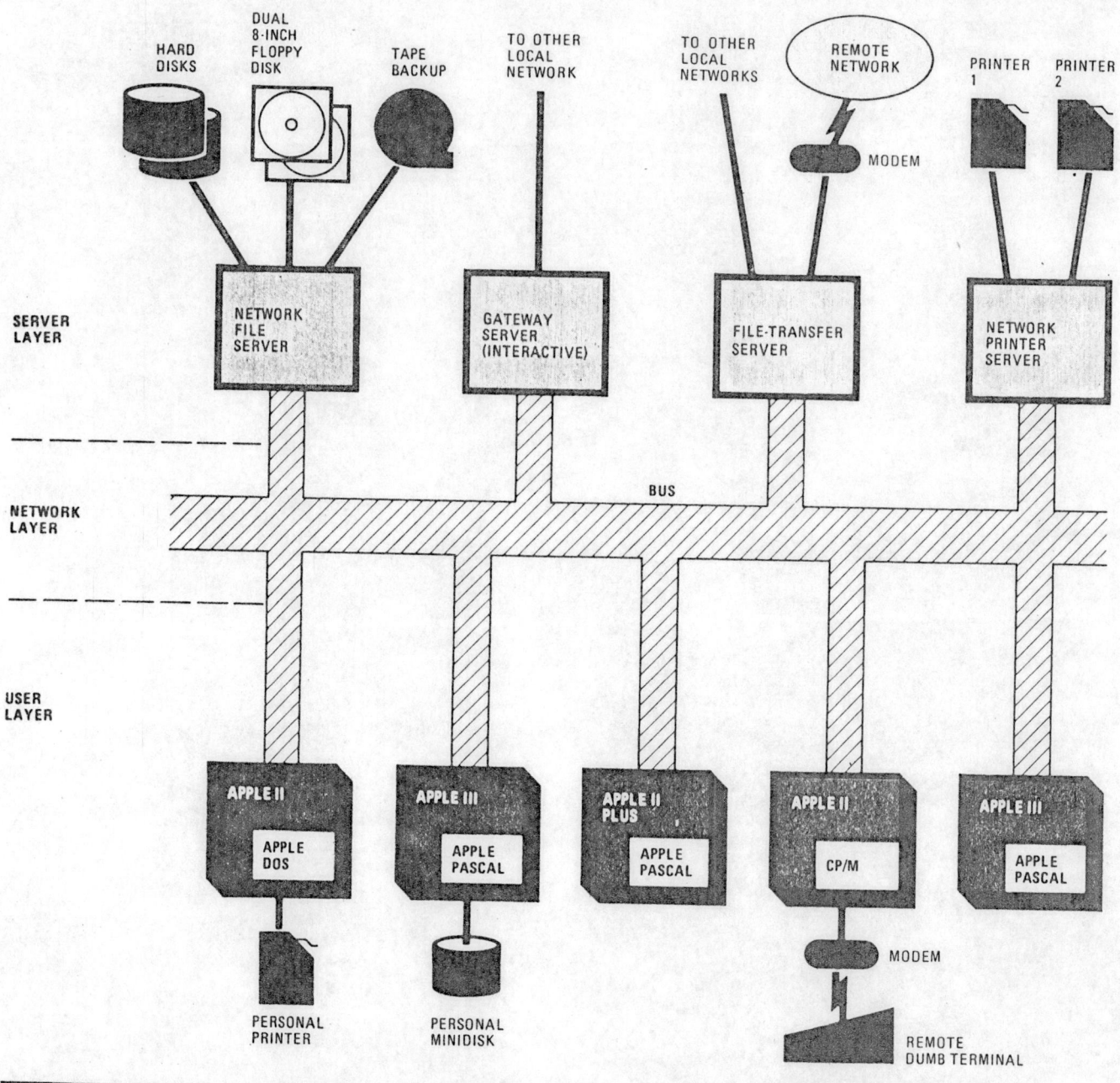

must be designed to cost much less than the personal computers themselves, while network speed and bandwidth must support the personal computer tasks.

These cost and performance factors lead naturally to the choice of simple, programmable hardware for interfacing chores, with most of an interface unit's function executed in software. If the network's software base is adequate, such a network is appropriate for use in office environments that require graphics and text processing, the automation of simple tasks, and strong interstation communications.

Nestar's Cluster/One Model A network is built

around as many as 65 Apple microcomputers (Fig. 1). Some function as user workstations; others are dedicated as file or print servers. The operating system may be Apple DOS, Apple Pascal, or CP/M from Digital Research, Pacific Grove, Calif. User Apples share mass storage and printers, but each machine is independent and can function as a standalone workstation, using its own minidisk drives and printers. The failure of any machine will not bring down the network. (Figure 1 does not show remote modems, which are assumed to be part of the remote interfacing devices.)

Stations are connected by 16-wire cable (flat ribbon,

twisted pairs, or round shielded bundle) and can be configured in any sequence and topology spanning 1,000 feet without repeaters. The addition of repeaters every 1,000 feet permits a total length of 3,000 feet. Straight-line bus, star, tree, and daisy-chain topologies are allowed. The fastest data transmission speed that can be used with these topologies is 240 kbit/s.

Each workstation accesses the cable through a printed-circuit interface card that contains network bus drivers, RAM (random-access-memory) buffers, and ROM (read-only-memory) code. This code is executed by the station's CPU to access the network. With an interface card in an I/O slot, commands that would ordinarily be sent to a local peripheral by the machine's operating system are sent instead to another, dedicated, Apple that receives the I/O commands and, for example, accesses a hard disk instead of a local floppy. This implementation of "virtual I/O" helps make the network transparent to users.

Design decisions
Cluster/One is Ethernet-like in its philosophy: It is a baseband network using carrier-sense multiple access with collision detection (CSMA/CD). The Apple was selected because it was judged the most economical and dependable off-the-shelf model.

The network file servers each support two 33-Mbyte hard disks and dual 8-inch floppy-disk drives. High-density streaming (continuous-loop) cartridge-tape drives, driven by Nestar software, are used for backup.

When a user-station Apple is turned on, the auto-start ROM on the computer's main circuit board searches the machine's peripheral slots for disk-controller cards. The Nestar interface card, disguised as a controller card, is discovered, and the Apple transfers control to it. The interface card notifies a designated file-server Apple on the network that the station is active, and a program is bootstrap-loaded (self-loaded and automatically sequenced) into the station's RAM.

User's choices
The loaded program is specified in a network file that contains a profile of each user station. Such profiles allow automatic startup of user-application programs. The default program allows the user to key in the name of the program to be loaded by identifying the virtual disk on the file-server disk to be bootstrapped. In this way, the user can also choose the local operating-system environment to be loaded.

The file server's shared hard disks and floppy disks are organized into a collection of directories and virtual disks. These may be bootstrap-loaded and are formatted for use in the operating systems available to Apple users. Virtual disks are created, "mounted," named and renamed, and otherwise manipulated using an application program executed from the local operating system. In this way, network operations are transparent to the user. Because network application programs and operations are accomplished via high-level languages, the user does not have to penetrate more than one level of software to reach his data.

When bootstrap-loading from a virtual disk, the network loads the required language and operating software into the local machine and follows any startup (HELLO) program instructions on the disk. If the disk is a DOS Basic type, for example, a Basic prompt will appear on the screen, just as with a standalone terminal. The local machine can then mount up to 255 variable-size (virtual) disks at multiple file servers, and code files, text files, and binary data on them can be accessed. Cluster/One currently supports up to 66 Mbytes of hard-disk memory per file server and up to six printers per print server. An arbitrary number of file servers and print servers may be used on a single network. The print server may be connected to multiple, separate networks.

In turnkey applications, both network and operating-system software must be transparent. In Cluster/One, at power on, network and operating-system bootstrap programs read files that may contain preset auto-startup instructions. The application program will then be downloaded into the machine automatically.

Security and the maintenance of data integrity are provided through a series of cooperative locks, password options, and the auto-start capability. Additionally, users can encrypt data at their stations before sending it to a file server. Application programs such as Visicalc (from Personal Software Inc., Sunnyvale, Calif.) and DB Master (from Stoneware Microcomputer Products, San Rafael, Calif.) are adapted to utilize network virtual I/O, which allows shared read-only and exclusive read/write access.

Electronic mail
Interstation communications, within a network and between networks, uses application programs written in Pascal. Electronic talk (terminal-to-terminal chat), staff scheduling, telephone messages, and interoffice and internetwork mail programs are examples. The Messenger, Nestar's electronic-mail program, is executed from the Pascal operating system. The user sends and receives workstation messages, files them according to class, forwards and answers them, and writes them to files or directs them to printers.

The network accomplishes this by creating and deleting files on the shared hard disks (Fig. 2). When a user composes and sends a message, the mail program creates a new mail file on a hard disk. This file contains the body of the message, preceded by a header with information such as the date and time the message was composed, the sender, the subject, and the recipient. When the recipient checks for new mail, the network reads the newly created file and places its contents in the workstation buffer. The message can then be filed, written to a permanent file, printed, forwarded, answered, or otherwise manipulated.

Modular software
Once created, the software that sends and receives messages exists as a module to be used over the network in various other application programs. In the same way, other modules are written, such as a "menu I/O" unit that causes a list of choices to be displayed to the user and input from the user to be accepted when var-

2. Carrying the electronic mail. *Interstation communications uses application programs written in Pascal. The user sends and receives messages, files them according to class, forwards and answers them, and writes them to files or directs them to printers. The network creates and deletes files on the shared hard disks.*

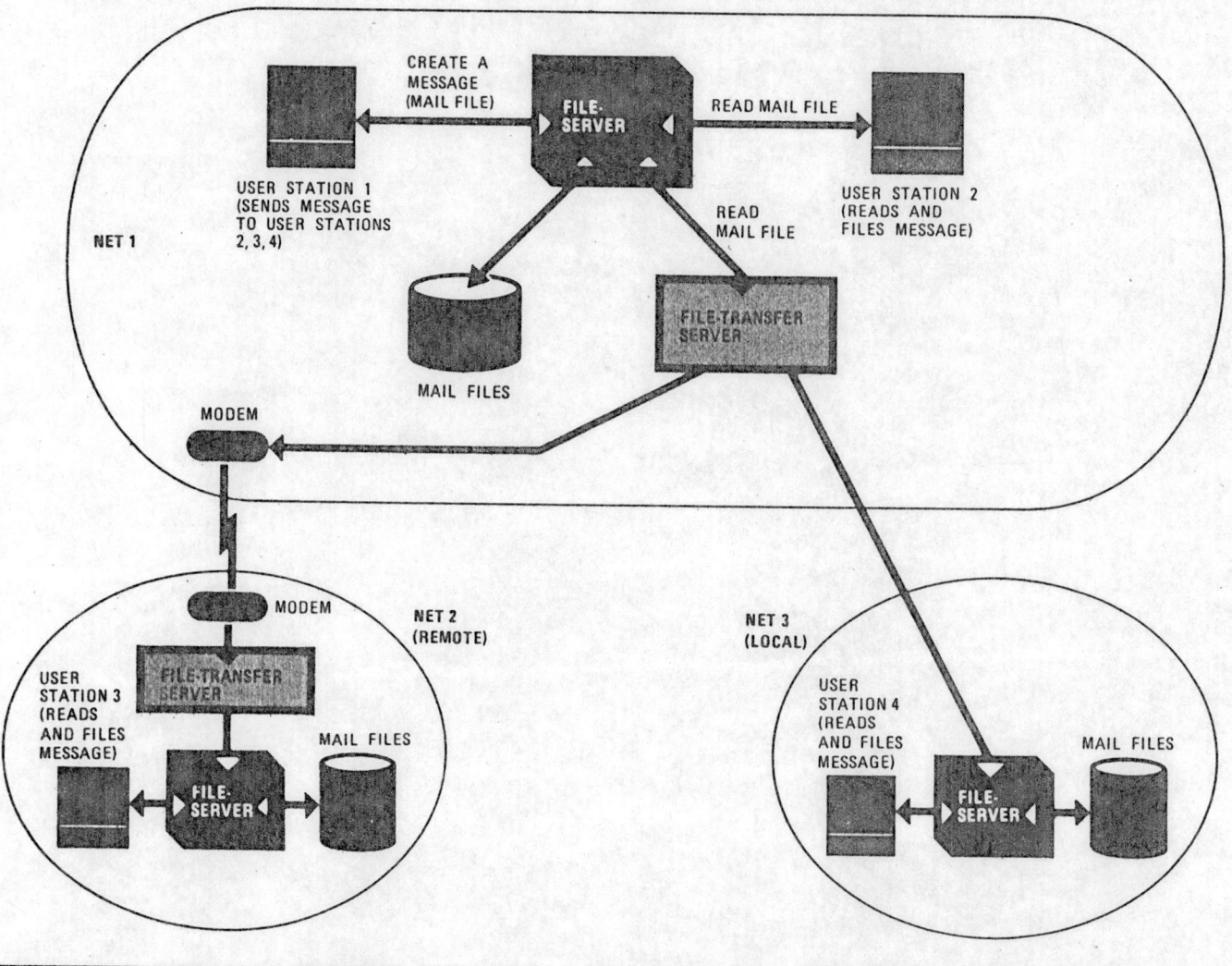

lous application programs are run. As the number of such available modules increases, the time spent to create new programs decreases.

There are two prerequisites for maximum modular program development: (1) network software that allows network transactions to be generated by a high-level operating system and (2) workstation machines sufficiently alike and sophisticated (with enough RAM and using a high-level language such as Pascal) to accommodate the software without being modified.

Nestar maintains a developmental multinetwork that currently links three networks at the company's Palo Alto facility with three networks at Zynar Inc., in Uxbridge, England, and a network at Morris Decision Systems, in New York City. The only additional hardware required for this implementation is a pair of comparatively inexpensive modems or acoustic couplers for the Uxbridge and New York connections. Remote dumb terminals (keyboards and screens) can also access assigned user stations via modems.

The networks interface in several ways. Application programs that rely on the manipulation of message and request files to transfer information between terminals operate as if on a single network: An Apple dedicated as a file-transfer server (FTS), connected to the three local networks, transfers the files from a file server/hard disk on one network to the file server on another. In this way, print requests and internetwork mail, for example, can move from one network to another. In a second, similar implementation, two FTS Apples communicate over the phone to exchange mail and other text and code files.

Interactive modes of interstation communications require a gateway server—a dedicated Apple running a packet-transfer program that moves transmissions between user stations on one network and file-server Apples on another. The gateway server handles digital data in real time. The user changes, by command, the server to which his network messages are sent. Instead of the file servers on his own network, he uses those of another. Of course, each network's password and locking security remain in force. ∎

247

A low-speed local net for under $100 per station

Robert Bosen, Zeda Computers International Ltd., Provo, Utah

If 25 kbit/s is fast enough for your applications, this local network—implemented around small business computers—may provide a solution.

Most publicity about local networks has been generated about the high end of the spectrum. Although Xerox Corporation's Ethernet, Wang Laboratories' Wangnet, and Network Systems Corporation's Hyperchannel enjoy the limelight, they are impossible to implement without expensive, exotic hardware.

Most of the expense and exotic techniques are made necessary by the very high speeds of these networks. In many cases, these networks' data rates actually exceed the internal, maximum, parallel data-transfer rates of the computers connected to them. A lower-speed, low-cost approach to local networks is sorely needed to enable microcomputer users to interconnect multiple systems at a more appropriate cost.

There will, of course, be a need for interfacing small, low-speed local networks with bigger, high-performance networks when the latter become available, just as it will be advantageous to link high-speed networks to international packet-switching networks for long-distance communications. But low-cost networks will always be sought to serve small businesses, educational institutions, and personal computer users.

One such network is Infinet, a common-bus, carrier-sense multiple-access with collision-detection (CSMA/CD) network vaguely resembling Ethernet but implemented at lower cost and with lower-speed hardware. It allows low-cost microcomputers to replace more expensive timesharing minicomputers by distributing workloads among inexpensive devices, each having access to large databases. Most important, such a network can be built for less than $100.

Infinet is currently implemented only on Zeda Computers International's small business computers, but its architectural concepts and low-end approach are applicable to nearly all microcomputer systems.

With the technology available today, the speed of data exchange on a local network has a significant impact on cost and reliability. Speeds beyond about 100 kHz are difficult to reach with low-cost MOS serial interface chips familiar to most microcomputer users, and speeds above about 1 MHz are unreachable even with exotic communications chips. Beyond a few MHz, the problem is compounded at both ends of the interface. Even with direct-memory-access (DMA) techniques, most microcomputers cannot supply or receive data fast enough to keep up with the network. Higher speeds also tend to be less reliable than their low-speed counterparts.

Speed also has an adverse effect on cable length—and therefore on the range of a network. As cable length increases, capacitance and propagation delay increase, resulting in the need for costly line drivers. Collision detection becomes more difficult at high speeds: If a network cable's end-to-end propagation delay exceeds a resolvable unit time (such as a byte-time), a collision occurring in the middle of the cable will go undetected. This can happen because the post-collision signal cannot return to its source before the unit time has expired. The limit in maximum cable length places restrictions on multiple-building or expansive single-building installations.

On the other hand, a data communications network

248

that operates too slowly for a given application is of no use. So network speed must be achieved by way of compromise. In cost-sensitive applications, the ideal network speed is kept as low as possible to do the job at hand. Looking at it another way, "fast enough" becomes the key phrase.

With regard to network size and its effect on speed requirements, Figure 1 points out that costs make local networks with many stations impractical when compared with modern timesharing minicomputers and multiple remote terminals. A ballpark estimate is that local networks offer advantages over timesharing minicomputers in installations of from 2 to 16 workstations. Interestingly, it is expected that most multiuser installations implemented within the next 10 years will fall within these limits.

Preamble
Designed around a multispeed philosophy, Infinet (Fig. 2) has a minimum data rate of 25 kbit/s. The protocols require all communications to be contained within packets and all packets, regardless of length and final data rate, to begin with a preamble of nine character times at 25 kbit/s.

This nine-character-time preamble and the remaining parts of a packet comprise the following fields (Fig. 3):

0 through 1	Break character marks beginning of each packet
2 through 4	Three-byte destination address
5 through 7	Three-byte source address
8	Command byte: any 8 bits for arbitrary use
9	Length of data field (in bytes)
10 up to 1st checksum	Data field: as many bytes as desired containing data to be delivered to destination
Last 2 characters	16-bit checksum character

By mutual agreement, any two stations can utilize the command byte to switch to a higher data rate or lengthen a packet's data field. So, although the basic Infinet can drive a 5-kilometer cable, and all packet communications is established with nine character times at 25 kbit/s, individual applications can control the speed versus cost versus distance trade-offs to increase the effective communications rate whenever appropriate.

Do's and don'ts
Certain rules exist for the orderly use of the network cable. For example, Infinet does not allow any packet to exceed 125 milliseconds in length. This prevents any one station from becoming a bus hog. Also, no new packet can be placed on the cable until 16 bit-times of silence have followed the previous packet.

A single exception to this is when a receiving station wishes to acknowledge proper receipt of a packet from a transmitter. It can place up to three characters of data on the bus immediately after receipt of the last character of the packet, without waiting for the cable to become available to the other stations on the net-

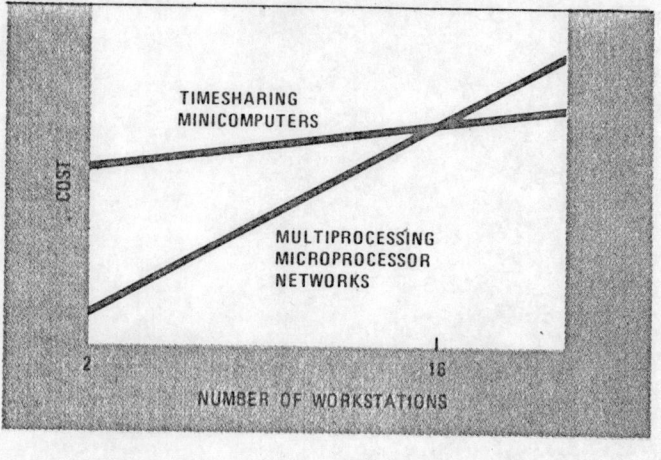

1. Costs. *A good estimate of the breakeven, or crossover, point in this comparison is approximately 16 workstations. Between 2 and 30 nodes can be configured.*

work. In this way, pack acknowledgment (or lack of it) can be added to a data exchange without the delays inherent in cable arbitration and collision resolution.

The basic packet format of data exchanged (Fig. 3) begins by placing the bus in a break condition for from 16 to 24 bit times. Destination and source addresses follow, along with packet control, length, and data fields. The last 2 bytes consist of a checksum character, which is the 16-bit sum of all preceding fields except the break.

Two character times are available immediately after transmission of a packet for the single addressee to respond with an acknowledgment. ACK acknowledges receipt and HOLD indicates that the packet was received and discarded because the application program is not ready for it. The lack of an acknowledgment indicates a reception error.

Standard
Infinet incorporates the lowest three levels of the International Standards Organization's open systems interconnection model in the following manner:

1. *The physical layer* of Infinet consists of a single twisted-pair cable, not longer than 5 kilometers, interconnecting all Infinet transceivers in parallel. Differential voltage levels on the cable conform to the conventions of RS-422. Characters are placed on the cable in UART (universal asynchronous receive transmit) fashion by LSI circuits using 1 star bit, 8 data bits, and 1 stop bit per character.

2. *The data link layer* is responsible for the construction of packets. This layer accepts data from higher levels, delivers formatted packets to the physical layer, and awaits acknowledgments. When receiving, this layer receives and acknowledges formatted packets from the physical layer, removes framing information, and delivers the contents of the data field to higher levels. Programs implementing this layer of Infinet have been embedded into CP/M (control program/monitor)-compatible operating systems. Such operating systems are widely employed by microcomputer users.

3. *The network layer* divides outgoing messages into packet-sized data fields and assembles incoming data fields into complete messages for higher levels. Several utility programs for transmission of disk files, printing files, and sharing disk drives are available for Infinet at this level.

Direct coupling

Infinet uses National Semiconductor's 8250 serial communications to interface directly with the microprocessor bus for parallel data transfers. The 8250 also provides serial I/O for connection with the network cable through its driving and detection circuits.

Detection of network-free and network-break conditions is accomplished by a pair of binary 16-bit counters, clocked at 25 kbit/s. One counter counts sequential 1s on the bus, and the other counts sequential 0s. Overflow of the 1s counter generates a network-free

interrupt, while overflow of the 0s counter generates a "break" interrupt.

The 8250 is programmed to pass these interrupts to the processor for service. Collision detection is accomplished by transmitting stations, which monitor their own transmissions and compare received data with transmitted data on a character-by-character basis. Any differences are interpreted as a collision. The 8250 allows different data rates by dividing the processor clock by programmable register values. This is done in two steps. First, the 8250 hardware performs an initial divide by 16, then it divides this quotient by the value of a programmable register. The basic 25-kbit/s data rate is attainable by dividing the 2-MHz CPU clock rate by 16 (inside the 8250), and then by 5. All popular central-processing-unit clock rates can be divided by simple counters and divisors to achieve the desired 25-kbit/s rate. ∎

2. UART and the microprocessor. *In the Infinet local network, the UART interfaces with the microprocessor, and the cable connects directly to it. The LSI circuit provides multiple data rates. Infinet has been implemented on a board that plugs into Zeda computers, but the design can be applied to machines. The unit costs under $100.*

3. Simple. *An Infinet cable directs RS-422-compatible logic to all parallel stations. Data is formatted into packets beginning with a break condition of from 16 to 24 bit times. Destination source addresses, command and length bytes, data, and checksums follow. Stations acknowledge a packet with a 3-byte message.*

250

Net/One's answer to packet and circuit switching

John M. Davidson, Ungermann-Bass, Santa Clara, Calif.

Ungermann-Bass's approach to local networking is flexibility. Its Net/One offers users both virtual-circuit and datagram schemes.

Data communications equipment is divided into two camps: intelligent and nonintelligent devices. Net/One is a local network that provides communications services for both kinds of devices. It does so at two levels, with a virtual-circuit and a datagram service.

The virtual-circuit service provides a means for dumb devices (such as teletypewriters) to exchange byte streams with other dumb devices in the network. Intelligent devices (such as hosts) can take advantage of the virtual-circuit service too. Datagram service provides the means for an intelligent device to exchange information packets with any collection of other intelligent devices in the network. Net/One consists of a single coaxial cable and from 2 to 100 network interface units (NIUs) placed at arbitrary locations along the cable (Fig. 1). The NIUs are essentially packet-switching computers.

They transmit on shared coaxial cable at 10 Mbit/s according to the DEC — Intel — Xerox Ethernet specifications. NIUs may be scaled to provide from 4 to 16 RS-232-C ports and from 2 to 8 parallel ports. Their means of gaining access to the shared cable is through a carrier-sense multiple-access/collision-detection (CSMA/CD) scheme. Both IEEE-488 and Digital Equipment Company (DEC) DR11-W interfaces are also available now, and others, such as RS-449, will be added in the future. Individual Net/One segments may be joined in an internetworking arrangement by gateway processors. All protocols employ internetwork headers to allow for needed future extensions.

Within Net/One, virtual circuits are implemented by software that switches packets of data on the shared cable. Although the physical end-points of the virtual-circuit service appear to the user to be devices, the logical end-points are actually processes (asynchronous software tasks that share the CPU) within the respective NIUs. These software processes control the devices at both the source and the destination sites.

Using software-controlled processes as the end-points for virtual circuits provides flexibility of service. For example, since process end-points can be individually tailored to accept or reject connection attempts, various types of access controls can be placed on a particular device. The use of processes also allows devices to establish circuits to services, as well as to other devices, so that as the local network grows, new services will be available to users.

Net/One provides three separate ways of establishing circuits:

- Direct command
- Implicit commands
- Administrative command

Direct command requires a software process to implement the functions of a command interpreter. Devices served by this process can issue commands directing it to open a connection to any remote device.

Interactive terminals are served by the direct-command-interpreter process so users can switch conversations among several destination devices. However, computers too can be served by the direct-command-interpreter process. This allows programs to command

251

1. Single cable. *Net/One's latest implementation relies on a single coaxial cable as the transmission medium and utilizes intelligent interface units as its logical backbone.*

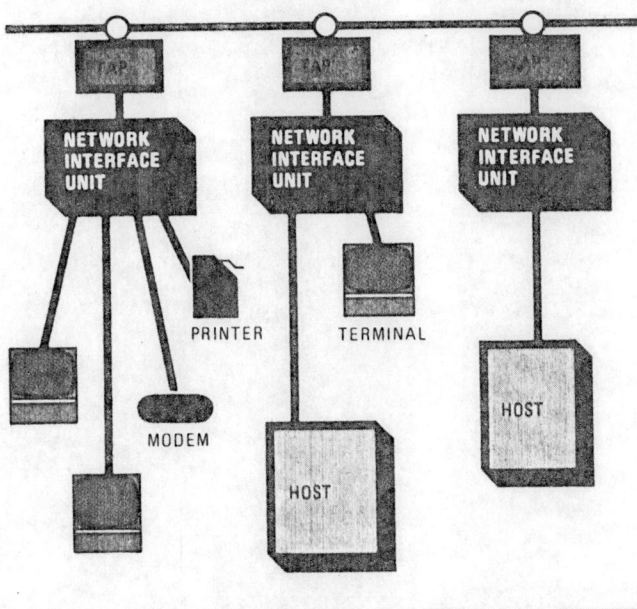

connection to various network devices (typically printers). Individual devices need the command-interpreter process only for placing outgoing "calls." If the device wants to receive incoming calls, it issues a command to the interpreter telling it to listen for a connection attempt. The device can resurrect the command-interpreter at any time by issuing another command.

Implicit commands require a software process that interprets circuit set-up information down-line loaded into the NIU when it is powered-on. Table entries in each NIU define which circuits should be created when that NIU is initialized. The process attempts to create these circuits and persists until they are completed.

One type of table entry describes a permanent circuit that is, in effect, a "wire replacement." The circuits are permanent only when the table entries in the NIU remain unchanged. Tools for changing the table entries associated with each NIU are provided to the network administrator through a utility program.

Other types of table entries describe initial and demand circuits. An initial circuit is created just like a permanent circuit, but it can be broken once it has served its purpose. Initial circuits are used generally to provide default connections for users who seldom need to establish connections to other devices. A demanded circuit is bound to a particular point but is created only when needed (for example, when a device is powered up or when a dial-up modem is answered). Demanded circuits take the place of permanent circuits when resource conservation is important.

A third type of virtual circuit can be dynamically created. Facilities are provided in the administrating NIU to connect or disconnect two arbitrary remote devices, as required, by simple commands.

Virtual circuits can be terminated in three ways: voluntarily, when either end decides to disconnect; invol-

untarily, when the network administrator commands a disconnect; and involuntarily, when the connection becomes inoperative.

A circuit may be voluntarily terminated whenever the device at either end of the circuit issues a "disconnect sequence"—an arbitrary string of from one to four characters—to its NIU.

The use of a disconnect sequence is mandated for compatibility with existing devices. Ideally, an out-of-band signal or special disconnect key would be provided on interactive devices so that users could unambiguously indicate their desire to close the connection, but such special functions (aside from artifacts like the "break" key, which is supported incidentally) are not generally available on most peripheral devices.

However, the character sequences associated with the special function keys available on many CRTs can be defined as disconnect sequences to give the effect of a disconnect key. Devices may also employ RS-232-C signals to indicate their desire to disconnect.

Devices using the command-interpreter process may redefine their disconnect sequence for each session so that one sequence can be used for different connections. Although the sequence is generally used only for a disconnect, techniques are provided for actually sending the characters of a disconnect sequence through the circuit when they occur as real data.

The second method of terminating circuits is by a special command from the network administrator. This has the effect of making each party think the other has hung up, forcing each to itself hang up.

Finally, circuits are terminated if either NIU involved in a connection "disappears." This may be due to an error condition, a reinitialization of an NIU (power-down or manual or remote reset), or a relocation or reloading of an NIU. The session or administrative circuits are closed for good; permanent circuits are re-established as soon as both NIUs are functional again.

Protocol

Net/One's virtual-circuit protocol (VCP) is used to carry data between the processes that serve as the endpoints of an external circuit.

VCP's flow-control algorithms automatically govern the rate at which either process can send data to the other. However, because the ultimate source and destination of the data is usually the devices to which the processes are attached, flow control between the two processes is not always sufficient to ensure a complete end-to-end transmission.

The reason for this is that data can be lost unless the source process can keep the source device from overrunning it with data. This requires some form of flow control between the source device and the source processing cases where devices' data bursts can exceed the buffering capacity of the virtual circuit.

Net/One uses several industry-standard flow-control techniques. An example is the X-on/X-off character strategy that a receiving party may use to turn on and off the other party's transmissions. As the receiver's buffers become full, the receiver sends an X-off character to its counterpart, telling it to suspend transmis-

sion. When space again becomes available, it sends an X-on. Many devices currently employ this kind of simple flow-control mechanism. Other types of flow control involve the manipulation of RS-232-C signals supported by the NIU.

Naming

Each device and each process-oriented service in Net/One can be given a name or an alias. These names are used in connection establishment. Connection end-points are specified by name in both user commands (for session-oriented circuits) and administrator commands (for administrative circuits). Names and aliases may be any arbitrary string of ASCII characters, such as "Unix port," "Tod's terminal," or "second-floor printer."

If two or more devices are assigned to the same name, a connection request specifying this name as an end-point will result in a connection to the first available named device. Such a "rotoring" capability is useful when equivalent services are available through a number of distinct NIU ports, as is the case for access to a timesharing host (see Fig. 2). Devices can be given both rotored and unique names. Whenever a rotored name is employed to establish a connection, a unique name is reported to the initiating device (user or administrator) in the event it later wants to re-establish its connection to the same port.

Name lookup employs a broadcast protocol. Each NIU maintains only a portion of the total name database—normally only the names that are associated with its own attached devices.

Datagram service

Besides providing virtual-circuit service for devices that send and receive bytes, Net/One provides a datagram service. Hosts that can implement their own protocols on top of the datagram service—including virtual-circuit strategies of their own—for talking among themselves. Examples of packet-switching hosts that might take advantage of this service are the Department of Defense (DOD) Arpanet hosts and Digital Equipment Corporation's (DEC) Decnet hosts.

The goal of the datagram service is to appear to hosts exactly like a shared-broadcast medium, with the following simplifications: (1) host datagrams are not subject to collisions, (2) host data rates do not need to be identical, and (3) hosts can employ conventional serial or parallel interfaces to send and receive their packets.

The datagram service requires the host to follow a simple datagram protocol (SDP) that causes the host to append a Net/One internet header to the front of any packet it sends (see "Virtual- and Circuit Datagram Protocol"). The header contains addressing information used by the NIU to select a route for the packet to traverse. The addressing information allows the host to invoke broadcast, multicast, or point-to-point routing strategies for its packets. When given special privileges, hosts are permitted to send packets to NIUs, as well as to other hosts.

SDP does not guarantee reliable delivery of host

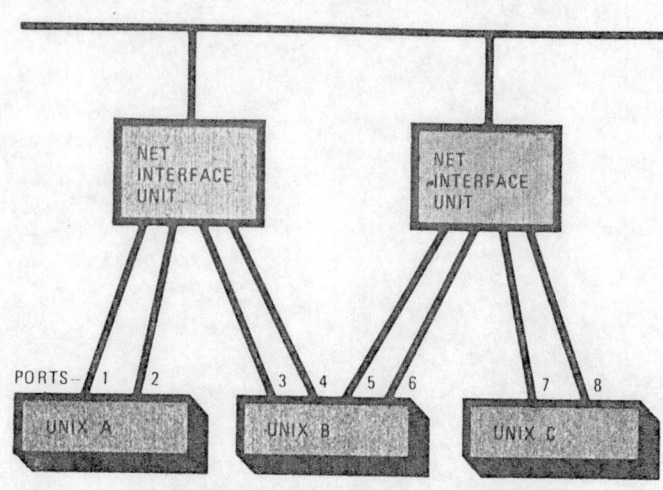

2. Names. *This kind of rotored naming system allows flexibility in information paths. For example, if port 8 is operating at 19.2 kbit/s, it can be called "high port."*

USING THESE NAMES,	YOU WILL GET ONE OF THESE PORTS							
	1	2	3	4	5	6	7	8
UNIX	●	●	●	●	●	●	●	●
UNIX A	●	●						
UNIX B			●	●	●	●		
UNIX C							●	●
UNIX A, TTY 1	●							
UNIX A, TTY 2		●						
UNIX B, TTY 1			●					
UNIX B, TTY 2				●				
UNIX B, TTY 3					●			
UNIX B, TTY 4						●		
UNIX C, TTY 1							●	
UNIX C, TTY 2								●

packets—just as a real cable does not guarantee error-free delivery of NIU packets. But in the normal course of events, the only errors that can affect reliable delivery of packets are real transmission errors and a deficiency of receive buffers at a destination host or NIU. Collisions are resolved by the NIU hardware, just as for any other type of packet entering the network.

Interestingly, although the channel presented to the user actually operates on a CSMA/CD network, the datagram service can be tailored to emulate other techniques for access control.

The datagram service is available to hosts via RS-232-C; 8-, 16-, and 32-bit parallel; DEC DR11-W-compatible; and IEEE 488 interfaces; a shared-memory interface is also possible for processors that can be tied to the NIU's internal bus. Since serial and parallel devices are commonly managed by existing host operating systems and are thus available to host application programs, the use of packet protocols is made available to user applications, and no major modifications to existing operating systems are necessary. For exam-

Virtual-circuit and datagram protocols

VCP was developed as a transport-layer protocol consistent with the International Standards Organization's open systems interconnection (OSI) model. The challenge for VCP is to provide as much functionality as possible without limiting the processing capabilities of the Z80 processors on which it executes.

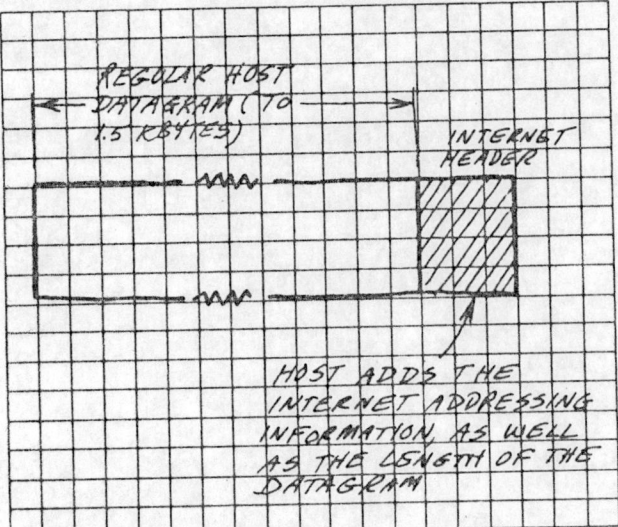

Unlike the Department of Defense's standard transmission control protocol (TCP), VCP sequences packets of bytes and not the bytes themselves. This reduces the per-packet processing overhead. In designing the Net/One local and internet headers, the trade-off

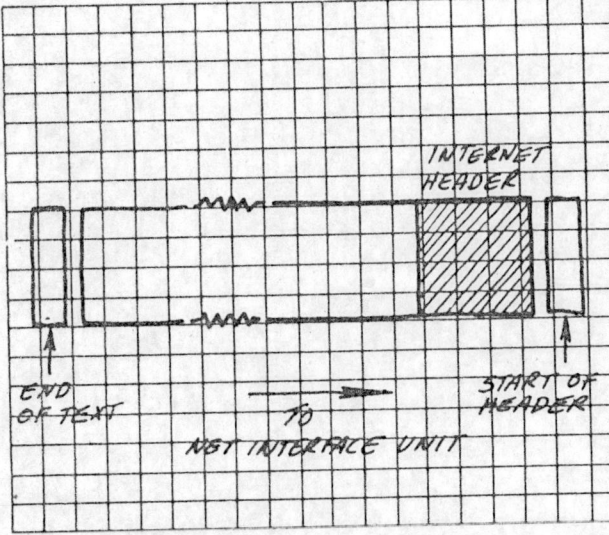

between channel efficiency and processor efficiency was always made in favor of the latter. Thus, per-port end-to-end data rates of up to 19.2 kbit/s are possible with the virtual circuit service.

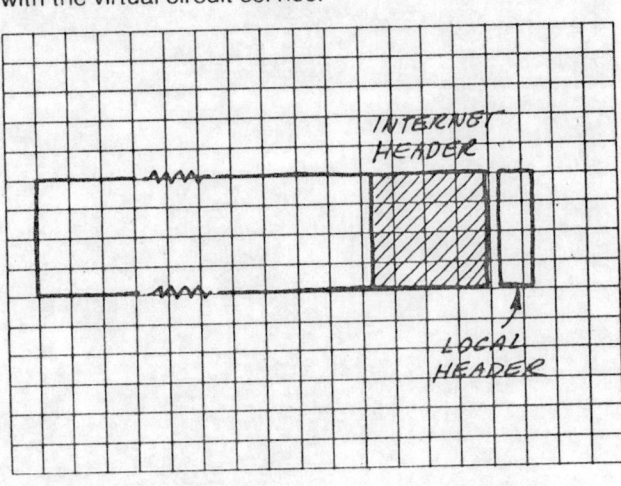

Datagrams. Hosts using SDP send internet packets just like those used by VCP. But hosts need only specify the internet header—the NIU appends a local header.

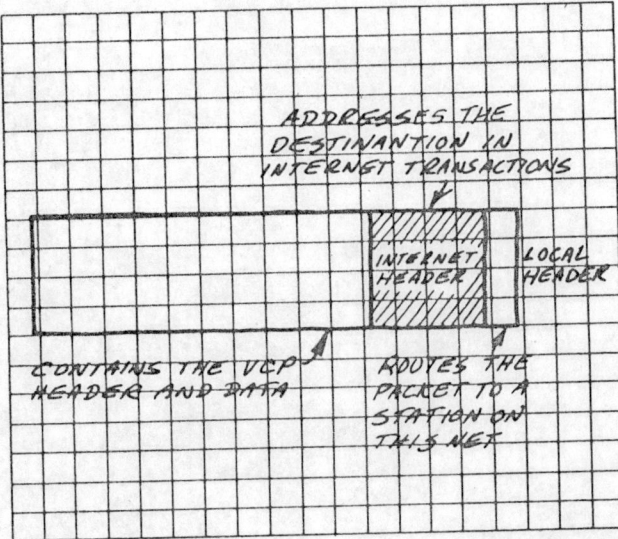

The host takes its own datagram, appends an internet header, and passes it via its serial port to the NIU with two framing characters to provide frame synchronization. The NIU adds the local header and launches the datagram on its way.

ple, a Basic application program running on a microcomputer-based system can send packets into or through the network, via its host's RS-232-C port.

To implement the datagram service, two software processes are required: (1) the packet mover forwards the user's packets between the host and the cable and (2) the controller maintains a database that reflects the operation of the packet-moving processes.

The database includes statistics on the operation of the packet mover and parameters that are used to control its operation. User hosts are permitted to send datagrams to any controller process for the purpose of reading or (interpretively) writing the database. This service is used primarily for statistics collection in support of host monitoring and measurement programs, but a variety of other services are planned. ■

Index

ABBS, 110
Accumulator, 103
ACS, 19
ADCCP, 20
Aloha, 3-4
Apollo Domain, 204
Apple, 112, 224-247
ARC (Datapoint), 223
Automatic rate detection, 105
Automatic fault detection, 8
Bank local networks, 213-219
Bell Labs network, 72
Bell Northern Research, 191
Belmac, 32, 76, 77
Bit encoding addressing, 26
BIU, 20
Broadband, 33-36
Bus, 32-36
C³, 157
Cambridge ring, 15
Card access, 145
Carry bit, 103
CATV, 17, 31
CBBS, 110
CBX, 179, 222
Coaxial cable, 31
Cobal, 78
Codex, 126-143
Com Design, 126-143
Compiler, 79-83
Compre Comm, 126-143
Control, 36, 37
Control Data Corp. (CDC), 17
Controller (cluster), 87
CP/M, 110
CRT blackboard, 203
Cyber, 17
Data General, 94
Datagram, 29
Datapoint, 98
DCA, 126-143
DCC, 126-143
DEC, 3, 11, 94
Demand port assignment, 123
DIX, (Fordnet), 24
DPLL timing (SDLC Chip), 168
Dynabus (Tandem), 14
Emulation (terminal), 99
End user (Fordnet), 60
Ethernet, 3, 15, 21, 52, 150-157, 224-227
Facsimile, 177
Fault recovery, 9
FDM, 31
FEP, 88
Flow control, 28
Fordnet, 2
Format (packet), 27
Fortran, 79
Gandalf, 126-143
Gateway, 54-60
GDC, 126-143
Halcyon, 126-143
HDLC, 20
Hewlett-Packard, 94
High-level protocol, 30, 87

Honeywell, 13, 96
Hyperbus, 225
Hyperchannel, 21-23
IBM's CTC adapter, 12
Idle line, 3
IEEE, 20, 84
Infinet, 248-250
Infotron, 126-143
Intel 8273, 166-169
Intercluster communications, 68
Internetworking, 60
Interpert, 83
IPC, 60
K68000 CPU (UH/CLC), 208
Key security, 145
Lightwave (Fiber optic), 17, 43-47
Local network vendors, 228, 229
Locking (a loop), 167
Logical ring, 49
LOG process (Fordnet), 7, 10
Loop mode SDLC, 165-172
Machine cycle, 103
Message, 60
Micom, 126-143
Microprocessor, 101-112, 189-201
Minicomputer, 86-100
MIT local network, 205
Mitrenet, 21-23
Multidrop, 2
NBS net, 31, 251-254
Nestar, 244-247
Net/One, 31, 251-254
Network layer process, 60
Network modeling process, 126
Network Systems Corp., 3, 16, 222, 224-227
NMU, 164
Non-persistent (contention), 3-5
Object code, 83
OCR, 177
Office automation, 174-188, 189-201
1-persistent (contention), 3-5
Operating system, 61-70
OSI, 54-56, 151
Passwords, 146
PBX, 222
PDP-11, 11, 12
Perkin Elmer, 97
Port, 60
Primenet (Prime), 97, 240-243
Process, 60
Programmers workbench, 73
Programming language, 78-84
Pseudo register, 103
PUP, 224
Ring, 2
Rixon, 126-143
RJE, 11, 12
Rolm, 22
Rome A.D. center, 192
Rotate, 103
Routing, 60
SBS, 19
SCU (Honeywell), 13
Series/1 (IBM), 96
Shift, 103

Slotted Aloha, 3-5
Source code, 83
Star, 2
Statistical multiplexers, 113-121, 126-143
Switching multiplexers, 121-125
TDM, 31
Terminal protocol, 100
Terminal security, 144-147
Texas Instruments, 97
3 Com, 151
Timeplex, 126-143
Token passing, 48-53
T-1, 162
TPL, 78-84
TPL compiler, 80
TRS-80, 112
Twisted pair, 32
Ubits, 157-160
UH/CLC, 61-65, 206-208
Ungermann-Bass, 31
University local networks 202-212
Unix, 71-77
Unix monitoring, 73
Unix on-a-chip, 76
Unix tree, 75
USART, 101
Virtual array, 80
Virtual memory 83
Voice, 178
Wangnet, 98, 234-239
Zero-bit insertion, 165
Znet, 230-233

Original Publication Dates

1 **SECTION I TECHNOLOGY**
2 Concepts, strategies for local data network architectures *R. H. Sherman, M. G. Gable, and G. McClure (July 1978)*
11 Local Networking: The missing link emerges *Ken Hardwick and William Federbusch (July 1980)*
20 Local networks consensus: High speed *Peter Hsi and Tsvi Lissack (December 1980)*
31 A user speaks out: Broadband or baseband for local nets? *Thomas E. Krutsch (December 1981)*
39 13 Often-asked questions about broadband *Edward Cooper (April 1982)*
43 How fiber optics reduces a private net's growing pains *Richard C. McCaskill (March 1981)*
48 Making a case for token passing in local networks *C. C. Kenneth Miller and D. M. Thompson (March 1982)*
54 Overcoming local and long-haul incompatibility *R. H. Sherman, M. G. Gable, and A. Chung (March 1982)*

61 **SECTION II SOFTWARE**
62 Dynamic reconfiguration by a local network's operating system *Robert Coyne (December 1981)*
71 Unix: An operating system that means business *Wendy Rauch-Hindin (October 1981)*
78 A programming language for networks *Paul A. D. de Maine (July 1981)*

85 **SECTION III EQUIPMENT**
86 Minicomputers' network roles *Edwin E. Mier (October 1980)*
101 Finesse versus force in bolstering micros' capabilities *John Wharton and Lionel Smith (August 1980)*
110 Microtalk's maxi applications could benefit companies *Frank J. Derfler (November 1980)*
113 The new network roles of the statistical mux *Joseph Visvader (June 1981)*
121 The new breed—switching muxes *Thomas H. Scholl (June 1981)*
126 A buyers guide to today's versatile statistical multiplexers *James H. Scharen-Guivel and A. A. Carlson (March 1982)*
144 How to keep terminal users honest *Alan Berman (May 1980)*

149 **SECTION IV IMPLEMENTATION**
150 Implementing Ethernet from soup to nuts *Jeffrey Mason and Gregory Shaw (December 1981)*
157 The first all-in-one local network *Didier S. Castueil, Domenic L. Giovachino, and Dennis L. Lengyel (August 1981)*
165 LSI devices control loop-mode SDLC data links *John Beaston (August 1978)*

173 **SECTION V APPLICATIONS**
174 Data Communications in the office *Edwin E. Mier and J. Peter Schmader (April 1980)*
189 Which technology will rule the automated office? *Wendy Rauch-Hindin (November 1981)*
202 Universities are setting trends in data communications nets *Wendy Rauch-Hindin (October 1981)*
213 Bank finds proven methods lead to successful network *Frederick S. Haines (February 1979)*

221 **SECTION VI SELECTION**
222 The many faces of local networking *Kenneth J. Thurber and Harvey A. Freeman (December 1981)*
230 Build a local network on proven software *Dale Way (December 1981)*
234 Inside Wang's local net architecture *Mark Stahlman (January 1982)*
240 Ring nets: Passing the token in local networking circles *Richard E. Sterry (December 1981)*
244 The microcomputer connection to local networks *Joe Malone (December 1981)*
248 A low-speed local net for under $100 per station *Robert Bosen (December 1981)*
251 Net/One's answer to packet and circuit switching *John M. Davidson (December 1981)*